AN INTRODUCTION TO CRIMINOLOGY

PAMELA DAVIES & MICHAEL ROWE

– AN –
INTRODUCTION
– TO –
CRIMINOLOGY

$SAGE

Los Angeles | London | New Delhi
Singapore | Washington DC | Melbourne

Los Angeles | London | New Delhi
Singapore | Washington DC | Melbourne

SAGE Publications Ltd
1 Oliver's Yard
55 City Road
London EC1Y 1SP

SAGE Publications Inc.
2455 Teller Road
Thousand Oaks, California 91320

SAGE Publications India Pvt Ltd
B 1/I 1 Mohan Cooperative Industrial Area
Mathura Road
New Delhi 110 044

SAGE Publications Asia-Pacific Pte Ltd
3 Church Street
#10-04 Samsung Hub
Singapore 049483

Editor: Alana Clogan
Assistant Editor: Eve Williams
Production Editor: Prachi Arora
Copyeditor: Audrey Scriven
Proofreader: Derek Markham
Indexer: Caroline Eley
Marketing Manager: Ruslana Khatagova
Cover Design: Francis Kenney
Typeset by: C&M Digitals (P) Ltd, Chennai, India

Editorial arrangement and Introduction © Pamela Davies and Michael Rowe, 2022

Chapter 1 © Linda Asquith, 2022
Chapter 2 © Eloise Moss, 2022
Chapter 3 © Jacki Tapley, 2022
Chapter 4 © Andromachi Tseloni and Elaine Duncan, 2022
Chapter 5 © Sarah Moore, 2022
Chapter 6 © Michael Rowe, 2022
Chapter 7 © Thomas Raymen, 2022
Chapter 8 © Loraine Gelsthorpe and Lucy Trafford, 2022
Chapter 9 © Tara Renae McGee, David P. Farrington and Darrick Jolliffe, 2022
Chapter 10 © Keith Hayward and Jairo Matallana-Villarreal, 2022
Chapter 11 © Max Travers, 2022
Chapter 12 © Francis Gaffney and Carl Wearn, 2022
Chapter 13 © Francis Gaffney, 2022
Chapter 14 © David Whyte, 2022
Chapter 15 © Xavier L'Hoiry and Jo Large, 2022
Chapter 16 © Angus Nurse, 2022
Chapter 17 © Laura Connelly, 2022
Chapter 18 © Neil Chakraborti and Stevie-Jade Hardy, 2022
Chapter 19 © Tina G. Patel, 2022
Chapter 20 © Nicola Groves, 2022
Chapter 21 © Murray Lee and Alex Simpson, 2022
Chapter 22 © Natasha Mulvihill and Marianne Hester, 2022
Chapter 23 © Pamela Davies, 2022
Chapter 24 © Ben Bradford, 2022
Chapter 25 © Joanne Clough, 2022
Chapter 26 © Kayliegh Richardson, 2022
Chapter 27 © Paul Biddle, Lyndsey Bengtsson and Aaron Amankwaa, 2022
Chapter 28 © George Mair, 2022
Chapter 29 © Kate Herrity and Jason Warr, 2022
Chapter 30 © Tim Bateman, 2022
Chapter 31 © Pamela Davies and Ian R. Cook, 2022
Chapter 32 © Jamie Harding, 2022
Chapter 33 © Michael Rowe and Pamela Davies, 2022

First published 2022

Library of Congress Control Number: 2021947247

British Library Cataloguing in Publication data

A catalogue record for this book is available from the British Library

ISBN 978-1-5264-8686-8
ISBN 978-1-5264-8685-1 (pbk)
eISBN 978-1-5297-6612-7

Contents

List of Figures, Tables and Case Studies

FIGURES

TABLES

CASE STUDIES

Notes on the Editors and Contributors

THE EDITORS

Pamela Davies Pam's research interests coalesce around gender, crime, harm, victimisation and justice. Combining her interest in victimology and social harm with a critical/feminist infused approach she has explored a range of contemporary social problems – both visible and hidden. Her early research focused on female offending and the interplay between women's offending patterns and experiences of victimisation. More recently she has examined tensions around social and environmental justice adopting a case study approach. She has led a number of research projects and evaluations of multi-agency innovations that tackle gendered forms of harm, including interpersonal violence, domestic abuse, the policing of serial perpetrators and support for victims. The ways in which gender mediates our life experiences continue to provoke new areas of inquiry and she is currently working with colleagues on 'gendering green criminology'.

Pam has published widely on the subject of victimisation and social harm, and on how gender connects to matters of community safety, public protection and well-being. Her most recent books are *Crime and Power* (authored with Tanya Wyatt) and *Victimology Research Policy and Activism* (edited with Jacki Tapley). She is the series editor of the Palgrave Macmillan 'Victims and Victimology' book series (with Associate Professor Tyrone Kirchengast, University of New South Wales, Sydney).

Michael Rowe Michael's research interests have tended to focus on accountability and governance in policing, and the changing organisation and delivery of policing in relation to diversity, professionalisation, the application of Evidence Based Policing and the challenges of policing in a digital age. A recent project has explored the changing nature of visible policing in relation to the impact of police buildings, material culture and social media on public perceptions of legitimacy and authority, as well as on police officer and staff professional culture and identity. Other projects have examined innovative police responses to domestic violence, organisational and cultural change in the policing of adult sexual assault investigations, and the ethical and governance challenges of using scientific research and AI technology in contemporary policing. He is currently developing work exploring the policing of Anthropocentric climate change.

He has published widely on these and related matters in the *British Journal of Criminology, Policing and Society, Public Management Review*, the *Journal of Contemporary Ethnography, Criminology and Criminal Justice* and many other journals. His books include *Policing the Police* (Policy Press, 2020), *Accountability in Policing: Contemporary Debates* (Routledge, 2015, edited with Stuart Lister) and *Introduction to Policing* (Sage, 2018, third edition). He is editor of the *International Journal of Police Science and Management*.

THE CONTRIBUTORS

Aaron Amankwaa is a Senior Lecturer in Forensic Science at Northumbria University. His primary research is focused on three key themes: the evaluation of the effectiveness of forensic science applications and technologies, development of forensic genetic testing, and development and evaluation of crime reduction initiatives.

Linda Asquith is the course director for the BA (Hons) Criminology course at Leeds Beckett University. She has worked in universities for over fifteen years and taught a very wide range of topics. Her PhD was awarded in 2015 and looked at life after genocide for those survivors who had migrated to the UK. Currently, Linda is researching the experiences of those people who have been wrongfully convicted, focusing on life after exoneration.

Tim Bateman is Reader in Youth Justice at the University of Bedfordshire. He has an extensive background in social work with children in conflict with the law and youth justice policy prior to taking up an academic position. Tim has written and researched widely on issues surrounding youth crime and has recently published 'The State of Youth Justice 2020'. Tim is co-editor of *Safer Communities* journal, News Editor for *Youth Justice* journal, and Chair of the National Association for Youth Justice.

Lyndsey Bengtsson is a Senior Lecturer and Solicitor Tutor within Northumbria University's Law School. Her research interests include out of court disposals, age discrimination in the workplace and clinical legal education. She is an editor for the *International Journal of Clinical Legal Education* and the *Journal of Legal Research Methodology*.

Paul Biddle is a Research Fellow in the Department of Social Sciences at Northumbria University. His research interests include the experiences of older prisoners, health service provision in prisons, police responses to domestic abuse, and the use and effectiveness of non-custodial punishments.

Ben Bradford is Director of the Institute for Global City Policing at University College London. Ben's research interests revolve around police-community relations and questions of identity, trust, legitimacy, cooperation and compliance in criminal justice settings.

Neil Chakraborti is a Professor of Criminology and Director of the Centre for Hate Studies at the University of Leicester. He has been commissioned by numerous funding bodies including the Economic and Social Research Council, Amnesty International and the Equality and Human Rights Commission, to lead research studies which continue to shape hate crime law making, policy, scholarship and activism. He is series editor of Palgrave Hate Studies, Chair of the Research Advisory Group at the Howard League for Penal Reform, and sits on the advisory boards of Tell MAMA, the International Network for Hate Studies, the British Society of Criminology Hate Crime Network and BLM in the Stix.

Joanne Clough is a former criminal defence solicitor who lectures on criminal law and evidence at the Ulster University, Belfast. She is a fee-paid First Tier Tribunal Judge and Deputy Judge of the Upper Tribunal.

Laura Connelly is a Lecturer in Criminology at the University of Salford. She has broad research interests around social inequalities, particularly around the intersections of gender, race, migration, and criminalisation. Much of her work to date has explored these issues within the context of the sex industry and/or in relation to human trafficking and modern slavery.

Ian R. Cook is a Senior Lecturer in Social Sciences at the Department of Social Sciences, Northumbria University. His research interests include sex work, the governance of cities, and the international circulation of policy models. His work spans criminology, geography and urban studies.

Elaine Duncan, MA (Hons), is a doctoral school-funded PhD candidate at Nottingham Trent University looking at police demand and decision making within force control rooms. Elaine is a fully accredited intelligence officer and criminal intelligence analyst, having previously worked with Police Scotland, The Gangmasters and Labour Abuse Authority and the National Crime Agency.

David P. Farrington, OBE, is Emeritus Professor of Psychological Criminology at Cambridge University. He has received the Stockholm Prize in Criminology and he has been President of the American Society of Criminology. His major research interest is in developmental criminology, and he is Director of the Cambridge Study in Delinquent Development, which is a prospective longitudinal survey of over 400 London males from age 8 to age 61. In addition to 867 published journal articles and book chapters on criminological and psychological topics, he has published 117 books, monographs and government publications, and 164 shorter publications (total = 1,148).

Francis Gaffney, PhD, has worked as an analyst in the risk management and international cyber security sectors for over 20 years with particular focus on strategic policy, geopolitical horizon-scanning, and threat intelligence. His current work focuses on strategic intelligence policy, the ethics of AI, quantum consciousness, and international cyber security. He is a Visiting Fellow of the Cranfield University in the Faculty of Defence & Security, and his current research primarily focuses on understanding psychological motivations and identifying methodologies that could strengthen young people's resilience to violent extremism, including cyber terrorism.

Loraine Gelsthorpe, PhD, is Professor of Criminology and Criminal Justice and Director of the Institute of Criminology, University of Cambridge. She has published extensively on matters relating to women, crime and criminal justice as well as on 'feminist criminologies'. Current research revolves around the meaning and impact of the arts in the criminal justice arena, deaths under community supervision, and community-based support for women in conflict with the law. Loraine sits on a number of government advisory bodies, and is also a UKCP registered and accredited psychoanalytic psychotherapist. She is a Fellow of Pembroke College, Cambridge.

Nicola Groves is a Senior Lecturer in Criminology at Leeds Beckett University. Her teaching and research interests include gender and crime and domestic abuse. She is the co-author of the book *Domestic Violence and Criminal Justice* (Routledge). Prior to becoming an academic Nicola worked in the voluntary sector primarily in the field of domestic violence.

Jamie Harding is a Senior Lecturer in Research Methods at Northumbria University and the joint programme leader of the Police Constable Degree Apprenticeship. He is the author of the textbook *Qualitative Data Analysis from Start to Finish* and two monographs on homelessness; *Making it Work: The Keys to Success Among Young People Living Independently* and *Post-War Homelessness in the UK: Making and Implementation*. He likes spending time with his grandchildren, running along to the level crossing to see the trains: this still provides lots of excitement (and the grandchildren enjoy it too).

Stevie-Jade Hardy is the Evidence and Evaluation Lead at the Violence Reduction Network for Leicester, Leicestershire and Rutland. She is an Honorary Fellow at the School of Criminology, University of Leicester. Over the past decade, Stevie has led complex, high profile research and evaluation projects for the public and private sector and not for profit organisations, which have shaped national and international policy relating to crime and justice.

Keith Hayward is Professor of Criminology at the Faculty of Law, University of Copenhagen. He is a leading figure in cultural criminology and has authored numerous books and articles on the subject. His research interests include criminological theory, crime and technological culture, spatial and social theory, and terrorism and extremism.

Kate Herrity is the Andrew W. Mellon and Kings College Junior Research Fellow in Punishment, University of Cambridge. She takes particular interest in researching at the edges both of criminology and epistemology, with a focus on sound and music in prison, punishment, sensory criminology and methodology. Her doctoral research explored the significance of sound in a local men's prison using aural ethnography, soon to appear in monograph. She moderates www.sensorycriminology.com which accompanies the recent Emerald publication, co-edited with Bethany Schmidt and Jason Warr, *Sensory Penalties: Exploring the Senses in Places of Punishment and Social Control* (2021).

Marianne Hester, OBE, FacSS, is Chair in Gender, Violence and International Policy and Head of the Centre for Gender and Violence Research at the University of Bristol, UK. Marianne has written extensively about many aspects of violence and abuse, including domestic and sexual violence, child contact, domestic abuse in LGBT+ communities and forced marriage. Much of her current work is on perpetrators of domestic abuse, on wider notions of justice for victim-survivors of gender-based violence, and on measuring coercive control. She is the Founder and Editor-in-Chief of the international Journal of Gender Based Violence.

Darrick Jolliffe is Professor of Criminology and Head of the School of Law and Criminology at the University of Greenwich, UK. He has published extensively in the areas of empathy, individual differences and offending, developmental life-course criminology, and punishment and offending. He has led large research studies for National and International Government Agencies.

Jo Large is a Senior Lecturer in Criminology in the School for Policy Studies, University of Bristol. Jo's research focuses on the connections between consumption and harm. This includes analysis of counterfeit markets and the overlapping nature of licit and illicit economies. More recently, Jo's interests have extended to examine the relationship between charity-based tourism and harm.

Murray Lee is a Professor in Criminology and Associate Dean Research at the University of Sydney Law School. He is the author of *Inventing Fear of Crime: Criminology and the Politics of Anxiety*, co-author of *Policing and Media: Public Relations, Simulations and Communications*, co-editor of *Fear of Crime: Critical Voices in an Age of Anxiety* and co-editor of *The Routledge International Handbook on Fear of Crime*. Murray's research focuses broadly on representations and perceptions of crime and how these lead to processes of criminalisation.

Xavier L'Hoiry is a Lecturer in Criminology and Social Policy at the Department of Sociological Studies, University of Sheffield. His research focuses on illicit entrepreneurship, the social embeddedness of organised crime, and the policing response to this type of criminal activity. He holds particular research interests in tobacco smuggling, human trafficking and commercial sexual exploitation, including the use of online environments to facilitate these illegal activities. He is an editorial board member for *Trends in Organized Crime* and *Urban Crime*.

George Mair recently retired as Professor of Criminal Justice and Head of Law at Liverpool Hope University. His research interests are community penalties, fines, the effectiveness of sentences and criminal justice policy.

Jairo Matallana-Villarreal is an independent researcher with extensive experience in the areas of rule of law, human rights, and crisis response in international development cooperation. His interests include policing practices, countermapping and participatory spatial analysis, theories of justice, and militarism and violence.

Tara Renae McGee is a Professor in the School of Criminology and Criminal Justice at Griffith University, Australia. She is founding co-editor of the *Journal of Developmental and Life-Course Criminology*, chairperson of the American Society of Criminology's Division of Developmental and Life-Course Criminology, and co-convenor of the Australian and New Zealand Society of Criminology's Thematic Group on Developmental and Life-Course Criminology.

Sarah Moore is a Senior Lecturer in the Department of Social and Policy Sciences at the University of Bath. She has published over 20 journal articles and book chapters, as well as four books, including *Crime and the Media* (2014) and *Detecting the Social: Post-1970s Detective Fiction* (2018). She is especially interested in socio-cultural processes of blame and responsibility. Her research is concerned with two questions. How and why are certain social groups made to feel responsible for their personal safety and well-being? And how do late modern social institutions make themselves accessible and accountable to the public? These questions have guided her research on a range of phenomenon, including courtroom broadcasting, the rise of the 'virtual' court, transparent justice initiatives, the cultural treatment of sexual violence, cultural amnesia in 'real life' crime drama, and post-1970s detective fiction as a form of critical sociological enquiry.

Eloise Moss is Senior Lecturer in Modern British History at the University of Manchester. Her first book, *Night Raiders: Burglary and the Making of Modern Urban Life in London, 1860–1968*, was published in 2019 with Oxford University Press. Eloise works on histories of crime, gender, sexuality and urban culture, and is particularly interested in historic systems of discrimination embedded within commercial sectors including the leisure and tourism industry.

Natasha Mulvihill is a Senior lecturer in Criminology and a member of the Centre for Gender and Violence Research at the University of Bristol, UK. She has written particularly on prostitution and sex work policy as well as victim-survivor experiences of domestic, sexual and 'honour'-based violence and abuse. Natasha's current interests include the intersections of popular and contemporary culture with gender, sexual harm and violence, as well as intersections of faith. She is Editor for the *Journal of Gender Based Violence*.

Angus Nurse is Head of the Department of Criminology and Criminal Justice at Nottingham Trent University. Angus has research interests in criminality, critical criminal justice, animal and human rights law, anti-social behaviour and green criminology. He is particularly interested in animal law and its enforcement and the reasons why people commit environmental crimes and crimes against animals. His books include *Policing Wildlife* (Palgrave Macmillan, 2015), *Animal Harm: Perspectives on Why People Harm and Kill Animals* (Ashgate, 2013). *Miscarriages of Justice: Causes, consequences and remedies* (Policy Press, 2018), co-authored with Sam Poyser and Rebecca Milne, *The Citizen and the State* (Emerald, 2020) and *Wildlife Criminology* (Bristol University Press, 2020), co-authored with Professor Tanya Wyatt.

Tina G. Patel is a senior lecturer in Criminology based at the University of Salford, UK. Tina is the author of a number of books, including *Race, Crime and Resistance* (2011, co-authored with David Tyrer) and *Race and Society* (2017). These examine continued racism in what is often referred to as a post-race society. Tina has widely presented and published papers on the subjects of race/ethnicity, post-race racism, and the experiences of minority ethnic groups with the criminal justice system.

Thomas Raymen is a Senior Lecturer in Criminology at Northumbria University, UK. His research has focused upon the social harms that emerge at the intersection of leisure and consumer capitalism and how moral, political, and continental philosophy can inform critical social harm perspectives. Currently, he is involved in an international ethnographic research project on luxury, corruption, and global ethics, in addition to developing a philosophy of social harm rooted in post-liberal ethics.

Kayliegh Richardson is a Senior Lecturer in law at Northumbria University. Prior to commencing her academic career in 2015, Kayliegh had a career in legal practice as a family law solicitor. Her research investigates the approaches of the family and criminal justice systems to victims and alleged perpetrators of domestic abuse, with a particular focus on barriers to accessing justice.

Alex Simpson is a Senior Lecturer in Criminology at Macquarie University. His research brings together inter-related themes of class, gender and performativity to examine the embedded, and often hidden, cultures of finance. Through ethnographic research methods, his work presents an 'on-the-ground' account of the everyday practices, thought process and common assumptions that both legitimise and neutralise the production of social harm connected to finance work.

Jacki Tapley is a Principal Lecturer in Victimology and Criminology at the School of Criminology and Criminal Justice, University of Portsmouth. Prior to joining the University of Portsmouth in 2000, she worked as a Probation Officer in Dorset. Her teaching and research focus on victims of crime, their experiences of the criminal justice system, and criminal justice professional practices and culture. Jacki is the course leader for the MSc Victimology and a postgraduate short course aimed at professionals working in the CJS. Jacki is a member of the national Victim Commissioner's Advisory Group, the Independent Facilitator for the Wessex CPS VAWG Scrutiny Panel, and a Trustee for Aurora New Dawn, a domestic abuse, sexual violence and stalking charity.

Lucy Trafford is a DPhil (PhD) student at the Centre for Criminology and Law Faculty at the University of Oxford. Her research explores police officers' understanding of intimate partner violence and how this informs decision making and discretion in IPV incidents, within an intersectional framework. Lucy is the Graduate Development Scholar for St Anne's College, Oxford, where she teaches undergraduate law students Jurisprudence. She is also an Associate Lecturer in Criminology at Oxford Brookes and a Leathersellers' Scholar, having completed her MPhil in Criminological Research at St John's College, University of Cambridge, and BA in Jurisprudence at Christ Church College, Oxford.

Max Travers is an Associate Professor of Sociology and Criminology in the School of Social Sciences at the University of Tasmania. He is the author of *The Reality of Law* (1997) and *The Sentencing of Children* (2012), and co-author of *Rethinking Bail* (2020). He has also co-edited *Comparative Criminology in Asia*, a collection that discusses the theoretical and methodological issues in conducting comparative research.

Andromachi Tseloni, BA (Hons), MA, PhD, is Professor of Quantitative Criminology at Nottingham Trent University with extensive research on criminal victimisation inequalities and the crime drop. She leads the Quantitative and Spatial Criminology Research Group which undertakes research that directly informs crime prevention and community policing. At the time of finalising the book she is also Academic Lead on the Administrative Data Research UK-funded Ministry of Justice Data First Project, and Subject Matter Expert on the College of Policing Safer Streets Fund Toolkit.

Jason Warr is a Senior Lecturer in Criminology and Criminal Justice at De Montfort University, with research interests in prisons, philosophy of punishment, sociology of power, the philosophy of science, criminological theory, and sensory criminology. His most recent book is concerned with forensic psychologists employed within the prisons of England and Wales and is titled *Forensic Psychologists: Prisons, Power, and Vulnerability*.

Carl Wearn works as a senior analyst in the cyber security sector and is a former specialist fraud and cyber crime investigator with particular interests in intelligence analysis, cyber crime investigation, and the development of resilience to cyber-attack campaigns.

David Whyte is Professor of Socio-legal Studies at the University of Liverpool where he teaches on, and researches, the relationship between law and power in capitalist societies. He is author of *The Corporate Criminal* (Routledge, 2015, with Steve Tombs), *Corporate Human Rights Violations* (Routledge, 2017, with Stefanie Khoury), and *Ecocide* (Manchester University Press, 2000).

Discover the Online Resources

An Introduction to Criminology is accompanied by online resources to support your teaching. Find them at: https://study.sagepub.com/daviesandrowe.

Lecturers can log in to access the following:

- **Essay Questions** Each chapter is accompanied by three Essay Questions which can be used by lecturers in teaching and exams. Also included are points to consider for students answering the essay questions.
- **SAGE Journal Articles** Access to three SAGE Journal Articles relating to each chapter is provided, which can also be shared with students.
- **SAGE Videos** and **Critical Thinking Questions** One SAGE Video per chapter offers valuable insights from a range of Criminology experts and can also be shared with students who can test their knowledge by considering and answering open ended questions related to each of the videos.
- **Testbank** Each chapter is accompanied by ten Multiple Choice Questions. Lecturers can use these questions in their teaching, for exams and to upload to their University's virtual learning environment.

Acknowledgements

EDITORS' ACKNOWLEDGEMENT

The Editors wish to thank all contributors for their engagement with this project and valuable perspectives on the discipline of criminology. We are extremely grateful also to Natalie Aguilera, Ozlem Merakli and colleagues at SAGE who have steered us along the way.

CONTRIBUTORS' ACKNOWLEDGEMENT

Eloise Moss would like to thank Thomas Verheyden and Adam Waddingham for their extremely useful feedback on earlier drafts of Chapter 2.

PUBLISHER'S ACKNOWLEDGEMENTS

The publisher would like to thank all of the lecturers who spoke to us and helped to review this book's content to ensure it is as useful as possible:

Gemma Birkett, City, University of London
Elisabeth Carter, University of Roehampton
Mark Connor, University of Leicester
Anne Ferguson, CQUniversity
Bianca Fileborn, Melbourne University
Maria Kaspersson, University of Greenwich
Anita Lavorgne, Southampton University
Giuseppe Maglione, Edinburgh Napier University
Melissa Mendez, Swansea University
Erin Sanders-McDonagh, University of Kent
Sarah Nixon, University of Gloucestershire
Rosie Smith, York St John University
Jemma Tyson, University of Portsmouth
Kate Williams, University of Wolverhampton
Suzanne Young, University of Leeds
Irene Zempi, Nottingham Trent University

The publisher would also like to extend a special thanks to Jay Heptinstall for his enormous contribution in creating the online resources that accompany this book.

Introduction

Although criminology is a relatively young academic discipline, not widely taught to undergraduates in UK universities before the 1990s, it has become a hugely popular subject and one that has grown both in size and scope. Emerging from sociological studies of deviance that developed in the UK and the US in the 1950s and 1960s, criminology has become a multidisciplinary subject drawing on traditions in politics, social theory, psychology, medical science, public administration, policy studies, and many others. This multifaceted character has led some to characterise criminology as a 'water cooler' discipline, in the sense that the central focus on crime, deviance, criminal justice and so on is approached from many and diverse perspectives. This is one reason why criminology is such an exciting, vibrant and diverse area of study. It combines complementary and competing perspectives, with links to a very broad range of topics of interest to scholars working in fields across the social and natural sciences, as well as the arts and humanities. Whether you have opened this book as a first-time student or an experienced scholar of criminology, you will quickly see that there is a wide variety of topics, perspectives, debates and connections with other disciplines that you might have encountered previously.

One of the central ambitions of this collection is to reflect the vibrancy of contemporary criminology. To this end the book addresses emerging perspectives and topics that have developed within the discipline in recent years. Cultural criminological approaches, questions of social harm, green criminology, the challenges of terrorism and state crime, and cybercrime are among the relatively recent themes to emerge within the discipline that are addressed in the chapters that follow. Equally, the book addresses historical and theoretical debates within criminology that have established the discipline in its current form. Readers will become equipped with a wide and deep appreciation of the roots of contemporary criminology, as well as a strong understanding of the 'green shoots' of academic enquiry likely to shape the future direction of our collective interests. Alongside these conceptual and issue-based discussions, the book provides you with a strong grounding in terms of the institutions and processes of the criminal justice system. In these chapters too, you will add to your knowledge of the development of these various practices and organisations as well as gain important insights into current challenges and innovations.

Another key priority that has informed the writing and preparation of the collection has been to develop chapters that provide both descriptive outlines of the various content areas and challenging analyses of continuing debates and controversies. Since many undergraduate students of criminology (in the UK at least) come to the discipline fresh for the first time as they begin university education, it has been a priority that the chapters provide an accessible entry point. However, we have sought to avoid the collection being 'introductory' in the sense that it offers only a descriptive oversight of the discipline. To this end authors provide rich and deep analysis that will serve as a continuing point of reference for scholars of criminology at all levels. Each chapter is authored by leading experts in the field and not only reflects their background knowledge of their subject, but also offers their insight into cutting edge themes and debates that will shape the continuing development of the discipline.

A further priority has been to provide you with a sense of what it means to practice as a criminologist, whether that will be as an undergraduate or postgraduate student, or as an academic or researcher, or within the many professional roles informed by criminology. Several of the chapters that follow are explicitly focused on what it means to develop a criminological imagination: a way of seeing the social world through a criminological lens and some of the ways that this can form intellectual and professional practice. The 'tools of the trade', in terms of research methods and approaches to data, are outlined throughout the book. The application of different methods, and the advantages of various methodological approaches, run through many of the chapters that follow, and provide insight into the ways in which research is practised and contributes to our understanding of real-world challenges and everyday debates. Reflexivity is central to developing your identity as a criminologist. In many ways the chapters give cause for us to rethink and question our perspectives in relation to the ethical, legal and policy questions that surround 'everyday' concerns about the nature and causes of offending, the appropriate responses to law-breaking, the rights of victims, and so on. As teachers of criminology we often find that an advantage is that people tend to have some insight and grasp of our core concepts and materials. Much of that, though, is gleaned from popular media sources and political debate that might not stand up well to scrutiny when considered against research evidence. Bridging this gap, between taken-for-granted assumptions and an evidence-based analysis, is central to becoming a criminologist. The content of each chapter encourages you to reflect on prior thinking and question your established perspectives. Additionally, each chapter is accompanied by questions, knowledge-check exercises, web resources, glossary terms, and suggestions for further reading (see the following section on 'How to Use This Book' for more information) that will help you develop your own criminological imagination.

Part 1 - Introduction to Crime and Criminology

The first five chapters of the volume will set the scene for becoming a criminologist. Part 1 serves as an extended introduction to the text as a whole. From the outset, the approach is to encourage you to adopt an evaluative approach to your studies and develop the ability to critically appraise political and social processes of victimisation and criminalisation. Chapters outline the historical development of criminology and identify central topics relating to the nature and extent of crime and victimisation. These chapters will delineate the ways in which the subject of criminology can be distinguished from other forms of understanding. You are encouraged throughout to develop a reflective approach and a critical awareness of the values of local cultures and local politics from the global North and South, and of the student's own values, biography and social identity, and how to bring these skills to bear in an informed response to crime and victimisation. Essentially the focus is on 'How to be a criminology student' with hints and tips for starting on the academic journey. In addition, these introductory chapters will address the construction and influence of representations of crime and victims, and of responses to crime, deviance and harm, as found in popular political debate, the mass media and public opinion. In contrast Chapter 4 will help you to identify scientific sources of data and information that can provide the potential for more robust analysis of crime. The recurring theme of Part 1, that crime is a socially constructed concept which needs to be understood in its historical global context, extends throughout the volume.

Part 2 - Theories and Concepts of Criminology

This run of six chapters examines a range of criminological concepts, perspectives, and theoretical approaches within criminology, starting with a history of criminological thought that sets the scene for the contemporary perspectives that follow. Having digested these chapters, you will be able to assess a range of perspectives and discuss the strengths of each for the understanding of crime, criminal justice, and victimisation. Chapter 7 provides a critical account of zemiology and the argument that criminology ought to focus on social harm, rather than limiting the scope of the discipline to actions and behaviour deemed by powerful elites to breach the criminal law. Broader conceptual discussion is continued in relation to feminist and cultural criminological theory, which are outlined along with the developmental 'life-course' perspective. All of these draw your attention to the connections between crime, injustice and wider patterns of power and social inequalities. The final chapter in this part addresses comparative criminology, and considers the impact of crime, social harm and criminal justice on populations that are marginalised in the global system.

Part 3 - Contemporary Challenges

The chapters in Part 3 cover an exciting range of contemporary challenges and crime types. This part of the book includes forms of crime that are stubbornly persistent – including violence in all of its manifestations (individual, physical and non-physical, coercive, structural and systemic, terrorist and state-sanctioned, and so on) – and those that have emerged in tandem with social, political and economic challenges of global concern. All are serious and complex types of crime and victimisation that continue to thrive in the twenty-first century. The range of crime types covered is far from exhaustive, those selected and foregrounded in these chapters are explored in ways that draw out the central approaches through which criminologists interrogate these subject areas. They allow us to foreground some of the most pressing contemporary challenges for criminologists to address. As mentioned earlier in this introduction, criminology is a discipline informed by many perspectives and you will notice that many of the forms of crime discussed in Part 3 can be addressed in terms of economics, political science, sociology, development studies, psychology, and other approaches. Once more you will develop your understanding of the ways in which victimisation – in relation to human trafficking, hate crime, gendered violence and environmental destruction – is linked to broader, often global, patterns of inequality and marginalisation.

Part 4 - Criminal Justice Practice

This part of the book encompasses the justice system not only in terms of the set of institutions involved in the processing of offenders and the administration of justice, but also in terms of approaches to justice and a range of wider practices related to that. The key elements of the criminal justice system – police, prosecution, courts and prisons – are all introduced, and you will develop insight into the ways in which these interact and are developing. This set of chapters will variously evaluate criminal justice agency practices and processes of governance, including human rights, which underpin the treatment of lawbreakers within UK criminal justice systems, and allied agencies that administer sentencing alternatives and variously manage offenders. In addition, you will read about over-arching styles of practice that cut across institutional boundaries. Multi-agency working, for example, is a widespread style of operating, and you will learn about the strengths and weaknesses of such community safety and crime prevention methods. Similarly, cutting across individual agencies, you will develop insight into the status of young people, victims and witnesses within the criminal justice system.

Part 5 - Becoming a Criminologist

The final two chapters of the book turn your attention to the various ways in which a criminological imagination can be applied to real-world contexts. If you are an undergraduate or a postgraduate student of criminology, it is likely that you will be expected to complete an independent research project – for a dissertation, for example – during your studies. In this part of the book you will learn about the design and implementation of research studies. Key to this is understanding how to formulate research questions, identify and design appropriate methods, and also consider the ethical implications of research practice. All of these matters are significant concerns for researchers in criminology in a number of post-education careers, and you will gain insight into the career experiences of various professionals in this part of the book. Incorporating reflections and testimonials from professionals in a wide range of careers, you will develop your understanding of how the study of criminology can inform working life within the criminal justice systems, as well as in a broad sweep of other roles that draw upon a criminological imagination.

Overall, throughout these five sections, the book offers breadth and depth in terms of increasing your knowledge of the development of criminology, the various debates and themes that will shape the future of the discipline, and ways in which you can develop personally and professionally. Written by leading experts and incorporating cutting-edge research and debate, the collection will be an important touchstone throughout your studies and is designed thereafter to encourage reflection and critical thinking skills that will be vital to you as you continue into your career.

PART I

INTRODUCTION TO CRIME AND CRIMINOLOGY

Being a Criminologist

Linda Asquith

Learning Objectives

By the end of this chapter you will:

- Understand the key elements of being a criminologist.
- Be able to identify and understand the key myths and realities of criminology.
- Understand the key skills of a criminologist.
- Be able to identify your motivations for studying criminology and how to access support to enable you to succeed in your studies.

Framing Questions
---

1. What do you think criminology is about?
2. What do you think criminologists do?
3. Where do you see yourself once you have graduated?

INTRODUCTION

Becoming an undergraduate student of criminology can be both an exciting and anxious time, and it may also be a time of great confusion, where you will receive a lot of information about your programme in a short space of time. This chapter will help you make sense of some of this information and give you some guidance on how to navigate your first few months as a student of criminology in a Higher Education Institution.

This chapter introduces you to the idea of studying criminology, and what criminology is as a subject. The chapter also aims to give you an insight into key areas of support that you may access during your programme of study. The final aim of the chapter is to consider the challenges you may face when studying criminology and how to deal with those challenges.

First, the chapter helps you to review your progress until now, and then moves on to thinking about getting started on your programme. We consider the myths and reality of studying criminology and the reasons why someone might choose to study criminology. The chapter then considers the key skills of reading, writing and **analysis** before thinking about what support you can access while at university. The chapter concludes by considering the challenges of *becoming and being a criminologist* and how we can respond to those challenges.

--- Pause for Thought ---

Why did you decide to study criminology?

MAPPING THE TERRAIN

We begin this section by reflecting on where you are right now. Taking this brief pause to review your reasons for studying criminology, and how you got to this point, can help prepare you for the year – or years – ahead.

Getting to This Point

First of all, congratulations, you have made it to university! You have made it through thirteen years of school, maybe an additional gap year, or perhaps you are returning to study following an access course, or a long break. However you got here, this is the start of an exciting and challenging time for you. You may have moved away from home for the first time and be living in halls or commuting to university from your family home. You may be 18 or 60, single, in a relationship, married or divorced. You may be going to university in the town you grew up in or have moved hundreds of miles to begin this new chapter of your life. Whatever your circumstances, starting studying at university can be a daunting time. You may have visited several universities, spent time visiting halls of residence and the university facilities. However much you have seen, it will feel very different now you are starting your studies. Your visits on open days may have taken place on sunny, warm days and now you are walking to your classes in sideways rain and gale-force winds. You have developed a bad head cold, your student loan payment is late, your flatmates were up until 4 a.m. singing, and you have got lost four times already, and suddenly the reality of university feels very different from your expectations. The main thing to remember is that you are not alone, and for every person posting on social media that they are 'living their best life', there are just as many who are wondering whether they have made the right choice or feeling out of place. This chapter will help you with making the shift to university, remembering why you chose your course and settling into your new role of criminology student.

Making the Shift to University

Studying at university can be very different from studying at school or college. You may be used to four or five hours of classes each day, with set homework, referring to your tutors as Miss/Sir, being given workbooks to complete, and your parents being involved in your education through parents' evenings or phone calls from your tutors. At university, you will likely have only a few hours a week of formal contact time (**lectures, seminars, tutorials**) and much more 'independent study' time. As you are over 18, your parents will not be involved with your studies unless you choose to involve them, and university staff cannot speak to your parents without your permission. If you have moved out of home for the first time, you will be getting used to living independently, choosing when, and what, to eat and how to spend your money. The first few months of university life can seem overwhelming at times, as you get used to a different way of living and studying. All too often, it is too easy to do too much of one thing and not enough of the other, whether that is drinking, studying, eating, exercising, partying, or any other behaviour. The key thing to focus on in your early days at university is balancing the demands of your course with the other demands on your time, whether those are work, friends or family. You need to find a way of balancing all those demands that works for you.

Getting Started, Getting Reading

Unlike your previous studies, you will not be directly handed everything to read, there will be no requirement to visit the library, buy some books or find information online though there will of course be help in finding such resources especially during your university induction period. This means one of your priorities is finding the library and where the criminology books are located. Your university may have a subject specialist librarian, so it is always worth finding out who they are and contacting them. They can save you a lot of time and energy further down the line when essay deadlines are looming. The modules you are studying will all recommend key readings, and these are likely to be provided in the library, either in physical or electronic form. Try to find these sources in the first couple of weeks of term, as again it will reduce your stress at essay writing time if you already know where the key sources are. If you are able, it is worth buying the core textbooks if you can afford them, as this guarantees you will be able to access these books at any time. Often bookshops close to universities will offer deals on a selection of core textbooks, so shop around to find the best one – secondhand bookshops can often be a treasure trove for the cash-strapped student. Generally, you will be given a set of readings for each week of each of your modules, so start your reading early, to help you develop your knowledge and understanding of what you are studying. We will return to the question of reading later in this chapter.

THE MYTHS AND REALITY OF CRIMINOLOGY

Criminology is a broad topic, but to begin with, it is worth pointing out what it is not, as there are many different understandings of what the subject is, and what people do within criminology. The term 'criminologist' covers many different behaviours and areas, so while two people may both be referred to as a 'criminologist', they will do very different things. There are also variances in different countries, and many European countries do not offer criminology as a degree-level topic to study. So, it depends on your background and previous experiences as to what you think criminology is.

Firstly, many people assume that criminology is mainly about forensic science and that people who get a degree in criminology will become forensic investigators, wearing white boiler suits, testing for DNA evidence, and dusting for fingerprints. Much of this supposition is due to television programmes such as *CSI* or *Bones*. In these very popular programmes, crimes are solved by scientists who examine a crime scene and solve the crime through the application of science. While some graduates with criminology degrees may become 'crime scene investigators', this is rare. This is because crime scene investigator roles require the individual to have a science-based degree (such as chemistry or biology) or equivalent practical experience. You can see the role requirements of a crime scene investigator in Figure 1.1.

Expertise in Role Required (At Selection – Level 1)	Essential Or Desirable
• Science based degree or equivalent practical experience in a relevant operational environment	Essential
• Basic knowledge of and ability to operate computer packages including casework management systems, crime systems Excel and Word	Essential
• Can demonstrate good communication skills and an aptitude for working in a diverse community	Essential
• Demonstrated understanding of H&S issues and legislation relevant to volume crime scene examination and attendance	Essential
• Demonstrated knowledge of the practical techniques used to examine volume crime scenes and understanding of the investigative response to such incidents	Essential
• Due to the nature of the role, must provide Biometric samples (fingerprints and DNA) for inclusion on the respective Police Elimination Databases for routine speculative searching purpose	Essential
• Basic knowledge of practical application of forensic science	Desirable
• Demonstrated competence and performance in attending and examining volume crime scenes as defined by the CSI National Occupational Standards	Desirable
Other (physical, mobility, local conditions)	
• Full current UK/European driving license	Essential
• Equitable contribution to the designated shift pattern covering 7am to 11pm 7 days per week	Essential
• Is able to complete a recognised manual handling course	Essential
• Flexible approach to working cross-border to ensure a full regional crime scene investigation service	Essential

Figure 1.1   Role Description for a Forensic Examiner

Source: West Yorkshire Police (2019)

So, criminologists are not generally crime scene investigators or have any involvement in crime scene processing or forensic investigation. They will, however, read about and understand the issues relating to forensic investigation to explore things such as wrongful convictions that occur due to poor forensic evidence (for example, the Birmingham Six case), or new ways of crime investigation that affect civil liberties, such as the national DNA Database. Forensic investigation and evidence are an important area of *study* for criminologists, but we do not generally *practise* it.

The other area that people assume criminology is involved in is offender profiling. The 1991 film *Silence of the Lambs* shows a young FBI agent, called Clarice Starling, interviewing the famous murderer Hannibal Lecter to help build the FBI's profile of a serial killer referred to as Buffalo Bill. Much more recently, we have seen the Netflix drama *Mindhunter*, based on the work of the FBI agent John Douglas. While offender profilers do exist in the UK, they are rare, and in all cases, their offender profiling role is in addition to their 'day job' of being an academic lecturer, or forensic psychologist, working in health-care facilities, universities, or prisons. To become a forensic psychologist, your undergraduate degree would first need to be accredited by the British Psychological Society (known as BPS accreditation). This recognition is not something that all criminology degrees offer, so if you are on a degree course that does not offer this, you would need to undertake a conversion course once you have completed your criminology degree. Following this, you would then need to undertake a Master's qualification in forensic psychology (or a conversion course which provides this), and then also undertake relevant work experience, and in some cases, a doctorate (PhD) in a relevant area. More information on this can be found on the British Psychological Society's website, www.bps.org.uk. The path to offender profiling, then, is a narrow and bumpy one, with little guarantee of success. Equally, like crime scene work, it bears very little resemblance to what is shown on television. So now we have considered the myths of criminology, we can think about what criminology *does* do.

The reality is that criminology is a multi-faceted, multi-disciplinary subject that seeks to understand crime from a range of viewpoints. As criminologists, we draw on a lot of ideas from sociology, law, and psychology, as well as thinking about what geography, history, medicine, and a wide range of other subjects can tell us about crime. The exciting part for us as criminologists is that this wide focus allows us to explore lots of different areas of study. Because of this, criminology is known as a 'rendezvous' subject, in part because of the varying backgrounds of researchers working in this field. You may find that your lecturers and tutors have qualifications in a range of subjects, from anthropology to political science and everything in between. As well as the usual topics of crime, law, victims and punishment, criminology also considers environmental harm, thrill-seeking behaviours, art fraud and theft, and international crime. Criminologists study crime in its broadest sense to improve society, reduce crime and victimisation, and change policy and practice.

Knowledge link: This topic is also covered in Chapter 6.

Graduates of criminology courses go into a wide range of careers. Some are obvious and relate to prisons, policing and probation, but some are less obvious. A degree in criminology, with its focus on critical thinking, analysis and in-depth exploration of a wide range of issues, equips students for a whole range of careers. Graduates of criminology programmes may find themselves working in housing, drug and alcohol work, and with young people or vulnerable populations, or even the security services. You can find out more about working in the security services and a range of other careers in the 'Go Further' section at the end of this chapter It is never too early to think about what you want to do once you have graduated, and thinking about it at the start of your degree will enable you to make the right choices with regard to your option modules, dissertation topics, and other opportunities whilst you are studying.

Knowledge link: This topic is also covered in Chapter 33.

In summary, criminology is rarely, if ever, about examining crime scenes or interviewing offenders in their cells to glean knowledge to catch another offender. So, after finding out that we do not do any of the things the public might expect us to do, why should someone choose to become a criminologist? You will have your own reasons for entering this exciting subject area. It will benefit you, however, to understand your fellow students' possible motivations for studying criminology.

WHY BECOME A CRIMINOLOGIST?

Many students choose to undertake a degree in criminology because they are fascinated by crime; why it happens, how it is responded to, and how it is prevented. Some of those students may have personal experiences of crime as a victim, and have chosen criminology because they want to understand their experiences. They may have had a negative experience as a result of being a victim of crime, or they may want to appreciate why they were victimised and understand an offender's motivation for offending to prevent future victimisation. By studying an issue from an academic, rather than a personal, viewpoint, a person might be able to understand their experiences and move beyond them, preventing the victimisation from having an ongoing influence over their lives.

Other students may have offended in the past or have members of their family who have committed criminal offences. In both cases, you may find that your fellow students may refer to this in seminar discussions or make no mention of it. Sometimes, students who have a personal or family experience of victimisation or offending choose to study criminology because they want to improve the system they have experienced. A particular area which has gained recognition over the past decade or so is the area of 'convict criminology'. This area of study has been defined by McLaughlin and Muncie (2013: 79) as a branch of criminology 'started by convict and ex-convict academics who were dissatisfied with mainstream criminological considerations of crime, crime control and justice'. So 'convict criminologists' are those people who were once convicted of an offence, and are now seeking to reform the system and research the system that they experienced. They offer an important contribution to criminological knowledge from first-hand experiences, and remind us of the human cost of imprisonment and the wider criminal justice system.

However, other students may have never experienced either offending or victimisation. Their interest may come from seeing an event in the media, and becoming interested in why that event happened, or hearing about a particular case from friends and feeling that there has been some unfairness, either through a wrongful conviction (where an innocent person is convicted of a crime they did not commit) or through the perceived leniency of a sentence. In other cases, students will have covered some of the topics we study in a criminology degree at 'A' level, or in their BTEC course, and as a result decide to focus on that particular area because they enjoyed learning about it. Some students may have watched a lot of documentaries about crime and want to understand the issues in more detail. A sense of social justice may motivate some people and they may want to develop their skills in this area so they can be part of creating a more just and fair society. Finally, some students may have decided on criminology because it sounded interesting when they went to a subject talk at a university open day. Whatever the reason for studying criminology, it is important to remember that everyone has a reason for doing so, and they will have different views and ideas about crime, victimisation, and offending.

In summary, your seminar and tutorial groups will be made up of a wide range of people, some of whom may have been victims, offenders and others who have a wide range of experiences. There will be people from a variety of backgrounds too and your personal biography and skills will add to that mix, and you will bring those experiences into your discussions in seminars and tutorials. As you will see below, people have many different motivations for studying criminology, and no one person's experience is more valid or important than another's.

Student Voice

The View from an Undergraduate Student

I first became interested in criminology when we did the 'crime and deviance' module in my A-level sociology course. I didn't realise I could study it at university until I had been to an open day when I attended a subject talk. I became fascinated by those who committed offences and their justifications for their criminal behaviour. Then I looked into the different types of criminology courses available and spent some time deciding on whether I wanted to study sociology and criminology, or just criminology. My first year at university consisted of some ideas I had already looked at during my A level, such as functionalist and interpretivist theories of crime, but also new things such as how the criminal justice system works. Some of my friends who had studied law had covered the criminal justice system in their A levels but hadn't covered theories of crime. This was great, as it meant we could help each other with the bits we understood and explain the ideas to each other. (Laura, Undergraduate student, BA (Hons) Criminology)

Hopefully, you will have realised by now that criminology brings together people from a wide range of backgrounds and experiences. While you and your fellow students will have had different experiences until this point, there will be several things that will unite you as you go through your course: deadlines, core modules, and social events amongst many others. You will also spend time working together and developing transferable skills, and we are now going to spend some time thinking about the key skills of a criminologist.

KEY SKILLS OF A CRIMINOLOGIST

Reading

In any social science degree, reading is an integral element of being successful. It is the main way you will find out information and learn the core arguments that have been made about the key issues within criminology. You will be given a reading list for each module, and one of the best things you can do to ensure your success on your course is to keep up to date with the set reading. Doing so will help you understand the lectures more but will also help you contribute more meaningfully to the discussions in your seminar and tutorials.

Your first step is to find the readings, either by buying the textbook yourself or finding it in the library. Sometimes, you may have digitised readings which you might be able to access through your university's Virtual Learning Environment (VLE). It is worth spending some time exploring the VLE so you are confident you can find the key information relating to your course and modules when you need it. At first, you will likely find the readings challenging. Don't worry if you do not understand something when you first read it. You will probably come across unfamiliar words. At this point, highlight or note these in some way and carry on reading. Once you have finished the reading, go back to the words you noted and look them up in a dictionary; for some words, a criminological dictionary rather than a general dictionary will be more helpful. Reading takes practice, so the more you read, the more comfortable you will be with the process, and the more confident you will become.

Another aspect of reading is engaging in wider reading. Like any habit, the more you read, the easier you will find it, and your reading speed will increase. Wider reading can include other criminology-related books, but can also include news reports from reliable media sources, blogs by academics, and short articles by academics such as those available in *The Conversation*; even reading fiction books of whatever genre will help you develop your comprehension, reading and writing skills. Try to set aside the same time each week to do your reading. Find somewhere that is distraction-free and comfortable and have the necessary things to hand around you so that you do not have to break off to find something you need. Spend some time scanning the reading for the central points and overall focus, then read the text carefully and make notes relating to important points and arguments. Make sure you note the details (author, year, title, place of publication and publisher) of the reading. When making notes, avoid copying or highlighting large amounts of text as this will not aid your understanding. Instead, take notes in your own words and think about whether you agree with the argument you are reading. If you do jot down a direct quote, remember to write it exactly as it appears in the reading, and indicate it using speech marks, and note the full reference details including the page number/s. This will save you a lot of time later, when you are writing your essay. If you struggle to understand the reading, return to your lecture notes from that topic. If you are still confused, write down any questions you have and take them to your next seminar so that you can ask your fellow students or the seminar tutor.

Writing

Another key element of your course is writing. You will, of course, need to complete essays as part of your assessments, but if that is the only time you write, you will not spend enough time developing and improving your writing skills. Writing lecture notes is an important skill that you will need to develop, and it is not as easy as writing down everything your lecturer says. You need to be able to develop skills in noting down the key parts of the lecture and identifying the fundamental issues. A research study by Mueller and Oppenheimer (2014) found that taking notes by hand enhanced students' understanding and recall of the topics being studied more than typing notes on a laptop computer. Students who typed notes were more likely to write verbatim (words as spoken by the lecturer) notes. This meant that students typing notes processed information at a shallower level than those handwriting notes. There was also evidence of distraction, where students writing notes on a laptop would check emails or social media during the lecture and therefore not be able to recall facts as easily as those who wrote handwritten notes. Many universities provide the PowerPoint slides of the lecture, so this means you do not need to copy down what is on the slides. If possible, download the slides before the lecture, and then make notes on the printed versions of these slides as this will help you structure your notes. Taking selective notes, rather than trying to write down everything your lecturer says, will help you develop skills to be able to choose the most relevant and important information. Some universities also provide 'lecture capture' where the lectures are recorded and available for students to access, and it can be beneficial to revisit the lecture at a later date, particularly if there were points in it that you did not fully understand.

One of the essential skills of writing is editing. Never submit the first draft of an essay; it will likely contain spelling, grammar and structure errors as well as omissions or irrelevant content. Write your first draft, then leave it alone for a couple of days. When you come back to it, you will be able to find errors and confusing points which you had not noticed before, and you can correct these before you submit your work. Read through your work critically and ask whether it answers the essay question. If there are parts which do not, delete or rewrite these. At this point, check your references: are they formatted correctly? Are all the references contained in your essay listed alphabetically in the reference list? Have you used good quality academic references? It is worth remembering that sources such as Wikipedia or A-Level revision websites should never appear in a university-level essay. Instead, focus on the sources recommended in your module reading lists. Doing so means your essay will be based on quality academic arguments that have good evidence supporting them.

Analysis and Evaluation

The most important skills to develop during your undergraduate studies are those of analysis and **evaluation**. These are skills which students often find very difficult, but the reality is that you will often analyse and evaluate in day-to-day life, such as judging the most appropriate clothing or when to eat and exercise. While on the face of it, it may not seem like you are analysing things when you are choosing an outfit or how to structure your day, but you are exploring the different options, and then making a choice based on several factors, such as the appropriateness of your clothes for an event and so on. For example, you would not normally choose to wear swimming kit to go out in a snowstorm. You may also include other variables, such as the cost of an outfit and the amount of money you have available. Additional to this, your values will come into play, i.e. how much value you place on clothes and your appearance in certain contexts. The good news then is that you already have these skills of analysis and evaluation, and you will need to shift the focus from your everyday tasks to your academic work. So, instead of deciding what clothes to wear, you decide which sources are the most useful, and within them, which arguments are the most convincing, and, furthermore, you need to be able to justify why they are the most convincing. As mentioned earlier, you can help yourself in this regard by only using quality sources when researching and reading for your essay.

Pause for Thought

1. Which of the skills mentioned above do you think is your strongest?
2. Which is your weakest?

Student Voice

The View from a Postgraduate Student

I returned to study after ten years working in the public sector. I wanted a new challenge, and to be able to move into a sector working with young people at risk of being involved in crime. I decided to apply to my local university as I have a family and my children are all in school and I didn't want to move them. I was really nervous returning to university, especially about essay writing as I hadn't written a long piece of work in a long time. I soon discovered that there was loads of support for me, from essay writing workshops to individual meetings with my tutor. All my tutors were incredibly helpful, and I knew I could go to them with any problem I was having, and they would be able to help me sort it out. The hardest challenge was managing the amount of work I had while also working and bringing up my children. I was lucky that my family were supportive and gave me time to study. I found that the more time I spent reading, the more I understood the issues, and discussing them with my course mates helped me understand them even more. (Ghazala, Postgraduate student, MA Criminology)

SOURCES OF SUPPORT AND WORKING WITH OTHERS

The good thing about studying at university is that you are not on your own. While you have significantly more independence than at school or college, there is a wide range of academic and support staff who are there to support and guide you throughout your programme of study. These people have a wide range of skills, from academic knowledge in different subject areas to understanding student finance, housing, disability or mental health issues. Although all these people are brilliant, the one thing they cannot do is read minds. This means that you need to speak to people to ask them for support or guidance, and this is particularly important if you are experiencing something which may affect your ability to complete your assessments, as there are specific rules about assessments which can have a significant impact on your progression and achievement at university.

Spend some time making a list of the key people to contact in case of problems, e.g. your personal tutor, course leader/director of studies, course administrator, study support, disability advice and student finance team etc. This means you will have a ready-made list of contacts should you need any help or guidance. It is a good idea to get to know your personal (sometimes called guidance) tutor. They will be able to help you with your academic issues but will also know who else to speak to in order to help you with any other problems. Your personal tutor is also the individual who will write references for the jobs, volunteering, study abroad or exchange schemes you apply for. Getting to know you makes this job a lot easier, so make sure you meet regularly with your personal tutor. Your course leadership team, which may include named administrative team members, can also be a valuable source of help. They have an excellent understanding of university regulations and procedures, and like your personal tutor, will know the best people to contact if you are having any problems.

—————————— **Hear from the Expert** ——————————

Course Administrator's View

I'm often the first port of call for many students who have queries or concerns. Some are relatively simple and can be resolved with a simple email or phone call. Others need more time or support, and I often refer students to disability services or our counselling service as well as providing help myself. The key thing that students need to remember is that I can only help if they tell me what's wrong. Sometimes students are afraid to come and speak to us because they are worried about what might happen, but in every case, the situation has been made worse or more difficult because the student has delayed contacting us. If you're struggling, tell someone! (Michael, Course Administrator)

Another valuable support system is your fellow students. While you will not necessarily form close bonds with all the students on your course, or even in your seminar groups, developing friendships is a key part of the three or four years you will spend at university. Seminars will often require you to work in groups for at least part of the time, and this can be daunting as a new student, but try to remember that everyone is in the same situation as you. If you struggle in social situations, speak to your seminar tutor or lecturer as they will be able to help you identify strategies that will help, or will direct you to a group you can be a part of. Many courses will include some form of group activity, such as a presentation as part of the assessment, so you will need to prepare for this and work together to produce your work. Sometimes, groups do not work effectively for a variety of reasons, such as some group members not engaging or responding to contact. If this happens, then the best thing you can do is contact your tutor or module leader as soon as possible to try and resolve the problems you are having. The key thing to avoid is getting to the point of submitting the assessment, and then complaining that a group member has failed to pull their weight as it will be too late to resolve the problems. Early communication (as mentioned earlier) is always the best course of action with any problem.

The other bonus of working with your student colleagues is the opportunity to study together. Sitting together and working out the best way to approach a problem can help you develop your understanding of an issue and increase your confidence and group work skills. While you should never share your written work with anyone else, working and discussing ideas with other students is very useful, and importantly, helps you develop work-related skills such as collaborative working and seeing different viewpoints.

In conjunction with group work, your own independent engagement and preparation are hugely important. Completing the set preparation work for your seminars and tutorials will allow you to construct a base of knowledge and understanding that the group work in your classes can build on. The more you engage with your studies, the better you will perform. Research undertaken by Lukkarinen, Koivukangas and Seppälä (2016) found that attendance is significantly related to performance in assessments. Obviously, attendance is not the only issue; if you attend, but do not engage, then this will potentially affect not only your overall assessment grades but also your happiness overall, as if you do not engage with your student colleagues and staff, you may well not enjoy your course as much and not feel as invested in your education. This means you need to prepare for your seminars through reading, note-making and thinking, and then continue to engage in the seminars and lectures and follow up on your classwork afterwards, by completing further reading or meeting with other students or your lecturers to discuss the issues. You will be helped in this area by reading the module handbooks provided, which will indicate the readings you need to complete and the reading lists, which will help you find the sources.

CHALLENGES OF BEING A CRIMINOLOGIST

Unsurprisingly, criminology discusses topics which some people might find difficult for several reasons. If you have been a victim of crime in the past, then discussing and reading about that crime or type of offence may be hard. If this applies to you, then seek support from your course tutors and the university wellbeing support (such as counselling). Your experiences can bring valuable insight into your academic study, but it should not mean you feel upset while studying. You could also seek help from victim charities such as Victim Support. In any event, you must seek help and support, which will allow you to continue your studies to the best of your ability. Whether you have been a victim of crime, or are struggling with other issues, all universities offer some form of personal support for students. The level of support will depend on your individual needs but do make use of these services if you need them. They are usually provided free of charge to all students and can help students at very difficult times in their lives. Also, remember to register with a medical practice if you have moved away from home. When 'Freshers' Flu' eventually hits, you will be glad that you have already registered with a GP.

While it is important that you commit to your degree fully, and engage as much as possible, there should always be some time that you have which does not involve working. This is particularly important if you are also working a part-time job as well as studying, and/or have caring responsibilities. Take some time to watch television (not a crime drama!), read a fiction book, go for a walk, play a sport, or anything else that you enjoy doing. Taking some regular time out for yourself will help you focus more effectively when you are working and ensure that you do not become unwell. To do this, you will need to ensure you prioritise your workload and manage your time effectively. Your university will offer guidance on this, but whatever guidance there is, you will need to adapt it to suit your personal circumstances. Some of your commitments may require specific times (such as childcare, work shifts, lectures and seminars). Others are more flexible (such as reading). The challenge for you will be to find out what works best for you and then to stick to your plan. It is all too easy to think you will do 'extra' another day, and then something unexpected happens (illness, or transport delays, for example) that prevents you from doing so. Always plan in extra time to allow for these sorts of events so that you do not become anxious or stressed because you have lost time.

If you do get ill, and you think it is going to affect your ability to devote time to your studies and complete your assessments, you must speak to your tutors or your student support team as soon as possible. You may be able to apply for an extension or extenuating/mitigating circumstances which would give you more time to complete your assessments. Importantly, most universities operate what is known as a 'fit to sit' policy, which means that if you submit work, or attend an exam, you are declaring that you are well enough to complete the work to the best of your abilities. Once you submit a piece of work, you cannot usually ask for your health/situation to be considered when marking that piece of work. So, if you are in any doubt about your ability to complete your assessments, then you must contact someone to discuss this as soon as possible.

You would likely need to provide some evidence for any extension or extenuating/mitigating circumstance, so do remember to get a doctor's note or confirmation from an official person giving the details of the issues that you have experienced. It is worth remembering that tutors and support staff help students with a range of issues on an almost daily basis, so do not be worried or embarrassed about seeking help. If you are worried about confidentiality, ask the person you are talking to about confidentiality and what happens to the information you disclose. Usually, the information relating to extensions and extenuating/mitigating circumstances is only disclosed to the people who need to know. Occasionally, you may be asked if you would like a referral to a specific support service, but this would generally be your decision.

Sometimes, within the first few weeks of the course, students realise that they have made the wrong degree choice. If you are concerned about this, get in touch with your course leader or personal tutor in the first instance. There are many reasons why someone begins to feel they have made the wrong choice, and talking to someone will help you think about what the issues are. You must speak to someone quickly as if you are thinking about changing course, as there are often time limitations in place that could affect your ability to transfer onto a different programme of study.

CHAPTER SUMMARY

Being a student of criminology is exciting, rewarding, challenging, and occasionally emotional, for many different reasons. This chapter has explored the motivations for and challenges of studying criminology in some depth, and highlighted the potential pitfalls you need to avoid and how you can succeed. The key things to remember are to:

- Engage fully with your course.
- Think about your career plans early.
- Talk to someone if you are struggling with anything.

You are at the start of an exciting journey. Like any journey, enjoy the sights along the way, take regular breaks, eat well, but do not lose sight of your overall goal – a good degree.

Review Questions

1. What are my motivations for studying criminology?
2. What are my strengths and weaknesses when it comes to studying?
3. Where do I see myself in five years' time?

GO FURTHER

Books

1. The *Sage Dictionary of Criminology* is a book that no criminology student can go without. It gives definitions of all the central concepts in criminology, and provides a short list of further readings for each topic.

   McLaughlin, E. and Muncie, J. (2013) *The Sage Dictionary of Criminology* (3rd edition). London: Sage.

2. Emily Finch and Stefan Fafinski's book on criminology skills provides students with guidance on study skills throughout their degree. This book contains information about writing essays, researching information, and a whole range of other important skills. It will help you throughout your degree.

   Finch, E. and Fafinski, S. (2019) *Criminology Skills* (3rd edition). Oxford: Oxford University Press.

3. James Treadwell's introductory book on criminology is clear and concise, and helps students begin their studies in criminology. It offers students advice on how to get the most out of their studies.

    Treadwell, J. (2013) *Criminology: The Essentials*. London: Sage.

Journal Articles

1. Anna Lukkarinen and colleagues' article was mentioned in this chapter, and it discusses the relationship between students attending class, and their performance in assessments.

    Lukkarinen, A., Koivukangas, P. and Seppälä, T. (2016) Relationship between class attendance and student performance. In J. Domenech, M. C. VincentVela, R. PenaOrtiz, E. DeLaPoza & D. Blazquez (eds), 2nd International Conference On Higher Education Advances. *Procedia Social and Behavioral Sciences*, vol. 228, Elsevier Science. pp. 341–347. International Conference on Higher Education Advances, Valencia, Spain, 21–23 June 2016.

2. Mueller and Oppenheimer's journal article discusses the advantages of taking notes by hand rather than on a laptop, and the positive impact taking notes by hand has on recall and retention of information.

    Mueller, P. A. and Oppenheimer, D. M. (2014) The pen is mightier than the keyboard: advantages of longhand over laptop note taking. *Psychological Science*, 25(6): 1159–1168.

3. Catherine Picton's article discusses how students perceive success in the first year of their degree.

    Picton, C., Kahu, E.R. and Nelson, K. (2018) 'Hardworking, determined and happy': first-year students' understanding and experience of success. *Higher Education Research & Development*, 37(6): 1260–1273.

Useful Websites

1. The MI5 Graduate Programme is one of many graduate programmes that someone with a degree in criminology may consider applying to: https://www.mi5.gov.uk/careers/opportunities/graduate-development-programmes
2. The Conversation is an independent source of news and views, sourced from the academic and research community and delivered direct to the public: http://theconversation.com/
3. Learning on Screen (also known as 'Box of Broadcasts') is a website which allows access to over two million radio and television broadcasts. Its academically focused system allows members of subscribing educational institutions to record programmes from many free-to-air channels, and view recordings from their extensive archive. If your institution is a subscribing member, you simply need to log in using your usual login details: https://learningonscreen.ac.uk/ondemand

REFERENCES

Lukkarinen, A., Koivukangas, P. and Seppälä, T. (2016) Relationship between class attendance and student performance; Procedia. *Social and Behavioural Sciences*, vol. 228: 341–347.

McLaughlin, E. and Muncie, J. (2013) *The Sage Dictionary of Criminology* (3rd edition). London, Sage

Mueller, P. A. and Oppenheimer, D. M. (2014) The pen is mightier than the keyboard: advantages of longhand over laptop note taking. *Psychological Science*, 25(6): 1159–1168.

West Yorkshire Police (2019) Crime Scene Investigator Vacancy. Available at: https://westyorkshirepolice.tal.net/vx/mobile-0/appcentre-External/brand-0/candidate/so/pm/6/pl/1/opp/765-RS264-Crime-Scene-Investigator-External/en-GB (accessed 22/07/19).

History and Crime

Eloise Moss

2

Learning Objectives

By the end of this chapter you will:

- Be able to critically examine how definitions of crime and criminal have changed over time.
- Understand different methodological approaches to the study of crime in the past, including using quantitative and qualitative forms of data, and intellectual trends such as 'social history' and 'cultural history' approaches.
- Be able to analyse how histories of policing and regulation are connected to histories of crime.
- Be able to assess the merits of a 'case study' approach, exploring the nature of 'criminal celebrity' in the past through the lens of Jack the Ripper.

Framing Questions

1. In what ways do historians analyse crimes and criminal behaviours? How far do their approaches differ from those used by criminologists?
2. Can historians and criminologists benefit from greater collaborative research into past instances of crime and its investigation?
3. Is it more useful to look for patterns of criminal behaviour, or to assess on a case-by-case basis?

INTRODUCTION

'We of the WSPU [Women's Social and Political Union] were women, fighting in a woman's war. Lord Coleridge, therefore, saw in us only reckless and criminal defiers of law.' Emmeline Pankhurst, *My Own Story* (1914), p. 248

The issue of what constitutes a crime, and which individuals and groups are categorised as criminal, varies dramatically over time, place, and space. The above reflections of suffragette leader Emmeline Pankhurst encapsulate this maxim. Writing at the outbreak of the First World War, having been imprisoned, force-fed, and released multiple times for acts of 'militant' suffragism for which she and her followers were treated as criminals rather than political protesters, Pankhurst's words were written just four years before the Representation of the People Act 1918 gave women over the age of 30 the right to vote. This legal shift ultimately rendered her 'criminality' part of a more acceptable history of civil rights agitation, demonstrating how malleable a concept crime can be. In order to delve deeply into the history of crime, therefore, it is worth becoming familiar with the social, cultural, political, and economic landscape of a particular place and time, as well as thinking about crime well beyond the confines of the criminal justice system.

Knowledge link: This topic is also covered in Chapter 4.

This chapter aims to provide an overview of the key themes and approaches used by historians to understand the role of crime in shaping society in the past, as well as the ways in which historians have studied crime and the criminal justice system. Historians and criminologists often work collaboratively on projects, seeking to understand patterns of crime in both past and present, and we can learn a lot by comparing each discipline's methods and approaches. In this chapter, we will first look at how the study of past crimes is useful to understand the history of social change. Second, we will examine how far historians and criminologists should be concerned with perceptions of crime in popular and official accounts, versus the accumulation of statistical 'data' (the collation of which has been subject to changing technological systems as well as the agendas of those charged with gathering such figures).

Finally, we will discuss whether it is possible for scholars to identify long-term patterns of behaviour in historical studies that shed light on criminality today. This chapter offers an introductory outline to these approaches, focusing particularly on how crime history has been studied in modern Britain (drawing on my own research expertise in histories of burglary). It also touches on the study of crime and 'deviance' in medieval and early modern periods, as well as broader global contexts. The chapter explores how 'crime' and the 'criminal' have never been fixed concepts, but have altered drastically according to time, space, and place. It discusses how you must remain alert to the changing relationship between crime, penal systems, culture, politics, and society when examining the nature and incidence of crime historically, foregrounding the significance of concepts of gender, race, and class in comprehending who was and is stigmatised as 'deviant.'

MAPPING THE TERRAIN

Pause for Thought

Why do scholars look at the history of crime in different ways?

What is the history of crime? Is it the study of patterns in criminal behaviour, or what environmental conditions tend to lead to particular types of crime (such as poverty and other forms of inequality)?

Does the history of crime simply serve as a lens onto broader subjects, giving us a snapshot of the dominant fears and anxieties of a past society? Scholars in the disciplines of history and criminology who research this subject tend to fall into three categories: 1) historians of a particular place and/or period; 2) historians of crime; 3) historical criminologists. The aims and approaches of these three groups are summarised below, although be aware that they do frequently overlap! Understanding that scholars may identify more strongly with a specific approach is important, however, because the perceived distance between historians and criminologists' intellectual agendas and methodologies has sometimes hampered constructive intellectual exchange between the disciplines (Godfrey et al., 2008: 6–10). This may stem from history's reputation as an 'Arts' discipline whereas criminology aligns more closely with the social sciences. Yet by recognising that *all* crimes have distinctive historical features, whether ancient or modern, both sets of scholars can bypass 'the need to choose between *either* continuity *or* change in historical interpretation', instead simply highlighting key points of interconnection to learn from (Churchill et al., 2017: 525).

1. *Historians of a particular period and/or place* (such as modern Britain, like myself) tend to use crime, and/or perceptions of crime, as a lens through which to examine changing social, cultural, political, and economic conditions in that context (see examples on the **Go Further** reading list at the end of this chapter. To give an example, my own research explores how iconic burglars such as Charles Peace (d. 1878) and fictional 'gentleman' burglar A. J. Raffles (created by E. W. Hornung in 1898) gained purchase in popular culture as embodiments of a glamorous, sexy 'criminal mastermind' archetype that, at particular historical moments, served to articulate broader antagonisms towards inequalities of class and wealth, and changing idealisations of working- and upper-middle-class masculinity in modern Britain (Moss, 2019). This takes a **cultural history** approach to understanding the impact that *perceptions* of crime in the past had in shaping media and legal responses to those tried for burglary, whilst identifying, through a **social history** lens, that the heroisation of burglars and their crimes tended to take place during periods of economic depression, hence giving a sense of the broader structural factors accounting for popular interest in crime during certain periods.

2. *Historians of crime* seek to understand the nature and recurrence of particular criminal behaviours in the past, the types of offenders most likely to commit them, and the environments in which certain crimes proliferated (see for example works by Meier, 2011, and Shore, 1999). This remit bears slightly closer relation to the aims of historical criminologists, which we shall look at next, though the primary concern of historians of crime remains the issue of understanding past crimes in historically specific ways (**historicising**).

3. *Historical criminologists* (i.e. criminologists who conduct research into crime in the past) endeavour to look at former instances of criminal activity and systems of regulation explicitly to give context to, or problem-solve, crimes in the present. This approach is somewhat problematic, often leading to rather simplistic analyses wherein past systems of crime, regulation, and punishment are used either to provide arbitrary starting-points for explaining how crime has evolved today, or to act as stark points of contrast to the present (highlighted by Lawrence, 2015, cited in Churchill et al., 2017: 524). This tends to lead to a 'flattening' of history whereby the specific historical conditions in which crimes were defined as such by law, criminals' motives, and modus operandi, as well as the complexities of delivering 'justice', are deemed worthy of analysis only in relation to modern trends.

The sections that follow showcase a range of analytical approaches and methodologies for 'doing' the history of crime using different sources, themes, and topics that aims to be of practical and intellectual use to students of both history and criminology. It is worth noting that if students wish to gain a further understanding of the development, and interaction, between the two disciplines since the nineteenth century (charting key methodological and ideological distinctions), an excellent overview is provided by Barry Godfrey et al. in the Sage textbook *History and Crime* (2008: 5–24), on the **Go Further** reading list at the end of this chapter.

Pause for Thought

What do you view as the strengths and weaknesses of the three approaches outlined above?

DEFINING 'CRIME' AND 'CRIMINAL'

The criteria for criminality or 'deviancy' exist, historically and today, in a constant state of flux (Emsley, 2007: 1–2). Thinking historically, those regarded as 'criminal' may either have broken the law, or transgressed prevailing religious doctrine, or have been viewed as having contravened any number of tacit, often unwritten social codes and expectations that one must understand sufficiently to explain why they were ostracised or even executed. For these reasons, a broader intellectual affinity with time and place is usually required to get to grips with why someone was 'criminalised' in a certain era of the past. Equally, though we may now recognise that a person was treated as a 'criminal', there are no guarantees that the specific legal term we recognise today was applied at the time (or if it was, in the same way we use it now), or even that the 'perpetrator' and their actions will feature in the *legal* record (though they may well appear elsewhere). Pinpointing the factors that have designated someone 'criminal' at a particular historical moment, requires a sensitive decryption of changing legislation, political imperatives, cultural beliefs and practices, gender, class, and racial stereotypes, social stigmas, economic conditions, space and geography, modes of policing, and concepts of 'justice'.

Knowledge link: This topic is also covered in Chapter 22.

One cannot always assume that the power to determine these factors has rested with the state (i.e. the government).

Let us analyse the partial decriminalisation of homosexuality in 1967 as an example. The Sexual Offences Act of 1967 legalised homosexual acts between two consenting men over the age of twenty-one in 'private' spaces (not including cubicles in public lavatories). Although this legislation was a landmark moment in the history of LGBTQ+ civil rights, historians have emphasised that it did not seek to eradicate the alignment of homosexuality with 'deviance', since public displays of affection between men remained illegal. Instead, the new law sought to constrain the visibility of homosexuality and protect the interests of so-called 'respectable' middle- and upper-class homosexuals, who were frequently subject to blackmail over their relationships and had the resources (in terms of property and access to other private space) to conduct their relationships away from public view (McLaren, 2002). The age of consent for homosexuals was five years older than that for heterosexuals (for whom the age of consent was sixteen), a clause that recalled Victorian fears over young men being 'corrupted' into homosexuality by predatory older men — most famously alluded to during the trial of Oscar Wilde for engaging in sexual acts with Lord Alfred Douglas, sixteen years his junior, in 1895. The differential age of consent reflects enduring ideas of homosexuality as a form of disease or learned behaviours rather than a natural sexual identity, even by the late 1960s. Whether someone was convicted of 'indecency' therefore depended more on *where* they had sex, and *with whom*, than the act of having sex itself.

Such nuances seem bewildering to us today. However, we can better understand (though not endorse) these distinctions if we reflect on the broader context of gender relations and the politics of the time. The 1960s witnessed the emergence of Second Wave Feminism, in which women increasingly campaigned for equal opportunities and rejected marriage and motherhood as offering their primary fulfilment and social status. Commensurately, it was no longer assured that men were to retain the forms of social, political, and economic power they had enjoyed to date, entwined with which were concepts of virility (reproduction) and other 'masculine' qualities viewed by socially-conservative commentators as incompatible with homosexual intimacy (Houlbrook, 2005). The post-war decades have also been characterised as a period of crisis for Christian religious observance in Britain, causing a reaction against forms of sexual behaviour deemed 'sinful' by the major religious denominations (again, to the detriment of those campaigning for the full decriminalisation of homosexuality). These are just some of the wider pressure-points that account for the partial nature of decriminalisation in 1967 ('history from below'), which we cannot identify if we exclusively examine the legislation or political discourse surrounding it ('history from above').

Hear from the Expert

How far did ordinary people have the power to change the law? The power (or 'agency') of ordinary people within the criminal justice system is sometimes difficult to uncover in the archive, since surviving texts were mainly produced by officials (for example, trial transcripts). However, Anindita Ghosh's fantastic book *Claiming the City: Protest, Crime, and Scandals in Colonial Calcutta, c. 1860-1920*, shows how even citizens oppressed under colonial regimes were sometimes able to change the way the criminal justice system worked. For example, Ghosh examines the way police officers and courts in late-nineteenth and early-twentieth century India responded with leniency towards thieves when urged to do so by their victims, recognising factors such as poverty or family honour in their treatment of offenders, and delivering sentences based on a very generous interpretation of the law (Ghosh, 2016: 235-236).

Ghosh also observes how popular crime writing by Calcutta's 'celebrity' detectives, such as Priyanath Mukhopadhyay, 'borrowed' from genres such as gothic horror and detective fiction, cultivating support for law and order through informal and entertaining stories rather than direct police action (Ghosh, 2016: 227-235). Such evidence challenges scholars to look beyond the structures of officialdom and embrace the way ideas about crime and policing circulated through popular culture. This approach, known as **poststructuralism**, encourages historians to 'reveal unquestioned assumptions and inconsistencies' particularly surrounding who holds agency and authority in political systems.

'Criminalisation' also takes the form of less formal or tangible features of social interaction, such as shame and stigma — including the act of 'shaming' those viewed as having transgressed acceptable behaviour. Though not encoded in law, these behaviours still need to be understood within the framework of histories of crime and criminal justice, as mechanisms by which societies create order and regulate others' behaviour and freedoms. The power of shame has been traced to early Judeo-Christian culture, specifically when directed at controlling women's sexuality and reproductive behaviour (Nash and Kilday, 2010: 7). This was extended during the medieval and early modern periods, when community-based punishment rituals known as 'charivari' or 'rough music' (in Britain) were observed across Europe and North America (Nash and Kilday, 2010: 7-10, 27). Charivari could be directed towards those whose marriage was viewed as transgressive, especially due to age disparity between the couple, or for actions we still recognise as 'criminal' such as theft and domestic violence (Zemon Davis, 1971; Thompson, 1972, 1992). Involving physical humiliation, taunts, the playing of loud music and other rituals designed to 'shame' the transgressor(s), charivari could be either a brutal or festive means of inculcating order at a local level.

The entwinement of prevailing religious doctrines, particularly Puritanism, with the identification and punishment of 'criminals' is perhaps best embodied in early modern witchcraft 'trials.'

Although, in sheer terms of historical distance, criminologists and historians of crime may rarely regard these phenomena as part of the lineage of the criminal justice system we recognise today, recent scholarship emphasises how accusers were often driven by a genuine belief in the supernatural as well as the desire to implicate enemies they felt 'wronged' by, in a highly complex set of drivers that legitimised mass executions over the centuries (Laskaris, 2019). Trials for 'modern' witchcraft were recorded in France during the early twentieth century (Pooley in Bell, 2019, forthcoming), whilst the force of 'shame' as a dimension of criminalising acts including homosexuality and abortion, or giving rise to libel, blackmail, and vigilantism, has remained a feature of our social worlds (McLaren, 2002; Pratten and Sen, 2008; Cohen, 2013; Nash and Kilday, 2017).

The meanings of 'shame', like the emotion itself, must be understood through careful historically- and geographically–contextualised analysis. What feels 'embarrassing' to one person at a particular place and time may be radically different from another, with the desire to avoid these situations serving as an important adjunct of the legal system. In this respect, deconstructing histories of crime, punishment, and victimhood among past societies requires students and scholars to embrace the field of the history of emotions, an important sub-discipline that is distinct from the modern discipline of psychology (Eustace et al., 2012: 1467–1511). Such theoretically informed work especially resonates when the crime being examined is psychological and/or sexual in nature. Domestic violence/abuse and rape have historically been underreported crimes, or in fact, disputed as crimes at all (for example, marital rape was only made a crime in law in England and Wales following the House of Lords ruling on the case of *R v R*, in 1991). At times, the only evidence we have for the occurrence and legacy of these crimes is in personal accounts of trauma, sometimes using coded or metaphorical language, since sexual knowledge itself has historically been constrained along lines of age, gender, class, and race (D'Cruze, 1998; Jackson, 2000; Bourke, 2007; Bingham et al., 2016). Official accounts are not always 'factual' accounts.

Likewise, penalties for these forms of assault have not always been delivered through the courts, where victims (predominantly women) have found themselves under hostile forms of scrutiny regarding their sexual histories, discouraging recourse to legal action. Instead, perpetrators have at times been contained through social ostracism, stigma, and loss of employment. For example, during the 1880s strikes occurred at cotton factories and mills throughout the North West of England after workers objected to the sexual exploitation of women spinners by foremen and employers (although the strikes were also partly motivated by male workers' desire to diminish competition for jobs by having those women removed on nominally 'moral' grounds) (Lambertz, 1985).

Pause for Thought

Has the criminal justice system always been the main system for creating law and order?

Case Study 2.1

Defining Burglary

In this example we are going to think in more detail about the way ideas about crime and criminals have been communicated among ordinary people. Consider the following extract:

'On Monday morning a further sensational discovery came to light. Behind a portière in Mr Davenheim's study stands a safe, and that safe had been broken into and rifled. The windows were fastened securely on the inside, which seems to put an ordinary burglary out of court, unless, of course, an accomplice within the house fastened them again afterwards. On the other hand, Sunday having intervened, and the household being in a state of chaos, it is likely that the burglary was committed on the Saturday, and remained undetected until Monday.' "Précisément," said Poirot dryly'. Agatha Christie, 'The Disappearance of Mr. Davenheim', *The Sketch* (28 March 1923)

Until the Theft Act 1968 collapsed the daytime crime of 'housebreaking' into the same category as burglary, the crime of burglary was defined in law as occurring only during the 'night-time' hours of nine p.m. until six a.m., and applied to thefts from a residential property ('dwelling house') in which some form of 'breaking' in or out had taken place. Burglary was deemed among the most serious forms of larceny as a result, incurring a maximum sentence of life imprisonment to recognise that victims may have been asleep, unawares, in proximity to the nocturnal criminal who might commit other forms of violence, including rape. Yet how do we assess whether this narrow legal definition was widely understood, or had an impact on broader social attitudes towards the crime? Were these criteria arbitrary, or did they reflect a popular consensus?

Read the extract above, from the short story 'The Disappearance of Mr. Davenheim' written by the hugely popular crime fiction author Agatha Christie in 1923. Detective Hercule Poirot is informed of a 'burglary' at the home of wealthy London banker Mr. Davenheim by Inspector Japp of the Metropolitan Police. The conversation carefully reflects on whether the theft meets the legal conditions to be termed a burglary, debating when it occurred, whether there was a 'break-ing', etc. This indicates the transmission of definitions of crime through middlebrow fiction of the era, since *The Sketch* was a relatively expensive magazine featuring fashion, Society news, short stories, and political features directed at a middle- and upper-class readership. Yet the story also affords scholars greater texture surrounding contemporary perceptions of the crime, performing what historian Shani D'Cruze has called 'the subjective appropriation of fiction into individual and shared cultural imaginaries', particularly associated with the genre of detective fiction (D'Cruze, 2004: 257). Japp's speculation over the possibility that the burglary had been effected with the assistance of a member of the household reflects the prevailing association between theft and servants. This was part of a broader criminalisation of the working classes that endured within social surveys and criminological discourse into the twentieth century (Davie, 2003; D'Cruze and Jackson, 2009: 36). Stereotypes of working-class criminality reflected enduring inequalities of wealth and access to education, the slow extension of political representation (after the First World War, the Representation of the People Act 1918 finally enfranchised all men over the age of twenty-one, and women over the age of thirty who met a property qualification or other cri-teria across the United Kingdom), and the control of the criminal justice system by upper-middle and upper-class white men. Hence a strong grounding in the specific historical and geographical context is vital to understanding which groups were imagined as criminal and disproportionately targeted as offenders in the past.

In this section, we have considered how the definitions and meanings of crime change over time. We have also analysed how ideas about crime circulate not only through criminal trials, but also through other forms of media (such as newspapers, fiction, and film).

Finally, we have identified that the regulation of certain behaviours deemed 'deviant', or the meting out of 'justice', has not always been delivered through legal institutions, but historically

Knowledge link: This topic is also covered in Chapter 5.

also took on less tangible forms of social ostracism such as stigma and shame. What this means for criminologists is that to understand what were regarded as 'crimes' in the past, you must develop a strong familiarity with the broader social, cultural, political and economic context, looking beyond the more obvious and familiar archive of the legal record. We will develop this point in the next section, when we reflect on how far popular concerns about crime and policing have correlated with statistical rates of criminal activity.

Pause for Thought

If you were to start writing an essay on the history of crime, what types of historical sources would you use?

'Lies, damned lies, and statistics'? A Social and Cultural History Perspective

We tend to regard the nineteenth century as an exciting new period in policing history when the rise of forensic science, fingerprinting, and photography laid the groundwork for the kinds of policing we associate with the modern world (Shpayer Makov, 2011). This era has been represented as one in which the fictional detective did battle with the master criminal. Indeed, Victorian England was a society that seemed almost saturated by narratives about crime. The first detective fiction was created in this era by authors Edgar Allan Poe, Wilkie Collins, and Sir Arthur Conan Doyle, introducing readers to the idea of the detective-as-hero. This new genre of fiction became even more popular after the murder and mutilation of five prostitutes in the East End of London during the autumn of 1888 by the first (reported) serial killer, Jack the Ripper, whose ultimate escape from capture seemed to encapsulate people's worst fears about a new breed of urban criminal (Walkowitz, 1992; Warwick and Willis, 2007). Fears about the criminality associated with the urban poor were raised again by Charles Booth, who described the 'lowest' class of the poor as 'semi-criminal' in his influential survey *Life and Labour of the People of London* in 1902.

However, this period is also characterised by historians such as V. A. C. Gatrell and Martin Wiener as witnessing the decline of theft and violence until 1914. Statistically, recorded crimes in England and Wales across the nineteenth- and early-twentieth century demonstrate a gradual *decrease* in the more 'serious' forms of crime. This is the case even when we allow for the so-called 'dark' figure of unrecorded crimes, and the fact that 'petty' crimes such as causing a public nuisance, drunkenness etc. increased (Gatrell, 1980; Wiener, 2004). So how do we reconcile the growing popular and often political focus on crime with its statistical decline? During the late 1990s and early 2000s, the historians Howard Taylor and Robert M. Morris renewed scholarly interest in the way criminal statistics were compiled and used prior to the First World War (after which crisis the long-term upward trend in recorded crime for the twentieth century was established). Taylor argued that crime statistics were used by successive governments primarily to persuade the public of declining rates of crime (Taylor, 1998).

Morris (2001) disputed Taylor's interpretation of the data, drawing attention to Sir Charles Edward Troup's preface to the 1893 edition of *Criminal Statistics for England and Wales* compiled by the Home Office:

The figures showing the numbers of crimes and consequently the proportions must be taken with a great deal of caution. The returns of the numbers of crimes committed depend to a considerable extent on the discretion of police; they are not certain and definite figures in the same way as the numbers of prosecutions and convictions are certain and definite. (Troup cited in Morris, 2001: 115)

Troup was a senior administrator at the Home Office who undertook a reform of how statistics were collated and analysed between 1893 and 1904, so that 'under his influence the judicial statistics changed from being the worst in Europe to among the best' (Bartrip, 2004). This example shows us that both the substance and silences of criminal statistics have, historically, been informed by the prejudices and preoccupations of police, lawyers, magistrates, politicians, and other officials. This is not to suggest that such data is therefore useless or 'biased' (a term I tend to ban amongst my own students). It is simply to recognise that statistics are 'technologies' of the state, a 'political arithmetic' that have been gathered, organised, and communicated in a way designed to sustain or service particular agendas (Poovey, 1995: 83, 115).

Knowledge link: This topic is also covered in Chapter 4.

Case Study 2.2

Burglary Cases

Perceptions of the incidence and danger posed by certain criminals may not, therefore, map squarely onto statistical data for a given period. Burglary again affords a useful example. During the period 1893 to 1938, burglary rose from 1,445 cases in 1893 to just 1,515 cases in 1938 (Moss, 2019: 25). This was a far smaller incidence of crimes than the number of 'housebreakings' (theft from a house during the daytime), or 'shopbreakings' (theft from a shop), cases of which numbered in the tens of thousands annually. Despite this, the burglary insurance and burglar alarm industry enjoyed huge commercial success in Britain from the 1880s, attesting to popular fear and fascination with burglary as a more dangerous and sinister form of night-time crime. Popular fears about burglary, as opposed to other types of theft, could also be seen in the numerous novels, plays, and films about 'cat' burglars created in this era and beyond (Moss, 2019).

In this section, we have considered how crime statistics have not always reflected popular concerns about criminal activity. We have also introduced the idea that statistics are shaped by the historical conditions in which they were created (including political agendas), so do not necessarily offer a 'factual' window onto crime in the past. In the next section, we will move to explore how historians analyse the changing character of policing and regulation.

HISTORIES OF POLICING AND REGULATION

Pause for Thought

What can the history of policing tell us about the relationship between citizen and state?

In Britain, London is regarded by historians as especially important to the history of policing. Timeline:

Knowledge link: This topic is also covered in Chapter 24.

1829: Sir Robert Peel, Home Secretary, creates the Metropolitan Police in response to the rapid expansion of London (both in terms of population and physical geography) during the late eighteenth and nineteenth century. Peel formed the Metropolitan Police to create a 'professional' state-controlled body of law-enforcers, the ethos of which was that it should be answerable to the public: policing by consent.

1842: Beyond the work of uniformed and highly visible police constables, a detective branch was introduced to the Metropolitan Police, replicated shortly thereafter within the City of London Police and provincial forces (Shpayer-Makov, 2011: 2). However, as historian Haia Shpayer-Makov asserts, detectives were not hugely popular, often being associated with spying.

1877: Four high-ranking Scotland Yard detectives were exposed as complicit in a series of frauds, forgeries, and of accepting bribes, in return for which they had warned perpetrators of impending police action against them (Shpayer-Makov, 2011: 38).

1878: The fall-out from this investigation led to the dissolution of the Detective Branch and the formation of the Criminal Investigation Department (CID) under direct command of Howard Vincent, who reported to the Home Secretary.

1880s: This did not mark the end of police woes however, as during the 1880s a number of bombs set off in London by the Fenians (an Irish Nationalist movement) included, in 1883, bombings of the London underground, and in 1884, more embarrassingly, a bomb set off directly beneath the CID itself at Scotland Yard (Porter, 1987: 35–50).

1888: The failure of police to apprehend Jack the Ripper marked yet another passage in a series of incidents that strained police–public relations, drawing attention to its investigative limitations and officers' inability to generate support among the impoverished citizens of Whitechapel in East London (Haggard, 2007).

Even when looking exclusively at the nineteenth century, therefore, we can comprehend that the extent to which police were viewed as protecting, or interfering with, civil liberties has been highly contested at particular moments and among certain groups and individuals. These tensions have arisen in part through the shifting constitution of 'the social', i.e. who has been included and excluded from the ranks of citizenship over time and space. As historian David Churchill has argued, scholars must be wary of succumbing to the idea of the 'state monopolisation thesis' or 'policed society', whereby it has been assumed that the nineteenth century witnessed the state assuming total control of the criminal justice system (Churchill, 2014). Other forms of policing co-existed with formal systems, for example, civilian apprehensions, the use of private detectives, and enduring cultures of social 'shaming', as well as the increasing influence of insurance and commercial security industries on the investigation of crimes (Churchill, 2014: 143–145). Coupled with these factors, public confidence in police efficiency and integrity needs historicising, being frequently impacted by successive corruption scandals and well-publicised failures.

Histories of policing and regulation also require scholars to take an **intersectional** approach (considering factors such as class, race, and gender combined). In the West, police officers have been a predominantly white, male body of law enforcers since their inception. In the United Kingdom, women police officers were only formally introduced in 1915. Throughout the twentieth century their responsibilities were heavily gendered towards 'soft' forms of welfare-oriented work, including 'the prevention and detection of child abuse, neglect and the "policing of families" … the befriending and referral of girls who were deemed "vulnerable" or in "moral danger" was a significant aspect of their work'

(Jackson, 2006: 1–2). The masculinisation of law enforcement historically, and the way it has been enmeshed within broader gender politics and cultures of authority premised on sexism, racism, and homophobia, are important dynamics to consider for any study of policing and regulation in the past.

─────────────── Pause for Thought ───────────────

Examining the changing nature and ideology of policing therefore offers another good place to start for analysing the conceptualisation and treatment of crime historically. Think about the following:

1. Systems of policing and regulation have developed at a local, regional, national, and transnational level.
2. Particular attention should be paid to the relationship between empire and the evolution of policing strategies and technologies, often (like the fingerprinting technique developed by Francis Galton in 1892) created through the desire to identify, categorise, and contain colonised 'subjects' along racialised lines (Anderson and Killingray, 1991; Thomas, 1994).
3. There has been a well-documented relationship between 'criminal anthropology' (the nineteenth-century attempt to identify a criminal on the basis of their physical appearance) and later systems of racial profiling (Panayi, 1996; Lahiri, 1998; Cole, 2009).

Similarly, the extent to which the technologies used by citizens to access police assistance, such as the telephone and CCTV, have been designed and distributed according to class, race, and gender (Manwaring-White, 1983; Williams, 2003; Klein, 2007; Moss, 2018).

In this section, we have charted how the history of policing and regulation has not been a linear story of improved organisation, efficiency, and authority over citizens. Instead, we have looked at how different models of policing emerged historically, and the way that citizens' relationship with police has depended on factors such as class, gender, and race, as well as geographical contexts.

Knowledge link: These topics are also covered in Chapters 8, 19 and 20.

We now move away from our broader examination of 'systems' of crime and policing to think about how focusing on a single, well-documented event can be useful for analysing the history of crime.

CRIMINAL CELEBRITY: THE MERITS AND PITFALLS OF THE CASE STUDY APPROACH

Let us now think about the meanings of 'celebrity' and 'notoriety' in relation to the fame accorded certain criminals historically. We will explore why transgressors and law-breakers could potentially be admired and romanticised as often as they were condemned and regarded as monsters in the 'evilness' of their acts. Focusing on individuals is a strategy often deployed by historians where particular high-profile cases might alone have generated a greater wealth of archival material left to analyse than a series of crimes (Frost, 2003; Bland, 2013; Houlbrook, 2016; Carter Wood, 2017). In this respect, scholarship on the history of crime is influenced by the imperatives of the media, and the decisions of editors, journalists, novelists and filmmakers to elevate particular criminals and cases to national attention due to their 'sensational' qualities (minimising the impact of others).

Knowledge link: This topic is also covered in Chapter 5.

Further, we must also pay attention to the politics of the archive, including acquisitions policies, conservation of certain records at the expense of others, and restrictions of access to certain files (often due to their sensitive nature). Whether or not such issues are going to shape the research can only be discovered through contact and familiarity with individual archival institutions, or through initial scoping exercises on the collections, especially where records may not yet have been fully catalogued.

These concerns aside, it is worth giving a brief history of the kinds of popular interest in certain narratives of crime and criminal examined by historians to date in order to put our discussion of 'criminal celebrity' into context. I will do so in relation to what the historian Gillian Spraggs calls the 'cult of the robber' in England from the medieval period to the present day (Spraggs, 2001). As Spraggs notes, various kinds of thief, whether real or fictional, have enjoyed a level of adulation and mythologising of their activities for centuries. Whether encountering fourteenth-century characters like Robin Hood (celebrated for 'robbing the rich to give to the poor', though his existence has never been verified) through real-life eighteenth-century highway robbers like Richard 'Dick' Turpin (hanged for horse-stealing in 1739) and Jack Sheppard (executed for robbery in 1724), the English have repeatedly chosen to celebrate such thieves as the subjects of ballads, songs, poetry, novels, and biographies.

During the late-nineteenth century, criminal 'celebrity' as a phenomenon can also be aligned with the rise of the 'new journalism' from the mid-1880s, i.e. the birth of the tabloid press. As Walkowitz (1992) notes, besides a more 'sensationalist' use of language this change in editorial style meant that newspapers emphasised visual content in a way that lent particular flavour to press articles dealing with both crime and celebrity, which relied heavily on the imagery of their subjects to capture readers' interest. More recently, both men and women thieves have proven enduringly popular characters in theatre and film since the Edwardian period, with historian Elizabeth Carolyn Miller analysing the success of a series of films about master-criminal 'Three-fingered Kate' created during the period 1909–1912 (Miller, 2008: 116–128; Moss, 2019). Recalled as morality tales on the perils of criminal lifestyles, or manifesting a popular discourse on the vicissitudes of wealth and economic hardship, stories about thieves have held a pronounced currency in the cultural life of the nation. Further, the identification of the robber with legitimised forms of resistance to the state has, at times, led to domestic idealisations of English men as 'braver' and more 'courageous' than men of other races and nationalities. Such metaphorical usage has, unsurprisingly, been pronounced during times of war or when other forms of social unrest have required an affirmation of the nation's racial and imperial strength (Spraggs, 2001).

In this section we have observed how focusing on an individual case study can offer an insight into the role of the media in creating the conditions for the mythologisation of certain perpetrators. We have also observed how the ability to do this kind of analysis rests on the fact that certain crimes leave greater archival traces than others. A case-study approach is useful, however, to illustrate how 'celebrity' criminals can embody popular ideas about national identity, political resistance, and/or gender relations in a particular historical moment. Let us explore this phenomenon in relation to Jack the Ripper.

Case Study 2.3

Jack the Ripper

In the autumn of 1888, London was gripped with fear by the well-publicised murder and mutilation of five women – Mary Ann Nichols, Annie Chapman, Elizabeth Stride, Catherine Eddowes, and Mary Jane Kelly – in Whitechapel, one of the poorest areas of East London. It is worth noting that although these murders constitute the five 'canonical' murders by the 'Ripper', there were in fact thirteen murders of other women, frequently working as prostitutes, in London's East End during the years

1887 to 1891, all of which may have possibly been committed by the same person. Accordingly, press reports of the Ripper 'striking again' continued to be published for many years after that autumn.

Why have these events remained the source of so much fascination?

> Historians are interested in these events, and the mythologisation of the murderer (who was never apprehended) because they crystallise a set of social tensions surrounding poverty, race, gender and crime in this era (Walkowitz, 1992; Haggard, 2007).
>
> The 'Jack the Ripper' murders highlighted the physically- and morally-degrading conditions of slum life in Victorian London's impoverished East End.
>
> The Ripper murders also arguably laid the foundations for the emergence of later community-based policing initiatives, due to the killer's escape being partly attributed to the reluctance of locals to work with police, with whom their day-to-day encounters were overwhelmingly hostile (Maguire in Newburn (ed.), 2003: 445).

Racism was also an important feature of the case. High levels of immigration of Russian and German Jews to Whitechapel, stemming from persecution on the continent and economic hardship, were at the root of a growing antisemitism within London and elsewhere in the country during the 1880s that led to the targeting of some Jews as suspects in the case (Haggard, 2007: 198-199). Publicised caricatures of the supposed murderer portrayed stereotypically 'Jewish' physiognomy and made suggestions about their sexual 'deviancy', appearing in publications including *The Times*, the *Pall Mall Gazette*, and the *Daily Star*. This gives us an insight into the role of the media in twinning high-profile crimes with racial tensions in this era (Walkowitz, 1992: 203-204).

The victims of the Ripper's attacks were similarly regarded as 'dangerous' women. Their association with prostitution effectively de-legitimised them from virtuous, 'innocent' idealisations of Victorian womanhood (Walkowitz, 1982; Mahood, 1990; Levine, 2003). Regarded as 'disease-carriers' whose work might imperil the health and strength of their clientele (men serving in the Armed Forces), the victims were subject to a level of prejudice that diminished the likelihood of finding them justice. As such, the 'Jack the Ripper' murders offer an unparalleled insight into the socio-political landscape of working-class lives in late-nineteenth century London, whilst retaining the lure of an unsolved mystery and a fascination with their horror that endures into the present.

CHAPTER SUMMARY

- There are three groups of scholars who study the history of crime: historians of a particular period/place, historians of crime, and historical criminologists.
- Definitions of crime change over time and space. Something viewed as illegal at one historical moment (such as the protests of the suffragette movement, or homosexuality) can be viewed only a few decades later as legal and worthy of celebration.
- Forms of social stigma and ostracism have historically effectively criminalised certain groups and individuals.
- Systems of policing and regulation have been shaped by historic prejudices, including racism, sexism, and homophobia, as well as by colonialism.
- Historians treat all evidence of the history of crime with a critical eye, including statistics, analysing what assumptions and political agendas underpinned their creation.
- The media has played an important role in determining attitudes towards crime historically, and in mythologising certain criminals as 'celebrities.'

Knowledge link: This topic is also covered in Chapter 11.

Review Questions

Through what types of sources do ideas about crime circulate through society historically, and should we treat some as more 'serious' or 'reliable' in nature than others – and if so, why?

Is a case-study approach better for understanding the relationship between crime and society?

What are the pros and cons of examining crime using criminal statistics?

In what ways were nineteenth-century attitudes to crime informed by class, race, and gender? How far were these concerns the by-products of broader developments such as urbanisation and empire?

Why should a criminological appreciation of crimes and criminal behaviours embrace historical perspectives?

GO FURTHER

Books

1. Emsley's seminal work in the history of crime and policing is a must-read for all interested in the subject; this book develops his earlier work to chart the policing and regulation of crime in a wider European context.

   Emsley, C. (2007) *Crime, Police, and Penal Policy: European Experiences 1750–1940*. Oxford: Oxford University Press.

2. Ghosh's book gives an extraordinarily rich social and cultural history of attitudes towards crime and deviance in colonial Calcutta.

   Ghosh, A. (2016) *Claiming the City: Protest, Crime, and Scandals in Colonial Calcutta, c. 1860–1920*. Oxford: Oxford University Press.

3. Nash and Kilday persuasively examine how shame was used to regulate behaviour in Britain from the early modern period to the start of the twentieth century, offering an alternative framework for looking at punishment in the past.

   Nash, D. and Kilday, A.-M. (2010) *Cultures of Shame: Exploring Crime and Morality in Britain 1600–1900*. London: Springer.

Journal Articles

1. Renowned sociologist and cultural theorist Stuart Hall uses the murder of Stephen Lawrence to explore systems of institutionalised racism in policing historically.

   Hall, S. (1999) Scarman to Stephen Lawrence. *History Workshop Journal*, 48: 187–197.

2. Laskaris' article helps us to better understand the emotional state of women who accused others of witchcraft in seventeenth-century America, as a neglected dimension of the trial process.

   Laskaris, I. (2019) Agency and emotion of young female accusers in the Salem witchcraft trials. *Cultural and Social History*. 16(4): 1–17. DOI: 10.1080/14780038.2019.1585316

3. Morris's important article responds to Howard Taylor's critique of the reliability of criminal statistics in the past, whilst highlighting the key contextual factors historians should take into account when analysing statistics.

    Morris, R. M. (2001) Lies, damned lies and criminal statistics: reinterpreting the criminal statistics in England and Wales. *Crime, Histoire & Sociétés/Crime, History & Societies,* 5(1): 111–127.

Useful Websites

1. Centre for the History of Crime, Policing, and Justice at the Open University: http://www.open.ac.uk/arts/research/policing/
2. 'Our Criminal Past' research network at Leeds Beckett University: https://www.leedsbeckett.ac.uk/ourcriminalpast/
3. Proceedings of the Old Bailey Online, London's Central Criminal Court, 1674–1913: https://www.oldbaileyonline.org/

REFERENCES

Anderson, D. & Killingray, D. (eds) (1991) *Policing the Empire: Government, Authority and Control, 1830–1940.* Manchester: Manchester University Press.

Anindita, G. (2016) *Claiming the City: Protest, Crime, and Scandals in Colonial Calcutta, c. 1860–1920.* Oxford: Oxford University Press.

Barry, G., Paul, L. & Chris, W. (eds) (2008) *History and Crime.* London: Sage Publications.

Bartrip, P. W. J. (2004) 'Troup, Sir Charles Edward, 1857–1941'. *Oxford Dictionary of National Biography.* Available at: https://doi.org/10.1093/ref:odnb/60141

Bland, L. (2013) *Modern Women on Trial: Sexual Transgression in the Age of the Flapper.* Manchester: Manchester University Press.

Bingham, A., Delap, L., Jackson, L. & Settle, L. (2016) Historical child sexual abuse in England and Wales: the role of historians. *History of Education,* 45(4): 411–429.

Bourke, J. (2007) *Rape: A History from 1860 to the Present Day.* London: Virago.

Christie, A. (1923) 'The Disappearance of Mr. Davenheim', *The Sketch,* 28 March.

Churchill, D. (2014) Rethinking the state monopolisation thesis: the historiography of policing and criminal justice in nineteenth-century England. *Crime, Histoire & Sociétés/Crime, History & Societies,* 18(1): 131–152.

Churchill, D., Crawford, A. & Barker, A. (2018) Thinking forward through the past: prospecting for urban order in (Victorian) public parks. *Theoretical Criminology,* 22(4): 523–544.

Cohen, D. (2013) *Family Secrets: Shame and Privacy in Modern Britain.* Oxford: Oxford University Press.

Cole, S. (2001) *Suspect Identities: A History of Fingerprinting and Criminal Identification.* Cambridge, MA: Harvard University Press.

Davie, N. (2003) Criminal man revisited? Continuity and change in British criminology, c. 1865–1918. *Journal of Victorian Culture,* 8(1): 1–32.

D'Cruze, S. (1998) *Crimes of Outrage: Sex, Violence, and Victorian Working Women.* London: UCL Press.

D'Cruze, S. (2004) 'Dad's back': mapping masculinities, moralities and the law in the novels of Margery Allingham. *Cultural and Social History,* 1: 256–279.

D'Cruze, S. & Jackson, L. (2009) *Women, Crime and Justice in England since 1660.* Basingstoke: Palgrave Macmillan.

Emsley, C. (2007) 'Historical Perspectives on Crime'. In M. Maguire, R. Morgan and R. Reiner, (eds), *The Oxford Handbook of Criminology*, 4th edition. Oxford: Oxford University Press. pp. 122–138.

Gatrell, V. A. C. (1980) 'The Decline of Theft and Violence in Victorian and Edwardian England'. In V. A. C. Gatrell, B. Lenman and G. Parker (eds), *Crime and the Law: The Social History of Crime in Western Europe since 1500*. London: Europa Publications. pp. 238–337.

Ginger, F. (2003) 'She is but a woman': Kitty Byron and the English Edwardian criminal justice system. *Gender and History*, 16(3): 538–560.

Jackson, L. (2000) 'Singing birds as well as soap suds': the Salvation Army's work with sexually abused girls in Edwardian England. *Gender & History*, 12(1): 107–126.

Jackson, L. (2006) *Women Police: Gender, Welfare and Surveillance in the Twentieth Century*. Manchester: Manchester University Press.

Klein, J. (2007) 'Traffic, Telephones and Police Boxes: The Deterioration of Beat Policing in Birmingham, Liverpool and Manchester Between the World Wars'. In G. Blaney (ed.), *Policing Interwar Europe: Continuity, Change, and Crisis, 1918–1940*. Basingstoke: Palgrave Macmillan. pp. 215–236.

Lahiri, S. (1998) Uncovering Britain's South Asian Past: the case of George Edalji. *Immigrants & Minorities*, 17(3): 22–33.

Lambertz, J. (1985) Sexual harassment in the nineteenth-century English cotton industry. *History Workshop Journal*, 19: 29–61.

Laskaris, I. (2019) Agency and emotion of young female accusers in the Salem witchcraft trials. *Cultural and Social History*, 16(4): 1–17.

Levine, P. (2003) *Prostitution, Race and Politics: Policing Venereal Disease in the British Empire*. London: Routledge.

Mahood, L. (1990) The Magdalene's Friend: prostitution and social control in Glasgow, 1869–1890. *Women's Studies International Forum*, 13: 1–2, 49–61.

Manwaring-White, S. (1983) *The Policing Revolution: Police Technology, Democracy and Liberty in Britain*. Brighton: Harvester.

Matt, H. (2005) *Queer London: Perils and Pleasures in the Sexual Metropolis, 1918–1957*. Chicago: University of Chicago Press.

Matt, H. (2016) *Prince of Tricksters: The Incredible True Story of Netley Lucas, Gentleman Crook*. Chicago: University of Chicago Press.

McLaren, A. (2002) *Sexual Blackmail: A Modern History*. Harvard: Harvard University Press.

Meier, W. (2011) *Property Crime in London, 1850–present*. London: Springer.

Miller, E. C. (2008) *Framed: The New Woman Criminal in British Culture at the Fin de Siècle*. Michigan: University of Michigan Press.

Morris, R. M. (2001) Lies, damned lies and criminal statistics: reinterpreting the criminal statistics in England and Wales. *Crime, Histoire & Sociétés/Crime, History & Societies*, 5(1): 111–127.

Moss, E. (2018) 'Dial 999 for help!': the three-digit emergency number and the transnational politics of welfare activism, 1937–1979. *Journal of Social History*, 52(2): 468–500.

Moss, E. (2019) *Night Raiders: Burglary and the Making of Modern Urban Life in London, 1860–1968*. Oxford: Oxford University Press.

Nash, D. & Kilday, A-M. (2010) *Cultures of Shame: Exploring Crime and Morality in Britain 1600–1900*. London: Springer.

Nash, D. & Kilday, A-M. (2017) *Shame and Modernity in Britain: 1890 to the Present*. London: Palgrave Macmillan.

Newburn, T. (2003) *Criminology*. London: Routledge.

Nicole, E., Lean, E., Livingston, J. & Plamper, J. (2012) Barbara Rosenwein, and William M. Reddy in an AHR Conversation: 'The Historical Study of Emotions'. *American Historical Review*, 117(4): 1467–1511.

Panayi, P. (1996) (ed.), *Racial Violence in Britain in the Nineteenth and Twentieth Centuries*. London: Leicester University Press.

Poovey, M. (1995) *Making a Social Body: British Cultural Formation, 1830–1864*. Chicago: University of Chicago Press.

Porter, B. (1987) *The Origins of the Vigilant State: The London Metropolitan Police Special Branch Before the First World War*. London: Boydell and Brewer.

Pratten, D. & Sen, A. (2007) *Global Vigilantes: Perspectives on Justice and Violence*. London: Hurst Publishers.

Robert, F. H. (2007) 'Jack the Ripper as the Threat of Outcast London'. In A. Warwick and M. Willis (eds), *Jack the Ripper: Media, Culture, History*. Manchester: Manchester University Press. pp. 197–214.

Shore, H. (1999) *Artful Dodgers: Youth and Crime in Early Nineteenth-century London*. London: Boydell Press.

Shpayer-Makov, H. (2011) *The Ascent of the Detective: Police Sleuths in Victorian and Edwardian England*. Oxford: Oxford University Press.

Spraggs, G. (2001) *Outlaws and Highwaymen: The Cult of the Robber in England from the Middle Ages to the Nineteenth Century*. London: Pimlico.

Taylor, H. (1998a) Rationing crime: the political economy of the criminal statistics since the 1850s. *Economic History Review*, 49(3): 569–590.

Taylor, H. (1998b) The politics of the rising crime statistics of England and Wales, 1914–1960. *Crime, Histoire & Sociétés/Crime, History & Societies*, 2(1): 5–28.

Thomas, R. R. (1994) The fingerprint of the foreigner: colonizing the criminal body in 1890s detective fiction and criminal anthropology. *ELH*, 61(3): 655–683.

Thompson, E.-P. (1972) Rough music: le charivari anglaise. *Annales. Histoire, Sciences Sociales*, 27(2): 285–312.

Thompson, E.-P. (1992) Rough music reconsidered. *Folklore*, 103(1): 3–26.

Warwick, A. & Willis, M. (eds) (2007) *Jack the Ripper: Media, Culture, History*. Manchester: Manchester University Press.

Walkowitz, J. (1982) *Prostitution and Victorian Society: Women, Class, and the State*. Cambridge: Cambridge University Press.

Walkowitz, J. (1992) *City of Dreadful Delight: Narratives of Sexual Danger in Late Victorian London*. Chicago: University of Chicago Press.

Wiener, M. (2004) *Men of Blood: Violence, Manliness, and Criminal Justice in Victorian England*. Cambridge: Cambridge University Press.

Williams, C. A. (2003) Police surveillance and the emergence of CCTV in the 1960s. *Crime Prevention and Community Safety*, 5: 27–37.

Wood, J. C. (2017) *'The Most Remarkable Woman in England': Poison, Celebrity and the Trials of Beatrice Pace*. Manchester: Manchester University Press.

Zemon, D. N. (1971) The reasons of misrule: youth groups and charivaris in sixteenth-century France. *Past & Present*, 50(1): 41–75.

Crime, Victimisation and Criminology

3

Jacki Tapley

Learning Objectives

This chapter will introduce students to those individuals and groups who experience the consequences of crime and criminal activity - the victims of crime.

By the end of this chapter you will:

- Be able to explore victimology as an academic discipline and its relationship with criminology.
- Identify the influence of competing victimology theories on our understanding of the processes of victimisation.
- Be able to critically appreciate the extent of victimisation and the tools used to measure it.
- Begin to examine the role of victims in the criminal justice system and the introduction of victim-centred policies and legislation.

Framing Questions

---

1. Who are the victims of crime?
2. What factors influence our perceptions of victimisation?
3. How do we know the extent of victimisation?
4. What role should victims play in an adversarial criminal justice process which was never designed with their interests in mind?

INTRODUCTION

Despite the fact that crimes are seldom victimless and the majority involve at least one victim, the study of crime victims has only relatively recently been acknowledged as a key element to the study of crime and criminology, even though the co-operation of victims and witnesses is indispensable for the effective functioning of the criminal justice system. This marginalisation of crime victims in the criminal process, however, has undergone a gradual yet extraordinary transformation during the last fifty years, due to a complex combination of factors, including academic scholarship, political activism and campaigning by victim advocate groups, and an increasing politicisation of crime victims. This has culminated in the development of a range of victim-centred policies and reforms, aimed at improving victims' experiences of the criminal justice system and impacting profoundly on criminal justice culture and professional practices.

As a consequence, **victimology** and victimisation have achieved unprecedented prominence in the study of criminology, and the minds of politicians and criminal justice policymakers, resulting in a substantial body of literature and research, and the development of victim-centred policies and increasing legislation. Due to the highly politicised nature of the subject, there are new reports, consultations and policies being published frequently, aimed at improving the criminal justice response to victims, so it is important to keep up to date with contemporary issues and debates, especially for those intending to become a criminal justice professional or work in a related field.

This chapter encourages you to: gain a greater knowledge of how processes of victimisation are understood and subsequently responded to; have a critical awareness of victims' experiences of the criminal justice system; understand professional practices and the role of victims in the criminal justice process.

MAPPING THE TERRAIN

Whilst two centuries ago victims of crime were the main protagonists in criminal matters, relying upon aggrieved individuals to take responsibility and initiate private action as the 'mechanism and impetus for legal proceedings' (Godfrey, 2018: 14), the expansion of a modern, interventionist and regulatory state usurped this once prominent role of the victim as a key party in the criminal justice process. As a consequence, the rise in the professional administration of criminal justice by judges, lawyers, police, prosecutors and criminal experts reduced the participation of the victim to that of prosecution witness only (Godfrey, 2018: 14). Victims of crime became a disenfranchised and disentitled group, as their conflict became the property of the state, and the concerns of the wider public interest subsumed the more particular needs of the victim (Christie, 1977, cited by Tapley, 2005a: 237). Thereby, the emergence of a modern criminal justice system resulted in the relationship between the state and the offender taking precedence over the responsibilities of the state and the offender towards the victim. The increased emphasis on the overriding issues of deterrence, detection, prosecution and punishment of the offender, resulted in the need for greater legal safeguards to ensure those accused of offences have the protection of the state prior to conviction and, if found guilty, to have the continued protection of the state and the opportunity of rehabilitation (Ashworth, 1983). In this scenario, with no longer a part to play, 'the victim became a legal non-entity, the forgotten figure of crime' (Shapland et al., 1985: 176).

However, from the mid-twentieth century onwards, a combination of complex social and political forces began to indicate that criminal justice reforms had gone too far in favour of the offender, resulting in the marginalisation and neglect of crime victims. Whereas offenders as citizens are entitled to the rights of a defendant against the power of the state, it became apparent that victims as citizens have very little redress from the state for its failure to protect them, and no right to participate in the proceedings to restore the harm done (Tapley, 2003: 30). At the forefront of attempts to acknowledge and redress this imbalance of power was the emergence of increasingly well-organised groups advocating on behalf of victims (Tapley, 2005a: 239), combined with a rise in crime and the fear of crime (Garland, 1996), and growing political concern over declining public confidence in the criminal justice process (Mirlees-Black, 2001; Tapley, 2005a: 248). The culmination of these disparate and often conflicting forces gave rise to debates regarding the needs and rights of victims of crime, resulting in the increasing politicisation of crime victims (Garland, 2000; Goodey, 2005). As a consequence of these activities, a range of victim-centred reforms have been introduced since the 1990s, aimed at improving the criminal justice response to victims and their experiences of the criminal justice process. Whilst these reforms have been widely welcomed, they have not been without controversy, including concerns regarding a perceived infringement of offenders' rights. Although a champion of reorienting the criminal justice system, Fattah (1986; 1997: 267) warned of the dangers of creating a false contest between the rights of offenders and victims, whilst other victims' advocates and scholars have described such reforms as merely 'tinkering with adversarialism' (Walklate, 2007: 11), rather than providing victims with specific rights and improving their status within the criminal justice process.

It is not an exaggeration to say, therefore, that one of the most profound influences upon criminology and criminal justice policy since the mid-twentieth century has been the extraordinary shift in emphasis from an offender-focused criminal justice system to an increasing recognition of the needs and rights of victims (Tapley and Davies, 2020). The development of victimology as an academic discipline has played a significant role in this process (Godfrey, 2018). Once described by a critic as 'the lunatic fringe of criminology' (Becker, 1981, cited by Rock, 2007: 42), **victimology** is now recognised as the scientific study of the extent, nature and causes of criminal victimisation, and its consequences for the persons involved. In addition to the impact and losses suffered, victimology explores the social and political processes that help us understand victimisation and how the public, the media and politicians view the plight of victims. Ultimately, the discipline examines how criminal justice professionals respond to victims, the development of victim-centred reforms, the impact on victims' experiences of the criminal justice system, and increasingly the influence of media representations on our understanding of victims and the processes of victimisation, which we explore next.

MEDIA REPRESENTATIONS OF VICTIMS AND VICTIMISATION

We hear the word 'victim' almost routinely now and there is seldom a day that passes without a media story focusing on victims and victimisation, either individually or as a collective group. Whilst victimisation can take a number of different forms resulting from 'natural' disasters, 'accidents' and state conflicts, the word 'victim' has become almost synonymous with debates around law and order and victims of crime. However, who these victims are, the causes of their victimisation and how we respond to them remains a controversial area for debate, informed by a range of competing theoretical perspectives. More specifically, how we define victims and who we readily acknowledge as a 'victim' of crime is influenced by how we understand the processes of victimisation and by multiple media representations of crime.

Knowledge link: This topic is also covered in Chapter 5.

Before examining the theoretical perspectives underpinning victimology, we will examine who the victims of crime are and why being a 'victim' is considered problematic.

Whilst media representations make it apparent who some victims of crime are, these stories only 'present a selective view of reality, as they are shaped by what and who is considered to be newsworthy' (Greer, 2017: 49). Consequently, only a partial reality is projected, reflecting and reinforcing existing social divisions and inequalities. Although the impact of the media on our views and attitudes is widely debated, a quote by Stanley Cohen (1972) still remains valid:

> ... while the media may not necessarily tell us what to think, they can be remarkably effective in shaping what we think about. (cited by Davies et al., 2017: 3)

Pause for Thought

Take a moment to think about stories in the news that focus specifically on a victim or victims of crime:

1. Which stories and 'victims' stand out in particular and do the victims you have identified share any common features?
2. What are these and what does this tell you about how crime victims are represented in the media?

Case Study 3.1

Sarah's Law and Clare's Law

You may have thought about media campaigns that take the name of the victim to push for new legislation, for example, Sarah's Law, relating to the sexual abuse and murder of eight year old Sarah Payne in 2000 by Roy Whiting, a convicted child sex offender; and Clare's Law, relating to the murder of Clare Wood in 2009 by her ex-boyfriend, George Appleton, who she had met on Facebook and who had, unbeknown to Clare, a history of domestic abuse against previous intimate partners. Both these cases resulted in the introduction of new legislation. Sarah's Law is a child sexual offender disclosure scheme that was introduced in England and Wales in 2011, which allows anyone to ask the police to check whether people who have contact with children pose a risk and have a previous record of committing child abuse offences. Clare's Law is the popular name given to the Domestic Violence Disclosure Scheme, introduced in England and Wales in 2014, which allows a person in a relationship (or a concerned third party) the 'right to ask' if a partner has a previous history of domestic abuse or violence; and the 'right to know', allowing statutory agencies to tell and advise a potential victim of a partner's previous history of abuse and violence if they believe there is a risk of harm. The introduction of these laws has caused controversial debates among legal and criminal justice professionals, victim advocates and academics, and as such they are a strong indicator of the politicisation of crime victims, demonstrating attempts by governments to be seen to be responding to public concerns and doing something to support victims of crime.

Knowledge link: This topic is also covered in Chapter 20.

Whilst newspapers and television channels have traditionally dominated how crime and victimisation has been represented in the media, the advent of digitisation and social media has to some extent challenged the nature of media representations of victims, by enabling the voices of marginalised individuals and groups to be more widely heard (for example, #everyday sexism; #MeToo, Black Lives Matter), thereby revealing other forms of previously hidden victimisation and encouraging others to share and call out their experiences.

Social media campaigns, such as #everyday sexism and #MeToo, have raised awareness of the extent of sexual harassment and violence experienced mainly by women, but which also can affect men and members of the LGBTQ+ communities.

In particular, the #MeToo campaign on Twitter has had a significant impact on public debates about sexual harassment in the workplace, encouraging previously silenced victims to speak up, and resulting in the infamous downfall of Harvey Weinstein, the Hollywood movie mogul, convicted of sexual assault offences in the US in March 2020 and sentenced to a total of twenty-three years' imprisonment. The latter high-profile case follows hard on the heels of sexual abuse by other powerful male figures including the prosecution and conviction of Bill Cosby, a popular Hollywood comedian and actor for most of the second half of the twentieth century. However, Cosby was released in 2021 when his conviction was overturned by Pennsylvannia's Supreme Court. Although the Judges admitted that their ruling was unusual, they said it had been based on a 'process violation' by the prosecutor, because Cosby's lawyer had made an agreement with a previous state prosecutor that he would not be charged in this case. This is an example of how the balance of rights within an adversarial criminal justice process, based upon procedural technicalities, can favour the defendant, subsuming principles of justice and ignoring issues related to wider public protection.

However, the influence of social media campaigns have expanded notions of victimhood to include those whose experiences would not normally be exposed by the mainstream media, and have also informed the subsequent development of legislation. For example, legislation introduced to address **image based sexual violence** (McGlynn and Rackley, 2017), more commonly referred to in the media as 'revenge porn', and 'upskirting', another form of sexual violence facilitated by developments in technology and predominantly perpetrated against women and girls (Sugiura and Smith, 2020). There have also been developments in **green victimology**, highlighting the plight of non-human species as victims of pollution and wider environmental harms (White, 2018; Weis and White, 2020).

Knowledge link: This topic is also covered in Chapter 16.

Having examined the influence of media representations of victims and victimisation, in the next section we examine how victims are defined in an official context.

DEFINING VICTIMS AND VICTIMISATION

An official international definition of a crime victim was first provided by the 1985 United Nations *Declaration of Basic Principles of Justice for Victims of Crime and Abuse of Power* (Goodey, 2005: 10). This definition makes it clear that in order to be defined as a victim, the act has to be a violation of a criminal law within a member state. In 2015, the European Union Directive (2012/29/EU: Article 1) came into force, establishing minimum standards on the rights, support and protection of victims of crime, and defining a 'victim' as (a) a natural person who has suffered harm, including physical, mental or emotional harm or economic loss which was directly caused by a criminal offence; (b) family members of a person whose death was directly caused by a criminal offence and who have suffered harm as a result of that person's death; (c) a 'child', meaning any person below eighteen years of age.

In England and Wales, the Code of Practice for Victims of Crime (Ministry of Justice, 2020: 3) defines a 'victim' as 'a person who has suffered harm, including physical, mental or emotional harm or economic loss which was directly caused by a criminal offence; a close relative of a person whose death was directly caused by a criminal offence'.

Knowledge link: This topic is also covered in Chapter 31.

In contrast to the official definitions above, many commentators argue that gaining the legitimate label of 'victim' is not a neat or absolute journey, but is instead part of a wider social process involving interactions with different actors in order to validate or deny the claim of victim. As observed by Rock (2002, cited by Goodey, 2005: 10):

> Victim, in other words, is an identity, a social artefact dependent, at the outset, on an alleged transgression and transgressor and then, directly or indirectly, on an array of witnesses, police prosecutors, defence counsel, jurors, the mass media and others who may not always deal with the individual case but who will nevertheless shape the larger interpretive environment.

Rock (2002) essentially captures the definition of 'victim' as a *process*. This is significant because it illustrates how attaining the label of 'victim' requires not only the person involved to recognise themselves as having been a victim, but also relies on many others to corroborate this in order for the victimisation to be recognised and appropriately responded to, including the incident being officially acknowledged as a criminal act. However, what behaviour is considered as acceptable and what is deemed a criminal act is dependent upon wider social and cultural factors and reflects the considerable power differentials that can exist between individuals and groups within different societies. Changes in society that subsequently alter the power balance between certain groups can result in previously accepted behaviour becoming criminalised (for example, marital rape and domestic abuse), whilst acts previously deemed as deviant can become legitimate (for example, the decriminalising of same sex and transgender relationships). As a consequence, changes in legislation can arise due to activism and campaigns, subsequent changes in social attitudes, and the introduction of new technologies, thereby creating new offences, new forms of victimisation and an increase in those we deem as legitimate victims (Tapley and Davies, 2020).

As the discussion above has begun to illustrate, determining 'who' and 'how' someone attains the legitimate label of 'victim' can be far more complex and problematic than initially assumed and remains a highly contested area (Walklate, 2017: 30). How victimisation is framed and understood is impacted by cultural influences and involves a process that often prioritises certain types of offences and victims, whilst marginalising the experiences of others. This creates a distinction between those individuals and groups easily able to attain the label of victim (**deserving victims**) and those individuals and groups who struggle or are unable to attain the label of victim (**undeserving victims**) (Mythen and McGowan, 2018: 366). The origins of the stereotypes and assumptions closely associated with acquiring the label will be examined next, as the development of victimology and its impact on our understanding of the processes of victimisation is explored.

EARLY PERSPECTIVES ON VICTIMS AND VICTIMISATION

In a review of the historical roots of victimology, Walklate (2001) locates the discipline's origins in the work of von Hentig and Mendelsohn. Both had backgrounds in law and criminology and both attempted to understand the relationship between the victim and the offender by constructing victim typologies. Von Hentig (1948) introduced the concept of 'victim proneness' based upon thirteen classes of victim who were considered to be either psychologically or socially more prone to victimisation, dependent mainly upon their ascribed characteristics. Mendelsohn's (1956) work, on the other hand, developed the concept of 'victim culpability' based upon a six-fold typology, ranging from the 'completely innocent' to the 'most guilty', which included the criminal who, having instigated the offence, then became the victim. Whilst such typologies, by their very nature, have been criticised for being anecdotal and lacking in empirical ratification, it was the later work within these traditional/ conventional perspectives that successfully translated victim culpability into the influential concept of 'victim precipitation' which subsequently determined 'what might be considered as reasonable and rational behaviour for a victim' (Walklate, 2001: 28). Based upon his study of homicide cases in Philadelphia, Wolfgang (1958) defined victim precipitated offences as those in which the victim is a direct, positive precipitator in the crime. By this, he was referring to those victims who may have started out as the instigator of the incident, perhaps by provoking the perpetrator and starting a fight. Or gang members, equally susceptible to being violent, but on this occasion becoming the victim. This concept was further developed by Amir's later and highly controversial study of rape in which he devised a typology of victim behaviour ranging from the 'accidental victim' to the 'consciously' or 'subconsciously seductive' victim (Amir, 1971). These ideas helped to fuel the powerful myths and stereotypes still associated with victims of rape and sexual violence, implying that the actions of the victim are to blame for the assault (for example, what they were wearing, whether they had been drinking alcohol, or flirting with the perpetrator prior to the assault, etc.), all of which reflect patriarchal expectations of what is reasonable and acceptable behaviour for men and women, all fiercely challenged by feminist activists and scholars (Davies, 2018).

As can be seen, victimology as an academic discipline emerged in the 1940s and 1950s, and focused specifically on individual risk and the situations where victimisation may occur. Introducing the concepts of victim proneness, culpability and precipitation, the early thinkers were the founders of positivist victimology, focusing on the role of the individual (human agency), whilst neglecting the role of the state which contributes to the wider social structural processes that create inequalities and impact upon vulnerability to and risk of victimisation (Davies et al., 2017: 12). Commonly referred to as conventional/traditional/positivist victimology, early theorising attempted to develop an understanding of victimisation by examining the relationship between the victim and offender in isolation from their wider social environments and, as observed by Francis (2017: 91), 'While never overtly "blaming" the victim for their own victimisation, such perspectives inadvertently draw attention towards the role victims play in their own misfortune, alongside their own responsibility for victimisation prevention'.

The stigma and negative connotations often associated with victimisation are closely linked to the ideas of these early scholars and help explain the suspicion around victimhood that persists today. Indeed, the early victimologists did nothing to improve the image of the victim, rather, victims became perceived 'as potentially dangerous and tainted people with a disturbing history and worrying associates' (Rock, 2018: 32). In fact, Rock (ibid) observes the extent to which criminologists went to avoid and ignore victims and mask the individual and social harms caused by victimisation. He contends they 'entertained almost no notion of rule-breaking as hurtful or distressing'. As such, victims were observed uneasily from afar with an uncomfortable air of the 'other' about them. The sole focus on the victim was on their own role in bringing about their own misfortune. Concepts of proneness, culpability and precipitation firmly place the blame upon the victims themselves, to the point that 'Victims were portrayed just as their perpetrators would have wished, as people who were causally and, indeed, often culpably complicit in their own downfall' (Rock, 2018: 36). Thus it was implied that victims provoked and conspired in their own victimisation and thereby deserved their fate.

This is reflected further in the 'just world' theory developed by Lerner and Simmons (1966, cited by Montada and Lerner, 1998: 1) whereby for the purposes of their own security and sense of autonomy, people believe they live in an essentially 'just' world where people get what they deserve. In other words, by believing that people who suffer misfortune or victimisation have somehow brought it upon themselves (i.e. they get what they deserve), this helps others to think they will avoid similar misfortune if they act in a way that cannot be considered as contributing to their own demise. By adopting this approach, it is easier and more convenient to blame the victim, rather than to consider the impact of other wider social, economic or political circumstances, which are harder to control than one's own behaviour and essentially removes any responsibility from more powerful individuals and groups and excuses the harmful behaviour. This gives powerful individuals and groups a sense of entitlement and privilege, to behave in unacceptable ways, but remain above the law. An example of this is the behaviour of Harvey Weinstein, referred to above, and further reinforced by the low conviction rates for rape and sexual violence because of powerful rape myths and rape myth acceptance by the public and criminal justice professionals (Davies, 2018: 114; Kim and Santiago, 2019). High attrition rates in rape cases have caused controversy and concern since the 1990's and a report by the HM Government (2021) reiterated the failures of the criminal justice system in its response to victims of rape, despite the introduction of policies, refoms and legislation. Here we see an example of entrenched social attitudes towards victims of rape, influenced by powerful myths and stereotypes, continuing to impact on the treatment of rape victims and their ability to access justice, despite the challenges of later theories.

We now consider those later theories that have challenged the early orthodoxy. Emerging ideas began to think beyond the role of the individual and critically examined the wider social structures that create and perpetuate many of the social inequalities that contribute to an individual and groups' vulnerability to and risk of victimisation.

RADICAL, CRITICAL AND FEMINIST VICTIMOLOGIES

The attribution of blame on the victim underpinning conventional victimology was later challenged by the rise of more radical perspectives within both criminology and victimology in the late 1960s and 1970s, emerging as a response to events in the larger world (Matthews and Young, 1992; Walklate, 1992). To gain an understanding of the wider social and political context that contributed to the intensity of this period and the subsequent increase in theorising about victims and victimisation, read Francis (2017: 85) who identifies four key factors; the impact of Second Wave feminism on raising awareness of the extent of male violence against women, particularly within the home; the inadequate response of criminology to the growing problem of crime, the causes and what to do about it; the introduction of the crime survey and its contribution to uncovering the nature, extent and impact of victimisation; and the growing mediatisation of crime and its impact on crime and victim representation, as discussed above.

In response to the criticisms of the early conventional theories, later theories emerged which focused on lifestyle and routine activities, although these remained positivist in nature. These approaches argued that differences in lifestyle impact on the risk of victimisation. Location, timing and contact with potential offenders were seen as important features of risky lifestyles (Hindelang et al., 1978; Gottfredson, 1981, and Cohen and Felson, 1979, cited by Spalek, 2017: 62). For example, young men involved in criminal activities from economically disadvantaged backgrounds will be most at risk of victimisation because of where they live and with whom they associate (see Green, 2007: 91), whereas an elderly married couple living in an affluent gated community will be at a significantly lower risk of victimisation, although may still be at risk of elder abuse by carers or relatives, or through local trader and financial scams. As observed by Goodey (2005: 71), 'where you go, what you do, and who you are, as determined by the limited choices in your routine daily activities, determines your victimisation proneness'. However, these theories remain focused on the individual, rather than acknowledging the impact of wider social structures that govern people's routine activities. Consequently, these theories fail to recognise the power differentials that exist between social groups, created by socio-economic status, education, occupation, gender, race, culture and age, thereby rendering some groups more prone to certain types of victimisation than others.

Knowledge link: These topics are also covered in Chapters 18, 19 and 20.

As a critique of these later positivist theories, which provide only a partial analysis of human agency and structural constraints, critical victimology set out to examine the 'processes that go on behind our backs, which contribute to the crime and victims that we see as opposed to that which we do not see' (Mawby and Walklate, 1994). By focusing on the role of the state in creating and perpetuating the social inequalities that contribute to victimisation, critical victimology adopted a policy approach based upon the principles of rights for victims. It challenged the individualistic and patriarchal assumptions underpinning government policy making and advocated the 'need for a gendered politics and a gendered debate around criminal justice policy' (Walklate, 2001: 187).

Exposing the gendered nature of crime, and in particular, the 'hidden' crimes we do not see, has been fundamental to the activism and campaigning of second wave feminist scholars since the late 1960s and early 1970s (Smart, 1976), challenging the failure of both criminology and victimology to acknowledge the importance of gender. In particular, feminist perspectives criticised the positivist, lifestyle and routine activity theories for being gender blind and started to reveal the extent of 'hidden' violence against women and girls in both the public and private spheres, sustained by male privilege and a patriarchal social structure which rendered women second class citizens, unequal to their male counterparts (Dobash and Dobash, 1980; Stanko, 1985). Davies (2017: 146) examines the features that contribute to the gender patterning of victimisation and the importance of considering the concepts of risk, vulnerability and victimisation through a gendered lens. The significant contribution of feminist perspectives to the development of victimology is widely documented (Walklate, 2001; Goodey, 2005: 53; Jordan, 2015).

Knowledge link: This topic is also covered in Chapter 8.

Davies (2018: 109) acknowledges the achievements of the different feminist approaches in the development of theories, policy, practice and research, raising awareness of the extent of female victimisation and the perpetrators. In particular, feminist perspectives eschewed the common assumptions that women should be fearful of the dangerous stranger lurking in public spaces, when the majority of women are victimised by men they know, with whom they are often in a familial or intimate relationship and within the walls of their own homes (Harne and Radford, 2008; Westmarland, 2015; Brennan, 2017). The Crime Survey for England and Wales (CSEW) (2018) demonstrates the gendered nature of domestic abuse, where the pattern of victimisation illustrates that men are overwhelmingly the perpetrators and women the victims. Statistics collected by the Office of National Statistics (2019) demonstrate that in cases of homicide, the majority of women are killed by a partner, ex-partner or somebody known to them, whilst men are more likely to be killed by strangers, acquaintances or others known to them.

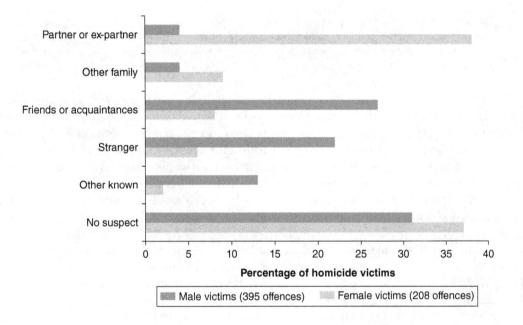

Figure 3.1 Suspects of Female Homicide Victims Aged 16 Years and Over (England and Wales: Year Ending March 2019)

Source: Homicide in England and Wales: year ending March 2019. Office for National Statistics. URL: https://www.ons.gov.uk/peoplepopulationandcommunity/crimeandjustice/articles/homicideinenglandandwales/yearendingmarch2019. Reproduced under the Open Government Licence v.3.0.

The report indicates that 'in almost 4 in 10 female homicide victims aged 16 years or over, the suspect was their partner or ex-partner (38%, 80 homicides). This was an increase of 17 homicides compared with the previous year. However, the 63 homicides in the previous year was the lowest number in the last 40 years. Over the last 10 years there was an average of 82 female victims a year killed by a partner or ex-partner' (ONS, 2019). See also the Femicide Census (2020) which provides a comprehensive study of the women killed by men in the UK, 2009–2018.

────────── Pause for Thought ──────────

Why do you think it has taken so long for violence and abuse within the home to be taken seriously and responded to as a real crime?

Despite radical, critical and feminist challenges since the last half of the twentieth century to the present time, and the introduction of policies and legislation specifically to address domestic abuse (Strickland and Allen, 2018), we still see the influence of positivist theories in the stereotypes and assumptions applied to victims of crime, especially victims of sexual violence and domestic abuse (Walklate, 2007; Walby et al., 2015; Jordan, 2015; Duggan, 2018). As with early criminology, early victimology theories were constructed by men, mainly from a legal perspective.

The critical and feminist theories sought to demonstrate how policies and laws introduced to protect the interests of the most powerful groups in society shape the prevailing social norms and values of a particular society, and those who do not conform to or contest those norms can be considered as deserving of the consequences. As observed by MacKinnon (1989: 161):

> The state is male in the feminist sense: the law sees and treats women the way men see and treat women. The liberal state coercively and authoritatively constitutes the social order in the interests of men as a gender – through its legitimating norms, forms, relation to society, and substantive policies.

As such, it is important to recognise that the agencies administering and implementing criminal justice are part of a wider system still operating within a deeply embedded patriarchal framework (Mawby and Walklate, 1994: 185; Jordan, 2015; Duggan, 2018). This can act to reinforce powerful myths and stereotypes that can influence whether individuals define themselves as a victim; their decision whether or not to disclose and/or report offences; and how victims are responded to by criminal justice professionals. In the context of sexual crimes, Davies (2018: 107) explores the existence of *'silencing agents'* (Jordan, 2012, cited by Davies, 2018: 114) that create barriers to accessing justice, and also examines the factors that contribute to the marginalisation of men as victims, including theorising masculinities (ibid: 119). As a consequence of feminist activities, Davies (2018: 117) observes that responses to victimisation are in the midst of a 'paradigm shift', impacting on criminal justice policies and professional practices. However, despite improvements in responses to victims of certain crimes, there remains significant evidence of failures in criminal justice processes due to the perpetuation of victim-blaming practices (Angiolini, 2015; Johnson et al., 2015), revealed further in HM Inspectorates' reports published by HMIC (2014a), HMCPSI (2016a; 2016b; 2017) and, HMICFRS (2021). It is important, therefore, to critically examine why such myths and stereotypes remain so powerful and to explore in whose best interests they operate. This is examined further below, as we start to explore the enduring concept of the **'ideal victim'**.

Knowledge link: This topic is also covered in Chapter 31.

THE ENDURING CONCEPT OF THE 'IDEAL VICTIM'

Nils Christie (1986: 18) introduced the concept of the 'ideal victim', defined as 'a person or a category of individuals who – when hit by crime – are most readily given the complete and legitimate status of being a victim'.

The concept of the 'ideal victim' remains a powerful and influential factor when determining which individuals gain legitimate recognition and access to formal support and those who do not. Put simply, those deemed as 'ideal victims' are often those considered to be the most weak and vulnerable (an elderly woman or child), completely innocent and blameless, and deserving of our sympathy as their victimisation is perceived as being unprovoked. Those considered less ideal are those who are considered more able to protect themselves (for example, men) or those who are deemed to have played a role in their own victimisation, for example, gang members, the homeless, and the careless (leaving valuables on show, windows or doors unlocked) (Duggan, 2018).

Building on this dichotomous framing of the victim, Bosma, Mulder and Pemberton (2018: 27–32) consider the role of the observers and how the victim is 'framed' within a wider social context, their status dependent upon the framer. Further, as observed by Scott (2018), empathy and sympathy for a victim may also depend upon who the perpetrator is and whether they can be considered as the **'ideal enemy'**, that is, 'a person who is easy to dislike and resent' (Christie, 1986, cited by Scott, 2018: xiv). For Scott (ibid), the concept of the 'ideal enemy' can be used by the populist press and politics to conform to fears and stereotypes and marginalise certain groups. This is evidenced in the Western politics of the early twenty-first century when considering the plight of refugees as a result of war and economic crisis. In fact, Christie's (1993, cited by Scott, 2018: xiv) argument that 'the appetite for "ideal enemies" grows as societies become more and more unequal as inequalities undermine social solidarity and create the conditions for social distance to widen' could perhaps be viewed as prophetic, given the far-right populist politics of Farage and Johnson in the UK and Trump in the US in the early decades of the twenty-first century. As such, perceptions of victimisation and who the victims and perpetrators are can rest upon perceptions of the respectability, power and status of both parties, not just the specific attributes of the victim (Duggan, 2018: 5).

Acknowledging the dichotomy between deserving and undeserving victims, Carrabine et al. (2009: 159) refer to a **'hierarchy of victimisation'**, with those most deserving of our sympathy at the top and those most blameworthy and undeserving placed at the bottom. As a consequence, attaining the legitimate label of victim for some is made difficult as they do not conform to the stereotype of the 'ideal victim', and especially difficult if the perpetrator does not conform to the stereotype of the 'ideal enemy'. The different categories of victim and their place on the hierarchy reveal power imbalances and how social inequality impacts on patterns of victimisation (see Davies et al., 2017: 2).

--- Pause for Thought ---

Taking the idea of a 'hierarchy of victimisation', which victims would you place at the top of the hierarchy (that is, which victims do you perceive as most deserving of our sympathy, the 'ideal victims') and who would you place at the bottom (those least deserving), and why?

In summary, this section has introduced you to the theoretical debates that have shaped and informed victimology, illustrating the links between theory, policy and practice. Whether as members of the public or criminal justice professionals, our perceptions of victimisation are informed by historical, cultural, political and media representations of who the 'victims' and 'perpetrators' are. By challenging the origins of the myths and stereotypes associated with victimisation, and providing a critical appreciation of the factors that influence individuals' vulnerability and risk to victimisation, victims have been moved from the margins to the centre of debates about crime and criminal justice policy, influencing the subsequent development of legislation and professional practice. Central to this analysis is our knowledge not only of who the victims are, but also of how much victimisation there is and who is most at risk. The next section examines the development of **victimisation surveys**.

Knowledge link: This topic is also covered in Chapter 4.

Initially introduced in the mid-1980s, they have since become the most influential tools used to measure the extent and patterning of victimisation, although the subsequent reliance upon them has not entirely been without criticism, as we will explore next.

UNDERSTANDING THE EXTENT OF VICTIMISATION

Traditionally the predominant indicators of levels of crime in England and Wales were official statistics produced by the Home Office based upon police recorded crime. However, recorded crime only represents the end product of a series of complex social processes, including victims' decisions to report an offence and the subsequent police response, and therefore this source does not provide a true or reliable reflection of the actual extent of crime and victimisation. Whilst there are Home Office counting rules to ensure crimes are recorded consistently and accurately, concerns have been raised regarding the accuracy of police recorded crime. A report by HMIC (2014b) examined crime data integrity and the recording of crime by the police in accordance with the Home Office Counting Rules and National Crime Recording Standards. The report revealed a lack of accuracy in crime-reporting patterns, a failure to record crimes and to inform victims of decisions made to no-crime their report. The report made clear the importance of ensuring crime data integrity in order to maintain public confidence and, most importantly, the confidence of victims to report crime. This is important when we consider historically why victimisation surveys were first introduced and what they revealed.

The primary objective of the first national British Crime Survey (BCS) in England and Wales in 1982, was to estimate the extent of crime independently of police recorded statistics, drawing from a representative sample of the population. One of the most significant findings of the first BCS was to identify the extent of crime and victimisation that went unreported (Hough and Mayhew, 1983), revealing what has become commonly referred to as the 'dark figure' of crime (Zedner, 1994). By identifying high levels of unreported crime, the victimisation survey helped to fuel increasing criminological interest in victims and has since emerged as an important source of information sitting alongside police recorded crime. Essentially, such surveys expose patterns of victimisation, identifying the factors associated with the likelihood of being victimised. Indicators of risk include gender, age, socio-economic status, environment and lifestyle, often reflecting significant social divisions and inequalities, thereby highlighting that 'vulnerability to crime, risk and fear of crime are exacerbated by social, economic and political exclusion' (Davies et al., 2017: 18). Whilst the data reveal that those most at risk of victimisation are men, in particular, the young and economically disadvantaged, those often most fearful of crime, older people and women, are actually at less risk of becoming victims.

Lee (2017: 132) has called this the 'risk-fear paradox' whereby 'many socio-demographic groups who are least likely to be victimised report higher levels of fear of crime in victim surveys'. However, Lee (2017:132) argues that the causal relationship between fear of crime and factors such as gender and age is far more complex than initially assumed. In particular, characteristics, such as age, gender and race, may increase feelings of vulnerability to crime, but do not necessarily correlate with actual risk. For example, very young or elderly women may feel more fearful of crime, yet statistically are less likely to become victims, whilst young men are less fearful, but statistically more likely to be victimised. However, these statistics can change when focusing on *specific* types of crime. For example, as we have seen above, it is women who are most likely to be victims of domestic abuse and sexual violence, whilst black, minority and ethnic groups are more likely to suffer hate crimes (Office for National Statistics, 2019).

It is important to consider the implications of the above, as information from the BCS has been used as a tool to inform the development of social and criminal justice policy. The term for the utilisation of crime survey data in this way became known as 'administrative criminology' (Young, 1994). In particular, this criminological perspective seeks to reduce the opportunities of committing crime and places a greater emphasis on the development of crime prevention strategies, which became a particular feature of criminal justice policy towards the end of the 1990s, associated with the dominant political ideology of individual responsibility (Pease, 2002). For example, the increased use of surveillance and widespread introduction of closed-circuit television (CCTV) cameras. This places greater responsibility upon individuals to protect themselves from crime (for example, to install window locks, house alarms, anti-theft devices in cars, and to avoid being in public spaces at night), but can be criticised for ignoring the socially divided nature of victimisation and the impact of wider social structures on people's risk and experiences of victimisation. In particular, it ignores people's *ability* to protect themselves from victimisation which requires money and resources.

Davies et al. (2017: 5) examine further the different tools and techniques used to find out about victims, crime and victimisation and highlight the two key methodologies employed – mass survey techniques, including national and international surveys, and smaller-scale qualitative studies including detailed case studies. They also examine the different types of victimisation survey and consider the limitations of such surveys (ibid: 8), including the difficulties of comparing survey data across different countries, and demonstrate the need for more qualitative studies. A key limitation is that the methodologies of such large-scale studies focus mainly on traditional crimes, for example, theft, burglary and violent crime in public spaces, thereby grossly undercounting what Stanko (1988) characterised as 'hidden violence'. Attempts were made to rectify this by introducing a self-completion survey to the BCS in 1996, in order to maximise victims' willingness to report domestic assaults and sexual violence (Myhill and Allen, 2002). However, criticisms have continued regarding the counting of incidents of domestic abuse. In particular, how official statistics mask the extent of domestic abuse by capping the number of incidents counted and underestimating the risk of harm (Walby et al., 2016).

Subsequent changes have been made to the BCS methodology in response to criticisms and the advent of new technology. In 2009, it started to include the experiences of 10–15 year olds, and from 2012, the BCS was changed to the Crime Survey for England and Wales (CSEW) to better reflect its geographical coverage. In the same year the publication of crime statistics moved from the Home Office to the Office for National Statistics (ONS). The ONS regularly publishes data and reports relating to crime and victimisation and the latest crime levels and trends for England and Wales can be found on the website (Allen, 2016).

In 2017, further changes were made to the CSEW as part of a cost-cutting exercise due to austerity measures, resulting in a reduction being made to the number of questions asked, particularly in relation to performance of the criminal justice system and victims' experiences of the criminal process. Instead, the collection of information relating to victim satisfaction is now the responsibility of the 41 elected Police and Crime Commissioners (PCCs) and the Mayor's Office for Police and Crime (MOPAC) in London, resulting in an inconsistent and unreliable measure of victim satisfaction across England and Wales.

In summary, we have examined the different sources of information that inform our views about the nature and extent of victimisation. As we have learnt, whilst these sources can provide us with some indication of levels of crime, there are also significant weaknesses in such methodologies rendering visible *all* victims of crime. This highlights the importance of examining *critically* all sources of information and using a range of tools to gain a greater appreciation and understanding of the nature of crime and victimisation. This information can then be used to influence the development of criminal justice policy to ensure the needs and rights of victims are considered and contribute to contemporary and often controversial debates regarding the role of victims in the criminal justice process, which we will start to examine next.

THE ROLE OF VICTIMS IN THE CRIMINAL JUSTICE PROCESS

As demonstrated above, the criminal justice landscape has altered significantly over the last four decades, with the crucial role victims play as gatekeepers to the criminal justice process more widely acknowledged in the literature and by successive governments. Without their willingness to report crime, co-operate with investigations and give evidence at trials, the criminal justice system would not be able to function and administer justice effectively. Their return to prominence at the end of the

Knowledge link: This topic is also covered in Chapter 31.

twentieth century has been hard fought and has involved a complex range of actors with often competing aims and ideologies, including activists, campaigners, academics, politicians and legal reformers (Williams and Goodman, 2007; Tapley and Davies, 2020). As a consequence, a plethora of legislative and policy reforms have been introduced in an attempt to improve the criminal justice response to victims, including the introduction of specialist police officers, prosecutors, and probation staff, a Witness Service and the implementation of special measures to assist witnesses to give their best evidence in court or remotely (Plotnikoff and Woolfson, 2013; Fairclough and Jones, 2018).

Significant changes have also been made to the way specialist support services are commissioned and delivered in attempts to meet the perceived needs of victims and witnesses (Wedlock and Tapley, 2016; Fohring and Hall, 2018). However, the development of these reforms has been piecemeal rather than strategic, and often as a politicised response to critical reports or specific high profile cases or incidents. For example, Sarah's Law and Claire's Law (as discussed above), or new legislation in response to key or signal crimes, e.g. 'Revenge porn' or 'Upskirting' referred to as image-based sexual violence. This is not to suggest that such legislation is not valid or required, but instead demonstrates that its development is not informed by a wider overall theoretical understanding of the social and political contexts in which these offences occur and a critically informed consideration of what the role of the victim should be in the criminal process that ensues.

Whilst reforms have attempted to reorientate the work of criminal justice professionals by placing greater responsibility upon them to work with victims, it remains that an adversarial system (designed to protect the defendant against the power of the state) denies victims a role with any substantive rights in the process. Without effective monitoring, evaluation and the provision of sufficient resources, such policies aimed at improving victims' experiences can become meaningless. More specifically, if they are not included in criminal justice performance measures they will not be considered a priority and unlikely therefore to be implemented as intended, resulting in an implementation gap (Wedlock and Tapley, 2016). Evidence from research continues to show that many reforms are not being implemented as intended due to a combination of factors, not all of them intentional, but as a result of insufficient resources, training, and inveterate professional cultures (Wedlock and Tapley, 2016).

An empirical study undertaken with victims of crime and support workers (Rossetti et al., 2017) validated the findings of previous studies that conclude more needs to be done to ensure that victims of crime are responded to as a priority and recognised for the crucial role they play in the criminal justice process. The research demonstrates that despite the political rhetoric, the majority of victims are not *'at the heart of the criminal justice system'*, but remain as observers on the periphery, marginalised by the increasing professionalisation of the criminal justice process and an emphasis on the rights of the defendant, as described at the beginning of this chapter. In spite of a number of key initiatives introduced to improve victims' experiences, including special measures, the Victim Personal Statement, Witness Care Unit, Victim Right to Review and compensation schemes, agencies are not routinely implementing their obligations and the service victims receive falls short of what is outlined in the Victims' Code of Practice (2020), most recently revised in 2020. Negative experiences with criminal justice professionals have an inimical impact on victim confidence and their willingness to engage with the process (Rossetti et al., 2017: 10).

Victim satisfaction relates to how they are responded to not only by the police, although they are likely to be the criminal justice professionals they have the most contact with, but also by other professionals working within the system, including the Crown Prosecution Service, Witness Care Unit, Witness Service and Court staff. However, as so few cases ever reach the prosecution stage, the majority of victim contact with the system starts and ends with the police, thereby highlighting how important the initial police response is and how it can determine victims' perceptions of the criminal justice process. Previous research has indicated high levels of satisfaction at the initial response, but has shown how levels of satisfaction steadily decrease as their case progresses, primarily due to a lack of information and being updated (Shapland et al.,1985; Tapley and Davies, 2020). This demonstrates how crucial responses to and on-going communication with victims of crime are and the importance of reforms being implemented as intended. As found by Wedlock and Tapley (2016), a factor that influenced victim satisfaction more often than the final outcome was how victims felt they had been treated throughout the process. This reflects the importance of **procedural justice** in victims' decisions to cooperate and engage with the criminal justice process.

Knowledge link: This topic is also covered in Chapter 22.

A review of the introduction and implementation of the Victim Personal Statement (VPS) scheme illustrates some of the points raised here.

VICTIM PERSONAL STATEMENTS

In England and Wales, despite the difficulties identified by the early pilot studies (Hoyle et al., 1998), Victim Personal Statements were introduced in 2001 amid claims that the scheme would be *'putting victims at the heart of the criminal justice system'* (Home Office, 2000). It is important to note that these should not be confused with Victim Impact Statements introduced in the United States in the 1970s and later in other jurisdictions, although many politicians and professionals still inaccurately refer to them as 'impact' statements.

As acknowledged above, in an adversarial process there is no role for the victim other than as a prosecution witness. All decisions regarding the investigation, charge, prosecution and punishment of offenders are made by criminal justice professionals with, up until recently, no consultation with the victim. In particular, victims or victims' families have had no opportunity to impart to the court the effect of the crime or to provide their own account. Because victims are not participants themselves, they are both practically and physically excluded from the business of the hearing. Whilst a defendant has a defence solicitor or counsel acting on their behalf to defend their rights, the Crown Prosecution Service is an independent prosecuting authority and represents the state, not the victim. As such, the victim has no representation and there is no opportunity for their interests or concerns to be heard. Victims are unable to tell the story they want, nor often in the manner they want, and this has proved to be a significant source of frustration and resentment for many victims (Walklate, 2006; Tapley, 2020). Instead, their story is edited and reframed to ensure the narrative is appropriate to the charges laid, which may already have been reduced to fit the evidence or accommodate a guilty plea by the defendant, however late in the process this is offered, which can be as late as the day of the trial.

Knowledge link: This topic is also covered in Chapter 25.

Therefore, the key purpose of the VPS is its expressive function. It is a mechanism designed to give victims a 'voice' in the adversarial process with potential therapeutic benefits. Providing victims with a voice enables victims to both 'speak' to and be 'heard' by the court, the offender and the community about their experiences of victimisation (Roberts and Erez, 2010). In a review of the expressive function of victim 'impact' statements in the Netherlands, Booth, Bosma and Lens (2018) state that it is the expressive function that is most important from a victim perspective and one of the major reasons for submitting a statement. In particular, 'many victims want to tell their stories and express their feelings about the crime … They want input in the process and feedback, evidence that someone has listened to them and engaged with their stories … [and] they want the harm they have suffered to be recognized and acknowledged' (Booth et al., 2018: 1481).

Under the VPS scheme in England and Wales, it is intended that police officers gain a VPS shortly after the offence, so that it can assist in identifying the needs of the victim and inform subsequent decisions regarding bail and charging. If a defendant is then prosecuted and convicted, the victim should be given an opportunity to update their VPS, and following conviction and prior to sentencing, the victim can choose to read their statement out in court or have an advocate read it out on their behalf. The cathartic benefit for victims is for the harm they have suffered to be recognised and acknowledged. The main conduit through which judges can demonstrate they have read or heard the VPS is through the formal sentencing judgement, where judges explain both the penalty imposed and the reasons for the decision, taking into account where appropriate the effect on the victim. However, despite revisions to the Victim's Code of Practice in 2015, a victim's entitlement to read their VPS in court remains at the discretion of the judge or magistrate and is not an enforceable right. Research by the Victim's Commissioner for England and Wales (2019a; 2019b) continues to show that not all victims are being given an opportunity to make a VPS, and those that do, do not always feel the manner in which their voice has been accommodated in legal proceedings has been done so fairly. Although the Victims Code of Practice (2020: 25) has since been revised and now states that victims have a 'right' to make a VPS, it still remains at the discretion of the judge or the magistrate to decide whether and what sections of the personal statement should be read aloud (or played), and who should read it. This puts into question the government's use of the term 'rights' and the fact that these remain unenforceable and the agencies responsible for implementing them unaccountable.

Whilst significant progress has been made to incorporate the needs and rights of victims into the criminal justice process, still more needs to be done to ensure practices are consistent, that all victims have access to enforceable rights and appropriate support, and all relevant agencies are held accountable. Instead of the ad hoc introduction of victim-centred reforms, critical commentators argue that what is required is a coherent and comprehensive review of the role of victims in the criminal justice process, supported by legislative rights to ensure the entitlements of victims are enforced and the relevant agencies held accountable (Wedlock and Tapley, 2016). Although the majority of political parties have pledged a commitment to introducing a Victim's Law (Strickland, 2016), such legislation has not yet been forthcoming.

The challenge for victimology, scholars, activists and politicians is to provide a theoretical and practical rationale for victims to have legislative rights and what these rights should be to enable them to participate in a criminal justice system that is not balanced in favour of either the offender or the victim. An effective and efficient criminal justice system should observe and respect the rights of all parties, work to acknowledge the harm done and resolve the conflict by punishing and rehabilitating the offender, whilst assisting the victims to recover. Whilst participatory justice will go some way in achieving this, if aspirations are to be realised, victims' entitlements need to be underpinned by legislative rights to ensure they are implemented consistently for all victims, as evidenced by the research and literature examined in this chapter.

CHAPTER SUMMARY

- This chapter has provided an alternative lens with which to view crime and criminology, that of the perspective of victims of crime.
- It has examined who the victims of crime are and how perceptions of crime victims are shaped by a range of actors, including the victim, academic scholars, the media, criminal justice professionals and practitioners, politicians and the public.
- It has explored the factors that have contributed to the significant shift in focus of the criminal justice system during the last four decades, with victims of crime having achieved a far greater prominence on the political and public agenda.
- However, it has highlighted that despite the introduction of victim-centred reforms, the status of victims within the adversarial process remains contested and finding effective and fair ways to incorporate a victim perspective within Western criminal justice processes remains aspirational and yet to be fully realised.

Review Questions

1. What contribution has victimology made to our understanding of crime and the extent of victimisation?
2. What factors influence our vulnerability to and risk of victimisation?
3. What role does the media play in who we perceive to be the 'ideal victims'?
4. What are the key challenges to developing a criminal justice system that provides victims with a key role in the process?

GO FURTHER

Books

1. This volume critically engages with the development of official policy and reform in relation to the support of victims of crime both within and beyond the criminal justice system of England and Wales. Utilising a combination of cultural victimological analysis, governance theory and legal scholarship, this book examines the fundamental questions concerning the drivers and impact of victim policy in England and Wales in the 21st century.

   Hall, M. (2019) *Victims of Crime: Construction, Governance and Policy*. London: Palgrave.

2. This book provides a comprehensive review of victimology, its historical and theoretical origins. It critically considers who counts as a victim and what counts as victimhood, and examines the problems and possibilities of developing victim-centred policies and legislation.

   Walklate, S. (ed.) (2018) *Handbook of Victims and Victimology*. Cullompton: Willan Publishing.

3. This book offers a critical examination of the range of complex factors that have impacted upon and altered the criminal justice landscape, shifting from the predominant focus on the defendant to the role and experiences of the victim in the criminal process. In particular, the book explores the interplay between victimology as an academic discipline, the creation and activism of special interest groups, and their impact upon policy making and professional practices.

   Tapley, J. and Davies, P. (eds) (2020) *Victimology: Research, Policy and Activism*. London: Palgrave.

Journal Articles

1. Underreporting has been a longstanding problem for criminal justice agencies, which masks the true scale of crime taking place and prevents victims from accessing justice and support. Using empirical evidence collected from more than 2,000 victims who came from different backgrounds and who had experienced different forms of crimes, this article proposes a new theoretical model to enhance our understanding of underreporting.

   Hardy, S. J. (2019) Layers of resistance: understanding decision-making processes in relation to crime reporting. *International Review of Victimology*, 25(3): 302–319.

2. This article examines rape myth acceptance and its predictors among criminology students who desire to work in law enforcement. Although CCJ majors took more classes on victimology, and they also evaluated positively the quality of such courses, the multivariate analysis found no significant positive educational effect on RMA among CCJ majors while controlling other

variables. The findings reiterate the need to make appropriate curriculum adjustments so prospective CJ practitioners will have the necessary tools to uphold a just criminal justice system.

Bitna, K. and Santiago, H. (2019) 'Rape Myth Acceptance Among Prospective Criminal Justice Professionals'. *Women & Criminal Justice*, DOI: 10.1080/08974454.2019.1664969

3. In this article, the author offers an insightful analysis of the perceptions and attitudes of police recruits in England as they transform into established officers over a four-year period. The article examines the power and discretion held by the recruits in their primary role as response and patrol officers, and the differential treatment individuals and groups received based upon their classification as either 'genuine' or 'ingenuine' victims.

Charman, S. (2020) Making sense of policing identities: the 'deserving' and the 'undeserving' in policing accounts of victimisation. *Policing and Society*, 30(1): 81–97.

Useful Websites

1. Crown Prosecution Service – this website outlines the roles and responsibilities of the CPS towards victims and witnesses: https://www.cps.gov.uk/victims-witnesses
2. Her Majesty's Inspectorate of Constabulary and Fire and Rescue Services – HMICFRS independently assesses the effectiveness and efficiency of police forces and fire and rescue services in England and Wales. This includes inspecting the police and their ability to fulfil their responsibilities towards victims of crime. To do this, HMICFRS publishes thematic reports focusing on specific types of crime and victims: https://www.justiceinspectorates.gov.uk/hmicfrs/
3. SafeLives is a UK-wide charity dedicated to ending domestic abuse, for everyone and for good. It provides support and advice to survivors of domestic abuse and advocates on behalf of victims through campaigns and the publication of research and reports: http://www.safelives.org.uk/

REFERENCES

Allen, J. (2016) *Crime Outcomes in England and Wales: Year Ending March 2016*. Statistical Bulletin. London: ONS.

Amir, M. (1971) *Patterns of Forcible Rape*. Chicago: University of Chicago Press.

Angiolini, Rt Hon Dame Elish (2015) *Report of the Independent Review into the Investigation and Prosecution of Rape in London*. London.

Ashworth, A. (1983) *Sentencing and Penal Policy*. London: Weidenfeld and Nicholson.

Bitna, K. and Santiago, H. (2019) Rape myth acceptance among prospective criminal justice professionals, *Women & Criminal Justice*, DOI: 10.1080/08974454.2019.1664969

Bosma, A., Mulder, E. and Pemberton, A. (2018) 'The Ideal Victim through Other(s') Eyes'. In M. Duggan (ed.), *Revisiting the 'Ideal Victim': Developments in Critical Victimology*. Bristol: Policy Press.

Booth, T., Bosma, A. and Lens, K. (2018) 'Accommodating the expressive function of victim impact statements: the scope for victims' voices in Dutch courtrooms', *British Journal of Criminology*, 58: 1480 –1498.

Brennan, D. (2016) *Redefining an Isolated Incident*. www.femicidecensus.org.uk

Button, M., Lewis, C. and Tapley, J. (2014) Not a victimless crime: the impact of fraud on individual victims and their families. *The Security Journal*, 27(1): 36–54.

Carrabine, E., Cox, P., Lee, M., Plummer, K. and South, N. (2009) *Criminology: A Sociological Introduction*. London: Routledge.

Christie, N. (1986) 'The Ideal Victim'. In E. Fattah (ed.), *From Crime Policy to Victim Policy*. London: Macmillan.

Crown Prosecution Service (2015) *Victim and Witness Satisfaction Survey*. London: NatCen Social Research and IFF Research.

Davies, P. (2017) 'Gender, Victims and Crime'. In P. Davies, P. Francis and C. Greer (eds), *Victims, Crime and Society: An Introduction*. London: Sage.

Davies, P. (2018) 'Feminist Voices, Gender and Victimisation'. In S. Walklate (ed.), *Handbook of Victims and Victimology*. Cullompton: Willan Publishing.

Davies, P., Francis, P. and Greer, C. (eds) (2017) *Victims, Crime and Society: An Introduction*. London: Sage.

Directive 2012/29/EU of the European Parliament and of the Council of 25 October 2012 establishing minimum standards on the rights, support and protection of victims of crime, and replacing Council Framework Decision 2001/220/JHA.

Dobash, R. and Dobash, R. E. (1980) *Violence Against Wives*. Shepton Mallet: Open Books.

Duggan, M. (ed.) (2018) *Revisiting the 'Ideal Victim': Developments in Critical Victimology*. Bristol: Policy Press.

Fairclough, S. and Jones, I. (2018) 'The Victim in Court'. In S. Walklate (ed.), *Handbook of Victims and Victimology*. Cullompton: Willan Publishing.

Fattah, E. A. (1986) *From Crime Policy to Victim Policy*. London: Macmillan.

Fattah, E. A. (1997) 'Toward a Victim Policy Aimed at Healing, Not Suffering'. In R. C. Davies, A. J. Lurigio and W. G. Skogan (eds), *Victims of Crime*. London: Sage Publications.

Fohring, H. and Hall, M. (2018) 'Supporting victims of crime in England and Wales: Local commissioning meeting local needs?', *International Review of Victimology*, 24(2): 219–237.

Francis, P. (2017) 'Theoretical Perspectives in Victimology'. In P. Davies, P. Francis and C. Greer (eds), *Victims, Crime and Society: An Introduction*. London: Sage.

Garland, D. (1996) The limits of the sovereign state: strategies of crime control in contemporary society', *British Journal of Criminology*, 36: 445–471.

Garland, D. (2000) The culture of high crime societies, *British Journal of Criminology*, 40: 347–375.

Godfrey, B. (2018) 'Setting the Scene: A Question of History'. In S. Walklate (ed.), *Handbook of Victims and Victimology*. Cullompton: Willan Publishing.

Goodey, J. (2005) *Victims and Victimology: Research, Policy and Practice*. Harlow: Pearson.

Green, S. (2007) 'Crime, Victimisation and Vulnerability'. In S. Walklate (ed.), *Handbook of Victims and Victimology*. Cullompton: Willan Publishing.

Greer, C. (2017) 'News Media, Victims and Crime'. In P. Davies, P. Francis and C. Greer (eds), *Victims, Crime and Society: An Introduction*. London: Sage.

Hamlyn, B., Phelps, A., Turtle, J. and Satter, G. (2004) *Are Special Measures Working? Evidence from Surveys of Vulnerable and Intimidated Witnesses*. London: Home Office Research Study 283.

Harne, L. and Radford, J. (2008) *Tackling Domestic Violence: Theories, Policies and Practice*. Maidenhead: McGraw-Hill/Open University Press.

HM Crown Prosecution Service Inspectorate (2016a) *Communicating with Victims*. London: HMSO.

HM Crown Prosecution Service Inspectorate (2016b) *Thematic Review of the CPS Rape and Serious Sexual Offences Units*. London: HMSO.

HM Crown Prosecution Service Inspectorate (2017) *Living in Fear - the Police and CPS Response to Harassment and Stalking*. London: HMCPSI.

HM Government (2021) 'The end-to-end rape review report on findings and actions' CP437 London: HMSO https://assets.publishing.service.gov.uk/government/uploads/system/uploads/attachment_data/file/994816/end-to-end-rape-review-report.pdf

HMIC (2014a) *Everyone's Business: Improving the Police Response to Domestic Abuse*. London: HMIC.

HMIC (2014b) 'Crime-recording: making the victim count: The final report of an inspection of crime data integrity police forces in England and Wales'. London: HMIC.

HMICFRS (2021) Police response to violence against women and girls: Final inspection report. London: Her Majesty's Inspectorate of Constabularies, Fire and Rescue Services.

Home Office (2000) 'Home Secretary announces national victims statements'. Home Office Press Release (147/20000). http://wood.ccta.gov.uk/homeoffice

Hough, J. M. and Mayhew, P. (1983) 'The British Crime Survey: First Report'. *Home Office Research Study* 76. London: HMSO.

Hoyle, C., Morgan, R. and Sanders, A. (1998) *Evaluation of the One Stop Shop and Victim Pilot Statement Projects*. London: Home Office.

Johnson, H., Fisher, B.S. and Jacquier, V. (2015) *Critical issues on violence against women*. London: Routledge.

Jordan, J. (2015) 'Justice for Rape Victims? The Spirit May Sound Willing, but the Flesh Remains Weak'. In D. Wilson and S. Ross (eds), *Crime, Victims and Policy*. London: Palgrave.

Lee, M. (2017) 'Fear, Vulnerability and Victimisation'. In P. Davies, P. Francis and C. Greer (eds), *Victims, Crime and Society: An Introduction*. London: Sage.

MacKinnon, C. (1989) *Toward a Feminist Theory of the State*. Harvard: Harvard University Press.

Matthews, R. and Young, J. (eds) (1992) *Issues in Realist Criminology*. London: Sage.

Mawby, R.I. and Walklate, S. (1994) *Critical Victimology*. London: Sage.

McGlynn, C. and Rackley, E. (2017) Image-based sexual abuse. *Oxford Journal of Legal Studies*, 37(3): 534–561.

Mendelsohn, B. (1956) Une nouvelle branche de la science bio-psycho-sociale: victimologie. *Revue Internationale de Criminologie et de Police Technique*, pp.10–31.

Ministry of Justice (2020) *Code of Practice for Victims of Crime*. London: HMSO.

Ministry of Justice (2018) *Victims Strategy*. London: HMSO.

Mirlees-Black, C. (2001) *Confidence in the Criminal Justice System: Findings from the 2000 British Crime Survey*. Home Office Research, Development and Statistics Directorate, Research Findings 137. London: Home Office.

Montada, L. and Lerner, M. J. (eds) (1998) *Critical Issues in Social Justice: Responses to Victimizations and Belief in a Just World*. New York: Plenum Press.

Myhill, A. and Allen, J. (2002) 'Rape and Sexual Assault on Women: The Extent and Nature of the Problem'. *Home Office Research Study* 237. London: HMSO.

Mythen, G. and McGowan, W. (2018) 'Cultural Victimology Revisited: Synergies of Risk, Fear and Resilience. In S. Walklate (ed.), *Handbook of Victims and Victimology*. Cullompton: Willan Publishing.

Office for National Statistics (2019) 'The nature of violent crime in England and Wales: year ending March 2018'. https://www.ons.gov.uk/peoplepopulationandcommunity/crimeandjustice/articles/thenatureofviolentcrimeinenglandandwales/yearendingmarch2018

Pease, K. (2002) 'Crime Reduction'. In M. Maguire, R. Morgan and R. Reiner (eds), *The Oxford Handbook of Criminology*. Oxford: Clarendon Press.

Plotnikoff and Woolfson (2013) 'Evaluation of Young Witness Support: Examining the Impact on Witnesses and the Criminal Justice System'. *Research Summary 2*. London: Ministry of Justice.

Roberts, J. V. and Erez, E. (2010) 'Communication at Sentencing: The Expressive Function of Victim Impact Statements', in A. Bottoms and J. V. Roberts (eds), *Hearing the Victim: Adversarial Justice, Crime Victims and the State*. Cullompton: Willan Publishing.

Rock, P. (2007) 'Theoretical Perspectives on Victimisation'. In S. Walklate (ed.), *Handbook of Victims and Victimology*. Cullompton: Willan Publishing.

Rock, P. (2018) 'Theoretical Perspectives on Victimisation'. In S. Walklate (ed.), *Handbook of Victims and Victimology*. Cullompton: Willan Publishing.

Rossetti, P., Mayes, A. and Moroz, A. (2017) *Victim of the System*. London: Victim Support.

Scott, D. (2018) 'Foreword: Thinking Beyond the Ideal'. In M. Duggan (ed.), *Revisiting the 'ideal victim': Developments in Critical Victimology*. Bristol: Policy Press.

Shapland, J., Willmore, J. and Duff, P. (1985) *Victims in the Criminal Justice System*. Aldershot: Gower.

Smart, C. (1976) *Women, Crime and Criminology*. London: Routledge and Kegan Paul.

Spalek, B. (2017) *Crime Victims: Theory, Policy and Practice*. London: Palgrave.

Stanko, E. (1985) *Intimate Intrusions: Women's Experience of Male Violence*. London: Virago.

Stanko, E. (1988) 'Fear of Crime and the Myth of the Safe Home: A Feminist Critique of Criminology'. In K. Yllo and M. Bograd (eds), *Feminist Perspectives on Wife Abuse*. London: Sage Publications.

Strickland, P. (2016) *A New Victims' Law in 2016? House of Commons Library Briefing Paper 07139*. London: HMSO.

Sugiura, L. and Smith, A. (2020) 'Victim Blaming, Responsibilization and Resilience in Online Sexual Abuse and Harassment'. In J. Tapley and P. Davies (eds), *Victimology: Research, Policy and Activism*. London: Palgrave.

Tapley, J. (2003) *From 'Good Citizen' to 'Deserving Client': The Relationship Between Victims of Violent Crime and the State Using Citizenship as the Conceptualising Tool*. University of Southampton. Unpublished PhD thesis.

Tapley, J. (2005a) 'Confidence in Criminal Justice: Achieving Community Justice for Victims and Witnesses'. In F. Pakes and J. Winstone (eds), *Community Justice: Issues for Probation and Criminal Justice*. Collumpton: Willan Publishing.

Tapley, J. (2005b) Public confidence costs – criminal justice from a victim's perspective. *British Journal of Community Justice*, 3(2): 25–37.

Tapley, J. and Davies, P. (eds) (2020) *Victimology: Research, Policy and Activism*. London: Palgrave.

Victim's Commissioner (2019a) 'Analysis of the offer and take-up of Victim Personal Statements 2018 to 2019'. London: Victim's Commissioner.

Victim's Commissioner (2019b) 'Victim Personal Statements and Defendants' Right to Censor' Statement from the Victims' Commissioner about Victim Personal Statements'. https://victimscommissioner.org.uk/news/victim-personal-statements-and-defendants-right-to-censor/12.07.19

von Hentig, H. (1948) *The Criminal and His Victim*. New Haven, CT: Yale University Press.

Walby, S. et al. (2015) *Stopping Rape: Toward a Comprehensive Policy*. Bristol: Policy Press.

Walby, S., Towers, J. and Francis, B. (2016) Is violent crime increasing or decreasing? A new methodology to measure repeat attacks making visible the significance of gender and domestic relations. *British Journal of Criminology*, 56(6): 1203–1234.

Walklate, S. (1992) 'Appreciating the Victim: Conventional, Realist or Critical Victimology?'. In R. Matthews and J. Young (eds), *Issues in Realist Criminology*. London: Sage Publications.

Walklate, S. (2001) *Gender, Crime and Criminal Justice*. Cullompton: Willan Publishing.

Walklate, S. (2007) *Imagining the Victim of Crime*. Cullompton: Willan Publishing.

Walklate, S. (2017) 'Defining Victims and Victimisation'. In P. Davies, P. Francis and C. Greer (eds), *Victims, Crime and Society: An Introduction*. London: Sage Publishing.

Wedlock, E. and Tapley, J. (2016) *What Works in Supporting Victims of Crime: A Rapid Evidence Assessment*. London: Victims' Commissioner, Ministry of Justice.

Westmarland, N. (2015) *Violence Against Women: Criminological Perspectives on Men's Violences*. London: Routledge.

White, R. (2018) Green victimology and non-human victims. *International Review of Victimology*, 24(2): 239–255.

Williams, B. (1999) *Working with Victims of Crime: Policies, Politics and Practice*. London: Jessica Kingsley Publishers.

Williams, B. and Goodman, H. (2007) 'The Role of the Voluntary Sector'. In S. Walklate (ed.), *Handbook of Victims and Victimology*. Cullompton: Willan Publishing.

Wolfgang, M. E. (1958) *Patterns in Criminal Homicide*. Philadelphia, PA: University of Pennsylvania.

Young, J. (1994) 'Incessant Chatter: Recent Paradigms in Criminology'. In M. Maguire, R. Morgan and R. Reiner (eds), *The Oxford Handbook of Criminology*. Oxford: Clarendon Press.

Zedner, L. (1994) 'Victims'. In M. Maguire, R. Morgan and R. Reiner (eds), *The Oxford Handbook of Criminology*. Oxford: Clarendon Press.

Tools of the Trade

4

Crime, Surveys and Big Data

Andromachi Tseloni and Elaine Duncan

Learning Objectives

By the end of this chapter you will:

- Be able to reflect on what 'crime' is.
- Understand how crime is measured.
- Know the main sources of crime statistics.
- Learn about police recorded crime.
- Learn about the Crime Survey for England and Wales.
- Have the tools for cross-national crime comparisons.
- Be familiar with administrative crime and justice data.

Framing Questions
---

1. How many crimes are in your postcode? Are they relatively many or few? Justify your answer.
2. Have burglary rates changed in England and Wales in the last three decades?
3. Have the risk factors for being burgled changed in England and Wales during the same period?
4. What are the advantages, if any, of existing data sources on crime to data collected by individual researchers?

INTRODUCTION

The study of criminology involves learning about theories of crime and how to prevent it including, but not exhaustive in, the role, history and structure of policing and the criminal justice system. A prerequisite for understanding and consequently preventing crime is measurement – appreciating the extent and nature of crime. This chapter will introduce you to the existing available tools for measuring crime, testing criminological theories, the effectiveness (both perceived and measurable) of the police and the criminal justice system, designing other crime prevention policies and evaluating their impact. It will first address the following questions:

- How is crime defined and documented?
- How is crime measured?
- What can we infer about victims and offenders from crime statistics?
- Which are the main sources on crime in the UK and internationally, and what are their strengths and limitations? For a spoiler, the main sources for measuring crime are police records and self-report offending and victimisation surveys. The discussion around sources of criminology statistics will first focus on police recorded crime and then, after a brief overview of crime surveys, on how to access and familiarise yourself with the Crime Survey for England and Wales (CSEW). Examples of tools for cross-national crime comparisons, big data and a brief mention of a new initiative in the UK to enhance research from administrative data will follow. The chapter ends with a summary. Examples of criminological theories and crime prevention strands that have been developed from analyses of crime data are mentioned throughout the chapter.

MAPPING THE TERRAIN

The study of criminology involves learning about theories of crime and how to prevent it including, but not exhaustive in, the role, history and structure of policing and the criminal justice system. With the field of criminology being around for around a century and a half and the proliferation of criminology and policing degrees in the last few decades, one may reasonably ask: Why is there still crime?

During your studies you will, if you have not already done so, become familiar with criminological theories that attempt to answer the above question. A good theory – and what distinguishes it from belief – is based on observation (seeing how the world functions), documentation (noting down those observations), and replication (getting the same results out of similar conditions). This chapter's focus is documentation. The documentation drawn upon for assessing whether a criminological theory is plausible and adequately answers why crime exists is typically police records and crime surveys (of which more to come). As they developed historically so did key criminological theories.

The routine activities theory was established based on police recorded crime and data on labour markets, national accounts on private consumption, and market data on sales prices and product characteristics (Cohen and Felson, 1979). The lifestyle victimisation theory was developed from the findings of the USA National Crime Survey (NCS) in the mid-1970s. Merged as the routine activities/lifestyle theory, it remains the predominant proposition of why individuals and/or households experience crime victimisation at all, and, if they do with a different frequency (Hindelang et al., 1978). Furthermore, the social disorganisation and repeat victimisation strands of victimisation theory started originally or significantly expanded from analyses of crime survey data (Osborn et al., 1992; Farrell and Pease, 1993). Cross-national explanations of the crime drop have relied on crime surveys, and police and criminal justice data (van Dijk et al., 2012).

──────── Hear from the Expert ────────

As a criminology student you would know that starting from the USA in the 1980s all **volume crime types** have fallen considerably in most industrialised countries (Tseloni et al., 2010). The number of burglaries per thousand households has fallen by more than 70% since 1993 in England and Wales. Research into 'which burglary security devices work for whom in what context?' relied exclusively on the Crime Survey for England and Wales (Tseloni et al., 2018a). This research provided a theoretical explanation of the burglary drop, the security hypothesis for the crime drop, and practical burglary prevention policies, all important contributions. For example, Tseloni et al. (2014) found that the most effective combination of security devices against burglary with entry is **W**indow locks, **I**ndoor lights on a timer, **D**oor double or deadlocks, and **E**xternal lights on a sensor (**WIDE**), giving 49 times more protection than no security. Police forces regularly advise householders to keep their homes safe by installing this WIDE security combination. Burglary prevention advice given by Gloucestershire Constabulary, for example, is shown in Figure 4.1.

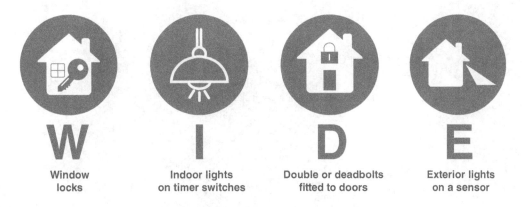

Figure 4.1 Gloucestershire Constabulary WIDE Leaflet

Source: https://www.gloucestershire.police.uk/police-forces/gloucestershire-constabulary/areas/gloucestershire/campaigns/campaigns/2019/burglary/

The analyses and ensuing knowledge that furnished this now WIDEly used crime prevention tool would not have been possible without the Crime Survey for England and Wales. For this research the first author of this chapter won the Office for National Statistics (ONS) Research Excellence Award 2019.

This section showed that a good understanding of what we mean by and measure with crime data is a vital prerequisite of criminology studies and careers. Let us now briefly explore this.

WHAT DOES CRIME DATA CAPTURE?

This section overviews the meaning of crime, data and their association. Firstly, human behaviour, acts and experiences, including crime, are the sum of numerous times (i.e. historical period, season and time of the day), personal (including development and socialisation), and environmental (for example, geography, community, place and circumstances) factors, and therefore entails to a larger or smaller extent a degree of randomness. Secondly, what is deemed as crime has also evolved over the years and differs considerably across societies. To complicate matters further, the prevailing view

Knowledge link: This topic is also covered in Chapter 2.

in a given society of what constitutes extremely unacceptable and punishable acts, and what is illegal according to the laws of the jurisdiction within which this same society operates, may diverge.

Before proceeding we need to introduce accurately the term 'data' which, as a familiar everyday word, might be prone to misinterpretation. The tools for measuring anything, including crime, are known as data: "'facts and statistics collected together for reference or analysis' and 'things known or assumed as facts, making the basis of reasoning or calculation' according to the *Oxford English Dictionary* (https://www.lexico.com/en/definition/data accessed 04.11.2019).

The main sources for measuring crime are police records and surveys. Figure 4.2 delineates how much of place- and time-specific crime can be measured by these two sources. Good police and survey data evolve to follow and reflect society's notion of crime. Survey-based crime statistics ideally enable comparisons with police statistics whilst incorporating tools for mapping it on existing legal definitions. Evidence from survey data may also inform changes in:, for example, the law to incorporate and define as crime objectionable by the society acts; and in the level of severity the police and the criminal justice system respond to particular crime types to match the level of distress they bring to society.

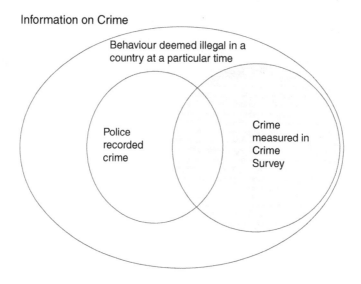

Information on Crime

Behaviour deemed illegal in a country at a particular time

Police recorded crime

Crime measured in Crime Survey

Figure 4.2 **Measuring Crime**

Pause for Thought

Try to find out:

a. whether rape in marriage is a crime in two countries of your choice;
b. the year it became a crime in England and Wales;
c. which set of CSEW questions allows identifying victimisation by this crime type; and
d. which year these questions were introduced in the CSEW - remember to search as far back as possible, for example, the questionnaires of the older version of the CSEW, i.e. the British Crime Survey (BCS).

Based on your findings please answer the following:

- Is rape in marriage a cross-nationally recognised crime?
- What came first in England and Wales – measuring rape in marriage or making it a crime?

Repeat the above exercise replacing rape in marriage with catcalling.

You may have by now (after reading the current and previous sections) realised that the job of criminologists which involves the triptych of measuring, understanding causes/opportunities and preventing crime, in this order, is a tricky one. It requires marrying theory and empirical observation together to develop continuously our understanding of crime (both as defined within a particular society, place and time and in a comparative perspective) and how to prevent it.

Knowledge link: This topic is also covered in Chapter 6.

The ultimate goal is to (inform how to) reduce crime-related harm and improve people's, including potential criminals', lives whilst always keeping in perspective that the goal posts are moving.

So, assuming a consensus on what behaviour, acts and experiences constitute crime, let us begin the main discussion of this chapter with an overview of how we get to know how much or how little crime exists in the society and/or across societies: crime measurements or **crime statistics**.

HOW IS CRIME MEASURED? CRIME STATISTICS, VICTIMS AND OFFENDERS

Measuring how much or how little crime there is relies on a set of crime statistics which have been developed over the years, in tandem with the development of criminological thought and the tools criminologists have at their disposal for analysis and crime prevention. We will now look at the various crime statistics and what they tell us about victims and offenders.

Knowledge link: This topic is also covered in Chapter 3.

Crime Counts

The earliest indicator of the extent of crime in a society is the total number of crimes, the **crime count**. Similarly, the *number of offenders/arrestees/convicted* and *the number of victims/targets* in a society have been among the earliest crime statistics. Counts of crimes, perpetrators and victims are available in crime surveys, police and court records. The last two were the only tools criminologists had (and in many parts of the world still have) at their disposal prior to the 1970s, and they invested a lot of time and effort to produce crime counts which nowadays are available online (see https://www.police.uk/). However, counts are misleading, especially for comparisons across jurisdictions and over time.

The number of crimes, perpetrators and victims is not informative without knowing the size of the society incurring these crimes and the total number of potential offenders and victims, respectively. Suppose that each of two towns, A and B, is the scene of five similar crimes. The population of town A is double that of town B, so the latter has double the crime problems that town A has. Over medium or long periods measuring crime changes based on counts is also suspect because the respective populations change too. Counts are, therefore, *unqualified* crime statistics. Unfortunately, crime is still heavily reported in the media via crime counts, arguably contributing to moral panics as in the case below.

—————————— Case Study 4.1 ——————————

Kent and Knife Crime

Kent, for example, witnessed the largest increase in knife crime in England and Wales between 2010-2018, increasing by 152% (*The Guardian*, 2019). The population of Kent has grown faster than the national average, increasing by 11.5% during the same period (ONS, 2019b). The growth in population and increase in knife crime are partially attributed to councils in London relocating homeless families out of the capital, leading to an increase in gangs from London travelling into Kent to sell drugs to newly recruited local gangs (*The Guardian*, 2019). There are various statistics available and you may be wondering which ones you should use. The Royal Statistical Society runs a number of programmes to promote greater awareness of the appropriate uses and pitfalls of various statistics which are available at https://rss.org.uk/ (accessed 17/4/2020).

Crime Rates

The earliest and most commonly used *qualified* crime statistic that with an additional piece of information greatly improves on and overcomes the pitfalls of crime counts, is the number of crimes per 100, 1,000, or 100,000 of the population or potential targets. This is the lay definition of the term **crime rate**. It is important to weigh the reported crimes considering who the potential targets for that offence are. For example, if the crime in question is infanticide its rate is the number of those killed for every 100,000 infants. However, thinking as criminologists, especially in the UK and other countries with crime surveys, we know that the above calculation gives the crime incidence rate, which is only one from a set of crime rates, as will be seen in the next paragraphs of this section. Further, dividing incidence rates by 100, 1,000, or 100,000 (the respective multiple of ten the basis refers to) gives the **mean number of crimes** per person or potential target.

Incidence rates and mean crimes are equivalent crime statistics since the only thing that differentiates them is the size of the basis to which they refer. To consider an extreme hypothetical case, an incidence rate of 900 crimes per thousand people, or a value of mean crimes of 0.9 (calculated as 900 over 1,000), implies that *on average* almost everybody has experienced a crime. This is not the same as saying that almost everybody has; in the same way that an average income of £30,000 in the UK does not mean that everyone earns this amount – some, usually the majority, earn less, and some, usually a small minority, much more. Incidence rates and mean crimes give a snapshot of overall crime in a society. They can be calculated from police, crime survey and other data. For many decades in the past and still in many countries of the world incidence rates were/are the only qualified crime statistic. Crime surveys, the tools for reliably measuring other aspects of crime, did/do not exist, thereby considerably limiting the field of criminology and crime prevention in those times and countries. Understandably, incidence rates have been referred to as crime rates (the generic term) since there have been no others.

With the advent of crime surveys since the late 1970s in the USA (Hindelang et al., 1978) and elsewhere (1981 in the UK, see Gottfredson, 1984) an entirely new set of crime statistics and different crime rates that measure the impact of crime on victims has gradually been introduced. The earliest of these are **prevalence rates**: the number of victims per 100, 1,000, or 100,000 of the population or potential targets. Dividing prevalence rates by 100, 1,000, or 100,000 (the respective multiple of ten that the basis refers to) gives the statistic of **victimisation risk**, i.e. the proportion of the population experiencing a crime. Victimisation risk and prevalence rates are equivalent measurements, since the only thing that differentiates them is the size of the basis to which they refer, e.g. a prevalence rate of 50 victims per thousand people is equivalent to a victimisation risk of 0.05 (calculated as 50 over 1,000). Prevalence rates and victimisation risk give a snapshot of who experiences crime in a society.

Knowledge link: This topic is also covered in Chapter 3.

These can be reliably calculated from reputable crime surveys but with questionable accuracy from police and other data.

The examples in the previous two paragraphs give the possible albeit implausible scenario that a society has respective crime incident and prevalence rates of 900 and 50 per 1,000 people. What does the juxtaposition of these two crime statistics mean? For every 1,000 people 50 crime victims experience a total of 900 incidents, so how is crime exactly distributed? At one end, victims are equally burdened by 18 crimes each. Conversely, a victim experiences the bulk of crimes, 851, whilst the rest (the other 49 victims) experience one crime each. Any combination between these two extreme situations is also possible. Therefore, in this example there is some degree of **crime repetition** – at least one victim experiencing at least two crimes. This discussion holds replacing victim with offender.

With the advent of crime surveys the phenomenon of **multiple victimisation** was observed and documented but not measured until another two decades had passed (Reiss, 1980; Sparks, 1981; for an overview see Farrell, 1992). In the 1990s additional crime statistics were developed to measure the distribution of crime in a society: **repeat crime rates, repeat victim rates,** and **crime concentration.** Repeat crime rates show the number of crimes which occurred against the same victim or target per 100, 1,000, or 100,000 of the population or potential targets. Repeat victim rates are the number of victims who, or targets which, experienced two or more crimes per 100, 1,000, or 100,000 of the population or potential targets. Finally, crime concentration is the number of crimes experienced by each victim on average. In effect, crime concentration is the ratio of incidence over prevalence; in the previous example of respective crime incident and prevalence rates of 900 and 50 per 1,000 people, this equals 18. However, to calculate repeat crime and repeat victim rates information about how many crimes each victim experienced is required.

Pause for Thought

Try to replicate calculating the different crime rates, following the working example in Tseloni (2014). Based on Tseloni and Pease (2005) which crime types had higher and which lower levels of repeat crimes in 2000? Based on the latest (at the time of writing) victimisation statistics published by the ONS (ONS, 2019a), have repeat crimes across different crime types changed since 2000?

The above crime statistics on repeats provide a picture of who experiences the bulk of crime (and associated harm) in a society and can be reliably calculated from crime survey data. Several studies provide further reading on various aspects and descriptive analyses of the phenomenon of repeat victimisation and its importance for crime prevention (Farrell and Pease, 1993, 2007; Pease, 1998; Tseloni and Pease, 2005, 2010). Crime statistics usually refer to a calendar or financial (April to March) year and are presented as annual rates. However, experts argue that annual repeat crime statistics, as currently presented, do not accurately reflect the magnitude of the problem. This is because the time period for the second crime is shorter than twelve months – it starts when the first incident occurred – that for the third incident starts when the second one happened, and so on and so forth (Farrell and Pease, 2014).

Victim and Offender Typology based on Crime Frequency

The above body of research concerned with crime measurement and repeat victimisation has also provided classifications of victim or targets in relation to crime victimisation frequency. Using this criterion, individuals, households and other potential targets, such as banks or wildlife, can be classified into the following categories:

- Non-victims with zero crimes in any given period, usually a year.
- Single victims experiencing one crime in any given period.
- Multiple victims experiencing at least two crime types in any given period, e.g. an assault and a burglary.
- Repeat victims with more than one incident of the same crime type in any given period, e.g. three unrelated burglaries.
- Series victims in the UK (the definition varies across countries) are those reporting two or more incidents of the same crime type and Modus Operandi (MO) that occurred under similar circumstances and possibly by the same offender(s) in any given period, e.g. two assaults in or outside the local pub perpetrated by members of the same gang after starting an argument on choice of music on jukebox; and as proposed by the first author of this chapter.
- Composite crime victim, whereby more than one offence was committed against the same victim or target in the same incident, e.g. violence during a burglary (Tseloni and Pease, 2010).

By now you should have a good grasp of the various ways of measuring crimes and resulting national crime statistics, victim and offender typology. Next we will look at the various sources of crime statistics.

SOURCES OF STATISTICS FOR CRIMINOLOGY

In this section you will learn about the main sources of crime statistics: police and criminal justice data, and self-report offending and victimisation surveys.

Police and criminal justice data

Police recorded crime data include basic information about crimes that have come to the attention of the police, such as the name of the victim, the time, date and place of incident. The crime classification must be recorded on all crime records, with protected characteristics documented, if known, such as the victim's age, gender, sexuality, ethnicity, religion, marital status and disability to allow for the analysis of trends and patterns amongst specific crimes.

Police recorded crimes figures have historically been the subject of criticism due to variations in police forces' recording procedures (Kershaw, 2008). Due to concerns about the reliability and consistency of recording practices a number of reports and reviews were published, resulting in significant improvements made to the way crimes and incidents are recorded across forces in England and Wales. The National Standard for Incident Recording (NSIR) ensures that all incidents are consistently recorded by police forces according to the National Incident Category List (see https://assets.publishing.service.gov.uk/government/uploads/system/uploads/attachment_data/file/116658/count-nsir11.pdf). The Home Office Counting Rules (HOCR) and National Crime Recording Standard (NCRS) both address the previous lack of statistical comparable crime data by ensuring that police forces across England and Wales record notifiable crimes in a consistent and accurate manner (Her Majesty's Inspectorate of Constabulary and Fire & Rescue Services (HMICFRS), 2017). The offence classification index provides a breakdown of offences and how they are classified. Some useful sources of crime statistics and crime recording practices can be found in Table 4.1.

Table 4.1 Sources of Crime Statistics and Crime Recording Practices

Source	Data Available	Website
Police.uk	Crime Statistics	https://www.police.uk/
Home Office/Scottish Office/Police Service of Northern Ireland	Official Records Police and Crime Statistics Admin Data	https://www.gov.uk/government/collections/crime-statistics https://www.gov.uk/government/collections/policing-statistics/ https://www.gov.scot/collections/crime-and-justice-statistics/ https://www.nisra.gov.uk/statistics/crime-and-justice/psni-statistics
Ministry of Justice/ Justice Directorate Scotland/ Department of Justice: Northern Ireland	Court Statistics Prison and Probation Statistics Offender Management Statistics	https://www.gov.uk/government/organisations/ministry-of-justice/about/statistics#latest-statistics/ https://www.gov.scot/collections/crime-and-justice-statistics/ https://www.nisra.gov.uk/statistics/crime-and-justice/justice
Home Office	The Offence Classification Index Counting Rules	https://www.gov.uk/government/publications/counting-rules-for-recorded-crime

The appointment of crime registrars, who oversee the crime recording processes, in forces across England and Wales was expected to improve the quality of crime data (Kershaw, 2008). However, although the practice of accurately recording crimes has improved, an interim report of the inspection of crime integrity in police forces in England and Wales indicated that not all forces were adhering to the guidelines, suggesting that 20% of crimes, approximately 800,000 per year, were not being recorded (HMIC, 2014). The most recent (at the time of writing) inspection reports, on the effectiveness and efficiency of force crime recording processes, indicate that several forces are still failing to record all crimes appropriately. Force inspection reports can be found at the HMICFRS website (https://www.justiceinspectorates.gov.uk/hmicfrs/publications/crime-data-integrity-force-reports/).

— Pause for Thought —

- Why do you think police forces don't record all reports of crimes?
- What are the implications of improving crime recording practices for crime statistics?
- Does the non-recording of crimes have any implications for victims?

Police and justice data are the only source of measuring homicides. In the short term recorded crime data are reliable indicators of crime levels and can help identify short-term changes in individual offences, such as burglary offences, which are believed to be largely well-reported and well-recorded (ONS, 2019c). To the extent crimes have been cleared up police and criminal justice data provide a wealth of information about offenders and their journey (Tseloni et al., 2018b). However, using recorded crime as a source for measuring crime across jurisdictions and/or over time has a number of limitations. Non-reporting crimes by the public, non-standardised recording practice across police forces and over time, as well as changes in offence classification and legal definitions over time, are some of the most common limitations of police recorded crime (van Dijk and Tseloni, 2012).

Survey Data:- Self-report offending and victimisation surveys

Knowledge link: This topic is also covered in Chapter 32.

Knowledge link: This topic is also covered in Chapter 9.

Surveys offer rich contextual information about crimes experienced by the general population, known as **crime victimisation surveys**, or crimes committed and experienced by young people, known as **self-report offending/delinquency surveys**. Sheldon and Eleanor Glueck collected the very first survey data in relation to chronic juvenile delinquents and conducted follow-up surveys of matched samples of juvenile delinquents and non-delinquents (Glueck and Glueck, 1950, 1968). Many self-report offending/delinquency surveys are **longitudinal**, i.e. the same respondents are surveyed at different periods of their lives. The data collected provide immense theoretical and policy insights on the onset of criminal careers, recidivism and desistence from crime. For additional examples of such longitudinal studies which greatly influenced criminological theory, please see Farrington et al. (2013) and Wikström et al. (2012).

Crime victimisation surveys, henceforth 'crime surveys', were developed in response to well-documented and widely acknowledged weaknesses in recorded crime data. They measure crimes that are omitted from recorded crime data and adopt a standardised methodology which allows comparisons between different jurisdictions. Crime surveys also ask follow-up questions on the details of at least some of the criminal incidents victims have suffered, and include additional 'modules' for sub-sets of respondents asking supplementary questions ranging from security measures to lifestyles and attitudes to the police and criminal justice system (Tseloni et al., 2018b).

Crime surveys provide more robust estimates of crime rates and trends, especially for high volume crimes, than police recorded crime. They also include rich supplementary information about: victims' crime experiences, police reporting and satisfaction; the general population's perceptions and attitudes about crime, disorder and the Criminal Justice System (CJS), including the police; and detailed demographic, socio-economic and other factual information about the survey participants, their household and neighbourhood. This information has provided the foundations for theory development, especially on the topics of victimisation, fear of crime, and legitimacy of and trust in the CJS. Many countries, such as England and Wales, the United States and Mexico, have victimisation surveys.

Pause for Thought

- Which criminological theories that you aware of have been instigated based on crime surveys?
- Which criminological theories have been tested via the use of crime survey data?

Summary

This section compared the main sources of crime statistics: police recorded crime and crime surveys. The introduction of a standardised approach to police crime recording improved the data only for specific crimes, such as homicides, theft of vehicles and burglary offences which are generally well reported and recorded. Surveys provide reliable national crime rates, comparisons both over time and across jurisdictions, and a wealth of theory development and crime prevention analyses. You can find some useful sources of crime surveys in Table 4.2.

The chapter will now provide more detail for the survey which you will undoubtedly encounter the most, both as criminologists and UK residents.

CRIME SURVEY FOR ENGLAND AND WALES

The Crime Survey for England and Wales (CSEW) currently furnishes the only national crime statistics in England and Wales. It is highly regarded internationally, easily accessible, and has been used widely by criminologists and crime prevention agencies. It also furnishes teaching tools and related documentation which you can freely access for practising and/or empirically supporting your arguments in assignments. Tutors in criminology/policing/ criminal justice courses and related modules in other courses, e.g. gender studies or political science, can also use it. The sample size and selection methods allow meaningful analysis of crime patterns nationally. For this reason, it has supported numerous studies and thus assisted in the development of criminological theory and crime prevention initiatives, especially in relation to crime experiences and perceptions and the public's assessments of the police and the criminal justice system.

Student Voice

View from a third year PhD student

'I enjoy working with CSEW data because it is the same data used by policy makers, which makes the research feel as though it has more potential for impact.'

'Working with secondary data allows you to get on with analysis much sooner than designing your own survey, and the CSEW is so varied, you can answer so many research questions.'

(Beth, third year student at Nottingham Trent University, Doctoral School-funded PhD candidate, and currently a Government Statistical Service (GSS) Statistician)

The CSEW is a nationwide crime survey for England and Wales administered by the ONS. In existence since 1982 – then known as the British Crime Survey (BCS) –- the CSEW occurred roughly every two years until 2000 and annually since 2001/02, using annual rotating samples with interviews occurring monthly throughout the year. Until 2000 it measured crimes that happened in the calendar year prior to the fieldwork period (for example, the 1992 CSEW measured crimes against individuals and households from January to December 1991). From 2001/02 the CSEW measured crimes within each financial year, i.e. from April to March of the following year.

Sampling and Coverage

The CSEW sample represents all England and Wales residents aged 16 or older (and since 2009/10 also children aged 10–15 years old), living in private accommodation. The CSEW sample size was roughly 20,000 respondents for the years prior to 2001/02 and since then around 35,000 per year. The CSEW sampling frame, a national 'catalogue' of the population from which the sample is selected, is the Postcode Address File. The CSEW uses a stratified multi-stage cross-section sample design with over-representation of low population density areas. The survey has consistent high response rates.

Knowledge link: This topic is also covered in Chapter 32.

A number of weights in the publicly available datasets adjust for sample design effects. Thereby the number of offences reported by victims in the sample can provide population estimates. These are reliable for volume crimes, but population estimates for relatively rare crime types, such as robbery or sexual assault, entail large sampling errors.

CSEW interviews, confidentiality and data access

The CSEW is conducted via face-to-face interviews using Computer Assisted Personal Interviewing (CAPI), and for sensitive questions, such as domestic violence and sexual assault, Computer Assisted Self-administered Interviewing (CASI) to preserve respondents' confidentiality and safety. For the same reason the CSEW data are available in two formats – end of user license and secure data. Secure CSEW datasets include, for example, small area identification, such as Middle Super Output Area (of about 10,000 people and 4,000 households) and Lower Super Output Area (of about 2,000 people and 800 households) and/or data on sensitive questions, such as sexual assault.

All BCS/CSEW datasets, whether end-user license or secure, are available via the UK Data Service, whilst the secure CSEW ones are also available via the ONS Secure Research Service. The end-user licence CSEW data provide publicly available information on all respondents and all recorded crime. Some CSEW Special Modules and geocoding identification of the area of residence of respondents are provided in the secure data. This can be accessed following established safeguards in relation to research projects, researchers' accreditation and the institutional credibility of researchers' affiliation and project funders.

--- **Student Voice** ---

View from a first year PhD candidate

'There is a lot to learn from the CSEW data, I am always surprised at the variety of criminological topics that can be researched from one dataset.'

'The large size of the dataset can be overwhelming at first, but the results are often robust and interesting.'

(Danielle, first year student at Nottingham Trent University, Doctoral School-funded PhD candidate)

CSEW Information and Questionnaires

Let's see now, as the student above testifies, examples of information pertinent to so many criminological topics that the CSEW holds. The CSEW questionnaire comprises different sections as follows: the sampled Household Details, the Main Questionnaire, the Demographics and Media Consumption Section, Special Modules covering themed topics, the Victim Forms, and ad hoc special topics modules. In order to cover as many themes as possible Special Modules are completed by a random sub-sample of the entire annual CSEW sample and/or alternate from year to year. The complete CSEW questionnaires for different years can be found in the UKDS website.

The CSEW survey includes questions relating to victimisation experiences by an array of crime types such as: domestic burglary and fraud; respondents' own offending and their drinking and illicit drug taking; questions relating to experiences and perceptions of the criminal justice system and other crime prevention public and voluntary agencies. It also contains background questions on household composition, employment, leisure activities, driving habits and a respondent's age, sex and ethnicity. Publicly available CSEW data pertinent to most research testing criminological theories on, for example, victimisation, crime perceptions, trust in the criminal justice system, and punitiveness, include households' and individuals' demographic and socio-economic characteristics, households' housing and residential stability, the area type and Government Office Region area identification of respondents' area of residence. Most important for applying criminological theory to develop crime prevention policies, the CSEW has questions about any precautionary behaviour, household security and vehicle security measures. To appreciate the value of information provided in the CSEW there are no less than 2,600 variables in the end-user dataset. This number excludes the information from sensitive special modules, such as self-reported drinking, drug taking and offending and the Victim Forms.

Respondents who report crime experiences in the screener questions of the Main Questionnaire are then given *up to six* further modules, the Victim Forms, to complete. Victim Forms are completed for crimes reported in reverse order of the screeners – that is the most serious crimes have priority over less serious ones. The descending order of crime seriousness is rape and sexual assault, robbery, assault, theft from person, burglary, theft from dwelling, vehicle theft and vandalism. Cyber-related and non-cyber-related fraud and computer misuse have been added since 2015 in a way that does not distort the historical series of traditional crime types. The CSEW classification of incidents' crime codes can be found at the ONS website (https://www.ons.gov.uk/peoplepopulationandcommunity/crimeandjustice/methodologies/userguidetocrimestatisticsforenglandandwales#appendix-2-crime-survey-for-england-and-wales-offences).

Out of the six Victim Forms (VF) per victim, the first three are long VFs. They collect detailed information about the crime incident, its circumstances, offenders' modus operandi, related loss and/or harm, reporting to the police and reasons for non-reporting, the criminal justice system response to the crime and victim satisfaction. A further three (short) VFs collect less detailed information but sufficient to classify the incident for counting purposes. Back office checks ensure that the reported incident is correctly classified into one of the crime categories which also resemble as much as possible the statutory definitions of offences. As already mentioned, some crimes, such as domestic violence, are recurrent events that cannot be clearly distinguished and which the CSEW classifies as series. The VF data amount to almost 1,900 variables. Based on the VFs, crime rates in the previous year are estimated by the ONS on: personal crimes (theft from person, robbery, assault, sexual offences); household crimes (domestic burglary, household theft, theft of/from car, criminal damage); and household cyber-related and non-cyber-related crime (fraud and computer misuse).

The 10–15 year olds' CSEW questionnaire has the same structure as the adults' one including the victimisation module. This however contains questions appropriate for this age group on schooling, perceptions of crime, and crime prevention and security. It also has a self-completion module covering: use of the internet; cyber-enabled victimisation and self-report offending; bullying; street gangs; school truancy; personal security; drinking; and cannabis use.

Pause for Thought

- Make a note of what you might like to investigate using the Crime Survey for England and Wales.
- Formulate one or more research questions that address your research topic.
- Access the CSEW questionnaire to find any questions and variables which, if analysed, will answer your research questions.

We will now briefly mention a few sources for cross-national crime comparisons.

TOOLS FOR CROSS-NATIONAL CRIME COMPARISONS

The spread of crime surveys world-wide encourages their use in cross-national comparisons. In spite of the above advantages, crime surveys can be different in ways that seriously compromise the comparability of the resulting data and care must be taken in using these data for comparative purposes. Using appropriate care is often contingent upon having the relevant information on instrumentation and procedures used in the surveys readily available. Much of the detailed information on instrumentation and procedures may exist on individual data producers' websites and/or the respective national surveys' technical reports. With this information, researchers can assess the implications of differences in the surveys for cross-national comparisons. A word of caution here is that adequate knowledge of the national language and social survey terminology by aspiring cross-national criminologists may be required for accessing this information across the countries to be compared.

Knowledge link: This topic is also covered in Chapters 3, 9, and 32.

International Crime Surveys

To overcome the problem of different survey methodologies and questionnaires when using national crime surveys for cross-national comparisons, international self-report crime victimisation and offending surveys have been developed. The most ambitious ones in terms of rigour, geographical coverage and continuity are the International Crime Victims Survey and the International Self-Report Delinquency Study.

Table 4.2 gives you some examples of well-documented national and international crime surveys.

Table 4.2 Sources of Key Crime Surveys

Crime Surveys	
Cross-National	
International Crime Victims Survey	http://www.unicri.it/services/library_documentation/publications/icvs/
International Self-Report Delinquency Study	https://web.northeastern.edu/isrd/
International Violence Against Women Survey	https://heuni.fi/-/international-violence-against-women-survey-ivaws
National	
British Crime Survey/Crime Survey for England and Wales	https://www.crimesurvey.co.uk/en/index.html https://ukdataservice.ac.uk/
Scottish Crime and Justice Survey	https://www.gov.scot/collections/scottish-crime-and-justice-survey/
Northern Irish Crime Survey	https://www.nisra.gov.uk/northern-ireland-crime-survey
Commercial Victimisation Survey	https://www.gov.uk/government/statistics/crime-against-businesses-findings-from-the-2018-commercial-victimisation-survey
Crime and Justice Survey [Longitudinal data (2003-2006)]	https://beta.ukdataservice.ac.uk/datacatalogue/series/series?id=2000042
Local - self-report offending/delinquency surveys	
Peterborough Adolescent and Youth Adult Developmental Study	https://www.cac.crim.cam.ac.uk/research/padspres
Edinburgh Study of Youth Transitions and Crime	https://www.edinstudy.law.ed.ac.uk/

| Crime Surveys | |
International	
USA - National Crime Survey/ National Crime Victimisation Survey (NCVS)	https://www.census.gov/programs-surveys/ncvs.html
France - Victimisation survey - living environment and security The Cadre de Vie et Sécurité (CVS)	https://www.insee.fr/en/metadonnees/source/serie/s1278 https://www.interieur.gouv.fr/Interstats/L-enquete-Cadre-de-vie-et-securite-CVS
Mexico - The National Survey of Victimisation and Perception of Public Security (ENVIPE)	https://www.inegi.org.mx/programas/envipe/2016/#

Next you will get a glimpse of data sources which were not created for criminological research but provide additional tools for criminologists.

NON-CRIME AND ADMINISTRATIVE DATA

A variety of other than police or crime survey data sources have been employed in criminological research to date. These are: local authority and other administrative data, including for example health, economic, and deprivation profiles; census data; other than crime social surveys; and observational data on neighbourhoods (Tseloni et al., 2018b). Geocoded information on land use (available, for example, within the Ordnance Survey points of interest data in England and Wales, street view Google maps, social media networking sites, and consumer data maps) is also useful when linked to, for example, the data on crime and crime perceptions.

Administrative data are data collected for an administrative purpose, such as running a company, a charity, a school, or indeed the criminal justice system. The use of administrative data in official statistics has grown considerably in recent years (Government Statistical Service, 2019). Linking various government and organisations' administrative data can help create new insights and allow for an in-depth analysis of social problems from various angles via collaborative work between policy makers, analysts and external experts (Office for Statistics Regulation, 2018).

The ONS and (at the time of writing) a new organisation, the Administrative Data Research UK (ADR UK), aim to ensure data provided by UK Government bodies are accessed in a safe and secure form with minimal risk to data owners or the public. One of ADR UK's flagship projects, MOJ/ADR UK Data First, is, as the title shows, in collaboration with the MOJ and therefore of great importance to criminologists and researchers from an array of other disciplines. It aims to create linked datasets across the justice system and associated departments, such as the Department for Education and the Department for Work and Pensions. By linking together data from civil justice, family justice, the Crown Courts and magistrates' courts, ADR UK aims to create a system-wide data inventory, enabling researchers to build a better understanding of users of the criminal, civil and family justice systems (https://www.adruk.org/our-research/crime-justice/). These data will be added to the armoury of future criminologists for theory development and policy.

CHAPTER SUMMARY

- Criminological research can use empirical data from police recorded crimes, crime surveys, justice and administrative data.
- Although the quality and accuracy of police recorded data have improved in recent years, it is important to understand that they do not provide a full count of crimes due to limitations in

the under-reporting and under-recording of particular crimes. Comparisons over time and across jurisdictions remain problematic due to respective recurring changes to categories of crimes and offence definitions.

- Crime surveys have a number of advantages over data from police reports of crime as they usually employ consistent behavioural descriptions of crimes (rather than official definitions of crime) which facilitate comparability. Since these surveys are collected specifically for research and statistical purposes and not as a by-product of service delivery, they are often very well documented.

- However, crime surveys do not estimate reliably the extent of rare crimes due to insufficient sample sizes, crime patterns at street networks (although this is possible with very local surveys), and timing of incidents. They usually omit highly vulnerable populations, such as the homeless or prison inmates.

- In line with big data for social research, such as social media geocoded data, the use of administrative data has grown considerably in recent years. A new MOJ/ADR UK Data First programme aims to provide a wealth of linked data for justice research and beyond.

Review Questions

1. What are the main sources for measuring crime?
2. Which non-crime or survey data sources can be useful when conducting criminological research?
3. What information can be gleaned from the Crime Survey England and Wales?
4. What are the issues with using crime counts as the only measurement of crime?
5. Can police recorded crimes provide a reliable picture of the nature and prevalence of crime across England and Wales?
6. What are the benefits of using crime surveys to measure crime rate and trends?

GO FURTHER

Books/Book Chapters

1. For a history and uses of the BCS up to that point, see:

   Maxfield, M. and Hough, M. (2007) *Surveying Crime in the Twenty First Century, Crime Prevention Studies*. Cullompton: Willan.

2. For specific examples of how survey data have contributed to environmental criminology, see:

   Tseloni, A., Tilley, N. and Farrell, G. (2018b) 'Victimization Surveys in Environmental Criminology'. In G. Bruinsma and S. Johnson (eds), *The Oxford Handbook of Environmental Criminology*. Oxford: Oxford University Press: pp. 277–296. DOI: 10.1093/oxfordhb/9780190279707.013.23.

3. For specific examples of how police recorded crime and crime survey data have contributed to the study of the crime drop internationally, see:

   Van Dijk, J., Tseloni, A. and Farrell, G. (2012) *The International Crime Drop: New Directions in Research*. Hampshire: Palgrave Macmillan. ISBN: 978-0-230-30265-5.

Journal Articles

1. For an overview of the CSEW and its potential uses for research and policy, see:

   Tilley, N. and Tseloni, A. (2016) Choosing and using statistical sources in criminology – What can the Crime Survey for England and Wales tell us? *Legal Information Management*, 16(2): 78–90. DOI: 10.1017/S1472669616000219.

2. For a history of self-report delinquency surveys, see:

   Kivivuori, J. (2014) 'History of Self-report Delinquency Surveys'. In G. Bruinsma and D. Weisburd (eds), *Encyclopedia of Criminology and Criminal Justice (ECCJ)*. New York: Springer-Verlag. pp. 2309–2319.

3. For a history of longitudinal crime surveys, see:

   Nguyen, H. and Loughran, T. A. (2014) 'Longitudinal Studies in Criminology'. In G. Bruinsma and D. Weisburd (eds), *Encyclopedia of Criminology and Criminal Justice (ECCJ)*. New York: Springer-Verlag. pp. 2960–2968.

Useful Websites

1. The ONS (undated) provides detailed information on the CSEW, its purpose, coverage and methodological rigour for the public and potential survey interviewees: https://www.ons.gov.uk/surveys/informationforhouseholdsandindividuals/householdandindividualsurveys/crimesurveyforenglandandwales
2. The UK Data Service, one of the DEA accredited data processors, is a national (safe) depository of social, economic and population data in order to make them available for analysis without compromising data confidentiality: https://ukdataservice.ac.uk/
3. The ONS Secure Research Service, another DEA accredited data processor, enables access to restricted microdata from ONS surveys and other confidential datasets, such as the MOJ/ADR UK Data First ones: https://www.ons.gov.uk/census/2011census/2011censusdata/censusmicrodata/securemicrodata

REFERENCES

Cohen, L. E. and Felson, M. (1979) Social change and crime rates and trends: a routine activity approach. *American Sociological Review*, 44: 588–608.

Farrell, G. (1992) Multiple victimisation: its extent and significance. *International Review of Victimology*, 2(2): 85–102.

Farrell, G. and Pease, K. (1993) *Once Bitten, Twice Bitten: Repeat Victimisation and its Implications for Crime Prevention*. Crime Prevention Unit Paper 46. London: Home Office.

Farrell, G. and Pease, K. (2007) 'The Sting in the British Crime Survey Tail: Multiple Victimisation'. In M. Maxfield and M. Hough (eds), *Surveying Crime in the Twenty First Century, Crime Prevention Studies*. Cullompton: Willan. pp. 33–53.

Farrell, G. and Pease, K. (2014) 'Repeat Victimisation'. In G. Bruinsma and D. Weisburd (eds), *Encyclopedia of Criminology and Criminal Justice (ECCJ)*. New York: Springer-Verlag, 4371–4381.

Farrington, D. P., Piquero, A.R. and Jennings, W. G. (2013) *Offending from Childhood to `Late Middle Age: Recent Results from the Cambridge Study in Delinquent Development*, Springer-Brief Criminology Series. New York: Springer. ISBN: 978-1-4614-6104-3 (Print) 978-1-4614-6105-0 (Online).

Glueck, S. and Glueck, E. (1950) *Unravelling Juvenile Delinquency*. New York: The Commonwealth Fund.

Glueck, S. and Glueck, E. (1968) *Delinquents and Nondelinquents in Perspective*. Cambridge, MA: Harvard University Press.

Gottfredson, M. R. (1984) 'Victims of Crime: The Dimensions of Risk', *Home Office Research Study No. 81*. London: HMSO.

Government Statistical Service (GSS). (2019) *Introducing the Administrative Data Methods Research Programme*. Available at: https://gss.civilservice.gov.uk/news/introducing-the-administrative-data-methods-research-programme/ [Accessed 15 November 2019].

The Guardian (2019) *County lines drugs blamed for Kent's big rise in knife crime*. Available at: https://www.theguardian.com/uk-news/2019/mar/10/county-lines-drugs-kent-knife-crime-rise-cuts/. [Accessed 14 November 2019].

Hindelang, M. J., Gottfredson, M.R. and Garofalo, J. (1978) *Victims of Personal Crime: An Empirical Foundation for a Theory of Personal Victimisation*. Cambridge, MA: Ballinger Publishing Company.

HMIC (2014) *Crime-recording: making the victim count. The final report of an inspection of crime data integrity in police forces in England and Wales*. London: HMIC.

HMICFRS (2017) Crime-recording process. Available at: https://www.justiceinspectorates.gov.uk/hmicfrs/our-work/article/crime-data-integrity/crime-recording-process/. [Accessed 14 November 2019].

HMICFRS (2019) Crime data integrity reports. Available at: https://www.justiceinspectorates.gov.uk/hmicfrs/publications/crime-data-integrity-force-reports/ [Accessed 14 November 2019].

Kershaw, C. (2008) Plans for a new crime statistics system for England and Wales. *Crime Prevention and Community Safety*, 10: 150–157.

Office for Statistics Regulation (2018) *Joining up Data for Better Statistics*. Available at https://www.statisticsauthority.gov.uk/wp-content/uploads/2018/09/Data-Linkage-Joining-Up-Data.pdf. [Accessed 14 Nov 2019].

Office for National Statistics (ONS) (2019a) *Estimating the extent of repeat and multiple victimisation using the Crime Survey for England and Wales* (14.10.2019). Available at: https://www.ons.gov.uk/releases/estimatingtheextentofrepeatandmultiplevictimisationusingthecrimesurveyforenglandandwales. [Accessed 04.11.2019].

Office for National Statistics ONS) (2019b) *Middle Super Output Area Population estimates*. Available at: https://www.ons.gov.uk/peoplepopulationandcommunity/populationandmigration/populationestimates/datasets/middlesuperoutputareamidyearpopulationestimates [Accessed 13/11/2019].

Office for National Statistics (ONS) (undated) *Crime Survey for England and Wales*. Available at: https://www.ons.gov.uk/surveys/informationforhouseholdsandindividuals/householdandindividualsurveys/crimesurveyforenglandandwales. [Accessed 07.11.2019].

Office for Statistics Regulation (2018) *Joining up Data for Better Statistics*. Available at: https://www.statisticsauthority.gov.uk/wp-content/uploads/2018/09/Data-Linkage-Joining-Up-Data.pdf. [Accessed 14 Nov 2019].

Osborn, D., Trickett, A. and Elder, R. (1992) Area characteristics and regional variates as determinants of area property crime levels. *Journal of Quantitative Criminology*, 8: 265–285.

Pease, K. (1998) *Repeat Victimisation: Taking Stock*. London: Home Office.

Reiss, A. J. (1980) 'Victim Proneness in Repeat Victimization by Type of Crime'. In S. Fienberg and A. J. Reiss (eds), *Indicators of Crime and Criminal Justice Quantitative Studies*. Washington, DC: Department of Justice. pp. 41–53.

Sparks, R. (1981) Multiple victimisation: evidence, theory and future research. *Journal of Criminal Law and Criminology*, 72: 762–778.

Tseloni, A. (2014) 'Understanding Victimisation Frequency'. In G. Bruinsma and D. Weisburd (eds), *Encyclopaedia of Criminology and Criminal Justice (ECCJ)*. New York: Springer. pp. 5370–5382.

Tseloni, A. and Pease, K. (2005) Population inequality: the case of repeat victimisation. *International Review of Victimology*, 12: 75–90.

Tseloni, A. and Pease, K. (2010) 'Property Crimes and Repeat Victimisation: A Fresh Look'. In S. Shoham, P. Knepper and M. Kett (eds), *International Handbook of Victimology*. New York: Taylor and Francis. pp. 127–149.

Tseloni, A., Thompson, R., Grove, L., Tilley, N. and Farrell, G. (2014) The effectiveness of burglary security devices. *Security Journal*, 30(2): 646–664. DOI: 10.1057/sj.2014.30.

Tseloni, A., Thompson, R. and Tilley, N. (2018a) *Reducing Burglary*. New York: Springer.

Wikström, P.-O.H., Oberwittler, D. and Hardie, B. (2012) *Breaking Rules: The Social and Situational Dynamics of Young People's Urban Crime, Clarendon Studies in Criminology*. Oxford: Oxford University Press.

Crime and the Media

5

Sarah Moore

By the end of this chapter you will:

- Recognise the media's role in constructing the problem of crime, and have begun to consider how this might be subject to historical change.
- Be able to identify some of the key developments in media depictions of crime in the post-1970s period.
- Have an understanding of the politicisation of crime in the news, the hyperviolence of media depictions, the acceleration of moral panics and cautionary tales, and the emergence of 'real life' crime programmes.
- Be able to describe and evaluate classical debates, such as those around moral panic theory, and more newly-emerged issues in the field, such as the role of cautionary tales, the rise of citizen journalism, and the increase in visual content.

—————— Framing Questions ——————

To start you thinking about all this, have a go at the following tasks and questions:

1. Spend a few minutes reviewing your consumption of media stories about crime and criminal justice. Jot down some notes detailing which media and formats you're especially likely to consume, when, and how. (And remember that this might include novels, magazines, blogs, YouTube videos, news platforms, podcasts, as well as television drama and film.)
2. Start to think about what these media accounts of crime and criminal justice have in common. Do they share certain themes, styles, or narrative devices? Do they prompt similar emotions (such as excitement, fear, anger)? What sort of crimes tend to be the focus of these media treatments? Are there any consistencies in terms of how criminals, victims/survivors, and criminal justice officials are represented?

INTRODUCTION

This chapter provides a wide-ranging discussion of media treatments of crime and criminal justice — from 24/7 crime news to *Making a Murderer*, from tabloid news about terrorism to nineteenth-century detective novels. A core aim is to place media depictions in a historical perspective, and to that end the chapter starts by going back in time to think about eighteenth-century newspaper coverage of a notorious highwayman. We think, here, about how and why the eighteenth-century problem of crime — as depicted in the news — was so very different from the picture of crime and criminality we get from twenty-first century media.

From there we jump forward to focus on a set of key developments in the post-1970s period: the emergence of a more sensationalised, adversarial form of print journalism, the increasingly graphic portrayal of violence, the proliferation of **moral panics**, and the turn towards **'real life' crime programming.** A key theme throughout is the idea that media depictions — though often firmly in the realm of fantasy and fiction — are 'real' in their effects, in as much as they create powerful and persistent myths about crime that inform public debate, politics and policy. As you read other chapters in this book you'll find, I hope, striking connections between the picture of crime conjured by the media in the post-1970s period and trends in criminal justice policy, punishment, and criminalisation.

MAPPING THE TERRAIN

Most of us have little direct experience of crime and the work of criminal justice agencies. For the most part, what we know — or think we know — is derived from media sources. We need only think about some of the most high-profile crimes of the twenty-first century to realise the power of the media in shaping our understanding of crime. Take, for example, the attacks on the World Trade Center Building in New York City in 2001. That event is inextricably linked — synonymous, even — with the photograph of a plane flying into one of the buildings, broadcast around the world almost instantaneously. Or think about the ongoing fascination with the O.J. Simpson trial, still a relevant example for my undergraduate students, despite the fact that the trial took place some ten years before they were born. This 'mega trial' has been kept alive by ongoing media interest — in the last year alone, a much-watched television series and documentary. Or — one final example — think about the #MeToo campaign, and its unprecedented mass-dissemination of personal stories of sexual harassment and abuse. This campaign was part of a tide-change in how we talk and think about sexual misconduct, a shift that has contributed to an unprecedented increase in historic cases of sexual violence across both North America and Europe. All of this helps explain why crime and the media has become one of the largest fields of criminological study in the twenty-first century. Its concerns are wide-ranging, as we'll see below. For now, and by way of introduction, I want to point out one of its foremost points of interest — the role of the mass media in defining crime. If, as others in the volume have pointed out, crime has no essential character, but is the product of time and place, then the media play a leading role in constructing crime for us. It does this in myriad ways. I started this section by pointing to a number of high-profile crimes. Although it might be tempting to think otherwise, it is not inevitably the case that highly impactful crimes garner the most media attention. The relationship works the other way round: we come to see crimes as highly impactful *because* of media attention. In other words, it is the media that define certain crimes as 'high-profile'.

Knowledge link: This topic is also covered in Chapter 4.

There is a huge amount of academic literature on this, and several distinct approaches to the question of why certain crimes come to be defined as high-profile. Many researchers are concerned with the media's role in distorting the 'reality' of crime by amplifying highly unusual one-off cases and obscuring the more regular features of crime. Ray Surette (2014) usefully refers to this as the 'law of opposites'. Where the media tells us that crime is a problem that affects the middle-classes, is spiralling out of control, and is typically violent; empirical data show that crime disproportionately affects the working classes, has declined overall over the last few decades, and is typically property-related. We can see this 'law of opposites' at work, too, in the persistent suggestion in the media that violence tends to be carried out by random strangers, rather than — as is more statistically likely — intimates or acquaintances. This is something that I'm especially interested in, too, and have written about in relation to the media depiction of rape (Moore, 2009; 2011; 2013). For me, and many other criminologists besides, the mass media play a key role in sustaining powerful myths about victimhood and criminality.

None of this is to suggest that what we get from the media is an unchanging diet of sensational violence and biased representation. When we look at cultural treatments of crime and criminal justice over time we can see distinct changes in tone, content, and format. With that in mind, let's spend some time thinking about media depictions of crime in their historical context before turning to key features of media depictions in the late twentieth, early twenty-first century.

Knowledge link: This topic is also covered in Chapter 2.

LOVEABLE ROGUES AND COOL-HEADED DETECTIVES: EXPLORING HISTORICAL MEDIA CONSTRUCTIONS OF CRIME

You might have heard the phrase 'the past is a foreign country'. Certainly, when we take a look at past media treatments of crime it often feels like we're in unknown territory. That sense of dislocation is important. It should prompt us to think about current media depictions afresh, with a deeper curiosity not just about why they tell us particular stories about crime, but *how* they tell those stories, and the overall picture of crime and criminal justice they set before us.

So we're going to start by taking a step back in time in a bid to sharpen our critical faculties. The news item below is a letter published in a 1774 edition of *The Public Advertiser*, a London newspaper. The letter concerns an initial court hearing for John Rann, a notorious highwayman who had evaded police capture for some years. The crime in itself is interesting. Highway robbery belongs firmly to a historical period so technologically different to our own, both in terms of transport and the fact that wealth came in material form. It's an excellent example of how crimes are a product of time and place — and here I mean both that technological change can usher in new crimes, and also that social change brings new concerns about crime. There are other striking differences between the picture of crime and justice conjured in this news item, and that constructed by twenty-first century news sources. Have a read of the item (Figure 5.1), and then have a go at answering the questions in the 'Pause for Thought' box that follows.

--- Pause for Thought ---

- How does the letter-writer characterise public sentiment towards John Rann?
- How does the letter-writer characterise the detention of Rann?
- In what respects is this account different from what we might expect today of the detention of a criminal?

There's so much we could say about this news item. You might have been struck by the curiously public nature of the event described — the scene conjured is pretty riotous. And then there's the criminal justice officials' seeming lack of authority in all of this. The letter-writer sees them as too laid-back about it all, too ready to turn a blind-eye to (as the writer sees it) Rann's attempts to boost his popular appeal. It's all too much for our letter-writer, who complains that '[i]t is really a pity that the people should not understand that there is something serious in justice'.

Sir —

I have observed in your paper a very proper reprehension(1) of John Rann, who exhibited himself last Wednesday in Bow Street with his irons(2) covered and decorated with blue ribbon tied in a bow, and with a huge nosegay(3) in his bosom made of myrtle and roses. His whole behaviour was daring and shocking beyond example, and I am sorry to say excited equally improper emotions in the audience, which apparently increased his impudence….[H]e was received with a general laugh, and everything he said and did occasioned merriment…I thought it would have become the Dignity of the Bench to have gravely rebuked and ferociously exhorted the poor wretch to reflect upon the solemnity of the occasion, and his awful condition and situation. I think too the gaoler ought to have been reprimanded for suffering a prisoner in his custody to be brought up in so indecent a manner to be exhibited in the public streets as an object of jollity, gaiety, and triumph…It is really a pity that the people should not understand that there is something serious in justice, and that something more is meant by apprehending highwaymen than being paid forty pounds for their apprehension.

(1) Reprimanding of
(2) Handcuffs and legcuffs
(3) A small bunch of flowers

Figure 5.1 News Item: Court Hearing for John Rann

Today, justice processes seem abundantly serious (even as media depictions make entertainment out of them — but more on that below). Or, at least, justice has become a bureaucratic, formal matter. Foucault (1979) makes this point too in *Discipline and Punish*, where he reviews the changing nature and meaning of criminal justice from the eighteenth to the twentieth century. He argues that where punishment was once corporal, spectacular, and public, modernity brought a sequestering of punishment so that it became more 'civilised' — that is, behind closed doors, more orderly, and directed towards reforming the mind rather than harming the body.

For Foucault, the public desire to see justice being done didn't go away with the advent of modernity, instead it got expressed in other ways. Foucault argues that where popular stories of crime in the eighteenth century focus on the exciting antics of anti-hero criminals — Rann is a great example of this — into the nineteenth century, we see the rise of narratives where the detective and official investigation become the focal point. So it is, he argues, that we see the birth of the detective novel in the nineteenth century, a genre that transferred audience attention 'from the execution to the investigation, from … physical confrontation to intellectual struggle between criminal and investigator' (Foucault, 1979: 69). Crime stories, in other words, came to focus more on the heroic endeavours of state officials and the extraordinary minds of their cunning criminal-counterparts — think Sherlock Holmes and his arch-nemesis Moriarty. Crime, in these popular accounts of the nineteenth century, tended to be planned, stemmed from evil intent, and was always a serious matter. This set of ideas might sound more familiar to us, but like the mythical stories about Rann, they too work to create a powerful fiction about crime, criminals, and justice.

Expand Your Knowledge

If you'd like to read more about historical media accounts of crime, the following are recommended for further reading:

- Churchill, D. (2016) Security and visions of the criminal: technology, professional criminality and social change in Victorian and Edwardian Britain. *British Journal of Criminology*, 56(5): 857–876.
- Thomas, R. (2004) *Detective Fiction and the Rise of Forensic Science*. Cambridge: Cambridge University Press.

Let's turn now to think about our own historical period, with a renewed sense that the media depiction of crime here is also a product of time and place. For the remainder of this chapter I'm going to focus on four defining features of media treatments of crime in the late twentieth, early twenty-first century period: the emergence of a law and order agenda in crime news, hyper-violent media depictions of crime, the acceleration of moral panics and **cautionary tales**, and the rise of as-live, 24/7, 'real life' programming.

BUILDING THE LAW AND ORDER AGENDA: CRIME IN THE NEWS

The tendency for crime news to sensationalise, simplify, and call for governments to clamp down on crime seems like a given. But it hasn't always been like this. Hall et al. (2013), in their classic study of crime news, *Policing the Crisis*, argued that the 1970s ushered in a new era of **'law and order' politics** in both the USA and the UK. The news, they suggested, was key to promoting the idea that there was an endemic problem of crime that required greater government control. They argued that this alarm around crime was manufactured — as states sought to shore up their authority during a period of economic downturn — and that one of the more evident signs of this attempt to push a law and order agenda was the acceleration in moral panics.

We'll return to discuss moral panics below, but for now I want to think about how, into the 1990s, law and order politics — and its accompanying news discourse — became increasingly entrenched. This is a period when economically-advanced countries around the world significantly increased their prison populations, undertaking what many criminologists describe as a project of mass incarceration. Newburn and Jones (2005) point out that, around this time, we can observe a political convergence in both the USA and the UK on the question of how to deal with crime. In the USA, a watershed moment came during the 1988 presidential election campaign. Newburn and Jones (2005) detail how the electoral hopes of the Democratic candidate, Michael Dukakis, were dashed after news organisations held him responsible for the violent crimes perpetrated by a prisoner, Willie Horton, allowed out of prison on day release. News outlets decried Dukakis — and the Democrats more generally — as 'soft on crime', and his opponent — George H.W. Bush — won by a landslide. Newburn and Jones (2005) point out that the longer-term impact was the emergence of a new assumption amongst politicians of all stripes that a clear, punitive line on crime was needed to win elections.

Around the same time, as Newburn and Jones (2005) note, the UK was going through a parallel political reorganisation. Too long out of government, the Labour party was re-imagining itself. In a much-quoted speech from 1993, Tony Blair (then Shadow Home Secretary) announced the party's new approach to crime — they would be 'Tough on Crime, Tough on the Causes of Crime'.

In both the USA and the UK, then, a new political consensus emerged around crime and criminal justice in the closing years of the twentieth century. As prison populations grew sharply — and with little political opposition — the 'law and order' agenda that had emerged in the 1970s became a consistent feature of political debate. News outlets in the USA and the UK played a key role in legitimising and reinforcing this discourse. Three factors are of particular importance here. Firstly, news organisations provided a ready vehicle for the simplistic, 'tough on crime' messaging that became a key feature of politics from the 1990s onwards. Pratt (2007) refers to this as the **'sloganization'** of criminal justice issues, and he suggests that this is one way in which the media has contributed to the rise of penal populism in the late twentieth, early twenty-first century.

Secondly, from the closing decade of the twentieth century onwards, crime news has tended to focus more on the impact of crime on victims and communities, and, as part of this, emphasises the emotional reactions of those affected (an especially insightful analysis of this shift is offered by Wardle, 2006). This is part of a broader shift wherein the news — especially broadcast news — has increasingly come to rely on conventions traditionally associated with entertainment formats, such as personalisation and sensationalism (Altheide, 1997).

Also of note — this is our third factor — is the increased tendency from the 1990s onwards for newspapers to model themselves as criminal justice campaigners and, more broadly, for news outlets to style themselves as anti-establishment (sometimes referred to in the literature as '**tabloid adversarialism'**). This too has given space and licence to an increasingly declamatory tone in news reporting on crime. A notable example here is the US and UK newspaper campaigns in the late 1990s and early 2000s pushing for government reform of child sex offence legislation. Spurred on by reporting on a single case — in the USA, the assault and murder of the seven year old Megan Kanka, and in the UK, of six year old Sarah Payne — certain newspapers campaigned for new legislation around sex offender registration. Far from being a simple conduit for official messages about crime and criminal justice, then, certain news organisations have sought to overtly influence government policy and action in this area, and this pressure has tended to be for more punishment, harsher sentences, and tougher policies.

Expand Your Knowledge

If you're interested in reading more about the role of crime news in reinforcing penal populism, the following are recommended as further reading:

- Greer, C. and Mclaughlin, E. (2018) Breaking bad news: penal populism, tabloid ad-versarialism and Brexit. *The Political Quarterly*, 89(2): 206–216.
- Jewkes, Y. (2013) Punishment in black and white: penal 'hell holes, popular media, and mass incarceration. *Atlantic Journal of Communication*, 22(1): 42–60.

BLOOD AND GUTS: HYPERVIOLENCE IN THE MEDIA

We tend to assume that 'if it bleeds, it leads', to quote an old saying in journalism. That's not always been the case, though. Violence became a more consistent feature of media coverage from the mid-1970s onwards, with a greater tendency for representations to be graphic and gratuitous. Reiner et al. (2003), in their review of British crime news in the post-Second World War period, note a steady shift so that news reporting has come to focus less on property-related crime and more on violent crime. Studies of sexual violence in the news tell a similar story. Discussing US and UK news coverage of rape, Kitzinger (2004) notes a shift in both the volume and tone of reporting in the 1970s:

> Prior to developments in the 1970s the mainstream media paid little attention to rape: journalists even avoided the word, preferring phrases such as "carnal knowledge". By the end of the 1970s, in the UK and the USA, news items on rape had doubled, and increased by a much larger proportion in certain publications. (Kitzinger, 2004: 15)

Not only has news reporting of violent crime increased, but it has also tended to frame these incidents as random and inexplicable. Best (1999) writes particularly well about this and suggests that crime news tends to reinforce a sense that anyone is potentially a victim of crime — that 'it could be you'. The effect is to amplify public fear and to obscure the fact that violence (both in terms of who does it, and who experiences it) is socially-patterned.

Criminologists studying fictional depictions of crime and criminal justice note similar trends. I've written recently about the shift in detective fiction in the post-1970s period, and here, too, there has been an evident move towards more graphic, and on occasion sickening accounts of violence (Evans et al., 2018). Criminologists point to a similar shift in fictional accounts of prison, perhaps most evident in the deeply violent 'prison horde' — seemingly animalistic and deeply depraved — as a recognisable motif of late twentieth, early twenty-first century films and television programmes (see, for example, Mason, 2006; Moore, forthcoming; O'Sullivan, 2001). In an analysis of *Oz*, the 1990s US television series set inside a fictional maximum security prison, Yousman (2009) notes the show's tendency to depict prison inmates as 'superpredators' given to unpredictable acts of **hyperviolence**. In making sense of this, he points out that *Oz* is by no means an isolated case. At the end of the twentieth century, there was an evident proliferation in television shows that depicted offenders as deeply violent — amongst them, *America's Most Wanted* and *Cops*. All of this amounts to a persistent suggestion that crime is a particular type of problem — predominantly, one of terrifying violence — requiring a particular type of official response — punitive and hard-line. As such, the trend towards hyperviolence in media depictions of crime is part of the broader cultural-political landscape sketched out in the section above.

Case Study 5.1

The Social Construction of Perpetrators and Victims

Criminologists have explored the ways in which cultural treatments of violence rely upon – and further entrench – social norms and assumptions about gender, age, social class, and ethnicity. A particular tendency is for offenders' ethnicity to be made into an explanatory frame in stories about violent crime. Yousman's (2009) study, mentioned above, notes this tendency in *Oz*: hyperviolence, he argues, is associated here with African-American masculinity, and there is a persistent suggestion that this group is especially prone to animalistic displays of hyperviolence. The result is to reinforce pernicious ideas about African-American men, and to legitimate the idea that certain social groups require particularly punitive forms of punishment and control.

In twenty-first century news items about terrorism, too, perpetrators and alleged perpetrators are customarily racialised – that is, their actions are seen through the lens of their ethnicity (and this, in turn, comes to be conflated in news reports with religion). This then obscures incidents' broader social and political context and contributes to a powerful cultural myth that those from particular religious and ethnic groups are – to use the tabloid phrase – 'evil-doers'. There has been much written about the islamophobic nature of news reporting on terrorism, but I'd particularly recommend taking a look at Bhatia et al's (2018) recent edited collection, titled *Media, Crime, Racism*.

It's not just the case that news reporting on violent crime depends on and entrenches stereotypical ideas about the perpetrators of crime. It can reinforce pernicious cultural myths about victims of crime, too. There is a substantial body of feminist research that explores the media's tendency to characterise victims of sexual violence as either blameless or blameworthy – as 'virgins' or 'vamps', as Benedict (1993) puts it – depending on their seeming adherence to norms of traditional femininity and their behaviour prior to the assault. More recent research, whilst tending to reinforce the idea that news reporting still broadly promotes this dichotomous thinking about victims of sexual violence, highlights more nuanced features of reporting. In an especially illuminating article, Nilsson (2018) examines Swedish news reporting, and points to the tendency to sensationalise and decontextualise sexual violence. She notes a reliance on familiar cultural tropes and categories (for example, 'lonely pervert' attacks, 'sex slave' attacks, and 'celebrity rape'). Nilsson argues that this serves to distract from the structural conditions that shape sexual violence by 'monstering' perpetrators and, on other occasions, calling into question the credibility of victims' accounts.

THE BLAME GAME: MORAL PANICS AND CAUTIONARY TALES IN THE MEDIA

'Societies appear to be subject, every now and then, to periods of moral panic,' observed Stan Cohen in his pioneering study of the societal reaction to altercations between two British youth subcultural groups in the early 1960s (Cohen, 1987: 9). Certainly, there are some excellent studies of British moral panics during the Victorian period that demonstrate their occurrence in historical periods other than our own (for example Barrow, 2015). Criminologists are apt to point out that moral panics appear to have intensified or accelerated in the last quarter of the twentieth century — including, as I noted above, Hall et al. (2013). This might help explain why the concept has become so very popular, both within criminology and public debate more broadly. With over-use comes analytical stretch. My advice is to think very carefully when you use the term 'moral panic', and bear in mind that not all periods of sustained, salacious media coverage are best thought of as this sort of phenomenon. Before we get into thinking about alternatives to the moral panic paradigm, let's explore how researchers define 'moral panic'.

Case Study 5.2

What are Moral Panics?

Many moral panic researchers are interested in the question of what constitutes a moral panic. Goode and Ben Yehuda (2009) offer one influential definition. They suggest that we see moral panics in terms of five criteria: public concern, hostility (a sense of 'them' versus 'us'), consensus that the problem is significant, disproportionality, and volatility (moral panics have a here-today, gone-tomorrow quality). Straightforward though it is, this set of criteria is open to debate. For one thing, as Lashmar (2013) points out, it's difficult to ascertain whether news coverage is 'disproportionate'.

Critcher (2017) usefully describes Goode and Ben-Yehuda's (2009) model as 'attributional', focused, as it is, on pinning down the essential criteria of this phenomenon. He contrasts this to Cohen's (1987) original model, which he describes as 'processual' – that is, focused on how moral panics unfold. Cohen's much-quoted definition of 'moral panic' reflects this interest:

'A condition, episode, person or group of persons emerges to become defined as a threat to societal values and interests; its nature is presented in a stylized and stereotypical fashion by the mass media; the moral barricades are manned by editors, bishops, politicians and other right-thinking persons; socially-accredited experts pronounce their diagnoses and solutions...'. (*Source:* Republished with permission of John Wiley & Sons, from Cohen, S. (© 1987) *Folk Devils and Moral Panics: The Creation of the Mods and the Rockers*, p.9. Permission conveyed through Copyright Clearance Center, Inc.)

In Cohen's (1987) classic formulation, the media is just one actor in a moral panic, along with other opinion leaders, politicians, and experts. In his schema – he refers to it as the '**deviancy amplification spiral**' – an initial act of deviance is responded to disproportionately by the media, with articles that exaggerate and distort. There is then an overly-harsh official reaction, leading to the **folk devil** – that is, the repository of anxiety and concern – feeling ever more alienated and liable to more serious acts of deviance. In other words, the actions of the police, courts, and legislature – Cohen refers to this as the 'control culture' – are all crucial in the making of a moral panic.

Pause for Thought

Spend a few minutes listing as many cases of moral panic that come to mind. Now, look back at your list and think: do these cases fit with Cohen (1987) and/or Goode and Ben-Yehuda's (2009) conception of moral panic? What further work would you need to do to find out to determine whether the cases fit?

As mentioned above, 'moral panic' isn't always the most relevant concept for studying peaks in media coverage of crime. This was my experience when studying the news coverage around drug-facilitated sexual assault at the turn of the twenty-first century. At the time, it looked like it fitted the conventional moral panic schema, in that the media coverage tended to be sensational and fear-provoking. Each time I spoke about the case — at conferences, in classrooms, to colleagues — I got the same reaction: well, it's a moral panic, isn't it? Except in many ways it wasn't. For one thing, there was no evident folk devil in this case — that is, no specific group that was marginalised and condemned. And much of the media coverage appeared in informal news sources, such as women's glossy magazines and urban legends circulated via email and social media. The more I read of these stories, as well as items in newspapers, the more it dawned on me that the focus was not so much the perpetrator of a crime, but instead the would-be victim; her perceived failure to 'watch her drink', to realise the risks of socialising, the need for all women — because the media generally directed these pieces at women — to be more self-aware, more alert, to take more care.

This is how the concept of the 'cautionary tale' was born. I use this term to describe intense periods of media coverage where the focus is the (usually female) victim of crime, rather than the (usually male) perpetrator of crime. Examples include media coverage of identity theft, festival assaults, and attacks by taxi-drivers (Moore, 2013). A broader range of media tend to be involved in the construction of a cautionary tale, partly because they rely less on official 'voices' of censure (a key feature of moral panics) and more on anecdotal warnings about the need to take self-protective measures. Cautionary tales are distinct from moral panics, but, as I argue elsewhere (Moore, 2013), they fulfil similar functions in allocating blame: the former, in such a way as to urge rule-adherence and the latter, in such a way as to censure rule-breakers. There's a broader lesson here. Crime stories play an important role in reinforcing moral boundaries and social rules. As criminologists, the deeper question about moral panics and cautionary tales is what compels a society, at a given point in time, to reinforce *these* boundaries, *these* rules, and *this* specific group or behaviour?

Pause for Thought

Hall et al. (2013) note an acceleration of moral panics in a post-1970s period. In my work on cautionary tales, I note that there are particular periods when this form of media coverage proliferates – including the post-1970s period.

- Why might moral panics and cautionary tales have proliferated in this period?
- What might connect moral panics and cautionary tales to the trends identified above (that is, the punitive, adversarial turn in crime news, and the tendency towards hyperviolence in media depictions of crime)?

CRIME 24/7, 'AS LIVE', IN 'REAL LIFE'

Above I mentioned that 'moral panic' is potentially an over-used concept. It's also subject to challenges concerning its ongoing relevance. This is McRobbie and Thornton's (1995) suggestion, in a still-influential article calling for moral panic theory to be updated to take account of key changes in news production and consumption. However idiosyncratic your patterns of news-consumption, it's probable that, like me, you select particular news stories to read, cross-reference information, interact with these sources (by clicking on links or adding comments), and receive live news updates. McRobbie and Thornton (1995) draw attention to some of these tendencies in news-consumption too, and argue that they fundamentally change the nature and meaning of moral panics. Of course, these changes have affected media treatments of crime and criminal justice more broadly in the post-1970s period. Let's think, now, about the factors driving these changes in media consumption, and as part of that consider how these factors might shape media depictions of crime. We'll focus on three key changes here — shifts in the media industry, technology, and culture.

Firstly, industry-level changes. McRobbie and Thornton (1995) point out that the massive expansion of media platforms and formats during the late twentieth century led to the proliferation of news sources. At the same time, the emergence of low-cost, online forms of news-transmission means that the amateur news-maker — so-called **citizen journalists** — can have as much reach as a national newspaper. As more voices join the media debate, the possibility for editorial control over media messaging decreases. The effect is to make moral panics more open to challenge and, more broadly, crime reporting more subject to contestation from those 'on the ground'. Social media plays a key role in all of this, and for many criminologists it has radically altered the public's ability to intervene in and reshape debates about crime (see, for example, Greer and McLaughlin, 2010).

Also important — and intimately connected to the expansion of the media — is a set of technological changes in the post-1970s period. The rise of satellite-enabled digital technology in the mid-1990s made it possible to instantaneously and cheaply transmit high-definition audio-visual material around the world. And the emergence of the Internet — and, with it, streaming — has provided further means for as-live media transmission. Today, we expect there to be an audio-visual record of an event, we expect that record to be part of the media story, and for it to be available in real-time.

An obvious effect of this is the rise of 24/7 news, a shift kick-started by the launch of CNN, the first 24-hour news channel, in 1980. A less direct effect of the huge increase in — and appetite for — as-live records of events is the rise of 'real life' accounts of crime, evident not just in the rise of citizen journalism, but also in the growing popularity of television programmes providing a seemingly direct, unvarnished view of crime and the work of criminal justice agencies. *Cops* and *America's Most Wanted* — launched in the 1980s, and amongst their network's most popular and long-running television programmes — were early examples of this trend. The hugely popular, critically-acclaimed criminal justice investigative documentaries of the early twenty-first century — *Making a Murderer, Jinx*, even the podcast *Serial* — are different in tone, but reflect, too, our interest in revealing, probing accounts of 'real life' crime and criminal justice.

There's so much to unpack here — and so much diversity in media treatments — but in the rise of 'real life' crime programming we can see an evident cultural shift (the third key shift under discussion here) wherein once-trusted social authorities tend now, in a post-1970s period, to be subject to greater scrutiny, much of it critical in nature. This is true not just of the work of criminal justice officials, but also of journalists: where, once, we might have trusted these as reputable and trustworthy, the greater tendency today is to see them as capable of exploitation, distortion, and corruption (as propagators of 'fake news'). This cultural current, too, has played a key role in shaping how we consume the media and the sorts of crime-stories that have become popular in the twenty-first century. It's not just that technological changes make it possible for us to surf the news, access the lay-person accounts of citizen journalists, and follow 'real life' crime shows. These reflect, also, the decline in public trust in sources of social authority that characterises the post-1970s period.

Pause for Thought

Towards the start of this chapter, I mentioned three high-profile cases/campaigns as evidence of the impact of media coverage of crime: the coverage of the 2001 attacks on the World Trade Center, the O.J. Simpson case, and the #MeToo campaign.

How might the developments discussed in this section – that is, the expansion of the media, the inclusion of a broader range of 'voices' in media debates, the rise of 24/7 media coverage, the interest in 'real life' and 'as live crime stories – have shaped the media construction of these cases?

CHAPTER SUMMARY

- This chapter started with an exploration of an eighteenth-century news item about a highwayman as our point of departure for thinking about how media constructions of crime are subject to historical change. This served to remind us that crime stories, including those we read and watch today, reinforce powerful fictions about crime and criminal justice.
- From there, we leapt forward in time, to think about the key features of media depictions of crime and criminal justice in the post-1970s period.
- We examined, in turn, the 'law and order' agenda in crime news, hyperviolence as a device and theme, the acceleration in moral panics and cautionary tales, and the emergence of 24/7, 'real life' media accounts of crime.

Review Questions

1. What does Surette (2014) mean when he suggests that media depictions of crime follow a 'law of opposites'?
2. What do Hall et al. (2013) mean by the 'law and order' agenda?
3. Identify one way in which crime news has helped reinforce penal populism.
4. What are the criteria of 'moral panic', according to Goode and Ben-Yehuda (2009)?
5. What is citizen journalism, and how has it shaped our consumption of crime news?

Framing Questions Revisited

1. At the start of the chapter I asked you to note down which crime-stories you consume, and then think about what these stories might have in common. Spend a few minutes now re-visiting your notes, and then think: how do the four key features of media coverage discussed above relate to your own media-consumption habits and preferences?

GO FURTHER

Books

1. If you want to read more about crime in the media, there are few better places to start than with Cohen's classic UK-based study of the societal reaction to altercations between two 1960s youth subcultural groups.

    Cohen, S. (2011) *Folk Devils and Moral Panics: The Creation of the Mods and the Rockers*. London: Routledge.

2. This fascinating book examines the history and meaning of serial killing in European films, and connects this cultural motif to consumerist logic of late modern societies.

    Dyer, R. (2015) *Lethal Repetition: Serial Killing in European Cinema*. London: British Film Institute.

3. Drawing upon an interesting mix of media-based analysis and first-hand interviews with practitioners, this book examines the impact of new media technology — principally social media — on crime and criminal justice.

    Hayes, R. M. and Luther, K. (2018) *#Crime: Social Media, Crime, and the Criminal Legal System*. Basingstoke: Palgrave Macmillan.

Journal Articles

1. This excellent article unpacks the media coverage of the murder of Marianne Vaatstra, and specifically how this was transformed into a high-profile case.

    Jong, L. and M'charek, A. (2018) The high-profile case as 'fire object': following the Marianne Vaatstra murder case through the media, *Crime, Media, Culture*, 14(3): 347–363.

2. Focused on one of the most popular criminal justice television documentaries of the last decade — *Making a Murderer* — this interesting article argues that the miniseries reinforces 'law and order punitivism'.

    LaChance, D. and Kaplan, P. (2020) Criminal justice in the middlebrow imagination: the punitive dimensions of *Making a Murderer*. *Crime, Media, Culture*, 16(1): 81–96.

3. This article is based upon a cultural analysis of the television series *Breaking Bad*, with a particular focus on the social and biological factors involved in violence. Recommended for its creative use of a television series to engage with and develop criminological theory.

    Wakeman, S. (2018) The 'one who knocks' and the 'one who waits': gendered violence in *Breaking Bad. Crime, Media, Culture*, 14(2): 213–228.

Useful Websites/Weblinks

1. A podcast exploring the allure and meaning of 'true crime' stories in the media:

    Murder Society — https://www.stmarys.ac.uk/research/areas/communications-humanities-social-policy/murder-society-podcast.aspx

2. A treasure trove of articles detailing the Library's world-leading collection of nineteenth century crime fiction, from penny dreadfuls to early detective fiction:

The British Library Collection on Crime and Crime Fiction — https://www.bl.uk/romantics-and-victorians/themes/crime-and-crime-fiction

3. This highly engaging, award-winning podcast re-examines criminal justice cases. A brilliant example of 'true crime' programming:

Serial — https://serialpodcast.org/

REFERENCES

Altheide, D. (1997) The news media, the problem frame, and the production of fear. *The Sociological Quarterly*, 38(4): 647–668.

Barrow, R. J. (2015) Rape on the railway: women, safety, and moral panic in Victorian newspapers. *Journal of Victorian Culture*, 20(3): 341–356.

Benedict, H. (1993) *Virgin or Vamp: How the press covers sex crimes*. Oxford: Oxford University Press.

Best, J. (1999) *Random Violence: How We Talk About New Crimes and New Victims*. Berkeley, CA: University of California Press.

Bhatia, M. et al. (eds) (2018) *Media, Crime, and Racism*. London: Springer.

Churchill, D. (2016) Security and visions of the criminal: technology, professional criminality and social change in Victorian and Edwardian Britain, *British Journal of Criminology*, 56(5): 857–876.

Critcher, C. (2017) 'Moral Panics', *Criminology and Criminal Justice: Oxford Research Encyclopedias*. Online.

Evans, M., Moore, S. and Johnstone, H. (2018) *Detecting the Social: Order and Disorder in Post-1970s Detective Fiction*. Basingstoke: Palgrave Macmillan.

Foucault, M. (1979) *Discipline and Punish: The Birth of the Prison*. London: Vintage.

Goode, E. and Ben-Yehuda, N. (2009) *Moral Panics: The Social Construction of Deviance*. Oxford: Blackwell.

Greer, C. (2017) 'News Media, Victims and Crime'. In P. Davies et al. (eds), *Victims, Crime and Society*. London: Sage.

Greer, C. and McLaughlin, E. (2010) 'We Predict a Riot?': public order policing, new media environments, and the rise of the citizen journalist. *British Journal of Criminology*, 50(6): 1041–1059.

Greer, C. and Mclaughlin, E. (2018) Breaking bad news: penal populism, tabloid adversarialism and Brexit. *The Political Quarterly*, 89(2): 206–216.

Hall, S. et al. (2013) *Policing the Crisis: Mugging, The State, and Law and Order*. London: Red Globe Press.

Hayes, R. M. and Luther, K. (2018) *Crime: Social Media, Crime, and the Criminal Legal System*. Basingstoke: Palgrave Macmillan.

Jewkes, Y. (2013) Punishment in black and white: penal 'hell holes', popular media, and mass incarceration. *Atlantic Journal of Communication*, 22(1): 42–60.

Kitzinger, J. (2004) 'Media Coverage of Sexual Violence Against Women and Children'. In K. Ross and C. M. Byerly (eds), *Women and Media: International Perspectives*. Oxford: Blackwell. pp. 13–38.

Lashmar, P. (2013) 'The Journalist, Folk Devil'. In C. Critcher et al. (eds), *Moral Panics in the Contemporary World*. Oxford: Bloomsbury.

Mason, P. (2006) Prison decayed: cinematic penal discourse and populism 1995–2005. *Social Semiotics*, 16(4): 607–626, 611.

McRobbie, A. and Thornton, S. (1995) Rethinking 'moral panic': the construction of deviance. *British Journal of Sociology*, 46(4): 559–574.

Mendes, K., Ringrose, J. and Keller, J. (2019) *Digital Feminist Activism: Girls and Women Fight Back Against Rape*. Oxford: Oxford University Press.

Moore, S. E. H. (2009) The cautionary tale: the British media's handling of drug-facilitated sexual assault. *Crime, Media, Culture*, 5(3): 305–320.

Moore, S. E. H. (2011) Tracing the life of a crime category: the shifting meaning of date rape. *Feminist Media Studies*, 11(4): 451–465.

Moore, S. E. H. (2013) 'The Cautionary Tale: A New Paradigm for Studying Media Coverage of Crime'. In J. Petley, et al. (eds), *Moral Panics in the Contemporary World*. Oxford: Bloomsbury. pp. 33–50.

Moore, S. (2014) *Crime and the Media*. Basingstoke: Palgrave Macmillan.

Moore, S. (forthcoming) From Alcatraz to Dannemora: 'flights from' and 'flights to' in prison escape stories, *Prison Service Journal*.

Newburn, T. and Jones, T. (2005) 'Symbolic politics and penal populism: The long shadow of Willie Horton', *Crime, Media, Culture*, 1(1): 72–87.

Nilsson, G. (2018) Rape in the news: on rape genres in Swedish news coverage, *Feminist Media Studies*, 19(8): 1178–1194.

O'Sullivan, S. (2001) Representations of prison in nineties Hollywood cinema: from *Con Air to The Shawshank Redemption*. *The Howard Journal*, 40(4): 317–334, 326.

Petley, J. et al. (eds) (2013) *Moral Panics in the Contemporary World*. Oxford: Bloomsbury.

Pratt, J. (2007) *Penal Populism*. London: Routledge.

Reiner, R., Livingstone, S. and Allen, J. (2003) 'From Law and Order to Lynch Mobs: Crime News Since the Second World War'. In P. Mason (ed.), *Criminal Visions: Media Representations of Crime and Justice*. Collumpton: Willan. pp. 13–32.

Seltzer, M. (2007) *True Crime: Observations on Violence and Modernity*. London: Routledge.

Surette, R. (2014) *Media, Crime, and Criminal Justice: Images and Realities*, 5th Edition. Belmont, CA: Wadsworth Press.

Thomas, R. (2004) *Detective Fiction and the Rise of Forensic Science*. Cambridge: Cambridge University Press.

Wardle, C. (2006) "IT COULD HAPPEN TO YOU": The move towards personal and societal narratives in newspaper coverage of child murder, 1930–2000. *Journalism Studies*, 7(4): 515–533.

Wright Monod, S. (2017) *Making Sense of Moral Panics: A Framework for Research*. Basingstoke: Palgrave Macmillan.

Yousman, B. (2009) Inside *Oz*: hyperviolence, race and class nightmares, and the engrossing spectacle of terror. *Communication and Critical/Cultural Studies*, 6(3): 265–284, 273.

PART II

THEORIES AND CONCEPTS OF CRIMINOLOGY

Approaches to Criminological Theory

6

Michael Rowe

Learning Objectives

By the end of this chapter you will:

- Be able to identify key schools, perspectives and theoretical traditions within the discipline of criminology.
- Outline key points of difference and similarity between different theories of crime through critical review and application to crime policy and practice.
- Explore underlying philosophical and scientific principles underlying different theories of crime.

Framing Questions

1. Is it conceivable to identify a theory that explains all forms of offending and crime?
2. Theoretically, how to do matters of political, social and economic power influence how crime is explained?
3. To what extent are offenders best understood as 'victimised actors'?
4. To what extent are offenders 'rational actors'?

INTRODUCTION

The discipline of criminology emerged in western societies against the broader context of the Enlightenment transformation of science and knowledge from the eighteenth century onwards. As Hall (2012) points out, the social sciences developed relatively recently and inherited a theoretical framework from older traditions in philosophy and political theory. The first 'modern' criminological study, still resonant in contemporary debates, is usually identified as Cesare Beccaria's study of punishment (published in the mid-eighteenth century), discussed at greater length below. Pre-classical thought had considered crime in metaphysical terms, perhaps with reference to divine intervention, and had considered punishment as a matter of redemption or in terms of retribution. As with the Enlightenment project more generally, the development of modern criminology was based upon fundamental assumptions about the possibility of understanding human behaviour on the basis of rational analysis and scientific validation. The diverse theories of crime explored in this chapter share a framework such that they can be tested and empirically examined: they are theories in the scientific sense that they can, in principle, be refuted or upheld. The theories outlined here are presented in broad schools of thought rather than in chronological terms. By organising the material in this way it is intended to avoid a teleological account that suggests progression from one perspective to another in an unending process of improvement and refinement. Instead you are asked to recognise that there is considerable overlap between the approaches and that many have existed co-terminously, and continue to do so. You will be encouraged to think about how these abstract perspectives can be applied to 'real world' criminology.

MAPPING THE TERRAIN

Criminology is usually defined as the study of the causes of criminal behaviour, and the nature of social responses to crime (Mannheim, 1965). Discussion of crime and criminality often starts from the relatively narrow perspective that criminal behaviour can be understood in terms of those actions, or non-actions, that do not comply with existing legal codes and can be understood as 'criminal'. This literal approach to the subject matter, however, raises many questions and is ultimately unsatisfactory. The 'crime as law-breaking' approach is complicated when changing legal codes prohibit or legalise certain activities as social concerns and mores develop and shift over time, and across societies. The consumption of alcohol, for example, was illegal in the United States during prohibition in the 1920s, in some societies it remains a criminal act, and in most countries consumption of alcohol is illegal below a certain age limit, although these proscriptions might not apply for children drinking alcohol in the home environment.

—————————————— Pause for Thought ——————————————

In conjunction with reading Chapter 3 on the history of crime, can you identify actions or behaviour that have been criminalised in some societies at some moments in time, but have not been illegal in other places or moments?

A 'black letter law' approach to defining crime becomes further complicated when the huge differences in enforcement are considered. Debate about the causes, and responses, to crime has been couched in terms of the 'harm' caused to individuals and to society. The 'harm' caused by crime, considered in terms of violation of the criminal law, however, might be significantly outstripped by the damage done by actions that do not violate the law and so technically are not criminal. Pollution and environmental damage, for example, might, or might not, be criminal offences. Often they are problems of a transnational character, which transverse jurisdictions, and so are difficult to investigate or prosecute. In any event, the harm caused is not necessarily reflected in law. Radical and critical criminologists point out that criminal codes are drafted by the powerful, and reflect established power relations. Definitions of crime focused upon infractions of the criminal law will reflect the power relations that underpin legal developments in the first place.

In order to present this short review of criminological theory in terms of helping your reading of the rest of this collection the discussion is organised into three parts. First, are accounts of offending premised on the perspective that offenders are rational actors who make calculated decisions to commit (or otherwise) offences on the basis of their understanding of the potential benefits they might secure compared to the potential costs that might follow. The focus of these approaches tends towards the individual person and the immediate circumstances in which offences occur. The second part explores a different set of approaches based on the idea that offenders are 'pre-destined' actors, whose behaviour is shaped (or even determined) by extraneous factors such as biological or psychological characteristics beyond their immediate control. The third section considers theoretical accounts that focus on social, political and cultural contexts that come to define some forms of behaviour as criminal, and so focus criminal justice and legal action disproportionally against groups and individuals who come to be regarded as threatening and problematic. Those otherwise powerless and marginalised in society are more likely than others to be defined and treated in these ways, it is argued. In each of the three sections, problems and implications of the various perspectives are noted, forming the basis for your critical reading of wider debates in criminology. Through identifying ways in which theoretical perspectives have been applied in practice it is hoped you can recognise links between concepts and applied policy responses, and that this can be carried through in your reading of other chapters in this collection. It should be noted that each section offers a simplified and truncated account of diverse, overlapping and contradictory bodies of work. Further reading is suggested that can develop a more nuanced understanding of criminological theory (and many of the issues that are touched upon here are expanded in other chapters in this book). The purpose here is to introduce you to key features and points of debate.

Knowledge link: This topic is also covered in Chapter 20.

Knowledge link: Chapter 8 in this collection examines the relation between crime, power and social harm in more detail and Chapter 27 explores this in respect of gender, crime and victimisation.

PART ONE - THE RATIONAL ACTOR MODEL

This model continues to inform much of our thinking about crime and policy responses to it. Here you are introduced to different approaches centred on this model, a classical school, more recent right realism, and routine activities theory.

The Classical School

The Classical School of criminology emerged during that period of intellectual ferment known as the European Enlightenment. The eighteenth century was a period of enormous change in terms of the development of scientific knowledge. The authority of the old aristocracies was challenged, both because of their claims to natural superiority and their corrupt political practices. Traditional conceptions of property and ownership were disrupted by these social changes. It was against this background that modern criminology emerged.

Earlier European judicial systems had been founded on the religious structures of the Middle Ages. Such law was mainly the product of judicial interpretation and whim. It was the gradual permeation of Enlightenment ideas that provided the basis to soften the rigor of this draconian Bloody Code (although as Emsley, (2005) has pointed out, the Code also waned because it became increasingly dysfunctional in ways that had nothing to do with changing punitive sensibilities). In the study of crime and criminal justice, Enlightenment perspectives are most often associated with the works of Cesare Beccaria, and in the jurisprudential and social reform writings of Jeremy Bentham.

Beccaria's major original contribution to criminological thought, first published in 1764, was the idea that criminals owe a 'debt' to society and punishments should be fixed strictly in proportion to the seriousness of the crime. Criminal justice policy was not simply a matter that could be left to private restitution between offender and victim, or to divine judgment, but was a matter of collective public interest. Beccaria argued that punishment ought to be administered on rational grounds, in proportion to the degree of social harm the crime had caused, and that all offenders be treated equally regardless of their social standing. First-time offenders and recidivists were treated exactly alike, solely on the basis of the particular act that had been committed. This avoided punishment being determined by extraneous factors relating to the imputed 'moral character' or social status of the offender. However, it became apparent that some personal characteristics, for example the age of the offender, should properly be taken into account in determining punishment and this was soon reflected in early modern criminal justice systems. Young (1983) noted that Beccaria paid attention to the specific rights of offenders to a greater degree than prevailing approaches to punishment, which had held that the sovereign retained the right to inflict strict sanctions to deter other offenders. Judges began to vary sentences to reflect different levels of individual culpability, relating to their capacity to act rationally. This breaks with the tenets of the Classical School, which operated on the basis that offenders were rational actors, and contributed to the development of neo-classicism.

The neo-classicists retained the central notion of a free will (or voluntaristic) model of human action, but with the recognition that certain structures, circumstances or accidents of biography may be less conducive to the unfettered exercise of free choice than others. Doctors, psychiatrists and, later, social workers testified before the criminal justice system about the extent to which individuals had acted in terms of calculated free choice or were conditioned or determined by outside factors. Essentially, this later perspective contributed to positivist approaches that explained criminal behaviour in terms of the biological, the familial, the environmental, or the social context that individuals found themselves in. The tension between the 'free will' and the 'determinist' explanations of criminal behaviour has dominated western criminology, as is reflected in much of the discussion that follows.

Knowledge Link: Approaches to offending drawing upon social and biological characteristics are discussed in more detail later, and in Chapters 9 and 11 in this collection.

Right Realism

Often associated with the emergence of 'new right' politics in the United States, Britain and elsewhere in the mid-1970s, right realism in criminology saw a revival of (neo)classical criminology, with an emphasis on rationality and deterrence. Right realism was partly a reaction to the perceived inability of the criminal justice system (or criminology) to identify the social, biological or environmental causes of crime. After a period of rising economic prosperity and untold public expenditure on crime reduction programmes and efforts to rehabilitate offenders, crime was, apparently, rising inexorably. If liberal welfare programmes were unable to diminish criminal behaviour, let alone prescribe treatment or interventions to prevent recidivism, the argument was made, then criminal justice ought to return to a 'cost-benefit' approach that might shape individual decisions to commit crime. From this perspective, offenders are understood as rational actors who weigh up potential benefits and possible costs before deciding whether or not to commit an offence.

This approach was particularly associated with the work of James Q. Wilson, who became crime advisor to President Reagan. In his 1973 text *Thinking About Crime*. Wilson argued, along classical lines, that criminal behaviour could be prevented by increasing the 'costs' of offending. Interestingly, he also argued that the benefits of pursuing legitimate lifestyles ought to be enhanced and that government intervention via social policy should be pursued, which put this approach somewhat at odds with neo-liberal conceptualisation of the minimal state. Wilson's right realism also differed from conservative political thought of the time as he did not endorse the perspective that extensive punishments ought to be pursued for their deterrent effect, arguing, in keeping with Beccaria, that punishment ought only to be determined by the characteristics of individual cases rather than an estimation of the broader social impact. Individual calculations of the potential costs of offending were not much influenced by the severity of punishment since most offenders felt it unlikely they would be brought to justice (Smith et al., 2002). Right realists argued that increasing the certainty of punishment had a greater deterrent effect than increasing tariffs. Wilson (1975: 21) demonstrated the rational choice basis of his utilitarian theory of the causes of crime in the following terms, highlighting the individualistic nature of decisions to offend:

> If the supply and value of legitimate opportunities (i.e. jobs) was declining at the very time that the cost of illegitimate opportunities (i.e. fines and jail terms) was also declining, a rational teenager might well have concluded that it made more sense to steal cars than to wash them.

Right realists also revived the notion that criminal acts transgressed the social contract and so were offences against the whole of society. Criminal behaviour reflected a decline in morality associated with liberal permissiveness. This approach regards the law as an expression of the moral community of the nation, and the punishment of transgressions demonstrates a more fundamental commitment to uphold common values and moral principles, and sends important symbolic signals. This reflects a Durkheimian approach such that the law ought to act to enforce social mores in order to maintain solidarity in an organic society (although Lukes and Prabhat, 2012 have argued this is a simplistic interpretation of Durkheim's argument). Enforcing the law not only demonstrates that particular types of behaviour are not tolerated by mainstream society, but, more generally, also demonstrates a commitment to apply a common normative framework.

While individual criminal acts entail decision-making by an offender, in terms of selecting a type of crime, a victim, a place, a time, and so on, the suggestion that these choices reflect rationality has been challenged. Just as economists have recognised that consumers rarely exercise their judgment as classic micro-economic models suggest, so too criminologists have argued that criminals, at best, operate with only a limited 'bounded' rationality. Few could name, for example, prevailing tariffs for different forms of offending or have much understanding of the chances of being apprehended. The evidence strongly suggests that many crimes are committed under the influence of alcohol or drugs, which further reduce rational thought (Smith et al., 2002).

Pause for Thought

What factors can you identify that might influence an individual's decision to commit a crime?

The notion that the criminal law is a symbolic expression of community, the enforcement of which signals a common value system that will be upheld, is well-established but does not always bear close

Knowledge Link: Chapters 23 and 27 explore hate crime and gender, crime and victimisation and develop understanding of the social context in which actions are held to contravene normative values.

scrutiny. Critics have argued that the selective enforcement of the law has often meant that the victims of certain forms of crime have been overlooked. The need to better respond to victims of domestic violence and hate crime, for example, has sometimes been couched in terms of the need to demonstrate that such offences transgress fundamental social values. While the communicative power of signalling social opprobrium in this way might be significant, there might remain consequences for marginalised groups that may find it difficult to gain the political recognition required to secure effective responses to their victimisation (Tatchell, 2002; Mason, 2014).

Case Study 6.1

Right Realism

Right realism has been central to the zero-tolerance policing strategy most associated with New York in the 1990s. A key component of the approach is that minor criminal infractions are vigorously policed such that the certainty of punishment is increased. Although the proponents of zero-tolerance policing have championed the success of the approach, and it has been credited with reducing crime rates in New York, there are doubts as to its impact. First, it is argued that crime rates fell in many American cities during this period, and many of those did not adopt zero-tolerance policing. Demographic changes and changing levels of use in crack cocaine might also have had a significant effect on levels of crime (Bowling, 1999). Moreover, zero-tolerance policing has been widely criticised for the negative impact that it has on police relations with the community. (McLaughlin, 2007)

There is considerable evidence about the lack of any association between length of sentence and recidivism, a central component of right realism. The case study above also draws attention to an apparent failure of 'tougher' enforcement to reduce crime rates. A meta-analysis of existing literature identified 111 studies that examined the association between various criminal justice punishments, incorporating studies of more than 400,000 inmates in all kinds of penal institutions (Smith et al., 2002: Public Safety Canada), and reached the stark conclusion that:

> ... criminal justice sanctions had no deterrent effect on recidivism. On the contrary, punishment produced a slight (3%) increase in recidivism ... longer sentences were associated with higher recidivism rates. Short sentences (less than six months) had no effect on recidivism but sentences of more than two years had an average increase in recidivism of seven per cent.

Routine Activities Theory

In common with the previous two approaches, routine activities theorists conceive of offenders as rational actors and avoid the search for macro-level explanations of criminal behaviour. Often associated with 'new administrative' criminology, routine activities theory focuses instead upon managing micro-level opportunities for crime. Although causes of crime are difficult to identify and rectify, interventions can be made that can prevent individual offenders making particular decisions to commit offences. Although the perspective shares with the previous two certain assumptions about crime being a rational choice activity, it recognises that such choices are exercised in strictly limited circumstances. Furthermore, deterrence is considered in terms broader than sanctions of the criminal justice system to include a host of interventions that can make the commission of a crime more difficult.

This approach is predominantly associated with the work of researchers such as Clarke (1983; 1992) and Mayhew et al. (1976), and its theoretical approach is well-summarised by Marcus Felson (1998) in his study *Crime in Everyday Life*. Felson argued that much crime was opportunist and that offenders did not tend to differ from the majority of the population in terms of their biological or sociological profile. Decisions to commit crime were based upon four key criteria, known by their acronym, VIVA.

Routine activity theory: VIVA dimension of crime

- **V**alue of target to offender (not simply objective financial value, but subjective value).
- **I**nertia of crime targets (i.e. the extent to which they are fixed or mobile, this applies to property but also victims of violent offences).
- **V**isibility of crime targets (property left on display, but also people present in areas and at times when violence might be more likely).
- **A**ccessibility (the ease with which the offender can get to, and exit from, the object or subject of the crime).

Rationality in this nexus informs the decision to commit a crime, but is shaped by immediate factors rather than more removed influences such as penal policy. The key to preventing crime is to intervene such that one or more of these factors is effected such that committing an offence becomes more difficult or less attractive. Methods to target-harden high-value property so that it is less subjectively valuable, more inert, less visible, or more inaccessible will reduce the incidence of crime, for example. Similarly, measures to increase physical or human controls might impact upon accessibility or other of these factors.

Pause for Thought

The extent to which interventions to limit the opportunities for offending may simply mean that crime is displaced has been the focus of criminological debate and research for many decades. Displacement is usually conceived of in four-fold terms, relating to the time, place, method, and type of crime. Simply put, the concern is that the prevention of an offence in one situation will mean that it reappears, perhaps in another form, in another context. Rossmo and Summers (2019) highlight the complexity of conceptualising and measuring displacement and note that these are often overlooked in the research literature. Nonetheless, the evidence tends to suggest that the extent of displacement varies in relation to different types of crime and different types of offender. Opportunist crime, whether it be theft, criminal damage, or much interpersonal violence, can be reduced with less displacement than other types of offending, such as domestic violence, or that which is committed by organised 'professional' offenders who are more likely to find other outlets for their activity, such as internet-based fraud, for example. Similarly, research suggests the relative decline in armed robbers targeting banks, which have been subject to considerable situational crime prevention, has meant instead that other businesses that might be 'cash rich' are targeted. Research with armed robbers, for example, has shown that rational choice is exercised but that when some targets become more difficult this does not mean that offenders opt for a non-criminal source of income so much as new opportunities for crime (Matthews, 2002). Even in circumstances where deterrence might prove effective in terms of reducing crime it might be that the costs of doing so are considered too large in terms of the financial imposition on society or on the freedom of the law-abiding to go about their legitimate business. Others have argued that the focus on routine activities, and situational crime prevention, amounts to a 'containment job', which ignores the wider social causes of crime, denies the possibility of rehabilitating offenders, and fails to engage in the moral landscape of crime (Young, 1986).

Case Study 6.2

Gill and Spriggs - Benefits of CCTV

The benefits of CCTV in deterring and preventing crime have been subject to an extended review, funded by the British Home Office and completed by Gill and Spriggs (2005) who examined the impact that systems had in fourteen different sites. Consistent with other findings relating to situational interventions, they argued that CCTV was most effective when used in specific circumstances. In the case of car parks, for example, they found that CCTV had a positive impact and that there was little evidence of significant displacement of car theft or damage to adjacent areas. This was attributed to the relative ease of monitoring an environment in which entry and exit points (the 'accessibility' of the VIVA model) are fixed and in which personnel can focus on a narrow range of problems. On the other hand, CCTV was less effective in terms of dealing with general crime problems in relatively open public areas, such as residential housing estates.

PART TWO - PRE-DESTINED ACTOR MODEL OF CRIME

The second set of approaches differ from those outlined above since they place less emphasis on the independent rational decision-making of the offender, focusing instead on various other factors that might lead to criminal behaviour. Some of these factors are 'internal' to the individual in terms of physical or mental characteristics, others are 'external' in the form of social, environmental or familial issues.

Biological, Genetic and Psychological Explanations

Consistent with developing scientific paradigms of the period, much criminological research and theorising that were developed in the late nineteenth and early twentieth century sought to identify criminological typologies, initially based around biological criteria. Often these explanations assumed that criminals were of a certain type distinct from the law-abiding majority of the population. While some of the scientific methods that underpinned such approaches can be questioned, it is significant that these models sought to develop an aetiology of crime based upon empirical criteria and so moved beyond pre-modern explanations couched in metaphysical notions that criminals were innately evil. For this reason these are regarded as early forms of positivist criminology.

Associated with the French theorist Comte, positivism holds that the study of society ought to be based around principles derived from the natural sciences. It was this aspect of his work that undoubtedly influenced Lombroso and the Italian School of Criminology, who used photographs of criminals and measured and catalogued their physiological characteristics, compared these with profiles of non-offenders, and developed typologies of criminals (Rafter, 2005). The categorisation was refined such that offenders who had committed different forms of crime were sub-divided according to more refined analysis of their physical characteristics. Although Lombroso is usually associated with biologically determinist explanations of crime – in his early work he argued that criminals were an atavistic throwback to an earlier stage of human evolution – he looked increasingly to environmental causes of crime later in his career.

Lombroso's method and conclusions have been widely criticised, and refutations of his crude evolutionary and biological explanations appeared soon after his studies were published in the 1890s, but his legacy continues to be apparent in on-going theorising about the causes of crime and claims that criminals are 'born and not made'. Heredity theories posit that criminality might be inherited in the same way as physical characteristics like height or hair colour. Genetic theories are linked to the concept of heredity through the recognition of abnormalities in genetic structure. Psychoses and brain injury research address the neurological and biochemical conditions that cause criminal behaviour (see Durrant, 2018 for a more detailed discussion).

Genetic explanations of offending are long-standing, and have been given enhanced currency more recently as efforts continue to map the human genome are often heralded, often very controversially, as the basis to explain all manner of human characteristics, including susceptibility to certain diseases, sexual preferences, and even artistic creativity. Since the mid-twentieth century heredity studies have examined criminal careers of identical twins, separated at birth, in an effort to control for genetic factors and isolate in analytic terms the influence of socialisation, environmental influences, and the like (Moffitt and Beckley, 2015). Other studies have sought to establish the genetic inheritance of criminal behaviour by examining generational patterns of offending among 'criminal families'. The balance of evidence from such studies, suggests that, as with other forms of human behaviour, biological or genetic factors can not be excluded from understanding the causes of crime. They have, however, limited explanatory power and need to be contextualised with reference to the wider social and cultural influences on human behaviour. A leading geneticist expressed these limitations by pointing out that a child who inherits skill at a musical instrument will still need to be nurtured and spend much time practising if they are to become a virtuoso performer (Jones, 2000).

Central to biological and genetic positivist conceptions of crime is the notion that criminality arises from some physical disorder within the individual offender. While some early proponents of these approaches advocated solutions that amounted to forms of eugenics, other interventions are also derived from biological explanations. From this perspective it is argued that by following a course of treatment, individuals can be cured of the predisposing condition that causes their criminality. Surgical intervention often meant pre-frontal leucotomy, a surgical technique which severs the connection between the frontal lobes and the thalamus. The very wide range of medical and psychological programmes designed to control problematic behaviour in young people and adults are often closely aligned to methods to prevent offending (MacKenzie and Farrington, 2015).

Also within the positivist tradition are those psychological perspectives focusing on identifying the 'criminal personality'. Contemporary debates about psychopathic or sociopathic offenders reflect a long-term approach to explaining the causes of crime (Durrant, 2018). Psychoanalytical theories originated with Freud whose ideas of childhood sexuality provided for a two-fold model of criminal behaviour. The first views certain types of criminal activity as essentially reflecting a state of mental disturbance or mental illness; the second proposes that criminals possess a 'weak conscience'. Psychoanalytic explanations have influenced modern psychiatric practice and the views of those responsible for the care of convicted offenders. John Bowlby, for example, proposed an explanation of offending behaviour which focused on maternal deprivation. Earlier, in the 1930s, a study of pairs of brothers argued that circumstances in which one had become delinquent, while the other had not, concluded that the delinquent brother had experienced maternal deprivation (cited in Vold and Bernard, 1986: 115).

Pause for Thought

You might note that the terms 'crime' and 'offenders' are often treated as unproblematic categories in much of the research and debate surrounding biological, genetic, or psychological explanations of criminal behaviour. Although the methodological weaknesses of early approaches, such as phrenology, have been overcome, much of the analysis is still flawed by a focus upon only certain types of behaviour that have come to be defined as 'crimes' or categories of individuals who have been so-classified.

There is a methodological problem in relation to many of the studies in this school. It is difficult to study the biological, genetic or psychological characteristics of the majority of offenders who do not come into contact with the criminal justice system. Analysis of prisoners, for example, might reveal something about those sentenced to jail but says nothing about (the majority) of law-breakers whose actions never become subject to legal sanction. Studies of 'delinquents', for example, have tended to treat uncritically the socio-cultural processes that identify certain behaviour as problematic (see Part Three). Efforts to treat homosexuality, which was only de-classified as a psychological disorder in the US in the mid-1970s, through combinations of shock and behavioural therapies, by drug treatments, and with surgical interventions, demonstrate not only how deviance, crime and delinquency are socially-constructed concepts but also that explanations of the causes of crime can raise important ethical concerns.

Knowledge link: see Chapter 11 of this volume.

Moreover, such studies assume that criminal behaviour is a fixed and unchanging characteristic, even though much of the evidence suggests that it is strongly associated with the life-cycle, such that the majority of those engaged in criminal behaviour 'grow out' of it as they reach adulthood. Clearly some psychological approaches might help explain this, but the biological and genetic character of these individuals does not change during this period. The case study below provides some evidence that biological components continue to pose significant questions.

Case Study 6.3

Mednick et al. - Data Relating to Conviction Rates

For all of the difficulties outlined above, there remains some important evidence that there might be biological components of offending (although you might consider whether these are causal or correlative relations). Mednick et al. (1987) studied data relating to conviction rates among nearly 14,500 people adopted in Denmark between 1924 and 1947. Their study compared the conviction rates of children and their biological parents, and so removed the impact of the child's socialisation. On this basis they noted:

> ... a relation between biological-parent criminal convictions and criminal convictions in their adopted-away children. The relation was particularly strong for chronic adoptee and biological-parent offenders ... this implies that biological factors are involved in the etiology of at least some criminal behaviour.

As with other arguments about the role of genetics and human behaviour, biologically determinist accounts of criminal behaviour are hugely controversial. First, it should be noted that this study, like many of its kind, suggested only 'a relation' between biology and offending and does not explain what that might be, or by what biological mechanism offending behaviour was transmitted between generations: the case study above, for example, sheds no light on this. Methodologically, it is of concern that only those convicted of offences are usually included in these studies. While this may have been for solid pragmatic reasons it does mean that nothing can be said about the biological determination of most offending behaviour that does not come before the criminal justice system.

Ecological Causes of Crime

Like those explanations focused on identifying biological or genetic causes of crime, ecological approaches seek to identify empirical factors that explain offending. However, ecological approaches suggest that causes of offending and deviant behaviour are found within the urban landscape, the neighbourhood, familial and social milieu in which crime occurs. Initial proponents of this approach were the sociologists that came to be known as 'the Chicago school' whose major work was carried out in that US city from the 1920s to the 1940s (Park and Burgess, 1925). Central to their approach was the notion that, just as the animal kingdom had evolved as a response to the changing natural landscape, so too human behaviour was shaped by the physical landscape of the city. Cities developed in ways that mimic changes in the balance of nature, and are influenced by economic competition for space. The urban environment was affected by a process of invasion, dominance and succession as different groups migrated and as economic activity changed and moved from different localities in the urban landscape. These perspectives were developed by the journalist-turned-sociologist Robert Park who charted the impact of waves of migration on that city and the influence that this had on the character and life of different neighbourhoods. Park argued that human behaviour, including criminality, could be understood with reference to the changing context in which people found themselves.

Park's approach was developed by Ernest Burgess, who conducted empirical work in Chicago that led him to a model of urban development based around concentric urban circles and, at their borders, various zones of transition.

Burgess's studies of Chicago found that the character of the various concentric zones changed over time: what had been industrial areas transformed to residential areas, the 'inner loop' of the central city had become less residential over time, and so on. Social problems, he argued, tended to arise in areas as they underwent transition in this way. Particular attention was paid to the 'zone in transition', which contained rows of deteriorating tenements, often built in the shadow of ageing factories. As the business district had expanded outward communities had been displaced. As the least desirable living area, the zone was the focus for the influx of waves of migrants who were too poor to reside elsewhere. Burgess observed that these trends weakened family and communal ties and resulted in 'social disorganisation'. It was this disorganisation which Burgess and the other Chicago sociologists believed was the primary source of criminal behaviour.

Shaw and Mackay (1972) used juvenile court statistics to test these theories and found that these crime rates could be mapped in ways consistent with the concentric zones and that offending rates bore an inverse relationship to levels of affluence. Moreover, Shaw and Mackay found that offending rates fell among populations in more affluent zones, even in those communities that were broadly similar in terms of other characteristics such as ethnicity. Shaw and McKay emphasised the importance of neighbourhood organisation in preventing or permitting adolescent offending. In more affluent communities, parents fulfilled the needs of, and carefully supervised, their children. In the zone of transition, however, families and other conventional institutions (schools, churches, voluntary associations) were strained, if not destroyed, by rapid urban growth, migration and poverty; 'social disorganisation' prevailed. As a consequence, adolescents received neither the support nor the supervision required for healthy development. Left to their own devices, young people were not subject to the social constraints placed on their contemporaries in the more affluent areas, and they were more likely to seek excitement and friends in the streets of the city.

Pause for Thought

You might notice that while the theorists mentioned seemed to show a strong association between criminality and the urban landscape, they said little about the precise mechanisms whereby criminality was transferred from the ecological context to human behaviour. How might you explain, for example, that many residents in such neighbourhoods do not commit crime?

The Chicago school often relied upon official criminal statistics. The focus of police, probation officer, and social worker attention on 'problem districts' would help to explain higher levels of recorded crime and deviance in those districts. Labeling theory, explored in Part Three, highlights serious concerns on these grounds. However, although these criticisms have some weight, the ecological perspectives epitomized by the Chicago school have been very important in the development of social and welfare policy responses to urban problems. In terms of understanding offending, they moved attention away from responses based upon providing medical or psychiatric interventions for 'disturbed' individuals and focused attention on the broader social and urban environment. The focus of approaches in this tradition has tended to pay little attention to the crimes of those living in affluent neighbourhoods.

Knowledge link: see Chapter 4 for a critique.

Case Study 6.4

Wilson and Kelling – 'Broken Windows' Thesis

One of the most influential crime prevention and policing strategies of recent decades is derived from the 'broken windows' thesis of Wilson and Kelling, whose work clearly owes a debt to the ecological approach. Wilson and Kelling argue that it is the minor signs of decay and damage that signals to residents and visitors that a neighbourhood is neglected. This in turn encourages further criminal and disorderly behaviour and a spiral of decline as the residential demographic shifts, the population turnover increases, and the ability of the community to exercise informal social controls is reduced still further.

The approach influenced the establishment of the Chicago Area Project (CAP), a decades-long programme which encompassed several approaches to crime prevention, including the creation of recreational programmes that would expose youth to a pro-social environment, efforts to improve the physical appearance of the area, and community policing (Skogan, 2009). Among other work, CAP staff members would attempt to 'mediate' on behalf of juveniles in trouble with school officials or the courts system. Furthermore, CAP staff provided 'curbside counseling' such that 'street credible' workers would provide informal guidance and support to youths otherwise at risk of offending. Clearly, the evaluation of such an ambitious and long-standing approach is challenging but one such effort concluded that there were grounds for '… a strong hypothesis that CAP has long been effective in reducing rates of reported juvenile delinquency'. (Schlossman et al., 1984: 46)

Sub-culture, Alienation and Anomie

In common with perspectives described in the previous section, sub-cultural explanations suggest that criminal and antisocial behaviour is associated with external factors that can be scientifically identified and examined. Unlike those perspectives, however, they couch causal explanations in terms of individuals' social associations and degree of adherence to prevailing social norms. The origins of these approaches are often traced to the work of Robert Merton (1938), who argued that deviancy *could* arise from a disjuncture between the dominant goals in a society and the legitimate means of achieving them (a state defined by Durkheim as 'anomie'). While achievement of economic success is a dominant goal in many societies, much of the population will be unable to achieve this goal through legitimate means. Merton suggested that this discrepancy led to a range of social reactions: first, an individual might take a *conformist* view by accepting the goals and the means (and accept their lot, as it were); second, an *innovative* response might arise, whereby the goals are accepted but the means rejected (and replaced by non-legitimate means); third, *ritualism* occurs if the individual rejects the goals but continues to observe the means; fourth, an individual might take a *retreatist* approach whereby both goals and means are

Table 6.1 Merton's Typology of Responses to Social Goals and Means

	Dominant Social Goals	Legitimate Means
Conformist	+	+
Innovative	+	−
Ritualist	−	+
Retreatist	−	−
Rebellious	+	+
	−	−

rejected; finally, a *rebellious* approach challenges the legitimacy of both goals and means and seeks to replace them with alternatives. This range of reactions is illustrated in Table 6.1.

It is important to recognise that Merton was seeking to explain deviance in general terms, and not all of the responses he describes would lead to behaviour of criminological interest. The ritualist, for example, might develop neuroses or psychological disorders that are non-criminal. Clearly though, the innovator might engage in illegitimate criminal behaviour in order to achieve the accepted social goal of economic wealth, the retreatist might withdraw into recreational drug use, and the rebel might engage in public disorder.

While these perspectives can provide a useful means of conceptualising criminal and deviant behaviour, they provide a poor framework for identifying individuals who are likely to become involved in such activity. Almost by definition, the deviant is anomic; while this aids understanding after an individual has been identified as deviant it is not useful as a means to highlight those who might be prone to engage in criminal or problematic behaviour. Sub-cultural theories seek to bridge this gap by using the idea of 'differential association' to explain ways in which individual responses such as those described by Merton are shaped and formed. Put simply, individuals do not select their reaction to established norms as a one-time rational decision. Acceptance or rejection, in various guises, develops in a particular context of social relations. Criminal behaviour, theorists such as Sutherland (1949) have argued, is learnt and communicated amid human relations, which explains why certain forms of criminal behaviour tend not to be spread randomly across the population but develop in clusters. Sutherland (1949) applied this approach to his study of white-collar offenders, as is outlined below. Differential association approaches suggest that criminal behaviour is learnt in two key respects. First, the content of criminal behaviour is learned, in the sense that techniques and opportunities for crime are developed and attitudes and justifications for such actions are also socially generated. In addition to the content of crime being communicated, differential association explanations stress that the processes by which learning takes place are also important factors. The frequency, depth, duration and intensity with which an individual socialises with other criminals, compared to non-criminal groups, will also determine the nature and extent of their own criminal behaviour. Most obviously associated with explanations of criminal gangs and 'juvenile delinquents' such theories of crime have been extended to consider corporate crime and a wide range of other forms of offending.

Pause for Thought

The various forms of subcultural explanations have been widely criticised on several grounds. You should consider why many individuals who experience difficulties adjusting to prevailing social norms do not engage in criminal or problematic deviant behaviour; why some individuals are lone or isolated offenders; why many subcultures that might be considered adaptive responses to social conditions are not centred on criminal activity; or why females have engaged in criminal subcultures to a much lesser extent than their male counterparts.

An important challenge to these approaches is the assumption that society shares a broad moral and normative framework, a set of values that highlight acceptable goals and the proper means to achieve them. By couching the behaviour of those who do not share in this consensus as 'deviant' they reinforce those dominant power relations which serve to define marginal groups as problems to be explained and confronted. Cultural criminologists note that 'rebellion' is a feature that has come to be incorporated into mainstream cultural, social and political discourse and that 'deviance' has been normalised and co-opted by dominant interests, as can be identified in relation to some of the sub-cultures mentioned in the case studies below.

Knowledge link: see Chapter 12.

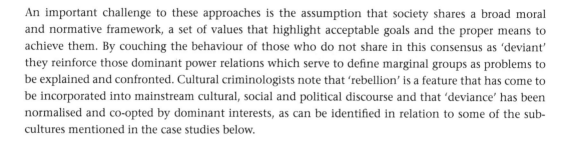

Case Study 6.5

Subcultural Approaches

Subcultural approaches have been used to explain the criminal and deviant activity of young people and 'delinquent' groups for many decades. In the 1950s these perspectives provided an explanation of 'street corner' gangs in US cities, in the 1960s they were applied to hippies and Hells Angels, in the 1970s to youth subcultures such as punks, in the 1980s to football hooligans in Britain, in the 1990s to anti-globalisation protestors, and more recently, they have reappeared in debates about gang culture, knife crime and the 'county lines' drugs trade.

It has been less widely noted that subcultural theories have also been used to explain offending among groups removed from the lower end of the social scale. Sutherland's (1949) seminal study that developed the concept of differential association was focused on white-collar crime. He examined processes by which professionals and executives came to justify embezzlement and the appropriation of company resources, in normative terms by arguing, for example, that they were under-paid, that their actions did not victimise anyone, and that many of their colleagues acted in similar ways.

Knowledge Link: This is discussed further in Chapter 18 where white collar and corporate crime is analysed.

PART THREE - THE VICTIMISED ACTOR MODEL OF CRIME

The focus of the perspectives included in the final section of this chapter draw your attention to the social, political, economic and cultural context in which some behaviours are defined as criminal. The emphasis here is less on the nature or characteristics of individual offenders and more on broader processes of criminalisation.

Labeling Theory

The perspectives noted in Part 3 focus upon ways in which core concepts such as 'crime' or 'delinquency' are socially-generated and reflect the prevailing political, social and economic power. Later the implications that these processes have in terms of social justice and the reinforcement of offending behaviour are highlighted. Although it is something of a caricature to regard this perspective as a 'victimised actor' model, it does focus attention on the marginalisation and criminalisation of those who come to be regarded as problematic for mainstream society.

Labeling theory (and related interactionist theory, societal reaction theory and transactional theory) originated with the work of Mead in the 1930s who argued that social identities and the meanings given to certain actions were not fixed phenomena associated with the properties or the individuals themselves. Instead, social identities and meanings emerge from the interactions between individuals in particular contexts. Deviance, it follows, is not a property *inherent* in certain forms of behaviour but is instead a status granted by audiences to that behaviour. Becker's (1963) famous study of marijuana users and musicians focused attention on the ways by which deviance is socially constructed, partly by the work of moral entrepreneurs: the political, social, religious, legal and criminal justice leaders who establish boundaries of 'acceptable' or 'normal' behaviour. Becker's (1963: 8–9) influential definition is outlined below.

Becker's 'central fact' about deviance

'… it is created by society. I do not mean this in the way it is ordinarily understood, in which the causes of deviance are located in the social situation of the deviant or in "social factors" which prompt his action. I mean, rather, that social groups create deviance by making the rules whose infraction constitutes deviance, and by applying those rules to particular people and labeling them as outsiders. From this point of view, deviance is not a quality of the act the person commits, but rather a consequence of the application by others of rules and sanctions to an "offender." The deviant is one to whom that label has successfully been applied.'

Labeling theory

Driving under the influence of alcohol is a good example of how the same behaviour comes to be labeled in different ways during different periods and among different sections of society. Until relatively recently, in many societies, such behaviour was considered neither criminal nor particularly deviant. Legal changes and policing innovations such as the breathalyzer, came to define driving under the influence as criminal. Public educational campaigns often seek to make drunk-driving normatively unacceptable and so label it as deviant.

─────────────── Pause for Thought ───────────────

What other forms of behaviour might be defined as deviant as a result of labeling processes, rather than as a consequence of its inherent features?

The criminological focus moves from the characteristics of the deviant or the circumstances in which they are found, and towards society's *construction* of certain acts as deviant. Not all individuals or agencies within society play an equal role in these processes of construction: the police, courts, psychiatrists, social workers and sections of the media will have a particularly powerful role in labeling processes (Rock, 1973). The relation between the labeled (as an 'offender') and the person or agency doing the labeling is one of profoundly unequal power relations. Radical theorists argue that these power differentials reflect broader structural inequalities.

Key to labeling theories is the notion that the stigmatisation of an individual as a criminal or a deviant will reinforce their marginalised status. This has consequences not only in terms of any efforts to rehabilitate or reform offenders that raise questions about reintegration and social justice, but also about the efficacy of criminal justice systems that further sustain offending behaviour. A study by Motz et al. (2019) found strong evidence that contact with the criminal justice system is a precursor to subsequent delinquency, an outcome they argue supports labeling theory.

--- Pause for Thought ---

Do we risk minimising the impact of crime by focusing on the ways in which offending behaviour is socially constructed?

By focusing on the social response to deviant behaviour, these theories say little about the nature, causes, or implications of that behaviour in the first instance. Realists (both of left and right) argue that these views ignore the impact that even relatively minor offences can have on the community. Left realists, in particular, argued from the 1980s, that the problem of crime is a real one, especially for deprived communities, and that it is simplistic to argue that crime is a phenomenon 'created' by powerful elites. Right realists argue that punishment is necessary since it sends signals about the moral community to which the majority of the population subscribe and that it is important to demonstrate that core values will be defended. Another concern is that labeling theory can provide a useful perspective on some types of offending, especially that of a relatively minor nature, and tells us something about the important ways that crime is socially constructed. Periodic concern about certain types of offending, for example, reveals important strains and anxieties of a more general nature, yet labeling theories reveal little about why some acts come to be defined as deviant, while others, which may be more harmful, do not. This is a key concern of radical criminologists and will be returned to later.

Knowledge link: see Chapter 9.

Moreover, as White and Haines (2000) noted, the impact of a label on an individual is difficult to predict. Not all who go into the juvenile justice system, for example, become confirmed entrenched offenders; for some, the imposition of a label seems to act as a catalyst for change. Life-course perspectives on criminal careers tend to confirm these concerns, since the advancing years seem to be a major factor in the desistance of (some types) of criminal activity: a point also made by control theorists who argue that the increasing stake that many people have in society as they get older means that they have more to lose (financially, socially, culturally, and so on) from engagement in criminal behaviour than they had at a younger age.

--- **Case Study 6.6** ---

Young - Study of Labeling

A classic study of labeling (and associated moral panic theory) was conducted in the early 1970s in relation to the criminal and deviant behaviour of cannabis smokers in London. Young (1971) argued that prior to their being labeled, the drug users were a loosely knit group for whom marijuana smoking was a peripheral aspect of their cultural, leisure and social identity, and whose involvement in criminal networks was occasional and often small scale as the drug was traded informally between casual users. Newspaper exposes of their 'lifestyle' led to calls for police interventions, pressure that meant that cannabis users became separated from 'straight' society, that their drug-use became a defining characteristic of their identity. Crucially, since the informal trading of the drug became more difficult, criminal drug gangs began to get involved and other, more harmful, drugs came onto the scene. The net effect, Young argued, was that the labeling of the group led to an increase in deviancy and enhanced problematic criminal behaviour.

Conflict and Radical Theories

Labeling theory demonstrates that crime is socially constructed, but remains relatively silent about which groups and types of behaviour come to be understood as criminal and deviant, and what broader social and political forces determine these processes. Traditionally, criminology has conceived of society in consensual terms, such that the offender transgresses commonly-held values about, for example, property ownership. The criminal act breaks the legal code that is itself an expression of consensus. Conflict theories, of whatever hue, rely on a fundamentally different perspective that regards social relations as inherently conflictual and competitive. The labeling of certain acts as criminal or deviant needs to be understood as an expression of wider power relations. Conflict theories differ in terms of their analysis of the nature, level and durability of conflict. For many pluralists conflict and competition is a permanent scramble for influence and power, but one that is entered into by changing configurations of different actors and groups. Scarce resources are sought by changing coalitions who use a range of devices in an effort to secure their interests. Among the resources available to them are the criminal law and processes of labeling and the construction of deviance. Companies that seek to develop natural resources, for example, might employ private surveillance techniques and suggest those who oppose their activities are criminal. The 'anti-social' activities of young people are often highlighted by sections of the community who seek to pressure the police to take action and 'move them on' from residential areas. Conflict can arise in relation not only to scarce material resources but also cultural and ethical issues (such as abortion or corporal punishment) or to authority, such as conflict over political legitimacy. A key proponent of conflict criminology in the United States has been George Vold, who argued (Vold and Bernard, 1986: 274):

> The whole process of law-making, lawbreaking, and law enforcement directly reflects deep-seated and fundamental conflict between group interests and the more general struggles among groups for control of the police power of the state. To that extent, criminal behaviour is the behaviour of *minority power groups*, in that these groups do not have sufficient power to promote and defend their interests and purposes in the legislative process.

Radical perspectives tend to consider conflict in more structured ways and relate it to fundamental contradictions of capitalism. Only change on a structural level, it is argued, can tackle the causes of crime. In the British context this tradition emerged in the early 1970s and was associated with the 'New Criminology' of Ian Taylor, Paul Rock, David Downes, and Jock Young, among others. A more recent example is provided in the case study below.

———— Case Study 6.7 ————

Hallsworth - Street Crime in London

Hallsworth's (2005) analysis of street crime in London is within the tradition of radical criminology. He argues that most perpetrators of street crime within London are young males, many of whom are of a minority ethnic background. Hallsworth criticises the criminological silence on this topic, which has been regarded as politically incorrect, and argues that this has allowed the radical right to dominate debates around these issues. Contemporary street crime, and other offending such as drug-dealing, Hallsworth argues, are best understood in terms of cultures of consumption which value conspicuous consumption and celebrate those who are able to demonstrate material wealth. These processes contribute to the development of youth subcultures that encourage people to own, display and celebrate valuable consumer goods and branded clothing, and this has a twofold impact as it enhances the need to secure high status items, in whatever way they can, while providing a readily available range of criminal targets.

In short, the New Criminology argued that crime is grounded in the material conditions of capitalism – it was not poverty in itself that caused property crime, they argued, but inequality. The New Criminologists considered that poverty, both in absolute and relative terms, was a product of the same iniquitous social relations that gave rise to crime. Consistent with labeling theory and conflict criminology, the New Criminologists considered that the power to criminalise, make laws and prosecute offenders, or particular groups that are perceived as offenders, was a function of the state. They went further, though, by linking this to Marxist debate about its nature and function within society. For the New Criminologists, the state is seen to vary in form during different historical periods, and the technique that it employs to maintain social discipline, ultimately in the interests of the powerful, also varies.

In summary, conflict and radical criminology offer structural approaches to explaining crime. Within this tradition the labeling perspective retains a great deal of importance. Indeed, it appears in the New Criminology to be at least as important as the underlying structural considerations that determine the nature of the labeling process – but this does have the advantage of ensuring that there is an appreciation that actors do possess a great deal of freedom of action within broad social circumstances – and decisions about these issues are left to the rationality of the actors themselves.

Pause for Thought

While it is important to recognise that much criminological theory relies upon untested and perhaps simplistic assumptions about the consensual nature of society, conflict theorists might travel too far in the opposite direction if they assume that there are no shared values or normative agreement about the order and purposes of social life. Even groups in conflict over particular issues are often likely to hold common perspectives on other broad matters. Conflicts might exist on some levels, but not be fundamental; for example, two groups might be in conflict over who holds the right to certain property but agree in general terms with the principle of property ownership.

Radical criminology is often criticised on two key grounds. First, it offers no prescriptions to intervene in crime problems short of the fundamental transformation or restructuring of capitalist society. If this is not attainable in the foreseeable future then it is hard to see where this perspective might lead. Second, as some of its proponents have subsequently recognised, the radical school often assumed that criminal acts were proto-revolutionary behaviour, an expression of broader class struggles. Victim survey findings have tended to show that crime is perpetrated within, rather than across, class divisions.

CHAPTER SUMMARY

- Even this brief review makes it abundantly clear that criminology is a broad church, and, to mix metaphors, has an appropriately light-fingered approach to borrowing concepts from other disciplines and intellectual traditions.
- The chapter has outlined a broad perspective on offending premised on the idea that offenders are rational actors who make calculated decisions to commit (or otherwise) offences on the basis of their understanding of the potential benefits they might secure compared to the potential costs that may follow. The focus of these approaches tends towards the individual person and the immediate circumstances in which offences occur.
- In contrast, a second broad tradition is based on the idea that offenders are 'pre-destined' actors, whose behaviour is shaped (or even determined) by extraneous factors such as biological or

psychological characteristics beyond their immediate control. The context in which the offender is located becomes an important part of the focus from this perspective.

- A further tradition is focused instead on the ways in which some forms of behaviour come to be regarded as deviant or criminal, and the legal and social consequences of this. Such processes, often focus criminal justice and legal action disproportionally against groups and individuals who come to be regarded as threatening and problematic.

- Although mid-twentieth century Western criminology continued in the belief that the development of scientific understanding of offenders could lead to a general solution to the problem of crime, contemporary perspectives are less ambitious. While interventions might be possible to prevent particular people from (re)offending or some crime from occurring, the notion that a fundamental 'cause' of crime could be found – a general theory of crime – let alone resolved, is barely even considered in contemporary criminological debates.

- Criminological theory should not be understood as a process of development toward a coherent unified theory of crime. A compelling reason why a single theory of crime is unlikely to emerge is that the concept of crime itself is too broad and is subject to variation in time and between places.

- Young's (1981) review of criminological perspectives argues that there are six key dichotomies that many theories about causes of crime tend to address. Although not providing a final statement about causality, they present a useful summary of the key policy implications that emerge from the discussion of the various approaches sketched here. Young lists these key points as:

1. Human nature: voluntarism vs. determinism?
2. Social order: consensus or coercion?
3. Definition of crime: legal or social?
4. The extent and distribution of crime: limited or extensive?
5. The causes of crime: individual or society?
6. Policy deductions: treatment or punishment?

Review Questions

1. How might different approaches to criminological theory apply to property crimes, such as theft or burglary?
2. How might different approaches to criminological theory apply to violent crimes, such as assault or murder?
3. Do biological positivist approaches suggest that offenders should not be held responsible for their behaviour?
4. Is offending the result of a conscious choice on the part of the perpetrator?

GO FURTHER

Books

There is a good range of useful books available that consider these issues further. Those used in developing the general themes of the discussion above are:

1. Hopkins-Burke, R. (2005) *An Introduction to Criminological Thought*, second edition, Cullompton: Willan Publishing, provides a comprehensive and engaging critical review of many of the themes discussed in this chapter.

2. Rafter, N. (2009) The Origins of Criminology: a Reader, Abingdon: Routledge, offers an excellent collection and of key traditions within the discipline and a strong narrative perspective.

3. Bernard, T., Snipes, J. and Gerould, A. (2018) Vold's Theoretical Criminology, Oxford: Oxford University Press, revisits the work of George Vold, who authored the classic text on criminological theory in the mid-20th century, combining empirical and conceptual analysis.

Journal Articles

1. The following provides an excellent example of the application of criminological theory to contemporary crime problems:

   Williams, M. L. (2016) Guardians upon high: an application of Routine Activities Theory to online identity theft in Europe at the country and individual level. *British Journal Of Criminology,* 56(1): 21–48.

2. Rocque and Posick critically review contemporary perspectives that seek to integrate traditions of biological and social positivist traditions, arguing that new models of bio-social criminology overcome some criticisms of the separate approaches:

   Rocque, M. & Posick, C. (2017) Paradigm shift or normal science? The future of (biosocial) criminology. *Theoretical Criminology*, 21(3): 288–303.

3. Sandberg explores how cultural theories need to be reconfigured to explain contemporary drug users, and remain crucial to understanding cannabis users:

   Sandberg, S. (2013) Cannabis culture: a stable subculture in a changing world. *Criminology & Criminal Justice*, 13(1): 63–79.

4. A 1988 (vol. 28, no. 2) special issue of the *British Journal of Criminology* explores the intellectual and theoretical development of criminology in Britain and contains many papers relevant to the discussion in this chapter.

Useful Websites

1. The SAGE Publications website provides a comprehensive and multi-media compendium of information relating to criminological theory, including many of the core concepts covered in this chapter and that informs discussion throughout this book: https://journals.sagepub.com/criminology-criminal-justice?

2. The website of the American Psychology Association includes a dictionary that gives useful summaries of some of the key terms used in this chapter: https://dictionary.apa.org/

3. Oxford Bibliographies is a useful online repository of information covered in this chapter, and much more of wider criminological interest: https://www.oxfordbibliographies.com/

REFERENCES

Becker, H. S. (1963) *Outsiders: Studies in the Sociology of Deviance*. New York: Collier-Macmillan.

Bowling, B. (1999) The rise and fall of the New York murder: zero tolerance or crack's decline, *British Journal of Criminology*, 39(4): 531–554.

Brooks-Gordon, B. M. and Bilby, C. (2006) Psychological interventions for treatment of sexual offenders. *British Medical Journal*, 333: 5–6.

Burgess, E. W. (1925/1967) 'The Growth of the City'. In R. E. Park and E. W. Burgess (eds), *The City*. Chicago: University of Chicago Press.

Clarke, R. V. (1983) 'Situational Crime Prevention: Its Theoretical Basis and Practical Scope'. In M. Tonry and N. Morris (eds), *Crime and Justice: An Annual Review of Research, Vol. 4*. Chicago: Chicago University Press.

Clarke, R. V. (ed.) (1992) *Situational Crime Prevention: Successful Case Studies*. New York: Harrow and Heston.

Currie, E. (1995) *Confronting Crime*. New York: Pantheon.

Durrant, R. (2018) *An Introduction to Criminal Psychology*, 2nd edition. Abingdon: Routledge.

Emsley, C. (2005) *Crime and Society in England, 1750-1900*, 3rd edition. London: Pearson Longman.

Fanslow, J. and Robinson, E. (2004) Violence against women in New Zealand: prevalence and health consequences. *New Zealand Medical Journal*, 117(1206).

Farrall, S., Bannister, J., Ditton, J. and Gilchrist, E. (1997) Questioning the fear of crime: findings from a major methodological study. *British Journal of Criminology*, 37(4): 658–679.

Felson, M. (1998) *Crime and Everyday Life*, 2nd edition. California: Pineforge Press.

Gill, M. and Spriggs, A. (2005) *Assessing the Impact of CCTV*, Research Study 292, London: Home Office.

Hall, S. (2012) *Theorizing Crime and Deviance: A New Perspective*. London: Sage.

Hallsworth, S. (2005) *Street Crime*, Cullompton: Willan Publishing.

Jones, S. (2000) *The Language of the Genes: Biology, History and the Evolutionary Future*. London: Flamingo.

Lea, J. and Young, J. (1984) *What is to be Done About Law and Order?* London: Penguin.

Lukes, S. and Prabhat, D. (2012) Durkheim on law and morality: the Disintegration Thesis. *Journal of Classical Sociology*, 12(3–4): 363–383.

MacKenzie, D. L. and Farrington, D. P. (2015) Preventing future offending of delinquents and offenders: what have we learned from experiments and meta-analyses? *Journal of Experimental Criminology*, 11: 565–595.

Mannheim, H. (1965) *Comparative Criminology*. London: Routledge & Kegan Paul.

Mason, G. (2014) Victim attributes in hate crime law: difference and the politics of justice. *British Journal of Criminology*, 54(2): 161–179.

Matthews, R. (2002) *Armed Robbery*. Cullompton: Willan Publishing.

Mayhew, P., Clarke, R. V., Sturman, A. and Hough, J. M. (1976) *Crime as Opportunity*. London: Her Majesty's Stationery Office.

McLaughlin, E. (2007) *The New Policing*. London: Sage.

Mednick, S. A., Gabrielli, W. F. and Hutchings, B. (1987) 'Genetic Factors in the Etiology of Criminal Behaviour'. In S. A. Mednick, T. Moffit and S. Stack (eds), *The Causes of Crime: New Biological Approaches*. Cambridge: Cambridge University Press.

Merton, R. K. (1938) Social structure and anomie. *American Sociological Review*, 3(5): 672–682.

Moffitt, T. E. and Beckley, A. (2015) Abandon twin research? Embrace epigenetic research? Premature advice for criminologists. *Criminology*, 53(1): 121–126.

Motz, R .T., Barnes, J. C., Caspi, A., Arseneault, L., Cullen, F. T., Houts, R., Wertz, J. and Moffitt, T. E. (2019) Does contact with the justice system deter or promote future delinquency? Results from a longitudinal study of British adolescent twins. *Criminology*, doi: 10.1111/1745-9125.12236.

Park, R. E. and Burgess, E. W. (eds) (1925) *The City*. Chicago: Chicago University Press.

Putnam, R. D. (2000) *Bowling Alone: The Collapse and Revival of American Community*. New York: Simon & Schuster.

Rafter, N. (2005) 'Cesare Lombroso and the Origins of Criminology: Rethinking Criminological Tradition'. in S. Henry and M. Lanier (eds), *The Essential Criminology Reader*. Boulder, CO: Westview/Basic Books. pp. 33–42.

Rock, P. (1973) *Deviant Behaviour*. London: Hutchinson.

Rossmo, D. K. and Summers, L. (2019) Offender decision-making and displacement. *Justice Quarterly*, DOI: 10.1080/07418825.2019.1666904.

Schlossman, S., Zellman, G. and Shavelson, R. (1984) *Delinquency Prevention in South Chicago: A Fifty-Year Assessment of the Chicago Area Project*, Santa Monica, CA: Rand.

Shaw, C. R. and McKay, H. D. (1972) *Juvenile Delinquency and Urban Areas*. Chicago: University of Chicago Press.

Skogan, W. (2009) *Police and Community in Chicago: A Tale of Three Cities*. Oxford: Oxford University Press.

Smith, P., Goggin, C. and Gendreau, P. (2002) *The Effects of Prison Sentences and Intermediate Sanctions on Recidivism: General Effects and Individual Differences (User Report 2002-01)*. Ottawa: Solicitor General Canada.

Sutherland, E. (1949) *White Collar Crime*. New York: Holt, Rinehart and Winston.

Tatchell, P. (2002) 'Some People are more Equal than Others'. In P. Ignazi (ed.), *The Hate Debate: Should Hate be Punished as a Crime?* London: Institute for Jewish Policy Research.

Vold, G. B. and Bernard, T. J. (1986) *Theoretical Criminology*, Third Edition, New York: Oxford University Press.

White, R. D. and Haines, F. (2000) *Crime and Criminology: An Introduction*, Oxford: Oxford University Press.

Wilson, J. Q. (1975) *Thinking About Crime*, New York: Basic Books.

Young, J. (1971) The Drugtakers: The Social Meaning of Drug Use, London: Judson, MacGibbon and Kee

Young, D. B. (1983) Cesare Beccaria: utilitarian or retributivist? *Journal of Criminal Justice*, 11(4): 317–326.

Young, J. (1981) 'Thinking Seriously About Crime'. In M. Fitzgerald, G. McLennan and J. Pawson (eds), *Crime and Society*. London: Routledge and Kegan Paul.

Young, J. (1986) The failure of criminology: The need for a radical realism. In R. Matthews & J. Young (eds), *Confronting crime* (pp. 4–30). London: Sage.

Young, J. (1992) 'Ten Points of Realism'. In J. Young and R. Matthews (eds), *Rethinking Criminology: The Realist Debate*. London: Sage.

Social Harm and Zemiology

Expanding the Horizons of Criminology

Thomas Raymen

7

Learning Objectives

By the end of this chapter you will be able to:

- Explain the difference between the concepts of crime, deviance and social harm and the relationship between social harm, critical criminology and zemiology.
- Illustrate how the concept of social harm expands the parameters of 'traditional' criminology and places some of the most pressing contemporary social challenges firmly within its disciplinary purview.
- Demonstrate an understanding of the various approaches to conceptualising social harm and their merits and limitations.
- Critically discuss the philosophical nature of the concept of social harm, the ambiguity surrounding its foundations and parameters, and the challenges this presents for criminology.
- Refer to specific thinkers, studies and research collectives focused upon social harm.

Framing Questions

A few questions for you to think about when reading this chapter are:

1. Can you think of some examples of social, political or economic processes and practices that, while legal, are nevertheless harmful?
2. On what basis do you call these practices harmful?
3. Is the concept of social harm 'objective'? How might the concept of harm attain greater objectivity?
4. What implications does the concept of social harm have for criminology as a discipline?

INTRODUCTION

The purpose of this chapter is to introduce you to the concept of 'social harm' and its use within the discipline of criminology. This chapter will begin by giving you a flavour of the kinds of topics to which the concept of social harm can be applied, topics that have until recently lain beyond criminology's crime-oriented purview. However, for the most part, this chapter will focus more closely on the concept of social harm itself. After the initial section which immediately follows this introduction, we will explore the historical criminological context from which interest in the concept of social harm emerged, specifically the dissatisfaction with the subjective and socially constructed nature of 'crime', and will consider the difficulties this poses for the concept of social harm. While ostensibly straightforward, the question of what constitutes 'social harm' is a notoriously slippery one, raising issues around how we establish foundations and parameters for the concept which can prevent it from drifting off into **relativism** and subjectivism (see glossary). Therefore, the chapter will conduct an overview of the most prominent attempts at conceptualising social harm and consider their respective merits and limitations. Indeed, in the pages that follow it is argued that the existing literature has fundamentally misconstrued the nature of the concept of social harm and what we are really doing when deliberating over what constitutes social harm. The chapter will then look at some more recent attempts at resolving these issues, before concluding by considering the implications that the concept of social harm raises for criminology's disciplinary boundaries and the kinds of knowledge required for criminologists to work from a social harm approach.

A SOCIETY OF HARMS

We are currently living in a society which is faced with a series of truly monumental and interconnected social crises. In the sphere of housing, the charity Shelter estimates that at least 320,000 people in Britain are currently homeless, with an 18% rise in homelessness within London in the last year. Housing prices and rental rates have become grossly inflated by a speculative real estate market and processes of urbanisation and **gentrification**, which concentrate wealth in particular areas and create 'super-prime' property enclaves for the super-rich (Atkinson, 2019; 2020). Housing is spiralling beyond the realms of reasonable affordability for increasing swathes of the population, making it difficult for the most socio-economically marginalised to access affordable and adequate housing, and casting many into an existence of perpetual financial and domestic insecurity (Madden and Marcuse, 2016).

While the cost of living has increased, the post-industrial West has seen enormous job loss, and real wages have also been in a state of stagnation and repression for over a decade (Winlow and Hall, 2013). Low-wage and precarious employment and under-employment are chronic (Lloyd, 2018). According to the latest figures from the Office of National Statistics, there were 1.8 million zero-hours contracts in the UK labour market, an increase of 100,000 zero-hours contracts from the previous year. Individuals working on these contracts cannot guarantee how many hours they will be working from one week to the next, with employers entitled to dismiss workers with no notice or in the middle of a shift. Many of you reading this textbook will likely be familiar with such employment, knowing that it makes any attempts at financial planning tenuous at best and futile at worst.

The finance industry has quickly capitalised upon this situation. To compensate for the rise in the cost of living and the stagnation of real wages, indebtedness through credit cards, bank loans and pay-day lenders has soared (Horsley, 2015). According to the Trades Union Congress, the average household debt – which excludes mortgage debt – currently stands at £15,400, a number that has been rising for over twenty years. For Britons, unsecured debt constitutes, on average, 30% of household income. This means that, on average, British people spend 30% of their income paying off debts, leaving an increasingly shrinking proportion of already-repressed wages to spend on housing, food, household bills, and leisure time. For many, the prospect of 'saving' for future financial comfort and security is only a fantasy.

Adverse mental health problems afflict a rising number of the UK population. At least 20% of the population suffer from depression and anxiety, with an accompanying 108.5% increase in the number of anti-depressant prescriptions in the UK between 2006 and 2016. It should be emphasised that mental health is not merely a psychological issue but is very often connected to underlying social, cultural, and political-economic conditions (Fisher, 2014). This issue is undeniably gendered as well. A 2018 Children's Society report estimates that one in four girls aged 14 self-harmed in the previous twelve months, with frequent references to concerns around their physical appearance and involvement with social media. It is not mere happenstance that the sharp rise in mental health conditions has coincided with the era of **neoliberalism**.

In the field of health more generally, the Institute for Public Policy Research (IPPR) recently calculated that since 2012 there have been approximately 132,000 deaths in the UK that could otherwise have been prevented if it were not for austerity measures. Austerity has been the dominant fiscal policy for at least the past decade in the UK, USA and supranational political and economic unions such as the EU (Mitchell and Fazi, 2017), and with the global COVID-19 pandemic in full swing at the time of writing, we have already seen under-funded and under-resourced health services approaching collapse under the pressure, with lives being lost and healthcare professionals operating in unsafe conditions without access to adequate protective equipment (Fazi, 2020). Shifting to a more global focus, climate change is rapidly making larger swathes of the world increasingly uninhabitable due to drought, flooding, bushfires, rapid sea-level change, and other extreme weather events. Violent confrontations have been emerging over dwindling resources such as food, water, livestock, and fertile land, in addition to growing concerns around the forced 'climate migration' of the global poor (Nixon, 2011; Parenti, 2011; White, 2018). I could go on, but the act of analysing the full range of social problems and crises facing contemporary society could take up the entirety of this textbook, let alone this chapter.

What is most interesting for our purposes is that none of the issues listed above are, in legal terms, 'criminal'. Nor are they 'socially deviant' in the sense that they transgress or *deviate* from dominant norms and social values. Rather, they stem from political, social, and economic practices and processes which are *hyper-conformist* to liberal capitalism's dominant socio-cultural and economic values of wealth accumulation, competitive individualism, and symbolic distinction (Hall et al., 2008; Hall, 2012a; Raymen and Smith, 2016). These practices are normalised in contemporary society, lying beyond the present prohibitive scope of criminal law. More problematically, they are *integral* to the continued functioning of the present political-economic, social, and cultural order of neoliberal global capitalism (Raymen, 2019).

However, this does not mean that such social problems are beyond the purview of criminology as an academic discipline. Over the past two decades, criminology has witnessed a concerted increase of interest in the study of *social harms*: the *systemic* processes and political, economic, and social practices that, while legal and normalised, are nevertheless detrimental and harmful to human beings, society, and the natural environment. In this period, scholars within criminology and the new field of **zemiology** have observed the limitations of the socio-legal constructions of 'crime' and 'social deviance', which exclude a wide variety of harmful processes, behaviours and practices. In doing so, they have attempted to develop a broader and more robust concept of social harm which enables criminologists to push beyond these limitations, and begin to justify the interrogation of various key social issues as legitimate subjects for criminological inquiry (Hillyard et al., 2004). The concept of social harm has been employed by criminologists to study issues as diverse as housing (Tombs, 2019; Atkinson, 2020); employment and work (Lloyd, 2018);

money-lending (Horsley, 2015); corporate harm (Tombs and Whyte, 2015); immigration and asylum policy (Canning, 2018); leisure and consumerism (Raymen and Smith, 2019); pornography (Dymock, 2018; Medley, 2019); climate change and environmental harm (White, 2013, 2018; Brisman and South, 2014); austerity (Cooper and Whyte, 2017), and many others.

MAPPING THE TERRAIN

When one looks at the historical genesis of the concept of social harm, it is useful to see it as part of a *tradition* of critical criminological scholarship. This is commonly conceived as a tradition of questioning the parameters of the concept of crime; of challenging the power dynamics involved in determining what and, just as importantly, *who* should and should not be deemed 'criminal'. Almost every major text on social harm locates the criminological origins of the social harm approach within the work of Edwin Sutherland in the mid-1940s. Sutherland's use of the notion of 'social injury' attempted to expand the definition of crime to incorporate the detrimental and injurious activities of corporations exposed through his work on 'white-collar' and corporate crime. It is equally well-documented that Sutherland's work was influential upon the Schwendingers' work (1970) who, twenty-five years later, drew upon the idea of basic human rights in order to analyse issues such as imperialism, poverty, homelessness, racism and sexism as crimes perpetrated and tacitly accepted by the State.

Naturally, then, much of the work conducted from a social harm approach since Sutherland and the Schwendingers has predominantly focused upon the 'crimes of the powerful', i.e. those harmful and injurious actions perpetrated by powerful actors such as corporations, the State, and the political-economic system of capitalism more broadly. The actions of these powerful groups often go unpunished, nor are they even recognised as crimes or harms for which corporations and the State were responsible. This is primarily a product of the power of the State to define what is deemed as criminal and the cosy relationship between the state and corporations due to the primacy given to elite economic interests and the preservation of a capitalist political economy over and above the wellbeing of the population more broadly.

This growing interest in a social harm approach resulted in the publication *Beyond Criminology* (Hillyard et al., 2004). As the first collective effort at rethinking the boundaries, parameters and very existence of criminology through the lens of social harm, it is frequently regarded as *the* seminal text in the development of a social harm approach within criminology. It has already been emphasised by many, including the editors of *Beyond Criminology*, that it would be misleading to position the text as a unified and coherent project. However, there was one issue which unified the broad range of positions found within the text. Namely, the unsatisfactory nature and perceived deficiencies of the concept of crime. *Beyond Criminology* gives nine interrelated reasons for why the concept of crime fails to cover the full range of socially mediated harms that the individual, the community, or the environment can experience. The purposes of space restrict a detailed discussion of each one of these reasons in turn. Therefore, for the purposes of our discussion here, I will prioritise three, i.e. their reasoning that crime consists of many 'petty events', that it excludes many serious harms, and most importantly, that 'crime has no ontological reality' (Hillyard and Tombs, 2004).

The first of these three reasons – that crime consists of many 'petty events' – is a relatively simple and to some extent misleading claim. Their argument is that much of what makes up the official statistics on 'crime' involves relatively trivial forms of anti-social behaviour and 'volume crime' which would 'not score particularly highly on a scale of personal hardship' (Hillyard and Tombs, 2007: 11). As Kotzé (2018: 92) has argued, this assertion 'pays little regard to the experiential reality of crime or the very real consequences for those who experience this reality as harm in the empirical domain of everyday life'. Moreover, global criminal markets often peddle life-threatening products (Hall and Antonopoulos, 2016) and are characterised by extreme forms of violence (Hall, 2012b); and the financial proceeds from a 'gross criminal product' which is now estimated to be in the trillions of dollars annually (Cribb, 2009) are diverted into tax havens and liquid assets like real estate and other forms of property (Shaxson, 2011; Atkinson, 2020), thereby coalescing with some of the harms (such as housing and austerity) which have interested social harm scholars rather than being distinct from them. Nevertheless, Hillyard and Tombs' (2004) critique that 'crime consists of many petty events' was also based upon a critique of politically influential strands of administrative criminology that have *not* focused on these forms of more harmful global criminal markets, and have instead disproportionately focused on relatively low-level forms of volume crime and anti-social behaviour. When compared to, say, the widespread impact of anthropocentric climate change, which threatens mass social and economic upheaval by making entire cities and regions uninhabitable, or the impact of the 2007/8 global financial crisis which caused two million people to lose their homes to foreclosure and left four million more at risk due to the deregulation of the banking sector (Harvey, 2010), the harms of these petty forms of volume crime do indeed pale in comparison. Moreover, as the issues and crises listed at the outset of this chapter demonstrate, the second related argument that the concept of 'crime' excludes many serious harms undeniably holds water. The driving motivation of social harm scholars was to move past the focus upon *individual acts* and pay closer attention to the harmful outcomes that stemmed from the systemic structures and processes of capitalism, and specifically neoliberal capitalism.

These critiques underpin first and foremost the critique shared by the editors of *Beyond Criminology* that 'crime has no ontological reality' (Hillyard and Tombs, 2004). Crime is indeed a socio-legal construction. The categorisation of various behaviours as 'crime' and of various groups as 'criminal', and the policing, prosecution and punishment are all informed by the arbitrary and subjective interests of *power*. Consequently, one of the many perceived benefits of utilising the concept of social harm was that it could push beyond the subjective and socially constructed, and power-mediated nature of crime. However, as numerous social harm scholars acknowledge, without adequate definitional foundations and criteria for determining whether certain practices or systemic processes are socially harmful, the broader nature of the concept of social harm could cause it to spiral into a catch-all concept and leave it as open to critiques of subjectivism and relativism as crime, if not more so given its broader focus. This concern regarding the potential for social harm to become a subjective 'catch-all' concept has nagged the approach since the Sutherland–Tappan debates of the 1940s, in which Tappan warned against Sutherland's notion of social injury as having the potential of 'damning as criminal almost anyone he pleases' (Tappan, 1946: 99, cited in Lasslett, 2010: 1).

The tradition of social harm scholarship and of attempts at conceptualising social harm can be read as a legacy of these earlier debates; an attempt to wrestle with the issues of subjectivism and relativism in determining what we call 'crime' and 'social harm'. As Yar notes, 'a lack of specificity leaves the concept [social harm] lacking the very same ontological reality that is postulated as grounds for rejecting the concept of crime ... nowhere in the writings is there a concerted attempt to give the concept analytical specificity i.e. to define what makes something a 'harm' or 'harmful' or what distinguishes the "harmful" from the "non-harmful"' (Yar, 2012: 59). Similarly, Millie (2016: 5) has argued that, '[l]ike crime, [social] harm is clearly a social construction', with no ontological reality whatsoever. Consequently, social harm scholars interpreted the task in front of them as self-evident. If social harm was to remedy crime's conceptual deficiency of subjectivity and address its own 'ontological deficit' (Yar, 2012), then academics must set off in pursuit of a more objective set of criteria which could act as both foundations and definitional parameters for the concept of social harm.

Pause for Review

1. The social harm approach was advocated due to perceived deficiencies with the concept of crime. Can you summarise, in your own words, the three main deficiencies with the concept of crime discussed above?
2. Is the argument that much of crime consists of 'many petty events' legitimate? Explain your reasoning.
3. Why is the issue of relativism such a problem? Does the concept of social harm resolve the issue of relativism, or enlarge it?

THE STATE OF THE CONCEPT OF SOCIAL HARM

While the study of social harm has undeniably exploded over the past two decades, the concept of social harm itself arguably remains in an underdeveloped state of disorder. We regularly *use* the language and the concept of social harm to shed light on some of the most important problems facing global society, and we do so in a manner which suggests that there exists some shared impersonal standard of criteria upon which we agree regarding what can and cannot be described as harmful. Yet when we begin to probe and penetrate deeper there remains a remarkable paucity of intellectual coherence or consensus around the conceptualisation of social harm which contradicts such confident use. There is palpable concern and uncertainty over how broadly the concept should be applied and how to establish some conceptual parameters which can make the most of its ability to push *beyond* legal definitions whilst avoiding the concept from becoming so nebulous that it loses all utility. As one of the pioneers and foremost advocates of using the concept of social harm, Tombs (2018) nevertheless acknowledges the conspicuous absence of any basis for determining whether a particular phenomenon should be deemed 'harmful' or classified as a 'social harm'. Pemberton (2016) offers an even more concerning observation, commenting that perhaps what is most remarkable about the concept of social harm is the relative scarcity of genuine attempts to define it within the criminological and zemiological literature.

Early attempts have provided mixed results, all of which have significant flaws which must be addressed. However, they also have crucial elements which are worth retaining and reworking to provide a better conceptualisation and framework for defining social harm. Hillyard and Tombs' (2004) initial efforts provided a typology of harms, grouping harms under categories of physical harm, financial/economic harms, emotional/psychological harms, and cultural safety. As Hall, Kuldova and Horsley (2020) argue, while such typologies are important, they are of little use to us in defining social harm absent of an established set of ontological, ethical and **epistemological** principles which can ground the concept, making these typologies somewhat premature. While Pemberton (2016) lists Hillyard and Tombs' approach as an attempt at defining social harm, it is questionable whether Hillyard and Tombs would do so themselves. Their only commentary on the matter argues that 'social harm is partially to be defined in its very operationalisation' (Hillyard and Tombs, 2004: 20). In short, what constitutes social harm will be defined by the practices and processes to which it is applied and the manner of this application. While there is some wisdom to this comment – which I will elaborate upon later in the chapter – without a wider ontological, ethical and epistemological framework, it is a somewhat lacklustre response to the definitional crisis of social harm that remains susceptible to the trap of relativism.

Independently of one another, and in different ways, Yar (2012) and Pemberton (2016) have attempted more robust definitions by rooting social harm within the **ontology** of the subject, conceiving social harm as an individual or systemic denial of fundamental human needs which compromises 'human flourishing'. Yar's approach grounds human needs, human flourishing, and social harm within a theory of recognition. Following the philosopher Hegel's notion of the master-slave relation, Yar argues that we are not independent self-subsistent entities as presented in standard liberal discourse. Rather, he argues that identities are always socially interdependent and reliant upon their recognition by the other. This recognition is a fundamental need for human wellbeing. As he writes:

> The individual comes to know himself, to recognise himself as a being with particular attributes or proper-ties, through the acknowledgement conferred by an 'other'. An individual's sense of worth remains mere 'subjective self-certainty', and hence uncertain of itself, unless that sense of worth (or 'idea-of-self') is affirmed by others. (Yar, 2012: 57)

To give a couple of simple examples, my enjoyment of a fancy Rolls-Royce and the symbolic status it conveys would be significantly diminished if it were mocked rather than admired or even envied by others; hence, perhaps, the trend in contemporary consumer culture of the conspicuous display of our lifestyles or new purchases on social media, which need to be validated by 'likes' and comments (Smith and Raymen, 2016). Equally, my identity and status as an academic with a certain level of expertise are reliant upon it being recognised by another. I must first complete a series of degrees, be awarded a PhD by an established university, and conduct academic research that is published in books and academic journals. In other words, I must first be *recognised* as an academic before I can legitimately claim to be one. Without this recognition, my claims would be empty and hollow. However, these are somewhat trivial forms of recognition. Yar's approach is concerned with far more elemental forms of recognition which, he argues, 'establish at a fundamental anthropological level the "basic needs" that comprise the conditions of human integrity and well-being (what Aristotelians call "flourishing")' (Yar, 2012: 59). These forms of recognition are 'love', 'rights' and 'esteem'. 'Each', Yar argues, 'corresponds to a basic element that is required to secure the subject's integrity in its relation to self and others … From this viewpoint, social harms can be understood to comprise nothing other than *the inter-subjective experi-ence of being refused recognition with respect to any or all of these dimensions of need*' (Yar, 2012: 59). While these are perhaps vague and inevitably subjective needs upon which to develop a more robust account of social harm, Pemberton (2007; 2016) is far more specific in his identification of fundamental human needs. Drawing on Doyal and Gough's (1984; 1991) theory of human needs, he argues that social harm constitutes the compromising of *human flourishing* through the systematic denial of access to the basic prerequisites for such flourishing such as healthcare, housing, education, safe working practices, employment, and financial security among others. Within this framework, it is clear how we could identify austerity, zero-hour contracts, or the privatisation of healthcare as systemic forms of social harm in a number of different ways.

The major positive of both of these approaches is that they situate social harm in terms of the com-promising of human flourishing. Their starting point is a consideration of what is good for human persons and working backwards from there. 'Human flourishing' is originally a term derived from Aristotelian moral philosophy, in which there was a collectively shared notion of the Good for human-kind – what Aristotle called the *telos* (MacIntyre, 2011). Therefore, if employed properly, 'human flourishing' could serve their stated aim of pushing past the negative and individualistic freedom of liberal ideology. For **liberalism**, there is no rightful moral, political, social or religious authority to which we should defer which can impinge upon or curtail the freedoms of the sovereign individual. There is only the negative liberty of the individual, in which the individual should have freedom *from* abuse, torture, oppression and so on. Liberty and moral authority are located within the sovereign individual, who should be free to pursue their privately defined and pluralistic notion of the good life.

Both Yar and Pemberton – along with the likes of Hillyard and Tombs (2017) – have argued that human needs approaches do indeed address the problems with liberalism's negative ideology. However, such an argument is specious. This is because both Yar and Pemberton use the term 'human flourishing' in a fashion that is completely divorced from Aristotle's conceptual scheme. The crucial shortcoming to each of their approaches is that they leave the content of what constitutes human flourishing relatively open-ended, failing to emphasise the necessity of a *shared and collective* understanding of what constitutes the good for human persons and society. Their notion of 'positive liberty' merely amounts to a slightly more ambitious, welfare-oriented and socialistic brand of negative liberty with a different name. It extends the traditional negative liberties of the right to life, freedom from torture, freedom of expression and so on, to include 'human needs' of equal access to physical and mental health services, education and personal development, and employment, among others. However, this does not constitute a radical departure from the negative ideology of liberal individualism. In much the same way as human rights approaches, they provide the crucial prerequisites for human flourishing, which can provide some broad starting point for thinking about social harm. But in failing to establish a shared collective understanding of the good for human persons, what constitutes 'human flourishing' (of what we should be doing and striving for) is still very much left open for the individual to decide, thereby allowing the term to work within the confines of liberal individualism quite comfortably. Under this framework, therefore, positive liberty is defined as the provider of basic material needs and services for individuals to enact their individual freedom to behave according to their sovereign view of 'human flourishing'. Positive and negative liberty thus collapse into one another, and 'human flourishing' in Pemberton and Yar's needs-based approaches is left in its individualised and pluralistic form. Without a shared notion of human flourishing, this term can be invoked in an individualised form and subjugated to arguments of negative liberty. This opens up questions regarding the limits to these pluralised notions of human flourishing, what happens when one individual's conception of human flourishing conflicts with and potentially damages another, and in the event of such a conflict, whose human flourishing is privileged and why, thereby disrupting the concept of social harm and plunging it back into the realms of individualistic relativism (Raymen, 2019; Hall et al., 2020).

In an effort to avoid these muddy waters and prevent the concept of social harm from becoming too nebulous, Lasslett (2010) has argued for a much more rigid ontological approach to conceptualising social harm. He critiques the likes of Pemberton for not conceptualising harm in a sufficiently objective and ontological manner, taking umbrage with their use of Doyal and Gough's (1991) theory of human needs and their notion of social harm as the compromising of 'human flourishing'. This, Lasslett argues, is not a properly 'ontological' approach because it is based upon a highly particular 'ethical conception of man' (ibid., 2010: 12). 'To define harm', Lasslett argues, 'we must make the transition from **ethics** to ontology, which is prior to ethics in philosophical terms' (Lasslett, 2010: 12). He therefore attempts to offer an approach which detaches harm from the question of ethics entirely. He advocates limiting the application of social harm to those processes, structures and relations which disrupt or fail to preserve the organic and inorganic reproduction of human beings or their environment. Such an approach, it is alleged, allows criminologists and social harm scholars to remain more strictly focused upon the most truly serious forms of harmful practice which threaten the organic and inorganic reproduction of human life: exposure to toxic chemicals, the creation of food, water or vital resource scarcity, the denial of access to vital medicines which help to preserve and reproduce the vital organic properties of the human body, and so on.

However, this is arguably far too prescriptive. There is a broad range of social processes and practices that are perhaps less drastic, but which in practice we do and arguably should call 'harmful'. For example, it is widely acknowledged that the intensely comparative and envy-inducing culture of contemporary social media is cultivating widespread forms of depression, anxiety, and body dysmorphia among many individuals within society, particularly among young people. Can we deny that this is immensely harmful and detrimental to the human condition and the social more generally, despite not *necessarily* threatening the organic and inorganic reproduction of human persons? Can we only call it harmful when it culminates in suicide or self-harm? Similarly, it was recently reported that FoxConn, a subsidiary company of Amazon, have been employing schoolchildren in China to produce Alexa smart speakers. Unsurprisingly, the working conditions for these schoolchildren have been poor, working up to ten hours per day, six days a week, with an explicitly mandated expectation to work night shifts and overtime. The physical demands have been deleterious to these schoolchildren's physical and mental wellbeing, and these schoolchildren (classified as 'interns') are paid a basic salary which is equivalent to £1.18 per hour (Chamberlain, 2019; China Labour Watch, 2019). But as a little thought experiment, what if the working conditions were quite good? What if these schoolchildren were paid fairly, given frequent breaks, with shift hours significantly reduced and restricted, and line managers who were supportive and nurturing towards their child employees? It does not matter that this scenario is entirely unlikely. What matters is that many people would arguably still balk at this idea, and still confidently assert that use of child labour was wrong, harmful to a child's development, and deprives them of the distinct life-stage of childhood. Yet all three of the 'ontological' frameworks we have explored thus far only allow us to denounce such child employment practices as 'harmful' if they were working in oppressive and dangerous conditions for poor pay, with managers who bullied and belittled them. They do not allow us to denounce child labour *as such*.

RETHINKING THE NATURE OF THE CONCEPT OF SOCIAL HARM

Is there a way out of the trap of individualist relativism on the one hand or an excessive restriction of the parameters of the concept of social harm on the other? This requires us to re-evaluate the nature of the concept of social harm at a deeper philosophical level. In attempting to combat the 'subjectivism' and 'relativism' of the concept of social harm, the concept has, at times, been treated as if it possesses a pure, timeless, and static reality that pre-exists and is independent of our social world and which we are striving to discover and articulate. Pemberton uses this precise language when reviewing the various attempts at defining social harm and attempting to provide a definition or conceptual framework of his own, acknowledging that 'up to this point, it remains difficult to discern what "social harm" actually *is*' (Pemberton, 2016: 18; emphasis added). However, as Hall et al. (2020: 6) emphasise, 'we cannot simply reach up and pluck the abstract essence of *zemia* [harm] out of Plato's realm of Ideal forms'. Social harm is a messy concept, born out of our social world. This is not to say that harm is merely a social construction. Harm is real, it is felt and experienced as real and, as Hall et al. (2020: 9) describe, 'If to some extent we know harms when we see them, we know them even better when we experience them and feel them receding'. Nevertheless, our understanding of social harm always rests upon a judgement that stems from and is 'the converse reality of an imagined desirable state' (Pemberton, 2016: 32). Social harm, therefore, is a fundamentally dialectical concept that, to borrow the phrasing of Hall and Winlow (2015), has 'one foot in reality'.

Consequently, Raymen (2019) and Lloyd (2018) have suggested that an initial step in the right direction is for social harm's ontology to be reconnected to a revived positive ethics. While the concept of social harm is certainly concerned with identifying social behaviours, practices and structural processes which produce outcomes that are universally regarded as undesirable, this is the concept's *purpose*, not its foundation. It is argued here that part of our difficulty with the concept of social harm can be located in the profound absence of a *shared idea of the Good* (Badiou, 2001). Social harm is an inherently evaluative and dialectical concept which functions as part of an historical sequence. As an evaluative concept, it is only intelligible and fully functional when it follows on the back of established criteria that are shared by the general population by which we evaluate a given social role, practice, structural process, or form of behaviour. To say that someone, something, or some group of people have been harmed is really to say that something has gone *wrong* with that person, thing, or group of people. But in order to establish that something has gone wrong there must be, by necessity, a shared and agreed-upon *goal*, purpose, or ideal state of things that the person, institution, or social practice is working towards. For example, in order for the statement that the present government is 'harmful' to be at all intelligible, there must also be some collective idea of the virtues, purpose, and responsibilities of the social practice of 'good' government which can act as a benchmark and a frame of reference against which the alleged 'harmful' government is measured and condemned.

At this point, one might object that such an approach is just as open to subjectivism. Arguably, what one deems to be 'good' government can quite easily be similarly pluralistic, subjective and individualist. This, however, is to mistake the nature of social practices. As MacIntyre (2011) argues, social practices must be thought of as socially established and *cooperative* human activities with *shared* purposes and goods *internal* to their practice. Healthcare, education, politics, news media, policing, parenting, housing and so on are all social practices with purposes and goods *internal* to them, the achievement of which are real and can be readily identified and understood. As the likes of Hall et al. (2020) and MacIntyre (1984) argue, relativism dies when we begin to deliberate and establish consensus around the proper ends and purpose of social roles, practices, institutions, and human life more generally. This is the true nemesis of relativism. I therefore argue that the question of harm is first and foremost a question of the shared and *collectively* understood goods internal to these practices and social roles, and their goals, purpose and associated ethical responsibilities in society (Raymen, 2019). In essence, what should we be striving for? By considering the goods internal to shared social practices, my stance takes inspiration from and re-works both Yar's and Pemberton's human needs approaches which focus on human flourishing, and Hillyard and Tombs' (2004) practice-oriented approach mentioned above, to provide a more robust and collective account of the Good and of human flourishing that is not as susceptible to relativism. Social harm, therefore, can be understood as the potentially detrimental outcomes which emerge from the systemic or individual failure to pursue and achieve the *shared and collectively agreed upon goods* internal to social roles, practices, and institutions.

Rather than attempting to establish a set of timeless criteria, my (Raymen, 2019) approach means that social harm's conceptual framework is never fully settled, but always a work in progress. Informed by continuous social research and philosophical reflection, it involves a continuous deliberation over the good for human persons, the environment, and the goods internal to these most crucial social practices. These will evolve and be carefully revised over time in accordance with changes in social reality. Climate change, for example, forces us to reconsider the goods internal to a variety of social practices. The practice of food production and distribution is one example. Under these environmental conditions, being a 'good' food producer and distributor involves producing nutritious food in a sustainable and environmentally friendly fashion, with greater emphasis placed upon growing, distributing, and consuming affordable food more locally rather than the global importation and exportation of food with all of its environmental consequences. This transforms social harm into a fundamentally positive concept which, in attempting to identify what is wrong with the world, is simultaneously involved in imagining a better society and 'constructing an imagination for the type of lives we want to lead, the society we want to live in, and the subjectivities we want to cultivate' (Raymen, 2019: 150).

However, there are significant barriers for such an approach to the concept of social harm. Through our previous discussion of liberalism, we have already seen how such deliberations are antithetical to postmodern liberalism's fundamental principles, in which the ultimate good is that of *negative liberty*. Negative liberty privileges the sovereign freedom of the individual to pursue their private conception of the Good and is simply the absence of constraint other than law and private conscience (Fawcett, 2014; Deneen, 2018). For the concept of harm, which includes but is not limited to the legal sphere and is an inherently social concept which necessitates wider public coherence than is demanded of private conscience, this is not a viable foundation. In lieu of deliberations over the shared goods, purpose and ends of social roles, institutions and social practices, political liberalism has put in place procedural rules and legalistic standards such as human rights to firmly establish the allegedly neutral 'ground rules' for 'fair play' between a plurality of individual freedoms in open competition with one another in the economic and cultural arenas (Rawls, 1971; Forrester, 2019). As Adrian Pabst (2019: 111) has written, 'In the name of neutrality that only liberal ground rules can secure, debates about the common human good and the shared ends of human flourishing have been banished from the court of public political discussion', effectively eliminating the concept of social harm's inherently dialectical nature.

Pause for Review and Thought

1. Pemberton (2016) argues that we should understand social harm as the compromising of human flourishing. What does he mean by this?
2. Why does Lasslett (2010) object to social harm being conceptually rooted in ethics? What are the strengths and weaknesses of Lasslett's more prescriptive 'ontological' approach?
3. What is meant by the term 'negative liberty'? Why is this understanding of freedom a problematic for establishing a more objective basis for social harm?
4. What does Raymen (2019) mean when he argues that we must base 'social harm' as a concept upon a shared conception of the Good? Can you think of your own examples of the 'goods' internal to social roles or practices, and how they have been harmed and corrupted?

My approach is also antithetical to the logic of our present political-economic system of neoliberal capitalism and its cultural variant of consumer culture. Capitalism and consumer culture are inherently geared toward the pursuit of external goods *for their own sake*, be it profit, wealth, fame, power, or social prestige and symbolic status. As capitalism seeks to expand existing markets and create new ones for the purpose of wealth accumulation and infinite growth, it has sought to place primacy upon these external goods in almost all spheres of life (MacIntyre, 2011). Take the example of housing, which has occupied much attention from criminologists interested in social harm (Cooper and Whyte, 2018; Atkinson, 2019; Tombs, 2019). Housing in late capitalism has become a speculative practice. Properties are increasingly used and understood for their exchange value (their external good) as opposed to its use value as a home (their internal good) (see Madden and Marcuse, 2016). This practice is what underpinned the real estate bubble which was a precursor to the global financial crash in 2007/8 (see the case study below).

Case Study 7.1

Mortgage-Backed Securities (MBS), the US Housing Bubble, and the 2007/8 Global Financial Crisis

The Global Financial Crisis (GFC) that came perilously close to collapsing the global economy in 2007-2008 is a perfect example of Raymen's (2019) point around the harms that occur when goods *external* to social practices such as housing are pursued over and above their internal goods. At the epicentre of the GFC was what Harvey (2010: 4) has described as 'the mountain of "toxic" mortgage-backed securities (MBS) held by Investment banks or marketed to unsuspecting investors all around

(Continued)

the world'. As a result of the GFC, 10% of Americans were unemployed, while 3.8 million Americans lost their homes due to foreclosure. This brief case study will attempt to explain, in very simplified and basic terms, what an MBS is and how it led to the crisis.

Under a so-called 'traditional' mortgage arrangement (demonstrated in Figure 7.1 below), a prospective homebuyer would request a loan from a commercial bank to buy a house. The homebuyer would then, over an established period (say 25 or 30 years), repay the initial loan in addition to an interest payment. Over that period, the bank recovers the initial money they loaned and profits from the additional interest. In a very basic way, this is how banks make money on mortgages. The downside of this, of course, is that the loans stay on the bank's balance sheets for that entire period. This ties up the capital they have available, as they are having to wait for a long period of time to see a full return on their initial loan.

To resolve this issue, banks came up with the idea of a mortgage-backed security (MBS). As depicted in Figure 7.2 below, in this scenario the bank acts as a 'middleman' or intermediary. A bank would take thousands of mortgages, bundle them together and put them into a single investment bond called a Mortgage-Backed Security. Shares in the MBS are then sold to individual investors and investment banks for a substantial fee. The bank benefits by immediately recovering the money they loaned out to homebuyers rather than having to wait decades to see a return, thereby freeing up their cash flow. The investors in the MBS, on the other hand, receive the mortgage and interest repayments from the homeowners whose mortgages are in the MBS, and it is divided up among them according to the percentage of shares each of the investors purchased.

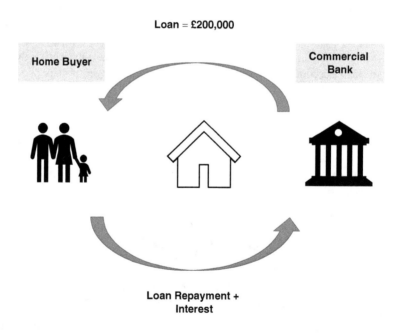

Figure 7.1 'Traditional' Mortgage Arrangement

These MBSs were considered secure investments as they consisted of low-risk mortgages which had relatively low interest rates, and were given to people who had secure incomes, strong credit histories, and a low likelihood of defaulting (failing to repay) their mortgages. However, there are only so many prospective property buyers with these characteristics. This of course places a limit on the number of mortgages that can be offered, which in turn restricts the number of MBSs banks could

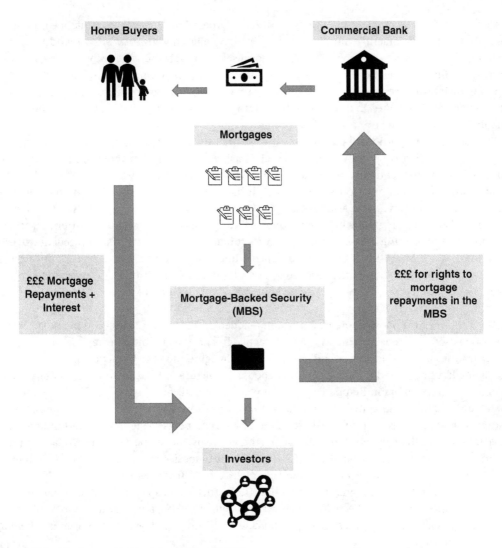

Figure 7.2 Mortgage-Backed Securities (MBS)

sell to investors, thereby constraining their potential profits. Consequently, banks began to lower their lending standards, offering large 'subprime' mortgages which had interest rates which increased significantly over time, and offered them to homebuyers with very low credit scores, deficient credit histories, and who often lacked secure, stable, or sufficient incomes, all of which increased the likelihood of defaults on repayments. These riskier subprime mortgages were then bundled together and put into MBSs. These MBSs were marketed and sold to investors as having higher profits (due to the higher interest repayments), *but they were being deliberately mischaracterised as low-risk investments* despite there being significant likelihood of payment defaults on the underlying mortgages within the MBS. In essence, to create a larger market in MBSs and make more money, banks engaged in irresponsible mortgage-lending and fraudulent marketing of MBSs.

In 2006, the housing bubble collapsed, and house prices began to decline rapidly. Homeowners found themselves in a situation where the debts they owed on their homes were substantially larger than what their homes were actually worth. Defaults on payments began to rise sharply as people either walked away from their mortgages or were unable to pay as interest rates increased, thereby making the MBSs sold to investors entirely worthless. Corporations, investment banks, pension funds, and municipal governments who had invested in these allegedly low-risk MBSs found themselves holding worthless pieces of paper. This sent shockwaves through the wider economy, as the losses accrued by investors rendered many of them unable to pay their employees or meet the costs of running their businesses and institutions, causing sharp rises in unemployment, and millions of foreclosures on people's homes. In many respects, this is an example of social harm that could and perhaps should be considered to be a 'crime of the powerful'.

By placing disproportionate primacy on the external financial goods of housing and turning it into a hyper-speculative profit-oriented financial business, the subprime mortgage industry almost collapsed the global economy, increased unemployment to levels not seen since before World War II, and cost 3.8 million Americans their homes. It has been pursued to such an extreme point that scholars such as Madden and Marcuse (2016) have seen it suitable to make distinction between 'real estate' and 'housing', in which the former attacks the latter. As they have written, '[t]he commodification of housing means that a structure's function as real estate takes precedence over its usefulness as a place to live. When this happens, housing's role as an investment outweighs all other claims upon it, whether they are based upon right, need, tradition, legal precedent, cultural habit, *or the ethical and affective significance of the home*' (Madden and Marcuse, 2016: 17; emphasis added).

The last line of the above quote is significant. Madden and Marcuse (2016) echo the broader sentiment proposed here that housing as a social practice has an integral moral component, with goods internal to its practice. In this regard, if we were to imagine the social practice of organising and regulating housing geared toward its internal goods, the picture of housing in contemporary society would look quite different. Emphasis would be placed upon all housing being affordable and well-maintained. Rather than cultivating the lifeless *non-spaces* (Augé, 1995) of gated communities and vacant neighbourhoods of 'prime real estate' in an effort to boost value, focus and funding would be geared toward the cultivation of genuine neighbourhoods and spaces for collective and intimate forms of public and private social life. These are the kinds of locales imagined by Jacobs (1961) in *The Death and Life of Great American Cities* – fundamentally ethical spaces which emphasise affective and emotional place-making through real human ties. The restrictions of space prevent me from providing further examples. These have been offered elsewhere (Raymen, 2019), and I invite you to think of your own examples. Nevertheless, these examples quickly reveal how the logic of capitalism is inherently conducive to harm.

CHAPTER SUMMARY

This chapter has endeavoured to show you the following:

- The importance of the concept of social harm in contemporary society, and how the concepts of crime are somewhat limited in addressing our most pressing social, political, economic and environmental challenges.
- How the concept of social harm expands the horizons of criminology and encourages us to critically analyse and evaluate wider social issues as a criminologist through the lens of social harm.
- That the concept of social harm is not simple or straightforward, and that various approaches have been taken to conceptualising social harm with their own specific merits and shortcomings, and none of these approaches should be dismissed outright.
- How we can look at these different conceptualisations as in a dialogue with one another and attempt to synthesise their respective approaches to develop a more robust concept of social harm that can identify, categorise and address the myriad crises we currently face.

Review Questions

Having read this chapter, think about the following questions:

1. Why do we need the concept of social harm? Why is the concept of crime deemed to be inadequate?
2. Can you think of five topics or issues of your own that might be looked at by criminologists using the concept of social harm?
3. What problems does the issues of 'subjectivism' and 'relativism' pose for the concept of social harm?
4. Can this problem be resolved? How have social harm scholars suggested we resolve this problem?

GO FURTHER

Books/Book Chapters

1. This is a seminal book which kick-started the social harm approach and the discipline of zemiology. It offers a range of chapters from experts in the field which reorient criminological issues toward a social harm approach, and explores how a social harm approach opens up new and important lines of critical enquiry.

   Hillyard, P., Pantazis, C., Tombs, S. and Gordon, D. (eds) (2004) *Beyond Criminology: Taking Harm Seriously*. London: Pluto Press.

2. Pemberton's book is a more advanced text which offers a more coherent and rigorous theoretical framework for understanding and applying the concept of social harm to contemporary social problems.

   Pemberton, S. (2016) *Harmful Societies: Understanding Social Harm*. Bristol: Policy Press.

3. This edited collection of chapters from experts in the field re-examines the relationship between crime and social harm, and offers theoretical and empirical insights which suggest that criminology and zemiology can and should be reconciled.

   Boukli, A. and Kotzé, J. (eds) (2018) *Zemiology: Reconnecting Crime and Social Harm*. London: Palgrave Macmillan.

4. An important introductory primer that offers a condensed version of some of the arguments made in Hillyard et al's book *Beyond Criminology*, this chapter provides an essential overview of the social harm approach and the discipline of zemiology to date.

   Hillyard, P. and Tombs, S. (2017) 'Social Harm and Zemiology'. In A. Liebling, S. Maruna and L. McAra (eds), *The Oxford Handbook of Criminology* (6th edition). Oxford: Oxford University Press.

Journal Articles

1. This article looks at the ambiguity and incoherence surrounding the concept of social harm, exploring the reasons for this ambiguity, and how we might develop firmer and more certain foundations for the concept of social harm.

   Raymen, T. (2019) The enigma of social harm and the barrier of liberalism: why zemiology needs a theory of the Good. *Justice, Power, and Resistance*, 3(1): 133–162.

2. An important critical article, which challenges the ethical basis on which social harm has been conceptually based and suggests a novel ontological foundation for social harm which, it is claimed, avoids the problems of relativism.

    Lasslett, K. (2010) Crime or social harm? A dialectical perspective. *Crime, Law, and Social Change*, 54: 1–19.

Useful Websites

1. Website and blog of the Harm and Evidence Research Collaborative (HERC), which aims to conduct high quality social harm research, and considers how harm can be evidenced, categorised and conceptualised. https://oucriminology.wordpress.com/
2. Website and blog of the deviant leisure research network; a group of academics who explore the normalised harms of contemporary leisure and consumer culture. www.deviantleisure.com
3. Website of the Journal of Contemporary Crime, Harm and Ethics. An open-access peer-reviewed journal that is the first criminology journal explicitly focused on issues of social harm, justice, and ethics. https://www.northumbriajournals.co.uk/index.php/jcche/index

REFERENCES

Atkinson, R. (2019) Necrotecture: lifeless dwellings and London's super-rich. *International Journal of Urban and Regional Research*. 10.1111/1468-2427.12707

Atkinson, R. (2020) *Alpha City: How London was Captured by the Super-rich*. London: Verso.

Auge, M. (1995) *Non-Places: An Introduction to Supermodernity*. London: Verso.

Badiou, A. (2001) *Ethics: An Essay on the Understanding of Evil*. London: Verso.

Boukli, A. and Kotzé, J. (eds) (2018) *Zemiology: Reconnecting Crime and Social Harm*. London: Palgrave Macmillan.

Brisman, A. and South, N. (2014) *Green Cultural Criminology: Constructions of Environmental Harm, Consumerism and Resistance to Ecocide*. Abingdon: Routledge.

Canning, V. (2018) 'Zemiology at the Border'. In A. Boukli and J. Kotzé (eds), *Zemiology: Reconnecting Crime and Social Harm*. London: Palgrave Macmillan. pp. 183–202.

Chamberlain, G. (2019) 'Schoolchildren in China work overnight to produce Amazon Alexa devices', *The Guardian*, 8th August. Available at: https://www.theguardian.com/global-development/2019/aug/08/schoolchildren-in-china-work-overnight-to-produce-amazon-alexa-devices

China Labor Watch (2019) *Amazon's Supplier Factory FoxConn Recruits Illegally: A Report*. Available at: http://www.chinalaborwatch.org/upfile/2019_08_07/Amazon%20English%20Report%2008.09.pdf

Cooper, V. and Whyte, D. (eds) (2017) *The Violence of Austerity*. London: Pluto Press.

Cooper, V. and Whyte, D. (2018) 'Grenfell, Austerity and Institutional Violence'. *Sociological Research Online*. DOI: 10.1177/1360780418800066

Cribb, R. (2009) 'Introduction: Parapolitics, Shadow Governance and Criminal Sovereignty'. In E. Wilson (ed.), *Government of the Shadows: Parapolitics and Criminal Sovereignty*. London: Pluto Press.

Deneen, P. (2018) *Why Liberalism Failed*. New Haven, CT: Yale University Press.

Doyal, L. and Gough, I. (1984) A theory of human needs. *Critical Social Policy*, 4(10): 6–38.

Doyal, L., Gough, I. (1991) *A Theory of Human Need*. Basingstoke: Palgrave Macmillan.

Dymock, A. (2018) 'A Doubling of the Offence? "Extreme" Pornography and Cultural Harm'. In A. Boukli and J. Kotzé (eds), *Zemiology: Reconnecting Crime and Social Harm*. Basingstoke: Palgrave Macmillan. pp. 165–182.

Fawcett, E. (2014) *Liberalism: The Life of an Idea*. Princeton, NJ: Princeton University Press.

Fazi, T. (2020) 'Could COVID-19 vanquish neoliberalism?', *UnHerd*, 6th April. Available at: https://unherd.com/2020/04/could-covid-19-vanquish-neoliberalism/

Fisher, M. (2014) *Ghosts of My Life: Writings on Depression, Hauntology and Lost Futures*. London: Zero Books.

Forrester, K. (2019) *In the Shadow of Justice: Postwar Liberalism and the Remaking of Political Philosophy*. Princeton, NJ:. Princeton University Press.

Hall, A. and Antonopoulos, G. (2016) *Fake Meds Online: The Internet and the Transnational Market in Illicit Pharmaceuticals*. London: Palgrave Macmillan.

Hall, S. (2012a) *Theorising Crime and Deviance: A New Perspective*. London: Sage.

Hall, S. (2012b) Don't look up, don't look down: Liberal criminology's fear of the supreme and the subterranean. *Crime, Media, Culture*, 8(2): 197–212.

Hall, S., Kuldova, T. and Horsley, M. (eds) (2020) *Crime, Harm and Consumerism*. Abingdon: Routledge.

Hall, S. and Winlow, S. (2015) *Revitalising Criminological Theory: Towards a New Ultra-Realism*. Abingdon: Routledge.

Hall, S., Winlow, S. and Ancrum, C. (2008) *Criminal Identities and Consumer Culture: Crime, Exclusion and the New Culture of Narcissism*. Abingdon: Routledge.

Harvey, D. (2010) *The Enigma of Capital*. Cambridge: Polity Press.

Hillyard, P., Pantazis, C., Tombs, S. and Gordon, D. (eds) (2004) *Beyond Criminology: Taking Harm Seriously*. London: Pluto Press.

Hillyard, P. and Tombs, S. (2004) 'Beyond Criminology?'. In P. Hillyard, C. Pantazis, S. Tombs, and D. Gordon (eds), *Beyond Criminology: Taking Harm Seriously*. London: Pluto Press. pp. 10–29.

Hillyard, P. and Tombs, S. (2007) 'From 'Crime' to Social Harm?' *Crime, Law and Social Change* 48: 9–25.

Hillyard, P. and Tombs, S. (2017) 'Social Harm and Zemiology'. In A. Liebling, S. Maruna, and L. McAra (eds), *The Oxford Handbook of Criminology*, 6th edition. Oxford: Oxford University Press. pp. 284–305.

Horsley, M. (2015) *The Dark Side of Prosperity: Late Capitalism's Culture of Indebtedness*. London: Ashgate.

Jacobs, J. (1961) *The Death and Life of Great American Cities*. New York: Vintage.

Kotzé, J. (2018) 'Criminology or Zemiology? Yes, Please! On the Refusal of Choice Between False Alternatives'. In A. Boukli and J. Kotzé (eds), *Zemiology: Reconnecting Crime and Social Harm*. London: Palgrave Macmillan. pp. 85–106.

Lasslett, K. (2010) Crime or social harm? A dialectical perspective. *Crime, Law and Social Change*, 54: 1–19.

Lloyd, A. (2013) *Labour Markets and Identity on the Post-Industrial Assembly Line*. London: Ashgate.

Lloyd, A. (2018) *The Harms of Work: An Ultra-Realist Account of the Service Economy*. Bristol. Bristol University Press.

MacIntyre, A. (2011[1981]) *After Virtue*. London: Bloomsbury.

MacIntyre, A. (1984) Relativism, power, and philosophy. *Proceedings and Addresses of the American Philosophical Association*, 59(1): 5–22.

Madden, D. and Marcuse, P. (2016) *In Defense of Housing*. London: Verso.

Medley, C. (2019) 'The Business of Resistance: Feminist Pornography and the Limits of Leisure Industries as Sites of Political Resistance'. In T. Raymen and O. Smith (eds), *Deviant Leisure: Criminological Perspectives on Leisure and Harm*. London: Palgrave Macmillan. pp. 237–258.

Millie, A. (2016) *Philosophical Criminology*. Bristol: Policy Press.

Mitchell, W. and Fazi, T. (2017) *Reclaiming the State: A Progressive Vision of Sovereignty for a Post-Neoliberal World*. London: Pluto Press.

Nixon, R. (2011) *Slow Violence and the Environmentalism of the Poor*. Cambridge, MA: Harvard University Press.

Pabst, A. (2019) *The Demons of Liberal Democracy*. Cambridge: Polity Press.

Parenti, C. (2011) *Tropic of Chaos: Climate Change and the New Geography of Violence*. New York: Nation Books.

Pemberton, S. (2007). Social harm future(s): exploring the potential of the social harm approach. *Crime, Law and Social Change*, 48(1–2): 27–41.

Pemberton, S. (2016) *Harmful Societies: Understanding Social Harm*. Bristol: Policy Press.

Raymen, T. (2019) The enigma of social harm and the barrier of liberalism: why zemiology needs a theory of the Good. *Justice, Power, and Resistance*, 3(1): 133–162.

Raymen, T. and Smith, O. (2016) What's deviance got to do with it? Black Friday sales, violence and hyper-conformity. *British Journal of Criminology*, 56(2): 389–405.

Raymen, T. and Smith, O. (2019a) Deviant leisure: a critical criminological perspective for the 21st century. *Critical Criminology*, 27: 115–130.

Raymen, T. and Smith, O. (eds) (2019b) *Deviant Leisure: Criminological Perspectives on Leisure and Harm*. London: Palgrave Macmillan.

Rawls, J. (1971) *A Theory of Justice*. Cambridge, MA: Harvard University Press.

Schwendinger, H. and Schwendinger, J. (1970) Defenders of order or guardians of human rights?, *Issues in Criminology*, 5(2): 123–157.

Shaxson, N. (2011) *Treasure Islands*. London: Bodley Head.

Smith, O. and Raymen, T. (2016) Deviant leisure: a criminological perspective. *Theoretical Criminology*. Available at: http://tcr.sagepub.com/content/early/2016/08/10/1362480616660188.abstract

Tombs, S. (2018) 'For Pragmatism and Politics: Crime, Social Harm, and Zemiology'. In A. Boukli and J. Kotzé (eds), *Zemiology: Reconnecting Crime and Social Harm*. London: Palgrave Macmillan. pp. 11–32.

Tombs, S. (2019) Grenfell: the unfolding dimensions of social harm. *Justice, Power, and Resistance*, 3(1): 61–88.

Tombs, S. and Whyte, D. (2015) *The Corporate Criminal: Why Corporations Must be Abolished*. Abingdon: Routledge.

White, R. (2013) *Environmental Harm: An Eco-Justice Perspective*. Bristol: Policy Press.

White, R. (2018) *Climate Change Criminology*. Bristol: Bristol University Press.

Wickware, C. (2020) 'Competition watchdog to monitor price hikes during COVID-19 outbreak as pharmacists report rising cost of drugs', *The Pharmaceutical Journal*, 9th March. Available at: https://www.pharmaceutical-journal.com/news-and-analysis/news/competition-watchdog-to-monitor-price-hikes-during-covid-19-outbreak-as-pharmacists-report-rising-cost-of-drugs/20207798.article?firstPass=false

Winlow, S. and Hall, S. (2013) *Rethinking Social Exclusion: The End of the Social?* London: Sage.

Yar, M. (2012) 'Critical Criminology, Critical Theory and Social Harm'. In S. Hall and S. Winlow (eds), *New Directions in Criminological Theory*. Abingdon: Routledge.

Feminist Criminologies

8

Loraine Gelsthorpe and Lucy Trafford

Learning Objectives

By the end of this chapter you will:

- Have been provided with a broad overview of how feminist thought has prompted developments in criminology.
- Understand how early feminism has impacted on mainstream criminology.
- Have explored more recent epistemological, international and intersectional dimensions of feminist criminologies.
- Be able to consider what future contributions feminism can make to criminology.

Framing Questions

---

1. How can we best characterise feminist perspectives in criminology?
2. How have feminist perspectives changed over time?
3. What are the key empirical and epistemological contributions?
4. Have feminist perspectives altered the terrain of criminology?
5. What features of feminist perspectives are relevant to twenty-first century thinking?

INTRODUCTION

Feminism and criminology have a complex but enduring relationship, and one which is rich with critical explorations of epistemology, methods, politics, policy and praxis. Gender-blind assumptions within criminology have been thoroughly questioned from early critiques in the 1960s and 1970s right through to more recent thinking which revolves around **intersectionality** and international perspectives. This chapter provides a critical overview of feminist contributions to criminology. If we think of feminist activity occurring in 'waves', there is a particular focus on second wave feminism (associated with challenges to mainstream criminology in the 1960s–1980s) and third wave feminism (associated with the 1990s and beyond) which highlights some of the limitations of second wave feminism, and recognises global issues common to women, and the need for an intersectional approach, combining constructions of gender with race, ethnicity, class, religion, and nationality, for instance (Crenshaw, 2017). Following a section which maps the terrain in terms of these 'waves', as well as defining feminisms and criminologies, we then outline and evaluate feminist contributions: the early critique, the substantive and political project (including equalising justice and recognising victims, as well as prompts for wider recognition of the construction of gender), **epistemological** developments and methodological adventures, and then new and emerging research agendas. The overall aim is to reflect the myriad ways in which feminist contributions to criminology have prompted changes to the contours of criminology.

MAPPING THE TERRAIN

The very term 'feminism' has an interesting history with origins in the mid-19th century. We can think of feminist 'waves' reflecting different time periods of activity in the western world. First wave feminism is associated with mid-19th and early 20th century activities to achieve equal rights for women, whether this be property rights, the right to vote, or the right to access education in the same way as men. Second wave feminism is associated with the 1960s–1980s, reflecting concern with issues of equality and discrimination; it is here that we see clear links with criminology, as early sociologists and criminologists critiqued the neglect of gender in criminological theorising and in criminal justice practice. Third wave feminism began in the 1990s and is perceived as a response to the failures of second wave feminism and as a backlash against some second wave initiatives relating to what was perceived as an exclusive focus on equality for white women. Thus, third wave feminism sees women's lives as intersectional, demonstrating how race, ethnicity, class, religion, gender, and nationality are all significant factors when discussing feminism. Third wave feminism also pushes issues into an international arena, recognising common oppressions as well as some differences.

As indicated above, over time feminist activity has reflected political, legal, cultural and economic movements to establish equal rights and legal protections for women. There have been numerous campaigns ranging from women's right to property, to vote, abortion and reproductive rights, maternity leave and equal pay, to protection from domestic abuse, sexual harassment and assault, workplace rights, and campaigns against all forms of discrimination that women encounter. The overall aim of this chapter is to examine feminist thinking and activity and their impact on criminological terrain. We do this by providing you with a broad overview of developments in criminology prompted by feminist thinking, from early inroads into mainstream criminology through to more recent epistemological, international and intersectional dimensions of feminist criminologies.

FEMINIST PERSPECTIVES

In order to address the relationship between feminism and criminology we need to acknowledge that there are many different versions of feminism. Rosemarie Tong (1989), for example, illuminates some of the key differences between alternative feminist perspectives by cataloguing the development of feminisms and the history of feminist thought. Tong (1989) identifies six main kinds of feminism:

Knowledge link: This topic is also covered in Chapter 20.

1. *Liberal feminism* – Involves a commitment to reforms concerning equal civil rights, equality of opportunity and the recognition of women's rights in welfare, health, employment and education; it is also associated with a particular methodological position which has been described as feminist empiricism and which includes not only the aim to focus more specifically on women, but also to include women in any data-gathering processes.

2. *Marxist feminism* – Involves describing the material basis of women's oppression and the relationship between the modes of production and women's status and applying theories of women and class to the role of the family.

3. *Socialist feminism* – Contends that women are treated as second-class citizens in patriarchal capitalism and that we need to transform the ownership of the means of production and women's social experience because the roots of women's oppression lie in the total economic system of capitalism. Socialist feminism is perhaps an outgrowth of Marxist feminism's dissatisfaction with the gender-blind concept of class.

4. *Existential feminism* – Existentialism is a philosophical theory which argues that individuals are free and responsible agents able to transcend their social roles and determine their own development. Feminist existentialism is perhaps epitomised by Simone de Beauvoir's (1949) *The Second Sex* in which she argues that women are oppressed because they are 'Other' to man's 'Self', and that as 'Other' they are 'not man'. Man is taken to be the 'Self', the free, self-determining agent who defines his own existence, whilst woman remains the 'Other', the object, whose meaning is determined by what she is not.

5. *Psychoanalytical feminism* – Whilst psychoanalysis has come under attack because of its seemingly inherent sexism (emphasising biology over social relations and taking masculine characteristics as the norm), a feminist psychoanalysis has been developed to show how prevailing norms of gender are imposed and structure the human mind. Feminist psychoanalysis is sometimes referred to as gender theory.

6. *Postmodern feminism* – Drawing on the general features of **postmodernism** as a major cultural phenomenon in the arts, architecture, philosophy and economics, and inter alia rejecting the idea of single explanations or philosophies, feminist postmodernism involves opposition to **essentialism** (the belief that differences between men and women are innate, rather than socially/experientially constructed), and a belief in more plural kinds of knowledge. Some of the roots of postmodern feminism are found in the work of Simone de Beauvoir (1949), as above. Emphasis on the positive side of 'Otherness' is a major theme in the associated deconstructionist approaches and in the celebration of a plurality of knowledges. 'Otherness' thus symbolises plurality, diversity, difference and openness. The so-called rationality and objectivity of contemporary science also comes under attack in feminist postmodernism and there are attempts to create fluid, open terms and language which more closely reflect women's experiences.

Radical feminism is perhaps the most commonly known form of feminism and one you may have come across already. It relates to understanding society as a patriarchy in which men dominate and oppress women. Thus, the aim of radical feminism is to liberate women from this oppression, including the sexual objectification of women. In this perspective there are attempts to raise public awareness of issues such as rape and domestic abuse, challenging the concept of gender roles and racialised and gendered capitalism which characterises many societies.

Two further feminist perspectives might be added to this initial list:

- *Black feminist thought* consists of ideas produced by Black women that clarify a standpoint of and for Black women. Black women possess a unique standpoint on, and experiences of, historical and material conditions. Black women's experiences uniquely provide an 'outsider-within' perspective on self, family and society which in turn serves to establish a distinctive standpoint vis à vis sociology's paradigmatic facts and theories.
- *Global feminism* recognises differences and similarities between feminisms in the West, East, North and South, encouraging movement away from Western-centric concepts. Global feminism is also known as 'world feminism' and 'international feminism'. Whatever the label, the intent is to align with post-colonial theory and post-colonial feminism, and to promote women's rights on a global scale (see Barberet, 2014).

Knowledge link: This topic is also covered in Chapter 16.

There are other kinds of feminisms you may come across, *Visionary feminism*, for instance is rooted in resistance to the idea of one gender being privileged over another. *Cultural feminism* is closely aligned to radical feminism and is embedded in the aim to build a women's culture. Collective efforts of radical and cultural feminists in the late 1970s had some positive social benefit: the creation of rape crisis centres, for example. One of the precepts of cultural feminism is that women are 'inherently kinder and gentler', though there is much to be debated in this. The assumption here perhaps needs to be questioned and explored, empirically. *Eco-feminism* relates the treatment of women to the treatment of the environment, animals or resources and argues for better treatment of all.

Pause for Thought

- Is it helpful for there to be so many different types of feminism?
- Why do you think that different feminist perspectives have developed?
- Does categorising feminism in this way help the cause of women's liberation?
- Are there any common themes across the different kinds of feminism?

Importantly:

In what ways have these different kinds of feminism promoted change regarding criminal justice policy and practice?

It is not that different kinds of feminism have followed each other in succession; rather they have accumulated and are sometimes overlapping in terms of both chronology and perspectives. At the same time, division exists between these feminist viewpoints. For example, there have been questions as to whether feminism neglects intersectionality, and whether 'feminism is dead', alongside accusations that feminism has perhaps lost a sense of public commitment. Martha Nussbaum, for example, in *The New Republic* declared that modern feminism '… is the virtually complete turning from the material side of life, toward a type of verbal and symbolic politics that makes only the flimsiest of connections with the real situation of real women' (1999: 38). Putting it another way, for all the feminist activity there has been, the sexual abuse of children continues, domestic abuse against women continues, serious sexual assaults of women continue – and so there have been serious questions as to the value of feminism. But before we question whether this kind of criticism is valid by looking at the relationship between feminism(s) and criminology, we should briefly acknowledge different kinds of criminology, although this book itself captures the rich variety of criminological perspectives.

A BRIEF LOOK AT CRIMINOLOGICAL PERSPECTIVES

Criminology has long since been described as a 'rendez-vous' subject; it is wide ranging and includes neuroscientific, sociological, biological, and psychological, historical and victimological perspectives. Big changes came when 'mainstream' criminology, based on assumptions about evidence produced from methods borrowed from the natural sciences, and assumptions that 'crime' is the result of a range of physiological, psychological, economic, or structural predeterminants, was challenged by more radical perspectives in the late 1960s. Mainstream criminology is largely individualistic in its focus (individual behaviour rather than societal context). Whereas those adopting radical perspectives (from Marxist perspectives in criminology to **Left Realism**) questioned notions of causation, and criticised positivist criminology as being little more than the servant of government, involving mere tinkering with the administration of criminal justice. Thus, criminology in the latter part of the twentieth century re-connected with the interplay between structure and agency. Criminologists began to develop a broader understanding of harms and a recognition that the power to define (and also ignore) certain acts was key to public understanding of crime and criminal justice. These days, criminology has expanded to include Green Criminology, Convict Criminology, Critical Race Theory, and, of course, Feminist Criminology. In other words, both 'feminism' and 'criminology' are dynamic concepts which continue to experience kaleidoscopic changes.

Knowledge link: This topic is also covered in Chapter 6.

Knowledge link: These topics are also covered in Chapters 16, 19, 20 and 29 respectively.

THE RELATIONSHIP BETWEEN FEMINISM AND CRIMINOLOGY (OR FEMINISMS AND CRIMINOLOGIES)

These complexities aside, there are some basic questions to ask:

- What does a feminist perspective mean in practice?
- Do feminist goals have to be explicit for thinking to count as 'feminist'?
- Might there be 'feminist research' which seemingly does feminism a disservice?
- What about the case of feminist research which is supportive of feminist goals?
- Does choice of research topic matter?
- Is feminist research necessarily gender-related, making women visible as victims and as people who have committed offences against the criminal law?
- Is feminist research necessarily 'on, by and for' women as Stanley and Wise (1983) once asked?

These are important questions, but perhaps none of these suggested criteria are adequate on their own as a test of whether something is 'feminist'. The key point is perhaps that holding a feminist perspective means accepting the view that women experience subordination on the basis of their sex, and it means working towards the elimination of that subordination. Perhaps it is more important to determine 'how, why and when' the 'by, on and for' criteria are relevant in social, political and cultural contexts. It can certainly be argued that it would be a mistake to exclude men from feminist scholarship (the more supporters the better), although involving men does not necessarily mean conceding the whole terrain and there are politically sensitive ways of describing men's involvement. For example, men might describe themselves as 'pro-feminist' rather than 'feminist'. The important thing is perhaps for there to be recognition of gendered subjectivity regarding the 'on, by and for'.

Moreover, it would be a mistake to assume a single relationship between feminism and criminology as there are a myriad of relationships. The criminology of the 1970s which prompted Carol Smart's 1976 critical text *Women, Crime and Criminology*, one of the first openly feminist critiques of criminology in Britain, is certainly not the criminology of today. The criminology of today is more diverse. Whether it is sufficiently diverse or open enough to accommodate some of the critical ideas of feminisms remains a matter for debate. Carol Smart (1990) made a strong case for abandoning criminology because she concluded that it was backward-looking. In a percipient conclusion to her 1976 text Smart suggested that criminology would have to reach beyond the usual study of men in order to fully participate in any transformation of existing social practices in the arena of criminal justice.

Her concern was that criminology, even in its more radical form, would be unchanged by feminist critiques. By 1990, she viewed criminology as the '**atavistic** man' in scholarship and wished to put it aside because she could not see what it had to offer feminism. Nevertheless, there are good reasons to pause before pursuing the abandonment option, given more recent signs of critical thinking in criminology. What are these contributions to criminology then, and how effective have they been? Let's begin with the early critique.

The early critique

The starting point for considering feminism and criminology is often the pioneering work of feminist scholars in criminology in the 1960s. Various criminology scholars, Frances Heidensohn (1987) included, have highlighted key theoretical deficiencies in mainstream criminology. Essentially there has been an absence of proper mention of women in criminological theorising, and where women have been mentioned there has been misrepresentation. For example, Eileen Leonard (1982) has described how Merton's USA-based strain theory is often seen as important in the panoply of criminological theories, but there is no concept of gender. If crime is the result of social and economic strain in society, then surely, we might expect more women to commit crime, given the added strain of gender-based oppression. The sociological subcultural theorists wrote about working-class culture amongst boys and young men; in which males rebel and respond to cultural strains and peer group pressure to achieve status, whilst young women and girls merely have walk-on parts in the drama of male lives. Even the Marxist inspired *New Criminology* (Taylor et al., 1983) with its reflection of critical and progressive criminology and its focus on the state, social and economic conditions and the state's capacity to define and confer criminality on others, fails to recognise the significance of gender. Thus, female criminality has largely been ignored in western criminological theorising.

The alternative is that where women do appear in theories, their behaviour is explained in terms of stereotypical assumptions about behaviour being biologically determined. Tracing the continuance of **sexist** assumptions from Lombroso to Pollak and beyond, Smart (1976) examined how assumptions of the abnormality of female offenders (biological and psychological) came to dominate both theory and criminal justice policy and practice. While analyses of class structure, state control and the political nature of deviance steadily gained credibility in mainstream criminology in the 1960s and 1970s, the study of women's crime remained rooted in notions of biological determinism and an uncritical attitude towards the dominant sexual stereotypes of women as passive, domestic, and maternal (Smart, 1976).

This is not to say that this early critique escaped criticism. It did not. Some writers rather naively assumed that a simple remedy to the deficiencies in theorising could be addressed by appropriating existing theories and inserting 'women' into them. One example here concerns the efforts to 'discover girl gangs' and consider girls in relation to subcultural theory; as discussed below this raised concerns about increased violence and masculinisation amongst women. It is also relevant to mention 'vengeful equity' here, whereby a quest for identical treatment overlooks the nuanced differences between males and females, leading to inappropriate outcomes and distortions in theory.

Case Study 8.1

Discovering Girl Gangs

During the late 20th and early 21st century a media scare occurred following a rise in the reporting of female violence, with cries that women were becoming as violent as men and media constructions of 'girl gangs', 'bad girls' and 'ladettes'. This concept of 'masculinisation' suggested that women were seeking equality in crime, as in the workplace. However, Chesney-Lind (2004) argued that the apparent rise in female crime was unrelated to a rise in female violence, with incidents that would previously have been ignored between females instead becoming criminalised - such as school playground fights.

Pause for Thought

- Why do you think these acts were previously overlooked?
- What role does the media play in public perceptions of crime?
- Why do you think fears arose that girls would seek equality in crime, through 'girl gangs'?

Thus, the early critique revolved around amnesia and misrepresentation. Eileen Leonard usefully summarised mainstream criminological theory by stating:

> Theories that are frequently hailed as explanations of human behaviour are, in fact, discussions of male behaviour and male criminality ... We cannot simply apply these theories to women, nor can we modify them with a brief addition or subtraction here and there. (1982:181)

It was within this early feminist critique of criminology that the notion of 'mainstream' (meaning 'malestream') emerged, reflecting a pointed critical focus on male domination of the subject of criminology.

The substantive and political project

In terms of substantive developments, feminist perspectives have contributed to the illumination of sexism in theory, criminal justice policy and practice. They have drawn attention to both explicit and implicit controls exercised over women, identifying links between informal social regulation of women's lives and policing through more formal mechanisms of social control (Cain, 1989). For example, feminists have highlighted social assumptions about women's behaviour, and explicit control of women by the medical and psychiatric professions, both in prisons and general medical care. There has also been a focus on the way in which women are subject to petty and coercive systems of control in prisons (more so than men). An oft-repeated claim within the criminal justice system is that women are often 'mad' or 'sad' rather than 'bad', although feminist scholars have highlighted the fact that the treatment of women in the courts has never been uniformly **chivalrous**. Indeed, feminist researchers have identified that women who do not occupy the appropriate gender role are often seen by the courts as 'doubly deviant'. Feminist scholars have pointed to the ways in which assessments, sentencing and the operation of the criminal justice system have been imbued with notions of 'good girls', 'good wives' and 'good mothers'. Many of these constructs remain prevalent in the criminal justice system today, especially perhaps in cases of sexual and physical violence against women.

Feminist academics have developed research in other critical directions. For example, Frances Heidensohn (2008) has given particular attention to gender and policing and to the ways in which female police officers survive in a predominantly masculine occupation. Indeed, it was not until the 1970s, following the Sex Discrimination Act 1975, that women police officers became fully integrated into police work, by working in the same departments and similar roles as male officers (rather than being tasked to work with juvenile offenders and victims). Heidensohn is also one of the key feminist researchers who has drawn attention to the harsh treatment experienced by groups of women who have frequent contact with the police. She notes that militant suffragettes were among the first to protest against the police's aggressive handling of them. Street prostitutes are another group who have frequently complained about sexual abuse and humiliation (with experiences being more marked among lesbian, Irish and Black women). One notorious event illustrating inappropriate treatment of women by police officers concerns the 'spy cops' scandal in 2018.

Pause for Thought

The 'Spy Cops' Scandal

Consider the enquiry into police infiltration of activist groups set up in 2018, following the apparent abuse of women within such groups through undercover police officers' relationships with them:

- What can you find out about the enquiry from newspaper reports?
- What concerns are raised from a feminist standpoint?
- How can police forces better protect vulnerable women and incorporate their perspectives?

Other achievements resulting from the influence of second wave feminism within criminology include a move to critique; the absence of women in criminal justice policy and assumptions that what works for men will work for women too, both a neglect of gender considerations in the courtroom *and* sexism in decision-making with judges and magistrates drawing on gender role stereotypes to shape sentencing, and similarly, a neglect of women's real needs in prisons which have been designed by men, for men. Subsequent attempts to gender 'criminal justice policy and practice' include reforms under the Labour Government of 1997–2010, with specific task forces to develop policy which would reflect more directly the needs of women in conflict with the law. The Women's Offending Reduction Programme created in the early 2000s, is just one example.

A second example comes in the form of a major commissioned review of vulnerable women in the criminal justice system, chaired by Baroness Jean Corston. The Corston Report was hard-hitting, offering trenchant criticism of the tendency to imprison women for non-violent offences and the treatment of women in prisons. Corston called for recognition of women's complex pathways into crime, their vulnerability and radical reform:

> It is timely to bring about a radical change in the way we treat women throughout the whole of the criminal justice system and this must include not just those who offend but also those at risk of offending. This will require a radical new approach, treating women both holistically and individually - a women-centred approach. (2007: 2)

Corston's challenging review prompted a new wave of feminist-inspired research and practice, looking not only at women's needs, but also at what might work in the community (Annison et al., 2015). The report also prompted further investment from the Government in regard to the support of community centres for women at risk of crime or already caught up in the criminal justice system.

Violence against women and the victims' movement

Another key achievement stemming from feminist research is the attention focused on female victims of crime and criminal justice processes, with recognition of women's fear of crime and sexism in the police's handling of offences against female victims (including serious sexual and violent assaults). A large body of empirical work drew attention to the experiences of female offenders and victims' experiences of criminal justice processes. Sandra Walklate (1995) and Betsy Stanko (1995) are among the key names to look for here to understand the significance of this work (see below). Stanko has brought to light hitherto hidden experiences of women by conceptualising how, within gendered societies, fear insidiously permeates everyday activities for women. Walklate has demonstrated the importance of female perspectives and conceptualisations of harm, as well as the severity of domestic abuse or rape and serious sexual assault in the home. Indeed, one key message in this work was that assumptions about rape being committed by strangers in dark alleys, were to be challenged, and violence within the home more fully recognised. Domestic violence has now become understood as including non-physical acts such as emotional and financial abuse, as exemplified in the key case of *Yemshaw v London Borough of Hounslow*. This greater appreciation of the harms caused by domestic violence to women and children has led to the creation of the Domestic Abuse Bill 2020 which seeks to codify UK laws against domestic violence for the first time.

Case Study 8.2

Key Writers to Look Out For

- S. Walklate (1995): 'One way in which feminist work has posed a very serious challenge to some of the myths attached to women who allege rape has been to document the quite complex and subtle distinctions women make between "pressurised sex", "coerced" sex', with men they know and the distinctions to be made between identifying an incident as rape with men they know as compared with rape by a stranger'. (*From Gender and Crime: An Introduction*, 1995: 82.) Walklate's work, alongside that of others, has thus made a significant contribution to legal reforms and changes in police practices by demonstrating subtle differences that women draw in understanding rape.
- E. Stanko (1995): '… women's anxiety about danger is largely a fear of men and reflects women's location in a gendered world. Confronting women's fear means confronting the danger women face at the hands of their partners, acquaintances, clients, and co-workers, as well as other potential violence from men inside and outside the home'. (From 'Women, Crime and Fear' in *The Annals of the American Academy of Political Science*, vol. 539: 46.)

Case Study 8.3

Continuing Concerns about Domestic Abuse

In response to the 2020/2021 Covid-19 pandemic, many countries across the globe enforced lockdowns which restricted movement and required people to stay at home. This highlighted just how dangerous the home environment is for women and their children, with a steep rise in domestic

(Continued)

homicides, as recorded by the *Counting Dead Women Project* (Smith, 2016). During the first five weeks of the UK Covid-19 lockdown fourteen women and two children were murdered in relation to domestic abuse, with domestic abuse helplines for victims and perpetrators receiving a record number of calls, increasing between 26.86% and 120% (Trafford, 2020). This greater understanding of the dangers of home environments for women and children led to the introduction of safe words in many shops, for women to communicate their need for help. This highlights the importance of considering victims' lived experience from a feminist perspective and of taking this into account when creating law and policy.

Pause for Thought

- Can you find other measures introduced to protect women and children during the 2020/2021 lockdowns?
- How does a feminist perspective help us understand victims' lived experiences?

Epistemological Developments and Methodological Adventures

In *Feminist Perspectives in Criminology* (1990) Gelsthorpe and Morris noted that creative feminist contributions to criminology go well beyond critique. The contributors to this edited collection both illustrated the **hegemonic** masculinity of most criminological work and set out the foundations for future gender-conscious work. Contributors gave particular attention to the ways in which feminist insights have changed the questions relating to violence against women. Traditional questions previously considered whether violent behaviour by individuals could be explained using pathological and structural approaches and focused on reasons why women might wish to stay in an abusive relationship. Instead, feminist criminologists posed questions that attempted to explain why men *as a group* generally direct their violence towards women, and what factors *inhibit* and constrain women's opportunities to leave violent men. We can see this as an attempt to reconstruct criminology.

Another push from feminist scholarship has been to problematise 'gender' and to recognise that gender is socially constructed. This applies to 'women' and 'men' and to non-binary forms of gender. A related strand in this reconstructive project has involved challenging assumptions about knowledge production and research processes. One of the key precepts of feminist perspectives in criminology has been to relate research to practice. In other words, research should benefit women's lives and involve them as participants. This has led to engaging more fully with 'the researched', recognising their subjectivity in a non-hierarchical way and using methods sensitive to the task. This means focusing more on 'experience' as a mode of knowledge, in contrast to conventional research methods, based on 'the scientific method' of testing hypotheses and so on, as in the natural sciences. In this way, feminist research has come to not only endorse qualitative research methods but also to celebrate them. The focus on women's experiences in research (with democratic insistence that women should be allowed to 'speak for themselves') has been used both to make women visible in criminological fields, and to link feminist ontology (beliefs about the nature of the social world) with feminist epistemology (beliefs about what counts as appropriate knowledge). Feminist beliefs about the social world, for example, relate to the idea that the social world is constituted by sets of structural constraints which subordinate and oppress women. The concept of patriarchy is critical here. At its base is the idea that power is unequally distributed between men and women to the detriment of women. Most forms of feminism characterise patriarchy as a present-day unjust social system whereby men subordinate, discriminate or are oppressive to women. Often, patriarchal values require women to conform to stereotypically domesticated roles and restrain their ability to partake in and contribute to the economy. Societal constructions of power and control are perceived as deeply gendered, reflecting hegemonic masculinity and sexuality (Connell, 2013). Sexism ingrained in society, as evidenced by 'the everyday sexism' project, is supported by patriarchy. Thus, patriarchy culminates in structural and systematic inequality for women.

Pause for Thought

In what ways, if any, do you think criminology has benefited from feminist contributions to knowledge production and methodology?

Is there anything you are critical of in terms of feminist contributions?

NEW AND EMERGING RESEARCH AGENDAS

As previously indicated, the main thrust of feminist research in recent years has focused on the injustices experienced by women in the criminal justice system as both offenders and victims, including women's experiences at the hands of the police and in prisons. There is much to do here. There continues to be concern about the police response to women (Heidensohn, 2008). In regard to women and criminal justice practice there have been steps forwards in creating community centres to support women at risk of committing crime, and to provide support for women under community supervision or recently released from prison, but a lack of consistent funding mars progress (Gelsthorpe and Russell, 2018). Moreover, notwithstanding the major report on the need to reduce the use of imprisonment produced by Baroness Corston (2007), later reviews of progress indicated unfulfilled promises (Annison et al., 2015; Moore et al., 2017).

It is arguable that feminist scholarship needs to maintain a *wide lens* so as to capture linkages between oppressions within the criminal justice system and other systems, such as education, welfare, poverty and the benefits system (noting that poverty is penalised in myriad ways). Other work which has gone beyond the traditional focus on criminal justice responses to women includes research on young women, victims of violence who are disabled, older women subject to violence, and violence in care homes. New agendas have included attempts to increase our understanding of the criminal justice system's intersections with other geographical sites (e.g. immigration and detention centres) and legal frameworks (focusing on human rights). Along with changing contours of 'crime' there has been increased attention given to gendered dimensions of terrorism. Some of these points are elaborated in Burman and Gelsthorpe (2017). Specific illustrations of new research agendas in criminology are given below in relation to cyberfeminism, human trafficking and migration.

Cyberfeminism

To demonstrate these new areas of research and third wave feminism within criminology, we consider a recent branch of scholarly work coined 'cyberfeminism' by philosopher and writer Sadie Plant. Plant and others aim to theorise, critique, and understand how gender impacts relations with the internet, cyberspace, and new media technologies (Hackworth, 2018). A new, as of yet unregulated, platform which can facilitate anonymous harassment and abuse.

Case Study 8.4

Cyber Abuse

Cyberfeminists have sought to document and analyse the gendered nature of online harassment and abuse experienced by highly visible women including: tweets directed at UK MPs leading up to the June 2017 General Election (Dhrodia, 2018); the #mencallmethings hashtag on Twitter in 2011; tweets received by Anita Sarkeesian during the height of #GamerGate; tweets aimed at Professor Mary Beard in 2013 after discussing immigration on BBC's *Question Time*; and harassment of women who use social media to participate in feminist debates (Lewis et al., 2017).

A focus on the rise of revenge porn, the publishing of sexual content without women's consent, has led to an analysis of how technology can facilitate further crimes against women. Including technologically facilitated stalking and domestic violence, to which feminist criminological lenses can be applied to understand the impact of these new crimes on women's lives (Marganski, 2020). The results of these studies have shown that online harassment directed toward women is common, and can be better understood as a form of gender-based violence that functions to exclude women from participating in the digital public sphere.

Feminists have thus drawn attention to hateful and **misogynistic** speech among online communities – and to focusing on online communication more generally. It is helpful to think about the concept of 'trolling' here (Phillips, 2015). Trolling involves a spectrum of behaviours that range from aggressive and hostile attacks which meet the legal threshold of harassment to more innocuous forms of trolling that include mischievous activities not meant to cause distress to the target. For example, '**Rickrolling**' is generally regarded as harmless internet trolling, which unexpectedly links users to the 1987 song 'Never Gonna Give You Up' by Rick Astley. However, cyberfeminists are critical of the notion that trolling is pointless or harmless with Bailey Poland (2016) noting that incidents of trolling targeting women are a form of online male domination. Arguably, misogynistic trolling ('gendertrolling'), is a very threatening phenomenon due to the sheer quantity and persistent nature of attacks, the use of gender-based insults designed to humiliate and ridicule women, vicious language, and credible threats of rape and death. In this way, gendertrolling bears similarities to offline instances of gender-based harassment and violence, particularly sexual harassment in the workplace and street harassment.

Pause for Thought

- What is the impact of online harassment?
- How can it be policed?
- What research questions emerge from feminist and criminological standpoints?

Knowledge link: This topic is also covered in Chapter 17.

Human Trafficking and Migration

A further illustration of feminist research which has been instructive for criminology is human trafficking, migration and criminal justice. Women and girls are reported to be victims of human trafficking in huge numbers. There are obvious problems in identifying victims, nevertheless, there has been some feminist (and non-feminist) focus on female trafficking victims subject to sexual exploitation and trafficking for forced labour (cleaning work, catering services work, domestic work, textile production, manufacturing cannabis, and work in nail salons and similar). There is also evidence of forced begging, baby selling, and forced marriages (UNODC, 2014). Siegel (2012) amongst others points to the seductions of foreign travel for quite young girls from Eastern Europe, and the way in which girls are 'groomed' with gifts before being trafficked. Whether there has been sufficient research into the gendered dimensions of human trafficking is a moot point; there is certainly scope to widen the usual 'lens' of men as perpetrators and women and girls as 'victims', with the UNODC (2014) observing that women comprise some 30 percent of convicted traffickers, though how many of the women convicted had themselves been subject to trafficking at some point is not clear. Becoming 'traffickers' could be a way of paying off debts incurred in the smuggling process, bearing in mind that smuggling (where individuals pay for unauthorised travel to another country) sometimes turns into 'human trafficking' mid-journey, when the costs are increased by a series of unscrupulous smugglers. Marie De Angelis's (2016) collected stories of women's experiences of trafficking give telling clues to the complexities here. A final point here relates to the sense in which human trafficking is often conceived as a 'security threat' to the state, leading to a quest for more effective border control. Feminist analyses have challenged this conception of the issues by prioritising the security and safety of trafficked persons and recognising the different ways in which victims are subject to both control via traffickers and the state (Lobasz, 2009).

Related to this are feminist observations regarding the gendered dimension of migration. A number of feminist writers have drawn attention to the 'gendering of borders'. For example, in a critical examination of issues relating to migration, Bosworth et al. have observed how gender informs what is perceived as legitimate and illegitimate:

> Gender works to delegitimise women as transnational migrants, especially in the face of increasing border control. The sorting of desirable from undesirable migrants at the border is heavily invested in 'civilising' tropes and 'gendered moralities'. (2015: 21)

Unauthorised mobility, of course, fosters gendered disapproval and, sometimes, criminalisation. Hales and Gelsthorpe (2012) have researched how women migrants have been criminalised, even though they may have been humanly trafficked and forced to work on cannabis farms or in other forms of labour.

Recent debate about the trade in human beings and migration in recent years has thus been conducted within feminist frameworks of analysis and advocacy. Whilst international feminism regards human trafficking as part of the political economy (cross-border prostitution, reproductive care and sex trafficking), transnational feminism focuses on the complexity concerning intersections of national identity, race, sexuality and economic exploitation within global capitalism. Global feminism emphasises that human trafficking is a form of violence against women, reflecting a dominant patriarchal culture.

Pause for Thought

- How do you think such issues can be researched from a criminological perspective?
- In what ways do you think feminist criminological research could be expanded here?

CHAPTER SUMMARY

- There have been several serious explorations of the relationship between feminism and criminology over the years whether nationally (Gelsthorpe and Morris, 1990), internationally (Hahn-Rafter and Heidensohn, 1995), or globally (Barbaret, 2014).

- During the past fifty years, feminism has helped criminology as a discipline to undergo a period of self-reflection, expanding to include those hitherto excluded from traditional criminology, with a greater emphasis on female criminality and women's experiences as victims, while questioning the traditional contours of criminological theorising and research methods.

- Feminist scholarship has revised theories applied to crime by considering how structural and social, rather than mainly pathological and sexist, theories affect women. It has incorporated a greater appreciation and critical analysis of how race, class and gender affect women's experiences, and highlighted the necessity of understanding male and female experiences differently.

- Feminist methodology has challenged assumptions about knowledge production and research processes. It has developed a focus on qualitative methods, studying women's experiences and preserving their voices as a mode of knowledge.

- Feminism has expanded research focuses by considering those in the global South and human global migration, areas less traditionally studied from Western criminological perspectives. Although, analysis beyond the western hemisphere remains scarce, with studies often originating from Southern criminological specialists.

- By increasing its scope and purview over the last three decades, feminism has more to offer in revisioning criminological tools, focus and policy. It is only when these distinct fields of feminist criminology are considered in unison and applied to increasing areas of society that we can use feminist criminology as a tool to develop truly insightful knowledge and policy.

- There are feminist-inspired awakenings in some quarters of criminology in the UK, in relation to theory, research and teaching, and there are some changes in policy developments too, with renewed attention shown towards gender-sensitive programmes in prisons and in relation to community penalties.

- New agendas emerging in feminist work are offering strong leads with scope to apply feminist criminology as a framework to understand new developments in crime, such as technologically facilitated cybercrime and its implications of harm for women and international criminalisation. Feminist criminology can reflect the growing demands and dangers in our society by acting as a tool to understand gendered aspects of emerging crimes including environmental crime and victimisation and gendered harms to human and non-human species.

- Overall, criminology has been invigorated and revised through feminist 'waves' in line with social, political and technological developments. Feminist criminology represents an inclusive understanding of female experiences and expands the traditional remits of criminology.

Knowledge link: This topic is also covered in Chapter 11.

Review Questions

1. What do you think are the major achievements of feminist criminology?
2. What should be the main focus for future feminist criminological research?
3. How can feminist criminology best be integrated into new areas of criminological study?
4. What are the hurdles to feminist research influencing mainstream criminology?

GO FURTHER

Books

1. The following title is a tour de force. It covers a broad range of topics which chart the development of feminist criminologies and show how feminist perspectives have extended the criminological gaze, including critical engagement with intersectionality and the dominance of global Northern perspectives.

    Walklate, S., Fitz-gibbon, K., Maher, J-M. and McCulloch, D. (eds) (2020) *Emerald Handbook of Feminism, Criminology and Social Change.*Bingley: Emerald Publishing.

2. Anne Logan's book provides a thoughtful excursion into history, between 1920 and 1970. The book challenges an oft-held assumption that feminist interest in criminal justice began with the emergence of campaigns to ensure better police and criminal justice treatment for victims of rape and domestic abuse in the 1970s.

    Logan, A. (2008) *Feminism and Criminal Justice*. Basingstoke: Palgrave Macmillan.

3. Carol Smart's title is a must-read classic. It offers a groundbreaking critique of conventional criminology and poses questions about the treatment of women in criminological theories and in the criminal justice system.

    Smart, C. (1976) *Women, Crime and Criminology*. Abingdon: Routledge.

4. The following title stretches criminology to examine the position of women and crime across the globe, with particular attention paid to the ways in which a human rights framework can help explain women's crime, victimisation and the criminal justice system. It also focuses on women's access to justice and the increased role of women in international criminal justice settings.

    Barbaret, R. (2014) *Women, Crime and Criminal Justice A Global Enquiry*. Abingdon: Routledge.

5. And finally, the following edited collection makes transparent the linkages between different forms of gender control in society, and poses critical questions about the world-wide increase in the use of imprisonment and seemingly benevolent developments which sometimes turn out to be oppressive. Drawing on a human rights perspective they suggest that even 'gender-informed' programes can be problematic.

    Malloch, M. and McIvor, G. (eds) (2013) *Women, Punishment and Social Justice*. Abingdon: Routledge.

Journal Articles

1. The following article outlines some key components of feminist thought and discusses their relevance for criminology. Three main areas of debate are covered: theories of gender and crime, ways of controlling men's violence towards women, and gender equality in the criminal justice system.

    Daly, K. and Chesney-Lind, M. (1988) Feminism and criminology. *Justice Quarterly*, 5(4): 497–538.

2. Dana Britton's article reflects back on twenty-five years of feminist research and how it has impacted criminology, before looking forward to consider the potential of emerging trends in feminist criminology.

Britton, D. M. (2000) Feminism in criminology: engendering the outlaw. *Annals of the American Academy of Political and Social Science,* 571(1): 57–76.

3. This article reflects backwards on the developments in criminal justice reform regarding women, identifies missed opportunities, and looking forwards argues for a consistent strategy derived from evidence-based research and experience.

Gelsthorpe, L. and Russell, J. (2018) Women and penal reform: two steps forwards, three steps backwards? *The Political Quarterly,* 89(2): 227–236.

Useful Websites

1. Prison Reform Trust – Works to improve conditions in prison so that they can be effective and humane: http://www.prisonreformtrust.org.uk/
2. Women in Prison – Focuses specifically on women's experience in prison, produced the Corston+10 Report to evaluate changes implemented following Baroness Corston's report: https://www.women inprison.org.uk/
3. Counting Dead Women – Records the number of women killed each year in the UK by men, or where a man is the main suspect, to ensure that victims are not forgotten: https://kareningala smith.com/counting-dead-women/

REFERENCES

Annison, J., Brayford, J. and Deering, J. (2015) Transforming rehabilitation: implications for women. *Women and Criminal Justice: From the Corston Report to Transforming Rehabilitation,* pp. 21–38.

Barberet, R. (2014) Women, Crime and Criminal Justice: A Global Enquiry. London: Routledge.

Bosworth, M., Pickering, S. and Fili, A. (2015) *Border Crossings and Gender in the Greek Detention System.* Available at: http://bordercriminologies.law.ox.ac.uk/border-crossings-and-gender-in-the-greek-detention-system/ [accessed 22.09.20].

Burman, M. and Gelsthorpe, L. (2017) 'Feminist criminology: inequalities, powerless, and justice' in A. Liebling, L. McAra, and S. Maruna (eds), *Oxford Handbook of Criminology,* 6th edition. Oxford: Oxford University Press.

Cain, M. (1989) *Growing Up Good: Policing the Behaviour of Girls in Europe.* London: Sage.

Chesney-Lind, M. (2004) 'Girls and violence: Is the gender gap closing?', *National Electronic Net-work on Violence Against Women.* Available at: http://www.vawnet.org/DomesticViolence/Research/VAWnetDocs/ARGirlsViolence.php [accessed 17.12.20].

Collins, P. Hill and Bilge, S. (2016) *Intersectionality.* Oxford: Polity.

Connell, R. W. (2013) *Gender and Power: Society, the Person and Sexual Politics.* Oxford: Wiley.

Corston, B. J. (2007) *The Corston Report: A Report of a Review of Women with particular Vulnerabilities in the Criminal Justice System.* London: Home Office.

Crenshaw, K. (2017) *On Intersectionality: Essential Writings.* New York: The New Press.

De Angelis, M. (2016) *Human Trafficking: Women's Stories of Agency.* Newcastle Upon Tyne: Lady Stephenson Library, Cambridge Scholars Publishing.

De Beauvoir, S. (1949) *The Second Sex (Le Deuxième Sexe,* published 1949). English translation published by Jonathan Cape (1953).

Dhrodia, A. (2018) Unsocial media: A toxic place for women. *Progressive Review (Special Issue: Forward March: The Next Destination for Feminism)*, 4: 380–387.

Gelsthorpe, L. and Morris, A. (eds) (1990) *Feminist Perspectives in Criminology*. Buckingham: Open University Press.

Gelsthorpe, L. and Russell, J. (2018) Women and penal reform: two steps forwards, three steps backwards?. *The Political Quarterly*, 89(2): 227–236.

Hackworth, L. (2018) 'Limitations of "Just Gender": The Need for an Intersectional Reframing of Online Harassment Discourse and Research'. In J. R. Vickery and T. Everbach (eds), *Mediating Misogyny*. Basingstoke: Palgrave Macmillan.

Hahn-Rafter, N. and Heidensohn, F. (eds) (1995) *International Feminis Perspectives in Criminology: Engendering a Discipline*. Buckingham: Open University Press.

Hales, L. and Gelsthorpe, L. (2012) *The Criminalisation of Migrant Women*, Cambridge: Institute of Criminology, University of Cambridge. Available at: https://citeseerx.ist.psu.edu/viewdoc/download?doi=10.1.1.448.56&rep=rep1&type=pdf [accessed 16.12.20].

Heidensohn, F. (1987) 'Women and Crime: Questions for Criminology'. In P. Carlen and A. Worrall (eds), *Gender, Crime and Justice*. Milton Keynes: Open University Press.

Heidensohn, F. (1992) *Women in Control? The Role of Women in Law Enforcement*. Oxford: Oxford University Press.

Heidensohn, F. (2008) 'Gender and Policing'. In T. Newburn (ed.), *Handbook of Policing*. Cullompton: Willan.

Leonard, E. (1982) *Women, Crime and Society*. New York: Longman.

Lewis, R., Rowe, M. and Wiper, C. (2017) Online abuse of feminists as an emerging form of violence against women and girls. *British Journal of Criminology*, 57(6): 1462–1481.

Lobasz, J. (2009) Beyond border security: feminist approaches to human trafficking. *Security Studies*, 18(2): 319–344.

Marganski, A. J. (2020) 'Feminist Theories in Criminology and the Application to Cybercrimes'. In *The Palgrave Handbook of International Cybercrime and Cyberdeviance*. London: Palgrave. pp. 623–651.

Moore, L., Scraton, P. and Wahidin, A. (2017) *Women's Imprisonment and the Case for Abolition: Critical Reflections on Corston Ten Years On*. Abingdon: Routledge.

Nussbaum, M. (1999) 'The Professor of Parody: The Hip Defeatism of Judith Butler', *The New Republic*. Available at: https://newrepublic.com/article/150687/professor-parody [accessed 16.10.20].

Phillips, W. (2015) *This is Why We Can't have Nice Things: Mapping the Relationship between Online Trolling and Mainstream Culture*. Cambridge, MA: MIT Press.

Poland, B. (2016) *Haters: Harassment, Abuse, and Violence Online*. Lincoln: University of Nebraska Press.

Siegel, D. (2012) The mobility of sex workers in European cities. *European Journal of Criminal Policy Research*, 18(3): 255–268.

Smart, C. (1976) *Women, Crime and Criminology*. London: Routledge and Kegan Paul.

Smart, C. (1990) 'Feminist Approaches to Criminology or Postmodern Woman meets Atavistic Man'. In L. Gelsthorpe and A. Morris (eds), *Feminist Perspectives in Criminology*. Buckingham: Open University Press.

Smith, K. (2016) *Counting Dead Women*. Available at: https://kareningalasmith.com/counting-dead-women/ [accessed 22.12.20].

Stanko, F. (1995) Women, crime, and fear. *Annals of the American Academy of Political and Social Science*, 539: 46–58.

Stanley, L. and Wise, S. (1983) *Breaking Out: Feminist Consciousness and Feminist Research*. London: Routledge and Kegan Paul.

Taylor, I., Walton, P. and Young, J. (1983) *The New Criminology*. London: Routledge.

Tong, R. (1989) *Feminist Thought*. London: Unwin Hyman.

Trafford, L. (2020) *The Importance of Combating Domestic Abuse During A Pandemic*. Available at: https://www.law.ox.ac.uk/centres-institutes/centre-criminology/blog/2020/04/importance-combatting-domestic-abuse-during-a-pandemic [accessed 17.12.20].

United Nations Office on Drugs and Crime (UNODC) (2014) *Global Report on Trafficking in Persons* (United Nations publication), Vienna. Available at: https://www.unodc.org/documents/data-and analysis/glotip/GLOTIP_2014_full_report.pdf [accessed 22.11.20].

Walklate, S. (1995) *Gender and Crime: An Introduction*. London: Prentice Hall/Harvester Wheatsheaf.

Developmental and Life-Course Criminology

Tara Renae McGee, David P. Farrington
and Darrick Jolliffe

Learning Objectives

By the end of this chapter you will:

- Understand why developmental and life-course criminology needs to use prospective longitudinal studies to examine the patterns in people's antisocial behaviour and offending over time.
- Recognise that these studies allow for patterns of offending, such as onset, persistence, and desistance to be compared to various risk factors.
- Appreciate that the different prospective longitudinal studies around the world have provided results that have led researchers to develop theories to explain the patterns that they observe in their data.
- Be able to critically evaluate the body of evidence produced by developmental and life-course criminology, and how this has informed prevention programmes, including both pre-school and family level programmes.

Framing Questions

1. What are the similarities and differences between the theories described in this chapter? How do they differ from other theories presented in this text book?
2. How would you determine when someone has desisted from crime? Consider whether you would use the last time they were convicted of an offence; the last time they were caught by police; the last time they self-reported committing an offence; or the last time they engaged in something that could be considered antisocial behaviour.
3. How does criminal behaviour develop? Are people born inherently selfish and become socialised into prosocial behaviour? Or are people born as a blank slate and become corrupted by poor parenting and social disadvantage?

Case Study 9.1

Communities That Care

Developmental and life-course criminologists have generated a wealth of knowledge about how to best ensure healthy human development and prevent offending; this work is also being done in other related disciplines. This knowledge is not useful unless it is translated into a practical framework where it can inform the work of those who are engaging activities to promote healthy human development. One of the best examples of this knowledge translation is Communities That Care (https://www.communitiesthatcare.net/research-results/).

INTRODUCTION

Developmental and life-course criminologists study the initiation and change in antisocial behaviour and offending using studies that follow-up the same individuals over time. This type of criminology is relatively new (it emerged in the late 1980s), but the studies have been around much longer. In this chapter, we describe the origins of this type of criminology and the key studies that have been used. Some of the key concepts that developmental and life-course criminologists examine are onset (when and why people start offending), persistence (why people continue offending), and desistance (what processes lead to the eventual termination of offending). They are also interested in the timing of offending, for example at what age do people commit the most offences (frequency), and at what age do more people commit offences (participation)? We will take a look at four of the most important developmental criminology theories that have been put forward and discuss some of the key findings of each of these. First, we will consider the background to this perspective and its importance for policy development.

MAPPING THE TERRAIN

Developmental and life-course criminology draws on many traditional theories of human behaviour (e.g. strain, labelling, rational choice) and as you will see from the discussion later in this chapter, these suggest that the causes of crime are a combination of individual characteristics, such as impulsiveness, interacting with environmental characteristics, such as parenting, families, schools, and neighbourhoods. Collectively developmental and life-course criminologists study the change in patterns over time in studies known as **prospective longitudinal studies**. In these studies, the same individuals are followed up over time and researchers ask them questions about their lives and/or link up government information on the same person (such as police arrests, court convictions, school records, and health records). The goal is to better understand how people's lives unfold and what factors might lead people to be more likely or less likely to commit offences. These are called **risk factors** and **protective factors** for crime. We will return to these again later in the chapter.

Researchers who are studying people's lives in these prospective longitudinal studies undertake statistical analysis of the numerical data they collect (such as scores on psychological tests), and also code and analyse the transcripts of interviews. In doing these analyses they look for patterns in these data and develop theories to explain the patterns that they observe. Developmental and life-course criminology draws on two main disciplines, psychology and sociology, and the differences between these disciplines provide some explanation for the debates that can be observed in the published research. Some explanations are more *psychological* in nature and researchers using these explanations tend to cluster under the 'developmental' category. In contrast, other researchers are more strongly *sociological* in nature and better identify with the 'life-course' part of the title. For example, two of the most influential and empirically tested theories in developmental and life-course criminology are Moffitt's (1993) theory of life-course persistent and adolescent-limited offending which is very psychological in nature, and Sampson and Laub's (1993) age-graded theory of informal social control which is more sociological.

─────────── **Hear from the Expert** ───────────

The Effects of Maternal Incarceration on Children
Professor Susan Dennison, Griffith University Australia

Rising rates of the imprisonment of females can be observed in many Western countries. (For more on the UK, see https://www.womeninprison.org.uk/campaigns/key-facts and also see https://www.prisonpolicy.org/global/women/2018.html for information on USA.)

In Australia, where I work, the prison population has decreased slightly for the first time in almost a decade, following a 40% increase over only a five-year period (Australian Bureau of Statistics, 2018). Nevertheless, the imprisonment rate continues to remain high, with 202 prisoners per 100,000 population (approx. 41,000 prisoners; Australian Bureau of Statistics, 2020). Although males make up the majority of prisoners (92%), females have been the fastest growing segment of the prison population, driven partially by a sharp rise in the imprisonment of Indigenous women. Female prisoners are also amongst the most disadvantaged and vulnerable groups in society, with the majority of women in custody having been victims of child sexual abuse, physical abuse, and/or domestic violence. Low education levels, sporadic employment, financial stress, periodic homelessness, poor mental health, and problematic substance use are also common amongst imprisoned women. The majority of women in custody are mothers with dependent children. Nationally, 85% of female prison entrants report having been pregnant at some stage in their lives (Australian Institute of Child Health and Welfare, 2018).

There is growing recognition that children with an incarcerated parent face many challenges and as a consequence, are at heightened risk of a range of poor life outcomes. Indeed, longitudinal studies have demonstrated that children who experience parental incarceration are more likely to engage in delinquent and offending behavior, and are also more likely to be incarcerated in adulthood. Various studies have also reported increased risks of child protection system contact, placement in out-of-home care, as well as grief and trauma, poor education and employment outcomes, social exclusion, substance use, and early pregnancies. These are all studied within developmental and life-course criminology, as well as other disciplines. Most studies focus on the effect of paternal incarceration on children, in order to obtain adequate samples of children in national longitudinal datasets. However, it is likely that maternal incarceration may be even more detrimental to children, not least because women are more likely than men to have dependent children at the time of entering prison (Australian Institute of Child Health and Welfare, 2018). Australian research shows that for children with a history of maternal imprisonment, more than half had child protection system contact by their second birthday. Rates of out of home placements were 27 times higher for Indigenous children and 110 times higher for non-Indigenous children, compared to children whose mothers had no prison history (Dowell et al., 2018). Child maltreatment, and out of home care in particular, are risk factors for later offending. Moreover, periods of risk are unlikely to be restricted to the time during which a mother is in prison, but be experienced as a package of family-level risks that are present throughout the young person's development and across generations (Giordano et al., 2019). This highlights the need for developing systems to support mothers and their children during and after periods of maternal incarceration, and this is a key focus of my work.

Read more about our current work here: https://www.transformingcorrections.com.au/

POLICY INFLUENCE

In the United Kingdom and elsewhere, developmental and life-course criminology has had a strong influence on the policy decisions of governments. For example, in the late 1980s the UK Home Office acknowledged evidence from the Cambridge Study in Delinquent Development in a press release that stated 'This work is evidence of the importance of responsible parenting in preventing crime. Its findings bear out the idea that the family is the first and most appropriate line of defence against delinquency'. Developmental and life-course approaches were only beginning to come into prominence in the 1990s. Rock (1994) analysed Home Office policy making in the early 1990s and stated 'Moreover, criminality prevention was attractive precisely because it was so *new*. It was a break from the "secondary" crime prevention of target-hardening and opportunity reduction whose experimental and political half-life was deemed to have expired' (Rock, 1994: 150–151).

Around the same time, in 1995, David Farrington was commissioned by the Rowntree Foundation to advise them about how to reduce crime. His monograph *Understanding and Preventing Youth Crime* (Farrington, 1996) influenced the Foundation to commit substantial funding to mount three major risk-focused crime prevention projects using the Communities That Care programme in Barnsley, Coventry, and Swansea. Subsequently, similar projects were implemented in over twenty sites in England, Scotland and Wales.

With the election of a Labour government in 1997, policies took on a very developmental focus. The White Paper entitled 'No More Excuses' (1997) (whose proposals were then included in the Crime and Disorder Act 1998) had a great emphasis on early prevention which was one of the key implications of developmental and life-course research. The White Paper stated, 'There will be a new focus on nipping crime in the bud – stopping children at risk from getting involved in crime and preventing early criminal behaviour from escalating into persistent or serious offending' (Home Office, 1997: 2). Also, it was stated in the White Paper that the prime minister would take the lead in tackling social exclusion. The Crime and Disorder Act 1998, for the first time, made it clear that the principal aim of the youth justice system was to *prevent* offending by young people. A number of British criminologists participated in meetings with Home Office policy makers and the Treasury in launching the multi-million-pound Crime Reduction Programme.

In the mid-2000s Prime Minister Tony Blair developed an Action Plan on Social Exclusion. This Action Plan proposed risk-focused prevention, including evidence-based programmes such as nurse home visiting, parent training, multi-systemic therapy and treatment foster care. The influence of developmental and life-course criminology can be observed in the prime minister's acknowledgment of research such as 'Childhood risk factors and risk-focussed prevention' (Farrington, 2007) as having influenced the Action Plan. Evidence-based approaches have become more and more popular, but the extent to which rigorous evidence is actually employed in policy is debatable.

ORIGINS OF THE DEVELOPMENTAL AND LIFE-COURSE PERSPECTIVE

Developmental and life-course approaches to the study of crime came to prominence in the 1980s but there were well-established prospective longitudinal studies around the world before then. These studies were undertaken as early as the 1940s and focused on aspects of key theoretical importance to DLC researchers. For more detailed information about all of the studies listed below, see Farrington (1979; 2013).

Most of the studies were conducted in the United States and these included:

- the Gluecks' study of 500 boys incarcerated in a youth reformatory and a comparison group of those who were not incarcerated in Boston, Massachusetts (Glueck & Glueck, 1968); they were also one of the few research teams of their time to study 'delinquent women';
- McCord's Cambridge-Somerville (Massachusetts) Youth Study – a large-scale experimental study started in 1939 and conducted on 506 boys who were nominated by schools as difficult or average (McCord, 1992);
- Werner's Longitudinal Study of 698 children born on the island of Kauai (Werner, 1993);
- Eron and Huesmann's Columbia County Study (New York) which began in 1960 interviewing 856 children in third grade and their parents (Huesmann et al., 2002);
- Wolfgang's Philadelphia birth cohort studies examined two birth cohorts born in 1945 and 1958 (Wolfgang et al., 1972);
- Kellam's Woodlawn project studied mothers and their 1,242 children in Chicago and took a wrap-around service delivery approach to supporting those who were struggling (McCord & Ensminger, 1997);
- Elliott's National Youth Survey national sample of 1,725 adolescents aged 11–17 who were interviewed in early 1977 concerning their involvement in delinquent behaviour during 1976 (Elliott, 1994).

Elsewhere in the world:

- West and Farrington's (1973) Cambridge Study in Delinquent Development of 411 working class boys aged 8–9 began in London in 1961;
- Miller and Court's (Kolvin et al., 1990) UK study of 1,142 boys born in Newcastle in 1947 was being conducted;
- Magnusson and Stattin's study of 1,027 children who were aged 10 in 1965, in Orebro, Sweden (Bergman & Andershed, 2009); and
- Pulkkinen's Jyvaskyla Longitudinal Study of 369 children aged 8–9 in 1968 in Finland (Pulkkinen et al., 2009).

As you can imagine, these studies had already delivered considerable new knowledge about the development of criminal behaviour, but it was in 1983 that this type of research came to prominence.

Pause for Thought

What differences would be observed, in the characteristics of participants, if you started a longitudinal study today?

That year the United States National Institute of Justice requested that the National Academy of Sciences convene a panel to examine research on criminal careers, setting them the task of evaluating the feasibility of predicting the future course of criminal careers, assessing the effects of prediction instruments in reducing crime through incapacitation, and reviewing the contribution of research on criminal careers (Blumstein et al., 1986). This resulted in the two-volume publication *Criminal Careers and 'Career Criminals'* (Blumstein et al., 1986). These volumes included the explication of a number of core concepts, such as onset and desistance, and the relationship between age and crime. We will go through each of these concepts below because when you understand them, you can better understand the purpose of the theories we will look at later in the chapter.

WHAT DO DEVELOPMENTAL AND LIFE-COURSE CRIMINOLOGISTS STUDY?

One of the first important concepts for you to understand is a **criminal career**. This is defined as 'the longitudinal sequence of offences committed by an individual offender' (Farrington, 1992). A criminal career describes the sequence of offences during some part of an individual's lifetime, with no necessary suggestion that offenders use their criminal activity as an important means of earning a living. Instead, the concept is intended as a means of structuring the longitudinal sequence of criminal events committed by an individual in a meaningful way. When you think about developmental and life-course criminologists conducting prospective longitudinal studies, the idea of a criminal career makes sense because they are interested in patterns of offending over the life-course. More broadly, the criminal career approach also incorporates an examination of the risk factors and outcomes of offending behaviour.

By now you will understand that developmental and life-course criminology researchers are very much focused on how people's lives unfold over time. Of course, it does not make sense to study the *crimes* of a child so it is often the broader spectrum of antisocial behaviour that these researchers examine in childhood. For some of these researchers, the ones who follow up children and their families from the prenatal period, they're interested in the development of children's behaviours as they grow up. Other researchers are more focused on criminal behaviours that have been detected by the criminal justice system. What they all have in common is their interest in the **onset** of these behaviours. Examinations of onset focus on when a particular behaviour started and more importantly what predicted this onset. Things that predict onset are referred to as **risk factors** for onset because they increase the likelihood, or risk, that a behaviour will occur. Table 9.1 provides a summary table of risk factors, from different studies, for different patterns of offending. In a review of all existing longitudinal studies from childhood or adolescence to at least age 30, researchers found that only eleven studies had ever been conducted that included measures of both official and self-reported offending (Jolliffe et al., 2017).

For example, Table 9.1 shows that parent cigarette use, high depression and high impulsivity were all associated with life-course persistent offending in the Seattle Social Development Study, while parent marijuana use, parent cigarette use and high depression were associated with adolescence-limited offending.

Researchers are particularly interested in **persistence**, i.e. why some people persist in their offending and for how long, and also study risk factors for persistence. Perhaps most importantly, especially for crime prevention efforts, developmental and life-course researchers also study when and why people stop offending, which is known as **desistance**.

Pause for Thought

What factors do you think would be related to someone stopping (desisting) from offending?

Table 9.1 Summary of Early Risk Factors for Different Types of Offending

Life-course persistent*	Adolescence-limited*	Late onset*
Seattle Social Development Project		
Parent cigarette use	Parent marijuana use	Parent marijuana use
High depression	Parent cigarette use	Parent cigarette use
High impulsivity	High depression	High anxiety
Pittsburgh Youth Study		
Lack of guilt	Lack of guilt	Child abuse
Child abuse	Hyperactivity	Lack of guilt
Low intelligence	Low intelligence	Low intelligence
Cambridge Study in Delinquent Development		
Convicted parent	High daring	Disrupted family
Poor supervision	Poor housing	Poor housing
Disrupted family	Convicted parent	Low school achievement

*These terms are defined and explained further below.
Source: Adapted from Jolliffe, D., Farrington, D. P., Piquero, A. R., MacLeod, J. F. and van de Weijer, S. © (2017) Prevalence of life-course-persistent, adolescence-limited, and late-onset offenders: A systematic review of prospective longitudinal studies. *Aggression and Violent Behavior*, 33: 4-14. Reprinted with kind permission of Elsevier.

Another key observation that underpins developmental and life-course criminology is the relationship between age and crime; the **age-crime curve**. The relationship between age and crime was observed in the early 1800s by Quetelet (1833). Since then many researchers studying the relationship between age and crime have observed that the aggregate pattern is such that criminal activity tends to rise to a peak in the late teens and then declines throughout adulthood (see Figure 9.1), based on the Cambridge Study. This peak is caused predominantly by more people participating in crime during adolescence (participation) rather than by the people who are engaging in crime committing more crimes (frequency). But those participating in crime also commit more offences more frequently during adolescence. Therefore, it can be observed that age is inversely related to criminality from the teenage years, with younger people being more likely to be involved in crime. Despite theoretical debates regarding why this peak occurs, all researchers observe that almost everyone ages out of crime eventually.

Since the 1990s we have seen precipitous drops in recorded crime in Western countries. At the same time the shape and nature of the age-crime curve (based on official records) have changed in current generations. For example, an examination of Scottish data showed that, over time, the shape of the age-crime curve has become less peaked and wider (Matthews & Minton, 2018). This is an important empirical fact that is only beginning to be reconciled with existing developmental and life-course theories. In 2020 the world experienced an unprecedented shutdown of systems that led to strains never before observed in terms of trauma, the death of family and loved ones, mass unemployment, interruption to schooling, new laws, and widespread poverty. Developmental and life-course criminologists know that these factors are all strong risk factors for crime, and that those who are already disadvantaged by the existing social structure will be most vulnerable to these new stressors. It remains to be seen what impact this has on the age-crime curve.

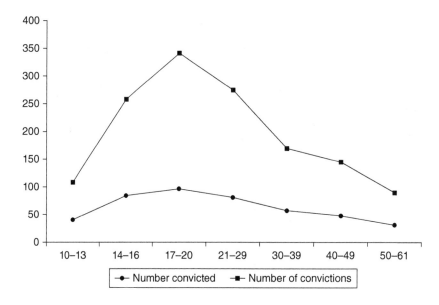

Figure 9.1 The Relationship Between Age and Crime

KEY THEORIES WITHIN DEVELOPMENTAL AND LIFE-COURSE CRIMINOLOGY

There is a tendency to think of theories as some old dusty things that live in textbooks, that some-one once came up with, and students have to memorise. But theories are 'living' things that explain how researchers think the world works. These theories need to have their key postulates tested, and on the basis of that testing theories are improved and refined. Collectively, developmental and life-course criminologists are pretty good at testing and refining their theories. While many of the theories in this tradition were originally articulated in the 1990s, they continue to be updated and revised over time. The most up-to-date collection of developmental and life-course theories can be found in the 2019 *Oxford Handbook on Developmental and Life-Course Criminology* (see the further reading section below). We provide you with a brief overview of just four of the theories here but you should look up more detailed descriptions of these and other theories if you want to under-stand their details.

Life-course Persistent and Adolescence-limited Antisocial Behaviour – Terrie Moffitt

Moffitt's (1993) dual taxonomy of *life-course persistent* and *adolescence-limited* antisocial behaviour was an attempt to reconcile what at first glance might seem to you like contradictory facts. The first is that there is a great deal of relative stability in antisocial behaviour (and related offending) across the life-course and the second is that there is a large peak in (absolute) offending during adolescence. She argues that these two observations are generated by two different groups of people: those who are antisocial across the life-course (life-course persistent group) and those who are antisocial only during adolescence (adolescence-limited group). These two groups are presented in Figure 9.2 and you can see that the prevalence of antisocial behaviour increases

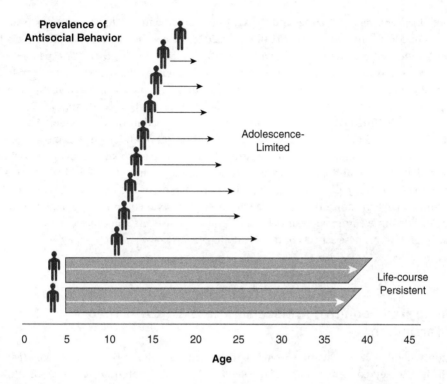

Figure 9.2 Pictorial Representation of Moffitt's (1993) Life-Course Persistent and Adolescence-Limited Groups

Source: David Farrington lecture, Life-Time Achievement Award, Division of Developmental and Life-Course Criminology (Moffitt, 2018).

during adolescence as the adolescence-limited group joins in. Also, there is the other group represented across the bottom, the life-course persistent group, participating in antisocial behaviour at all ages.

Moffitt's theory also includes groups of *low-level chronics* whose early antisocial behaviour leads to experiencing problems throughout their lives. She also identified *abstainers*, i.e. those who never participate in antisocial behaviour. She argues that those who abstain may not experience what she calls the 'maturity gap' due to a late onset of puberty and an early onset of adult roles, may possess pathological characteristics which exclude them from peer networks, and may have a lack of opportunities for social mimicry of antisocial peers. More recent research has identified two types of abstainers, one type with poor adjustment and the other with good adjustment (Mercer et al., 2016).

Pause for Thought

- Do you think adolescent delinquency is normative?
- Or given the flattening of the age-crime curve (as mentioned earlier in the chapter) do you think abstaining from delinquency is normative?

The theory has been very influential and the subject of much empirical testing and revision, including reviews by Moffitt herself (2006; 2018). In her 2018 review she discussed adult-onset offenders; those who were first arrested or convicted as adults. Moffitt argued that these people had been offending previously and had just not been caught. Adult onset offenders do commit offences that are less likely to be detected and that require access to adult roles, compared to those who were first detected by the criminal justice system in adolescence (McGee & Farrington, 2010). McGee and Farrington (2010) concluded that about half of detected adult-onset offenders had previously committed undetected offences but half were true adult-onset offenders. In her most recent review Moffitt (2018) also identified the need for future empirical research to address recent changes in crime (e.g. digital crime and the changing nature of the age-crime curve) and scientific advances in human development (e.g. neuroscience and genetics). One of the other challenges for Moffitt's theory is that a large proportion of the population are 'unclassified' in her typology and this group has received very little empirical examination by criminologists. As you can see there is lots of scope for those interested in these aspects of the theory to conduct new research – maybe you will do that later in your career.

The Integrated Cognitive Antisocial Potential (ICAP) Theory – David Farrington

Farrington's theory is called the Integrated Cognitive Antisocial Potential (ICAP) theory (Farrington, 2005). In it, the key concept is *antisocial potential*. Antisocial potential refers to an individual's propensity to commit antisocial acts and is further divided into long-term and short-term antisocial potential. When you look at Figure 9.3, start at the middle and focus on the long-term antisocial potential box and short-term antisocial potential box and work outwards from there. To explain short-term within-individual variations in antisocial potential, the theory draws attention to short-term situational factors and the motivation of the individual to engage in antisocial behaviour. This focus on situational and motivational factors illuminates *why some people commit certain types of offences at specific times and places*. In contrast, long-term between-individual differences are explained by long-term persisting factors such as an individual's impulsiveness and strain, modelling, and socialisation influences. This line of inquiry explains *why a person becomes an offender*. As you can see, these explanations for antisocial potential draw on a range of preexisting theories. This theory also focuses on the long-term impact of risk factors and, similar to other developmental and life-course theories, draws attention to the importance of distinguishing between those factors that are causal rather than correlational.

We have tested the theory using data from the Cambridge Study in Delinquent Development (Farrington & McGee, 2017) and in that study we showed that antisocial potential scores were relatively stable (in the ordering of individuals) from age 18 to age 48, and that they tended to decrease over time (there was absolute change). As expected, based on the theory, these scores correlated with and predicted convictions of the males in the study, at different ages. Deductions from the ICAP theory in regard to age 8–10 risk factors predicting antisocial potential scores at age 18 were also tested. As expected, socio-economic, school achievement, child-rearing, and impulsiveness factors were significant independent predictors of high antisocial potential scores. The most surprising result was that a convicted parent was not a significant independent predictor of antisocial potential scores, and neither was attending a high delinquency-rate school. And yet having a convicted parent was the strongest predictor of convictions at ages 10–18. So parental convictions predict offspring convictions, but not offspring antisocial potential (possibly because of official labelling).

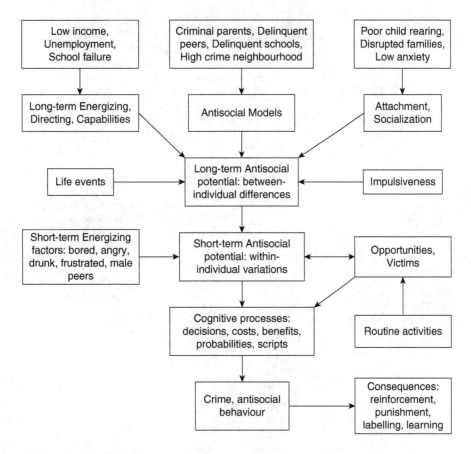

Figure 9.3 The Integrated Cognitive Antisocial Potential (ICAP) Theory

The Age-Graded Theory of Informal Social Control – Robert Sampson and John Laub

Sampson and Laub's theory is focused on how informal social controls, such as families, schools, and employment, exert control over human behaviour and lead to conformity. Over their lives people accumulate something called social bonds from their participation in these informal social control networks. Those with lower levels of social bonds are more likely to engage in criminal behaviour. You might notice as you read the description here of Sampson and Laub's theory, that it is very sociological in nature. It stands in contrast to the theories above which are more psychological in nature. To explain the *onset* of offending, they argue that a complex mixture of risk factors leading to crime in adolescence (individual differences, structural variables, family, school, and peers; see Figure 9.4). Crime occurs as an interplay between social bonds and an individual's choices to engage in offending. Remember that one of the things that developmental and life-course criminologists try to do is explain *desistance*. Sampson and Laub have a really interesting explanation for this, focusing on 'turning points'.

Turning points are life changes such as employment, marriage and attachment to a spouse, joining the military, being sent to reform school, and changes in neighbourhood/residence. They usually increase social bonds and lead away from crime (see how social bonds are theorised to relate to crime in Figure 9.4). Think about your own life; it may have taken a very different path if you had

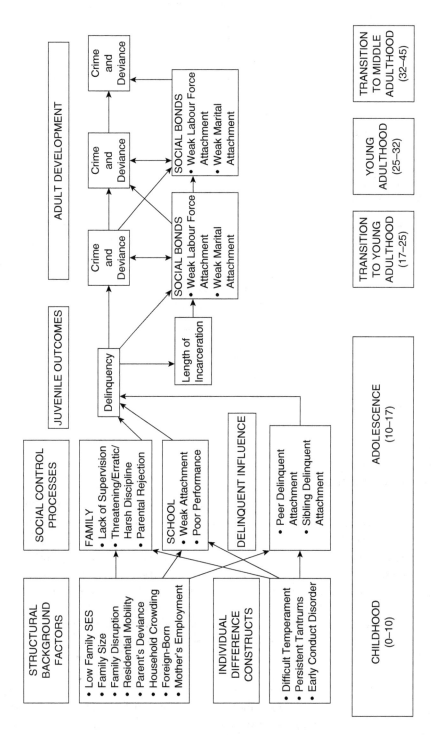

Figure 9.4 Age Graded Theory of Informal Social Control

Source: Sampson & Laub (1993) pp. 244-245.

not come to study at university at this stage in your own life-course. Turning points for crime need to be understood within the context of criminogenic environments. For some people, turning points create a 'knifing off' of individual offenders from their past and their immediate environment. A positive engagement with turning points brings about a change in and gives structure to routine activities, which allows for identity transformation, and ultimately leads to *desistance* from offending behaviour. In terms of creating opportunities for *persistent* offending, a turning point such as a job opportunity may provide the opportunity to engage in theft from work, and a marriage may create opportunities for engaging in intimate partner violence. So turning points can lead both towards and away from crime depending on the criminogenic environment. If you want to read more about their research and theory, their book *Shared Beginnings, Divergent Lives* (Laub & Sampson, 2003) is a really great summary of an amazing study.

Pause for Thought

Do you think the turning points identified by Sampson and Laub are relevant to current generations of adolescents and young adults? Why/why not?

Situational Action Theory of Crime Causation – Per-Olof Wikström

One of the key additions that Wikström makes to developmental and life-course theories of crime, in Situational Action Theory, is a focus on moral rule breaking. His fundamental argument is that 'people are moved to action ... by how they see their action alternatives and make their choices when confronted with the particularities of a setting' (Wikström, 2006: 61). In Figure 9.5 you can see that in this theory, when people are presented with a temptation or provocation, they will decide whether or not crime is an option based on their moral filters.

Situational Action Theory explains crime as resulting from interactions between people with certain crime propensities and settings with certain criminogenic features (Wikström & Treiber, 2018). Of all the developmental and life-course theories, this is most similar to the Integrated Cognitive Antisocial Potential (ICAP) theory in that it draws attention to the ways in which the interaction

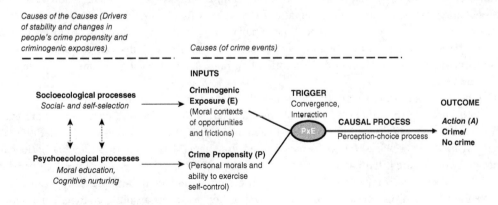

Figure 9.5 Model of Situational Action Theory

Source: Figure provided by Professor Per-Olof H Wikström.

between individual experiences and situational and environmental features leads to criminal acts. There are also parallels with Sampson and Laub's theory, which highlights the ways in which the individual interacts with opportunities for change (turning points) in fostering desistance or persistence.

The focus of Situational Action Theory, however, is on moral rules. Wikström takes a step back from just examining the causes of crime and instead identifies the 'causes of the causes' which include both socioecological and psychoecological processes. He argues that all crimes break moral rules that define what is acceptable in a given setting (see Figure 9.5) and whether or not crime is an option. Laws are viewed as codified moral rules, and crimes are breaches of these moral rules. The greater the extent to which one's moral rules correspond with the moral rules enacted in laws, the lower the likelihood of offending. Wikström acknowledges that self-interest and rational choices have a role to play in explaining human action, but also argues that a better foundation for understanding human action is to consider it in the context of moral rules and moral contexts. The choice of crime, according to this theory, can only be made when the individual perceives that crime is a viable option for action. By drawing attention to moral rules, the theory focuses on explaining *why individuals perceive crime as an option*, not just why they choose crime.

KEY DEBATES IN DEVELOPMENTAL AND LIFE-COURSE APPROACHES TO UNDERSTANDING CRIMINALITY

Despite the widespread adoption of developmental and life-course approaches and the large volume of research being conducted within the criminal career tradition, there are many competing explanations of criminality. In contrast to developmental and life-course theories of crime, there are models which propose that there are persisting individual differences between people that explain their delinquency and criminality (Wilson & Herrnstein, 1985; Gottfredson & Hirschi, 1990). These theorists view crime at any stage of the life-course as having the same underlying causes. For example, Hirschi and Gottfredson (1995: 135) argue that crime at all ages depends on the time-stable trait of self-control. An individual's level of self-control, according to this model, is acquired via socialisation and fixed by about the age of eight years.

One of the goals of theory development is parsimony; finding the simplest explanations for observed phenomena. And while using what is argued to be a stable trait of self-control to explain behaviour achieves parsimony in its explanation, it is problematic because there is research that shows there are changes in self-control in individuals in childhood (Tremblay, 2003), adolescence (Moffitt et al., 1996), and later in life (Laub & Sampson, 2003). Self-control when studied over time does not appear to be stable. These observations raise questions about *relative* versus *absolute* stability in the causes of crime. Over time it is possible to have relative stability in the rank ordering of people (the most antisocial people are the most antisocial at all stages of the life-course) but also absolute change in the level of different variables (offending rates decrease with age from late adolescence through to death).

Competing theoretical viewpoints are intensely debated in the academic literature (for example see: Gottfredson & Hirschi, 1986, 1988; Blumstein et al., 1988a, 1988b). These debates are exemplified in the ongoing discussion between Hirschi and Gottfredson (Gottfredson, 2005; 1995), and Sampson and Laub (1995; 2005). As we have argued elsewhere (McGee & Farrington, 2015), the competing viewpoints are often based on theorists talking at cross-purposes. For example, Gottfredson and Hirschi focus on the relative stability in rank ordering of individuals, arguing that absolute levels of offending depend on opportunities. In contrast, others focus on absolute change. For example, Moffitt focuses on individual changes in the level of offending over time. Both of these arguments have empirical support as seen in the earlier discussion of the ICAP theory.

DEVELOPMENTAL AND LIFE-COURSE PREVENTION PROGRAMMES

The most effective prevention programmes target risk factors for offending and the best evidence about the effectiveness of these programmes comes from randomised experiments with long follow-ups, that also include a cost-benefit analysis component (Farrington, 2018). Impulsiveness and low empathy are risk factors that are targeted by cognitive behavioural skills programmes and preschool programmes. Preschool programmes also address the risk factors of low intelligence and school failure; good preschool programmes set up children for later schooling success. Family level risk factors such as poor parental discipline and supervision are delivered via family training programmes such as the nurse home visitation programme (Olds et al., 2010). Another successful parent training programme is Triple-P which was developed in Australia and has been implemented in many other countries since then (Sanders et al., 2000). It has also become evident that prevention programmes work best when administered in a prevention delivery support system such as those being used in the USA (Fagan et al., 2018) and Australia (Homel et al., 2019). There is a strong body of evidence regarding what works and shows promise in developmental prevention of antisocial behaviour and offending. This evidence should be drawn on when making decisions about how to support young people and their families (Farrington et al., 2016; Farrington et al., 2017).

CHAPTER SUMMARY

As you may have noticed reading this chapter, even though developmental and life-course research has expanded rapidly over the past three decades, there still remain many questions and gaps to be explored. One of the key things to remember about this type of criminology is that those working in this tradition study the ways in which people's lives unfold over time and they do this by undertaking prospective longitudinal studies. In this chapter we have given you an overview of the core aspects of criminal careers that are investigated by developmental and life-course researchers, such as onset, persistence, and desistance. We also provided you with an overview of four of the theories but there are many more so check them out in the sources identified in the additional reading below. Perhaps you might even become a developmental and life-course criminologist in the future! To date, most studies in developmental and life-course criminology have examined between-individual differences in risk factors and offending, but in more recent work there has been a shift to examining within-individual differences over time (some notable examples are Farrington et al., 2002; Jolliffe et al., 2019). There needs to be more of this in the future. One of the key benefits that prospective longitudinal studies can offer is the ability to examine changes within individuals over time in order to establish the causes of crime. It is important to understand the *causes* of crime and not just the *correlates*.

Future research and theory development in developmental and life-course criminology needs to strive to identify the causes of crime. Developmental and life-course theories postulate causal effects of factors such as poor parental supervision and low socio-economic status. In order to establish causal effects, it is necessary to demonstrate that a change in a factor such as parental supervision is reliably followed by a change in offending. In turn, this requires longitudinal studies with regular repeated measures of presumed causal factors such as parental supervision and outcomes such as delinquency. For example, in the Pittsburgh Youth Study, there were yearly measures from age 7 to age 19 for one cohort of 500 boys, and yearly measures from age 13 to 25 for another cohort of 500 boys (Loeber et al., 2008). These enabled Farrington and his colleagues (2002) to demonstrate that changes in parental supervision within individuals reliably predicted changes in delinquency within individuals. More longitudinal studies of this nature are needed, as well as more analyses of changes within individuals, in order to demonstrate whether risk factors have causal effects on offending.

GO FURTHER

Books

There are a number of detailed books available that will give the reader a more in-depth understanding of developmental and life-course criminology.

1. The most comprehensive and up-to-date volume on developmental and life-course criminology is the text below. In this volume, the editors have brought together chapters by all the key theorists so that you have the most recent articulations of their theories all in one place. This book also provides chapters on key dimensions of developmental and life-course criminology, correlates and risk factors, turning points, and developmental prevention:

   Farrington, Kazemian, and Piquero's (2019) *Oxford Handbook on Developmental and Life-Course Criminology*. Oxford: Oxford University Press.

2. The following book provides an overview of developmental and life-course criminology, its background, and chapters on key concepts such as onset, persistence, and desistance:

   Carlsson, C. and Sarnecki, J. (2016) *An Introduction to Life-Course Criminology*. London: Sage Publications.

3. The following title provides overviews and empirical tests of a number of developmental and life-course theories. It also provides empirical examinations of a number of key developmental and life-course criminology concepts:

   Blokland, A. and van der Geest, V. (eds) (2016) *The Routledge International Handbook of Life-Course Criminology*. Abingdon: Routledge.

4. The final recommendation for further reading is the following title. This volume brings together theoretical statements, empirical tests and debates on these major theories within the developmental and life-course criminology perspective:

   McGee, T. R. and Mazerolle, P. (2015) *Developmental and Life-Course Theories of Crime*. Abingdon: Routledge.

Journal Articles

1. We will start with a classic. This is one of the early papers that comprehensively examines the relationship between age and crime; a key focus of developmental and life-course criminology:

   Farrington, D. P. (1986) Age and crime. *Crime and Justice, 7*: 189–250.

2. This is an encyclopedic review of criminal career research, including criminal career parameters such as frequency, duration and desistance, issues such as specialisation versus versatility, relevant theories, psychopathy and biosocial criminology. It ends by discussing 16 key criminal career issues that should be addressed in the future:

   DeLisi, M. & Piquero, A. R. (2011) New frontiers in criminal careers research, 2000–2011: A state-of-the-art review. *Journal of Criminal Justice, 39*: 289–301.

3. This is one of the most read and cited papers in developmental and life-course criminology. Note that it has had many revisions and updates as Moffitt revises her theory based on empirical testing, but this is the original publication:

Moffitt, T. E. (1993) Adolescence-limited and life-course-persistent antisocial behavior: a developmental taxonomy. *Psychological Review*, 100: 674–701.

Useful Websites

1. This is the website of the American Society of Criminology's Division of Developmental and Life-Course Criminology. Here you will find out information about the Division, awards given, and the latest developments in the discipline in the Division's newsletter: https://dlccrim.org/
2. The latest research is developmental and life-course criminology is published in the *Journal of Developmental and Life-Course Criminology*. You should be able to access the papers through your university library. If not, don't be afraid to contact the author directly and they will be happy to send you a copy: https://www.springer.com/journal/40865
3. Finding longitudinal data when you're first starting out as a criminologist can be tricky. You can collaborate with existing criminologists but you can also access publicly available data. This website is a good place to start: https://www.icpsr.umich.edu/

Review Questions

1. What type of studies do developmental and life-course criminologists undertake?
2. When looking at the age crime curve, what is the difference between frequency and participation?
3. How does Moffitt explain the peak in age-crime curve?
4. What are Sampson and Laub referring to when they talk about informal social controls?
5. Turning points provide opportunity for a change in a criminal pathway. What are three turning points that an individual may experience?
6. What has happened to the age-crime curve in recent times?
7. What is Farrington referring to in his theory when he talks about an individual's long-term antisocial potential?
8. Which family and parent training programmes have good evidence of success in preventing offspring antisocial behaviour?
9. What is the purpose of moral filters according to Wikström's theory?
10. What are some of the things that still need more research in developmental and life-course criminology? (And are you going to be the one who does them?)

REFERENCES

Australian Bureau of Statistics (2018) *Prisoners in Australia*, 2018.

Australian Bureau of Statistics (2020) *Prisoners in Australia*, 2020.

Australian Institute of Health and Welfare (2019) *The heath of Australia's prisoners 2018*. Cat. no: PHE 246 Australian Government.

Bergman, L. R. & Andershed, A.-K. (2009) Predictors and outcomes of persistent or age-limited registered criminal behavior: a 30-year longitudinal study of a Swedish urban population. *Aggressive Behavior*, 35: 164–178.

Blokland, A. & Van der Geest, V. (eds) (2016) *The Routledge International Handbook of Life-Course Criminology*. Abingdon: Routledge.

Blumstein, A., Cohen, J. & Farrington, D. P. (1988a) Criminal career research: its value for criminology. *Criminology*, 26(1): 1–35.

Blumstein, A., Cohen, J. & Farrington, D. P. (1988b) Longitudinal and criminal career research: further clarifications. *Criminology*, 56(1): 57–74.

Blumstein, A., Cohen, J., Roth, J. & Visher, C. (1986) *Criminal Careers and 'Career Criminals'* (Vol. 1 & 2). New York: National Academy Press.

Carlsson, C. & Sarnecki, J. (2016) *An Introduction to Life-course Criminology*. London: Sage.

Dowell, C. M., Mejia, G. C., Preen, D. B. & Segal, L. (2018) Maternal incarceration, child protection, and infant mortality: a descriptive study of infant children of women prisoners in Western Australia. *Health and Justice*, 6 (2). DOI 10.1186/s40352-018-0060-y

Elliott, D. S. (1994) 'Serious violent offender: Onset, developmental course, and termination', The American Society of Criminology 1993 Presidential Address. *Criminology*, 32(1): 1–21.

Fagan, A. A., Hawkins, J. D., Catalano, R. F. & Farrington, D. P. (2019) *Communites That Care: Building Community Engagement and Capacity to Prevent Youth Behavior Problems*. Oxford: Oxford University Press.

Farrington, D. P. (1979) Longitudinal research on crime and delinquency. *Crime and Justice*, 1: 289–348.

Farrington, D. P. (1986) Age and crime. *Crime and Justice*, 7: 189–250.

Farrington, D. P. (1992) Criminal career research in the United Kingdom. *British Journal of Criminology*, 32(4): 521–536.

Farrington, D. P. (1996) *Understanding and Preventing Youth Crime*. York: The Joseph Rowntree Foundation.

Farrington, D. P. (2005) 'The Integrated Cognitive Antisocial Potential (ICAP) Theory'. In D. P. Farrington (ed.), *Integrated Developmental and Life-Course Theories of Offending: Advances in Criminological Theory* (Vol. 14, pp. 73–92). London: Transaction.

Farrington, D. P. (2007) 'Childhood Risk Factors and Risk-focussed Prevention'. In M. Maguire, R. Morgan and R. Reiner (eds), *The Oxford Handbook of Criminology* (4th edition, pp. 602–640). Oxford: Oxford University Press.

Farrington, D. P. (2013) Longitudinal and experimental research in criminology. *Crime and Justice*, 42(1): 453–527.

Farrington, D. P. (2018) 'Origins of Violent Behavior over the Life Span'. In A. T. Vazsonyi, D. J. Flannery and M. DeLisi (eds), *The Cambridge Handbook of Violent Behavior and Aggression*. Cambridge: Cambridge University Press.

Farrington, D. P., Gaffney, H., Lösel, F. & Ttofi, M. M. (2017) Systematic reviews of the effectiveness of developmental prevention programs in reducing delinquency, aggression, and bullying. *Aggression and Violent Behavior*, 33: 91–106. https://doi.org/10.1016/j.avb.2016.11.003

Farrington, D. P., Kazemian, L. & Piquero, A. R. (eds) (2019) *The Oxford Handbook of Developmental and Life-Course Criminology*. Oxford: Oxford University Press.

Farrington, D. P., Loeber, R., Yin, Y. & Anderson, S. J. (2002) Are within-individual causes of delinquency the same as between-individual causes? *Criminal Behaviour and Mental Health*, 12: 53–68.

Farrington, D. P. & McGee, T. R. (2017) 'The Integrated Cognitive Antisocial Potential (ICAP) Theory: Empirical Testing'. In A. A. J. Blokland and V. V. D. Geest (eds), *The Routledge International Handbook of Life-Course Criminology* (pp. 11–28). Abingdon: Routledge.

Farrington, D. P., Ttofi, M. M. & Losel, F. A. (2016) 'Developmental and Social Prevention'. In D. Weisburd, D. P. Farrington and C. Gill (eds), *What Works in Crime Prevention and Rehabilitation: Lessons from Systematic Reviews*. London: Springer.

Giordano, P. C., Copp, J. E., Manning, W. D. & Longmore, M. A. (2019) Linking parental incarceration and family dynamics associated with intergenerational transmission: a life-course perspective. *Criminology*. https://doi.org/10.1111/1745-9125.12209

Glueck, S. & Glueck, E. (1968) *Delinquents and Non-delinquents in Perspective*. Cambridge, MA: Harvard University Press.

Gottfredson, M. R. (2005) Offender classifications and treatment effects in developmental criminology: a propensity/event consideration. *Annals of the American Academy of Political and Social Science*, 602(1): 46–56.

Gottfredson, M. R. & Hirschi, T. (1986) The true value of lambda would appear to be zero: an essay on career criminals, criminal careers and selective incapacitation, cohort studies and related topics. *Criminology*, 24: 213–234.

Gottfredson, M. R. & Hirschi, T. (1988) Science, public policy, and the career paradigm. *Criminology*, 26(1): 37–55.

Gottfredson, M. R. & Hirschi, T. (1990) *A General Theory of Crime*. Stanford, CA: Stanford University Press.

Hirschi, T. & Gottfredson, M. R. (1995) Control theory and the life-course perspective. *Studies on Crime and Crime Prevention*, 4(2): 131–142.

Home Office (1997) *No More Excuses – A New Approach to Tackling Youth Crime in England and Wales* (White Paper, CM 3809). London: HMSO.

Homel, R., Branch, S. & Freiberg, K. (2019, Feb) Implementation through community coalitions: the power of technology and of community-based intermediaries. *Journal of Primary Prevention*, 40(1): 143–148. https://doi.org/10.1007/s10935-019-00541-8

Huesmann, L. R., Eron, L. D. & Dubow, E. F. (2002) Childhood predictors of adult criminality: are all risk factors reflected in childhood aggressiveness? *Criminal Behavior and Mental Health*, 12: 185–208.

Jolliffe, D., Farrington, D. P., Brunton-Smith, I., Loeber, R., Ahonen, L. & Palacios, A. P. (2019) Depression, anxiety and delinquency: results from the Pittsburgh Youth Study. *Journal of Criminal Justice*, 62: 42–49.

Jolliffe, D., Farrington, D. P., Piquero, A. R., Loeber, R. & Hill, K. G. (2017, Mar-Apr) Systematic review of early risk factors for life-course-persistent, adolescence-limited, and late-onset offenders in prospective longitudinal studies. *Aggression and Violent Behavior*, 33: 15–23. https://doi.org/10.1016/j.avb.2017.01.009

Jolliffe, D., Farrington, D. P., Piquero, A. R., MacLeod, J. F. & van de Weijer, S. (2017) Prevalence of life-course-persistent, adolescence-limited, and late-onset offenders: a systematic review of prospective longitudinal studies. *Aggression and Violent Behavior*, 33: 4–14. https://doi.org/10.1016/j.avb.2017.01.002

Kolvin, I., Miller, F. J. W., Scott, D. M., Gatzanis, S. R. M. & Fleeting, M. (1990) *Continuities of Deprivation? The Newcastle 1000 Family Study*. Ashgate: Avebury.

Laub, J. H. & Sampson, R. J. (2003) *Shared Beginnings, Divergent Lives: Delinquent Boys to Age 70*. Cambridge, MA: Harvard University Press.

Loeber, R., Farrington, D. P., Stouthamer-Loeber, M. & White, H. R. (2008) *Violence and Serious Theft: Development and Prediction from Childhood to Adulthood*. Abingdon: Routledge.

Matthews, B. & Minton, J. (2018) Rethinking one of criminology's 'brute facts': the age–crime curve and the crime drop in Scotland. *European Journal of Criminology*, 15(3): 296–320.

McCord, J. (1992) 'The Cambridge-Somerville Study: A Pioneering Longitudinal Experimental Study of Delinquency Prevention'. In J. McCord and R. E. Tremblay (eds), *Preventing Antisocial Behavior: Interventions from Birth through Adolescence*. New York: Guilford Press.

McCord, J. & Ensminger, M. E. (1997) Multiple risks and comorbidity in an African-American population. *Criminal Behaviour and Mental Health*, 7: 339–352.

McGee, T. R. & Farrington, D. P. (2010) Are there any true adult onset offenders? *British Journal of Criminology*, 50(3): 530–549.

McGee, T. R. & Farrington, D. P. (2015) 'Developmental and Life-Course Theories of Crime'. In A. R. Piquero (ed.), *Handbook of Criminological Theory*. Oxford: Wiley-Blackwell.

McGee, T. R. & Mazerolle, P. (eds) (2015) *Developmental and Life-Course Theories of Crime*. Abingdon: Routledge.

Mercer, N., Farrington, D. P., Ttofi, M. M., Keijsers, L., Branje, S. & Meeus, W. (2016) Childhood predictors and adult life success of adolescent delinquency abstainers. *Journal of Abnormal Child Psychology*, 44(3): 613–624.

Moffitt, T. E. (1993, Oct) Adolescence-limited and life-course-persistent antisocial behavior: a developmental taxonomy. *Psychological Review*, 100(4): 674–701.

Moffitt, T. E. (2018) *Child-to-adult life-course multidisciplinary research studies to inform prevention*, David Farrington lecture American Society of Criminology Annual Meeting, Atlanta, GA, USA.

Moffitt, T. E., Caspi, A., Dickson, N., Silva, P. & Stanton, W. (1996) Childhood-onset versus adolescent-onset antisocial conduct problems in males: natural history from aged 3 to 18 years. *Development and Psychopathology*, 8: 399–424.

Olds, D., Kitzman, H., Cole, R., Hanks, C., Arcoleo, K., Anson, E., Luckey, D., Knudtson, M., Henderson, C., Bondy, J. & Stevenson, A. (2010) Enduring effects of prenatal and infancy home visiting by nurses on maternal life course and government spending. *Archives of Pediatrics & Adolescent Medicine*, 164(5): 419–424.

Pulkkinen, L., Lyyra, A.-L. & Kokko, K. (2009) Life success of males on non-offender, adolescence-limited, persistent, and adult-onset antisocial pathways: follow-up from age 8 to 42. *Aggressive Behavior*, 35: 117–135.

Quetelet, A. (1833) *Research on the Propensity for Crime at Different Ages* (2nd edition). M. Hayez, Printer to the Royal Academy.

Rock, P. (1994) The social organisation of a Home Office initiative. *European Journal of Crime, Criminal Law and Criminal Justice*, 2: 141–167.

Sampson, R. J. & Laub, J. H. (1993) *Crime in the Making: Pathways and Turning Points through Life*. Cambridge, MA: Harvard University Press.

Sampson, R. J. & Laub, J. H. (1995) Understanding variability in lives through time: contributions of life-course criminology. *Studies on Crime and Crime Prevention*, 4(2): 143–158.

Sampson, R. J. & Laub, J. H. (2005) A life-course view of the development of crime, *Annals of the American Academy of Political and Social Sciences*, 602(1): 12–45.

Sanders, M. R., Markie-Dadds, C., Tully, L. A. & Bor, W. (2000) The Triple P - Positive Parenting Program: a comparison of enhanced, standard and self-directed behavioural family intervention for parents and children with early onset conduct problems. *Journal of Consulting and Clinical Psychology*, 68: 624–640.

Tremblay, R. E. (2003) 'Why Socialization Fails? The Case of Chronic Physical Aggression'. In B. B. Lahey, T. E. Moffitt and A. Caspi (eds), *The Causes of Conduct Disorder and Juvenile Delinquency* (pp. 182–224). New York: Guilford Press.

Werner, E. E. (1993) Risk, resilience, and recovery: perspectives from the Kauai Longitudinal Study. *Development and Psychopathology*, 5: 503–515.

West, D. J. & Farrington, D. P. (1973) *Who Becomes Delinquent?* New York: Heinemann.

Wikström, P.-O. H. (2012) 'Does Everything Matter? Addressing the Problem of Causation and Explanation in the Study of Crime'. In J. M. McGloin, C. Sullivan and L. W. Kennedy (eds), *When Crime Appears: The Role of Emergence*. London: Routledge.

Wikström, P.-O. H. & Treiber, K. (2018) 'The Dynamics of Change: Criminogenic Interactions and Life-Course Patterns in Crime'. In D. P. Farrington, L. Kazemian and A. R. Piquero (eds), *The Oxford Handbook on Developmental and Life-Course Criminology*. Oxford: Oxford University Press.

Wilson, J. Q. & Herrnstein, R. J. (1985) *Crime and Human Nature*. New York: Simon and Schuster.

Wolfgang, M. E., Figlio, R. M. & Sellin, T. (1972) *Delinquency in a Birth Cohort*. Chicago: University of Chicago Press.

Cultural Criminology

10

Keith Hayward and
Jairo Matallana-Villarreal

---------------- Learning Objectives ----------------

By the end of this chapter you will:

- Appreciate the contested cultural meanings that often underpin crime and its control.
- Understand the relationship between cultural criminology and late modernity.
- Understand the importance of meaning, power, and emotional affect in the study of crime, deviance and control.
- Be familiar with the key criticisms of cultural criminology and how cultural criminologists have responded.
- Have explored recent developments in cultural criminology and how the field will evolve in the future.

---------------- Framing Questions ----------------

1. What are the main propositions of cultural criminologists? How can these propositions be used to expand our understanding of crime and control?
2. What criminological traditions do cultural criminologists draw on, and how have cultural criminologists adapted this earlier work to fit the context of late modernity?
3. What can we learn about the discipline of criminology from the debates that surround cultural criminology?

INTRODUCTION

We are all of us shaped and influenced by culture. It is a, perhaps *the*, lens through which we see the world and establish social relations. Although a complex term to pin down, 'culture' is a set of practices, habits, norms and beliefs that enable us to navigate the social world and make sense of our selves within collective formations. Certainly, for cultural criminologists, culture is very much the stuff of collective meaning and collective identity; within it and by way of it, the government claims authority, the consumer decides what to purchase – and the criminal, as both person and perceived social problem, comes alive. From this starting position, cultural criminology develops its principle claim: that crime, the criminal justice system, and the myriad social responses to deviance, are all cultural products, creative constructs, and as such must be read in terms of the *meanings* they carry. It is vital therefore that if we are to understand (and ultimately control) crime we must situate it within its cultural and spatial context. This, essentially, is cultural criminology's raison d'être.

Knowledge Link: This topic is also covered in Chapter 6.

As a distinct school of thought, cultural criminology brings together an array of different theoretical and disciplinary perspectives to understand crime and crime control as cultural constructions intersected by power relations (see Hayward and Young, 2004; Hayward and Young, 2012; Ferrell et al., 2015 for detailed introductions). Its foundations can be traced to two traditions of criminological theory. First, the American legacy of interactive and interpretive sociological criminology, with its emphasis on symbolic interactionism, labelling perspectives, and subcultural practice and meaning – a rich body of work that spans the research produced by members of the Chicago School of sociology, and later sociological luminaries such as Robert Merton, Howard Becker, David Matza and Erving Goffman. Second, research undertaken in the UK in the 1970s by scholars associated with the Birmingham School of cultural studies and the 'New Criminology' allied with the National Deviancy Conference. However, cultural criminology is much more than a simple reboot of these well-known traditions. Since its emergence at the turn of the twenty-first century, cultural criminology has sought to expand criminology's imagination by drawing on a host of new developments in areas such as cultural geography, urban studies, media studies, digital sociology, and science and technology studies. At the same time, it has also worked hard to integrate *inter alia* feminist, anarchist, and global and 'Southern' epistemologies into its analyses. In this sense, rather than a stand-alone theory, cultural criminology is best described as an evolving analytical perspective, 'a triadic [criminological] framework concerned with meaning, power and existential accounts of crime, punishment and control' (Hayward, 2016: 300).

Knowledge link: These topics are also covered in Chapters 8 and 11.

But what does all this mean for you as a new student of criminology? No doubt your interest in criminology will have been stimulated by popular culture representations of crime and violence. By engaging with news media reportage, crime-related TV boxsets, and other forms of factual and fictional crime content, you will have been exposed to a range of 'crime explanations' and 'solutions to crime', many of which will have been proffered by supposed 'experts' who in reality have all sorts of reasons for presenting crime in the way they do. Cultural criminology urges you to take a step back from many of these accounts and instead pose a series of questions about crime and harm that are often neglected in the mainstream media. Why, for example, are certain types of predatory street crime over-represented on our screens, while other forms of illegal behaviour such as corporate crime/corruption or environmental exploitation are largely ignored? Why do some countries view certain human activities as normal or harmless, while elsewhere the very same actions are socially condemned and harshly punished by criminal sanctions? What is the role of traditional and social media in victim-blaming and the reproduction of stereotypes? Likewise, given that many of today's crime 'solutions' involve the deployment of new technology and heightened forms of physical security, shouldn't we also be asking questions about what all this technology means for the future of an open, plural society – and, more importantly, who stands to profit from the imposition of all these new measures? Such uncomfortable questions frequently drive cultural criminologists' research, and as such it should be seen as an interrogative approach that brings to bear philosophical, sociological, and political perspectives on the analysis of crime.

Knowledge link: This topic is also covered in Chapter 5.

The aim of this chapter is to provide you with a general introduction to cultural criminology and some of the debates that surround this paradigm. The chapter is structured in four sections. We start by presenting the foundations of cultural criminology, explaining the context in which it emerged and how it is, to a large extent, a response to under-contextualised and over-simplistic theories of crime and deviance. Second, we introduce some of cultural criminology's key themes and concepts and explain their application to real-world criminological problems. Third, we briefly discuss some of the criticisms of cultural criminology and provide a response to each of these in turn. Finally, we outline some of cultural criminology's latest lines of analysis, including linkages with other perspectives both past and present.

CONTEXTUALISING CULTURAL CRIMINOLOGY

Cultural criminology's insistence that the meaning of crime and crime control is always under construction comes into especially sharp focus when we consider the times in which we live – a period often referred to by social theorists as *late modernity*.

Late modernity is a shorthand term that encapsulates the way space and time are being compressed by the forces of economic and cultural globalisation (Giddens, 1990; Harvey, 1990; Young, 1999). Under these conditions, culture breaks loose from locality, a never ending stream of images and cultural referents reshape personal identities and destabilise social values, and new vectors of interconnectivity – information technology, social networks, mass tourism etc. – offer up putative alternative lifestyles and new 'ways of being'. But while a late modern, globalised world in flux opens up all sorts of opportunities for innovation, creativity and personal development, it does so at a cost. In many communities, transformations and fluctuations in the old constants of work, family and community cause profound upheaval. Similarly, the diasporas and flows of immigration associated with globalisation often bring to the surface cultural and racial tensions, as established populations are forced to deal with the diversity of values associated with hyper-pluralism.

Building on the ideas of David Harvey, Ulrich Beck and Zygmunt Bauman, cultural criminologists have highlighted several characteristics of the late modern era that have a bearing on crime and crime control (Hayward, 2004; Young, 2007; Ferrell, 2018). First, the erosion of stable structures – long-term employment, a sense of locality and community – needed to sustain everyday life. Second, a growing sense of disillusionment and lack of trust in the institutions of the state – increasingly even the very concept of the nation state itself. Third, a tension that develops within many individuals as they are forced to confront the fact they lack the necessary skills or resources to function effectively in a late modern society that places a premium on entrepreneurship, individual accomplishment, and self-realisation. In urban settings such feelings are often further exacerbated by a second tension between the dreams and aspirations provoked by lifestyle consumerism, and the material constraints of poverty and marginality (Nightingale, 1993; Hayward, 2004). These and other emotional, psychosocial states brought on by the disembeddedness and disappointments of late modernity, were neatly captured by the late British criminologist Jock Young in his concept of '**ontological insecurity**':

> We now live in a much more difficult world: we face a greater range in life choices than ever before. Our lives are less firmly embedded in work relationships, our everyday existence is experienced as a series of encounters with risk either in actuality or in the shape of fears and apprehensions. We feel both materially insecure and ontologically precarious. (Young, 1999: vi)

Finally, the complexity and ambiguity of late modern life are further intensified by the fast-changing, omnipresent and increasingly interactive contemporary 'mediascape' and its associated digital technologies.

Often promoted by tech companies and Silicon Valley insiders as liberating and transformative, this brave new technological world also brings with it the spectre of overwhelming surveillance and control. For example, social media sites enhance connectivity and creativity, but at the cost of undermining privacy, as corporations and governments can use this same technology to monitor individuals and record their interests and political preferences.

Late modernity is also characterised by *neoliberal* forms of governance (Harvey, 2007). Primarily associated with free market reforms and the deregulation of capital markets, neoliberalism (as an economic and political sensibility) also manifests itself in the sphere of social control (Deflem, 2019). By this we mean that many countries such as the UK, USA, Australia, and Canada have shifted the focus of social regulation and order maintenance from welfare policies based around inclusion and rehabilitation, to more control-oriented approaches based around risk management, security, surveillance, and crime prevention – a strategy for dealing with deviance and social malaise that David Garland famously described as a 'late modern culture of control' (Garland, 2001). This conflation of neoliberal values with totalising systems of surveillance and control is exemplified in the various 'wars' on crime, drugs, terrorism, illegal migration etc. that have, over the last few decades, functioned to normalise the application of military tactics and security technologies in everyday crime control (Sadowski, 2019). This 'new military urbanism' (Graham, 2011) manifests itself in the way security personnel view the city as a battleground, the diffusion of boundaries between police and military forces, and the construction of internal social groups as enemies that must be neutralised.

In a similar vein, late modernity is also characterised by the consolidation of a security assemblage underpinned by the growing participation of the private sector in the criminal justice system and the expansion of private security (Zedner, 2009). This commodification of security has led to an exponential increase in sales of an array of technological solutions to the crime problem, including everything from face, iris and now even gait recognition camera systems (Hayward and Maas, 2020), to police robots (Danaher, 2018), to Wide Angle Motion Imagery (WAMI) surveillance platforms (Michel, 2019). Importantly, while these services and technologies are always sold to the public as 'objective' and 'value free', in reality they represent the further incursion of private interests and global corporatism into the fabric of city life (e.g. Kitchin, 2014; Hollands, 2015).

Given there is every chance you are reading this chapter as a student of criminology, it is interesting to reflect on the fact that higher education is also subject to the sort of managerial neoliberalism and privatisation that is such a prominent feature of late modernity. Today, university departments and individual academics are subjected to frequent monitoring as a result of the pressures of national and international university ranking tables and other 'impact' metrics. This, alongside the colonisation of research agendas where many criminologists and sociologists now undertake so-called 'client-led criminology', sees research funding tethered to orthodox 'criminal justice' outcomes. Cultural criminologists actively resist the pressure of blindly serving the demands of the criminal justice system, developing a series of epistemological approaches and research methods that stand in sharp contrast to both the managerialism that courses through contemporary higher education, and the growing battery of academic rules now functioning to narrow theoretical fields and restrict research vistas (see Winlow and Hall, 2012; Ferrell et al., 2015: chs. 7 and 8).

It is against this late modern backdrop that cultural criminology undertakes its analysis of crime, deviance, and control. It is a criminological approach designed explicitly to resonate with the contemporary world, and thus penetrate its obfuscations and critique its injustices. It is for this reason that cultural criminology is often referred to as a 'criminology of now', an exciting, interdisciplinary mode of analysis that constantly strives to revitalise criminology in such a way as to attune it to the shifting dynamics associated with the late modern condition.

Pause for Review

- What are the main characteristics of late modernity and why are they important for the study of crime and control?
- Why do cultural criminologists believe it is important to question many of criminology's dominant assumptions about crime, deviance and control?

CONCEPTUALISING CULTURAL CRIMINOLOGY

By emphasising culture, cultural criminologists recognise the decisiveness of meaning in matters of crime and justice, arguing that crime and crime control take shape through a contested process of representation and interpretation. In this section we offer you a selection of key themes and concepts associated with cultural criminology – including an introduction to some of the main research methods cultural criminologists employ when conducting their studies. The following short subsections are intended simply as precursor resources to prime you for a wider engagement with the constantly evolving project of cultural criminology.

Emotion, Edgework and Affect

One of the main appeals of cultural criminology is that it often challenges dominant, orthodox criminological approaches (Ferrell, 2004; Young, 2011). This is especially apparent when it comes to the issue of **aetiology**. Unfortunately, it remains the case that, for too many criminologists, the goal today is simply to 'manage' crime and criminals in a similar way to which economists attempt to risk-manage the economy. Consequently, fundamental questions about *why* offenders break the law or how offenders *feel* when undertaking particular crimes are neither asked nor rarely even considered. For cultural criminologists, this impoverished approach to causality is highly problematic. In contrast, cultural criminology prioritises a distinctly human approach to the study of criminality that rejects attempts to reduce crime and punishment to an abstract technical or (pseudo) 'scientific' problem.

Inspired by existentialist philosophy and phenomenological sociology, cultural criminology reinstates the importance of *emotionality* and *affect* in the study of crime and punishment. Rather than mechanistic individuals operating through an endless sequence of cost benefit analyses, cultural criminology recognises that humans are greatly influenced by emotions and the immediacy of the sensorial experience. From the thrills and sense of adrenalin that come from activities such as drug taking, football hooliganism, and even terrorism (Cottee and Hayward, 2011), to the fear and anxiety that often drive punitive political responses to crime and violence, criminality and its control are saturated with emotion and expressive dimensions that transcend rational and instrumental explanation. Likewise, as cultural criminologists such as David Brotherton (2004) and Jody Miller (1995) have long-since identified, collective actions of transgression associated with subcultural practices are not simply about disobedience, opportunity, or the rational calculation of pleasure versus pain, but rather about creating alternative meanings and reasserting identities in response to perceived injustices or barriers to achieving success. Hence cultural criminology's emphasis on the expressive aspects of subcultures beyond their instrumental character: being part of a street gang or an organised crime syndicate is about much more than simply making a living – it is wrapped up with honour, humiliation, gendered identity, discontent, shrewdness, and a host of other affect-laden motivations and justifications.

The central text in this recuperation of emotion within criminology is Jack Katz's *Seductions of Crime: Moral and Sensual Attractions of Doing Evil* (1988), a work that served as a touchstone for numerous subsequent cultural criminological studies into the feelings of the perpetrator and the bodily experience of the offence (e.g. Morrison, 1995 (ch. 15); Fenwick and Hayward, 2000; Presdee, 2000; De Haan and Vos, 2003; Jackson-Jacobs, 2004; Van Hellemont, 2012). According to Katz, criminology has long been constituted back to front – built, that is, on an assumption that background structural factors can predict the nature of crime and criminality. Consequently, criminology has been overwhelmingly preoccupied with these background factors, while largely ignoring the situational context of crime and crime control as emergent phenomena in their own right:

> Somehow in the psychological and sociological disciplines, the lived mysticism and magic in the foreground of criminal experience became unseeable, while the abstractions hypothesised by "empirical theory" as the determining background causes, especially those conveniently quantified by state agencies, became the stuff of "scientific" thought and "rigorous" method. (Katz, 1988: 311-2)

In a similar vein, the concept of *edgework* (Lyng, 1990; 2005) is also a key component of cultural criminology's thinking about the role emotions play in the commission of crime. Edgework denotes acts of voluntary and often illicit risk-taking – activities such as urban exploration (Kindynis, 2016), BASE jumping (Ferrell et al., 2001), and graffiti writing (Ferrell, 1996). But beyond this, edgework is conceptualised as a distinct response to the accumulating degradations of late modernity. Voluntary engagement in high-risk activities reverses the logic of contemporary risk management, instead embracing risk for its sensual pleasures and transgressive possibilities. Because edgework is most easily applied to high-risk, physically-dangerous activities, some critics have suggested that cultural criminology's application of this model is limited only to so-called 'prototypically masculine' pursuits (Naegler and Salman, 2016). Yet in reality, the concept of edgework has been used on numerous occasions by criminologists to explain women's involvement in a host of activities that involve the interplay of emotion, risk, adrenaline and (gendered) identity (see e.g. Lois, 2005; Rajah, 2007; Worthen and Abby Baker, 2016).

The stress placed by cultural criminologists on emotion and affect can also be valuable when it comes to understanding the criminal justice system and the mentality and behaviour of certain state agents (e.g. Aiello, 2014; Linnemann et al., 2014). Likewise, paying attention to the feelings and sensations associated with victimisation can also aid our understanding of how to improve the criminal justice system by enhancing harm reparation measures and emotion-based reintegrative shaming programmes (Braithwaite, 1989).

As the originator of the edgework concept, Stephen Lyng (2005: 5) reminds us, understanding the complex conflation of existential motivation and emotionality that drives many forms of illicit transgression is likely to become an ever more crucial task as risk-taking gathers further momentum within the social and institutional structures of late modernity.

Power, structure, and everyday crimes – large and small

City life has always been a central focus of cultural criminology (Ferrell, 2001; Hayward, 2004; 2012). This abiding interest in the underlife of urban space has generated a large body of research that explores forms of low-order, everyday criminality like loitering, graffiti writing, shoplifting, and dumpster diving, while also documenting the legal responses and public controversies that surround such street-level criminality (Ferrell and Ilan, 2013). For cultural criminology's critics, this interest in 'small crimes' is a problem (O'Brien, 2005). They see in this focus on everyday law-breaking and everyday people a failure to deal with the more serious, socially harmful forms of crime associated with political economy. Yet, as has been made clear in several statements over the years, for cultural criminologists, unchecked capitalism is the wellspring of many of the ugliest examples of contemporary criminality – big or small:

> Tracing a particularly expansionist trajectory these days, late modern capitalism continues to contaminate one community after another, shaping social life into a series of predatory encounters and saturating everyday existence with criminogenic expectations of material convenience. All along this global trajectory, collectivities are converted into markets, people into consumers, and experiences and emotions into products. So steady is this seepage of capitalism into social life, so pervasive are its crimes - both corporate and interpersonal - that they now seem to pervade most every situation. (Ferrell et al., 2008: 14)

This passage makes clear that the boundary between everyday crime and more serious criminal projects is often a blurred one. Take mobile phone theft. To make sense of this street-based form of acquisitive crime, one must also consider both the global black market for stolen handsets and their internal components, and the way corporations use sophisticated lifestyle advertising to tether customers' sense of identity to the latest digital device. Such examples illustrate a cultural criminological truth – that to effectively study crime, one must always analyse it *across* structural, contextual, and micro levels. This more comprehensive, constitutive synthesis of explanatory levels allows cultural criminologists to locate structural dynamics within the domain of lived experience and thus overcome the blunt dualism of agency and structure (Young, 2003).

Importantly, this does not mean that cultural criminology overlooks the various ways in which power (in the form of social structure) restricts individuals by limiting life opportunities and moulding the way people see the world. Background factors such as race or gender (that are themselves culturally constructed and socially reproduced) profoundly affect economic opportunities and shape exclusionary processes. But power is a slippery thing. It has the capacity to take many forms, some of which are immediately apparent, some of which are only ever partially glimpsed.

Case Study 10.1

Arbitrary Detentions of Young People in Colombia

As an illustration of the way cultural criminologists study the relationship between power, structure, and everyday life, consider Matallana-Villarreal's (2017) study of arbitrary detentions of young people in Colombia. (Until very recently, the Colombian army would regularly raid poor urban neighbourhoods and involuntarily conscript young men and women into military service, uprooting them from their families, sometimes for years). In this study, Matallana-Villarreal explores the normalisation and neutralisation processes that allowed this practice to remain unsanctioned for decades – and sometimes even accepted and welcomed by communities that had grown accustomed to living under the yoke of a military culture. But the complex dynamics that connect power and culture do not only flow in one direction. This study also draws attention to the emergence of nonviolent resistance practices against the extra-legal use of force by the Colombian military. In doing so, he affirms another of cultural criminology's maxims: exploring power also means studying responses to power, from acquiescence to resistance. To this end, cultural criminologists also focus a good deal of attention on the creative/productive nature of political resistance (Ferrell, 2001) - and importantly how to differentiate meaningful community action from the type of pseudo 'rebellion' that too often passes for political protest today (Hayward and Schuilenburg, 2014).

Crime, media and representation

Given its focus on meaning, it should come as no surprise that cultural criminology places considerable importance on the mediated *representation* of crime and punishment (Hayward and Presdee, 2010; Jewkes, 2017). It is an area of study that has occupied cultural criminologists since the field's inception in the mid-1990s, as this quote from the very first book on the subject makes clear:

> Criminal events, identities, and styles take life within a media-saturated environment, and thus exist from the start as a moment in a mediated spiral of presentation and representation … Criminal subcultures reinvent mediated images as situated styles, but are at the same time themselves reinvented time and time again as they are displayed within the daily swarm of mediated presentations. In every case, as cultural criminologists we study not only images but images of images, an infinite hall of mediated mirrors. (Ferrell and Sanders, 1995: 14)

For some, this interest in the 'crime-media nexus' is nothing new; the salacious nature of certain criminal acts having ensured a ready audience for crime for well over a century. This is certainly true, but today the situation is far more acute. We now inhabit a world where 'the screen scripts the street and the street scripts the screen' (Hayward and Young, 2004: 259), where power is increasingly exercised through mediated representation and symbolic production, and where battles over image, meaning, and cultural representation are an everyday feature of late modern reality.

How, then, to make sense of this expanding tangle of digital technologies and visual platforms, this enveloping world of media festival and digital spectacle? Perhaps the first thing to state is that within the late modern 'mediascape' a fundamental inversion is taking place. Today, as images and memes bleed from one medium to the next, as videos are uploaded and downloaded, copied and cross-posted, and as 'fake news' and 'deep fakes' are Facebook-ed and PhotoShop-ped, images of crime and its control are becoming almost as 'real' as crime and criminal justice itself – 'if by "real" we denote those dimensions of social life that produce consequences; shape attitudes and policy; define the effects of crime and criminal justice; generate fear, avoidance and pleasure; and alter the lives of those involved' (Ferrell et al., 2004: 4). For example, as Teresa Cladeira (2001) makes clear in her account of social segregation in São Paulo, Brazil, politically-charged news stories and televisual crime messaging are not simply titillating forms of information and entertainment; they fuel fear and create stereotypes that have radically transformed the city into a latticework of fortified enclaves characterised by private security and self-interested 'neighbourhood rights' groups. In a bid to capture such dynamics, cultural criminology developed a theory of media 'loops' and 'spirals' (Ferrell et al., 2015: 154–161) – interrelated concepts that trace the way various images of crime and justice play off and reproduce one another, while at the same time seeping from one context to the next:

Knowledge link: This topic is also covered in Chapter 5.

> In this world perpetrators and witnesses post images of crime and violence to YouTube and Instagram; politicians formulate criminal justice policy to ensure that it will 'play in the media'; attorneys take acting lessons and repackage evidence so as to sway juries steeped in television crime dramas; and advertisers and marketers utilize images of crime and transgression to sell everything from energy drinks to family cars. (Ferrell and Hayward, 2018: 27)

Cultural criminology's work on crime and the media encompasses many other theories and insights, from Majid Yar's (2012) notion of 'the will to representation', to Alison Young's (2009; 2010) thoughtful work on how visceral crime images affect us both bodily and sensually. It is through this type of innovative visual analysis that cultural criminology traces the contours of a late modern world where crime and crime control are increasingly inseparable from the politics of representation (see McClanahan, 2021 for a recent introduction).

Crime, Technology and Virtuality

From sensor-laden robotic police platforms to remote-controlled biometric lasers capable of identifying protestors by individual heartbeat signatures, each month brings with it an array of new technologies linked to smart systems and autonomous machines. Often referred to as disruptive networked technologies (Greenfield, 2017), these fast-emerging, hyper-connected innovations are redrawing the contours of the existing late modern order with profound implications for crime, disorder and social control. So significant is this technology that it is not an exaggeration to say that, when viewed collectively, these disparate technological incursions into everyday life herald the emergence of a new computational order in which social equilibrium and civic harmony will be established and maintained by a combination of data management, digital/biometric surveillance, and intelligent self-organising systems.

From a criminological perspective, networked technologies also provide an array of new opportunities for criminal activity, including everything from the emergence of adversarial/malicious Artificial Intelligence, to the use of cryptocurrencies by terrorist organisations. As our society becomes evermore reliant upon interactive devices and interconnected data architecture, we accelerate further into a world where the greater the connectivity, the greater the attack surface or vulnerability vector. Yet, so far criminology has been slow to address this situation. Criminology's established methods and (causal) theories, based as they are on utilitarian models of human behaviour and mid-twentieth century notions of deviance, are not sufficient for a world in which data-behaviourism is supplanting human agency, and where traditional notions of discipline and control are being superseded by dissipative systems that curate individuals within restricted terrains (Krivý, 2018). Consider the cybercrime literature. While important, this field tends to focus on either internet regulation, computer forensics, or the diffusion of online victimisation (e.g. phishing/scamming). As such, it upholds a series of false dichotomies (between online/offline criminality and datafied object/agent), rather than understanding networked crime as a phenomenological exchange or dialogue *between* people and technology. Consequently, not only has criminology neglected potentially useful digital sociology concepts like virtuality, convergence and digital presence, it has also failed to prioritise the inequalities associated with the digital divide and related cyber harms with respect to gender, race and sexuality (Gilbert, 2010; Magnet, 2011).

Knowledge link: This topic is also covered in Chapter 12.

However, things are beginning to change. For some time now, cultural criminologists have been saying that the prefix 'cyber' is no longer sufficient for covering the ever-expanding mass of crimes – old and new – that are being reconfigured by the digital era (see Yar, 2017). Indeed, they have already begun the task of developing a more rounded, interdisciplinary, and importantly tech-literate criminology capable of dealing with the societal disruptions and realignments caused by radical new technologies (e.g. Schuilenburg and Pali, 2019; Hayward and Maas, 2020). Moreover, a growing body of culturally-inspired work is emerging that understands not just the digital harms associated with the social networks, crypto-markets, and darkweb platforms that constitute the new criminological frontier, but also how these new spaces lead to entirely new collective criminal imaginaries. Consider Goldsmith and Brewer's (2015) compelling concept of 'digital drift', and how the blurring of the real and the virtual results in a new 'criminal interaction order' characterised by anonymous pathways into crime that are more episodic, unstable, and unpredictable than was the case with more traditional crime forms. Likewise, research by the likes of Judith Aldridge, Thomas Holt, Gavin Smith, Lyria Bennett-Moses, Jacob Demant, Mike McGuire, Rasmus Munksgaard, and Kevin Steinmetz on *inter alia* encryption, crypto-markets, illicit trade and 'dropgangs' on the dark web, 'stalkerware', gender-based 'sextortion', and a host of other 'technocrimes' (Steinmetz and Nobles, 2017) hints at the exciting possibilities that exist as cultural criminology expands to include the technosocial practices associated with digital crime – and, of course, its corollary, digital control and anticipatory surveillance (Hayward, 2021; Smith and O'Malley, 2020).

——————————— **Case Study 10.2** ———————————

A New Vision of Criminology

In their excellent recent book *Digital Criminology*, Anastasia Powell, Gregory Stratton and Robin Cameron (2018) present a new vision of criminology, one specifically attuned to the technological world and the many challenges it presents. Powell et al's primary aim is to push beyond a relatively siloed cyber-oriented criminology towards a better understanding of the disruptive networked technologies (complex and mundane) that are currently reshaping crime, deviance, criminalisation, victimisation, and community justice. Importantly, in an earlier article, the same authors acknowledge the value of cultural criminology for achieving this task:

> A notable exception lies in the emerging work of cultural criminologists who have sought to explore how the social web may be changing the culturally constructed nature, and socially constituted practices, of crime and deviance.

(*Source*: Stratton et al. (2017: 23). Reproduced under the Creative Commons Attribution 4.0 International License (CC BY 4.0). URL: https://creativecommons.org/licenses/by/4.0/)

On Knowledge and Methodology

Since its inception, cultural criminology has been deeply sceptical of the type of fake scientism that characterises much mainstream quantitative criminology (e.g. Young, 2011). This critique of rigid determinism also extends to official crime statistics and definitions of crime and crime control reproduced by the criminal justice system, the media, and the crime control industry (Ferrell et al., 2015: ch. 8). In contrast, cultural criminology aims to generate criminological knowledge that prioritises the lived realities of groups within the crime-control spectrum whose voices are often neglected or subject to politicisation. So how do cultural criminologists go about gathering their data?

From its earliest days, cultural criminology has been closely associated with the ethnographic study of crime (see the edited collection *Ethnography at the Edge* by Ferrell and Hamm, 1998), and a series of book-length participant-observation studies by the founder of cultural criminology, Jeff Ferrell (1996; 2001). Partly due to its interest in **phenomenology**, and partly as a direct challenge to the abstracted positivism that dominates criminology today, cultural criminologists favour interacting with people in their everyday environments in an effort to elicit qualitative 'thick description' about the subjective emotions and ways of being that drive (criminal) behaviour and shape (sub)cultural formations. This goal of gaining deep cultural and emotional knowledge is embodied in the concept of 'criminological **verstehen**'. Introduced by Ferrell, 'criminological *verstehen* denotes a researcher's subjective understanding of crime's situational meanings and emotions – its moments of pleasure and pain, its emergent logic and excitement – within the larger process of research' (1997: 10). It is for this reason that Mark Hamm and Jeff Ferrell described ethnography as a 'methodology of attentiveness'; a way for cultural criminologists to immerse themselves within situations and cultures that often defy simple explanation.

At this point it is important to stress that cultural criminology is not simply a criminologically-informed mode of ethnography. As we saw above, it has always maintained a keen interest in representation, aesthetics, and the scholarly deconstruction of media images and cultural texts (Altheide, 1996). Given cultural criminology's abiding focus on the symbolic, the aesthetic, and the visual, how could it be any other way? Interestingly, as the field developed, cultural criminologists started to meld these methods in the form of two techniques known as 'instant' and 'liquid' ethnography (Ferrell et al., 2015: 215–221): the former concerned with single 'decisive moments' of phenomenological serendipity that illustrate or embrace something of cultural criminology's progressive mandate; the latter a research strategy perfectly aligned with the shifting nature of late modernity and thus sensitive to the type of interplay of images outlined above. Whether in the form of a meaning-laden photograph, a short video clip, or even a fieldwork-based blogpost, adopting an instant/liquid approach to ethnography can be an incredibly powerful way to capture meaning's momentary construction.

As the project has developed over the last two decades, a host of other research methods have been added to cultural criminology's arsenal. Given its strong commitment to interdisciplinarity, many of these have been incorporated from other fields, including approaches based on empathy, reflexivity, and positionality that stem from feminist methodology and epistemology, and action-oriented techniques associated with protest groups, journalists, artists, and other actors operating beyond academic circles. Thanks to this mélange of intellectual and interdisciplinary influences, cultural criminologists are today as likely to employ research methods like participative action research, critical digital cartography, netnography, or narrative analysis as they are more established tools of ethnography or discourse analysis. And this reimagination of criminology's traditional methods shows no sign of slowing down. In recent years, cultural criminology's abiding interest in the visual and the symbolic has resulted in a range of new ways of recording data and studying the media, including auto-ethnographic diary photography, semiotics, iconology, and other indexical film studies techniques, and most significantly, 'documentary criminology' (Hayward, 2018) – a filmmaking technique pioneered by David Redmon (2015) predicated on cultural criminology's focus on ethnographic and phenomenological immersion.

Pause for Review

- Think of gender-based violence: can it be properly explained using theories based on cost-benefit calculations? Why do we need to understand power dynamics, affects, and cultural norms to properly analyse violence and crime?
- Cyber criminologists assert that information and communication technologies generate new opportunities for "online crime". Why do cultural criminologists argue that this is a reductionist view?

CRITIQUING CULTURAL CRIMINOLOGY

Over the last two decades, cultural criminology has become the leading theoretical orientation concerned with the convergence and contestation of cultural, criminal, and crime control processes. But during that period it has also generated its fair share of criticism. For example, some commentators have accused cultural criminologists of being confused about the concept of culture (O'Brien, 2005). Their main concern is that cultural criminology over-emphasises individual subjectivity at the expense of the more shared elements of culture such as routines, patterns, and other forms of collective practice. This criticism is the product of engaging only with cultural criminology's early works, which, in a bid to address mainstream criminology's failure to consider the emotions, tended to prioritise the role of affect and aesthetics in certain forms of transgression. It is unfair, however, to suggest that cultural criminology's later works disregard the underlying framework of cultural practice. For example, consider this quote by David Brotherton on the analysis of resistance in American street gangs:

> Essentially, we see the street organizations both generating and transforming their traditions as they respond to the specifics of their transnational marginality. As organizations, the emphases on dignity, identity, and self-renewal and the structure that provides them with roles and statuses are perfect for youth and adults looking to make sense of their transnational social and cultural locations. (2008: 66)

Throughout his article, Brotherton focuses on the interplay *between* cultural practices, socio-economic structures, and the expressive aspects of gang life, including the continuous process of contestation and renegotiation of identity. Brotherton's work is therefore a good example of how cultural criminology attempts to situate human agency – including, importantly, the decision to engage or disengage from crime – *within* the cultural practices and norms that facilitate the social navigation of everyday life. Or as the authors of the statement book, *Cultural Criminology: An Invitation* (2015: 3) make clear:

> Culture suggests the collective search for meaning, and the meaning of the search itself; it reveals the capacity of people, acting together over time, to animate even the lowliest of objects - the homeless person's bedroll, the police officer's truncheon, the gang member's bandana, the Guy Fawkes mask - with importance and implication ... Cultural forces, then, are those threads of collective meaning and understanding that wind around the everyday troubles of social actors, animating the situations and circumstances in which their troubles play out.

Cultural criminology has also been criticised for having little interest in policy making, even conveying a certain romanticism towards the subjects of its study (Matthews, 2014). For cultural criminologists, however, this is (yet again) a matter of emphasis: uncovering and analysing the motives and representations of deviant behaviour and its criminalisation – or legal toleration – is as important as acting upon it. When the root causes of problems are meagrely understood, the typical response is to resort to traditional crime control practices, such as targeted containment or harsh punishment, none of which effectively address the underlying structural or cultural causes of crime.

The issue of emphasis inevitably spills over into a related concern about cultural criminology's supposed failure to analyse state formations and state agents. Implicit in both these criticisms is the view that cultural criminologists study *the wrong type of criminals*. Yet, even the most basic review of the literature reveals a considerable amount of work on state crime and various agents of state control (see e.g. Morrison, 2006; Wender, 2008; Klein, 2011; Wall and Linnemann, 2014). Likewise, if cultural criminologists were uninterested in improving policy/criminal justice practice, why would they undertake lengthy research projects such as those on policing practice in Rio de Janeiro (Pauschinger, 2020), drug policy in rural America (Linnemann, 2016), or the regulation of sex workers (O'Neill, 2010)?

Finally, and on the subject of harm, cultural criminology has been labelled by some critics as a criminology of 'thrills and risks', an overly-romantic perspective that fails to pay sufficient attention to the wider political economy of crime or the impact of predatory violence on victims. Hall and Winlow (2007), for example, claim that cultural criminology should concentrate more on serious and harmful crime across the capitalist social fabric, rather than focusing on minor illegalities and misdemeanours. Yet, here again, such readings of cultural criminology are both superficial and selective, failing to acknowledge that cultural criminologists have written almost as much about boredom (Ferrell, 2004; Bengtsson, 2012), resentment (Presdee, 2004), and the mundane nature of crimes such as online scamming and phishing (Steinmetz, 2015) or counterfeit good manufacture (Yar, 2005), as they have about graffiti or street brawling. Furthermore, as cultural criminology gains traction in other parts of the world, it is now being used as a framework for analysing everything from transnational drug smuggling operations to police extermination squads.

CULTURAL CRIMINOLOGY CONTINUED

As we made clear at the start of the chapter, the crimes and controls of late modernity are a central concern of cultural criminology. However, it is important to acknowledge that, as a sociological construct, the 'late modern condition' is largely a product of the European and North American intellectual imagination. Elsewhere in the world, very different social realities exist. In the Global South, for example, although late modernity partially describes the hyper-connectivity and cosmopolitanism of major metropolises like Sao Paulo, Bangkok, Manila, or Lagos, in many cities and regions around the world, late modernity coexists alongside modern and even pre-modern conditions. In such places, an altogether different clash of values, lived realities, and aspirations takes place. Importantly, and in contrast to the oversimplification of the stable/failed state binary, in many countries different (and often highly uneven) levels of state control coexist. In such places, while the monopoly of force is typically not challenged in the main centres of power (capital cities, seats of government), peripheral and rural regions often experience oligopolies of force, or in extreme cases, a monopoly of coercion by warlords and organised crime syndicates who thrive in these unregulated zones.

As cultural criminology has developed over the last decade or so, it has slowly expanded to include such concerns (e.g. Kahled, 2018; Matallana-Villarreal, 2020; Pauschinger, 2020). Drawing on its aforementioned interest in state crime and the crimes of state agents, cultural criminologists combine the study of macro structures and geopolitical questions, with mid-level subcultural theories, and micro-level accounts of violence, in an attempt to overcome the dualism of agency and structure, and thus discard the false dichotomy between crimes large and small. Beyond the legal analysis of state crime, this approach can help explain how crime and violence (whether perpetrated by state agents or non-state actors) are normalised by the population and neutralised by aggressors (Khaled et al., 2020). It is an approach that requires criminologists to view power from multiple angles, not only in terms of how oppression is organised and exercised, but also how civil nonviolent resistance is often criminalised and undermined. By stressing the importance of culture, and importantly by folding into its research agenda the work of indigenous scholars (Tauri, 2013), cultural criminology is able to question the euro-centric lenses of traditional criminological schools. Here, the criticism levied against cultural criminology regarding its focus on small-scale transgression can be answered by embracing the challenge of analysing the varied troubles and struggles around the world – including recognising the non-monolithic concept of the state, and thus the plural typologies and uneven gradients of criminal justice that constitute the lived reality of life outside the organised folds of Western modernity.

—— Hear from the Expert ——

Some thoughts on violence, crime and culture in the Global South

Violence and crime are learned, transmitted, and normalised. Violence and criminal behaviours are learned and transmitted in spaces of socialisation, regardless of social condition, and occasionally normalised across generations. In Bogota, Colombia, there are families where the head of the household regards crime as work, and that belief is transmitted down to children and grandchildren. The wider communities and social circles in which these families live may also consider criminal activity a normal everyday practice.

Violence is a form of communication that lays bare power and submission. In many households, domestic violence is a commonly-used tactic to communicate and reinforce gender/family power dynamics

(Continued)

with the aim of establishing relationships accordingly. Likewse, within the Colombian public sphere, a massacre that involves dumping beheaded bodies in front of a courthouse is a message that seeks to subdue communities and/or institutions. Intimidation is a normalised and often extremely effective form of non-verbal communication.

There is no necessary correlation between violent or criminal acts and legal sanctions. Crimes that entail lesser personal and social consequences are often punished more rigorously than serious violent offences. For example, theft or low level drug offences are often taken more seriously than systemic corruption or rape. And here we are talking not only about the criminal justice system, but about how crime is perceived and normalised by the general public.

There is no obvious assessment of what society should protect and sanction. Institutionally and socially, in many cases, the greatest efforts are made to protect and defend property, rather than life and integrity. For example, in the 1990s in Bogota, the internal reward system of the police assigned greater value to recovering stolen cars than reducing homicide. This led then-mayor, Antanas Mockus, to put life protection as the central objective of his security policy. He even went as far as to publicly declare that 'it did not matter if thefts increased, as long as victims or perpetrators did not die as a result'. A focus on human life and upholding human freedom should be the priority of any legal system – sadly, this has not always been the case in parts of Central and South America.

The 'anything goes' widespread logic privileging ends over means generates violence and crime. Getting richer or gaining prestige regardless of means is at the core of both street-level and white-collar criminality – but this is not simply an individual venture. It is sustained at community level by the inculcation of values that tacitly accept illegal and morally reprehensible means as normal route to achieve 'higher' culturally instantiated goals.

(Hugo Acero, former Secretary of Security,
Bogota City Government, Colombia)

Knowledge link: This topic is also covered in Chapter 7.

Relatedly, in recent years, cultural criminologists have also started the process of integrating social harm into their analyses. This developing interest in **zemiology** can be traced to two ongoing developments. First, a growing relationship between cultural criminologists and scholars working in the emerging field of *deviant leisure* (see e.g. Hayward and Smith, 2017; Hayward and Turner, 2019). Defining deviant leisure is not an easy task – indeed the term itself is constructed from two of the broadest concepts in the social sciences. Yet, for shorthand purposes we can state the following: deviant leisure is concerned with expanding the concept of deviance beyond the simple contravention of laws and norms to a position capable of encompassing activities and subjectivities that, through their engagement with the cultural values inscribed by consumer capitalism, have the potential to result in harm (Smith and Raymen, 2018). With its focus on the harm caused by activities like gambling or the transgressive excesses associated with the alcohol-based night time economy, deviant leisure clearly resonates with early cultural criminological research on the 'crime-consumerism nexus' (Hayward, 2004), but beyond that it also allows for a more thorough-going appraisal of how environmental harms are structurally embedded within many accepted forms of normalised behaviour. Environmental concerns are also evident in a second area of zemiological interest within cultural criminology. Developed by Avi Brisman and Nigel South, 'green cultural criminology' (2013) is a new approach based around three interrelated lines of cultural enquiry: the exploration of contestation and resistance to environmental harms; the analysis of media constructions and representations of environmental crime and harm; and the attention given to patterns of consumerism and their impact on the environment. For cultural criminology, these two new approaches are both

Knowledge link: This topic is also covered in Chapter 16.

extremely valuable when it comes to understanding how serious environmental crimes are made almost banal by the everyday patterns of life within consumer societies (Ilan, 2019).

Finally, a word about research methods and how cultural criminology's methodological toolkit might develop in the future. As mentioned earlier, cultural criminology is against the 'scientism' and obscurantism of much orthodox, empirical criminology. However, it is not against numbers per se. Nor does it reject the use of new technology for undertaking quantitative studies about crime and deviance (Hayward, 2016). On the contrary, given society's increasing dependence on technology, ignoring important developments in computational (Williams et al., 2017) and Big Data-era criminology (Chan and Bennett Moses, 2017; Smith et al., 2017) would be short-sighted indeed. It is therefore essential that cultural criminology continues to embrace new research methods of all stripes, including 'quali-quant' approaches capable of capturing and interpreting both aspects of the 'techno-social'. To some extent this process is already well underway, with cultural criminology's interest in spatio-statistical tools and alternative forms of digital mapping (Dorling, 1998) that, rather than simply documenting geographic or physical features, focus instead on the cartography of population flows, event 'moments', and even the psycho-geographic notion of 'affective landscapes' (Kindynis, 2014; 2019).

Elsewhere, other new developments such as the critical repurposing of forensic science techniques to help identify and interrupt state crimes and human rights violations (Weizman, 2014); the emergence of participatory action research and its association with new forms of critical pedagogy; and the ongoing use of innovative visual methods such as diary/autoethnographic photography and documentary criminology, all suggest that cultural criminology will continue to adapt and develop in pursuit of its goal of making criminology a more meaningful enterprise in a world shaped by meaning.

CHAPTER SUMMARY

This chapter has provided you with:

- an introduction to cultural criminology and the many exciting possibilities that exist when studying crime, deviance, and social control through the lens of culture. For a fuller understanding of the subject we urge you to explore the further readings (below) and the many references that accompany this chapter.
- a brief snapshot of some of cultural criminology's main features. We hope this has whetted your appetite, maybe even to the point where you might consider undertaking your own cultural criminological project. After all, as the authors of *Cultural Criminology: An Invitation* once stated – 'you've heard our story, now let's hear yours'.

Review Questions

1. Draw up a random list of crimes and identify the emotions that are integral to each. How does each crime differ in terms of its emotional dimensions?
2. What do you understand by the term 'the phenomenology of transgression'?
3. In what ways are the methods employed by cultural criminologists different from more mainstream criminological research?
4. Why do some of its critics claim that there is nothing inherently new about cultural criminology? How would cultural criminologists challenge such criticism?

GO FURTHER

Books

1. Replete with images and even a filmography, the following text is the most accessible and comprehensive introduction to cultural criminology. Suitable for both undergraduate and postgraduate students:

   Ferrell, J., Hayward, K. and Young, J. (2015) *Cultural Criminology: An Invitation.* London: Sage.

2. This classic work is not only a theoretical tour de force, but a foundational cultural criminological title on the phenomenological meanings and emotional motivations that drive criminality:

   Katz, J. (1988) *Seductions of Crime.* New York: Basic Books.

3. The first book to announce cultural criminology as a distinct criminological approach, this collection of essays on crime and culture includes chapters on criminal subcultures, media representations of crime, and various criminalised forms of music and style. It represents the early North American formulation of cultural criminology:

   Ferrell, J. and Sanders, J. (eds) (1995) *Cultural Criminology.* Boston: Northeastern University Press.

4. Our final recommendation is a definitive four-volume collection on cultural criminology. Eighty chapters are organised under the following subheadings: 'Precursor Resources', 'Core Readings', 'Key Themes', 'Research Methods and Critical Approaches', and 'New Directions':

   Hayward, K. J. (2018) *Cultural Criminology: Critical Assessments in Criminology.* London: Routledge (Major Works series).

Journal Articles

1. The following article provides compelling responses to some of the main criticisms of cultural criminology:

   Hayward, K. J. (2016) Cultural criminology: script rewrites, *Theoretical Criminology,* 20(3): 297–321. doi:10.1177/1362480615619668.

2. This paper considers how cultural criminology is being shaped by various (late modern) political and social developments and what this means for the project going forward:

   Ilan, J. (2019) Cultural criminology: the time is now. *Critical Crimiminology,* 27: 5–20. https://doi.org/10.1007/s10612-019-09430-2.

3. The following article serves as a useful introduction to cultural criminology's early ideas and in particular how cultural criminologists conduct fieldwork that is sensitive to other's actions and motivations:

   Ferrell, J. (1997) Criminological verstehen: inside the immediacy of crime. *Justice Quarterly,* 14(1): 3–23. doi: 10.1080/07418829700093201.

Useful Websites

1. The website of *Crime, Media and Culture: An International Journal.* Published three times a year, *Crime, Media, Culture* is a great place to access journal articles about cultural criminology and related subjects: https://journals.sagepub.com/home/cmc

2. You can access a number of key cultural criminology publications on this site hosted by the University of Kent, UK: https://blogs.kent.ac.uk/culturalcriminology/key-papers/
3. Carnivalesque Films, the website of filmmakers David Redmon and Ashley Sabin. Often inspired by the theories of cultural criminology, Redmon and Sabin's poignant documentaries tell stories about how disruption, celebration, excess, and transgression play out in everyday life: http://carnivalesquefilms.com/
4. A repository of criminological articles by the late Jock Young: http://www.malcolmread.com/JockYoung/

REFERENCES

Aiello, M. F. (2014) Policing the masculine frontier: cultural criminological analysis of the gendered performance of policing. *Crime, Media, Culture*, 10(1): 59 –79.

Altheide, D. (1996) *Qualitative Media Analysis*. Thousand Oaks, CA: Sage.

Bengtsson, T. (2012) Boredom and action: experiences from youth confinement. *Journal of Contemporary Ethnography*, 41(5): 526–553.

Braithwaite, J. (1989) *Crime, Shame and Reintegration*. Cambridge: University of Cambridge Press.

Brisman, A. and South, N. (2013) A green-cultural criminology: an exploratory outline. *Crime, Media, Culture*, 9(2): 115 –135.

Brotherton, D. (2004) 'What Happened to the Pathological Gang?'. In J. Ferrell et al. (eds), *Cultural Criminology Unleashed*. London: GlassHouse.

Brotherton, D. C. (2008) 'Beyond social reproduction: Bringing resistance back in gang theory'. *Theoretical Criminology*, 12(1): 55–77.

Burnap, P. and Williams, M. L. (2016) Us and them: identifying cyber hate on Twitter across multiple protected characteristics. *EPJ Data science*, 5(1): 11.

Cladeira, T. P. (2000) *City of Walls: Crime, Segregation, and Citizenship in São Paulo*. Berkeley: University of California Press.

Chan, J. and Bennett Moses, L. (2016) 'Is big data challenging criminology? *Theoretical Criminology*, 20(1): 21–39.

Cottee, S. and Hayward, K. J. (2011) Terrorist (e)motives: the existential attractions of terrorism. *Studies in Conflict and Terrorism*, 34(12): 963–986.

Danaher, J. (2018) The automation of policing: challenges and opportunities. Available at: https://philosophicaldisquisitions.blogspot.com/2018/10/the-automation-of-policing-challenges.html

De Haan, W. and Vos, J. (2003) A crying shame: the over-rationalized conception of man in the rational choice perspective. *Theoretical Criminology*, 7(1): 29–54.

Deflem, M. (2019) *The Handbook of Social Control*. Hoboken, NJ: John Wiley.

Dorling, D. (1998) Human cartography: when it is good to map. *Environment and Planning A*, 30(2): 277–288.

Fenwick, M. and Hayward, K. J. (2000) 'Youth Crime, Excitement and Consumer Culture. In J. Pickford (ed.), *Youth Justice*. London: Cavendish.

Ferrell, J. (1996) *Crimes of Style*. Boston: Northeastern University Press.

Ferrell, J. (1997) Criminological verstehen: inside the immediacy of crime, *Justice Quarterly*, 14(1): 3–23.

Ferrell, J. (2001) *Tearing Down the Streets*. New York: Palgrave.

Ferrell, J. (2004) Boredom, crime, and criminology. *Theoretical Criminology*, 8(3): 287–302.

Ferrell, J. (2018) Drift: Ilicit Mobility and Uncertain Knowledge, California University Press.

Ferrell J. and Hamm, M. S. (1998) *Ethnography at the Edge*. Boston: Northeastern University Press.

Ferrell, J. and Hayward, K. (2018) 'Cultural Criminology Continued'. In P. Carlen and L. Ayres França (eds), *Alternative Criminologies*. London: Routledge.

Ferrell, J., Hayward, K., Morrison, W. and Presdee, P. (2004) *Cultural Criminology Unleashed*. London: GlassHouse.

Ferrell, J., Hayward, K. and, Young, J. (2008/2015) *Cultural Criminology: An Invitation*. Los Angeles, CA: Sage.

Ferrell, J. and Ilan, J. (2013) 'Crime, Culture, and Everyday Life'. In C. Hale, K. Hayward, A. Wahidin and E. Wincup (eds), *Criminology*. Oxford: Oxford University Press.

Ferrell, J., Milovanovic, D. and Lyng, S. (2001) Edgework, media practices, and the elongation of meaning. *Theoretical Criminology*, 5(2): 177–202.

Ferrell, J. and Sanders, C. (1995) *Cultural Criminology*. Boston: Northeastern University Press.

Garland, D. (2001) *The Culture of Control*. Chicago: University of Chicago Press.

Gilbert, M. (2010) 'Theorizing digital and urban inequalities: critical geographies of "race", gender and technological capital', *Information, Communication, Society*, 13(7): 1000–1018.

Giddens, A. (1990) *The Consequences of Modernity*. Cambridge: Polity Press.

Goldsmith, A. and Brewer, R. (2015) Digital drift and the criminal interaction order. *Theoretical Criminology*, 19(1): 112–130.

Graham, S. (2011) *Cities Under Siege*. London: Verso Books.

Greenfield, A. (2017) *Radical Technologies*. London: Verso Books.

Hall, S. and Winlow, S. (2007) Cultural criminology and primitive accumulation. *Crime, Media, Culture*, 3(1): 82–90.

Harvey, D. (1990) *The Condition of Postmodernity*. London: Blackwell.

Harvey, D. (2007) A Brief History of Neoliberalism, Oxford: Oxford University Press.

Hayward, K. J. (2004) *City Limits*. London: GlassHouse.

Hayward, K. J. (2012) Five spaces of cultural criminology. *British Journal of Criminology*, 52(3): 441–462.

Hayward, K. J. (2016) 'Cultural criminology: script rewrites', *Theoretical Criminology*, 20(3): 297–321.

Hayward, K. J. (2018) 'Documentary criminology: a cultural criminological introduction'. In M. Brown and E. Carrabine (eds), *The Routledge International Handbook of Visual Criminology*. London: Routledge.

Hayward, K. J. (2020) 'Five Smart City Futures'. In M. Schuilenburg and R. Peeters (eds), *The Algorithmic Society*. London: Routledge.

Hayward, K. J. and Maas, M. M. (2020) Artificial intelligence and crime: a primer for criminologists. *Crime, Media, Culture*, 1741659020917434.

Hayward, K. J. and Presdee, M. (2010) *Framing Crime: Cultural Criminology and the Image*. London: Routledge.

Hayward, K. J. and Schuilenburg, M. (2014) To resist = to create? Some thoughts on the concept of resistance in cultural criminology. *Tijdschrift over Cultuur and Criminaliteit*, 4(1): 22–36.

Hayward, K. J. and Smith, O. (2017) 'Crime and Consumer Culture'. In *The Oxford Handbook of Criminology*, pp. 306–328. Oxford: Oxford University Press.

Hayward, K. J. and Turner, T. (2019) '"Be More VIP": Deviant Leisure and Hedonistic Excess in Ibiza's "Disneyized" Party Spaces'. In T. Rayment and O. Smith (eds), *Deviant Leisure*. London: Palgrave Macmillan.

Hayward, K. J. and Young, J. (2004) Cultural criminology: some notes on the script. *Theoretical Criminology*, 8(3): 259–273.

Hayward, K. J. and Young, J. (2012) 'Cultural Criminology'. In M. Maguire, R. Morgan and R. Reiner (eds), *The Oxford Handbook of Criminology*. Oxford: Oxford University Press.

Hollands, R. (2015) Critical interventions into the corporate smart city. *Cambridge Journal of Regions, Economy and Society*, 8(1): 61–77.

Ilan, J. (2019) Cultural criminology: the time is now. *Critical Criminology*, 27(1): 5–20.

Jackson-Jacobs, C. (2004) 'Taking a beating: the narrative gratifications of fighting as an underdog'. In J. Ferrell, K. J. Hayward, W. Morrison and M. Presdee (eds), *Cultural Criminology Unleashed*, London: Cavendish.

Jewkes, Y. (2017) *Media and Crime*. London: Sage.

Katz, J. (1988) *Seductions of Crime*. New York: Basic Books.

Khaled Jr, S. H. (2018) Crime e Castigo. Ensaios de Resistência, Controle Social e Criminologia Cultural, Belo Horizonte: Letramento.

Khaled, J. R. S. H., Oxley Da Rocha, A. and Baziewicz, G. (2020) Votando com armas nas eleições presidenciais brasileiras de 2018: a vontade de representação e a transgressão como performance repleta de significado na modernidade tardia. *Revista de Direitos e Garantias Fundamentais*, 22(1).

Kindynis, T. (2014) Ripping up the map: criminology and cartography revisited. *British Journal of Criminology*, 54(2): 222–243.

Kindynis, T. (2016) Urban exploration: from subterranea to spectacle, *British Journal of Criminology*, 57(4): 982–1001.

Kindynis, T. (2019) Persuasion architectures: consumer spaces, affective engineering and (criminal) harm. *Theoretical Criminology*. ISSN 1362–4806.

Kitchin, R. (2014) The real-time city? Big data and smart urbanism. *GeoJournal*, 79(1): 1–14.

Klein, J. R. (2011) Toward a cultural criminology of war. *Social Justice*, 38(3): 86–103.

Krivý, M. (2018) 'Towards a critique of cybernetic urbanism: the smart city and the society of control', *Planning Theory*, 17(1): 8–30.

Linnemann, T. (2016) Proof of death: police power and the visual economies of seizure, accumulation and trophy. *Theoretical Criminology*, 21(1): 57–77.

Linnemann, T., Wall, T. and Green, E. (2014) The walking dead and the killing state: zombification and the normalization of police violence. *Theoretical Criminology*, 18(4): 506–527.

Lois, J. (2005) 'Gender and Emotion Management in the Stages of Edgework'. In S. Lyng (ed.), *Edgework*. New York: Routledge.

Lyng, S. (1990) Edgework: a social psychological analysis of voluntary risk-taking. *American Journal of Sociology*, 95(4): 876–921.

Lyng, S. (2005) *Edgework: The Sociology of Risk-taking*. New York: Routledge.

Magnet, S. (2011) *When Biometrics Fail: Gender, Race, & the Technology of Identity*, Durham: Duke University Press.

Matallana-Villarreal, J. (2017) *Countermapping state crime: A cultural criminological exploration of arbitrary conscription in Bogotá*. Doctoral dissertation, University of Kent/ELTE University.

Matallana-Villarreal, J. (2020) Conscription or constriction? Military policing of urban youth. *Environment and Planning D: Society and Space*, 38(3): 453–471.

Matthews, R. (2014) *Realist Criminology*. London: Palgrave-Macmillan.

McClanahan, B (2021) Visual Criminology, Bristol: Bristol University Press.

Michel, A. H. (2019) *Eyes in the Sky*. Boston, MA: HMH Books.

Miller, J. (1995) 'Struggles over the symbolic: gang style and the meanings of social control'. In J. Ferrell and C. Sanders (eds), *Cultural Criminology*, Boston: Northeastern University Press.

Morrison, W. (1995) *Theoretical Criminology*. London: Cavendish.

Morrison, W. (2006) *Criminology, Civilization and the New World Order*. London: GlassHouse.

Naegler L. and Salman, S. (2016) 'Cultural Criminology and Gender Consciousness: Moving Feminist Theory From Margin to Center'. *Feminist Criminology*. 11(4): 354–374.

Nightingale, C. (1993) *On the Edge*. New York: Basic Books.

O'Brien, M. (2005) What is cultural about cultural criminology? *British Journal of Criminology*, 45(5): 599–612.

O'Neill, M. (2010) Cultural criminology and sex work. *Journal of Law and Society*, 37(1): 210–232.

Pauschinger, D. (2020) Working at the edge: police, emotions and space in Rio de Janeiro. *Environment and Planning D: Society and Space*, 38(3): 510–527.

Powell, A., Stratton G. and Cameron, R. (2018) *Digital Criminology*. London: Routledge.

Presdee, M. (2000) *Cultural Criminology and the Carnival of Crime*. London: Routledge.

Presdee, M. (2004) 'The Story of Crime: Biography and the Excavation of Transgression'. In J. Ferrell, K. Hayward, W. Morrison et al. (eds), *Cultural Criminology Unleashed*. London: Cavendish.

Rajah, V. (2007) Resistance as edgework in violent intimate relationships of drug-involved women. *British Journal of Criminology*, 47(2): 196–213.

Redmon, D. (2015) Documentary criminology: expanding the criminological imagination with 'Mardis Gras – Made in China' as a case study. *Societies*, 5(2): 425–441.

Sadowski, J. (2019) 'The captured city: the "smart city" makes infrastructure and surveillance indistinguishable', realifemag.com, 12 November.

Schuilenburg, M. and Pali, B. (2019) Fear and fantasy in the smart city. *Critical Criminology*, https://doi.org/10.1007/s10612-019-09447-7

Smith, G. J. D., Bennett Moses, L. and Chan, J. (2017) The challenges of doing criminology in the Big Data era: towards a digital and data-driven approach. *British Journal of Criminology*, 57: 259–274.

Smith, G. J. D. and O'Malley, P. (2017) Driving politics: data-driven governance and resistance. *British Journal of Criminology*, 57(2): 275–298.

Smith, G. and O'Malley, P. (2020) ''Smart' crime prevention?: digitization and racialized crime control in a smart city', *Theoretical Criminology*, November 2020. doi:10.1177/1362480620972703

Smith, O. and Raymen, T. (2018) Deviant leisure: a criminological perspective. *Theoretical Criminology*, 22(1): 63–82.

Steinmetz, K. F. (2015) Craft(y)ness: an ethnographic study of hacking. *British Journal of Criminology*, 55(1): 125–145.

Steinmetz, K. F. and Nobles, M. R. (2017) *Technocrime and Criminological Theory*. New York: Routledge.

Stratton, G., Powell, A. and Cameron, R. (2017) Crime and justice in digital society: towards a 'Digital Criminology'? *International Journal for Crime, Justice and Social Democracy*, 6(2): 17–33.

Tauri, J. M. (2013) 'Indigenous Critique of Authoritarian Criminology'. In K. Carrington et al. (eds), *Crime, Justice and Social Democracy* (pp. 217–233). London: Palgrave Macmillan.

Van Hellemont, E. (2012) "Gangland Online: Performing the Real Imaginary World of Gangstas and Ghettos in Brussels", *European Journal of Crime, Criminal Law and Criminal Justice*, 20(2): pp. 165–180.

Wall, T. and Linnemann, T. (2014) 'Accumulating atrocities: Capital, State Killing and the Cultural Life of the Dead'. In D. Roethe and D. Kauzlarich (eds), *Towards a Victimology of State Crime*. New York: Routledge.

Weizman, E. (2014) 'Introduction: Forensis'. In *Forensis: The Architecture of Public Truth*, pp. 9–32. Berlin: Sternberg Press.

Wender, J. (2008) *Policing and the Politics of Everyday Life*. Champaign: University of Illinois Press.

Williams, M. L., Burnap, P. and Sloan, L. (2017) *Crime sensing with big data: The affordances and limitations of using open-source communications to estimate crime patterns. The British Journal of Criminology*, 57(2): pp. 320–340.

Winlow, S. and Hall, S. (2012) What is an "ethics committee"? *British Journal of Criminology*, 52(2): 400–416.

Worthen, M. and Abby Baker, S. (2016) 'Pushing up the glass ceiling of female muscularity: women's bodybuilding as edgework', *Deviant Behavior*, 37(5): 471–495.

Yar, M. (2005) The global 'epidemic' of movie 'piracy': crime-wave or social construction? *Media, Culture & Society*, 27(5): 677–696.

Yar, M. (2006) *Cybercrime and Society*. London: Sage.

Yar, M. (2012) Crime, media and the will to representation. *Crime, Media, Culture*, 8(3): 245–260.

Yar, M. (2017) 'Toward a Cultural Criminology of the Internet'. In K. F. Steinmetz and M. R. Nobles (eds), *Technocrime and Criminological Theory* (pp. 132–148). New York: Routledge.

Young, A. (2009) *The Scene of Violence*. London: Routledge.

Young, A. (2010) 'The Scene of the Crime: Is There Such a Thing as Just Looking?'. In K. Hayward and M. Presdee (eds), *Framing Crime*. London: GlassHouse.

Young, J. (1999) *The Exclusive Society*. London: Sage.

Young, J. (2003) Merton with energy, Katz with structure: the sociology of vindictiveness and the criminology of transgression. *Theoretical Criminology*, 7(3): 389–414.

Young, J. (2007) *The Vertigo of Late Modernity*. London: Sage.

Young, J. (2011) *The Criminological Imagination*. Cambridge: Polity Press.

Zedner, L. (2009) *Security*. London: Routledge.

Southern and Comparative Criminology

11

Max Travers

--------- Learning Objectives ---------

By the end of this chapter you will:

- Understand the development of comparative criminology since the nineteenth century, and the emergence of Southern Criminology as a contemporary approach.
- Be able to summarise and discuss the key concepts in Southern Criminology.
- Be able to apply the approach to criminological topics, such as violence against women and imprisonment.
- Understand criticisms by those contributing to this emerging field.

--------- Framing Questions ---------

1. Why is it important to understand crime and criminal justice comparatively?
2. How is Southern Criminology a critical perspective?
3. How are cultural differences important in understanding responses to crime?
4. What do you understand by the 'crimes' of colonialism? Why should these interest criminologists?

INTRODUCTION

When you study subjects such as criminology and sociology, it is understandable to focus on problems in your own country, such as poverty or crime. But even if you are half-aware of international events, you will know there are much greater economic problems, and more disturbing conflicts, in many countries. To give one example, at the time of writing, thousands of students are protesting on the streets in Hong Kong. Some students have been arrested for unlawful conduct and may spend several years in prison. Whatever you feel about this political issue, it suggests the need for thinking about criminal justice in broader comparative terms.

The aim of this chapter is to introduce you to a relatively well-established field of comparative criminology though one that is still marginal in undergraduate criminology teaching (Nelken, 2010; Pakes, 2015), and the emerging field of Southern Criminology (Carrington et al., 2016; 2018; 2019). The connection between the two is that Southern Criminology as a critical theory is strongly opposed to some varieties of comparative criminology, and yet Southern Criminology has been criticised for not being sufficiently radical.

There are three significant challenges for you as criminology students, and for us as teachers, when engaging with these approaches. The first is that it is difficult to overcome **ethnocentrism**, and develop a comparative outlook. Ethnocentrism is the tendency to assess other cultures using values and standards in your own society. The second is that these are complex interdisciplinary fields. The third is that Southern Criminology is a critical theory, meaning that it seeks to challenge received views about crime. For the most part criminology has focused on, and you will have been taught to view crime, in terms of individual offences that harm fellow citizens. Whereas Southern criminologists argue that developed nations, including the United Kingdom, committed war crimes while acquiring overseas colonies.

My approach in teaching criminology, and the approach adopted in this chapter, is to encourage you to engage with debates, rather than asking you to accept a conservative or critical orthodoxy. This short introduction to this field starts with an overview of the intellectual terrain, and then seeks to explain key ideas and applications. I start with a brief review of comparative criminology, using studies about the Netherlands and Italy as my main examples. I have given most space to Southern Criminology, a new sub-field of comparative criminology.

MAPPING THE TERRAIN

It is important that you get a sense of the field as a whole before looking at particular traditions. You may find this challenging, since the terrain in comparative criminology (sometimes called international criminology) is quite complex.

The comparative tradition that still has most influence in teaching programmes today, especially in the USA, is **modernisation theory**. This theoretical tradition in sociology believes that the whole world must develop like industrialised, Western societies (Shahidullah, 2014). Modernisation theorists have been unashamedly positive about globalisation and development. They see the USA as the most advanced society in the world and believe that other countries will eventually become industrialised, urbanised societies, based on **individualism** as a central value, as they develop and modernise.

Comparative criminology is also a scientific endeavour conducted by quantitative and qualitative researchers. The quantitative tradition originates in the methodology developed by Emile Durkheim to investigate the causes of suicide in late nineteenth century Europe. Durkheim (1895/2006) pioneered the use of statistical measures to compare suicide rates. He also sought to develop a scientific theory to explain variations. The objective of anthropological and qualitative research is to appreciate and understand cultural differences. Researchers have achieved some comparative insight through obtaining policy documents, interviewing informants and observing legal practices in other countries.

A recent addition to comparative criminology is **transnational crime**. Transnational crime is an attempt to refashion criminology in an age of globalisation (Aas, 2013). Globalisation is the process through which the world is becoming more interconnected economically and through the mass media. Instead of examining crime and criminal justice inside nation states, researchers in transnational crime examine global processes. Examples are crimes by corporations and states, international organised crime, and people trafficking.

Southern Criminology (Carrington et al., 2018) is theoretically distinctive in being explicitly opposed to modernisation theory, placing more emphasis on cultural and **epistemological** differences, and viewing the treatment of **Indigenous peoples** by developed countries as crimes. Raewyn Connell (2005) has advanced these ideas forcefully (see 'Hear from the Expert' below).

There have been several intellectual influences on Southern Criminology from **postcolonial theory**. Older influences include the African postcolonial writer Franz Fanon (1952). Recent influences include Boaventura de Sousa Santos (2016), a theorist from Brazil, who used the terms Global North and Global South to describe postcolonial relations.

Although this is a fragmented field, there are many points of contact and room for cross-fertilisation between different traditions. Comparative criminologists, and Southern criminologists, are each opposed to ethnocentric, national research, and recognise the importance of globalisation.

Knowledge link: This topic is also covered in Chapter 15.

Knowledge link: These topics are also covered in Part 3.

———— Hear from the Expert ————

Raewyn Connell and Southern Theory

Raewyn Connell is Professor Emerita at the University of Sydney. She is well known for her work on class divisions in education, and for problematising gender relations. In recent years, she has advanced a case for a radical rethinking of social science developed in the Global North:

> Metropolitan social theory comfortably talks about the constitution of society, about the building blocks of social processes, and about the reproduction of social structures. It has been much less keen – and perhaps lacks the concepts – to talk about the destruction of social relations, about discontinuity and dispossession, about the bloodshed and suffering in creating the world in which we currently live. (Connell, 2007: 215)

Researchers around the world use metropolitan ideas, without considering alternative perspectives. Connell reviews thinkers from the South, for example Africa and Latin America, who offer a different way of thinking about modernisation and knowledge.

COMPARATIVE CRIMINAL JUSTICE

After mapping out the field, we will now turn to an area of comparative research that has seen some contributions by British criminologists: differences in imprisonment rates in Western societies. There have been attempts to explain statistical variation for youth and adult imprisonment in relation to institutional cultures (see for example, Muncie and Goldson, 2006).

The comparative statistics collected by international organisations are certainly interesting. The USA has a very high imprisonment rate compared to those of European countries. Within Europe, Britain has a higher imprisonment rate compared to that of France or Italy. The Scandinavian countries and the Netherlands have much smaller prison populations (World Prison Brief, 2019). How can these differences be explained?

An approach pursued by the British criminologist David Nelken (2010) is influenced by anthropology. The aim of the comparativist should be to understand cultural differences, preferably by spending a long time in a different country. Nelken has worked for some years in Italy. This has enabled him to appreciate that the criminal justice process is much slower than in the United Kingdom. From a British perspective, we might view this as a problem through employing our own criteria of fairness to defendants and victims of crime. But this is ethnocentrism. In Italy, slow justice is seen as positive: it makes possible reconciliation and social healing through informal processes. There have also been attempts to explain the low imprisonment rate in the Netherlands compared to the United Kingdom (see Case Study 11.1).

Case Study 11.1

Falling Imprisonment in the Netherlands

According to World Prison Brief (2019), the number of prisoners in the Netherlands fell from 20,436 in 2010 to 10,102 in 2016. The rate of imprisonment is currently 59 prisoners per 100,000 people. By contrast, the United Kingdom has 82,617 prisoners. This is a rate of 139 per 100,000. These countries are geographically close and have similar legal and political systems. Yet the United Kingdom imprisons two-thirds more people than the Netherlands.

The challenge for the comparativist is to explain such differences. Commentators on the Netherlands point to a relaxation of drug laws, a greater emphasis on rehabilitation, and a willingness to use electronic monitoring as an alternative to prison (Smith, 2018).

Pause for Thought

- How would you design a research project that investigates a stage of the criminal justice process in two European countries?
- How would your project employ quantitative and qualitative methods?

SOUTHERN CRIMINOLOGY: MAIN IDEAS

Southern Criminology offers a deliberately provocative mix of comparative criminology and critical theory. I will explain the main ideas under the following headings: geographical terms; cognitive justice; and crimes of colonialism. Then I will look at two applications: violence, gender and the Global South; and Southern penalties. I will conclude with a summary of some criticisms and responses.

Geographical Terms

The first step towards understanding Southern Criminology as a theoretical approach is to consider how it uses the geographical terms North and South. There is an older postcolonial literature that contrasts Western developed countries with their colonies in the East. Western countries, including Britain, France and Germany, acquired colonies in Africa and Asia from the sixteenth century. Many colonies achieved independence in the mid-twentieth century, particularly when European powers were weakened by two world wars. Independence movements and postcolonial theorists have argued that having a low standard of living results from economic exploitation over a long period.

The Brandt Report (1980) provided a different terminology. It divided the world into developed and developing countries. Developing countries were in the Global South, although placing the line somewhat above the equator, and then making some rather imaginative adjustments, allowed the report to recognise both Japan and Australia as developed countries. The world according to Southern Criminology is different again. It places Australia in the South, as an ex-colony. This might seem strange, since most Australians enjoy a high standard of living. We will consider this criticism later in the chapter. In addition, it is not always clear how Southern Criminology classifies countries that have rapidly developed since the 1970s. China (an economic superpower) is located in the North, but often describes itself as a developing country. India and Brazil, located in the South, have rapidly industrialised.

Anticipating such criticisms, those promoting Southern Criminology have argued that it has most value as an analytic tool that identifies relations of economic dominance. This has some similarities to **Dependency Theory** that explained global inequalities during the 1960s through unequal trade relationships and exploitative investments. There can be developed regions in the South, and developing regions in the North. Despite these apparent inconsistencies in employing geographical terms, Southern Criminology is helpful in making visible global economic inequalities.

Cognitive Justice

The geographical terms used by Southern Criminology ask us to consider economic inequalities. Yet this is only one aspect of inequality. The term 'cognitive justice' was coined by Boaventura de Sousa Santos (2016). He argues that, in addition to achieving economic justice (equal treatment in the world economy), those living in the South should also campaign for recognition of their distinctive cultures and values.

The importance of cognitive justice is perhaps most clearly expressed by Franz Fanon (1952) in a powerful critique of the psychological effects of colonialism. Fanon argues that colonialism involves not only economic exploitation but also cultural dispossession. Worse, those colonised come to accept the culture and way of life of the colonising power as superior, and to see themselves as backward in comparison. Elites send their children to study in metropolitan countries, appreciate Western art and music, and forget their own cultures. This also applies to academic disciplines. It is assumed that ideas from the North have universal relevance. Criminologists from countries in the South are expected to learn about theory and methods through postgraduate study in Northern universities. The best journals, although they claim to produce universal knowledge, publish articles about a few metropolitan countries.

There is, however, more political bite to this cognitive critique than simply appreciating diversity. Firstly, it is suggested by de Sousa Santos that the Northern bias in criminological research arises from a power imbalance. Secondly, it is implied and sometimes explicitly suggested, that there are knowledges, values and ways of life in the South that are opposed to modernisation. Connell (2007) argues that Indigenous peoples, who suffered most harm from colonisation, have collective rather than individualist values. De Sousa Santos (2016) sees rural communities across the South as having greater ecological awareness than those of us living in Northern industrialised societies.

In discussing these differences in relation to Asia, it is difficult not to revert to East/West as a contrast device. Here, it is interesting to report on experiences from attending conferences of the Asian Criminological Society. Many Asian criminologists have studied on postgraduate programmes in the

USA. They have learnt universal theories, and returned home to test these in their own countries. Yet some researchers have been surprised to find that the concepts do not seem to explain criminal behaviour in Asia (see Case Study 11.2). This suggests the need for Asian criminologists to develop new theories and concepts that recognise collective social values (Liu et al., 2017).

Case Study 11.2

Is Crime Different in Asia?

A postgraduate student from South Korea who was studying in the USA reported how he found American behaviour quite strange. This cross-cultural observation points to an underlying difference between individualistic and collectivist values. There may also be a related difference between criminal justice systems. There seems to be a reluctance to use the formal legal system in Asian countries. Instead, informal procedures are employed to resolve disputes within families and communities (Yun, 2008).

Pause for Thought

- What do you understand by the term 'cognitive justice' in relation to criminology as an academic discipline?
- Why is it important to represent different viewpoints in what are currently recognised as the best journals?

Crimes of Colonialism

Raewyn Connell (2007) has perhaps done most to advance a postcolonial viewpoint in recent years (see 'Hear from the Expert' above). Yet she has been accused of engaging in a 'sociological guilt trip' by a distinguished American sociologist (Collins, 1997). This critic may have meant that there is no point dwelling on the wrongs of the past if they cannot be remedied. Nevertheless, exposing or remembering the wrongs of the past is central to Southern Criminology. Let me give two examples that illustrate how Southern criminologists think about such issues.

The first example is from Australia, a country in which the Indigenous inhabitants, Aborigines and Torres Strait islanders, were dispossessed after European settlement. Many died from imported diseases, and others were massacred by European settlers. Today, numbers have increased. However, in many parts of Australia Aborigines are living in remote settlements with low standards of health and education. In recent times, the government imposed martial law to address high levels of child abuse (Cunneen, 2018).

In my own state of Tasmania, the history is even more distressing. There was a genocide that wiped out almost the entire Indigenous population. When the British colonised Tasmania in the early nineteenth century, there was resistance from Indigenous nations (Ryan, 2012). This led to the Black Wars in which two thirds of the estimated 6,000 population were killed, and many also died through influenza. Eventually, a small number were put on a reservation by benevolent British authorities to protect them from extinction. Today, only a few descendants remain. Sometimes they make the international news in their campaigns to repatriate remains from British museums.

The second example is from the United Kingdom. This country was responsible for the dispossession of Indigenous peoples in Australia, although cannot be blamed for subsequent ill-treatment after independence. The UK was also the largest participant in the slave trade from the sixteenth to the eighteenth century, in which African slaves, purchased with British manufactured goods, were shipped to work in plantations in the Caribbean and South America (Yorke, 2017). By the 1790s, 480,000 people were enslaved in the British Colonies. Many of the forced migrants died in the holds of ships. In America, families were broken up when they were sold at auction. Freed after the civil war (1861–1865), black Americans remain economically disadvantaged and subject to racism and discrimination. In 2007, the British Prime Minister Tony Blair expressed 'deep sorrow' for Britain's role, although he did not offer a full apology or financial compensation.

Although some would argue that the normal rules of civilised conduct do not apply in wars, most jurists would agree that these are crimes against humanity. The slave trade and mass murders committed by states continue today. Should we recognise these as crimes? On any moral compass, they might seem worthy of more attention than the minor offences that come before national criminal courts. The crimes took place in plain sight. Slaves were traded from commercial buildings, since converted into shops and cafes in the city centres of Liverpool, Bristol and Glasgow. The Wills Memorial Library in Bristol University is an example (see Case Study 11.3). Southern criminologists argue that they should be viewed as 'crime scenes', or at least that we should acknowledge this dark part of our history.

Case Study 11.3

A 'Crime Scene' in a British University?

Some readers studying at Bristol University may have their graduation ceremony in the Wills Memorial Tower, a central historic part of the campus. Yet in 2017 there was a campaign to rename the building, because it is named after Henry Overton Wills III. He was the founding Chancellor of the university, but had also made his fortune out of African slaves working in the tobacco plantations in the Caribbean. Wills could not even claim that slavery was viewed as normal at the time. Critics claim that his family continued to import slave-grown tobacco from American plantations up until the American Civil War in 1865 – more than three decades after slavery was abolished under the 1833 Abolition Act (Yorke, 2017).

Bristol university listened sympathetically to the objections, but decided to keep the name (Yorke, 2017).

Pause for Thought

Can historical wrongs justify crime?

There is a further aspect to this critique of colonialism that is equally contentious. This is the argument that crimes committed by ethnic groups today can be explained or excused by the historical offences committed against them. Southern criminologists have noted that levels of violent crime in the USA are highest among black people who have experienced economic disadvantage and discrimination (Carrington et al., 2018, ch. 2). From this perspective, their geographical location in Southern cities is not accidental. One could argue that this reflects both discrimination towards them by law enforcement agencies and social disintegration following transportation.

APPLYING SOUTHERN CRIMINOLOGY

Having mastered the main ideas, you may be wondering how Southern Criminology can be applied to conventional topics in criminology. It is worth giving a short summary of two thematic discussions. First, I consider gendered violence and this is followed by a discussion about Southern penalties.

Violence, Gender and the Global South

Criminology as a discipline is concerned with crime and disorder in modern, industrialised societies, and state responses to these problems. Yet these are peaceful and orderly compared with most developing countries that do not have strong states (Carrington et al., 2019: 32).

Southern Criminology sees colonisation and its aftermath ('coloniality') as responsible for violence. Firstly, theorists argue that the most destructive forms of violence, civil wars and ethnic cleansing, are caused by colonisation and the decolonisation process. Secondly, poverty and inequality cause violence. To give one example, 'of the 50 most violent cities in the world, 46 are in the Global South and only four are in the Global North' (Carrington et al., 2019: 35). Thirdly, levels of violence against women are considerably higher in Southern countries.

An example is the Mexican side of the border with the USA in which there have been mass disappearances of women. Campaigners have suggested that these killings were perpetrated by male workers at risk of losing their jobs. Such crimes are also made possible by 'machismo', an aggressive form of masculinity that celebrates violence. Southern criminologists believe that violence against women partly arises as a product of colonisation:

> The coloniality of power has arguably had a role in the making of these very violent border masculinities. Beneath the cultural representation of machismo resides an inferiority, a vulnerability, an imperfection that is magically cast aside by the exaggeration of a gun-toting manliness. (Carrington et al., 2019: 44)

Violence against women is a complex, multi-faceted issue in which it is difficult to establish an effective national or international response. Universal concepts such as patriarchy are good at explaining the experiences of women in modern, industrialised societies. But Southern criminologists argue that these concepts are inadequate:

> this body of knowledge also needs to broaden its conceptual and spatial horizons by globalizing research agendas to add voices from the Global South. (Carrington et al., 2019: 40)

—————————————————— Pause for Thought ——————————————————

- Are high levels of violence in Southern countries caused by historical experiences of dispossession?
- How would a modernisation theorist respond to this argument?

Southern Penalties

The second example, I have chosen to illustrate how Southern Criminology makes us think differently about crime and criminal justice as imprisonment (Carrington et al., 2019: ch. 4). Textbooks given to students in the United Kingdom present a familiar narrative of modernisation, advanced most recently by Michel Foucault (1975/1991). This theorist argued that wrongdoers were tortured and executed during the Middle Ages but today they are confined in prisons. Yet this historical narrative may only tell half the story of punishment. For one thing, the dominant type of punishment for colonial powers was **transportation**. The convicts sent to Australia were flogged (a form of torture) but given their freedom quite quickly, and even became model citizens, challenging assumptions about crime and punishment. Carrington et al. (2019: ch. 4) have also drawn attention to parallels with immigration detention today (what some term 'crimigration'). They argue that the objective of each form of border regulation is to maintain or defend white populations.

An emphasis on detention rates can be misleading in other ways. It is often assumed by comparative researchers in the critical tradition that imprisonment is growing worldwide, and this is caused by **neoliberalism** (Wacquant, 2009). Neoliberalism is a set of policies through which governments reduce state regulation over market forces in an attempt to stimulate economic growth. In the USA, the policy has resulted in high unemployment and the expansion of prisons, yet there are problems in applying this argument to the South. For one thing, there are lower imprisonment rates in the Pacific Islands, in the Torres Strait islands in Australia, and in many East Asian countries. In these countries, **restorative justice**, in which offenders apologise to victims, has been widely practised as a means of diverting people from prisons.

These two examples illustrate that conventional topics in criminology, as addressed in this book, are mostly concerned with a limited number of Northern countries. They will make you think critically about a subject that claims to have found universal truths about crime and criminal justice.

CRITICISMS AND RESPONSES

After reviewing the main ideas in Southern Criminology, I will consider two criticisms. The first is that Southern Criminology does not go far enough in recognising epistemological differences. The second is that it advances too positive a view of the pre-modern world.

Does Southern Criminology Go Far Enough?

Southern Criminology champions marginal voices from the South, and repeatedly charges colonial powers with committing crimes against humanity. Nevertheless, like any leftist position it has been criticised by those who see themselves as further to the left. This is because theoretical statements have rather cleverly presented the approach as not fundamentally challenging criminology. A statement published in the British Journal of Criminology (Carrington et al., 2016) suggested that Southern Criminology was simply an addition to 'the criminological tool box'. This paper also distanced the approach from those claiming there are fundamental epistemological differences between North and South. This has made the approach seem less threatening, and may even explain why the statement was accepted in this mainstream journal. But it has made it possible for critics to identify what they see as compromises, and to engage in identity politics.

Although this is a complex literature, I will distinguish between three related arguments. The first advanced by Mark Brown (2018) in relation to Southern India is that Southern Criminology may become a means of disseminating metropolitan ideas and approaches rather than transforming the discipline (see 'Hear from the Expert' below). What though does Brown mean by transformation? Although this is not explained with examples, he is talking about epistemological differences. He believes that there is a different way of thinking about crime and criminal justice in the subcontinent, and perhaps even of 'being human' (Brown, 2018: 102).

─────── # Hear from the Expert ───────

Mark Brown on Southern Epistemologies

What I have attempted to do … is to set out at least the contours of a solution to the key epistemological threat facing Southern criminology: that it will simply replicate metropolitan approaches, making it little more than a branch office of the metropolitan master discipline. What this would demand of Southern criminology is a quite new epistemological and thus methodological approach, although without necessarily discarding all that has gone before.

(*Source*: Brown, M. (2018) 'Southern Criminology in the Post-colony: More than a "Derivative Discourse"?'. In K. Carrington, R. Hogg, J. Scott and M. Sozzo (eds), *The Palgrave Handbook of Criminology and the Global South* (p. 100). Reprinted by permission of Springer Nature.)

A related criticism is that Southern Criminology is rather timid or modest politically. It is good at discussing the crimes of the past, but does not sufficiently campaign against the wrongs of the present. Chris Cunneen (2018: 32) argues that respecting and acknowledging the culture of Indigenous peoples is important. However, there also needs to be political action that gives 'genuine self-governance based on Indigenous laws and values' (see 'Hear from the Expert' below).

─────── # Hear from the Expert ───────

Chris Cunneen on Indigenous Demands

Indigenous demands place criminology (in all its variations) inextricably within a political paradigm … It is inconceivable that criminological research involving Indigenous people can be anything but political because it must take a position. Either it supports the principles of Indigenous rights … or it fundamentally ignores Indigenous political aspirations.

(*Source*: Cunneen, C. (2018) 'Indigenous Challenges for Southern Criminology'. In K. Carrington, R. Hogg, J. Scott and M. Sozzo (eds), *The Palgrave Handbook of Criminology and the Global South* (p. 35). Reprinted by permission of Springer Nature.)

A third related criticism is that Southern Criminology does not go far enough because the main proponents are from metropolitan countries. Leon Moosavi (2019) has noted that, in Carrington et al. (2018), many of the chapters are by Australian authors. Since Australia is one of the most affluent countries in the world, perhaps the Brandt Report (1980) was right to assign it to the global North. There are, however, two reasons why Australia should, arguably, be considered part of the South. The first is that it is an ex-colony, founded by transported convicts. Australian intellectuals, like Connell (2007), even though they are mainly white, suffer from a similar inferiority complex in relation to metropolitan theories as intellectuals (Fanon, 1952) in black African countries. The second is that Australia is a country in which Indigenous peoples have been dispossessed. This is why white, privileged Australians have taken a lead in writing about these issues, as part of a larger postcolonial movement.

You may have noticed that Southern Criminology cannot please everyone! It is too tame politically for some internal critics, but sympathetic outsiders ask difficult questions about central assumptions. You should try to engage with these debates, and form your own view about this emerging field.

--------- Pause for Thought ---------

- What do you understand by the criticism that Southern Criminology should do more in campaigning against the wrongs of colonialism?
- Should academics get involved in political struggles?

Is Southern Criminology based on Romanticism?

The Romantic movement was a critical response to industrialisation associated with artists and poets, and has influenced many intellectuals. Those influenced by **Romanticism** tend to forget that people lived shorter lives without modern medicine, or the services provided by the state, including the criminal justice system. They have a nostalgic, idealised view of the pre-modern world.

Anticipating this criticism, Southern criminologists have attempted to distance themselves about claims to epistemological difference, and certainly the moral superiority of Southern cultures. Nevertheless, it is difficult to remove or downplay these ideas and maintain a distance from mainstream criminology. There are two critical issues that need discussion. The first is whether there are fundamental differences in epistemology and culture, or aspirations for a different way of life, between North and South. Many people living in traditional societies aspire to the standard of living enjoyed by those in industrialised countries, especially the USA. Those studying criminology are actively looking for ideas, models and methods from Northern countries (Brown, 2018).

The second more philosophically challenging issue is whether one would wish to live in a traditional society, once the rose-tinted spectacles are removed. Is this a price you might wish to pay for living in harmony with the environment? Indigenous communities, and arguably powerful states such as China, have no place for individuals or democracy. This is why protests by students in Hong Kong, influenced by Western values, are criminalised. Is this a price you might wish to pay for a reduction in crime? To give an example, despite the aspiration of de Sousa Santos (2016) to build an international progressive coalition, there is still considerable prejudice in many traditional societies against sexual freedom, including homosexuality.

FUTURE DIRECTIONS

Thinking about the criminological traditions reviewed in this chapter leads into difficult questions to which there are no clear cut answers. Comparative criminology invites reflection about the relationship between quantitative and qualitative methods, and the nature of comparison (Nelken, 2010; Pakes, 2015). Southern Criminology makes us think about the nature of crime, globalisation and even future directions for the modern world (Carrington et al., 2018).

The two perspectives raise difficult questions about how to conduct research outside your own country, and how to teach criminology both in Northern countries and across the world. In terms of research, it has always been difficult to conduct international research for both financial and practical reasons. Ideally, you have to visit one or more countries for extended periods, working with local researchers. There is, however, some scope for armchair research, especially in the internet age. In addition, it is possible to address comparative questions through attending meetings and events (Merry, 2016; Liu et al., 2017).

In terms of pedagogy, there are also challenges. At present, most textbooks in Britain have a national focus. In the USA, comparative criminology is taught in some criminology and law programmes, but is still informed unreflectively by modernisation theory (see for example Shahidullah, 2014). Perhaps the natural home for Southern Criminology will be critical criminology. It can be viewed as the latest variety of critical theory, and leads into similar debates about the epistemology of subordinate groups and political objectives.

Teaching Southern Criminology in the South has different challenges. In some countries, criminology is an applied discipline, concerned with policing and crime control. Critics have complained that it is implicated in the crimes of **colonialism** (Cohen, 1988). It is ironic that one way criminology students in different parts of the world may learn about Southern Criminology is through textbooks written for students in Northern countries.

Despite the challenges, there is considerable potential, especially through Southern Criminology, to revitalise criminology. Those behind recent theoretical statements, and particularly Connell (2007), can be congratulated for not ghettoising the approach, either through making it too complex, or too difficult and politically challenging, for the mainstream discipline. Brown (2018: 100–101) notes that Southern Criminology 'is a high bar and it seems likely that many criminologists who would wish to identify with the idea of Southern Criminology would have neither the interest nor the inclination to rework radically what criminology currently looks like'. Nevertheless, even if it only adds to the existing tool box, it raises important questions about a globalising world.

CHAPTER SUMMARY

Here is a summary of the main points in this chapter:

- There is much to be learnt from researching how crime is understood, and the workings of criminal justice, in different countries.
- Comparative criminal justice has existed for some years as a reflective field that employs quantitative and qualitative methods of comparison.
- Southern Criminology is an emerging critical approach that draws on insights from postcolonial theory in the human sciences, and focuses on the relationship between crime and global inequality.
- Southern Criminology sees criminology, currently practised, as reflecting the bias and needs of developed countries. Controversially, it aims to correct this by including voices and alternative epistemologies from the Global South, and by recognising the crimes of colonialism.

Review questions

1. Consider the similarities and differences between criminal justice in two industrialised societies. Examples could be the United Kingdom and the USA, or the United Kingdom and the Netherlands.
2. What is distinctive about the response to crime in modern societies?
3. What do you understand by the terms 'North' and 'South'?
4. What do you understand by the term 'crimes of colonialism'? What measures have been taken to apologise, and compensate, victims?

GO FURTHER

Books

1. The following book provides a useful introduction to comparative criminology:

    Pakes, F. (2015) *Comparative Criminal Justice*, 3rd edition. London: Routledge.

2. The following is another good introduction, critical towards modernisation theory:

    Nelken, D. (2010) *Comparative Criminal Justice: Making Sense of Difference*. London: Sage.

3. This third text brings together different literatures, with a focus on transnational crime:

    Aas, K. (2013) *Globalization and Crime*. London: Sage.

Journal Articles

1. The following is a short statement of the main ideas and arguments of Southern Criminology:

    Carrington, K., Hogg, R. and Sozzo, M. (2016) Southern criminology. *British Journal of Criminology*, 56(1): 1–20.

2. This second article is a critical review of Southern Criminology:

    Travers, M. (2017) The idea of a Southern Criminology. *International Journal of Comparative and Applied Criminal Justice*, pp. 1–12 , doi: 10.1080/01924036.2017.1394337.

3. And the third article below is a critical review of Southern Theory:

    Collins, R. (1997) A sociological guilt trip: comment on Connell. *American Journal of Sociology*, 102(6): 1558–1564.

Useful Websites

1. The United Nations Office on Drugs and Crime website contains statistical reports on global crime: https://www.unodc.org/unodc/en/data-and-analysis/statistics.html
2. The World Health Organisation: Intimate Partner and Sexual Violence collects international information on violence against women: https://www.who.int/violence_injury_prevention/violence/sexual/en/
3. Raewyn Connell's website, which contains theoretical discussion and reviews of Southern Theory: http://www.raewynconnell.net

REFERENCES

Berlin, I. (1999) *The Roots of Romanticism*. London: Chatto and Windus.

Brandt, W. (1980) *North-South: A Programme for Survival*. London: Pan Books.

Brown, M. (2018) 'Southern Criminology in the Post-colony: More than a "derivative discourse"?'. In K. Carrington, R. Hogg, J. Scott and M. Sozzo (eds), *The Palgrave Handbook of Criminology and the Global South* (pp. 83–104). London: Palgrave.

Carrington, K., Hogg, R., Scott, J. and Sozzo, M. (eds) (2018) *The Palgrave Handbook of Criminology and the Global South*. London: Palgrave.

Carrington, K., Hogg, R., Scott, J., Sozzo, M. and Walters, R. (2019) *Southern Criminology*. London: Routledge.

Cohen, S. (1988) Western crime control models in the third world: benign or malignant? *Research in Law, Deviance and Social Control*, 4: 85–119.

Connell, R. (2007) *Southern Theory: The Global Dynamics of Knowledge in Social Science*. Crows Nest, NSW: Allen and Unwin.

Cunneen, C. (2018) 'Indigenous Challenges for Southern Criminology'. In K. Carrington, R. Hogg, J. Scott and M. Sozzo (eds), *The Palgrave Handbook of Criminology and the Global South* (pp. 19–41). London: Palgrave.

de Sousa Santos, B. (2016) *Epistemologies of the South: Justice against Epistemicide*. London: Routledge.

Durkheim, E. (1895/2006) *Suicide*. Harmondsworth: Penguin.

Fanon, F. (1952) *Black Skin, White Masks*. New York: Grove Press.

Foucault, M. (1975/1991) *Discipline and Punish*. Harmondsworth: Penguin.

Liu, J., Travers, M. and Chang, L. (eds) (2017) *Comparative Criminology in Asia*. New York: Springer.

Merry, S. (2016) *The Seductions of Quantification: Measuring Human Rights, Gender Violence, and Sex-Trafficking*. Chicago: University of Chicago Press.

Moosavi, L. (2019) A friendly critique of 'Asian criminology' and 'Southern criminology'. *British Journal of Criminology*, 4: 85–119.

Muncie, J. and Goldson, B. (2006) *Comparative Youth Justice*. London: Sage.

Ryan, L. (2012) *Tasmanian Aborigines: A History Since 1803*. Sydney: Allen and Unwin.

Shahidullah, S. (2014) *Comparative Criminal Justice Systems: Global and Local Perspectives*. Burlington, MA: Jones and Bartlett.

Smith, R. (2018) 'Dutch prisons are so empty they're being turned into homes for refugees', *World Economic Forum*, 2 February. Available at: https://www.weforum.org/agenda/2018/02/netherlands-prisons-now-homes-for-refugees/ [accessed February 2020].

Wacquant, L. (2009) *Punishing the Poor: The Neoliberal Government of Social Insecurity*. Durham, MD: Duke University Press.

World Prison Brief (2019) http://www.prisonstudies.org/world-prison-brief-data [accessed June 2019].

Yorke, H. (2017) 'Students inspired by Rhodes Must Fall campaign demand Bristol University change name of Wills Tower over "slave trade" links', *Daily Telegraph*, 28 March. Available at: https://www.telegraph.co.uk/education/2017/03/28/students-inspired-rhodes-must-fall-campaign-demand-bristol-university/ [accessed June 2019].

Yun, I. (2008) Wengu Zhisxin: review the old and know the new. *Asia Pacific Journal of Police and Criminal Justice*, 6(1): 3–23.

PART III

CONTEMPORARY CHALLENGES

Cyber Crime

12

Francis Gaffney and Carl Wearn

--------- Learning Objectives ---------

By the end of this chapter you will:

- Develop an understanding of the concept of cyber crime and be able to outline the complexities of the term.
- Explore the aims and diverse characteristics of cyber threat actors.
- Familiarise yourself with cyber crime methodologies.
- Explore the main features of investigative responses, as well as some of the challenges faced.
- Be able to identify key approaches to mitigating the threat of cyber crime.

--------- Framing Questions ---------

- Why is it so hard to articulate a definition of cyber crime?
- What are the challenges to investigating cyber crime?
- Why is it so difficult to attribute activities to actors?

INTRODUCTION

The Internet has transformed how we interact, do business, and share information. In addition to the advances in technology, it has had a range of effects on contemporary society. These influences have been manifested in all domains – political, governmental, social, industrial, and the media. Furthermore, as these domains drive towards increased mobility and increased digitisation, they have become more dependent on such technologies as an enabler.

This increased demand has driven the formation of its own industry with the moniker 'cyber' being used to describe the aspects associated with it, e.g. cyber security, cyber insurance, cyber hacktivists, cyber landscape, and the cyber domain. Cyber can be defined as *'involving, using, or relating to computers, especially the Internet'* (Cambridge English Dictionary, 2019).

Cyber threats are complex and dynamic, and network defences often have trouble keeping up with them. Highly sophisticated and targeted attacks continue to exploit the evolution of technology and the increased drive towards digital transformations, easing the process of the exfiltration of data from networks. An increased variety and volume of attacks is inevitable given the desire of financially- and otherwise criminally-motivated actors to obtain personal and confidential information (Yar & Steinmetz, 2019).

Mitigating cyber crime remains a critically important policy area due to two key elements. First, is the current economic, reputational, and personal impacts that nefarious cyber activity has on society – businesses, public services, and individuals. Second, is the potential impact of a cyber threat based on the levels of reliance that people have, both individually and collectively, on information integrity.

This chapter will present an overview of the current challenges and threats within this domain. It will also provide a narrative detailing what cyber crime is, the features of cyber threat actors (CTAs), the methodologies employed in conducting cyber crime activities and campaigns, how cyber crime is investigated and the challenges to **attribution**, and how the threats are currently mitigated.

MAPPING THE TERRAIN - WHAT IS CYBER CRIME?

The term 'cyber crime' (also referred to as 'e-crime', 'electronic-, or digitally-based crime') has evolved in common parlance to cover previously identifiably different types of crime now commonly considered to be associated with the use of computers, the Internet, or information technology systems. For example, computer crime is defined, in UK law, to be those offences associated with the use of a computer for illegal purposes, e.g. accessing a device without the owner's consent; modifying, deleting, or exfiltrating data from a device; introducing **malware** onto a device; or using a computer to commit an offence (such as fraud) (see HM Government (A), 1988, or HM Government (B), 1990).

Computer crime was initially viewed as distinct from what was then referred to as 'e-crime' because the latter included an element of the usage of the Internet or communications' technologies. However, media reporting often referred to these crimes as 'cyber' (having discarded the use of 'e-crime' also in preference to the moniker 'cyber'), perhaps to sensationalise the offending behaviours in order to increase the circulation or 'views' of the respective reporting. Over time, the difference between what is a computer crime, or a **cyber crime**, has become blurred to all but legal and law enforcement entities or academics.

The UK has an international reputation for taking the lead on regulation and legislative implementation with regard to offences relating to the Internet and wider societal issues. However, the rapid growth of the Internet and its user bases, has rendered it increasingly difficult for legislators/policymakers to keep up to date and manage the increasingly sophisticated nature of cyber threats, the ever-changing interpretation of related legislation, and the inventiveness of CTAs.

The overarching aim of such legislation is to keep individuals' personal data safe. The CIA triad – **c**onfidentiality, **i**ntegrity, **a**vailability – is a useful model to assist in how one should think comprehensively about the individual's information security (Neumann et al., 1977):

- *Confidentiality*: Protecting confidentiality is dependent upon being able to define and regulate the access / permissions to information. This could involve having separate data centres, limited permissions to edit or access data records via control lists or applying levels of sensitivity to data via encryption.
- *Integrity*: Data integrity prohibits the ability to copy, move, or alter any data unless they are logged, or there are appropriate permissions to access them.
- *Availability*: This refers to the actual availability to authorised person(s) when they need access. Authentication mechanisms and access systems have to ensure that hardware/software failures, upgrades, or power outages are mitigated against.

The continuous evolution of cyber technologies, and the increased drive to mobility and digital transformations, have facilitated threats from CTAs who use these same enablers to gain access to target networks (to identify weaknesses in the architecture, infrastructure, or defences), exfiltrate personally identifiable information (often referred to as PII), and to exploit any potential vulnerabilities (see, for example, Chowdhry et al., 2020).

Definition

For the purposes of this chapter, the differences will be acknowledged, and the definition used will be 'the use of networked computers or Internet technology to commit or facilitate the commission of crime'.

This includes the following:

a. 'Pure' online crimes, where a digital system is the target as well as the means of attack. These include attacks on computer systems to disrupt IT infrastructure, and stealing data over a network using malware (the purpose of the data theft is usually to enable further crime).
b. 'Existing' crimes that have been transformed in scale or form by their use of the Internet. The growth of the Internet has allowed these crimes to be carried out on an industrial scale.
c. Use of the Internet to facilitate drug dealing, people smuggling and many other 'traditional' types of crime. (House of Commons Select Committee, 2013)

This definition is intentionally broad enough to recognise the continuously altering nature of cyber crime and the evolving nature of traditional offences which invariably increasingly incorporate cyber elements over time. Furthermore, this definition must be subject to regular review to ensure that it covers this dynamic process as well as incorporating any significant changes in legislation and any legal definition (including other developing international frameworks), and therefore, remains fit for purpose.

US Jurisdiction

The Federal Computer Fraud and Abuse Act 18 USC, Section 1030 (CFAA, 2008), is the key statutory means relating to the prosecution of cyber crime in the US. It provides criminal and civil penalties and prohibits the following (Cornell Law School, 2008):

a. Obtaining National Security Information.
b. Accessing a Computer and Obtaining Information.

c. Trespassing in a Government Computer.
d. Accessing to Defraud and Obtain Value.
e. Damaging a Computer of Information.
f. Trafficking in Passwords.
g. Threatening to Damage a Computer.
h. Attempt and Conspiracy.

This is supplemented by legislation under the Electronic Communications Protection Act and the Wiretap Act 18 USC Section 2511 in relation to the interception, disclosure and use of intercepted communications. In practice these federal laws are, however, also supplemented by an extensive framework of state-specific legislation which varies widely (Jarrett & Bailie, 2015). The US is a signatory to the European Convention on Cyber Crime.

European Convention on Cyber Crime 2001

Lastly, the European Convention on Cyber Crime (Council of Europe, 2001) deserves additional mention as the only enforceable multilateral framework to deal with the cross-border issues cyber crime presents. This convention is aimed at harmonising the substantive domestic criminal law in relation to cyber crime across jurisdictions, thereby enabling an effective regime of international co-operation given the trans-national nature of cyber crime and the criminal groups involved in it. There is likely to be increased harmonisation of international laws related to cyber crime and this may well in future lead to clear and widely agreed definitions of e-crime and various cyber crimes. Cyber crime is constantly evolving, with new methods of offending occurring as new technologies develop.

AIMS AND FEATURES OF CYBER THREAT ACTORS

Threat actors generally fall into one or more of five broad categories:

- Cyber criminals.
- Issue-motivated groups or 'hacktivists'.
- Trusted insiders.
- Nation state-supported groups.
- And/or nation state actors.

These threat actors generally seek to achieve one or more desired outcomes, including financial gain, highlighting a cause or gaining attention, unauthorised access to information or intellectual property, exfiltration of data, or denying, disrupting, or degrading access to systems or information (Wall & Yar, 2010).

Threat actors undeniably exploit times of confusion or global events to conduct cyber attacks and email phishing campaigns. These actors are opportunistic and inventive – often taking advantage of an organisation's own information and using it against them. They assess how well a company secures its networks to identify vulnerabilities in its infrastructure and defences, which they then use to improve their attack methodologies. If an organisation is well protected, they may pursue third-party stakeholders or those in the 'supply chain' – such as business partners, accountants, or outside law firms, whose defences may not be as robust, and use these external networks as alternate means by which to gain access to a more secure network.

Further considerations are the threat of state-sponsored actors, which is not merely limited to information exfiltration; digital attacks can now have kinetic effects. Physical destruction requires a great deal more coding sophistication and target intelligence than simple information theft, and the cost involved in developing effective attack tools is far higher than the hacking toolkit that forms many current cyber threats, but the number of countries with the necessary skills is increasing (Lewis, 2014).

CYBER CRIME METHODOLOGIES

Over 90% of cyber crime exploits begin with email, making it the single biggest threat vector to organisations and the data they manage (Fruhlinger, 2020). Furthermore, not only are emails a common vehicle to share and exchange personal data but also email servers are prime repositories for data such as names, email addresses, and associated contact information. CTAs employ a number of methodologies to exploit a target's vulnerabilities which include:

- Phishing, including spear-phishing, whaling, spear-whaling, SMShing, vishing, and Deepfake (audio and video).
- Ransomware attacks.
- Password attacks.
- Denial-of-Service attacks.
- Drive-by downloads/rogue software.
- Malware (including adware, exploit kits, viruses, worms, trojans, botnets, blended threats, and remote access).
- Spyware (for IP theft, credentials harvesting, corporate espionage, exfiltration of data).
- AI-enabled attacks.
- Impersonation attacks.
- Data-in-transit attacks.
- Electronically communicated fraud (i.e. impersonation, false invoicing).
- Possession or sharing of any images which could be considered *grossly indecent.*
- Possession or sharing of any images which show the abuse of children.

Case Study 12.1

Ransomware (Maze)

Ransomware has developed into a significant threat to all organisations and sectors in the past two years and increasing numbers of CTAs are entering the 'market', using various iterations of ransomware to attack an increasingly wide range of sectors globally. There are typically two types of ransomware. The first type encrypts the files on a computer or network. The second type locks a user's screen. Both types require users to make a payment (the 'ransom') to be able to use the computer, or access data, normally again. Ransomware infections are particularly problematic as they can take weeks or months to remediate if the ransom is not paid and adequate back-ups have not been made. Although there are recognised CTAs, these are now supplemented by newer groups seeking to exploit the perceived success of those who are more established.

A key group concerned in ransomware development, and the most active in 2020, from the sheer volume of open source reporting in relation to their activities, is known to deploy the Maze ransomware (previously known in the community as 'ChaCha ransomware'), having been active since the end of 2019. Initially attempting compromise via spoofed government documents as

(Continued)

malicious attachments to emails, this group has taken the lead in a number of key developments to ransomware threat groups' tactics throughout 2020. They were the first to exfiltrate information in order to threaten to leak data, which was not previously standard practice for ransomware groups, and have been instrumental in promoting this to other ransomware operators. This tactic, employed to add pressure to compel payment of any 'ransom' demand, poses additional challenges to organisations due to the complexity of having to report a data breach in many jurisdictions, and the increased likelihood of a potentially significant reputational loss.

Over the course of 2020, their tactics have developed to include enhanced collaboration with other criminal groups operating ransomware, to the extent that they have shared other groups' leaked data on their own leak site. Furthermore, although previously attempting ransomware delivery via an email compromise or exploit kit, the group is now more heavily focused on the exploitation of Remote Desktop Processes (RDP) and known server vulnerabilities, particularly those related to Virtual Private Networks (VPNs) and other remote working applications or processes.

The Maze malware takes the following actions (Mundo, 2020) to encrypt the files, (redacted):

- Check the existence of the file/software the malware is looking to exploit.
- Reserve memory to the file.
- Create a file mapping.
- Generate a random key, IV, and a new random file for the victim file.
- Encrypt the file with the ChaCha algorithm, the key, and IV.
- Rename the file (making it hard to use forensic tools to recover the file).
- Repeat for the encryption of more files.
- When the malware finishes all the files, it changes the desktop wallpaper to display the ransom note.

Maze has a 'chat' function not only to exchange information on how to obtain the cryptocurrency (Bitcoin) required to make payment, but also to discuss the opportunity for the decryption of three images for free to verify the process will work.

Having previously targeted key enterprises, in common with other ransomware threat actors, this ransomware has been observed to target and/or compromise a far wider range of industries than traditionally has been the case for ransomware operators. Their targeting has become far more opportunistic. This has included a large number of medical and healthcare-related organisations, particularly in the United States (CISAa, 2020). This is a rational, although highly repugnant choice, as these organisations will feel additional significant urgency and compulsion to pay any ransom, given the circumstances of the COVID-19 pandemic and their ongoing critical importance to any national pandemic response.

The group have shown a rapid evolution in their tactics to effectively compromise organisations and insert ransomware, but also an increasingly highly organised and collaborative evolution, with a willingness to work with other criminal groups to increase their notoriety and reach. Part of the apparent drive for exposure from this particular group, in common with legitimate businesses, will inevitably be the promotion of their 'brand'.

As Maze operates on a ransomware-as-a-service (RaaS) model, through affiliates who employ their malware to launch attacks and paying a percentage of any monies extorted to the developers, notoriety aids in marketing their 'service'. With an ever-expanding range of threat actors and malware for hire entities competing to insert ransomware, an effective marketing strategy through the accrual of notoriety and a projected perception of capability and expertise, is almost certainly an intentional strategy to dominate the ransomware space. It also ensures significant returns through a widely distributed network of affiliates who conduct additional attacks on their behalf and then pay a percentage to them.

This particular group restricts access to non-English speakers and is highly active on Russian language forums. Their ransomware also checks the language on the target's machines/networks to avoid some countries within the Commonwealth of Independent States (CIS); if detected the malware fails to initiate. It can, therefore, reasonably be assumed that the group's development activity likely originates from an unspecified CIS or 'sanctuary' region, and that they are thereby seeking to avoid the retribution or complication of law enforcement activity within that particular region, or any political impact.

Social engineering (most commonly through impersonation) remains a key tactic for CTAs with their activity constantly evolving and techniques changing on a frequent basis to continue to trick their targets (Hatfield, 2018). This leads to further activity, including the impersonation of domains, subdomains, landing pages, websites, mobile apps, and social media profiles. All of these are used, many times in combination, to trick the target organisation and/or its employees into surrendering credentials and other personal information or installing malware.

Case Study 12.2

Social Engineering and Pattern of Life Analysis

Social engineering is one of the most successful methods by which CTAs get their target to interact with their attack methodology (by volume, opportunistic attacks are the most observed). Research has identified that humans are the single biggest exploitable focus. Human error accounts for over 90% of cyber incidents, with at least 90% of breaches involving email as a delivery vector at some stage. Methods will vary depending on the target, but these are usually related to common functions like document access, voicemail retrieval, or clicking on a link.

By getting the intended victim to empathise, relate to, or be interested in the 'lure' (the text or image the victim receives with malware attached, embedded, or with a link to click on), the CTAs have a greater chance of the victim engaging and the malware being successfully delivered.

In order to get the victim to be interested, the CTAs often research their target's interests, hobbies, political/religious/sexual preferences, and identify their network of friends (or work colleagues) via their social media presence. This is referred to as a 'pattern-of-life-analysis' as it allows for the identification of the victim's behaviours and activities, and also for the prediction of how the victim might interact with a well-scripted communication. It is worth noting here that not having a social media presence is also an advantage to the CTAs as it is now possible to impersonate their target (and they will not know they have been impersonated).

Once the CTAs have sufficient information about their target, they craft and prepare the communication to accompany the malware. There are many examples in the media of these types of attacks exploiting the victim's familiarity with the content of the communication. For example, the target receives a correspondence where they are presented with a voucher offering 15% off at their favourite restaurant (where they may have tagged themselves, given a review, or have photographs of them there). The voucher could have the malware embedded in it (and will be downloaded with the voucher) or it could be activated via a link to a spoofed website for the restaurant and the victim is invited to enter their credentials to obtain the voucher.

Pause for Thought

How could we make ourselves more resilient to social engineering /pattern-of-life analysis in an increasingly technologically-dependent society?

Further activity includes successful phishing e-mails (exploiting social engineering techniques) leading to data breaches or the insertion of spyware, ransomware, and other forms of malware. CTAs are also increasingly expanding their activities by stealing computer resources (e.g. crypto-jacking).

The bushfires in Australia in early 2020 caused significant destruction in the two most populous states of New South Wales and Victoria; businesses, infrastructure, wildlife, and livestock were impacted. However, at the same time the number of malicious attempts to exploit this increased significantly as criminal entities sought to take advantage of human vulnerability. This was observed through spoofed emails, cloned websites, and fictitious charity campaigns. As has been observed in many previous campaigns, malicious actors have sought to exploit the uncertainty and confusion associated with geopolitical events and natural disasters, to further their own ambitions against both individuals and businesses.

Case Study 12.3

Fraud

The COVID-19 pandemic has given rise to a global surge in cyber-enabled, but otherwise traditional, fraud. As would be expected, criminal groups, both organised and more opportunistic offenders, have sought to take advantage of the developing international crises by a variety of means (NCSC, 2020). This has included the advertising of 'cures' for COVID-19, for a price, and the sale of substandard items experiencing any significant demand, such as a wide variety of essential personal protective equipment (PPE), toiletries, and various purported but dubious means to 'kill' the virus, or to apparently prevent any infection at all. These offers of goods are primarily delivered via spam email campaigns and social media messages, advertising or posts, and range in complexity from the very basic to the well-presented and credible (Action Fraud, 2020).

Given the spam or basic volume email delivery methods of many of these campaigns, they are highly likely indicative of increased opportunistic criminal activity for monetary gain, almost certainly reflecting the activity of a wider range of criminal individuals and groups seeking to utilise the circumstances of the pandemic for monetary gain. Many early campaigns were very clearly simple attempts at fraud and included spelling errors and poor presentation. These forms of fraud are unlikely to represent significant monetary loss to an individual but could potentially be used to gain the credentials in order to exploit the end user (or their network) through the deployment of other forms of malware.

Additionally, previously employed tactics, such as those exploiting the annual return of tax documentation/refunds, have been repurposed to exploit the processes involved in the payment of monies in support of businesses or individuals due to the pandemic. Any proposed tax refund or payment has invariably been subject to widespread spoofing and exploitation by criminals as they seek to get ahead of, or supplant, any official or government messaging in relation to such schemes (CISAb, 2020). These primarily operate in order to gain funds fraudulently through spoofed emails, text messages, websites and domains.

There also continues to be a thriving global market for *zero-day attacks*, with researchers in many countries offering their discoveries of unknown vulnerabilities for sale to cyber criminals, governments, or sometimes even the company that produced the software. Zero-day attacks are readily available and let attackers use new and undetectable software tools to siphon off cash, IP, PII, or disrupt networks. As technology advances and is updated, new vulnerabilities will continue to be exploited.

Cyber-criminal activity is often financially motivated, but it can also be politically focused. The greatest source of risk in cyberspace comes from groups with the resources and commitment to continuously target a company or government agency until they succeed in compromising the entity targeted and then exfiltrating data out. These attackers are known as Advanced Persistent Threats (APTs).

Advanced Persistent Threats (APTs)

Advanced persistent threats (APTs) are often well-financed and possess sophisticated hacking skills that they will constantly evolve. APTs have the resources, persistence, financing, and skills needed to design complex attacks, overcome most defences, and more importantly, avoid detection (Schultz & Du, 2016).

While APTs used to only target organisations with high-value intellectual property portfolios, they have most recently been observed to target any organisation/individual with useful information, intellectual property, or money. Targets of such threat actors have been found to be in almost every industry sector, from small companies to large, and in almost every country. The most advanced APT groups operate from 'sanctuaries' where they face little risk of arrest or prosecution. These are often specific national jurisdictions which are perceived as having poorly regulated cyber crime (and related offending) processes, or in some cases, actively promote, condone, or are complicit in the offending behaviours, as it is seen to serve its own political purposes.

Attacks Via Third Parties

Organisations that are regularly compromised are usually done so via outside vendors or third-party service providers. CTAs have slowly shifted their attack patterns and posture, to exploit third-party stakeholders or those in the 'supply chain' or partner environments. This methodology permits CTAs to gain entry to target systems, even in the most secure of industries with mature cybersecurity standards, frameworks, and regulations.

Sophisticated 'upstream' attacks are also becoming more commonplace. Attackers first go after a company that makes information technology products that other companies use to secure their networks, such as the Secure Socket Layer (SSL) certificates used to authenticate a transaction. They then use the stolen technology to attack other companies or to deceive end users.

For victims of upstream attacks, the use by hackers of digital credentials that are indistinguishable from the bona fide product can often easily bypass many security measures.

HOW IS CYBER CRIME INVESTIGATED/ATTRIBUTED?

The *general* methodologies to be employed to conduct all initial investigations of cyber crime involve investigative activity through the interrogation of data to ascertain the origin of a communication and achieve the aim of attributing it to an individual. This is called attribution.

To conduct even a basic investigation requires access to the full unforwarded email header of any email related to a crime. Using the header detail, the investigator can identify an IP address and, in most cases, resolve this to an Internet Service Provider (ISP) that the email will appear to originate from.

The majority of cases will be unattributable beyond an individual ISP but may provide limited insight into the geographic origins of an attack. The other avenues of investigation will routinely include the use of sandboxing and other online resources such as hash resolution, to witness the behaviour of malware within a controlled environment and then ascertain if a specific form of malware has been used which is already attributable to a specific APT.

Digital Evidence Gathering

Gathering evidence to prove and prosecute cyber offences differs by jurisdiction but is almost certain to become more consistent across many Western jurisdictions in the coming years due to moves by a number of governments, including the USA, to facilitate the operation of the European Convention on Cyber Crime internationally. That particular treaty framework aside, the principles related to and the process of gathering digital evidence are also subject to the industry ISO/IEC standard 27037 (ISO 27037, 2016), which is recognised internationally. This standard covers the key points critical to the effective management of digital evidence and the maintenance of its integrity. By adhering to the principles and practices detailed in this standard, evidence can be gathered, and an investigator's actions detailed, or explained, in a way which seeks to ultimately preserve the integrity of that digital evidence.

ISO 27037 provides guidance on the activities undertaken in handling digital evidence, the key processes being the identification, collection, acquisition, and preservation of potential digital evidence. These processes would be required in any investigation that is designed to maintain the integrity of digital evidence – contributing to its admissibility in legal and disciplinary actions, as well as other circumstances. It also aims to assist those interrogating that evidence by providing a recognised procedure which can be referred to in relation to any digital evidence presented.

In most jurisdictions digital evidence is governed by three fundamental principles, i.e. relevance, reliability and sufficiency. These three principles are, however, key to all investigations, not just those related to digital evidence and its admissibility in court. Digital evidence is 'relevant' when it goes towards proving or disproving an element of the case being investigated. Although the detailed definition of 'reliable' varies across jurisdictions, the general meaning of the principle is *'to ensure digital evidence is what it purports to be'* and this is considered to be widely held. It is not always necessary to collect all data or to make a complete copy of the original digital evidence. In many jurisdictions, the concept of sufficiency denotes the collection of enough potential digital evidence to allow the matter to be adequately investigated.

There are then four key aspects critical to the handling of digital evidence itself: auditability, repeatability, reproducibility, and justifiability. It should be possible for an independent assessment to justify any decision-making process utilised by the evidence gatherer, and to ascertain if an appropriate method or procedure was used. The process of gathering the information or evidence should be repeatable, utilising the same procedure/processes and equipment, and which must be documented by the evidence gatherer to ensure repeatability.

To ensure reproducibility the same test results should then be obtainable at any time after the original examination, using the same measurement methodology, and even using different instruments under different conditions. Lastly, the evidence gatherer should be able to justify the means and actions taken in handling any digital evidence, essentially by illustrating that the decision made represented the best choice to obtain the digital evidence. Another evidence gatherer should be capable of validating this by successfully reproducing these actions.

ISO 27037 covers the initial handling process in detail – noting that digital evidence can be particularly fragile or volatile and, therefore, special attention has to be paid by the evidence gatherer to minimising the handling of any device or evidence, accounting for any changes made and documenting them, complying with local rules of evidence, and not taking actions beyond their competence or training.

ISO 27037 goes further to provide detailed parameters for an initial collection process, broken down into the further key stages of identification, collection, acquisition, and preservation. Conducting a search for digital evidence, the evidence gatherer needs to identify the digital evidence present by systematically searching for devices that may hold evidence. Collection of the evidence should be conducted by the most appropriate means and is hugely dependent on whether devices are 'off' or 'on' when located. Any actions taken have to be fully documented and particular care given to ensuring evidence is not lost or destroyed during the collection process.

The acquisition of evidence is where an evidential copy of the evidence is produced, and as actions have to be carried out to do this, this process has to be fully documented, as with the previous one, as changes to data states are likely unavoidable at this stage. Means of verification between the copy and original are undertaken at this stage to ensure integrity. Lastly, steps are taken and documented to preserve the digital evidence from modification, loss, or damage, again contributing to the integrity of the evidence gathered.

Within all of these processes the '**chain of evidence**' remains critical throughout, requiring the evidence gatherer to also consider the chain of custody in relation to any evidence, and essentially demands the detailing of any individuals who checked, accessed, or changed the data and the reasons why. The times and dates of these events must be recorded. This particular process is notably applicable beyond the lifetime of the evidence.

These processes cover the key principles directly covering the gathering and integrity of digital evidence. Further detailed guidance is given within ISO 27037 in relation to ensuring that the evidence gatherers are appropriately trained, and that any decision-making process is reasonable and guided by processes in relation to the various different types of media and the state it is in, including video evidence, and whether devices are in an 'on' or 'off' state.

By employing ISO 27037 as a baseline for the gathering of digital evidence, it is possible to ensure that the evidence gathered will be as trustworthy as possible and potentially admissible in jurisdictions outside of the country it is gathered in. This will become increasingly important due to the global reach of cyber criminals exploiting the Internet and the inevitable transnational nature of cyber crime offending and the individuals perpetrating it.

Pause for Review

What international instrument could investigate, enforce, or prosecute offences in this transnational, interconnected, and interdependent environment? And just as importantly, what framework would they employ?

Challenges When Attributing

By definition, any activity that relates to malware, any form of cyber-enabled crime, or the communication of messages which could be considered fraudulent or related to extortion, is evidence of a crime. Any attribution for these alleged offences must consider that it has the potential to compromise any existing and long-standing criminal investigation being conducted by law enforcement or the security services.

Increasingly, this investigative activity could well be taking place over multiple jurisdictions and may involve significant law enforcement resources. Therefore, if attribution is made, both correct (and incorrect attributions) have the potential to seriously adversely affect any criminal investigation, and any subsequent prosecution that may ensue.

Non-law enforcement entities (e.g. cybersecurity media) would, rightly, be subject to significant criticism (or legal action) if they compromised or impacted an ongoing investigation by regularly speculating on the attribution of attacks.

Another key consideration in any effort to attribute the source of a crime must be the confidence level which you have in making that attribution. For any attribution to be *high confidence* it would require a chain of, and continuity of, communication evidence which can reliably and unequivocally attribute the origin of a message or communication to a single user or machine in a distinct location. This is the level of confidence which is required to confidently attribute an offence to an individual or group to enable an additional follow-up or law enforcement-related action.

Attributing attacks to specific groups, or threat actors, based solely on the techniques or methods used is inherently flawed, as nation state actors (or the more sophisticated organised crime entities) use a wide range of means to obfuscate the true origins of their own activities. With nation state actors, or organised crime groups in particular, there is a significant likelihood of intentional activity to mis-represent the origins of an attack and even to falsely flag it or mimic known campaigns and methods, which have previously repeatedly been attributed by well-known security vendors, in order to obfus-cate its origins (see, for example, Berghel, 2017 or Tsagourias, 2012).

This activity further complicates any attempt to accurately and confidently attribute a crime. To take this a step further, there have been repeated examples of CTA or espionage groups having their infra-structure compromised and used by other groups in the last year. This activity is incessant between a number of commonly attributed groups, given the current geopolitical background globally.

Reliable attribution can only be made through following the origins of a specific email communica-tion. The IP address will normally resolve to an ISP of origin. This will only differ if it uses an established network, whether via a compromised account or a criminally operated domain. If related to private indi-viduals, most IP addresses are temporarily leased to individuals from a pool of addresses and, therefore, only enquiry with the ISP can ascertain the specific location of the communication's origin.

Attempts can be made to obtain this information, but it is at the discretion of any ISP to refuse any request from an entity other than from a law enforcement authority and this request can clearly relate to personal data. In the case of Western ISPs most will have an established formal process to obtain this information and which is intended solely for the use of law enforcement.

Further complications which limit the investigator's ability to correctly, or accurately, attribute a communication include, but are not limited to the following:

- The stripping and replacement of header details by individual ISP or mail services.
- The use of VPNs.
- The use of proxy servers.
- Or the use of TOR services.

Many cases may well be unattributable beyond an individual ISP but might provide limited insight into the geographic origins or concentration of effort in relation to an attack.

Hear from the Expert

Jonathan Miles, Cyber Security Consultant and Intelligence Analyst

The COVID-19 pandemic that has shaped global events since late 2019, has also accelerated the existing trends for criminality to be conducted online, enabled threat actors' capabilities, and added to the volume of observed attacks. With more people across the globe being restricted to working remotely, there has been a move by some criminals away from offending in the physical domain leading to an escalation in cyber crime (using malware-as-a-service software).

Additionally, although cyber crime is often seen as a borderless crime, the same cannot be said for the geographical (physical) and human (cognitive) situation. For example, in Europe, and the UK, these entities are diverse not only in their geography and languages, but also in their business practices, legal frameworks, and cultural interpretations; one must also consider that the infrastructure in both traditional on-premises and cloud topologies has a physical component. These physical devices, servers, relays, and cabling are at risk of attack not only from cyber threat actors, but also physical damage from natural disaster, fire, theft, and vandalism which can also affect the integrity and availability of data to the end user.

Finally, it must be noted that the evidential principles detailed throughout the ISO 27037 standard have evolved from long-established principles in relation to the gathering of physical evidence. These principles are intended to maintain the integrity and chain of custody for key items of evidence so as to provide the best opportunity for the successful investigation and prosecution of offences in the cyber domain.

MITIGATING THE THREAT OF CYBER CRIME

Good cyber hygiene does not occur in a technological, social, or cultural vacuum. CTAs exploit times of confusion or global events to conduct cyber attacks and email phishing campaigns. This has been seen most recently in repeated campaigns themed specifically in relation to the Australian bushfires (January 2020), the postponed Olympic Games (Japan 2020), the postponed Euro 2020 Football tournament, and other geo-political events, such as the *Black Lives Matter* demonstrations, and most notably the COVID-19 pandemic.

To have the confidence and assurance that good cyber hygiene processes and advice are being followed, a robust monitoring mechanism should be developed (at home as well as at work). These monitoring mechanisms could take a number of forms:

- Reviewing and updating information management policies.
- An ongoing auditing process.
- Maintaining records of processing activities (for accidental or unauthorised alteration, anonymising data, copying, moving, or deleting data).
- Maintenance of information security controls – including a robust patching regime.
- Ensure basic requirements for physical security of hardware, records, or information processing facilities (access control).
- Business continuity management processes, reviews, and exercises.
- Provision of targeted awareness training for end users.
- Establishing and fostering a proactive information governance culture.
- Monitoring compliance with regulatory bodies and appropriate legislation.
- Sharing best practice, updates on new innovations, or ensuring compliance with standard procedures.
- Liaising with third parties (such as contractors or those in supply chain) to ensure familiarity with cyber hygiene policy and compliance with it.

CHAPTER SUMMARY

The focus of this chapter was to:

- Deepen our understanding and insight into the 'how' and 'which' individuals become engaged in cyber crime activity.
- Explore the types, features, and methodologies for those engaged in cyber crime activity.

- Explore the challenges in this rapidly changing environment and technologies – such as the sheer scale of the problem, the complexity of the malware and campaigns, and the transnational element of the offending.
- Explore the challenges of policing, hampered by the difficulty in attribution, as well as the inherent difficulty in dealing with cyber crime activity through discrete national jurisdictions.
- Propose potential mitigating measures.

Review Questions

1. What are the challenges to defining what cyber crime is in the global setting?
2. Recall the types of cyber crime activity.
3. What are the generic features of cyber crime activity?
4. Outline the key features of digital data gathering.
5. How could you be more resilient to pattern-of-life analysis?

GO FURTHER

Books

1. This book provides a comprehensive overview of the tactics, techniques, and procedures many threat actors employ to compromise target networks, organisations, and end users. It does not require a deep technical understanding and so is easily accessible to readers of all skill levels:

Erickson, J. (2008) *Hacking: The Art of Exploitation,* 2nd edition. San Francisco, CA: No Starch Press.

2. This book provides a useful overview of the most current methods used to influence potential victims. The insights offered in the book are from experienced practitioners in this field and so provides credibility and authenticity to those not fully cognisant of activities:

Hadnagy, C. (2018) *Social Engineering: The Science of Human Hacking*, 2nd edition. London: Wiley.

3. Geoff White is an investigative journalist and his book, *Crime Dot Com*, provides a great narrative of the history of malicious cyber activity. It provides great insights into this domain of criminality, easily accessible to readers of all levels of experience in this arena:

White, G. (2020) Crime Dot Com: From Viruses to Vote Rigging, How Hacking Went Global. London: Reaktion Books.

Journal Articles

1. Social engineering methodologies are used increasingly in malicious cyber activity – often for significant financial gain. Research on social engineering frameworks and methodologies is still at an early stage. This article explores the evolution of this attack vector:

Hatfield, J. M. (2018) Social engineering in cybersecurity: the evolution of a concept. *Computers & Security,* 73: 102–113.

2. Attribution on cyber activity is a significant challenge for those engaged in law enforcement and criminal investigation. This article explores the issues with attribution:

    Berghel, H. (2017) On the problem of (cyber) attribution, *IEEE*, March. Available at: http://www.berghel.net/col-edit/out-of-band/mar-17/oob_3–17.pdf

3. This article develops concept and explores the challenges of attempting to attribute malicious cyber activity to a specific threat actor:

    Tsagourias, N. (2012) Cyber attacks, self-defence and the problem of attribution. *Journal of Conflict and Security Law*, 17(2): 229–244.

Useful Websites

1. The Computer Misuse Act 1990 deals specifically with offences relating to the unauthorised accessing or modification of data stored on a computer: https://www.legislation.gov.uk/ukpga/1990/18/contents
2. The Malicious Communications Act 1988 details the offence of communicating a message containing indecent or grossly offensive information, threats or false information by way of letter or electronic communication: https://www.legislation.gov.uk/ukpga/1988/27/contents
3. The Federal Computer Fraud and Abuse Act (CFAA) 2008 outlines the key statutory means relating to the prosecution of cyber crime in the USA: https://www.nacdl.org/Landing/ComputerFraudandAbuseAct
4. The only enforceable multilateral framework to deal with the cross-border issues cyber crime presents: European Convention on Cyber crime 2001: https://www.coe.int/en/web/conventions/full-list/-/conventions/treaty/185

REFERENCES

Action Fraud (2020) *COVID-19 Related Scams - News and Resources*. Available at: https://www.actionfraud.police.uk/covid19

Berghel, H. (2017) On the problem of (cyber) attribution. *IEEE*, March. Available at: http://www.berghel.net/col-edit/out-of-band/mar-17/oob_3-17.pdf

Cambridge English Dictionary (2019) *Cyber*. Available at: https://dictionary.cambridge.org/dictionary/english/cyber

CFAA (2008) *The Federal Computer Fraud and Abuse Act (CFAA)*. Washington, DC. Available at: https://www.nacdl.org/Landing/ComputerFraudandAbuseAct

Chowdhry, D. G., Verma, R. and Manisha Mathur, M. (2020) *The Evolution of Business in the Cyber Age: Digital Transformation, Threats and Security*. Florida: Apple Academic Press.

CISA (a) (2020) *APT Groups Target Healthcare and Essential Services*. Alert (AA20-126A). Available at: https://us-cert.cisa.gov/ncas/alerts/AA20126A

CISA (b) (2020) *Malicious Cyber Actor Spoofing COVID-19 Loan Relief Webpage via Phishing Emails*. Alert (AA20-225A). Available at: https://us-cert.cisa.gov/ncas/alerts/aa20-225a

Cornell Law School (2008) *Section 1030. Fraud and related activity in connection with computers*. Legal Information Institute. Available at: https://www.law.cornell.edu/uscode/text/18/1030

Council of Europe (2001) *Details of Treaty No.185* - Convention on Cybercrime, Budapest. Available at: https://www.coe.int/en/web/conventions/full-list/-/conventions/treaty/185

Fruhlinger, J. (2020) *Top Cybersecurity Facts, Figures and Statistics For 2020*, CSO. Available at: https://www.csoonline.com/article/3153707/top-cybersecurity-facts-figures-and-statistics.html

Hatfield, J. M. (2018) Social engineering in cybersecurity: the evolution of a concept. *Computers & Security*, 73: 102–113.

HM Government (a) (1988) *The Malicious Communications Act 1988*. London: TSO. Available at: https://www.legislation.gov.uk/ukpga/1988/27/contents

HM Government (b) (1990) *The Computer Misuse Act 1990*. London: TSO. Available at: https://www.legislation.gov.uk/ukpga/1990/18/contents

House of Commons Select Committee (2013) 'E-crime'. House of Commons Home Affairs Committee, Fifth Report of Session 2013–14. London: TSO. Available at: https://publications.parliament.uk/pa/cm201314/cmselect/cmhaff/70/70.pdf

ISO 27037 (2016) Information Technology — Security Techniques — Guidelines for Identification, Collection, Acquisition and Preservation of Digital Evidence. BSI Standards Limited, 2016.

Jarrett, H. M. and Bailie, M. W. (2015) *Prosecuting Computer Crimes*, 2nd edition. Washington, DC: Computer Crime and Intellectual Property Section, Criminal Division, Office of Legal Education Executive Office for United States Attorneys. Available at: https://www.justice.gov/sites/default/files/criminal-ccips/legacy/2015/01/14/ccmanual.pdf

Lewis, J. A. (2014) *Cyber Threat and Response Combating Advanced Attacks and Cyber Espionage*. Washington, DC: Center for Strategic & International Studies. p. 4. Available at: http://csis-website-prod.s3.amazonaws.com/s3fs-public/legacy_files/files/publication/140313_FireEye_WhitePaper_Final.pdf

Mundo, A. (2020) *Ransomware Maze*, McAfee Blog. Santa Clara: California. Available at: https://www.mcafee.com/blogs/other-blogs/mcafee-labs/ransomware-maze/

NCSC (2020) *COVID-19 Exploited by Malicious Cyber Actors*, NCSC Advisory. London: TSO. Available at: https://www.ncsc.gov.uk/news/covid-19-exploited-by-cyber-actors-advisory

Neumann, A. J., Deege, L., McLellan, P. M., Sopko, M. J., Statland, N., Stone, R. and Webb, R. D. (1977) *Part XI: Post-Processing Audit Tools and Techniques*, Computer Science & Technology: Audit and Evaluation of Computer Security Proceedings of the NBS Invitational Workshop, Miami Beach, Florida, March. *National Bureau of Standards Special Publication 500-19*. Washington, DC: US Department of Commerce. pp. 11.1–11.21. Available at: https://nvlpubs.nist.gov/nistpubs/Legacy/SP/nbsspecialpublication500-19.pdf

Schultz, E. E. and Du, C. (2016) 'Managing Advanced Persistent Threats'. In H. F. Tipton and M. K. Nozaki (eds), *Information Security Management Handbook*, 6th edition. Florida: CRC Press.

House of Commons Select Committee (2013) 'E-crime', House of Commons Home Affairs Committee, Fifth Report of Session 2013–14. London: TSO. Available at: https://publications.parliament.uk/pa/cm201314/cmselect/cmhaff/70/70.pdf

Tsagourias, N. (2012) Cyber attacks, self-defence and the problem of attribution. *Journal of Conflict and Security Law*, 17(2): 229–244.

Wall, D. S. and Yar, M. (2010) 'Intellectual Property Crime and the Internet: Cyber-Piracy and Stealing Information Intangibles'. In Y. Jewkes and M. Yar (eds), *Handbook of Internet Crime*. London: Routledge.

Yar, M. and Steinmetz, K. F. (2019) *Cybercrime and Society*, 3rd edition. London: Sage.

Terrorism

Francis Gaffney

13

———— Learning Objectives ————

By the end of this chapter you will:

- Understand what terrorism is.
- Understand the aims of and features of terrorist activity.
- Understand the motivations to engage in terrorist activity.
- Explore group ideologies and group dynamics.
- Understand countering terrorism.

———— Framing Questions ————

1. Why is it so hard to articulate a definition of terrorism?
2. Is terrorist activity driven by the cause or the destruction of those who oppose it?
3. What motivates an individual to cause harm to another?

INTRODUCTION

Terrorism continues to be a high profile and critical issue in many contemporary societies. It is a complex phenomenon and so are the potential factors that motivate people to carry out associated terrorist activity. Such violence, or threat of violence, is usually intended to attract a wider audience than the immediate victims. Society faces a number of threats from distinct themes of radical groups: animal rights activists; nationalists; religious extremists; right-wing extremism; and political extremism. At present there is no reliable or extensive theoretical framework for comprehending terrorist motivations, but an appreciation of the contributing factors involved is essential to developing such an understanding. This requires analysis of the 'how' as well as the 'why' people resort to terrorist activity.

This chapter will present an overview of the current research in this field contextualizing it within global responses to terrorist activity. It will also provide a narrative on the development of counter-terrorist policy and processes before finally discussing, UK, Europe, and global responses to terrorist/extremist activity.

MAPPING THE TERRAIN

Often, the field of terrorism research is hampered by the sheer scale, complexity, and sensitivity of the issues. Furthermore, research published in this field previously relied on secondary and tertiary source material. For example, Lum et al. (2006) found only 3% of the 6,041 peer-reviewed articles between 1971 and 2003 were based on any kind of empirical data. However, it would appear that this is being addressed as evidenced in a recent work (Schuurman, 2018) where a review of all the articles submitted to nine key journals between 2007 and 2016 showed the use of first-hand data had increased to 53.8%.

Terrorism, and the problems associated with the ambiguity of its definition, are applied to diverse groups with different origins and goals. Terrorism can (and does) occur in both wealthy and poor states, in democracies as well as in authoritarian states. Terrorists are generally not drawn from the poorest segments of their societies. Typically, they are at average or over-average levels in terms of education and socio-economic background.

DEFINITION

A number of terms referred to in this chapter are often misunderstood, or their purpose misinterpreted. Such misunderstanding can be very unhelpful when one is attempting to introduce measures and strategies to counter terrorist behaviours because there are often political or polemic stigmas associated to some.

The word 'terrorism' (and associated activity) is understood across the world but still has limited agreement in terms of a common definition. The word 'terrorism' entered into European languages in the wake of the French Revolution of 1789 and was defined as a 'system or rule of terror' and 'terroriste' as 'an agent or partisan of the Terror that arose through the abuse of revolutionary measures' (*Dictionnaire de l'Académie Française*, 1798: 775). Whilst any such proposed definition may be useful in the legal realm as a measure for defining terrorism it does not in itself give an insight into what motivates individuals to involve themselves in terrorist activity.

Unhelpfully, the use of the term is sometimes intended to be polemical or to act as a derogatory label, meant to condemn an opponent's cause as illegitimate rather than as a description of an individual's behaviour. Politicians in countries affected by terrorism often make political use of the definition of terrorism by attempting to emphasize its brutality. One of the prevalent ways of illustrating the cruelty and inhumanity of terrorists is to present them as harming 'the innocent' (Netanyahu, 1985: 18):

The idea that one person's 'terrorist' is another's 'freedom fighter' cannot be sanctioned. Freedom fighters or revolutionaries don't blow up buses containing non-combatants; terrorist murderers do. Freedom fighters don't set out to capture and slaughter schoolchildren; terrorist murderers do.

As Netanyahu's quote demonstrates those involved in these sorts of activities cannot readily 'hide' behind the defence that they are 'freedom fighters' attempting to overthrow 'oppressive regimes'. If this were the case, it could be argued that their targeting selection should only include instruments of such a regime – police, interior forces, the military, or parliamentarians. By targeting 'innocents' such as children or non-combatants, it could be argued that they are not actually interested in political change as their primary focus, but rather instilling fear to a wider audience.

Pause for Review

If indeed one accepts that such activity could be accepted as the actions of 'freedom fighters', should these actors be held accountable under the Law of Armed Conflict (and basis of the Geneva Convention and Additional Protocols)? This provides protection for the victims of conflict such as 'Persons hors de combat' and those who do not take a direct part in hostilities are 'entitled to respect for their lives and their moral and physical integrity. They shall in all circumstances be protected and treated humanely without any adverse distinction'. Therefore, shouldn't the killing of innocents be treated as a 'war crime'?

Modern parlance and media reporting equate (violent) radicalism and extremism with terrorism, while at the same time using terrorism as shorthand for anti-state political violence in general. For example, Schmid (2013: 13) proposes:

as there exists legal acts of warfare and illegal war crimes in armed conflicts, it makes sense to differentiate normless and criminal terrorism from illegal but sometimes (more) legitimate forms of political violence (although the parallel only goes some way).

As evidenced during the popular resistance of the Arab Spring of 2011, not every use of political violence is a '*terrorist*' or '*extremist*' action. Though illegal under national laws, political violence has been justified by the wider international community (under international humanitarian law) when it is perceived to be against highly repressive and undemocratic regimes.

When observing any society there will always exist an extreme view at either end of the spectrum of opinion. These 'extreme' views are only viewed as such when compared to the respective societal norm and are not always illegal or involve violence.

Without a clear (and concise) definition of what terrorism is (and isn't), it is impossible to formulate or enforce international agreements against terrorism because the Member States of the UN sometimes disagree on whether certain movements are, or are not, terrorist in nature. Some progress was made in UN Resolution 1566 in formulating such a definition, capable of serving as a basis for international counter-terrorist activity that satisfied the majority of stakeholders, but not all.

For the purposes of this chapter, the UK definition taken from the Terrorism Act, 2000 (HM Government, 2000: Chapter 11) and amended in the Terrorism Act, 2006, is the one to be used – although it is acknowledged here, and was noted by Lord Carlile of Berriew (HM Government, 2007) that the creation of this definition presented its own problems and difficulties and is still not without ambiguity:

... 'terrorism' means the use or threat of action where ... it involves serious violence against a person, serious damage to property, endangers a person's life, other than that of the person committing the action, creates a serious risk to the health or safety of the public or a section of the public, or is designed seriously to interfere with or seriously to disrupt an electronic system ... (and) the use or threat is designed to influence the government or to intimidate the public or a section of the public, and the use or threat is made for the purpose of advancing a political, religious or ideological cause.

Source: HM Government (2007) *The Definition of Terrorism: A Report by Lord Carlile of Berriew Q.C. Independent Reviewer of Terrorism Legislation*. Reproduced under the Open Government License v3.0. URL: https://www.nationalarchives.gov.uk/doc/open-government-licence/version/3/

This definition articulates the aims as well as the features of terrorist activity. The aim (or intention) of an activity is often, under law, as important as the activity itself.

AIMS AND FEATURES OF TERRORIST ACTIVITY

The aim of a terrorist group is *normally* political even if the language used is indicative of religious belief or other motivation, because any terrorist activity will demand a response from the government/international community, but the features of such activity are often highly diverse and encompass a wide variety of phenomena. Furthermore, the aims of the individuals and groups participating in such activity can be equally wide-ranging. Terrorism is often sustained for reasons other than those that spawned it in the first place. It is, therefore, not certain that terrorism will end even if the grievances that gave rise to it, or the root causes, are somehow dealt with.

Terrorist groups may sometimes have vested interests in continuing their actions long after they realize that their political cause is lost because profitable criminal activities, used to finance their political and terrorist campaigns, are too valuable to give up. Alternatively, some continue even if many of their political demands have been met

--------------- **Case Study 13.1** ---------------

FARC Narcoterrorism

The *Fuerzas Armadas Revolucionarias de Colombia* (Revolutionary Armed Forces of Colombia – FARC) evolved to be the dominant actor in Colombia and South America and the growth of the illicit drugs trade, combined with their use of terrorism, facilitated this significantly. The FARC initially prohibited the growth and cultivation of illicit drugs as this was deemed counter-revolutionary, but in 1982 it changed its doctrine to tax the peasant growers and facilitate the trafficking of drugs.

This was part of a calculated strategy to prevent the loss of their peasant community support, increase their influence and control within the regions they operated in, and to obtain essential funds to sustain their terrorist activity. By protecting coca farmers, the FARC reportedly brought security, justice, and welfare programmes to once impoverished areas.

Although the motives for the association between the FARC and drug producers may have initially differed, their common objective was to undermine the Colombian Government's infrastructure, creating instability, and so the illicit drugs trade could not have expanded as rapidly as it did without this association.

Those who plan terrorist acts are usually thinking about what they want to accomplish. They aim to inflict long-term costs on their enemy and gain long-term advantages for themselves. Many factors, including the structure, ideologies, and aims of such groups, add to the complexity of identifying motivation for causing harm.

Terrorist action aims to:

- Create mass anxiety and fear.
- Promote a sense of helplessness and hopelessness.
- Reveal the incompetence of the authorities.
- Erode one's sense of security and safety.
- Have psychological repercussions beyond the immediate target.
- Provoke extreme reactions from individuals or the authorities (e.g. repressive legislation or the excessive use of force against suspected individuals).

Common features include:

- Political aims and motives.
- The use of illegal force that is violent or threatens violence.
- Being conducted/inspired by an organization with an identifiable chain of command or structure.
- Being perpetrated by a sub-national group or non-state actors.
- Unconventional methods.
- Attacks against 'soft' civilian and passive military targets.
- Acts aimed at purposefully affecting an audience.

Terrorist methodologies include the following:

- Bombing (including mass-casualty bombings of high-profile symbolic targets).

  o Suicide bombings (including proxy), (additional methodology)

- Hijacking.
- Arson.
- Assault (including punishment beatings).
- Kidnapping and the taking of hostages (in order to pressure governments to accede to specific political demands).
- Assassinations.
- Social and welfare provision (activities used by Hizballah and DAESH).
- Propaganda, coercion, and repression in areas under their control.
- Cyber terrorism (spam/worm/trojan bombs, hacking of websites/systems, etc.).
- Eco terrorism.
- Narcoterrorism.
- Other organized crime activities (including drug, weapon, and human trafficking).

Another significant factor for motivating individuals to participate in terrorist activity is some sort of **'trigger' event**. Such a trigger could include an extreme act committed by the perceived enemy, unjust acts, massacres, contested elections (i.e., Iran 2009), or other provocative events that call for revenge or action. It is worth noting that it is probable that no universal model is feasible because no two people experience the same events and are impacted differently by 'trigger' events.

Target selection is determined by a number of factors, and the terrorists' ideology is central to this process, not only because it provides the original impetus for the terrorists' actions, but also because it can set out the moral agenda within which they operate. Targets can fall into two categories: discriminate or indiscriminate. Targets are often selected primarily for their symbolic value.

For many terrorists, the technicalities of the activity are often less important than the symbolic message of the action. It is not an insignificant role the media plays in achieving the terrorist group's goal in its bid to broadcast their message and images. In addition to the symbolic value, terrorists typically consider a range of other political and logistical issues in target selection; factors include accessibility, vulnerability, publicity value, financial implications, probability of success, and possible retribution/censure.

Individuals are also more likely to engage in violence if they are able to obscure, or distort, the relationship between their actions and the effects they cause (i.e., if the perpetrator de-humanizes the victim). This propensity to cause harm to another is explored now.

Propensity to Cause Harm

When an individual is permitted to overcome moral inhibitions by diffusing responsibility and weakening self-restraints, the link between behaviour and its consequences is obscured. For example, an individual may engage in violent acts if a legitimate (or recognized) authority accepts responsibility for the consequences of their conduct. Under such conditions, it is perceived that the authorities are liable for the actions rather than the individual; because they are not the actual agents of their actions, they are spared self-prohibiting reactions.

Essentially, people tend to conform to what others have said if they are aware of others' judgements. This conformity is greater when those others are physically present, and experiments have shown that people will conform even against their own judgement. This is powerfully evidenced in the research studies of Milgram, and separately, Zimbardo (see the two Case Studies below).

There does not appear to be a universal model for explaining aggressive tendencies. A reason for this could be the multitude of types of aggression, with each one having a different root cause. Although psychologists recognize a number of root causes/theories for aggressive tendencies, because of the diversity in terrorist activity, it is proposed that terrorist aggression has a basis in a number of these theories, but any one theory does not satisfy all activity. If one were to focus on a particular group or activity, then a specific theory could be formulated to understand the motivations for their respective activity.

―――――――――――― **Case Study 13.2** ――――――――――――

Milgram Obedience Experiment

The Milgram Obedience Experiment (Milgram, 1963) was conducted between 1960 and 1964 by Stanley Milgram, a social psychologist at Yale University, and aimed to investigate what level of obedience would be shown when participants were told by an authority figure to administer electric shocks to another person.

This was shortly after the trial of the World War II criminal Adolf Eichmann had begun. Eichmann's defence was that he was simply following orders when he ordered the deaths of millions of Jews. Milgram wanted to know if 'following orders' was a genuine explanation and justification for actions that individuals would not ordinarily perform independently.

Essentially, participants were led to believe that they had been 'randomly' assigned the role of 'teacher' whilst another 'participant' (an actor involved in the study) had been assigned the role of 'pupil' (the assignment of roles was fixed so that the participant was always selected as the teacher and the pupil role was taken by one of the actors in the study).

The task was for the participant-teacher to teach a list of words to the actor-pupil for a test of memory. Whenever the actor-pupil answered incorrectly, the participant-teacher was instructed to activate one of the switches, starting at the lowest voltage and progressing to the higher voltages (no shock was actually delivered – but the participant-teacher did not know this). The level of shock that the participant-teacher was willing to deliver was used as the measure of obedience.

Of the 40 participants in the study, 26 delivered the maximum shocks while 14 stopped before reaching the highest levels. It is important to note that many of the participants became extremely agitated, distraught, and angry with the experimenter, yet they continued to follow orders all the way to the end.

Milgram's experiment showed that people would obey others, even when such obedience causes them to act against their own conscience and harm others. Interestingly, later experiments conducted by Milgram indicated that the presence of rebellious peers dramatically reduced obedience levels. When other people refused to go along with the experimenter's orders, 36 out of 40 participants refused to deliver the maximum shocks.

Case Study 13.3

The Stanford Prison Experiment

The 1971 Stanford Prison Experiment, conducted by the psychologist Philip Zimbardo and his colleagues (Haney et al., 1973), set out to create an experiment that further investigated the impact of situational variables on human behaviour. Zimbardo was a former classmate of Stanley Milgram and was interested in expanding upon the latter's research.

In this study, the researchers set up a mock prison and then randomly selected 24 undergraduate students to play the roles of both prisoners and guards. While the Stanford Prison Experiment was originally timetabled to last fourteen days, it had to be stopped after six because, while the prisoners and guards were allowed to interact in any way they wanted, the interactions were generally hostile or even de-humanizing; the guards began to behave in ways that were aggressive and abusive toward the prisoners, while the prisoners had begun to show signs of extreme stress and anxiety and became passive and depressed.

The study showed that the behaviour of the 'normal' students (who had been randomly allocated to each role) was affected by the assigned role to the extent that they seemed to believe in their allocated positions. An individual's expectations about others can become a self-fulfilling prophecy – the individual lives up to those expectations and so they are reinforced – thus causing the individual to live up to them more.

Pause for Review

Do such studies – as referred to above – potentially exonerate some actors' behaviours as part of group activity? How could such studies support/dismiss the models of radicalization of youth and their involvement in terrorist activity?

The complexity of defining terrorism, identifying motivations, classifying what is considered normal behaviour etc., means that there are advocates on both sides of the argument for the opposing theories on the mental state of actors in terrorism. In fact, terrorist organizations avoid recruiting people with diagnosed mental illnesses; such organizations need members that will be cooperative and loyal to the group. An individual without such lasting qualities may endanger missions or betray the group. Terrorists may follow their own rationalities based on extremist ideologies or particular terrorist logics, but they are not irrational.

It is more useful to see terrorists as rational and intentional actors who have developed intentional and premeditated strategies to achieve political objectives (Hoffman, 1999). They make their choices between different options and tactics, on the basis of the limitations and possibilities of the situation.

Three components that can lead to an individual participating in terrorist activity are the motivation of the individual, the group ideology, and, the group dynamics. The chapter will now look at each of these in turn.

MOTIVATIONS TO ENGAGE IN TERRORIST ACTIVITY

A basic tenet of psychology is that one's belief system influences and informs a person's thinking and actions (Bandura, 1999). Influences could include family, community, immigration, economics, identity, youth culture, ideology, religion, ethnicity, and politics. It follows that the concept of good or evil is thus dependent upon the subjective moral values and antecedents of that person.

For an individual to feel aggrieved (potentially due to cultural alienation as a migrant or displaced population, economic marginalization, perceived victimization, or a resentment towards a respective state's foreign policy) can take some time to develop. It can, however, be a fairly rapid process if participation in extremist activity is in response to a 'trigger event' (although there remains the question of a predisposition to being susceptible to responding to such events).

A key idea is whether the ideology is driven more by the promotion of the 'cause' or the destruction of those who oppose it. People do not ordinarily engage in such action until they have justified to themselves the morality of their actions. Finding ways to dehumanize the enemy can erode the powerful barriers that inhibit human killing:

> By declaring your enemies 'non-persons' and by denying their human qualities, you block moral scruples right from the beginning. (Wasmund, 1986: 215)

This in turn could provide sufficient impetus to lead an actor down the path to participating in terrorist activity and form their views as to who, or what, may be seen as a legitimate target, and to an extent it allows them to de-humanize the people they intend to harm. As an individual becomes increasingly committed to an ideology there appears to be a growing inhibition of their other concerns/behaviours, and therefore a greater degree of radicalization.

The range of participation of the individuals could be from passive support (non-kinetic roles, e.g., fundraising, administration) to those willing to sacrifice themselves as suicide bombers in support of the ideology. Horgan (2008) found that people who are more open to terrorist recruitment tend to:

- Feel angry, alienated, or disenfranchised.
- Believe that their current political involvement does not give them the power to effect real change.
- Identify with perceived victims of the social injustice they are fighting.
- Feel the need to take action rather than just talking about the problem.
- Believe that engaging in violence against the state is not immoral.

- Have friends or family sympathetic to the cause.
- 'Believe that joining a movement offers social and psychological rewards such as adventure, camaraderie and a heightened sense of identity'. (Horgan, 2008: 84–85)

Some individuals may be true believers – those who are motivated by ideology and political goals – whereas others get involved for purposes of self-interest, or because belonging to a strong group is important for their identity. This last incentive is of importance as the influence of others (such as the presence of charismatic leaders), able to translate injustices and frustrations into a political agenda for violent struggle, can be the key factor that permits people to overcome their moral inhibitions.

The past fifteen years have seen the publication of many models depicting the process of radicalization. Research on radicalization increased in 2004 in response to the reaction by Islamic extremist groups following the Western Coalition intervention in Iraq in 2003. The London bombings in 2005 generated further interest in the phenomenon of 'home-grown terrorism', where apparently self-starting cells of 'radicalized' individuals mobilized against their host countries (as a justification of their argument of alienation and disenfranchisement) with little or no material support from foreign terrorist entities.

Academics and practitioners in this field recognize a number of models for pathways to radicalization. Predictably new models will likely emerge, or existing ones will be refined, as our understanding and primary research develops. The most dominant/influential are shown in chronological order in Table 13.1.

Table 13.1 Models of Radicalisation

Name	Author
Four Stage Model of the Terrorist Mindset	Borum 2003
Wiktorowicz	Wiktorowicz 2003
Four-Stage Process	Sageman 2004
Eight-Stage Recruitment Process	Taarnby 2005
Staircase Model	Moghaddam 2005
The Prevent Pyramid	ACPO 2007 to date
NYPD Four-Stage Radicalisation Process	Silber & Bhatt 2007
Pathway Model	Gill 2007
Sinai 2012	Sinai 2012
12 Mechanisms Model	McCauley and Moskalenko 2008
Quest for Significance Model of Radicalisation	Kruglanski et al 2014

Introducing counter-radicalization programmes, before an individual has committed any crime, requires an understanding of personality traits in individuals allegedly predisposed to terrorist activity. Such traits could predict future behaviours and aim to divert those who are already on their way along the radicalization process away from extremist ideologies that are potentially mobilizing them to become violent.

Personality Traits

It is well-documented that some individuals may be predisposed toward certain types of behaviour, and this could include individuals having different motives for involving themselves in terrorist activity irrespective of the overall aim of the group. Violent extremist ideologies tend to provide a set of beliefs that justify and mandate certain behaviours. Those beliefs are often regarded as absolute, and the activity seen as serving a noble cause.

However, it has become increasingly apparent that there is no common personality profile that characterizes most terrorists (who appear to be relatively normal individuals) making the identification of them well nigh impossible before they can act. Early attempts to articulate a 'terrorist personality' have largely been abandoned (Horgan, 2003) in favour of identifying the radicalization pathways, but most researchers agree that the majority of terrorists are not irrational in their activity:

> Neither psychological nor other research has revealed qualities unique to those who become involved in terrorism, or the existence of singular pathways into (and out of) terrorism. Though terrorist profiles exist in a broad sense, no meaningful (i.e., having predictive validity) psychological profile has been found either within or across groups. (Horgan, 2017: 200)

Despite such academic criticism, the efforts to find 'personality traits' in terrorist/extremist activity are still sought by respective nation state's security services. This presents a problem for nation states to identify and profile subjects of interest associated with terrorist activity.

What is agreed upon in the current research in radicalization methodologies, is that as an individual becomes increasingly committed to an ideology there appears to be an increasing inhibition of their other concerns/behaviours, and therefore a greater degree of participation and radicalization.

This range of participation (and radicalization) of the individuals could be from passive support (non-kinetic roles, e.g., fundraising, administration) to those willing to sacrifice themselves as suicide bombers in support of the ideology. The next section will now explore the power and influence of groups in enabling the acceptance of extremist ideologies.

GROUP IDEOLOGY

As expected in such a complex field of research, where there are many factors and triggers that could lead to the radicalization of individuals, most research proposes there is no single cause but a composite mix of influences. Individuals join extremist groups for different reasons. These groups' ideologies tend to provide a set of beliefs that justify and mandate certain behaviours. Those beliefs are sometimes regarded as absolute, and the activity is seen as serving a noble cause.

Trujillo et al. (2009) suggest there are two proposed recruitment pathways to terrorist activity. The first is self-recruitment where a group will 'exchange knowledge and practices and reinforce ideological positions' (Trujillo et al., 2009: 723). The second witnesses an individual attracted to extremist activity by a charismatic leader or mentor and is

> the process of systematic directed and conscious psychological manipulation, very similar to that produced by sectarian or totalitarian groups. (Trujillo et al., 2009: 724)

Most groups identify with suffering some sort of injustice or harm by an outside entity. This entity then becomes the focus of the group's activity to right this perceived injustice (often justifying its activities through some sort of morality or teaching). By dehumanizing their enemies (and thereby justifying violent activity against them), they are able to incentivize sacrifice (on whatever scale is palatable) by promising redemption and heroic accolades.

A group's **ideology**, however ill-defined or misguided, provides the individual with a moral and political compass that inspires their actions, informs the way they interpret the world, and defines how they judge the actions of others. The beliefs, ideologies, and narratives of terrorist groups consist of culturally-specific descriptions of the way in which societies or groups maintain their vision of their collective selves through different historical and projective narratives. It is through the influence of such narratives that societies and groups produce different types of terrorism and different terrorists.

Common ideologies that have underpinned terrorist organizations or movements have included to varying degrees:

- Marxism (that range from South American revolutionaries, Baader Meinhoff, and Palestinian Organisations).
- Self-determination (IRA, ETA).
- Right-wing groups (National Action, British Nationalist, SKD (Sonnenkrieg Division)).
- Environmental groups (Earth First, Earth Liberation Front).
- Animal rights' groups (SPEAC (Stop Primate Experiments At Cambridge), SHAC (Stop Huntingdon Animal Cruelty)).
- Faith-based ideologies (AQ, DAESH).

Whereas terrorists' indoctrination, recruitment, and training used to rely primarily on physical meetings between recruits and recruiters (which often required time, coordination, and travel), the Internet can now provide these connections quickly, easily, remotely, and anonymously. Terrorist groups are using this to their advantage and are employing a wide array of online platforms to disseminate a variety of content. Many terrorist organizations utilize the Internet to varying degrees as a tool for reaching out to their followers or potential supporters, and in recent years that use by terrorist groups has proliferated rapidly.

Case Study 13.4

DAESH's Use of the Internet

DAESH (from the Arabic ad-Dawlah al-Islāmiyah fī 'l-'Irāq wa-sh-Shām) is an extremist Islamic organization that grew out of a violent insurgent group that has changed its name a number of times to reflect its geographic ambitions (DAESH is also referred to as 'Islamic State' (IS); 'Islamic State in Iraq' (ISI); 'Islamic State in Iraq and al-Sham' (but also 'Islamic State in Iraq and Syria' – ISIS); and, 'Islamic State in Iraq and the Levant' (ISIL)). It is a transnational Sunni terrorist group that claimed three strands of activity (terrorist activity, state-building/governance, and insurgency) which have required significant support.

DAESH's influence outside of the Middle East was due to its perceived strong ideological religious appeal that represented different things to different audiences – claiming the religious legitimacy for its actions was based on an extreme Salafist/takfiri interpretation of Islam that essentially meant anyone who opposed its rule was, by definition, either an apostate ('murtad') or an infidel ('kafir').

DAESH's publicity apparatus (both the Internet and its *Dabiq* publication) enabled this increased awareness and its proficiency and appeal surpassed other jihadist originations in its global reach and sophistication. As the group's use of the Internet has flourished, it has tailored its online platforms to specifically attract youth audiences promoting a radical ideology and violence through cartoons, games, and videos posted online.

DAESH initially had been immensely successful in its recruitment of fighters and radicalization to its jihadist ideals via its use of the Internet (especially social media sites and apps). Whereas terrorists' indoctrination, recruitment, and training used to rely primarily on physical meetings

(Continued)

between recruits and recruiters (which often required time, coordination, and travel), the Internet provided these connections quickly, easily, remotely, and anonymously. Furthermore, by employing a wide array of online platforms to disseminate a variety of content this meant radicalization times became shorter, with networks expanding rapidly, and spreading to countries previously unaffected by Islamist extremism.

The core narratives and ideologies identified with terrorist movements are often mediated through other more specific narratives of relevance to the context of the group in question. In addition to the respective group's ideology, the dynamics of the group can have a powerful influence on the individuals within it.

GROUP DYNAMICS

Being part of a group's ideology (whether or not the individual goes on to join the group or acts as a 'lone wolf'), is one of the most reported findings in the research in this field. Empowering environments that can advance group dynamics, include both the physical (training camps, social groups) and virtual domains (i.e., the Internet), and can be a source of radicalizing material for individuals as well as satisfying a psychological quest for significance. Congruently, an individual being part of a social network (including online groupings) that espouses terrorist activity can lead to the development of extreme ideologies and radicalization.

The idea of **social identity** is where being regarded as a member of certain groups provides an important part of the self-concept of individuals. Most individuals belong to many groups (family, co-workers, religion, country) and as described above each of these groups has some influence on the beliefs and behaviour of the individual. The extent to which group membership contributes to a sense of self varies depending upon the level of group orientation present in the native culture.

When a group evidences a high degree of cohesion, there are powerful internal, as well as external, pressures to conform to group norms, thereby developing a loyal support of past decisions. Each member is then under significant pressure to maintain their commitment to the group's decisions and to support (often unquestionably) the arguments and justifications they have worked out together to explain away obvious errors in individual judgement.

Given this shared commitment, the members put pressure on each other to continue with the status quo and to insist that, sooner or later, everyone will toe the line. They become inhibited about expressing doubts to each other with regard to the ultimate success and morality of their policies. Janis (1971) termed this behaviour **groupthink**, i.e., behaviour that reinforces and is in turn reinforced by the shared beliefs of the group members, when consensus seeking becomes so dominant that it tends to override individual thinking:

> Terrorism is not a consequence of individual psychological abnormality. Rather it is a consequence of group or organizational pathology that provides a sense-making explanation to the youth drawn to these groups. (Post, 2001: 18)

The influential power of this group now extends to every kind of personal and moral judgement. Group actions can overcome moral inhibitions by diffusing responsibility and weakening self-restraints, thereby obscuring the link between behaviour and its consequences. This can make violence against the enemy not just acceptable but also necessary.

To complicate the process of classifying such groups is the fact that nation states can themselves be involved in terrorism in different ways in order to achieve political aims. This could be in the form of: providing general support for terrorist organizations (such as financial support, supply of weapons, harbouring suspected terrorists, or ideological support); providing operational assistance (such as military or operational assistance), by initiating or directing attacks, i.e., 'state-sponsored terrorism' (through groups outside their own associations); or by the perpetration of terrorist attacks by official state agencies (by perpetrating terrorist acts via their own security forces or intelligence services). Such involvement is often used as a political tactic, e.g., a rival state accusing another, or organizations using it against states acting against them.

COUNTERING TERRORISM

We now turn to explore counter terrorism (and de-radicalization programmes) in the UK, EU, and globally through the lens of countering terrorist activity. Introducing programmes that intervene earlier in the process, before an individual has committed any crime, allows the prevention of the radicalization of individuals in the first place (or diverts those who are already along the radicalization process) away from extremist ideologies which could potentially mobilize them for terrorist activity.

Arguably, the most significant of all was the **CONTEST** Strategy which was introduced in 2003 and was arranged around four themes:

- **Prevent** (preventing individuals from participating in terrorist activity).
- **Protect** (protecting the general public and critical infrastructure by reducing susceptibility to attack).
- **Pursue** (pursuing, investigating, and prosecuting terrorists, disrupting their planning, movement, and communications, and preventing access to funding and material) and
- **Respond** (responding in a coordinated way when developing resilience).

The **Prevent** programme initially focused on primarily Muslim communities and their youth/community programmes before expanding across the entire UK.

The UK's **CONTEST 3** document (HM Government, 2011) readily acknowledged that some factors that facilitated international terrorism would continue to exist despite the international community's best efforts to curtail them. These factors include the following:

- Radicalization.
- The many conflicts and regional disputes that terrorist groups exploit show little, or no, sign of straightforward resolution.
- There will always be states that have weak control or are viewed as failing that these groups can take advantage of.
- The ever-developing technologies that facilitate terrorist activity (making attacks more lethal) and evasion of detection by security services are likely to continue to be used.
- The existence of those willing to support or even participate in terrorist activity, including financing, logistical support, training, harbouring, or perpetrating violent acts.

Counter-terrorism methods are usually introduced as a temporary measure with limited deviations from the 'normal' functioning of the state's laws and norms. These methods tend to have an air of permanency; the UK was in a declared 'state of emergency' for eight years (the time it derogated from the *International Covenant on Civil and Political Rights* (ICCPR) and European Convention on Human Rights (ECHR)) that has left an enduring and damaging effect on the UK's human rights' freedoms.

Terrorist groups exploit human rights' freedoms as part of their strategies to compensate for their material weakness; the right to free speech and association allows them to raise awareness of their cause and attract supporters (radicalize new recruits?) whilst concealing their real intent; and the right to privacy limits the state's ability to conduct surveillance operations easily. This results in the government limiting those rights to conduct more effective counter-terrorism campaigns.

The use of the military in response to terrorism, whether domestic (Northern Ireland) or in the pursuit of alleged terrorist safe-havens (Iraq and Afghanistan conflicts), has demonstrated that it has created the parallel judicial systems that are lacking in impartiality. This could be in the form of military courts, detention, and deviation from international norms and safeguards. This has led, on numerous occasions, to serious violations (such as the right to a fair trial/liberty/access to legal counsel). A military response can become so dominant that other methodologies are neglected. resulting in human rights' freedoms and the 'normal' rule of law being undermined.

European Context

Although the European Union (EU) has had some disagreement on their manner of countering terrorism (i.e., some countries supporting the US in their military action against terrorism, whilst others are strongly opposing it), the EU has established a number of measures aimed at countering this threat. Some of these measures included a common (albeit broad) definition of terrorism and legislation that make it possible to apprehend terrorists or freeze their assets anywhere in the EU.

The most useful of its legislation included:

- The European Convention on the Suppression of Terrorism (1977).
- The Council of Europe Convention on the Prevention of Terrorism (2006).

The possibilities afforded by the Lisbon Treaty 2007 could provide further development such as the coordination and interaction between traditional external policy apparatus and internal aspects of counter-terrorism activities, but this remains to be seen.

In 2005, the EU adopted a strategy, similar in structure to the UK's **CONTEST** Strategy (it, too, was arranged around the four themes described above) to combat the perceived global terrorist threat.

Middle East Context

Many Middle East countries have been the subject of scrutiny by the wider global audience for many years. These countries have often undergone significant change in their national identities and in finding their place in the global family which has also involved conflict – with both internal and external threat actors. As a result, their interpretation of what is understood as terrorist activity is experienced through the lens of their own histories and experiences. This can be evidenced in some states reportedly engaging in 'state terrorism' for the purposes of facilitating their own strategic and economic interests.

Global Context

Terrorism opposes the central foundation of the Charter of the UN and its international instruments, namely the rule of law, respect for human rights, and peace and tolerance among nations. The UN has developed its own Global Counter-Terrorism Strategy (UN, 2005) that was adopted by Member States in September 2006. It has also issued a significant number of Resolutions (both in its General Assembly (44) and Security Council (33), related to terrorist activity since 11 September 2001). The key Resolutions include:

- 1269 (1999) – Calling for international cooperation in the fight against terrorism.
- 1267 (1999) & 1333 (2000) – Introducing measures against the Taliban.
- 1373 (2001) – Introducing measures relating to combating international terrorism.
- 1566 (2004) – Introducing measures relating to combating international terrorism (non-AQ/Taliban).

UNSCR 1373, whilst affirming previous Resolutions, expressed concern at the increase in acts of terrorism in the various regions of the world and required Member States to:

> Refrain from providing any form of support, active or passive, to entities or persons involved in terrorist acts, including by suppressing recruitment of members of terrorist groups and eliminating the supply of weapons to terrorists. (UN, 2001: 2)

UNSCR 1373 also established the Counter-Terrorism Committee (CTC) to monitor the implementation of this Resolution and to offer technical advice to Member States. However, the weakness of one country in dealing with terrorist activity is highlighted when it impacts on the security of other countries. This is clearly illustrated where ineffective airport security in one country could cause a terrorist attack in another. It follows that global security can be seen to rely on the co-dependency of numerous counter-terrorism strategies in the world's nation states.

There can be many potential obstacles to different countries cooperating with each other in terrorist-related issues. The key obstacle is centred on the issue of the definition. A major stumbling block to consensus on a definition is where a state interprets the line between terrorism and legitimate acts of resistance, including political opponents. A precise definition can have the effect of limiting the scope of criminal sanctions under international law, whereas overbroad definitions can have significantly adverse effects on human rights' freedoms and hamper international cooperation in counter-terrorism operations. Moreover, the lack of a definition can create state counter-terrorism measures outside the remit of international law norms.

Other obstacles could include:

- The nationalities of the individuals involved with the activity (these can present jurisdictional or extradition complications).
- The location of the incident or base of operations (again, these can present jurisdictional or extradition complications).
- The target or victim may have a multinational interest with jurisdictional or political implications (i.e., the 1988 bombing of a US aircraft by Libyan nationals over Lockerbie, Scotland, with many different nationalities on board).
- The sanctuary, funding, training, and arming of the individuals involved with the activity can present jurisdictional, political or extradition complications.
- The population support/diaspora (i.e., the targeting of funding or support activity may present political complications).

CHAPTER SUMMARY

The focus of this chapter was to:

- Understand the contested definition of terrorism.
- Deepen our understanding and insight into 'how' and 'why' individuals could potentially become engaged in terrorist activity.

- Explore the ideologies and dynamics of terrorist groups.
- Explore the aims, features, and motivations for those engaged in terrorist activity.
- Explore the UK, European, and global responses to terrorist activity and countering terrorism.

—————————— Review Questions ——————————

1. What are the challenges to defining what terrorism is?
2. What are some aims of terrorist activity?
3. What are the generic features of terrorist activity?
4. Outline the key outcomes of the Milgram Obedience and Stanford Prison Experiments.
5. What do counter-terrorism programmes aim to achieve?

GO FURTHER

Books

1. Bruce Hoffman's work on terrorism is essential reading for all students of this concept. He has shared insights and assessments in the field of terrorism for over four decades at strategic and international level (including work with the FBI and being a former CIA 'scholar in residence') so has a great wealth of experience. This book is a comprehensive account of terrorism and associated activity:

   Hoffman, B. (1998) *Inside Terrorism*. New York: Columbia University Press.

2. John Horgan is another thought leader in this field. His recent research mainly focuses on disengagement and counter-radicalization activities. This book provides an in-depth critical analysis of the motivations and characteristics of 'how' and 'why' individuals participate in terrorist activity.

   Horgan, J. (2014) *The Psychology of Terrorism*, 2nd edition. Abingdon: Routledge.

3. Andrew Silke is another thought leader in this field. His primary research interests include terrorism, conflict, crime and policing, and he is internationally recognized as a leading expert on terrorism and low intensity conflict. He has worked with a wide variety of government departments and law enforcement and security agencies as part of his research. This book provides excellent insights into the motivations and psychology of terrorists and associated activity.

   Silke, A. (2010) *The Psychology of Counter-terrorism*. Abingdon: Routledge.

Useful Websites

1. The Milgram Obedience Experiment (Documentary) is a useful account of the experiments conducted by Stanley Milgram and his team: https://www.youtube.com/watch?v=rdrKCilEhC0
2. The Stanford Prison experiment (BBC documentary) is a useful account of the experiments conducted by Philip Zimbardo and his team (following on from Milgram's research): https://www.youtube.com/watch?v=F4txhN13y6A
3. The United Nations Security Council Resolutions website is a useful resource to research and explore UN Security Council Resolutions: https://www.un.org/securitycouncil/content/resolutions-0

Journal Articles

1. Martha Crenshaw's research here, although dated, still has relevance on how terrorist activity should be viewed, and how the resilience and responses are managed:

   Crenshaw, M. (2014) The long view of terrorism. *Current History*, 113(759): 40–42.

2. This following research article is one of the most widely accepted interpretations of how the pathway to radicalization is realized:

   Kruglanski, A., Gelfand, M., Bélanger, J., Sheveland, A., Hetiarachchi, M. and Gunaratna, R. (2014) The psychology of radicalization and deradicalization: how significance quest impacts violent extremism. *Political Psychology*, 35(1): 69–93.

3. This next piece of work by Marc Sageman challenges current researchers to 'add' to the collective understanding of terrorism and associated activity with original, first-hand accounts rather than reviewing legacy research:

   Sageman, M. (2014) The stagnation in terrorism research. *Terrorism and Political Violence*, 26(4): 565–580.

REFERENCES

Bandura, A. (1999) 'A Social Cognitive Theory of Personality'. In L. Pervin and O. John (eds), *Handbook of Personality*, 2nd edition (pp. 154–196). New York: Guilford Publications.

Borum, R. (2003) Understanding the terrorist mindset. *FBI Law Enforcement Bulletin*, 72(7): 7–10.

Dictionnaire de l'Académie Française (1798) Paris, vol. 2, p. 775.

Gill, P. (2007) A multi-dimensional approach to suicide bombing. *International Journal of Conflict and Violence*, 1(2): 142–159.

Haney, C., Banks, W. C. and Zimbardo, P. G. (1973) A study of prisoners and guards in a simulated prison. *Naval Research Review*, 30: 4–17.

HM Government (2000) *Terrorism Act 2000*. London: TSO. Chapter 11.

HM Government (2007) *The Definition of Terrorism: A Report by Lord Carlile of Berriew Q.C. Independent Reviewer of Terrorism Legislation*. London: TSO.

HM Government (2011) *CONTEST: The United Kingdom's Strategy for Countering Terrorism*. London: TSO.

Hoffman, B. (1999) The mind of the terrorist: perspectives from social psychology. *Psychiatric Annals*, 29(6): 337–340.

Horgan, J. (2003) 'The Search for the Terrorist Personality'. In A. Silke (ed.), *Terrorists, Victims and Society* (pp.3–27). Hoboken, NJ: Wiley.

Horgan, J. (2008) From profiles to pathways: the road to recruitment. ANNALS, AAPSS, 618 (July).

Horgan, J. (2017) Psychology of terrorism: introduction to the special issue. *American Psychologist*. 72(3): 199–204.

Janis, I. L. (1971) 'Groupthink among Policy Makers'. In N. Sanford and C. Comstock (eds), *Sanctions for Evil* (71–89). San Francisco, CA: Jossey-Bass.

Kruglanski, A., Gelfand, M., Bélanger, J., Sheveland, A., Hetiarachchi, M. and Gunaratna, R. (2014) The psychology of radicalization and deradicalization: how significance quest impacts violent extremism. *Political Psychology*, 35(1): 69–93.

Lum, C., Kennedy, L. W. and Sherley, A. J. (2006) *The Effectiveness of Counter Terrorism Strategies, Campbell Systematic Reviews*. citeseerx.

McCauley, C. and Moskalenko, S. (2008) Mechanisms of political radicalization: pathways toward terrorism. *Terrorism and Political Violence*, 20(3): 415–433.

Milgram, S. (1963) Behavioural study of obedience. *Journal of Abnormal and Social Psychology*, 67: 371–378.

Moghaddam, F. M. (2005) The staircase to terrorism: a psychological exploration. *American Psychologist*, 60(2): 161–169.

Netanyahu, B. (1985) *Terrorism: How the West Can Win*. New York: Farrar, Straus and Giroux. p.18.

Post, J. M. (2001) *The Mind of the Terrorist: Individual and Group Psychology of Terrorist Behavior*, prepared for Subcommittee on Emerging Threats and Capabilities, Senate Armed Services Committee, 15 November. pp.1–44.

Sageman, M. (2004) *Understanding Terror Networks*. Philadelphia: University of Pennsylvania Press.

Schmid, A. P. (2013) *Radicalisation, De-Radicalisation, Counter-Radicalisation: A Conceptual Discussion and Literature Review*, ICCT Research Paper, ICCT. p.13.

Schuurman, B. (2018) Research on terrorism, 2007–2016: a review of data, methods, and authorship. *Terrorism and Political Violence*, 32(5): 1–16.

Silber, M. D. and Bhatt, A. (2007) *Radicalization in the West: The Homegrown Threat*. New York: NYPD Intelligence Division.

Sinai, J. (2012) Radicalisation into extremism and terrorism: a conceptual model. *The Intelligencer*, 19(2): 22–23.

Taarnby, M. (2005) *Recruitment of Islamist Terrorists in Europe: Trends and Perspectives*, Danish Ministry of Justice, IPT.

Tajfel, H., Turner, J. C., Austin, W. G. and Worchel, S. (1979) An integrative theory of intergroup conflict. *Organizational Identity: A Reader*. pp. 56–65.

Trujillo, H., Ramirez, J. and Alonso, F. (2009) Evidences of coercive persuasion for indoctrination of jihadist terrorists: towards violent radicalization. *Universitas Psychologica*, 8(3): 723–724.

UN (2001) *UN Resolution 1373*. S/RES/1373. New York: United Nations.

UN (2005) *The UN Global Counter-Terrorism Strategy - Plan of Action*. New York: UN.

Wasmund, K. (1986) 'The Political Socialization of West German Terrorists'. In P. H. Merkl (ed.), *Political Violence and Terror: Motifs and Motivation* (p. 215). Berkeley: University of California Press.

Wiktorowicz, Q. (2003) *Radical Islam Rising: Muslim Extremism in the West*. Lanham: Lowman & Littlefield.

Youth Justice Board (2012) *Process Evaluation of Preventing Violent Extremism Programmes for Young People*. London: Youth Justice Board.

Corporate Crime and the Regulation of Ecocide

14

David Whyte

Learning Objectives

By the end of this chapter you will:

- Understand the crime of 'ecocide' and the types of ecocide that corporations are responsible for.
- Have examined how the concept of crime applies to corporations and the legal issues that arise when dealing with corporate wrongdoing.
- Understand the issues involved in regulating corporations and the structural limitations on regulation in capitalist societies.
- Explore why regulators can be said to *encourage*, as well as control, corporate crime and harms.
- Be able to think critically about what could be done to prevent environmental crimes and harms caused by corporations in the future.

Framing Questions

---

1. How should we respond to the problem of corporate crime, when it is threatening the future of the eco-system and the human species?
2. Can the regulation and punishment of corporations help in dealing with the environmental catastrophe?
3. Does criminology have a role in challenging corporate ecocide?

INTRODUCTION

Corporations are the key agents in climate change. It is estimated that the oil, coal and other carbon fuel produced by just 100 companies are responsible for 71% of greenhouse gas emissions. The biggest offenders are ExxonMobil, Shell, BP and Chevron (Griffin, 2017). Almost all of the plastic that is choking our oceans is produced by corporations for profit. Greenpeace has listed the biggest offenders as Coca-Cola, PepsiCo, Nestlé, Danone, Mondelez International, Procter & Gamble, Unilever, Perfetti van Melle, Mars and Colgate-Palmolive. Most ambient air pollution – the air pollution caused by particles released into the environment which is estimated by the World Health Organisation to cause 4.2 million early deaths every year – is produced by corporations (Tombs and Whyte, 2015).

For anyone studying criminology, all of this raises fundamental questions about the role that the law and the regulatory system plays in protecting us and the planet from corporate crime. But is this a question for criminology? After all, the products described above are generally not illegal; in general the production of pollution is licensed and permitted by governments. In this context, asking questions about the role of the law in protecting us from those types of corporate activities seems rather abstract. After all, it does look like the law is *encouraging*, not controlling, the most harmful impacts on our environment.

MAPPING THE TERRAIN: ECOCIDE

Knowledge link: This topic is also covered in Chapter 16.

We have recently seen a revival of a relatively old concept in international law: the crime of **ecocide**. Calls to re-establish the crime of ecocide seek new forms of control aimed at ameliorating the impending climate and **biodiversity** crisis (Higgins et al., 2013). In general, proposals seek to implement a new offence through the mechanisms of the International Criminal Court and in national legal systems. Some states (including Armenia, Belarus, Moldova and the Ukraine and Georgia) have incorporated some version of Falk's crime of ecocide in their penal codes. Georgia's penal code specifies a jail term of eight to twenty years in length for ecocide (Gauger et al., 2012).

The term 'ecocide' entered the political lexicon in 1972 when Olof Palme, the Prime Minister of Sweden, described the Vietnam War as an ecocide. Palme, along with other leaders including the Indian Prime Minister Indira Gandhi, called for ecocide to be an international crime. The world had watched when almost 20% of Vietnam's forests were wiped out by chemical herbicides, including the notorious Agent Orange. Those herbicides had been sprayed to clear crops and target civilians as a tactic of war. It is estimated that up to 400,000 people died from the immediate effects and that a million people were disabled or suffered severe health problems. People in Vietnam are still being born with congenital disorders caused by the presence of the chemical in the ecosystem.

International lawyer Richard A. Falk's Ecocide Convention was drafted in 1973, directly in response to the interventions made by Olof Palme and Indira Gandhi (Falk, 1973). It set out a new offence that sought the abolition of the use of chemical substances in wartime or peacetime that had the effect of clearing people from the land. But this offence was never adopted by the international community.

Nine different private chemical companies, led by Monsanto, had been given the job of developing and manufacturing Agent Orange for the US military (Monsanto, 2017). There have been a number of legal actions taken against those companies, specifically Dow, Monsanto, and Diamond Shamrock. Those companies have, like the US military, continued to deny any relationship between health effects on claimants and their chemicals. Most of the **class actions** have been settled out of court. The US government continues to deny the effects of Agent Orange on the Vietnamese people and the persistent poisoning of land and water supplies (US Department of Veteran's Affairs, n.d.). The fact that corporations played a central role in the Vietnamese ecocide is not peripheral or coincidental; it cannot be reduced to a footnote in history.

The renewed call for a crime of ecocide raises some vital questions about the role of law in capitalist societies, not least law's role in protecting them from corporate activity. Corporations have continued to play a central role in ecocide, and, as the introduction to this chapter indicates, are perhaps most often criticised for their active promotion and organisation of a fossil fuel economy in an era of climate change. This raises a fundamental question for us as we begin this chapter: can we say that those corporations, and by implication, the senior managers that control them, and the investors that profit from them, are responsible for climate change? We begin to address this question in the following section.

PREMEDITATED CORPORATE CRIMES

In the discussion that follows, we will discover that corporations and their senior managers are responsible for acts that, if they were committed by individuals in any other context, would be regarded as serious crimes.

The key test that needs to be met in a criminal court to determine if someone is guilty or not is known as **mens rea**. This latin phrase means 'guilty mind'. If someone is aware of their actions (or inactions) and this leads to a criminal act, then the person can be found guilty of that act. There are a number of different mental states captured by *mens rea*: intention, knowledge, recklessness, and criminal negligence. If someone intends to commit an act that is criminal, this can be criminal conduct. If someone has knowledge of a criminal act occurring and has the power to prevent it but does nothing, this can be criminal conduct. And if someone is reckless and it is a reasonable expectation that a crime will be committed as a result, this can be criminal conduct. It is at this point that we begin our schematic investigation of the culpability of corporate actors in serious environmental harms.

There is convincing evidence that the major oil companies have had knowledge of the extent of the damage they are doing to our ecosystem for decades, and at least since the 1970s. Executives at the international oil and gas company Exxon were presented with evidence of the industry's impact on climate change by its own scientists in 1977. This evidence estimated that 'a doubling of the carbon dioxide concentration in the atmosphere would increase average global temperatures by 2 to 3 degrees Celsius' (Banerjee et al., 2015). The company then embarked on an intensive programme of research that sampled carbon dioxide emissions and conducted rigorous climate modelling. In 1981, the research programme concluded that '[a]n expanded R&D program does not appear to offer significantly increased benefits' and was quietly ditched (Exxon Research and Engineering Company, 1981: 2). From the early 1990s onwards corporate funding by Exxon and the fossil fuel industry charity Koch Family Foundations directly financed groups that attacked climate change science and policy solutions. This research sowed enough polarisation and doubt around climate change science to ensure that political recognition of the problem of climate change was significantly downplayed (Farrell, 2016).

Case Study 14.1

CFCs

One of the first major chemical products that raised the alarm about climate change was chlorofluorocarbons (CFCs), chemicals used in a range of products including aerosols, fridges and air conditioning units. The main brand was a coolant that General Motors made in partnership with the

(Continued)

chemical company DuPont as 'Freon'. In 1974, two significant scientific studies demonstrated that a build-up of CFCs was responsible for depleting the ozone layer, essential for absorbing the sun's ultraviolet radiation and cooling down the earth. The DuPont-developed coolant, once released into the environment, was damaging this essential natural cooling process of the earth and heating the atmosphere. It is highly unlikely that DuPont and the rest of the chemical companies manufacturing CFCs knew, or could have known, their irreversible environmental effects before 1974. Yet as soon as the findings were published, the US Chemical Manufacturers Association, led by DuPont, initiated a research programme by academic investigators. The industry urged caution, and promising it would step up the search for a safe alternative chemical, did everything it could to delay a regulatory ban on CFCs (Maxwell and Briscoe, 1997). In 1980, as it became more likely that a global ban would be implemented, DuPont withdrew all research funding for its safe alternative (Weisskopf, 1988). It was not until 1986 (when British scientists had discovered a gaping hole in the ozone layer over Antarctica) that DuPont recommitted to finding an alternative, and later the company was to support a phase-out of CFCs by 2000. James Lovelock, the British scientist that had discovered the problem of CFC build-up in 1971, noted with regret almost fifty years later:

> Manufacturers were determined to deny they had any effects on the global environment, notably the depletion of the ozone layer in the atmosphere. (Lovelock, 2019)

The manipulation of the science of climate change and ozone depletion reveals a pattern of corporate denial and deliberate cover-up that seems to prevail, even when the evidence becomes irrefutable. This is a pattern that has typified the production of our most persistent and damaging chemicals. Case Studies 14.1 (above) and 14.2 (below) are very clear examples of this. But there are countless more, including, to name but a few: Leaded Petrol; Bisphenol A (BPA); Polychlorinated biphenyl (PCB); Polyvinyl chloride (PVC); Organophosphates and Glyphosate (best known as the 'Roundup' brand of weedkiller). To those cases, we might also add the better known examples of tobacco and asbestos (Whyte, 2020).

In each of those cases, the corporations were involved in a process of 'denial'; they used a range of techniques to justify the continuation of their deadly activities. The executives that wilfully ignored and actively sought to bury the evidence of the devastating effects of their products on human health and the eco-system, were fully aware of the consequences of what they were doing but did it anyway. And we can observe precisely the same process in countless other industries. The same process of corporate denial and distortion surrounding the fatal nature of their products can be found in food production and sales, in pharmaceuticals, in agricultural products, in textile and clothing production, in electronics production, and on and on and on (Stauber and Rampton, 1995; Lubbers, 2002; Pellow, 2007; Michaels, 2008).

Case Study 14.2

'Dieselgate'

The Volkswagen 'dieselgate' case which broke in 2015 involved the use of software to fraudulently understate deadly NOx emissions from 11 million cars. The real level of NOx emissions in Volkswagen, Audi and Porsche cars was up to 40 times more than the test results showed, and research subsequently showed that this pollution led to around 1,200 premature deaths (Massachusetts Institute of Technology News Office, 2017). One of the first things that Volkswagen did after the news stories began to emerge in summer 2015 was to commission its own engineers to test other brands (McGee, 2018). The company's executives knew that one way of deflecting attention and mitigating the blame was to dish the dirt on the whole industry. Volkswagen put their research team on the job because they assumed something that the rest of us didn't, i.e. that the falsification of diesel emissions had been common practice across the industry for years. The aim was to show that cheating was normal across the industry and therefore would mitigate Volkswagen's guilt and reduce its exposure to damages – and of course its assumption was correct. As well as the Volkswagen brands, we now know that 'defeat' devices were used by Fiat Chrysler, Nissan, Renault, Mercedes and Mitsubishi, amongst others (BBC News, 19th January 2016; Nikkei Asian Review, April 20th, 2016; Iwoamoto, 2016; BBC News, 11th June, 2018; BBC News, 9th July 2018; Shubber, 2019).

A clear pattern emerges in the Volkswagon case that is replicated in all of the cases discussed in this section. On close inspection, we see that all of them develop through the same five phases. Those phases are summarised in Table 14.1.

Table 14.1   Five Phases of PreMeditated Corporate Crime

Phase 1	Major corporations manufacture products that they either know or don't know are deadly.
Phase 2	As soon as the medical and scientific evidence emerges, they dispute this evidence.
Phase 3	Instead of prioritising action to mitigate environmental hazards and/or avoid causing deaths, corporations take action to ensure the market for its products expands.
Phase 4	As part of this response, scientific evidence and academic studies are dismissed and demeaned.
Phase 5	Corporations fund think tanks, scientific studies and even scientific institutes to fabricate an alternative evidence base about the health impacts, and ensure there is enough doubt for their industry to survive and thrive.

This is a pattern that seems to pervade all industries that are hazardous to the environment. Corporate executives have known at an early stage about the extent of the damage they are doing to humanity, animals and the environment. In a very broad sense, we can therefore say that they had full knowledge of what they were doing and of the consequences of their actions.

Pause for Review

Can you think of a similar case? Do they follow the same five phases as shown in Table 14.1?

But the analogy of criminal process should not end there. Those corporate executives have gone to great lengths to deny and distort any knowledge that causes us to avoid their products. They have actively prevented us knowing about them, let alone being able to do anything about them, long before much of the harm done had actually occurred. In the context of street offending, or the crime caused by relatively low-status individuals, the process outlined in Table 14.1 would be described as **premeditated crime**.

Think about the notion of 'premeditated crime'. In most jurisdictions, if a crime is planned or designed in any way, then this is taken to be something that aggravates or makes it worse. In the US, for example, the most serious category of murder is first degree murder. The premeditated nature of a killing is something that would render it serious enough to be considered first degree murder, or first degree manslaughter. From a criminal lawyer's perspective, the prior knowledge that corporate executives had about the deadly effects of the substances they sold makes what they did much more serious.

It is precisely this type of offending that the crime of ecocide seeks to capture. Yet it may not be so easy. As the remainder of this chapter will show, there are a number of deep structural problems embedded in the organising concepts of criminal law that limit its implementation. We begin to uncover those **structural limitations** in the section that follows.

THE PROBLEM OF DEFINING CORPORATE CRIME AS CRIME

If we explore the rules that determine criminal guilt a little more, there is no reason not to regard those executives as criminal killers. In other words, it is not difficult to see how each and every one of the scenarios in the previous section could be unambiguously prosecuted as crimes. Indeed, on rare occasions, some were. In Porto Marghera, Italy, for example, the managers of a chemical plant were put on trial for killing 157 workers and poisoning the Venice lagoon with polyvinylchlorides. Eventually a technicality prevented prosecution, but the court did hear the case, something of a rarity in this type of crime (*Independent*, 9th November 2001).

The problem with *mens rea* is that it has been developed in law to be applied to the guilty mind of *individuals*. Within a corporate boardroom of course a number of different decisions are made, very often *collectively*. This is one legal reason why working within a corporation reduces the potential criminalisation: as a collective entity, senior level decisions which impel action or inaction are generally not reducible to any one individual; moreover, it is often harder to identify the lack of action on the part of boardroom – or a series of negligent or reckless acts occurring at different points in the hierarchy of the organisation – than it is to identify a particular *act* which led to crime or a conspiracy to commit a series of criminal *acts*. Yet elsewhere, laws have been developed to capture just this type of collective crime. It's just they are not normally applied to corporate executives.

A highly controversial criminal law doctrine in the UK, known as **joint enterprise**, was developed to criminalise people who contributed to the offence, but were not necessarily directly involved in the physical act. The law does not even require the offender to be present. The key test is whether the offender could have foreseen that their participation in preparing or encouraging something to happen might lead to the primary offender committing an unlawful act. It is for this reason that this law fits very closely the types of crimes described in the previous section. The principle of 'joint enterprise' could easily be applied in, for example, the case of a corporate executive who was grossly negligent in not recognising or acting on the risks of a deadly substance. If we wanted to criminalise corporations in the UK for this type of crime, this might well be a legitimate legal route to take.

However, this is where we need to be a little bit careful about our understanding of how and why the criminal justice system does what it does. We know from almost eighty years of corporate crime research that criminal law is generally not used to target the powerful, even when there is no legal barrier to do so (Sutherland, 1983). Joint enterprise is a criminal offence that is used almost exclusively against those who are labelled as gang members. The campaign organisation JENGbA estimates that over 80% of those convicted using this legal principle are from black and minority ethnic communities (House of Commons Library, 2018). The offence is mainly used to convict young black men who can be found guilty of an offence by association, even when they were not at the scene of the crime.

There are other, more theoretical reasons for thinking that it is appropriate to apply criminal legal concepts to corporate crime. **Deterrence** theory remains the single most significant rationale underpinning the use of punishment in criminal justice systems. This is not to say it is the only rationale. There are a number of different rationales familiar to every criminology student that stand behind different forms of punishment (incapacitation, rehabilitation, reintegration and so on). Insofar as the dominant punishments are largely based on the expectation of a deterrent effect, it remains the dominant rationale. The problem with deterrence theory is that it doesn't work against the population that criminal punishment is used against the most.

Knowledge link: These topics are also covered in Chapters 28 and 29.

Deterrence theory is based upon the idea that individual conduct – the decision whether or not to commit a criminal act – is shaped by the costs and benefits that might arise from the conduct. Individuals are therefore supposed make a rational calculation or choice that weighs the chances of being caught and the severity of the punishment against the 'benefits' of committing a crime. Yet there are two reasons why this constitutes a flawed basis on which to punish. First, rational choice depends upon the subject having perfect knowledge of the risks of being caught and what the consequences might be if they are caught. Second, rational choice depends upon individuals being capable of exercising rational judgement. Generally, the model is applied to those who are least capable of acting rationally. As sociologist Pierre Bourdieu has argued, the people that punishment tends to target (people with a relatively low social status and few resources to draw upon to weigh up a rational decision) are not in the best position to judge either the chances of being caught, or the severity of the punishment (Bourdieu, 1998). More importantly, they are less likely to care, because they don't have much to lose. The ability to act rationally, in other words, is severely compromised where people do not have any control over the social conditions that shape their present and their future.

Knowledge link: This topic is also covered in Chapter 6.

However, in theory, deterrence is much more likely to work against corporations and executives. Indeed, corporate crime scholars have used the critique of deterrence theory to observe that it may well be more applicable to corporate crime (Chamblis, 1967). Corporations and the senior managers that run them do have some motivation to consider the long-term consequences of their decisions, and the costs of punishment to their business and their social position. They are much more likely to commit crime only after making a reasoned assessment and the choice to act rationally. In other words, corporations, unlike the usual targets of criminal justice systems, are 'future oriented' (Braithwaite, 1989). Moreover, although most individuals do not possess the information necessary to calculate rationally the probability of detection and punishment, large bureaucratic organisations do have the resources to deploy sophisticated information-gathering systems and to call upon lawyers and accountants. Both companies and their directors do make calculated decisions, not based upon perfect knowledge, but upon a range of knowledge resources available to them which allow them to make calculated decisions.

We have a difficult question to answer then: if concepts like 'joint enterprise' and theories like deterrence work best when applied to corporations and senior managers, then why are they so rarely applied to them? After all, it would not take a major stretch of the imagination to adopt criminal law categories to fit this purpose. Again, this is a major motivation behind the proposal of a new crime of ecocide. Yet when we think about how to fit the criminal law to this task, we come up against a different kind of structural limitation: the capacity of states to intervene. It is a discussion of this structural limitation that the chapter turns to next.

REGULATORY DEGRADATION

The first point to make is that the task that environmental regulators and legal reformers have on their hands is gargantuan. Take the issue of particulate air pollution, mentioned in the introduction to this chapter. As we saw, it is estimated to kill more than four million people each year across the globe. In addition to the Kyoto and Paris Agreements on climate change, the international community has numerous separate treaties that set out the targets to reduce particulate pollution, such as the 1979 UN Convention on Long-range Transboundary Air Pollution. In order for those treaties to be enforced, national governments have to take action. But this pollution is produced by hundreds of thousands of corporations worldwide, some very small and some very large; some of those will seek to minimise those emissions as far as possible and others will not. Sometimes minimising emissions as far as possible won't be enough to allow governments to reach their targets. This is the first dilemma that the problem of environmental regulation faces, i.e. how the huge task of ensuring legal limits are not breached can be enforced.

As a rule, corporations are rarely prosecuted for pollution offences, and corporate executives are prosecuted even less frequently (Whyte, 2010). In the case of environmental pollution-related deaths, for example, it is highly unlikely that any will result in prosecution. This is partly because cases of deaths 'brought forward' by pollution are not generally subjected to any process of investigation, and partly because of the complexities of investigating and prosecuting such cases.

This partly explains why, when regulators impose legal limits, corporations may or may not comply. And normally this depends on a very wide range of conditions, some of which states retain direct control of and others – like market conditions – that they might decide to retain less control over. States determine how regulatory regimes work. How often will a company's management be visited and inspected, and how will its senior management's legal compliance be monitored and enforced?

Those are questions that are progressively becoming more politically difficult for regulators to answer. Since the 1980s, the major international economic institutions, along with the most powerful national governments, have enthusiastically adopted policies that seek to undermine a whole range of social protections, including environmental regulation. This political strategy bemoans regulation as a 'burden on business', promotes the privatisation of public services, seeks further restrictions on workers' rights, and encourages the rolling back of a whole array of limits placed on corporations. The project to bring market discipline to the public sector on a grand scale – with its British origins in the Thatcher governments of the 1980s and its US origins in the Reagan administration – has always contained a militant anti-state ideology at its core. The consequence for environmental regulation is one of the great tragedies of the neoliberal period. Since the 1990s, most environmental regulatory authorities have faced tightening budgets and been unable to do a job that was already incredibly complex and difficult.

Take the UK as an example. There are over five million registered businesses that might potentially breach the law. Yet the main UK regulator employs little more than 1,000 frontline officers dedicated to law enforcement across those sectors. This is probably little more than the number of traffic wardens in London. Yet the task faced by those regulators – to ensure millions of businesses are complying with the law – is Sisyphean. In the UK, the annual budget for the Environment Agency is just 0.13% of annual government spending. The UK is not an outlier in this respect. The UK's approach is broadly comparable with other advanced industrial states (Farmer, 2007). Spending on the US Environmental Protection Agency (EPA), for example, accounts for just 0.2% of the annual federal budget in the US (Environmental Defense Fund, 2020).

Globally, the pressure on regulatory agencies has certainly intensified in the post-2008 financial crisis. The UK environment agency has faced in excess of 40% cuts in funding – again a feature of advanced economies that is not unique to the UK. Funding for the US Environmental Protection

Agency (EPA), for example, is now at a forty-year low. And this, combined with a series of political attacks on the Agency by the Trump administration, is having a major effect on enforcement. The *Washington Post* recently reported that US prosecutions have fallen to their lowest level in a decade (Eilperin and Dennis, 2019).

The preservation of a viable system of regulation in the neoliberal era is more difficult when we consider that other policies, such as privatisation, have intensified the demand on the need for effective regulators. The UK Environment Agency has faced major problems with the regulation of water quality since the privatisation of water provision in England. A recent investigation by the *Financial Times* revealed that most water companies were failing in their legal responsibility to keep Britain's waterways safe. A particular problem is the dumping, or failure to control the flow of, raw sewage into public waterways. None of England's rivers are safe enough to swim in because of the risk of people getting sick (Plimmer, 2019).

The capacity of states to intervene and protect us from corporate activity, as this section has shown, is already difficult in societies that do not prioritise control infrastructures. It is getting progressively worse in an era of regulatory degradation. What this means is that even if we have a new law on the statute books, major questions would remain about how that law might be effectively implemented and enforced. The effort needed to control corporate activities is certainly beyond the capacity of regulatory systems as they are currently configured.

Let us say, for the sake of argument, that we did have well-funded regulatory agencies, or at least agencies that were allocated more than a fraction of 1% of the annual budget, there would still be major questions about how we could change the overall effect of regulation. As we shall see in the following section, regulation is not only about the task of trying to control damage to the environment; the process of regulation also gives corporations permission to pollute within particular limits.

Pause for Review

As this section argues, the regulation of pollution is made more difficult by the concentration of corporate power in our neo-liberal era. Apart from the scale of the task, what else prevents states from taking tough action on environmental pollution?

LICENCED TO KILL

The issuing of licences that stipulate the levels that a particular industrial site can pollute air or waterways forms an important part of any regulator's work. The UK Environment Agency, for example, issues 14,000 pollution licences every year that allow corporations to produce waste, or to discharge substances into the air or into waterways (Environment Agency, 2018). A similar system is used in most advanced democracies. Even the deadliest forms of pollutant are very often produced under the conditions of a licence granted by a regulatory authority.

In the 1990s, just two chemical facilities run by Associated Octel and Ineos were permitted to emit four tonnes of dioxins into the English air every year (Whyte, 2014). Those factories alone accounted for 40% of the UK's carcinogenic chemical pollution. And they were licenced and encouraged by the British government to do so. One of those plants, in Ellesmere Port in North West England, is now said to be the last factory in the world producing lead additives for petrol. The facility is licenced for this purpose, and exports the chemical to Algeria, despite a worldwide ban (Johnston, 2017).

At the same time as setting the parameters for its 14,000 live licences to pollute, the Environment Agency also prosecutes breaches of those licences. This is the way that regulation works. States play an expansive 'regulatory' role that enables and facilitates corporate activities. This is the paradox that lies at the heart of the regulatory process. Corporations are licenced to kill, but within acceptable limits. Increasingly those limits are not determined by the extent to which they threaten public safety, or indeed the future of the planet, but by the sustainability of the corporate system.

In 2015, the UK government introduced a new duty for all regulatory agencies. This 'growth duty', introduced into law in the Deregulation Act 2015, requires regulators to 'have regard to the desirability of promoting economic growth' (UK Government, 2015). What this meant was that frontline inspectors at the Environment Agency and every other regulatory agency (including the Health and Safety Executive, the Financial Conduct Authority and the Serious Fraud Office) would have to consider the impact of their decisions on the economic health of a business before they enforce the law. UK government rules now require regulators to formally report on the effect that the growth duty has on how they enforce the law.

The problem here is that regulators have a dual function, and those functions have opposite aims. On one hand, the function demands the promotion of the growth of an industry, and on the other hand, the control of its harmful and criminal activities. All of this makes crimes against the environment appear as abstract crimes, i.e. they are very often not crimes at all, but things we define as harmful that the state fails to develop appropriate opprobrium against, things that the state declines to criminalise. And this abstraction makes the crime of 'ecocide' even more difficult to make workable. Indeed, as the commentary to Falk's original formulation declared:

> the State system is inherently incapable of organizing the defence of the planet against ecological destruction. (Falk, 1973: 20)

STRUGGLES AGAINST THE ECOCIDAL CORPORATION

Falk highlights, as we must, the structural limitations that we face when we expect states to place necessary controls on corporations. Our discussion of the way that states regulate corporations – the organisations that are now in control of the greatest threats to our planet – must therefore make us question the extent to which we could ever rely on international or national authorities to enforce the law of ecocide. In any case, as this chapter shows, national systems of regulation *legalise* and *encourage* almost everything that would count as ecocide.

States are culpable for their toleration and legalisation of much of this harm, their failures to develop adequate law and regulation which might mitigate these, their failures to enforce adequately such laws as do exist, and their failures to impose effective sanctions where violations of law are proven. This is not to say that we should ever abandon arguments for the criminalisation of the things that truly present a threat to us and the future of the planet. As researchers and as human beings, we must demand every effort to hold shareholders and directors of corporations to account for their actions and inactions.

Yet the deep paradox that faces us as students of corporate crime is that we can never rely on a capitalist state to enforce crimes that are committed in the name of **capitalism**. Criminologists who are minded to argue that solutions are to be found in the criminal justice system should reflect that even the very worst forms of corporate ecocide have, to use Kit Carson's concept, become 'conventionalised' (Carson, 1979).

Where can we look for change then, in a context in which the state is complicit in ecocide and the criminal justice system has proven to be less than useless at controlling corporate crime? One point that a number of corporate crime scholars make is worth repeating. Advances in law only happen when there is an organised popular demand. None of our social protections would have been possible unless people struggled for them outside the state. There would be few regulatory protections in the workplace without trade unions and without workers having taken action to demand those protections. It is therefore significant that the current demand for a law of ecocide is coming from the direct action campaigns on the streets that have been organised by school students and by organisations like Extinction Rebellion. If they are insisting on change, and if they are strong enough, then it is a possibility that ecocide might be taken seriously as a criminal offence.

───────── Hear from the Expert ─────────

As I research the topic discussed in this chapter, I am always amazed that explicit recognition of the corporation's central role in bringing us this close to the extinction of the human remains absent from most significant scientific reports on climate change and global pollution. Pick up any of the reports by the UN or the international financial institutions, or indeed any of the global health organisations, and you will not see any serious discussion of the corporation's role in the growing environmental catastrophe. The same goes for the international treaties on climate change. The Paris Agreement, for example, includes no acknowledgment of the key role that profit-making corporations play in climate change. In the extensive documents accompanying the Kyoto Protocol, corporations are only mentioned in the articles setting out their permission to trade in carbon credits. In other words, the corporation is only ever seen as the solution to the problem. This matters a lot to researchers and to students, because international organisations set the agenda and set the parameters of what are considered legitimate issues and therefore legitimate questions to ask. It is only very rarely that UN bodies or inter-governmental organisations ask about how we should deal with the corporation as a *problem*. Moreover, when the corporation is seen as a problem to be addressed, UN bodies or inter-governmental organisations almost never confront the problem of the corporation in relation to climate change. That means it's up to us to keep asking this questions and to place corporations under proper scrutiny.

CHAPTER SUMMARY

- Corporations are key agents in climate change.
- Calls to re-establish the crime of ecocide seek to implement a new offence through the mechanisms of the International Criminal Court and national legal systems.
- The renewed call for a crime of ecocide raises some vital questions about the role of law in capitalist societies, not least law's role in protecting them from corporate activity.
- There is a pattern that seems to pervade all industries that are hazardous to the environment: corporate executives have known from an early stage about the extent of the damage they are doing to humanity, animals and the environment.
- The prior knowledge that corporate executives had about the deadly effects of the substances they sold makes what they did much more serious.
- When we think about how to fit the criminal law to this task, we come up against a number of structural limitations: the conceptual foundations of the criminal law; the capacity of states to intervene; the dual function of regulation that simultaneously controls corporate activity and gives corporations the permission to pollute.
- Criminalisation of the corporate activities that present a threat to us will not be enough to protect the future of the planet, but this doesn't mean we should not demand every effort to hold shareholders and directors of corporations to account for their ecocidal actions and inactions.

Review Questions

1. What is the crime of 'ecocide'?
2. What types of environmental harm are corporations responsible for?
3. What are the structural limitations that make a law of ecocide difficult to implement and enforce?
4. What could be done to prevent the environmental crimes and harms caused by corporations in the future?

GO FURTHER

Books

1. The following book develops the themes in this chapter, fully placing the arguments in the context of theories of the corporation, the colonial history of the corporation, and the global regulatory process:

   Whyte, D. (2020) *Ecocide: Kill the Corporation Before It Kills Us*. Manchester: Manchester University Press.

2. This second title explores the history of the corporation through the lens of international law, offering a radical analysis which explains why corporations cannot be held accountable by law.

   Baars, G. (2020) *The Corporation, Law, and Capitalism: A Radical Perspective on the Role of Law in the Global Political Economy*. Chicago, IL: Haymarket.

3. The title below uses a number of case studies (Palestine, Sri Lanka, Australia and Alberta, Canada) to analyse the relationship between colonialism, capitalism, and the ecological crisis:

   Short, D. (2016) *Redefining Genocide: Settler Colonialism, Social Death and Ecocide*. London: Zed.

Journal Articles

1. This article contains Falk's original statement on ecocide, and his proposal for a new law:

   Falk, R. (1973) Environmental warfare and ecocide — facts, appraisal, and proposals. *Bulletin of Peace Proposals*, 4(1): 80–96.

2. This article explores how close Falk's proposal for a new law and similar proposals have come to being introduced. It reinforces his argument for a law of ecocide, conceptualising it as the '5th Crime against Peace':

   Higgins, P., Short, D. and South, N. (2013) Protecting the planet: a proposal for a law of ecocide. *Crime, Law and Social Change*, 59(3): 251–266.

3. This article analyses how the neo-liberal phase of capitalism has sought a move away from social and environmental protection at a time we need it most:

   Tombs, S. (2016) Making better regulation, making regulation better? *Policy Studies*, 37(4): 332–349.

Useful Websites

1. UK Corporate Watch produces detailed briefings on corporate wrongdoing, with a particular emphasis on their impact on the environment and the failure to regulate: Corporate Watch (UK): https://corporatewatch.org/
2. Although they are not part of the same organisation, US Corporate Watch does the same thing as its UK namesake and is an excellent source of information on the environmental impact of corporate activity: https://corpwatch.org/
3. The Bureau of Investigative Journalism is a good source of reportage on corporations with a mission to 'hold power to account': https://www.thebureauinvestigates.com/projects/corporations

REFERENCES

Banerjee, N., Song, L. and Hasemyar, D. (2015) 'Exxon's Own Research Confirmed Fossil Fuels' Role in Global Warming Decades Ago', *Inside Climate News*, 16th September. Available at: https://insideclimatenews.org/news/15092015/Exxons-own-research-confirmed-fossil-fuels-role-in-global-warming

Bourdieu, P. (1998) *Acts of Resistance: Against the Tyranny of the Market*. New York: New Review Press.

Braithwaite, J. (1989) *Crime, Shame and Reintegration*. Cambridge: Cambridge University Press.

Carson, W. G. (1979) The conventionalization of early factory crime. *International Journal of the Sociology of Law*, 7: 37–60.

Chamblis, W. (1967) Types of deviance and effectiveness of legal sanction. *Wisconsin Law Review*, no. 3, Summer: 703–719.

Eilperin, J. and Dennis, B. (2019) 'Under Trump, EPA inspections fall to a 10-year low', *Washington Post*, 8th February.

Environment Agency (2018) *Regulating for People, the Environment and Growth*. Bristol: Environment Agency.

Environmental Defence Fund (2020) Deep EPA cuts put public health at risk. Available at: https://www.edf.org/deep-epa-cuts-put-public-health-risk

Exxon Research and Engineering Company (1981) Internal memo dated February 5th: 2. Available online at:http://insideclimatenews.org/sites/default/files/documents/Exxon%20Review%20of%20Climate%20Research%20Program%20%281981%29pdf

Falk, R. (1973) Environmental warfare and ecocide — facts, appraisal, and proposals. *Bulletin of Peace Proposals*, 4(1): 80–96.

Farmer, A. (2007) *Handbook of Environmental Protection and Enforcement: Principles and Practice*. London: Earthscan.

Farrell, J. (2016) Corporate funding and ideological polarization about climate change. *Proceedings of the National Academy of Sciences of the United States of America*, 113(1): 92–97.

Gauger, A., Rabatel-Fernel, M. P., Kulbicki, L., Short, D., Higgins, P. (2012) *The Ecocide Project: 'Ecocide is the missing 5th Crime Against Peace'*, London: School of Advanced Study, University of London.

Geis, G. (1996) 'A Base on Balls for White Collar Criminals'. In D. Shichor and D. Sechrest (eds), *Three Strikes and You're Out: Vengeance as Public Policy*. Thousand Oaks, CA: Sage.

Griffin, P. (2017) *The Carbon Majors Database: CDP Carbon Majors Report 2017*. London: CDP UK.

Higgins, P., Short, D. and South, N. (2013) Protecting the planet: a proposal for a law of ecocide. *Crime, Law and Social Change*, 59(3): 251–266.

House of Commons Library (2018) *Joint Enterprise Debate Pack Number CDP-2018-0014*, 23rd January. London: House of Commons Library.

Johnston, I. (2017) 'UK company sells lead to last place on Earth where leaded petrol is legal', *The Independent*, 22nd August. Available at: https://www.independent.co.uk/environment/leaded-petrol-algeria-still-legal-innospec-cheshire-uk-sale-export-tel-tetraethyl-lead-a7907196.html [accessed 5th August, 2019].

Kentaro Iwoamoto (2016) 'Mitsubishi Motors rigged fuel economy tests for more than 600,000 cars', *Nikkei Asian Review*, 20th April. Available at: https://asia.nikkei.com/Business/Companies/Mitsubishi-Motors-rigged-fuel-economy-tests-for-more-than-600-000-cars

Lovelock, J. (2019) *Novascene: The Coming Age of Hyperintelligence*. London: Allen Lane. p. 38.

Lubbers, E. (ed.) (2002) *Battling Big Business: Countering Greenwash, Infiltration and Other Forms of Corporate Bullying*. Dartington, Devon: Green.

McGee, P. (2018) 'Car emissions scandal: loopholes in the lab tests', *Financial Times*, 7th August.

Massachusetts Institute of Technology News Office (2017) 'Study: Volkswagen's excess emissions will lead to 1,200 premature deaths in Europe', press release, 3rd March. Available at: http://news.mit.edu/2017/volkswagen-emissions-premature-deaths-europe-0303

Maxwell, J. and Briscoe, F. (1997) There's money in the air: the CFC ban and DuPont's regulatory strategy. *Business Strategy and the Environment*, 6(5): 276–286.

Michaels, D. (2008) *Doubt is Their Product*. Oxford: Oxford University Press.

Monsanto (2017) 'Agent Orange: Background on Monsanto's Involvement', 7th April. Available at: https://monsanto.com/company/media/statements/agent-orange-background/

Pearce, F. and Tombs, S. (1998) *Toxic Capitalism: Corporate Crime in the Chemical Industry*. Aldershot: Ashgate.

Pellow, D. N. (2007) *Resisting Global Toxins*. Cambridge, MA: MIT Press.

Plimmer, G. (2019) 'Can England's water companies clean up its dirty rivers?', *Financial Times*, 12th June. Available at: https://www.ft.com/content/5c1a33e4-8939-11e9-97ea-05ac2431f453

Short, D. (2016) *Redefining Genocide: Settler Colonialism, Social Death and Ecocide*. London: Zed.

Shubber, K. (2019) 'Fiat Chrysler agrees to pay $800m to settle emissions cheating case', *Financial Times*, 10th January.

Stauber, J. and Rampton, S. (1995) *Toxic Fudge is Good for You*. New York: Common Courage.

Sutherland, E. (1983) *White Collar Crime, The Uncut Version*. New Haven, CT: Yale University Press.

Tombs, S. and Whyte, D. (2015) *The Corporate Criminal: Why Corporations Must Be Abolished*. New York: Routledge, Taylor & Francis Group.

UK Government (2015) *Deregulation Act 2015*, Section 108. London: HMSO.

US Department of Veteran's Affairs (n.d.) *Birth Defects in Children of Women Vietnam Veterans*. Available at: https://www.publichealth.va.gov/exposures/agentorange/birth-defects/children-women-vietnam-vets.asp

Weisskopf, M. (1988) 'CFCs rise and fall of chemical "miracle"', *The Washington Post*, 10th April.

Whyte, D. (2004) All that glitters isn't gold: environmental crimes and the production of local criminological knowledge. *Crime Prevention and Community Safety*, 6(1): 53–63.

Whyte, D. (2010) 'An Intoxicated Politics of Regulation'. In H. Quirk, T. Seddon and G. Smith (eds), *Regulation and Criminal Justice*. Cambridge: Cambridge University Press.

Whyte, D. (2020) *Ecocide: Kill the Corporation Before It Kills Us*. Manchester: Manchester University Press.

Organised and Transnational Crime

15

Xavier L'Hoiry and Jo Large

Learning Objectives

By the end of this chapter you will:

- Be able to critically explore the nature and dynamics of transnational and organised crime.
- Examine three broad law enforcement responses to organised crime.
- Challenge popular and political narratives around transnational organised crime, in relation to mafias, diversification of offenders and the nature of victimhood.
- Examine key issues that have emerged from research on transnational organised crime.
- Be able to highlight the culturally and socially embedded nature of transnational organised crime activities, including its causes and drivers such as the importance of demand.

Framing Questions

1. Why do you think transnational organised crime is a topic that attracts so much media and political attention?
2. What are the main approaches law enforcement agencies have used to respond to transnational organised crime? For what reasons might they be problematic?
3. In what ways does academic research on transnational organised crime challenge popular depictions?

INTRODUCTION

Transnational organised crime has been a subject of fascination for decades. From highly stylistic and romanticised Hollywood films to governmental depictions emphasising danger and violence, a considerable mythology has arisen around this form of criminality. Many of these depictions tend to portray organised crime as the domain of ruthless criminals operating within groups defined by some form of societal 'otherness' – be it their ethnicity, nationality or socio-economic background. These outsiders are said to carry out their illicit activities in a murky underworld characterised by notions of honour, respect and extreme violence. Although all of this may make for exciting television, much academic research has sought to rebut these popular representations. These depictions are criticised as being far too narrow and simplistic, framing what is a complex social problem as one which can be solved by relatively simple means – such as providing law enforcement with greater resources and powers.

This chapter takes a critical stance in exploring the nature and dynamics of transnational organised crime and, in doing so, encourages you to challenge narratives presented by the State and mainstream media. We will explore various illicit marketplaces and consider how these examples of organised criminality problematise popular understandings of this phenomenon. The chapter begins with a brief overview of definitional debates concerning organised crime as well as outlining State-led efforts to combat organised crime. The chapter then considers four key areas of discussion in organised crime:

1. The presence of mafia groups.
2. The diversity of offenders in illicit marketplaces.
3. The ambiguity of victimhood.
4. The role of demand as the driver of illicit markets.

These themes are intended to help you become more critical of dominant discourses concerning organised crime and move you towards more nuanced understandings of this form of criminality, its social and cultural embeddedness, its causes and drivers, and ultimately, what might be done about it.

MAPPING THE TERRAIN

The following section introduces you to ongoing debates surrounding definitions of organised crime before exploring governmental attempts to respond to this phenomenon.

What is Organised Crime?

Perhaps the key debate concerning organised crime – for academics and practitioners alike – is how exactly this term should be defined. Should definitions focus on types of offences? Should they concentrate on offenders? How should we differentiate organised crime from other types of criminality? Should the focus be on the transnational dimensions of organised crime or would it be more worthwhile to examine the local context which facilitates this type of offending? Many different answers exist to these questions, leading to the creation of hundreds of different definitions of this phenomenon. German criminologist Klaus von Lampe (2019) has attempted to track these many definitions and estimates that there are now over 200 different definitions of organised crime across the globe.

One key area of ongoing debate amongst those concerned with organised crime and how to define it is the extent of its transnationality. In the late 1990s, governments around the world grew more and more concerned with what they deemed to be the increasingly transnational nature of organised crime, and the ways in which criminals exploited advancements in technology and communications to cross international borders. In response, the United Nations (UN) created the UN Convention against Transnational Organised Crime, known as the Palermo Convention since the resolution was signed in Sicily's capital. The Palermo Convention envisioned organised crime as a transnational phenomenon in which 'the enemies of progress and human rights seek to exploit the openness and opportunities of globalization for their purposes' (United Nations, 2004: iii). But while contemporary illicit markets undoubtedly operate across national borders, researchers have warned against ignoring the local dimensions of organised crime, particularly 'local trading networks, [in which] commercial viability is assured by the continual realignment of local precedents in the context of global markets, coordinating relations between individuals and groups, and involving constant mediations and renegotiations within culturally complex social systems' (Hobbs, 2013).

Definitional debates are complex, and as such we do not have space to do them justice here, though we return to discussions of organised crime definitions in later sections of this chapter. However, it is worth highlighting how these debates are generally not helped by depictions of organised crime relentlessly promulgated by mainstream media which paint such activities as (depending on the film or television series in question) extremely violent, laced with romanticism, predatory, bound by codes of honour and respect, highly organised and exceptionally sophisticated. These depictions have become indelibly attached to popular understandings of organised crime, to the extent that, as Woodiwiss (2000) argues, their presence has served to 'dumb down' what should be intricate and meticulous discussions concerning a complex socio-economic and political issue.

Knowledge link: This topic is also covered in Chapter 5.

Pause for Thought

Thinking of a recent film or television series about organised crime, what impact has this had on your own, perhaps unconscious, perceptions of this type of criminality? Think also about whether these depictions situate organised crime in the context of socio-economic or political developments. Or rather, does the film or television series in question tend to focus on the violent or otherwise dramatic aspects of organised crime at the expense of unpicking the complex forces and processes which shape this type of crime?

As we will see next, a consequence of defining organised crime along narrow criteria reliant on media depictions is that this has shaped State-led responses to this type of offending in ways which may not always be particularly useful or progressive.

Responding to Organised Crime

Despite multiple and at times conflicting understandings of organised crime, governments around the world and their respective law enforcement agencies have tended to deploy broadly similar measures in responding to this type of criminality. The dominant approaches tend to originate in the United States before being adopted by other jurisdictions. These might be broadly categorised as a) fight fire with fire and b) follow the money. In recent years however, rather more innovative approaches have also emerged.

Fight fire with fire

Governmental understandings of organised crime have often conceptualised those involved in such activities as operating within highly organised, rigid hierarchical groups with the ability to deploy sophisticated means to achieve their criminal ends. In many ways, this understanding of organised crime dates back to American discourses in the mid-twentieth century which overwhelmingly focused on Italian-American groups as the dominant organised crime threat to the nation. Having understood the problem in this way, the logical response for governments has been to fight fire with fire and to create dedicated agencies which mirror the perceived size, structure and means of the threat they allegedly face. This explains the decision in the 1950s to assign the Federal Bureau of Investigation as the leading agency tasked with tackling organised crime in America. In the UK, a similar desire to mirror the perceived scale and means of the organised criminal threat has been demonstrable in the successive amalgamation and ongoing nationalisation of law enforcement agencies tasked with combatting organised crime – from Regional Crime Squads (1964), to the National Crime Squad (1998), to the Serious Organised Crime Agency (2006), to the National Crime Agency (2013).

Knowledge link: This topic is also covered in Chapter 13.

Though the work of these agencies has undoubtedly led to notable successes, concerns remain as to the rationale which has underpinned these responses to organised crime (Woodiwiss and Hobbs, 2009), not least the danger of ignoring the critical local context for this type of activity.

Follow the money

Given the financial motives which are said to underpin organised criminality and the belief that money laundering facilitates much of these activities, governments have become increasingly concerned with finance-based strategies to combat organised crime. These approaches include the creation of legislation which empowers governments to seize the assets of convicted organised criminals, such as the US Racketeer Influenced and Corrupt Organizations Act in the US, the Proceeds of Crime Act in the UK, and the Criminal Code in the Netherlands. Alongside these powers of forfeiture, many jurisdictions around the world have introduced instruments variously known as 'currency transaction reports', 'suspicious transaction reports' or 'suspicious activity reports' – all of which compel so-called financial intermediaries (such as banks, accountants and lawyers) to report suspicious financial activity. Despite some successes, finance-oriented strategies to combat organised crime have not been without their criticisms. It has been argued, for example, that there remains insufficient evidence demonstrating the successes and value of these strategies, partly because little is known about the true scale of the organised crime/money laundering problem in the first place. Moreover, there are questions as to the sustainability of these approaches in the longer term, particularly in light of the ongoing rise of cryptocurrencies and the extent to which current strategies – and those tasked with delivering them – are equipped to tackle this new challenge.

Innovative approaches

In recent years, new and innovative approaches to combatting organised crime have emerged, particularly in Italy where the problem of organised crime might be considered deeply culturally embedded in certain regions. For instance, grassroots movements in places like Sicily have attempted to encourage forms of resistance to mafia activities through what has been called '**critical consumption**' (Forno and Gunnarson, 2010). This involves educating local consumers about which suppliers are affiliated to mafia groups and which are not – and encouraging locals to resist organised crime by shopping with non-mafia affiliated suppliers. Moreover, Sergi (2018) has discussed the use of child protection measures to separate the children of mafia members from their families. Such approaches seek to disrupt the transmission of mafia cultures from parents to siblings which are said to sustain mafia activities from one generation to the next. By removing children from familial settings, it is hoped these cycles can be broken.

The following sections explore key issues in organised crime debates, considering who commits organised criminal offences, who the victims of such offending may be, and the extent to which the public can be considered complicit in the proliferation of illicit marketplaces.

TRANSNATIONAL ORGANISED CRIME AND MAFIAS

Discussions of transnational organised crime seemingly always involve some mention of *The Mafia*. It is difficult to talk about organised crime without conjuring up images of shadowy gangsters in pin-stripe suits smoking big cigars and making offers you can't refuse. But research shows that we should be careful how we treat this phenomenon both conceptually and practically. This section explores mafia groups and considers the extent to which it can be said that such groups continue to play a central role in contemporary transnational organised crime. It is worth remembering that while the following discussion focuses on Italian examples of mafia groups, non-Italian mafia groups exist in different parts of the world.

What is actually meant by the term 'mafia'? The word itself originates from Italy, but scholars disagree on exactly what it means. Over time, the term 'mafia' has been increasingly used to describe criminal behaviour, particularly that perpetrated by groups of men in Southern Italian regions such as Sicily and Calabria. In 1982, Italian law formally adopted this latter understanding of the term by enacting the famous Article 416 of the Italian penal code which legally recognised mafia groups as criminal associations. But while this understanding of the term is now legally enshrined, specific definitions of mafia groups remain contested insofar as what the criteria for such a criminal association should be. In other words, some would argue that not all organised crime groups can be called mafias. Italian criminologist Letizia Paoli (2014) proposes a four-pronged criterion for 'true' mafia groups:

1. Longevity – mafia groups have a long lineage and trace their origins back several decades and centuries. This means they are deeply socially and culturally embedded into the fabric of their home towns, cities and regions.
2. Organisational and cultural complexity – mafia groups are comprised of highly complex organisational systems composed of hierarchical structures, divisions of labour and ruling bodies. They also display complex cultural practices which emphasise the exclusivity of mafia membership and the dominance of the mafia group over all other aspects of members' lives. This cultural code invokes notions of honour and secrecy, with pre-modern rituals such as blood oaths used to initiate new members into mafia groups.
3. Political dominion – mafia groups seek to exercise some form of political dominion. Exercising political power remains at the heart of their activities and they often do this by controlling voting blocs which are highly influential in local and regional elections.
4. Control of markets – mafia groups attempt (but are not always successful) to control markets, establishing monopolies or duopolies in both legal and illegal sectors.

If these criteria are used, simply being a well-organised, hierarchical group engaging in criminal activities does not necessarily mean that such a group would constitute a mafia. Instead, only a select few groups can be termed 'mafias' with scholars proposing that these might include, for instance, the Sicilian Cosa Nostra, the 'Ndrangheta, the Japanese yakuza and some Chinese Triads (Paoli, 2008; 2014). Other organised crime groups might be very successful, such as some South American drug cartels, but they cannot be categorised as mafias since some aspects of their activities do not meet the full criteria as set out by Paoli. Describing any organised crime group as a mafia is an error often made by the media who tend to equate all organised crime with mafias and are quick to warn of the dangers of various mafias, be it from Eastern Europe, Africa or South America (Woodiwiss and Hobbs, 2009).

This is yet another example of the way in which complex debates about organised crime are stripped of their nuance and instead, contested terminology is erroneously and haphazardly used. Finally, it is also important to note that research has not found evidence of a singular, monolithic mafia operating across the globe, exerting control over illegal markets. In this sense, the idea of *The Mafia* as a single, shadowy conspiracy is a fallacy. Instead, there are several different mafia groups of different shapes and sizes, some of which are well-known and others less so; some are involved in multiple commodities whereas others focus on specific markets; and some operate across the world while others prefer to leave a smaller geographical footprint.

There is little doubt that mafia groups have been heavily influential in the development of organised crime in some parts of the world. In Southern Italy, mafia-type organised crime traces its lineage across several centuries, as far back as the end of feudalism when a vacuum of governance and power in regions such as Sicily emerged. Groups of local men filled this vacuum, acting as protectors and de facto rulers of their local areas, sometimes operating as go-betweens mediating disputes between landowners living in the north and local peasants in the south. Italian social scientist Diego Gambetta (1993) has called these processes Protection Theory, in which so-called 'men of honour' carried out what would usually be State functions such as protecting local populations and collecting taxes as payment for their services. These activities continued for centuries, embedding these mafia groups deeply in their local communities and giving birth to what was to become organised crime in Italy, carried out by mafia groups across regions of Southern Italy such as Sicily, Campania and Calabria (Paoli, 2008).

However, despite this evident historical presence, there are questions as to the enduring influence of mafia groups today. Some groups appear to be growing and enjoying considerable success in their criminal endeavours. The 'Ndrangheta, for example, is said to have a worldwide network of members and associates while the Camorra, which originated in Campania, appear to be increasingly prosperous in recent years. The Camorra's criminal activities have been documented to range from extortion, drug trafficking, counterfeiting and waste disposal, involving criminal networks extending across Europe, South America, and parts of Africa.

In contrast, there are reports that perhaps the most well-known mafia group, the Sicilian Cosa Nostra, is struggling to retain its influence (Asthana, 2019). The Sicilian Cosa Nostra is often said to have given birth to Italian-American organised crime groups following the mass migration of Southern Italians to the USA in the early twentieth century. Scholars suggest that the Sicilian Cosa Nostra is one of the oldest mafia groups in the world, a testament to its fiercely insular code of conduct and the depth with which the group has embedded itself into parts of Sicily (Paoli, 2008). But more recently, this group is said to have entered a period of decline for a number of reasons. Firstly, law enforcement efforts against the Sicilian Cosa Nostra have intensified in the past few decades, culminating in the arrest of the group's powerful 'boss of bosses' Salvatore 'Toto' Riina in 1993. Riina's replacement, Bernardo Provenzano, was himself arrested in 2006 in another blow to the group's activities. Aside from law enforcement activities however, the Sicilian Cosa Nostra might be said to have suffered as a result of non-crime related developments, such as underpopulation in some Sicilian towns and villages. This serves as another reminder that organised crime groups live in the real world and are subject to many of the same socio-economic conditions experienced by everyone else. It might also be argued that the Sicilian Cosa Nostra's own codes of conduct which emphasise secrecy and exclusivity work against the group in some ways. The Sicilian Cosa Nostra place an emphasis on strong ties, exercising 'extreme rigidity' (Paoli, 2008: 19) in their recruitment practices and demanding absolute loyalty and secrecy from their members. The group has even created a self-imposed rule decreeing that Sicilian families should not re-settle outside of the region, a move designed to 'strengthen the cohesion of the mafia consortium' (Paoli, 2008: 20). But while this might seem a sound approach in order to avoid the gaze of law enforcement, it also makes it difficult to create connections with actors outside of the group's immediate circle. The Sicilian Cosa Nostra, who have for so long relied on pre-modern rituals to secure their survival over several centuries, may therefore be struggling to adapt their insular cultural practices to an increasingly globalised world.

Research therefore suggests that mafia groups retain considerable involvement in contemporary organised crime. Equally, however, it is important to remember that these groups are just one type of actor in the broader spectrum of those involved in organised crime, many of whom are disorganised, non-ideological and principally motivated by making a quick profit. While some mafia groups have undoubtedly prospered in recent years, others are struggling to retain their previous influence and power. It is important therefore not to over-estimate their presence in illicit marketplaces and to avoid falling foul of media-led depictions of some mythical, omnipresent mafia exerting control over criminal markets from the shadows. The next section moves away from focusing on the understandings of organised crime that focus the role of mafias (or other highly organised criminal groups) in order to emphasise the diverse nature of offenders who are involved in organised crime activities.

DIVERSIFICATION OF OFFENDERS IN TRANSNATIONAL ORGANISED CRIME

In his critique of terms such as 'transnational organised crime', Hobbs (2019: 42) argues that we must consider the 'chaotic nature of the multiple groups and individuals who are immersed in illegal markets' and further, emphasises the 'disparate range of entrepreneurial activity' that takes place. This section will explore research case studies that challenge the 'Othering' we see in organised crime discourse and highlight the mundane and varied actors involved in organised crime activities.

Much like the difficulties in capturing what organised crime is through a clear and meaningful definition, capturing a meaningful description of who organised crime offenders are, remains difficult. This is largely because the diversification of offenders – or actors – involved in organised crime activities is variable; in terms of size of organisations, how they are structured, how they are organised, and the kinds of illegal markets they are involved in. Several attempts to categorise organised crime actors and networks have been made. These challenge media depictions of organised crime and highlight the range of offenders and actors involved.

Part of the issue stems from challenges in defining what we mean by organised crime in the first place and what types of characteristics we look for in terms of who the offenders are, what illegal markets/activities are involved, how the organisation is structured – and especially for *transnational* organised crime, how these groups operate across borders. Hagan (2006: 135), who differentiates between 'organised crime' (activities or crimes that require a degree of organisation) and 'Organised Crime' (groups or organisations that commit crime) suggests an Organised Crime Continuum that can be used to identify primary and secondary characteristics of Organised Crime. This means we can identify different levels of Organised Crime groups:

- Level 1 – 'fully fledged groups'
- Level 2 – 'semi Organised Crime groups that lack full development of some characteristics'
- Level 3 – 'street gangs and others that are lower level in exhibiting full development'

Some authors are critical of these kinds of descriptions, as they can bring individual groups under one umbrella term, with no clear rationale for why a single descriptive or demographic characteristic is selected as most important.

Regardless of attempts to categorise actors involved in organised crime activities, there is clear consensus on the need to recognise the variety of different groups and individuals involved. Wider economic changes are reflected in organised crime structures. This is through increasing flexibility, less rigidity and networking between different – and disassociated – groups. Groups that were once identifiable through particular social and cultural characteristics have changed. Using drug markets as an example, Antonopoulos and Papanicolaou (2018) describe how contemporary British organised crime groups are not only more flexible, but also cross ethnic and social class boundaries. However, this is not to say that ethnicity or locality should be discounted from relevance (Antonopoulos and Papanicolaou, 2018).

Taking the illicit trade in drugs as an example, it is clear to see the extent of diversity in how individuals and groups involved are connected – and disconnected in terms of their structure and size. How different actors work, and who the offenders are in terms of their demographic characteristics, also vary considerably. This is perhaps unsurprising when you consider the diverse nature of drug markets which exist within a competitive and rapidly evolving context (see Antonopoulos and Papanicolaou, 2018: 53). Ethnographic research on the cocaine market, by Hall and Antonopoulos (2017), found 'a fragmented business dependent on networks of individual entrepreneurs and groups. At the core of collaborations often lie family, ethnic or kinship relationships and relationships forged within legal businesses and in prison'.

The emphasis on *transnational* organised crime threats in official and policy discourse, and the resulting position these activities hold on the international law enforcement agenda, suggests a very structured picture. However, it is argued that in illegal markets such as drugs and counterfeits, this emphasis fails to recognise that the diverse range of people involved are not necessarily being manipulated and controlled by organised crime groups (Antonopoulos and Papanicolaou, 2018). In fact, research highlights the entrepreneurial nature of much activity in these markets and the quite unusual range of those involved. In their study of the illicit trade in counterfeit, falsified and illicit medicines, Hall and Antonopoulos (2016) highlight the numerous actors and different structures that are needed. They found that some individuals may be linked to organised crime groups, however the trade was facilitated by a much wider range of actors. This is like the trade in counterfeit products more generally.

Hear from the Expert

Professor Georgios Antonopoulos

Generally, manifestations of 'organised crime' are based on small, opportunistic networks. Illegal markets are highly competitive environments involving mostly horizontal (rather than hierarchical) structures. A close look at the profiles of drug marketers, for instance, can reveal the participation of bouncers, youngsters, teenagers 'having a good time' in the night-time economy, transporters, couriers, respectable professionals (legal entrepreneurs, lawyers, celebrities), 'user-dealers', and many other 'ordinary' people. Similarly, in my research on the illicit tobacco trade, I came across university students and pensioners supplementing their income from smuggling from major holiday destinations.

The diversity of offenders in illegal markets such as counterfeits and tobacco are well illustrated at the distribution end of the process. Here we see examples of street sellers, who are often socially and economically marginalised migrants, but also those who are from a much more secure socio-economic background. This variation challenges the notion of the 'hardened criminal' in these markets; violence is often not a desirable feature given it is likely to be 'bad for business' (Antonopoulos and Papanicolaou, 2018: 67). Technology is also changing the accessibility of illegal markets to a broader range of actors. Here we see not only expansions in existing markets, but also opportunities for newer markets. For example, digital technology has impacted on markets in illicit lifestyle drugs, creating **prosumers** (those who are both producers and consumers) who are part of a complex new era of **multifunctional actors** in markets that are opened up to people across socio-economic and cultural boundaries.

Making distinctions and generalisations about offenders, therefore, becomes challenging. This is partly due to bias that results from the reliance on case files and law enforcement data to shape our understanding of who is involved in organised crime (Antonopoulos and Papanicolaou, 2018), but further, assumes a consensus around what constitutes organised crime. Adding the term 'transnational' into this mix further exacerbates these issues. This is because it over-emphasises the abstract global element, neglects the importance of local context and experiences, and suggests a false sense of structure (see Hobbs, 2019).

As the next section shows, it is not only organised crime offenders who are frequently and erroneously portrayed within narrow definitional parameters; the same can also be said concerning victims of organised crime.

VICTIMHOOD AND TRANSNATIONAL ORGANISED CRIME

Transnational organised crime undoubtedly leads to people being victimised, be it as victims of modern-day slavery, by becoming addicted to harmful substances, or by experiencing other forms of violence. But State-led discourses of organised crime together with popular media depictions often present the relationship between offenders and victims as straightforward and linear. In contrast, research has sought to problematise the offender-victim dichotomy in organised crime and scholars have called for more critical approaches to understanding the multifaceted nature of victimhood in this context (Zhang, 2009). This section considers examples of organised criminal activities in which victims clearly exist, but the nature of their victimhood necessitates further analysis in order to appreciate the dynamics of illicit marketplaces.

Knowledge link: This topic is also covered in Chapter 17.

Human smuggling and trafficking marketplaces are useful examples through which to explore the ambiguity of victimhood.

The market in human smuggling has a long history but has certainly grown in recent years as a result of socio-economic and political developments. Natural disasters, civil wars and economic declines have all pushed large amounts of people to seek moves away from their home regions and countries. With the political climate seemingly turning against welcoming migrants into Western countries, those wishing to relocate are increasingly turning to illegal means to do so. Hence, human smuggling is enjoying a boom. As an aside to this discussion, these developments are a useful reminder that illicit marketplaces are responsive to developments in the licit socio-economy and do not simply operate in a mythical underworld cut off from the rest of society. Transnational organised crime reacts to political, legal and social processes and illicit markets are very much shaped by events which on the face of them may seemingly have nothing to do with organised crime.

Victimhood in human smuggling is particularly ambiguous since this type of criminal activity is often characterised by mutual consent between the smuggler and the individual being smuggled (Kleemans and Smit, 2014). The presence of consent may be one way of distinguishing smuggling from human trafficking and exploitation, i.e. the person being smuggled is aware of what's happening and consents to take part. In this sense, the relationship might be akin to a business transaction: a customer desires a service and the smuggler will, for a fee, provide this service. The fact that consent is present between all parties may therefore problematise the notion of victimhood in this criminal market. While no one doubts that the many thousands of people who have died during perilous sea and other crossings in recent years are of course victims, the existence of consent makes the victim-offender relationship more complex than is often presented. What the example of human smuggling perhaps demonstrates is the nuanced nature of consent. Consent may be present between the parties involved in human smuggling, but this consent is not always freely given in the sense that it is highly dependent on the broader context of socio-economic and political developments across the world. In the case of people requesting and consenting to be smuggled, these individuals often come from desperate situations, escaping warfare, famine, persecution and many more dangers. Moreover, at times of refugee crises and mass migration movements, demand for illegal border crossings far out-strips supply, creating an asymmetry of power in favour of smugglers. This means that while those asking to be smuggled might consent to this activity in principle, they often do so out of desperation, with no alternatives and thus with little bargaining power to negotiate the cost or request basic safety measures. As a result, they are often forced to acquiesce to dangerous smuggling conditions for which they are, of course, charged extortionately. In this sense, the notion of mutual consent as part of business transactions becomes problematic.

Human trafficking is another salient example. Unlike human smuggling, definitions of trafficking emphasise that individuals cannot consent to being trafficked. The victim-offender relationship therefore appears to be less ambiguous here. However, research in this field has challenged popular understandings of victimhood in this illicit market. Sheldon Zhang (2009) suggests that we have come to rely on simplified understandings of victimhood, dominant amongst which is the so-called 'Natasha story'. This narrative, according to Zhang, can be summarised as such:

> A young woman, naïve and desperate to escape poverty or to help her families, answered an advertisement promising jobs in a foreign country - waitressing, modelling, or bartending. No out-of-pocket payment was required, but she was asked to pay back her travel expenses once she started working. Then she embarked on a journey entrusting her life in the hands of strangers. Either during the journey or after she arrived at the destination, she found herself held against her will, her travel documents taken and her movement restricted. She was sold to a brothel and told to sleep with as many men as possible to pay off her debt, which often multiplied for various reasons. Physical violence and gang rape were used to break her will. When ... Natasha sought help from the authorities, detention and deportation were often the outcome.

> *Source*: Zhang, S. X. (2009) Beyond the 'Natasha' story - a review and critique of current research on sex trafficking (181), *Global Crime*, Taylor and Francis. Reprinted by kind permission of Taylor & Francis Ltd.

This scenario is of course often true (Surtees, 2008), but victims of trafficking may also undergo many different experiences which fall outside of this narrow understanding of victimhood. For one thing, trafficking includes forms of exploitation which do not involve sex – domestic servitude, manual labour and organ removal, for instance. Rather than explore the vast variety of victims' experiences however, governmental and popular understandings of trafficking appear to have become inexorably wedded to the Natasha story.

———— Case Study 15.1 ————

Nail Salons and Trafficking

Growing attention has been paid in recent years to instances of trafficking and exploitation occurring in nail salons. Academic and journalistic investigations have uncovered widespread abuses of undocumented migrants - often of Vietnamese or other South East Asian backgrounds - working in exploitative conditions in nail salons. The rise of this type of trafficking and exploitation has been linked to the public's 'cheap manicure habit', with British women estimated to spend up to £450 per year on such treatments (Llewelyn Smith, 2019). Reports also argue that nail salons are sometimes used as brothels outside of regular business hours, with the same women also sexually exploited. This example demonstrates firstly the diversity of exploitation in trafficking processes and, while reminding us that sexual exploitation is common, other types of forced labour are also present. Secondly, this also demonstrates that illicit markets are fluid and, crucially, responsive to consumer sensibilities. As the public's desire for cosmetic services such as nail treatments increases, organised criminals are able to offer consumers a cheap option for those ignorant of or indifferent to the signs of exploited workers. Once again, this emphasises the public's complicity in driving this form of organised criminality.

Even if we focus only on trafficking for the purposes of sexual exploitation, research suggests that the reality is rather more nuanced than that presented in the Natasha story. Rebecca Surtees' work focusing on trafficking in South-Eastern Europe (2008) has found that the narrative of nefarious strangers preying on ignorant victims may be slightly misleading. Her analysis reveals that recruitment of victims relies 'heavily on a trafficker's existing relationship with the victim' (2008: 52), with boyfriends and families frequently acting as recruiters. Surtees has also found that victims of sexual trafficking are often implicitly aware that that they will be expected to work as sex workers upon arrival in a new country. One may suggest that this is a compromise some victims may be willing to make in order to secure passage to a new country, particularly if they are escaping life-threatening conditions in their home regions. This awareness or acceptance of their fate of course does not equate to consent, and these individuals are still victims even if they consider this form of exploitation the best of a series of bad options. This finding does however present another rebuke to simplified narratives such as the Natasha story. Another concern with victimology discourses such as the Natasha story is that they are highly gendered, presenting offenders as male and victims as female. Such approaches are riddled with pitfalls. Firstly, they potentially ignore the existence and experiences of male victims of trafficking and exploitation. Secondly, they obfuscate understandings of female offenders in illicit markets. Human trafficking research has shown that women are commonly involved as offenders in roles as diverse as the recruitment of victims, in supporting or acting as partners to male offenders, and as leaders of exploitation rings and brothels. Indeed, it has been argued that women are involved precisely because popular understandings of trafficking focus only on men as offenders, meaning women are less likely to arouse the suspicion of potential victims and law enforcement (Surtees, 2008). Narrowly casting men as offenders and women as victims using discourses predicated on moral crusading therefore fails to appreciate the wide spectrum of offender and victim profiles in trafficking and in organised crime more broadly.

It is critical for you to note that all these conclusions do not seek to deny the victimhood of those who have been smuggled, trafficked and exploited. Rather, research which problematises victimhood in human smuggling and trafficking challenges us to think more critically about victimhood and to try to understand the nuanced nature of consent and awareness. What narrow discourses of victimhood such as the Natasha story might be doing is performing a disservice to many victims of organised crime. By implicitly demanding that they follow pre-framed narratives, victims are stripped of their individuality and the complexity of their experiences. This runs the risk of ignoring or somehow blaming all the other victims of organised crime who do not fit these simplified preconceptions, potentially exacerbating their victimhood. Once more therefore, we must question government and media-led narratives of transnational organised crime and the nature of victimhood in these contexts.

The next section continues to problematise the offending/victimhood dichotomy in organised crime by exploring the complicity of the general public in driving many illicit markets via demand for certain goods and services.

Pause for Thought

Think about the goods and services you consume – how much do you know about the people who provide these goods and services to you? Have you ever had a manicure in a nail salon? Have you taken your car to a car wash? Have you had food delivered from your local takeaway? There are reports that these and other activities are often performed by individuals exploited by organised crime actors. Would this knowledge make you reconsider using these services?

As we will see in the next section, consumer demand is a central pillar of illicit markets which enables organised criminals to prosper. It is important for everyone to confront their own role and complicity in contributing to the forces which support organised crime.

ROLE OF DEMAND IN DRIVING ILLICIT MARKETS

The size and scale of profits generated from illicit markets form one of the primary concerns of official discourse on organised crime. This is perhaps most commonly recognised within representations of illegal drug markets. Illegal drug markets are considered as the most profitable of all illicit markets, with the United Nations Office on Drugs and Crime (UNODC) estimating that the global trade is worth more than $100 billion. Organisations such as Europol emphasise the role of organised crime groups and hardened criminals who prey on the innocent public. Similar discourses exist in relation to other illicit markets, including counterfeit goods, tobacco and arms smuggling. At the same time, with goods such as counterfeits, there is an increasing emphasis in enforcement policy on consumers to be more aware about buying fake goods. Despite this, much of the discourse around demand and illicit markets tends to reinforce stereotypical assumptions around sellers, buyers, victims and offenders. Research on illicit markets challenges some of these ideas and highlights the role of demand as an important driver in sustaining illicit markets. This section considers examples of illicit markets that challenge the idea of the law-abiding public ('us') and hardened organised criminals ('them') and examines the public's role as central to that of organised crime.

Illicit markets are considered as demand driven (Naylor, 2003; Antonopoulos and Papanicolaou, 2018). This has lead Naylor (2003: 98) to propose that 'the customer is, in that sense, more guilty than the supplier'. Counterfeit goods, illicit tobacco and illegal drugs are all good examples of markets that have a broad variety of consumers who actively engage with them. For example, with drugs, if we consider those who have used drugs recreationally or on occasion, and likewise counterfeits, i.e. those who have both knowingly and unknowingly bought fake handbags, or iPhone chargers for example, it is possible to see just how diverse the consumer market is. Those engaging with these illicit markets, are those who we would consider usually, as *law-abiding* citizens.

However, to what extent does the role of demand as a driver of illicit markets, actually make the consumer of the product or service more guilty than those supplying? Here, it is important to think about the broader context of demand and remember that illegal markets are not just driven by demand for the illicit product. Illegal markets, arguably, are fundamentally created via criminogenic asymmetries of the State, by high taxation or prohibition, for example.

Case Study 15.2

The Heroin Trade

In the nineteenth century the trade in heroin was a lucrative legal marketplace and heroin was sold as a medicine for numerous illnesses, including minor coughs and colds. The name 'heroin' was in fact trademarked by pharmaceutical giant Bayer in 1895 with the drug sold over-the-counter and marketed as being a non-addictive alternative to morphine. In the USA however, heroin developed a negative reputation partly due to its association with opium-addicted Chinese railroad workers which fed into fears about new migrant arrivals. Moral, religious and health concerns eventually led to the prohibition of heroin in the USA in the early twentieth century. As evidence of the drug's pervasive impacts on health continued to grow, countries around the world followed suit and criminalised the trade in heroin. However, it is worth noting that as late as 1955, *The Times* newspaper in the UK ran an editorial entitled 'The Case for Heroin' in an attempt to defend the sale and consumption of this substance. By the time governments around the world began to criminalise heroin however, many users had developed chronic addiction and dependency issues. From the supply side too, it was clear that this marketplace offered significant potential for enormous profits. Rather than eliminate the market therefore, the decision to prohibit the manufacture, sale and consumption of heroin redirected demand underground, towards the illicit economy. Today, the illicit trade in heroin is one of the most lucrative and violent marketplaces in organised crime, with heroin addiction an endemic problem across the world.

Figure 15.1   A Bottle of Heroin Sold as Medicine

This case study is useful as it reminds us that illegal markets or activity are spatially and temporally constructed. There are many examples, both within legal markets and illegal markets, where licit and illicit activity may overlap or be co-dependent. At what point organised crime intersects with these, within the context of global (and local) economies, may be challenging to pick apart. Examples of the role of organised crime in urban development, exploitation of natural resources, clothing – amongst numerous others – all point towards the symbiotic relationships between legal and illegal including the role of the State.

In addition to recognising the construction of illegal markets within the context of legal ones, it is also useful to remember other factors that influence the nature of organised crime, and the structures and demand for illegal markets. Aas (2013) describes the nature of the contemporary world and describes how the structural, political and economic conditions that exist also 'proliferate' opportunities for illegal markets. Supporting this wider context of understanding organised crime and illegal markets, scholarly research such as work on counterfeit medicines (Hall and Antonopoulos, 2016), illegal drugs like cocaine (Hall and Antonopoulos, 2017) and various other illicit markets, has emphasised the importance of both the broad demographic spectrum of those willingly and actively consuming these items, and the broader cultural, technological, economic and political factors affecting consumer demand.

Therefore, despite government and regulatory organisations' depictions of 'pusher' markets and organised criminals preying on innocent victims, we know from research that consumer demand is a key driver of illicit markets. It is, of course, not always as simple as consumers *knowingly* engaging with illegal markets. However, academic research does directly challenge the 'them versus us' discourses of organised crime and the public should be situated as central to the existence of organised crime. As noted by Aas (2013: 133), 'deviant supply is therefore essentially driven by deviant demand'.

CHAPTER SUMMARY

This chapter has sought to encourage you to become more critical of the ways in which transnational organised crime is presented to you, particularly by the State and popular media. The examples discussed above demonstrate a number of important features about the contemporary organised crime landscape, and we suggest that the key points to take away from the discussions above are as follows:

- That narrow visions of organised crime as the work of an all-powerful 'Mafia' are misguided.
- That many ordinary and mundane individuals habitually partake in organised criminality.
- That simplified discourses of victimhood in organised crime must be avoided in order to avoid further victimisation of some individuals and groups.
- That demand is often more important than supply in driving illicit markets.

Taken together, these examples show that organised crime and criminals do not simply exist in some detached underworld operating in the shadows of civil society. Instead, organised crime is deeply embedded in the real world and illicit marketplaces are shaped by the same market forces and socio-economic and political conditions as their licit counterparts. All of this reminds us that we must continue to carefully consider whose interests are served by narrow depictions of organised crime, which strip nuance from what are in fact complex debates about legal regulation, politics, economic policy, and international trade.

Review Questions

1. How might you characterise the type of actors involved in organised crime?
2. Why are understandings of victimhood which rely on the 'Natasha story' limited?
3. Which example(s) might you draw on to explain the idea that demand is more important than supply in organised crime?

FURTHER READING

Books/Book Chapters

1. The following book remains a seminal piece of work which has considerably advanced under-standings of organised crime as a form of illicit enterprise:

   Reuter, P. (1983) *Disorganized Crime: Illegal Markets and the Mafia*. Cambridge, MA: MIT Press.

2. Cressey's book has been much-criticised but this work is nevertheless important in understanding how and why the mythology of the Italian-American mafia was cemented in the US during the mid-twentieth century:

   Cressey, D. (1969) *Theft of the Nation*. New York: Transaction Publishers.

3. This book chapter provides a very useful overview of key theoretical perspectives developed by scholars in organised crime studies:

   Kleemans, E. R. (2014) 'Theoretical Perspectives in Organized Crime.' In L. Paoli (ed.), *The Oxford Handbook of Organized Crime*. Oxford: Oxford University Press.

Journal Articles

1. The following paper offers an excellent analysis of the development of organised crime discourses in the US and the UK as a form of moral panic:

   Woodiwiss, M. and Hobbs, D. (2009) Organized evil and the Atlantic Alliance: moral panics and the rhetoric of organized crime policing in America and Britain. *British Journal of Criminology*, 49(1): 106–128.

2. The following paper is a very good critique of discourses on victimhood and offending in human trafficking:

   Zhang, S. X. (2009) Beyond the 'Natasha' story – a review and critique of current research on sex trafficking. *Global Crime*, 10(3): 178–195.

3. The following paper is a useful analysis of existing attempts to define organised crime and explores the distinction between 'Organized Crime' and 'organized crime'.

   Hagan, F. E. (2006) 'Organized Crime' and 'organized crime': indeterminate problems of definition. *Trends in Organized Crime*, 9(4): 127–137.

Useful Websites

1. The following website hosts a fantastic collection of the hundreds of definitions of organised crime around the world:

   von Lampe, K. (2019) Definitions of Organized Crime. Available at: www.organized-crime.de/organizedcrimedefinitions.htm

2. The following podcast is an interesting discussion about the difficulties faced by the Sicilian Cosa Nostra in recent years:

   Asthana, A. (2019) 'Is this the end for the Sicilian mafia?', *The Guardian*, 18 December 2018. Available at: https://www.theguardian.com/news/audio/2018/dec/18/is-this-the-end-for-the-sicilian-mafia.

3. The following media article is an excellent analysis of how organised crime actors are able to infiltrate licit marketplaces to maximise their profit-making:

Roberts, H. (2018) 'How the mafia got our food', *Financial Times*, 8 November. Available at: https://www.ft.com/content/73de228c-e098-11e8-8e70-5e22a430c1ad#comments-anchor

REFERENCES

Aas, K. F. (2013) *Globalization and Crime*, 2nd edition. London: Sage.

Antonopoulos, G. A. and Papanicolaou, G. (2018) *Organized Crime: A Very Short Introduction*. Oxford: Oxford University Press.

Forno, F. and Gunnarson, C. (2010) 'Everyday Shopping to Fight the Italian Mafia'. In M. Micheletti and A. S. McFarland (eds), *Creative Participation: Responsibility-Taking in the Political World*. London: Paradigm Publishers.

Gambetta, D. (1993) *The Sicilian Mafia*. Cambridge, MA: Harvard University Press.

Hagan, F. E. (2006) 'Organized crime' and 'organized crime': Indeterminate problems of definition. *Trends in Organized Crime*, 9(4): 127–137.

Hall, A. and Antonopoulos, G. A. (2016) *Fake Meds Online: The Internet and the Transnational Market in Illicit Pharmaceuticals*. London: Palgrave.

Hall, A. and Antonopoulos, G. A. (2017) 'Coke on Tick': exploring the cocaine market in the UK through the lens of financial management. *Journal of Financial Crime*, 24(2): 181–199.

Hobbs, D. (2013) *Lush Life*. Oxford: Oxford University Press.

Hobbs, D. (2019) 'Faces in the Clouds: Criminology, Epochalism, Apohenia and Transnational Organized Crime'. In T. Hall and V. Scalia (eds), *A Research Agenda for Global Crime*. Cheltenham: Edward Elgar.

Kleemans, E. R. and Smit, M. (2014) 'Human Smuggling, Human Trafficking, and Exploitation in the Sex Industry'. In L. Paoli (ed.), *The Oxford Handbook of Organized Crime*. Oxford: Oxford University Press.

Llewelyn Smith, J. (2019) 'Are Britain's nail bars abetting people trafficking?', *The Times*, 16 November 2019. Available at: https://www.thetimes.co.uk/article/are-britains-nail-bars-abetting-people-trafficking-fsmqqn5ff (last accessed 26.11.19).

Naylor, R. T. (2003) Towards a general theory of profit-driven crimes. *British Journal of Criminology*, 43(1): 81–101.

Paoli, L. (2008) 'The Decline of the Italian Mafia'. In D. Siegel and H. Nelen (eds), *Organized Crime: Culture, Markets and Policies. Studies in Organized Crime*, vol. 7. New York: Springer.

Paoli, L. (2014) 'The Italian Mafia'. In L. Paoli (ed.), *The Oxford Handbook of Organized Crime*. Oxford: Oxford University Press.

Sergi, A. (2018) Widening the antimafia net: child protection and the socio-cultural transmission of mafia behaviours in Calabria. *Youth Justice*, 18(2): 149–168.

Siegel, D. and de Blank, S. (2010) Women who traffic women: the role of women in human trafficking networks – Dutch cases. *Global Crime*, 11(4): 436–447.

Surtees, R. (2008) Traffickers and trafficking in Southern and Eastern Europe. *European Journal of Criminology*, 5(1): 39–68.

United Nations (2004) 'United Nations Convention Against Transnational Organized Crime and the Protocols Thereto'. Available at: https://www.unodc.org/documents/middleeastandnorthafrica/organised-crime/UNITED_NATIONS_CONVENTION_AGAINST_TRANSNATIONAL_ORGANIZED_CRIME_AND_THE_PROTOCOLS_THERETO.pdf [last accessed 26.11.19].

Woodiwiss, M. (2000) 'Organized Crime – The Dumbing of Discourse', The British Criminology Conference: Selected Proceedings, Volume 3. *Papers from the British Society of Criminology Conference, Liverpool*, July 1999. Available at: http://citeseerx.ist.psu.edu/viewdoc/download?doi=10.1.1.127.1915&rep=rep1&type=pdf [last accessed 8 August 2019].

Zhang, S. X. (2009) Beyond the 'Natasha' story – a review and critique of current research on sex trafficking. *Global Crime*, 10(3): 178–195.

Green Crimes and Green Criminology

16

Angus Nurse

By the end of this chapter you will:

1. Have a firm understanding of what is meant by green crime and also understand the principles of **green criminology**.
2. Understand the causes and nature of green crimes and the challenges for justice systems in dealing with these types of crime and the associated environmental harm.
3. Understand the core theoretical concepts of **environmental justice**, **ecological justice**, **species justice** and environmental harm that are of importance in understanding green criminology's approach to green crimes.
4. Understand the concept of the **Anthropocene** and how human actions cause environmental crime and environmental harm.
5. Understand the eco-global perspective on criminology and the need to consider green crimes in the context of debates on transnational crime.

———————— Framing Questions ————————

1. Why do we need a green criminology and what can it add to our understanding of crime and deviance?
2. In what ways are green crimes different from 'mainstream' crimes and how should they be dealt with by justice systems?
3. What differences in approach might there be in considering green *harms* as opposed to green *crimes*?

INTRODUCTION

While much of criminology is concerned with mainstream concerns of street crime, violence and contemporary security concerns such as terrorism, green crimes have emerged as an area of concern over the last thirty years or so. Holley and Shearing (2018: 13) suggest that criminology 'will be defined by environmental crimes and environmental harms in the age of the Anthropocene', indicating also that criminology may require some rethinking in a contemporary era of human-caused harm. Tombs and Whyte (2015: 47) identify a range of contemporary crimes such as 'illegal emissions to air, water and land; hazardous waste dumping; and illegal manufacturing process' that cause considerable harm to the environment and that arguably should draw the attention of criminological inquiry. Criminologists have increasingly become involved and interested in environmental issues to the extent that the term 'Green Criminology' is now recognised as a distinct subgenre of the field. Within this unique area of scholarly activity, researchers consider not just harms the environment, but also:

Knowledge link: This topic is also covered in Chapter 15.

- the links between green crimes and other forms of crime, including organised crime's movement into the illegal trade in wildlife
- corporate environmental crime such as illegal pollution
- the links between domestic animal abuse and domestic violence, and serious forms of offending such as serial killing.

Knowledge link: This topic is also covered in Chapter 20.

In this chapter you will examine the importance of studying green crimes, the application of criminal laws to environmental harms, environmental criminality, and the abuse and exploitation of nonhuman animals as a form of crime. The chapter also examines how green criminology provides a mechanism for rethinking the study of criminal laws, ethics, crime and criminal behaviour (Situ and Emmons, 2000; Lynch and Stretesky, 2003). You will read about the importance of green criminology and how green crimes are defined in law and policy. You will also examine some theoretical concepts on green crime that help to develop our understanding of how and why green crimes may occur. In addition, you will examine how green crimes are policed and some of the ideas on how enforcement of green crimes can be improved and linked to mainstream crime and justice practices. The chapter also encourages you to think about some global perspectives on green crimes and the arguments for bringing green crimes into mainstream law and order policy and practice.

First, we will start by looking at the importance of green criminology as a subdiscipline of criminology.

MAPPING THE TERRAIN: THE IMPORTANCE OF GREEN CRIMINOLOGY

Discussion of green crimes within green criminology frequently concerns the transnational nature of such crimes and the extensive harm caused by green crimes. For example, Lynch and Stretesky (2014: 94–95) identify thousands of elephants lost to illegal poaching as part of the transnational trade in illegal ivory and wildlife trafficking. They also indicate that green victimisation 'due to air pollution exposure is 33.6 billion times more likely than a violent street crime victimisation' (2014: 88). Lynch and Stretesky conclude that 'humans are much more likely to be the victims of violent green victimisations than they are to be the victims of criminal acts of violence' (2014: 92). Green criminology considers such issues, drawing together several different theoretical and ideological conceptions within a criminology concerned with the general neglect of ecological issues within mainstream criminology (Lynch and Stretesky, 2014: 1). As Lynch and Stretesky state:

Knowledge link: This topic is also covered in Chapter 15.

> As criminologists we are not simply concerned that our discipline continues to neglect green issues, we are disturbed by the fact that, as a discipline, criminology is unable to perceive the wisdom of taking green harms more seriously, and the need to reorient itself in ways that make it part of the solution to the large global environmental problems we now face as the species that produces those problems. (Lynch and Stretesky, 2014: 2)

This lack of attention to environmental crimes within criminology is something you are invited to reflect on as you read through this chapter. Criminologist Rob White (2007; 2012a) observes that, given the potential for environmental harms to extend far beyond the direct impact on individual victims that are the norm with 'traditional' crimes of interpersonal violence and property crime, green crimes should be given importance if not priority within justice systems. Eco-global crimes such as the illegal trade in wildlife, pollution crimes, and actions such as deforestation and illegal timber trafficking that cause environmental harm are of significance. This is not just because they are crimes that have a global reach and impact on both existing communities and future generations, but also because they affect and involve a range of nation states and different justice systems. By considering these matters, green criminology examines complex issues in criminological enquiry and extends beyond the focus on street and interpersonal crimes to encompass consideration of how human activities can have destructive impacts on local and global ecosystems. By examining green crimes, green criminology goes beyond crime as defined by a strict legalist/criminal law conception (Situ and Emmons, 2000). While the manner in which we define crime is discussed later in this chapter, green criminology also examines issues concerning rights (both human and environmental), justice, morals, victimisation, criminality and the use of administrative, civil and regulatory justice systems. Green criminology also examines the actions of non-state criminal justice actors such as Non-Governmental Organisations (NGOs) and civil society organisations. This is particularly important in the area of enforcement and policy development as NGOs and civil society organisations can be heavily involved as enforcement bodies and in pursuing policy and new environmental protection laws. As leading green criminologist Nigel South once wrote, addressing environmental harms and injustice requires 'a new academic way of looking at the world but also a new global politics' (2010: 242).

White and Heckenberg (2014: 7) describe green criminology as a distinctive critical form of criminology that can either refer to specific forms of environmental crimes or harms or can instead incorporate a conceptual approach that includes ideas such as ecological justice or species justice (referred to elsewhere in this chapter). Green criminology may also apply conventional criminological theory such as strain theory or relative deprivation, that can be applied to environmental harms such as climate change or the illegal trade in wildlife.

Arguably green crimes should not be separated from our consideration of other crimes and criminal activity and there is a need to consider how green crimes can be incorporated into contemporary criminal justice. Examining green crimes helps in reappraising more traditional notions of crimes, offences and deviant or harmful behaviours as well as the role that societies (including corporations and governments) play in generating environmental degradation. You should, therefore, consider why green crimes and mainstream crimes are still often dealt with differently and why green crimes still largely fall outside of the gaze of mainstream criminology. Potter (2010: 10) argues that the link between environmental issues and criminology takes place on three levels:

1. First, it identifies a range of crime and criminal justice activity relating directly to environmental issues.
2. Second, green criminology allows the study of environmental harm in general as an extension of the well-established (and indeed fundamental) tradition within both sociology and criminology of critically questioning the very definition of crime and the core subject matter of criminology.
3. Finally, it is possible to identify a number of areas where environmentalists can benefit from the experience of sociologists and criminologists working within more traditional notions of crime.

Potter (2010) suggests that green criminology is concerned not just with distinctly environmental crimes but also with how studying green crimes can help to improve criminology. Similarly, Sollund identifies that 'because of the multivariate character of problems relating to eco-global crimes, it is necessary to expand the boundaries of criminology as a discipline' (2012: 3). In summary, green criminology is concerned not just with what you might think of as 'purely' environmental crimes because they only affect the environment and non-human nature. Green criminology also considers how green crimes and mainstream criminology are linked and how our understanding of crime needs to expand to also consider the harm caused by crime and deviance. In the next section you will examine this issue in more detail by considering how green crimes are defined.

DEFINING GREEN CRIMES

This section explores the different ways that we understand and categorise green crimes. You will examine how green crimes are defined by legal systems as well as how society creates an understanding of green crimes.

White has argued that environmental harms often 'transcend the normal boundaries of jurisdiction, geography and social divide' (2012a: 15). Much green crime is transnational in nature, affecting more than one country and possibly requiring action by more than one legal system, police force and policy approach. Examining green crimes has importance as scientific and academic study is concerned not solely with mainstream 'cops and robbers' crimes of interpersonal violence and individuality, but also with addressing wider concerns with harms of a global nature and which have long-lasting consequences for human and non-human animals and the biosphere. White thus identifies eco-global (green) criminology as a discipline requiring transnational and comparative research to identify differences and commonalities between nation-states 'whether related to pollution wildlife or other issues' (2012a: 25). You will see that while green criminology takes a critical look at the issue of environmental harms and abuse of animals, not all things considered to contravene environmental protection norms or offend notions of green morality are classified as 'crimes' as the next section illustrates.

Legal Definitions of Green Crime

The reality is that many forms of environmental harm that cause concern to NGOs, environmental activists and others are the result of legal activity. Thus, one way that you can look at this is to consider that only those things defined by criminal law as offences can really be classed as green crimes. Situ and Emmons (2000) define this as follows:

> The strict legalist perspective emphasizes that crime is whatever the criminal code says it is. Many works in criminology define crime as behaviour that is prohibited by the criminal code and criminals as persons who have behaved in some way prohibited by the law. (2000: 2)

This explanation identifies green crimes by a strict legalist view that argues that crime is whatever the criminal law defines it as being and only those actions specified as prohibited under the law should be seen as crimes. However, an alternative approach to green crimes sometimes advocated by activists is the social legal perspective which argues that some acts, especially by corporations, 'may not violate the criminal law yet are so violent in their expression or harmful in their effects to merit definition as crimes' (Situ and Emmons, 2000: 3). This approach reflects the reality that the construction of crime definitions is determined by various segments of society, and a political process that means that some definitions of crime are accepted and become 'embodied in the law' whereas others may not (Situ and Emmons, 2000: 3). Green crimes sometimes fall outside of our mainstream understandings of crime and some green crimes take place away from urban society and may not directly affect most citizens. As a result, they may be considered less important even though green criminology would argue that this is a flawed perspective given the harm some green crimes cause.

Knowledge link: This topic is also covered in Chapter 4.

Crime versus Harm

A central focus of green criminology is the notion of environmental *harm*, a conception which incorporates the victimisation and degradation of environments and harm caused to nonhuman animals. Lynch and Stretesky (2014: 8) argue that environmental harms are more important than the personal harms of street and property crimes in terms of both being more extensive and damaging. While such crimes may have a severe impact on the individuals who experience them, most people luckily do not suffer the direct effects of crime. By contrast Lynch and Stretesky argue that 'the environment around us is under expanded assault, that is it is routinely harmed and damaged by humans' (2014: 9). Holley and Shearing (2018: 3) refer to the period known as the Anthropocene which they broadly define as the post-Holocene period of human interference as a driving force in the planetary system. They identify that a key criminological challenge is addressing the intractable problems of the Anthropocene, which include: climate change; overexploitation of natural resources; related human security and fortressed spaces; and the rise of new risks and social harms. Many of the problems of the Anthropocene relate to the type of green crimes discussed within this chapter. However, debate continues over when the Anthropocene began, and arguably there are at least three different definitional dimensions to consider: firstly, a new geological epoch/history that has not yet been fully and formally validated; secondly, an Earth-system science perspective that the Earth is experiencing a shift from its Holocene state; and thirdly, the impact of humanity as one in which the relationship between humans and the environment has changed by virtue of the fact that human action and Earth dynamics have converged so that it is no longer possible to distinguish between distinct activities and processes.

Knowledge link: This topic is also covered in Chapter 7.

These discussions reinforce the idea of green crimes as being human-caused and a social construction influenced by:

- social locations: Global North perspectives and those of wealthier societies that determine which green crimes we are concerned with and especially which harms are defined as crimes by the criminal law
- power relations in society: powerful actors in society such as companies and politicians influence our understanding and classification of crime
- definitions of environmental crimes: some types of pollution are legal and permitted despite the environmental harm they may cause (such as a contribution to global warming or poor air quality).
- media: for example the media may report on harm caused to charismatic wildlife like the rhino and the tiger but pays less attention to less attractive species like the pangolin and shark which may be equally threatened
- political process: for example, environmentally damaging oil extraction or mining operations may fall outside of definitions of crime because of the political power that these industries have to prevent politicians from regulating their industry too closely.

This social-legal perspective also allows for consideration of symbiotic green crime which grows out of the flouting of rules that seek to regulate environmental disasters. There are, for instance, numerous major and minor examples of governments breaking their own regulations and contributing to environmental harms. Another example of the kind of secondary crime that would be classed as symbiotic green crime would be where Mafia-style groups help corporations to ignore pollution and waste regulations. In this example, the company pays the Mafia-style group to take the waste away without asking questions about what will be done with it. However, the company is aware that it is really their responsibility to ensure safe and legal disposal of the waste. Green criminology, by examining the social construction of green crimes, considers changing social notions of the acceptability of environmental harm. For example, many forms of animal abuse that historically were legal have now been criminalised. The recent examples of the abolition of hunting with dogs in the UK (via the passing of the Hunting Act 2004), and the introduction of new or revised animal abuse laws in various US states, illustrate changes in how animals are perceived and treated within contemporary society. But they also allow criminologists to study new aspects of criminality as new offences are created; resistance to criminal laws as those who oppose such laws react negatively or continue their offending behaviour; and the effectiveness of policing and better understanding of how and why people come to stop their offending (this is known as desistance).

To summarise, in one sense green crimes are primarily those acts prohibited by the law and defined as crime, but green crimes can also incorporate regulatory offences; these are 'technical' breaches of the law which may not be defined as crimes but which nevertheless are the subject of some form of sanction and punishment. The reality of environmental harm is that its consequences are wide-reaching, affecting more than just the direct victims of street crime and impacting negatively on ecosystems, future generations, and the survival of many human and nonhuman animal species. Hall (2013) identifies that environmental harm has the potential for long-term negative impacts on human health (citing examples such as the Bhopal chemical disaster, the Chernobyl nuclear reactor explosion and the Deepwater Horizon Gulf oil spill where direct human harm was a consequence). Environmental harm also has negative long-term economic, social and security implications, and is thus worthy of consideration by criminologists as both a direct and indirect threat to human populations. Both Hall (2013) and Lynch and Stretesky (2014) identify that environmental harm is often caused by continued production and consumption within a market-based economy where natural resources are exploited by corporations and states in order to produce and consume products (e.g. wood for home furniture). This theme is explored by a range of other writers (see for example Walters et al., 2013) and is a core part of green criminology's claim for developing justice systems and research enquiries that extend beyond concentrating on criminal justice systems and the use of the criminal law. The case study on the Gulf Oil Spill later in this chapter illustrates these issues. The next section discusses some of the theoretical concepts that help develop our understanding of how and why green crimes occur.

THEORETICAL CONCEPTIONS ON GREEN CRIMES

Green criminology considers the link between crimes against the environment and nonhuman animals and mainstream criminology and critically evaluates what is known about environmental criminality. However, green criminology also considers the moral dimension of harms against animals and exploitation of natural resources that are legal, but which should arguably be made illegal. As a result, green criminology provides a means for examining fringe areas of policing and criminality and applying critical thought to these areas. Green criminologists are therefore often in the position of challenging contemporary criminal justice ideas and their theories provide a new way of looking at contemporary criminal justice problems. We will now look at a few key theoretical concepts.

Green Crimes and Green Criminological Concepts

Environmental justice is human-centred and refers to the distribution of environments in terms of access to and use of natural resources. This broad term can be split into several different aspects of justice for the environment which include ecofeminism, environmental racism and the Red-Green Movement, summarised as follows:

Ecofeminism was originally conceived as connecting ecology and women in a manner that integrates environmental feminism and women's spirituality concerns (Spretnak, 1990). The paradigm criticised capitalist profit-growth orientation and the patriarchy, where male concerns often lead to environmental harms. It also connects the domination and exploitation of nature with the domination and exploitation of women, arguing that women are more concerned with survival than men. Ecofeminism would argue that all forms of dominance are connected, and that environmental equality could be achieved by returning to small-scale local economies and grassroots democracy, and reorienting cultural values.

Environmental racism considers discrimination and marginalisation in access to environmental resources. In doing so it simultaneously advocates for environmental justice and the elimination of racial discrimination in environmental decisions. This perspective argues that toxic factories, pollution and waste sites affect communities of colour more than Caucasians and that people of colour have a long history of struggling for environmental justice (Turner and Pei Wu, 2002). Within this perspective, criminology examines the conception that environmental protection exists primarily for the benefit of the elite who predominantly have access to rural areas and the benefits of a healthy environment; something often denied to poorer groups in which ethnic minorities are disproportionately represented. Critical perspectives on environmental racism thus contend that positive environmental developments and enhanced protection often 'disproportionately benefit white and upper-class people' (Turner and Pei Wu, 2002: 4), reinforcing white privilege while further marginalising ethnic minorities through denial of their environmental justice rights. The short-term goals of environmental racism discourse are race-linked theory and action, which means considering positive racially-oriented action to combat discrimination. Long-term goals are the elimination of exposure to dangerous products and practices for all.

The **Red-Green Movement** associates economic oppression with environmental degradation. It applies a Marxist contextualisation to environmental harms arguing that environmental problems disproportionately affect the working class and poor as a product of the class society. Red-green perspectives on environmental justice consider methods of production and decision making that exclude the working class, effectively disengaging them from environmental concerns. Thus, any green revolution must begin in the workplace and empower workers with environmental responsibility and a tangible interest in protecting the environment.

Ecological justice is more ecocentric and acknowledges that human beings are only one part of the planet and that any system of justice needs to consider the wider biosphere and species which depend on nature. **Species justice** discourse falls within ecological justice and considers the responsibility that humans owe to other species as part of broader ecological concerns. Humans, as the dominant species on the planet, have considerable potential to destroy nonhuman animals, or through effective laws and criminal justice regimes, to provide for effective animal protection. This includes animal rights, aspects of animal protection, and criminality which impacts negatively on a range of nonhuman animals. Benton suggests that 'it is widely recognized that members of other animal species and the rest of non-human nature urgently need to be protected from destructive human activities' (1998: 149). If this is true then contemporary criminal justice needs to extend beyond traditional human ideals of justice as a punitive or rehabilitative ideal, to incorporate shared concepts of reparative and restorative justice between humans and nonhuman animals. In effect, the criminal justice system needs to be modified to provide for a broad criminal justice perspective, justice for all sentient beings, not just for humans.

--------- Pause for Thought ---------

What challenges might there be in extending criminal justice to green crimes and the protection of animals and the environment?

We will now look at the policing of green crimes and examine enforcement approaches to green crimes.

POLICING GREEN CRIMES

How the justice system should deal with green crimes and criminality is a core concern of green criminology, particularly given the lack of attention paid to these crimes within general criminal justice policy discourse. White (2007) identifies the following three approaches:

1. **The socio-legal approach** – which emphasises use of the current criminal law and attempts to improve the quality of investigation, law enforcement, prosecution and conviction of illegal-environmentally related activity.
2. **The regulatory approach** – this has an emphasis on social regulation, using many different means as the key mechanism to prevent and curtail environmental harm. This attempts to reform existing systems of production and consumption using enforced self-regulation and bringing NGOs into the regulatory process.
3. **Social action approach** – this has an emphasis on the need for social change predominantly through democratic institutions and citizen participation.

White's categorisations of the approaches reflect the fact that most jurisdictions have environmental regulations which seek to address actions harmful to the environment but this does not mean a unified approach. Enforcement practice varies across jurisdictions and green criminology's critical evaluation of enforcement and policy effectiveness from both a theoretical and practical perspective has identified significant failings in the implementation of environmental and ecological justice concerns (Nurse, 2013). For example, the Convention on International Trade in Endangered Species of Flora and Fauna (CITES) is generally considered to be the main international law addressing wildlife trafficking. Yet CITES arguably allows continued trade in wildlife and simply regulates this rather than prohibiting wildlife trade and is limited in how it considers the welfare of wildlife in trade. As a result, it fails to provide the strict prohibition on exploitation of wildlife that an ecological justice perspective might require.

Environmental laws (broadly defined) are often dealt with via administrative or civil law systems rather than criminal justice ones, which means that the enforcement of green crimes is often not a core responsibility of mainstream criminal justice agencies like the police. For example, wildlife law is often a fringe area of policing whose public policy response is significantly influenced by NGOs (Nurse, 2012; 2015) and which continues to rely on NGOs as an integral part of the enforcement regime (Nurse, 2011). For example, the enforcement of legislation banning hunting with dogs in the UK (primarily the Hunting Act 2004) continues to rely on the enforcement activities of NGOs like the League Against Cruel Sports. The RSPB maintains a role in the enforcement of wild bird legislation, albeit working with the police and other agencies. White (2012b) identifies that third parties such as NGOs often play a significant role in investigating and exposing environmental harm and offending, and have become a necessity for effective environmental law enforcement. Environmental harm caused by corporations is also largely dealt with by environmental regulators such as the Environmental Protection Agency (US) or the Environment Agency (UK). Arguably this reflects the notion that environmental crimes are not 'real' crime, and in practice environmental regulations are often poorly enforced by under-resourced agencies whose job is to regulate corporate activity. In the wildlife arena of green crimes, animal protection legislation may protect animals only in certain circumstances and from certain activities while retaining their subservience to human interests. Thus, while the need for improved standards of animal protection legislation has generally been adopted at least by western legislators, criminal justice systems often fail to afford priority to effective enforcement of wildlife legislation. Instead this becomes the responsibility of NGOs or civil justice agencies and the level of enforcement is heavily dependent on NGOs' ideological concerns and availability of resources (Nurse, 2013). There is a need to arouse public consciousness about harmful environmental activities. Even where the state has a range of environmental enforcement tools available, public engagement is a vital tool in changing attitudes towards compliance. Without public monitoring and disapproval the social destruction caused by environmental harm will continue, especially where corporate profit motives encourage this, and weak regulation allows corporate environmental criminality to continue.

Several green criminologists argue that conceptually there should be a wider definition of crime that incorporates harms not currently defined as crimes. As Lynch and Stretesky state, 'the form of criminal justice criminologists ordinarily examine to discuss the control of crime is a narrow form of justice' (2014: 7). Conceiving an effective form of justice means considering more than just individual human victims of crime (Benton, 1998), and requires exploration of a wider range of criminal behaviour than just that of the rationally driven offender (Nurse, 2013). Green criminology attempts this both in theory and in practice by reconceptualising definitions of crime to focus on the impact of behaviour on the environment. Green criminology also considers the extent to which actions which infringe existing legislation are deserving of a response commensurate with the idea of what criminal sanctions are intended to achieve, i.e. punishment, reparation and rehabilitation or changed behaviour.

Knowledge link: These topics are also covered in Part 4.

Green criminology routinely goes beyond the personal to consider the wider context of crimes. White's (2009) notion of fusing the global and the local is illustrated by the green crime of wildlife trafficking, arguably one of the most prevalent forms of green crime existing today (Wyatt, 2013; Nurse, 2015). Wildlife law has developed to a stage where animal protection through integration of legally enforceable animal welfare standards is now firmly enshrined in environmental policy and legislative systems (Schaffner, 2011; Nurse, 2013). The incorporation of international law mechanisms such as the CITES (mentioned earlier) into national legislation also means that, at least in principle, wildlife are protected from *certain* illegal activity (e.g. the illegal trade in wildlife) and illegal activity affecting wildlife is also subject to criminal sanctions. Yet the extent to which such mechanisms are enforced is as much a political decision as a moral one based on acceptance that humans owe a duty towards other inhabitants of the planet (Benton, 1998). Where human and nonhuman or ecological interests are in conflict, governments generally calculate that animal/ecological interests should be seen as secondary, resulting in animal law that primarily reflects animals' status as property. Thus, compliance with animal welfare legislation is very much a mixed bag and some industries such as the industrial agriculture industry arguably continue to suffer from a disregard for legislation and non-transparency in respect of their compliance with legislation:

> Animal abuse (and wildlife crime) concerns risk remaining at the fringes of green criminology and being dominated by debates about the case for legal animal rights rather than embracing species justice principles into an integrated justice approach. White (2007) identifies a main concern of species justice as being 'the rights of other species (particularly animals) to live free from torture, abuse and destruction of habitat'. (2007: 38)

The global operations of Multi National (business) Entities (MNEs) can have significant negative consequences for the communities in which they operate and the wider environment. While businesses may in principle embrace the concept of ethical operations and human rights compliance, claiming to implement these in their Corporate Social Responsibility (CSR) policies, the extent to which they do so, the content of those policies and their applicability to the concepts of environmental compliance varies considerably. Corporations who break environmental laws are also not always dealt with by criminal justice systems, but may only be subject to civil or administrative sanctions that do not always deal adequately with the harm caused by corporations or directly address their criminal behaviour. This combination of sanctions is illustrated in the Case Study 16.1 below in relation to the response to the Deepwater Horizon oil spill of 2010.

—————————————— Case Study 16.1 ——————————————

Deepwater Horizon (the Gulf Oil Spill)

The Gulf Oil Spill (also known as the Deepwater Horizon Spill) is considered one of the worst environmental disasters of the early twenty-first century and illustrates the challenges of dealing with green crimes committed by corporations. On April 20, 2010, the Mississippi Canyon 252 Deepwater Horizon oil well owned by Transocean, and leased by major oil corporation BP, exploded, linked to a failure in the blowout preventer system. Eleven people were killed in the explosion and the rig eventually sank on 22 April 2010. Oil flowed from the site for 87 days, following several unsuccessful attempts to stem the flow by a number of methods, including: attempting to close the blowout preventer valves; placing a containment dome over the largest spill; pumping drilling fuels into the spill and attempting to seal it with concrete; and diverting the flow to a containment seal. Eventually a relief well was drilled, and a replacement blowout preventer was installed. The resultant oil spill covered 28,958 square miles, an area the size of South Carolina. Goldstein et al. (2011) suggest that the Gulf Oil Spill's 'magnitude, duration of release, source of emission (the deep-sea floor), and management techniques used (dispersants and controlled burns)' put the spill in a different category than other spills (1334).

In addition to the harm caused to marine wildlife, the oil spill in the Gulf of Mexico posed a direct threat to human health from inhalation or dermal contact with the oil and dispersant chemicals, and indirect threats to seafood safety and mental health. BP was considered to be 'grossly negligent' in respect of the offshore rig explosion that killed eleven workers and caused a 134-million-gallon spill.

The case involved both civil and criminal issues. Civil claims related to claims made by businesses and persons affected by the oil spill with the spill and subsequent pollution having destroyed the livelihoods of several businesses relying on the marine environment. Transocean who owned the rig were the subject of class actions for financial losses under the Oil Pollution Act of 1990, commonly referred to as the Oil Spill Pollution Act. Seventy-seven cases, including those brought by state governments, individuals, and companies, were eventually heard in the US District Court for the Eastern District of Louisiana under Multi-District Litigation docket MDL No. 2179, captioned *In re: Oil Spill by the Oil Rig "Deepwater Horizon" in the Gulf of Mexico, on April 20, 2010*. In September 2014 a federal judge ruled that BP was primarily responsible for the oil spill as a result of its deliberate misconduct and gross negligence. Criminal cases included a Department of Justice claim that sought to establish that BP 'was grossly negligent and engaged in wilful misconduct in causing the oil spill'. The government's investigation concluded that BP had operated 'a culture of corporate recklessness' and indicated that the company took risks with pressure tests that if conducted correctly could have stopped the oil flow before the blowout.

The case was eventually the subject of an estimated $20 billion settlement, which included $5.5 billion in civil Clean Water Act penalties, and billions more to cover environmental damage and other claims by the five Gulf states and local governments. At the time of writing, BP agreed to plead guilty to 14 criminal counts, including manslaughter, and will pay $4 billion over five years in a settlement with the US Justice Department. Transocean Deepwater also agreed to plead guilty to violating the Clean Water Act and to pay a total of $1.4 billion in civil and criminal fines and penalties.

Pause for Thought

Consider the penalty identified in the Deepwater Horizon case. How effective do you think this penalty would be in changing the behaviour of a major oil company?

THE LEGAL AND THE ILLEGAL: GLOBAL PERSPECTIVES AND GREEN CRIMES IN THE MAINSTREAM

As you can see, the Deepwater Horizon case study illustrates how particularly in the area of exploitation of natural resources (including animals) green crimes identify the link between the legal and the illegal. The oil company's actions in drilling for oil were lawful, but the consequence of their alleged governance failures and the explosion on the oil rig resulted in several deaths and damage to the marine environment that will likely require decades to fully remediate. In addition, the loss of livelihood to fishermen in the area and health problems caused to those affected by the oil spill are arguably green crimes although they will be addressed primarily through civil justice mechanisms (e.g. compensation schemes and claims for loss of earnings). As Holley and Shearing (2018) identify, in the age of the Anthropocene the human element of environmental crimes requires environmental policy to consider human behaviour both collectively and individually as a major source of environmental harm. Humans have an interest in maintaining a healthy environment, but the full consequences of human behaviour are not always considered as we continue to consume natural resources. The lack of effective global enforcement, and little or no integrated enforcement activity in respect of transnational crimes and crimes which are subject to multiple regulatory structures, are also raised as an issue. Corporations have the option of moving their operations to 'pollution havens', i.e. those jurisdictions with weak enforcement regimes providing environments where large corporations are subject to less stringent regulation than they might find in western, environmentally conscious jurisdictions. As the Deepwater Horizon case study shows, corporate environmental responsibility, while accepted in principle, is a concept subject to varied interpretation with no clear definition. As a result, clearly identifying the precise nature of the wrongdoing is problematic.

Green criminology's strength is its ability to apply ideas about mainstream crime to green issues, whilst also applying green perspectives to mainstream criminological concerns. In doing so it develops criminological discourse. Techniques of neutralisation (Sykes and Matza, 1957) that allow a corporation to distance itself from the consequences of its actions are an integral factor in corporate environmental crime, thus applying core criminological theory directly to an environmental problem. So, in applying these neutralisations, corporations caught breaking the law often deny responsibility for their actions or claim to be victims while also behaving in a way that demonstrates little acceptance of the legitimacy of, or need for, the enforcement regime. Enforcement of environmental crimes can be problematic where criminal justice systems prove inadequate to the task of dealing with particular types of offending. Corporate crimes are of particular concern given the difficulty of either identifying specific individuals within the corporation who are culpable for the offence or in taking enforcement action against a corporate body. You can hopefully see that the enforcement conception is an important one; arguably a lack of enforcement has often aided the emergence of new forms of corporate environmental crime such as the illegal trade and disposal of e-waste.

CHAPTER SUMMARY

- The term 'green crimes' covers a wide range of offending and can often extend to environmental harms that go beyond the pure socio-legal consideration of crime as being that which is defined by the criminal law.
- The term 'green crimes' brings both green crimes and green harms within criminological attention. Lynch and Stretesky argue that 'green harms are the most important considerations in modern society because they cause the most harm, violence, damage and loss' (2014: 7).
- There is a relationship between legal and illegal actions. Much corporate environmental damage (e.g. pollution) is entirely legal – it does not violate the law – but can have long-term harmful consequences, e.g. damage to water courses, acceleration of global warming and exposing citizens to harmful toxins. Only when the permitted emission limits are exceeded or an 'upset' incident such as a chemical spill or other discharge occurs might the incident constitute a crime.
- There is a need to consider crime *and* harm. Many environmental offences are dealt with as regulatory breaches and are not seen as crimes. As a result, they only attract fines or administrative sanctions rather than the punitive response of the criminal justice system. Incidents of global importance and which affect human, nonhuman animals, plants and ecosystems can sometimes be treated more 'leniently' than interpersonal crimes which have less far-reaching consequences.
- Actual green crimes such as illegal wildlife trafficking, illegal dumping of toxic waste and illegal destruction of natural resources meet most definitions of 'crime'.

———————— Review Questions ————————

1. What do we mean when we talk about green crimes and what difficulties exist in ensuring that green crimes are considered by criminal justice systems?
2. What is green criminology and why is it important when examining how criminology considers green crimes?
3. To what extent is environmental crime ignored by mainstream policing agencies? Give reasons for your answer and explore why mainstream justice agencies might not consider environmental crimes to be important.
4. In what ways is climate change and dealing with environmental disasters a criminological issue?
5. To what extent is harm caused to the environment by the activities of major corporations a criminological issue?

GO FURTHER

Books

1. The following book addresses a number of important green crime topics including: victimisation waste and corporate crimes; agri-business and food crimes; biomedical research and illegal wildlife trafficking:

Sollund, R. (ed.) (2015) *Green Harms and Crimes: Critical Criminology in a Changing World.* Basingstoke: Palgrave Macmillan.

2. This second book contains contributions from a range of scholars to contemporary issues in green criminology, providing cutting-edge discussions on topics such as ecocide, environmental activism, environmental enforcement, human rights and green criminology and wildlife harms:

Hall, M., Maher, J., Nurse, A., Potter, G., South, G. and Wyatt, T. (2017) *Greening Criminology in the 21st Century: Contemporary Debates and Future Directions in the Study of Environmental Harm.* London: Routledge.

3. The following book is one of the first major explorations of environmental criminology and ecological justice setting out the scope of a green criminology and assessing how environmental harms and environmental crimes should be dealt with:

White, R. (2008) *Crimes Against Nature: Environmental Criminology and Ecological Justice.* Cullompton: Willan.

Journal Articles

1. The following article is of importance in exploring the meaning of the term 'green' from a criminological perspective and examining a definition of environmental justice:

Lynch, M. J. and Stretesky, P. B. (2003) The meaning of green: contrasting criminological perspectives. *Theoretical Criminology, 7*(2).

2. This next article examines how international legal agreements continue to allow the exploitation of natural resources whilst criminalising aspects of traditional ways of life which effectively enables a socially harmful land-grabbing process:

Ruggiero, V. and South, N. (2010) Critical criminology and crimes against the environment. *Critical Criminology,* 18(4): 245–250. https://doi.org/10.1007/s10612-010-9121-9.

3. The final article is of importance in highlighting some of the methodological problems in the study of global environmental harms which are beyond the scale and scope of traditional crimes:

White, R. (2009) Researching transnational environmental harm: toward an eco-global criminology. *International Journal of Comparative and Applied Criminal Justice,* 33: 229–248.

Useful Websites

1. The following link is the online home of CITES, the international agreement between governments that aims to ensure that international trade in specimens of wild animals and plants does not threaten their survival. Convention on International Trade in Endangered Species of Wild Fauna and Flora (CITES): https://www.cites.org/

2. This second weblink is an online resource for environmental news stories. The site also contains an email newsletter that delivers environmental news stories from around the globe free to its subscribers. Environmental News Network (ENN): http://www.enn.com

3. The final link takes you to the US governmental agency with a remit to ensure that the US federal laws protecting human health and the environment are enforced fairly and effectively. Environmental Protection Agency (US): http://www.epa.gov

REFERENCES

Benton, T. (1998) Rights and justice on a shared planet: more rights or new relations?. *Theoretical Criminology*, 2(2): 149–175.

Goldstein, B., Osofsky, H. and Litchveld, M. Y. (2011) The Gulf Oil Spill. *New England Journal of Medicine*, 364: 1334–1348.

Hall, M. (2013) 'Victims of Environmental Harm. In R. Walters, D. Westerhuis and T. Wyatt (eds), *Emerging Issues in Green Criminology: Exploring Power, Justice and Harm*. Basingstoke: Palgrave Macmillan.

Holley, C. and Shearing, C. (2018) 'Thriving on a Pale Blue Dot: Criminology and the Anthropocene'. In C. Holley and C. Shearing (eds.), *Criminology and the Anthropocene*. Abingdon: Routledge.

Linzey, A. (ed.) (2009) *The Link Between Animal Abuse and Human Violence*. Eastbourne: Sussex Academic Press.

Lynch, M. J. and Stretesky, P. B. (2003) The meaning of green: contrasting criminological perspectives. *Theoretical Criminology*, 7(2).

Lynch, M. J. and Stretesky, P. B. (2014) *Exploring Green Criminology*. Farnham: Ashgate.

Nurse, A. (2009) 'Dealing with Animal Offenders'. In A. Linzey (ed.), *The Link Between Animal Abuse and Human Violence* (ch. 19). Brighton: Sussex Academic Press.

Nurse, A. (2012) Repainting the thin green line: the enforcement of UK wildlife law. *Internet Journal of Criminology*, October.

Nurse, A. (2013) *Animal Harm: Perspectives on Why People Harm and Kill Animals*. Farnham: Ashgate.

Nurse, A. (2015) *Policing Wildlife: Perspectives on the Enforcement of Wildlife Legislation*, Basingstoke: Palgrave Macmillan.

Potter, G. (2010) What is Green Criminology? *Sociology Review*, November: 8–12.

Schaffner, J. (2011) *An Introduction to Animals and the Law*. Basingstoke: Palgrave Macmillan.

Situ, Y. and Emmons, D. (2000) *Environmental Crime: The Criminal Justice System's Role in Protecting the Environment*. Thousand Oaks, CA: Sage.

Sollund, R. (2012) 'Introduction'. In R. Ellefsen, R. Sollund and G. Larsen (eds), *Eco-global Crimes: Contemporary Problems and Future Challenges*. Farnham: Ashgate.

Sollund, R. (2015) *Green Harms and Crimes: Critical Criminology in a Changing World*. Basingstoke: Palgrave Macmillan.

South, N. (2010) 'The Ecocidal Tendencies of Late Modernity: Transnational Crime, Social Exclusions, Victims and Rights'. In R. White (ed.), *Global Environmental Harm: Criminological Perspective*. Cullompton: Willan.

Spretnak, C. (1990) 'Ecofeminism: Our Roots and Flowering'. In I. Diamond and G. F. Orenstein (eds), *Reweaving the World: The Emergence of Ecofeminism* (pp. 3–14). San Francisco, CA: Sierra Club Books.

Sykes, G. M. and Matza, D. (1957) Techniques of neutralization: A theory of delinquency. *American Sociological Review*, 22: 664–673.

Tombs, S. and Whyte, D. (2015) *The Corporate Criminal: Why Corporations Must Be Abolished*. Abingdon: Routledge.

Turner, R. L. and Pei Wu, D. (2002) *Environmental Justice and Environmental Racism: An Annotated Bibliography and General Overview Focusing on US Literature 1996–2002*. Berkeley: University of California.

Walters, R., Westerhuis, D. and Wyatt, T. (eds) (2013) *Emerging Issues in Green Criminology*, Basingstoke: Palgrave Macmillan.

White, R. (2007) 'Green Criminology and the Pursuit of Ecological Justice'. In P. Beirne and N. South (eds), *Issues in Green Criminology*. Cullompton: Willan Publishing.

White, R. (2009) Researching transnational environmental harm: toward an eco-global criminology. *International Journal of Comparative and Applied Criminal Justice*, 33: 229–248.

White, R. (2012a) 'The Foundations of Eco-global Criminology'. In R. Ellefsen, R. Sollund and G. Larsen (eds). *Eco-global Crimes: Contemporary Problems and Future Challenges*. Farnham: Ashgate.

White, R. (2012b) NGO engagement in environmental law enforcement: critical reflections. *Australasian Policing*, 4(2): 7–12.

White, R. and Heckenberg, D. (2014) *Green Criminology: An Introduction to the Study of Environmental Harm*. Abingdon: Routledge.

Wyatt, T. (2013) *Wildlife Trafficking: A Deconstruction of the Crime, the Victims and the Offenders*. Basingstoke: Palgrave Macmillan.

Trafficking and Exploitation

17

Laura Connelly

--- Learning Objectives ---

By the end of this chapter you will:

- Better understand the challenges associated with defining and measuring trafficking and exploitation.
- Be able to think critically about how trafficking and exploitation may be used in the pursuit of other moral and political agendas.
- Have considered trafficking's recent rebrand as modern slavery and the implications of this new framing for the human rights of people who migrate.
- Be aware of how anti-trafficking efforts can cause harm, as well as helping trafficked and exploited people.

--- Framing Questions ---

1. Why are trafficking and exploitation such contentious issues?
2. How are trafficking and exploitation used to pursue other policy agendas?
3. Are current anti-trafficking efforts effective? Can they have (unintended) harmful consequences?

INTRODUCTION

Although once the concern of only a handful of non-governmental organisations (NGOs), trafficking and exploitation have risen up the political agenda in recent decades across much of the world. Trafficking is in fact often framed as one of the foremost human rights issues of the twenty-first century. This is irrespective of the contention that exists both around the prevalence and the definitions of trafficking and exploitation, and disagreement over the degree to which anti-trafficking mechanisms have a positive impact upon human rights. Indeed, many of the claims made about trafficking by governments, state agencies, NGOs and some academics are unsubstantiated or, at the very least, contested. Furthermore, while trafficking research has burgeoned in recent years, there remains a lack of empirically, methodologically and theoretically rigorous research into trafficking and exploitation upon which to base evidence-informed policy.

With this in mind, the chapter encourages you to think about the topics of trafficking and exploitation with a critical criminological mind. The next section introduces you to the definitional difficulties surrounding trafficking, how trafficking and exploitation have been used to justify other policy agendas, and a key legislative development of recent years, the Modern Slavery Act 2015. In the main part of the chapter, we develop these themes in more detail and drill down upon some key issues. We first explore some of the challenges associated with measuring the extent of trafficking, before considering anti-trafficking responses in the UK context under the broad themes of prevention, protection and prosecution. We will then interrogate both how the **modern slavery** agenda and the **Rescue Industry** have gained traction in recent years, despite having some harmful consequences for people who migrate.

MAPPING THE TERRAIN

In this section, we will begin to consider some of the definitional difficulties surrounding trafficking and exploitation, as well as key policy and legislative developments. Although there are no universally agreed definitions of trafficking and exploitation, for the 173 states that have ratified the **United Nations Trafficking Protocol**, the definition of trafficking outlined in article 3a) is a key legal reference point:

> Trafficking in persons shall mean the recruitment, transportation, transfer, harbouring or receipt of persons, by means of the threat or use of force or other forms of coercion, of abduction, of fraud, of deception, of the abuse of power or of a position of vulnerability or of the giving or receiving of payments to achieve the content of a person having control over another person, for the purpose of exploitation. Exploitation shall include ... forms of sexual exploitation, forced labour or services, slavery or practices similar to slavery, servitude or the removal of organs. (UN, 2000: 2)

It is generally understood that human trafficking has three constitutive elements:

1. The action (recruitment, transportation, transfer...).
2. The means (threat or use of force, coercion, abduction ...).
3. The purpose (sexual exploitation, forced labour, slavery ...).

All three elements must be present in cases involving adult victims of trafficking. In cases involving children, the means element is not required because it is not necessary to establish that a child has given informed consent.

Although the UN Trafficking Protocol was initially considered an attempt to alleviate some of the historical contention around the definition of trafficking, it did little to prevent trafficking being used by a range of state and non-state actors in the pursuit of their own political and moral agendas. Some scholars have, for example, drawn attention to how states frequently conflate trafficking with smuggling. By doing so, draconian border policies can be framed as a way of preventing trafficking and exploitation, and therefore enacted with seeming legitimacy (O'Connell Davidson, 2015). Yet there is ample evidence that rather than preventing trafficking and exploitation, anti-immigration practices force migrating people to pursue illegal mechanisms of entry and unregulated forms of employment, both of which leave them at greater risk of exploitation. Other scholars have highlighted how trafficking for sexual exploitation is routinely conflated with voluntary sex work in the pursuit of an anti-prostitution agenda. This is in spite of compelling counter-evidence which suggests that more often than not, migrant women involved in the sex industry have made rational decisions to sell sex (Mai, 2009). Debates over the relationship between sex trafficking and sex work are, therefore, vehemently polarised and have dominated discussions of human trafficking. This has meant that historically there has been an overwhelming focus on trafficking for sexual exploitation, both in academic literature and in policy and practice, to the neglect of other forms of trafficking and exploitation.

Student Voice

"Trafficking is a challenging yet compelling subject matter, and one I urge every criminology student to familiarise themselves with. Its complexities in relation to real life situations differ greatly to the widely believed stereotypes, thus dissecting it carefully is imperative." (Nazia Shah, LLB Law with Criminology student)

Yet it is **forced labour** that is in fact the most common type of exploitation in the UK. According to the International Labour Organisation, forced or compulsory labour is 'all work or service which is exacted from any person under the menace of any penalty and for which the person has not offered himself voluntarily'. Although forced labour is not restricted to particular labour markets, sectors susceptible to exploitation include agriculture, factory work, construction, domestic work and hospitality. There is also increasing awareness around trafficking for forced criminality in the UK, particularly in relation to drug trafficking and cultivation. The Modern Slavery Act 2015 introduced a new statutory defence to protect against the inappropriate prosecution of victims of trafficking for crimes committed as part of their exploitation. Yet there is evidence to suggest that victims of trafficking may still be misidentified by the police as offenders and prosecuted by the Crown Prosecution Service (CPS).

The Modern Slavery Act – which received royal assent in England and Wales on 26 March 2015 – groups various phenomena together under the umbrella of modern slavery. Trafficking is but one possible outcome of modern slavery, alongside slavery, servitude, and forced or compulsory labour. These offences are not explicitly defined in the Act, although Table 17.1 outlines the definitional guidance provided by the College of Policing (2017). Whilst the Act was welcomed by many for consolidating existing offences related to trafficking and slavery, it has been the subject of much criticism (see for example Craig et al., 2019). Anti-trafficking NGOs, for example, have argued that the Act focuses on policing to the neglect of protecting and supporting victims. An independent review in 2016 – the Haughey Review – also found that the operationalisation of the Act was hindered by patchy training for criminal justice agencies. Furthermore, although a key provision of the Act was the introduction of an Independent Anti-Slavery Commissioner, the first Commissioner, Kevin Hyland, resigned citing government interference. We will return to thinking about the Act, and the broader modern slavery discourse, a little later. For now, we will focus on some key issues in relation to trafficking and exploitation, starting with the problem of measurement.

Table 17.1 Definitions of Offences Under the Modern Slavery Act 2015

Offence	Definition
Slavery	"...the status or condition of a person over whom any or all of the powers attaching the right of ownership are exercised."
Servitude	"Servitude is linked to slavery but is much broader than slavery... It includes, in addition to the obligation to provide certain services to another, the obligation on the 'serf' to live on the other's property and the perceived impossibility of changing his or her status."
Forced or compulsory labour	"Section 1 of the Forced Labour Convention, 1930 (No. 29) defined forced or compulsory labour as being 'all work or service which is exacted from any person under the menace of any penalty and for which the said person has not offered himself voluntarily'... indicators of forced or compulsory labour include recruitment by deception, coercion and/or abuse, exploitation at work, and coercion at destination."
Human Trafficking	"This states that a person commits an offence if they arrange or facilitate the travel of another person, to exploit them. It is irrelevant whether the exploited person, adult or child, consents to the travel."

Source: (College of Policing, 2017)

THE EXTENT OF TRAFFICKING: MEASURING THE IMMEASURABLE?

The prevalence of trafficking and exploitation is notoriously difficult to measure and as such, there is little agreement about the scale of the problem. Attempts at quantification vary enormously, commonly from 4 million up to 27 million. Although many estimates are based upon unreliable and ambiguous data sources, they have been repeated so often that they have become somewhat unquestioned. As Weitzer (2014: 14) notes, the figure of 27 million slaves worldwide derives from the work of Kevin Bales, who calls it 'a good guess' but offers little indication of how he arrived at the figure. Nonetheless, it has been portrayed as factual by the media, some non-governmental organisations, and by some government sources, including in the high-profile US State Department's Trafficking in Persons Report 2017 (Weitzer, 2014). There appear to be few reliable estimates of the magnitude of trafficking and statistics are too often inflated in order to attract funding donations, media coverage and the attention of the public and/or policy makers. Indeed, the conflation of trafficking with smuggling and/or prostitution operates to inflate estimates in the service of particular policy agendas. Assessing the prevalence of trafficking therefore essentially remains guesswork.

Knowledge link: This topic is also covered in Chapter 4.

The difficulties associated with measuring trafficking and exploitation are, in large part, understandable. After all, they are mainly clandestine activities. Consistent with most forms of crime, the under-detected, under-reported and under-prosecuted nature of trafficking means that official crime statistics represent a significant underestimate of the problem.

The cross-border nature of trafficking compounds the problem of measurement, since it dictates that different states around the globe must share information effectively in order to accurately measure its prevalence. This represents a challenge in practice since there are significant differences between countries in the counting rules they employ, as well as their reporting practices, monitoring systems and criminal codes.

In the UK, the **National Referral Mechanism** (NRM) is often cited as a central point for the identification, support and systematic counting of victims of trafficking. The National Crime Agency (2019) indicates that there were 6,993 potential victims of trafficking referred into the NRM in 2018, an 80% increase on the previous two years. It is important that we recognise, however, that NRM statistics reveal little in reality. Many victims of trafficking are not referred into the NRM, either because they do not come to the attention of the agencies that can make a referral or because they do not wish to be processed in this manner. Furthermore, the notable increase in referrals is likely to be the result of improved awareness of trafficking rather than an increase in this type of crime per se. We must therefore think critically about any attempt to measure the prevalence of trafficking and not simply repeat unverifiable statistics. Let us now turn our critical criminological minds to anti-trafficking responses in the UK, under the broad themes of prevention, protection and prosecution.

Pause for Thought

Why is it difficult to measure the extent of trafficking and exploitation?

ANTI-TRAFFICKING RESPONSES: THE '3PS' OF PREVENTION, PROTECTION AND PROSECUTION

States around the world often categorise their anti-trafficking responses within the strategic framework of the '3Ps', i.e. prevention, protection and prosecution. This framework was first used by the US Government in its annual Trafficking in Persons Report and then taken up latterly within the UN's Trafficking Protocol. In UK domestic policy, the '3Ps' featured explicitly in the 2007 UK Action Plan on Tackling Human Trafficking, and its updates in 2008 and 2009, and remained integral to Human Trafficking: The Government Strategy in 2011. Whilst the current Modern Slavery Strategy does not cite the '3Ps' explicitly, the goals of prevention, protection and prosecution remain central. In practice, however, it does not appear that the '3Ps' have been taken up by states in equal measure. The goal of prosecution often seems to be prioritised over victim protection. Of course, the '3Ps' are not mutually exclusive – that is to say, prevention, protection and prosecution efforts can crosscut. Let us bear that in mind as we now consider in turn how each of the '3Ps' are operationalised in the UK context.

Prevention of Trafficking

Preventative efforts have been operationalised in several ways in the UK. Firstly, a range of state and non-state anti-trafficking actors – such as representatives from the National Crime Agency and the police, Police and Crime Commissioners, and NGOs – have sought to improve understandings of trafficking amongst the general public, as well as amongst officials who may come across trafficked people, and latterly amongst businesses. One of the key ways in which NGOs have sought to 'improve' public awareness around trafficking and exploitation is through anti-trafficking campaigns. Simplified storylines and visceral imagery are, however, key components of many of these campaigns. Scholars have therefore argued that these campaigns, although well-intentioned, may in fact have harmful consequences for people who migrate. Indeed, they delimit so narrowly the category of victim that many exploited migrants may not recognise their victimisation. Simplistic campaigns may also discourage would-be migrants from crossing borders and thus serve nationalistic border regimes, as well as legitimising the deportation of trafficked people. Another key way in which institutions such as the police and immigration authorities, as well as NGOs, have sought to raise awareness is by encouraging the public to 'spot the signs' of trafficking. This can be understood within the context of a broader shift towards responsibilising the public for crime prevention since the 1990s. Yet the 'signs of trafficking' often apply to migrants working voluntarily in the UK. Thus, members of the public concerned with trafficking become, in effect, tasked with identifying undocumented migrants, who may then be detained and deported by the Home Office. Furthermore, it does not hold true that once a member of the public has 'spotted' a trafficked person that person will be legally entitled to victim status, a point we will return to later.

A second way in which preventive efforts are operationalised is by targeting 'demand'. This may involve appealing to consumers of products produced or services performed by victims of trafficking and/or targeting the employers of trafficked people. Traditionally, demand efforts have been focused on one particular type of trafficking, i.e. trafficking for sexual exploitation. Radical feminist/abolitionist individuals and organisations argue that laws should be introduced to criminalise those who purchase sex. They argue that if clients were deterred from buying sex, there would no longer be a demand, thus eliminating victims of sex trafficking. Yet it is both problematic and ineffective to advocate for the eradication of an entire industry as a way of dealing with exploitation. Indeed, the criminalisation of sex work clients in Sweden (as well as Northern Ireland, France, Norway and a host of other countries) has led to: increased competition between sex workers and therefore greater difficulties in terms of negotiating safer sex work; an increase in violence against those who sell sex; and a deterioration in the relationship between police and sex workers (Levy, 2015).

Thirdly, preventative efforts may take the form of addressing the 'supply' of victims of trafficking by engaging in anti-trafficking work in 'origin countries' and through border control. Much of the preventative work in origin countries focuses upon identifying individuals who may be at risk of being trafficked. Risk-focused and early-intervention crime prevention of this sort is, however, widely criticised. The high level of subjectively involved means that the 'science' of prediction is likely to yield both false positives and false negatives. Furthermore, who is identified as 'at risk' is likely to be informed by gendered and racialised stereotypes. In relation to the other key 'supply side' measure, i.e. border control, the UN Trafficking Protocol requires states to strengthen their borders in order to tackle human trafficking. In the UK, increasingly restrictive immigration policies have been accompanied by anti-immigration sentiments which construct migrants as undesirable. Sentiments of this nature, in turn, justify the implementation of draconian border policies. Yet there is growing awareness that preventive measures will likely fail if they focus solely upon the individual-level risk factors associated with trafficking and the closing of legal routes of immigration. Instead, as criminologists, we should also consider the socio-structural factors that create and maintain the conditions that give rise to trafficking and exploitation.

Protection from Trafficking

In relation to the second strategic aim, protection, the Ministry of Justice contracts The Salvation Army to provide victim support provisions in England and Wales under the National Referral Mechanism (NRM). Of course, other anti-trafficking NGOs provide support outside of the NRM but we will focus on the state-funded system here. The NRM was established in 2009 as a framework for identifying potential victims of trafficking and ensuring they receive government-funded support. As Figure 17.1 depicts, once a referral is made into the NRM, the Single Competent Authority (SCA) first makes a Reasonable Grounds decision to determine if it suspects the person to be a potential victim of trafficking. The burden of proof at this point is relatively low, at least lower than the criminal standard of proof (i.e. beyond reasonable doubt). A positive Reasonable Grounds decision entitles the potential victim to a government-funded **Recovery and Reflection period** of a minimum of 45-days, in accordance with the UN Trafficking Protocol. During this period, potential victims of trafficking are entitled to support (*recovery*) provisions via The Salvation Army's sub-contractors. The period is also intended to give potential victims time to *reflect* on whether they would like to cooperate with law enforcement agencies. A Conclusive Grounds decision should then be made by the SCA as soon as possible after 45 days to determine, 'on the balance of probabilities', that there is sufficient evidence

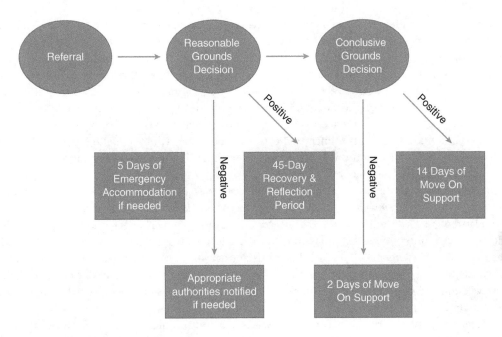

Figure 17.1 The National Referral Mechanism Process

that the individual is a victim of trafficking. A positive Conclusive Grounds decision will trigger an additional 14 days of 'move on' support, whilst those granted a negative Conclusive Grounds decision receive only two days of additional support. It is, however, often argued that the 45-day Recovery and Reflect period is not long enough to address the complex needs of many victims of trafficking, and that government-funded 'move on' support is inadequate. This may be particularly so for victims who are pursuing immigration applications, or are embroiled in complex legal cases or compensation claims (Roberts, 2018).

Prosecution of Trafficking

The third strategic aim pursued by anti-trafficking actors is that of 'prosecution'. Despite being a key anti-trafficking priority in the UK, there have been relatively few prosecutions for human trafficking offences. According to the UK Government's Modern Slavery Report 2018, 309 defendants were prosecuted under the Modern Slavery Act 2015 in 2017, whether or not modern slavery was the principle offence. That is to say, in some cases the defendant may have been charged with other offences alongside modern slavery. This represents an increase from 2016, when 155 defendants were prosecuted. It is important to remember, however, that under the Modern Slavery Act 2015, modern slavery offences include not only human trafficking but also slavery, servitude, and forced and compulsory labour. It is also important to recognise that there have been far fewer convictions under the Act. In 2017 there were 63 convictions, although only 22 of these convictions were on a principle offence basis. In other words, the majority of those convicted under the Modern Slavery Act were convicted of another offence (under different legislation), for which they received a higher penalty.

One of the key challenges involved in securing successful convictions for trafficking offences is that victims are often reluctant to engage with the criminal justice system. Without victim testimonies, it can be more difficult to secure a conviction in a trafficking case. It is widely documented in the academic literature that victims' reluctance to engage with the police or provide testimony in court may be based upon a fear of reprisal. Other victims lack trust in the criminal justice system. This may be due to bad experiences of the police in their countries of origin but it may also be the result of negative experiences of the police in destination countries. There is evidence to suggest that victims of trafficking find police 'rescue raids' to be traumatic events that leave them feeling confused about what is happening and concerned about possible arrest and deportation (Boff, 2012). It may also be the case that victims of trafficking or exploitation do not wish to engage with the criminal justice system because they do not consider themselves to be victims. Some victims of trafficking are understood to develop emotional attachments to their trafficker, whilst others may be willing to pay a debt bondage and endure exploitative conditions because they deem that preferable to the circumstances in which they found themselves previously.

Knowledge link: This topic is also covered in Chapters 3 and 31.

In other cases, victims may be deemed by the police or the CPS as not suitable to provide testimony in court. Instead, the involvement of a victim may be considered a threat to their own wellbeing and/or understood as likely to jeopardise the success of the case. My own research indicates that before allowing a victim to provide testimony in court, the police and CPS often assess whether the victim appears 'believable', are able to construct a consistent narrative about their experiences, and/or able to withstand cross-examination. Judgements about the 'credibility' of trafficking victims are often, however, quite arbitrary and may be informed by the 'ideal victim' stereotypes we will examine later in the chapter.

Furthermore, another key barrier to securing a conviction in trafficking cases relates to the challenges associated with evidence-gathering to build a case. It can, for example, be difficult to draw a line between forced labour and labour that is performed willingly. Trafficking cases can also be exceptionally expensive for police forces to investigate, particularly if they involve large policing operations (such as in the Rooney case: see Case Study 17.1) or are cross-border in nature. Given the challenges associated with proving a suspect's guilt (beyond reasonable doubt) in trafficking cases, the CPS appear to routinely choose to prosecute under a statute with which they believe they are more likely to secure a conviction (e.g. for fraud or grievous bodily harm). This can lead to a distortion in the official statistics. The introduction of the Modern Slavery Act in 2015 was intended to make it easier to prosecute traffickers, although there is not yet enough evidence to assess whether this has been successful. Nonetheless, we will now turn to think some more about the broader modern slavery agenda that was both constitutive of and constituted by the Modern Slavery Act 2105.

Case Study 17.1

Operation Pottery

In one of the biggest modern slavery cases in English legal history, eleven members of the Rooney family were jailed in 2017 for exploiting at least eighteen victims of modern slavery offences. Across a series of trials at Lincolnshire Crown Court, jurors heard how the Rooney family targeted men between the ages of 18 and 63 who were 'vulnerable': some were homeless, had learning difficulties, mental health problems, and/or suffered from alcoholism. The Rooneys promised their victims paid work via their tarmacking and paving business, and food and accommodation in caravans on the Drinsey Nook Traveller site upon which the Rooney family lived. However, Operation Pottery – an exceptionally costly police investigation – found that the Rooney family had subjected their victims to violence and intimidation, squalid living conditions, and made them work for little or no pay. In 2019, twelve members of the Rooney family were ordered to pay their victims £1,000,000 under the Proceeds of Crime Act 2002.

What are some of the challenges associated with implementing the 3Ps of Prevention, Protection and Prosecution?

THE REBRANDING OF TRAFFICKING AS MODERN SLAVERY

In the UK, the term 'trafficking' has been largely replaced by the term 'modern slavery' in debates around severe forms of exploitation in recent years. This is, in no small part, one of the consequences of the Modern Slavery Act 2015, but the term 'modern slavery' had been gaining traction in the years leading up to the Act too. Although the Act indicates that trafficking is but one possible outcome of modern slavery, the terms often appear to be used interchangeably in political discourse, and by a range of state and non-state actors. This shift is understood by academics to represent something more than simple linguistic slippage and they have raised a number of concerns about the modern slavery agenda (see Craig et al., 2019). Indeed, as criminologists, it is important that we think about why the modern slavery discourse has gained traction, how it is used to justify particular policy responses, and what effects these policy responses have. It is these issues that we now turn to.

In large part, the modern slavery agenda has gained significant traction in recent years not only because of concerns about human rights but also, because of its successful deployment of highly emotive language and imagery. The modern slavery agenda relies heavily upon a link drawn – either explicitly or implicitly – between contemporary forms of exploitation and the trans-Atlantic slave trade. Indeed, the adjective 'modern' functions to set apart 'new' slavery from 'old' by implying that slavery has re-emerged in recent years, whilst retaining the powerful imagery the trans-Atlantic slavery metaphor evokes. Bravo (2011: 562) argues that the trans-Atlantic slave trade serves as an 'emotional and historical touchstone' – that is to say, the visceral imagery it commands resonates powerfully across the globe. She argues that the emotions the analogy generates – shock, shame, guilt, horror – when cultivated effectively, can be used to mobilise action. Yet some critics argue that the link drawn between 'old' and 'new' slavery trivialises the trans-Atlantic slave trade by failing to recognise that while 'old' slavery involved the forced movement of African peoples, those labelled as contemporary victims of trafficking almost invariably make conscious decisions to migrate (O'Connell Davidson, 2015). In this sense, the gradual inclusion of a range of forms of exploitation under the umbrella of modern slavery is a form of exploitation creep in which the seriousness of slavery risks becoming diluted. Equating contemporary forms of exploitation with trans-Atlantic slavery is viewed by some, therefore, to appropriate the suffering of Black people to serve a contemporary political agenda.

Other criticisms of the modern slavery agenda focus on how it justifies particular policy responses. For example, scholars have drawn attention to how the modern slavery agenda has arisen from, and further enables, neo-conservative moral agendas on prostitution (see for example Agustín, 2007). In both the UK and US, abolitionist feminists – those opposed to the sex industry – have found an uneasy alliance with religious conservatives around the issue of trafficking for sexual exploitation. Despite historical differences in their gender and sexuality politics, these two groups have joined efforts to lobby for the criminalisation of the purchase of sex as a way of preventing trafficking and exploitation. Yet they have faced significant criticisms for conflating the voluntary sale of sex and 'sexual slavery' and in so doing, denying the agency of sex workers and legitimising (anti-prostitution) policy and practice that is reported to harm those who sell sex. As noted by the expert below, the conflation of sex work and sex trafficking may also occur in policing responses to trafficking and exploitation. The modern slavery agenda has also been criticised for encouraging the practice of 'rescuing' people constructed as 'sex slaves' – even if those people do not view themselves as victims of modern slavery – a practice considered by some to be both ineffective and paternalistic. We will return to think more about 'rescue' practices and their consequences shortly.

Hear from the Expert

The conflation of sex work and sex trafficking as part of the modern slavery agenda

Professor Teela Sanders works closely with the police to develop evidence-based policy around the sex industry. She notes that:

> "Working with the police to disseminate research knowledge and make evidence-based policy around sex work related issues is often tricky because the government (and therefore targets; taskforces; resources; intelligence) focuses largely on the 'modern slavery agenda'. Often, police forces have individuals who are responsible for safeguarding, child sexual exploitation, modern slavery, as well as sex work/prostitution. As these roles become conflated, the nuances of context and individual agency/circumstances are often not understood, or where they are, police have little time/resources to act according to nuance. A classic example is the idea that 'pop up brothels' are the harbourers of trafficked migrant women, when the reality is that many people work within their own ethnic groups, move around, and are making rational choices - within a set of circumstances - to make a living through selling sex."

Scholars have also drawn attention to how the modern slavery agenda also works in the interests of crime control and immigration agencies. Indeed, modern slavery has tended to be conceived of narrowly and within a simple narrative of good and evil. This operates to perpetuate stereotypical understandings of trafficking, in which victims are constructed as those who have been kidnapped or otherwise moved against their will by an evil individual or organisation, much like the victim in the 2008 film *Taken* starring Liam Neeson. According to Chuang (2015: 146), this framing 'creates a simple moral imperative with enormous popular appeal'. Yet in so doing, it operates to direct the blame for modern slavery towards the individual criminal and away from the role the state plays in creating and maintaining the socio-structural conditions that give rise to exploitation (O'Connell Davidson, 2015). Therefore, through institutions like the police, the state can be seen to be 'doing something', i.e. punishing traffickers and 'rescuing' victims, whilst in effect doing very little to address the real causes of trafficking and exploitation. Furthermore, the evil trafficker is almost invariably constructed as the foreign 'Other' within the broader criminalisation of migrants – or at least particular migrants – in much of the Western world. Thus, draconian border controls can be 'justifiably' implemented under the guise of tackling so-called modern slavery. Anti-immigration policy and practice is not only legitimised through the modern slavery agenda but also via the Rescue Industry, and so we will now move on to examine what the Rescue Industry is and does, and how it simultaneously helps and harms trafficked and exploited people.

THE RESCUE INDUSTRY

A growing body of literature draws attention to how a burgeoning and highly profitable industry has emerged around fighting trafficking for sexual exploitation. Agustín (2007) calls this the **Rescue Industry**: a growing network of 'social helpers' who seek to 'rescue' women from, what they perceive to be, the horrors of the commercial sex industry. For many anti-trafficking actors within the Rescue Industry, their approach is characterised by benevolence, i.e. a well-meaning aspiration to improve the lives of migrant women. As such, they no doubt represent an important source of support for some women involved in the sex industry, providing safe-housing, health care and other victim services. The provision of these services is particularly important in light of government funding cuts in recent years, which have meant that NGOs play a crucial role in plugging the gaps in victim support left by a retreating welfare state. Yet critics of the 'rescue' approach argue that it can cause harm, as well as helping victims of trafficking and exploitation (see for example Connelly, 2015). It is important, therefore, that we now look with a critical criminological eye at how the Rescue Industry can simultaneously help and harm.

Within the Rescue Industry, the brothel raid – sometimes framed as a 'welfare visit' – has become a key anti-trafficking instrument. Very often a partnership-approach is adopted during these 'visits'; that is to say, the traditional police practice of raiding is combined with NGO outreach, and they are sometimes joined by immigration authorities. Together these agencies enter, typically by force, premises believed to be occupied by victims of trafficking, in order to 'save' them from exploitation. Whilst the practice has no doubt led to the identification of some victims of trafficking, 'raid and rescue' has been widely criticised by academics and NGOs that support the movement for sex workers' rights. Notably, the practice fails to recognise that not all migrants involved in the sex industry require or desire to be saved. With limited access to formal labour markets, undocumented people may perceive sex work to represent a viable and flexible form of employment. Sex working may provide an income that enables 'dignified living standards in the UK, while dramatically improving the conditions of their families in the country of origin' (Mai, 2009: 1). Furthermore, there is ample evidence that 'raid and rescue' practices place sex workers in positions of vulnerability, leaving them homeless, displaced and unemployed. Premises known to be occupied by migrant sex workers may be targeted for raiding in particular, with the guise of rescue used to justify their arrest, detention and/or deportation.

My own research indicates that it is common practice within the Rescue Industry to conflate migrancy, trafficking and prostitution. This conflation can, in some cases, result in the over-application of trafficking victim status, and in others, it can result in the denial of trafficking victim status. At first glance, this idea seems somewhat contradictory, so let us unpack it some more. On the one hand, individuals and organisations oriented by radical feminist/abolitionist goals assume that all migrants involved in the sex industry are victims of trafficking since they believe that no one would sell sex willingly. On the other hand, others involved in the (broadly-defined) Rescue Industry – particularly, although not exclusively, police and immigration officials – routinely engage in a systematic disbelieving of trafficking victimhood, assuming that an ulterior motive exists behind victim claims. It seems that some **subaltern** women – a term used by Gayatri Chakravorty Spivak to refer to those who are socially, politically and geographically marginal from the hegemonic power structure – struggle to acquire victim status and instead are treated as immigration offenders. Thus, a seemingly paradoxical situation exists within the Rescue Industry. However, both approaches in fact serve a similar purpose in that they justify the deportation of migrating peoples. By constructing migrants involved in the sex industry as victims, they can be 'justifiably' deported under the guise of protection, and by constructing them as illegal immigrants, exploited migrants can be 'justifiably' arrested, detained and deported under the guise of protecting national security. In this sense, the Rescue Industry can be understood as another tool through which to suppress the movement of 'undesirable' bodies.

It is clear then that victimhood is not an objective experience. One does not simply acquire trafficking victim status based solely upon the interaction(s) that have taken place with an 'offender' or because one has experienced something that violates a criminal law. Instead, the label of victim is more readily conferred upon some people than others and therefore involves some kind of socio-political judgement from those in positions of relative power. With this in mind, it is important that we think about the construction of the 'ideal victim' in relation to trafficking (Christie, 1986). The ideal trafficking victim is constructed as entirely blameless, i.e. the victim's account will be more readily accepted if they have displayed little or no agency in their movement across borders nor in the sale of sex. This construction of the ideal trafficking victim is based upon, and works to reaffirm, a false dichotomy between agency and coercion. This dichotomisation is inherently problematic. Few victims of trafficking have exercised no agency at all and as such, they often face significant challenges to having their victim claims believed by the authorities. Those who are seen as being in some way 'complicit' in their exploitation may not be seen as real victims but instead regarded as (immigration or prostitution) offenders. Thus, while the Rescue Industry is commonly understood to be built upon good intentions, it can operate to exert social control, as well as offering care to those who are granted the (heavily politicised) label of victim of trafficking.

Knowledge link: This topic is also covered in Chapter 3.

Student Voice

"I found studying the topic of trafficking very interesting yet a little upsetting. As a female, it triggered a sense of rage within me as it shows the power relations that exist within the sex industry and how victims of trafficking can be portrayed as an 'offender' rather than, as a 'victim'." (Lydia Carruthers, Psychology and Criminology student)

CHAPTER SUMMARY

This chapter has introduced you to the topics of trafficking and exploitation, encouraging you to think about these complex and timely issues with a critical criminological mind. It is important to remember the following:

- While responding to trafficking (or 'modern slavery') has become a political priority in recent years, there remains significant disagreement about: what it is; how prevalent it is; how best to respond to it; how it links to and can be used in service to agendas surrounding other issues, such as immigration and/or prostitution; and the extent to which anti-trafficking efforts actually have a positive impact upon people who migrate. A key message to take away then is that trafficking and exploitation are highly contentious issues.
- Trafficking's recent rebrand as 'modern slavery' has only muddied the waters further, raising concerns that the seriousness of slavery risks becoming diluted in order to serve particular (conservative) moral and political agendas and in turn, that the human rights of people who migrate are undermined.
- Anti-trafficking efforts – although often well-intentioned – can be used as a guise through which to pursue harmful anti-prostitution practices and a draconian immigration agenda. It is therefore essential that we, as criminologists, draw attention to how seemingly benevolent anti-trafficking policy and practice can cause significant harm, as well as helping those labelled as victims of trafficking.

Review Questions

1. Why is it difficult to measure the extent of trafficking and exploitation?
2. What challenges do anti-trafficking actors face when implementing anti-trafficking policy and practice through the framework of the '3Ps'?

3. What are some of the problems associated with reframing trafficking as modern slavery?
4. How have trafficking and exploitation been highjacked in the pursuit of an anti-immigration agenda?
5. To what extent does the Rescue Industry help and/or harm migrants involved in the sex industry?

GO FURTHER

Books

I recommend the following three books that develop in more detail the issues touched upon in this chapter:

1. The below text provides a clear and accessible introduction to the topic of human trafficking, and the contentious forms of social control, regulation and surveillance that have been enacted to combat it:

   Lee, M. (2011) *Trafficking and Global Crime Control*. London: Sage Publications.

2. For those interested in the relationship between trafficking and the modern slavery agenda, Davidson's ground-breaking text below challenges popular and policy discourses and modern slavery:

   Davidson, J. O. (2015) *Modern Slavery: The Margins of Freedom*. London: Palgrave Macmillan.

3. Agustín's text below, remains the authoritative source on how the conflation of voluntary migrant sex work and sex trafficking operates to disempower women and justify interventions into their lives:

   Agustín, L.M. (2007) *Sex at the Margins: Migration, Labour Markets and the Rescue Industry*. London: Zed Books.

Journal Articles

The following three journal articles expand on the key themes underpinning this chapter.

1. Chuang's excellent article examines the rebranding of trafficking as modern slavery and the problems associated with it:

   Chuang, J. (2015) The challenges and perils of reframing trafficking as 'modern-day slavery. *Anti-Trafficking Review*, 5: 146–149.

2. For an analysis of how the Rescue Industry operates in the UK context, my own short article will serve as an accessible introduction:

   Connelly, L. (2015) The rescue industry: the blurred line between help and hindrance. *Graduate Journal of Social Science*, 11(2): 154–160.

3. Nandita Sharma's (2003) article remains an authoritative source on how anti-trafficking efforts operate to reinforce restrictive immigration practices and those rendered illegal:

   Sharma, N. (2003) Travel agency: a critique of anti-trafficking campaigns. *Refuge*, 21(3): 53–65.

Useful Websites

Finally, the following online resources will also be of use to those interested in learning more about the topics of trafficking and exploitation.

1. *It's Time for the Anti-Trafficking Sector to Stand Up for Decriminalisation of Sex Work* (2019) is an anonymous blog by an anti-trafficking actor for the Beyond Trafficking and Slavery Open Democracy series. It makes the case for a shift away from the anti-prostitution ideology that dominates the anti-trafficking sector: https://www.opendemocracy.net/en/beyond-trafficking-and-slavery/its-time-for-the-anti-trafficking-sector-to-stand-up-for-decriminalisaton-of-sex-work/
2. Karen Bravo's (2014) blog for Open Democracy on *Trans-Atlantic Slavery and Contemporary Human Trafficking* offers an accessible analysis of how 'old' slavery is invoked in contemporary anti-trafficking efforts and the consequences of its invocation: https://www.opendemocracy.net/en/beyond-trafficking-and-slavery/transatlantic-slavery-and-contemporary-human-trafficking/
3. Luke De Noronha's (2015) blog for Open Democracy entitled *'Foreign Criminals' and Victims of Trafficking – Fantasies, Categories and Control* examines how simple constructions of trafficking 'victims' and 'villains' legitimise an anti-immigration agenda: https://www.opendemocracy.net/en/beyond-trafficking-and-slavery/foreign-criminals-and-victims-of-traffickingfantasies-categories-an/

REFERENCES

Agustín, L. M. (2007) *Sex at the Margins: Migration, Labour Markets and the Rescue Industry*. London: Zed Books.

Boff, A. (2012) *Silence on Violence. Improving the Safety of Women: The Policing of Off-street Sex Work and Sex Trafficking in London*. London: Mayor's Office.

Bravo, K. (2011) The role of the transatlantic slave trade in contemporary anti-human trafficking discourse. *Seattle Journal for Social Justice*, 9(2): 555–597.

Christie, N. (1986) 'The Ideal Victim'. In E. Fattah (ed.), *From Crime Policy to Victim Policy: Reorienting the Justice System*. London: Macmillan. pp. 17–30.

Chuang, J. (2015) The challenges and perils of reframing trafficking as 'modern-day slavery. *Anti-Trafficking Review*, 5: 146–149.

College of Policing (2017) Major investigation and public protection: Definitions Available at: www.app.college.police.uk/app-content/major-investigation-and-public-protection/modern-slavery/definitions

Connelly, L. (2015) The rescue industry: When help becomes a hindrance. *Graduate Journal of Social Science*, 11(2): 154–160.

Craig, G., Balch, A., Lewis, H. and Waite, L. (eds) (2019) *The Modern Slavery Agenda: Policy, Politics and Practice in the UK*. Bristol: Policy Press.

Levy, J. (2015) *Criminalising the Purchase of Sex: Lessons from Sweden*. Abingdon: Routledge.

Mai, N. (2009) *Migrant Workers in the UK Sex Industry: Full Research Report*. Swindon: ESRC.

National Crime Agency (2019) *National Referral Mechanism Statistics: End of Year Summary 2018*. London: National Crime Agency.

O'Connell Davidson, J. (2015) *Modern Slavery: The Margins of Freedom*. London: Palgrave.

Roberts, K. (2018) Life after trafficking: A gap in UK's modern slavery efforts. *Anti-Trafficking Review*, 10: 164–168.

United Nations (2000) *Protocol to Prevent, Supress and Punish Trafficking in Persons Especially Women and Children*. Geneva: United Nations.

Weitzer, R. (2014) New directions in research on human trafficking, *The ANNALS of the American Academy of Political and Social Science*, 653(1): 6–24.

Hate Crime

18

Neil Chakraborti and
Stevie-Jade Hardy

Learning Objectives

By the end of this chapter you will:

- Understand the underlying factors that have given rise to increasing levels of hate crime around the world.
- Be familiar with definitions of hate crime and the challenges associated with the development of a consistent policy framework.
- Be able to identify the range of groups and communities who are affected by hate crime.
- Have explored the motivations behind the perpetration of hate crime.
- Be in a position to assess the effectiveness of criminal justice responses.

Framing Questions

1. In what ways do hate crimes hurt more than ordinary crimes?
2. Should hate crime policy be reframed in order to cover a wider or narrower set of identity characteristics or has an appropriate balance been struck?
3. What factors are likely to generate higher levels of satisfaction amongst victims in relation to criminal justice responses?

INTRODUCTION

Hate crime is a term that has assumed particular relevance within academic and political spheres in recent times. As societies across the world have become increasingly diverse, and within a context of profound political and economic change, concerns about intolerance, **prejudice** and hostility have escalated. A growing body of hate crime scholarship has promoted collective awareness and a shared understanding of extreme and 'everyday' acts of hate amongst a range of different actors, including law-makers, non-governmental organisations, activists and professionals within and beyond the criminal justice sector. While much progress has been made in terms of improving levels of practical support for victims, a number of conceptual and operational challenges remain which have diluted the impact of empirical research and policy development.

Within this chapter, we consider a series of important questions that form the central debates around hate crime. What does the term 'hate crime' mean and is there a universal definition? Who is affected by hate crime and what harm does it cause? Who are the perpetrators of hate crime and what are their motivations? How is hate crime addressed and are current responses effective? As we shall see, hate crime is a complex, highly subjective and pervasive phenomenon which has a range of implications for victims, their families and wider communities.

MAPPING THE TERRAIN

Let's first turn to recent contextual developments which help to illustrate the significance of hate crime. The rise in levels of hate crime amidst a backdrop of an increasingly polarised social climate has contributed to its ascendency upon political and academic agendas. Within the UK the 2016 EU Referendum was a catalyst for an upsurge in reports of hate crime. Over 14,000 hate crimes were recorded by police forces in England and Wales between July and September 2016, with three-quarters of forces reporting record levels of hate crime during that period (Hardy and Chakraborti, 2017). The UK has also observed a rise in popularity amongst far-right movements in recent years such as Britain First, the Democratic Football Lads Alliance (DFLA) and National Action, which have inflamed social tensions as hateful narratives gain traction in mainstream discourse. Across Europe, populist political parties in countries such as Austria, Denmark, France, Germany, Hungary and the Netherlands have been exploiting anti-immigrant sentiment, fuelling the scapegoating of particular minority groups and stoking up widely held anxieties. Similarly, spikes in hate crime were seen in the USA following a build-up of tensions during and after the 2016 presidential campaign, alongside numerous hate-motivated attacks, including the 2018 Pittsburgh and 2019 Poway synagogue shootings. The growth of hate and **extremism** in online and offline environments paints a worrying picture, and illustrates the need for effective and meaningful responses to deal with hate crime.

There is now a substantial body of empirical evidence which demonstrates the multiple layers of harm associated with hate crime (see Iganski and Lagou, 2015). This form of victimisation has the capacity to inflict greater psychological and emotional damage when compared to non-hate motivated crimes (Home Office, 2018; Paterson et al., 2019). These harms have been described by the Office for Democratic Institutions and Human Rights (ODIHR, 2009) as harms which violate human rights between members of society; intensify the level of psychological hurt experienced by the individual victim; transmit an increased sense of fear and intimidation to the wider community to whom the victim 'belongs'; and create security and public order problems as a result of escalating social tensions.

The additional harms associated with hate crime have been central to its prioritisation. Within the UK we have seen a succession of hate crime laws introduced by consecutive governments, a significant volume of criminal justice policy and related guidance and resolute campaign group activism. The most recent iteration of the UK Government Hate Crime Action Plan, published in October 2018, reinforces commitments to tackle hate crime through a series of actions and priority areas, identifying good practice across all forms of hate crime (HM Government, 2018). Similarly, the volume of theoretical and empirical advancement in hate crime scholarship over recent years means that we now know more about hate crime than ever before: more about the people who suffer hate crime as well as those who perpetrate hate crime; more about the nature, extent and impact of victimisation; and more about the effectiveness, or otherwise, of different interventions. These developments have shaped thinking across a number of academic disciplines, including criminology, psychology, sociology, history, political science and legal studies; within statutory, voluntary and private sectors; and amongst senior figures in political and criminal justice spheres 'down' to activists, campaigners and community volunteers working at a grassroots level.

Annual hate crime statistics have shown year-on-year increases in police recorded hate crime within England and Wales since 2012/13. In 2018/19, the police in England and Wales recorded 103,379 hate crimes, an increase of 10% compared with the previous year (Home Office, 2019). While attributable to improved reporting rates and recording practices, the upsurge is thought to also reflect a genuine increase in the prevalence of hate crime. Recent estimates from the 2017/18 Crime Survey for England and Wales, which takes account of those experiences of victimisation which have not been reported to the police, suggest that approximately 184,000 hate crimes were committed in the same timeframe (Home Office, 2018). The 'real' figure is likely to be far greater, as many cases of hate crime are simply not recognised by criminal justice agencies, non-governmental organisations or by victims themselves. A growing body of evidence highlights that decision making within the context of reporting incidents of hate crime is influenced by a wide range of structural, social, situational and individual factors, all of which create and reinforce layers of resistance to reporting.

DEFINING HATE CRIME

This next section outlines some of the ways in which academics and policy makers have conceived of hate crime. Coined in the United States during the 1980s to describe bias-motivated violence against Jewish, African-Americans and lesbian, gay and bisexual people, the term 'hate crime' gained common currency in the UK following the racist murder of Stephen Lawrence in 1993 and the ensuing publication of the Macpherson Report in 1999. Before considering some of the challenges around hate crime in greater depth, it is important to reflect upon what we mean by the term itself. When asked to define hate crime, we might naturally suggest offences which are motivated by hatred. However, 'hate' is an emotive and conceptually ambiguous label which can mean different things to different people, and the presence of 'hate' is not a prerequisite for an offence to be classified as a hate crime. Rather, most academic definitions consistently refer to a broader range of factors to describe the motivation which lies behind the commission of a hate crime (see Chakraborti and Garland, 2015). In particular, terms such as 'prejudice', 'bias' and 'targeted hostility' have been used interchangeably by criminologists as a way of highlighting that 'hate' is not central to the commission of hate crime.

In the absence of a single, universally agreed definition, the framework proposed by Canadian criminologist Barbara Perry (2001: 10) is often referred to as the most comprehensive interpretation of hate crime within contemporary academic literature. According to Perry:

> Hate crime ... involves acts of violence and intimidation, usually directed towards already stigmatised and marginalised groups. As such, it is a mechanism of power and oppression, intended to reaffirm the precarious hierarchies that characterise a given social order. It attempts to re-create simultaneously the threatened (real or imagined) hegemony of the perpetrator's group and the 'appropriate' subordinate identity of the victim's group. It is a means of marking both the Self and the Other in such a way as to re-establish their 'proper' relative positions, as given and reproduced by broader ideologies and patterns of social and political inequality.

There are several significant elements to Perry's framework:

- Firstly, it acknowledges the complexity of hate crime victimisation by highlighting the relationship between structural hierarchies, institutionalised prejudice and acts of hate. It gives primacy to the idea that violence is different when motivated by bigotry and directed towards already marginalised populations. For Perry, hate crime emerges as a response to threats posed by 'others' when they attempt to step out of their 'proper' subordinate position within the structural order. In other words, it is a mechanism whereby violence is used to sustain the hegemonic identity of perpetrator, as well as the boundaries between dominant and subordinate groups by reminding the victims of their place.
- Secondly, Perry places emphasis on the group instead of the victim's individual identity. Within this context, acts of violence and intimidation are directed not simply towards the individual victim, but towards the collective wider community to whom the victim is perceived to belong. As such, a message is sent to the victim's community that they are 'different' and 'do not belong', thereby transmitting a sense of fear and apprehension which has ripple effects beyond the immediate victim and their family. Within this framework, hate crime is part of a process of repeated or systemic victimisation influenced by wider social, political and historical factors.

Despite the strengths of Perry's definition and its influence upon the field of hate studies, there is scope to think of hate crime in a more expansive fashion than conceived of within Perry's framework. For instance, we advocate a simpler, and in some ways wider-ranging definition, which sees hate crimes as acts of violence, hostility, and intimidation directed towards people because of their identity or perceived 'difference' (see also Hardy and Chakraborti, 2019). This definition covers forms of verbal abuse, anti-social behaviour and intimidation which might not be criminal acts in themselves, but which can have equally significant impacts upon the victim, their family and wider communities. Whilst this definition is deliberately concise, it acknowledges that some victims can be subjected to hate not exclusively because of their membership of a particular identity group, but also because they are seen as vulnerable or somehow 'different' in the eyes of the perpetrator. Moreover, and crucially from the perspective of making hate crime an operationally viable concept, the more long-winded definitions that academics are inclined to use sometimes feel rather complex, too ethereal and detached from the everyday realities confronting those who deal with hate crime cases in the 'real world'.

Pause for Thought

What do you think are the key features within academic definitions of hate crime?

Hear from the Expert

"As a child I was a regular victim of what is now called hate crime. I had no knowledge of how the UK legal system would evolve to recognise hate offences. Now, as I research disability hate and become involved with the victims of it, I can make links with the past. I realise that studying hate crime is not an isolated academic pursuit. Instead it reveals the deep psychological distress, fear and loneliness caused by attacks on personal identity. The victims of hate deserve our attention."

Dr David Wilkin, Honorary Fellow at the School of Criminology, University of Leicester and Lead Coordinator of the Disability Hate Crime Network

Within the UK the College of Policing provides a crucial source of policy guidance on hate crime. As the professional body responsible for setting professional development standards across English and Welsh police forces, their interpretation of hate crime is especially relevant to the present discussion. This is because it offers a broad application of the hate crime concept and outlines practical ways in which criminal justice agencies can respond to any conceptual ambiguity. For example, the guidelines include a requirement for all hate incidents to be recorded by the police, even if they lack the requisite elements to be classified as a notifiable offence later in the criminal justice process. This means that at the recording stage, any hate incident, whether a *prima facie* 'crime' or not, is to be recorded if it is perceived by the victim or any other person (such as a witness, a family member or a carer) as being motivated by hostility or prejudice (College of Policing, 2014). This interpretation of hate crime enables the police to respond to the 'everyday' forms of targeted hostility which many victims are routinely subjected to, in addition to violent expressions of hate.

The College of Policing guidance also stipulates that the police are obliged to record an offence as a 'hate crime' if the incident was motivated by hostility on the grounds of any one of **five monitored strands**:

- Disability
- Race
- Religion
- Sexual orientation
- Transgender

This recording procedure enables police forces to collate statistics which can then be used to identify trends and facilitate regional and international comparisons. Importantly, there is a degree of flexibility in how the boundaries of hate crime are framed within UK policy. Official guidance states that the five monitored strands 'are the minimum categories that police officers and staff are expected to record', and thereby police forces are able to record other forms of targeted hostility as hate crime if there are legitimate localised grounds for doing so (College of Policing, 2014: 7). For instance, in 2016 Nottinghamshire Police began recording misogynistic incidents as hate crimes in a bid to tackle the abuse and harassment suffered by women on a daily basis (Mullany and Trickett, 2018). This policy has been developed as a result of tragic cases and an emerging body of research highlighting the targeting of 'other' identities who have not routinely been considered as hate crime victims (see below for examples).

It is worth pausing for a moment at this stage to reflect upon what we know about hate crime from this inspection of definitions. As this section has illustrated, a universally accepted definition of hate crime does not exist, and the elasticity of the concept invariably results in some degree of subjectivity and ambiguity when it comes to generating a shared understanding and framing policy responses. It is also evident from the definitions presented above that the presence of 'hate' is not central to the commission of a hate crime, and that the label itself is an inaccurate descriptor of the majority of incidents which blight the lives of hate crime victims. We now move on to consider the experiences of those victims in more detail.

HATE CRIME VICTIMS

As with attempts to define hate crime, the process of determining which groups of victims to protect through policy and law is highly subjective. Unsurprisingly, there has been much debate among scholars and professionals with regard to people's identity or lifestyle characteristics, which should be recognised within hate crime legislation and therefore afforded special protection. Recent figures

Knowledge link: This topic is also covered in Chapter 3.

collated by the Office for Democratic Institutions and Human Rights (ODIHR) demonstrate that race and ethnicity is the most commonly monitored type of identity, with a total of 23 countries recording data on racist or **xenophobic** crimes. This level of recognition is predictable, given that racist hate crime remains the strand of hate with which commentators are most familiar. One of the shortcomings of existing literature within the field of hate studies has been a tendency to rely upon simplistic and naïve constructions which depict ethnic minorities as one seemingly homogeneous victim group. This approach dismisses, or at best underplays, the differences in experiences and needs between people clustered under a 'catch' all category, as well as those who are typically excluded from such frameworks altogether. A notable example is mixed-race families and relationships, with what little research evidence there is suggesting that those from a mixed heritage background face a higher risk of racist victimisation. There are also many other victim groups, including Gypsies and Travellers, **foreign national**s, **refugee**s, **asylum seeker**s and **migrant worker**s who suffer racist violence and abuse on a regular basis, but still remain peripheral to academic and policy debates about racially motivated **hate crime**.

Over the past decade religiously-motivated hate crime has occupied a more significant role within political and academic thought. The escalating level of prejudice directed towards Muslim communities in particular has raised the profile of religiously motivated hate crime and has been a significant factor in the formulation of explicit legislative protection against attacks upon religious identity across several countries (see Case Study 18.1). However, Muslim communities are not the only faith group to have experienced an increase in hate crime. Research suggests that anyone ostensibly 'looking Asian', for instance through wearing a turban, sporting a beard or simply by virtue of being 'dark-skinned', has become increasingly susceptible to the risk of physical assault or verbal abuse (Awan and Zempi, 2018). This is why it is important to consider the role of intersectionality within the context of victim selection. Conceiving of hate crimes simply as offences directed towards discrete strands of a person's identity, fails to give adequate recognition to the interplay of identities with one another and with other personal, social and situational characteristics. Research by Chakraborti et al. (2014) found that more than half of the victims surveyed within their research had been targeted on the basis of more than one identity or lifestyle characteristics. Indeed, many felt that they had been victimised because of their race *and* religion; their mental ill-health *and* physical or learning disability; or their **sexual orientation** *and* dress and appearance.

——— Case Study 18.1 ———

Hanane Yokoubi

On 13 October 2015 Hanane Yakoubi – who was 34 weeks pregnant – was travelling on a bus in north-west London.* Unprovoked, a passenger on the bus started berating Hanane and her two family members for talking in their native language. For the next five minutes, Simone Joseph subjected Hanane and her family to a vile barrage of abuse, calling them 'sand rats' and 'ISIS bitches', and accusing them of supporting Islamic State and hiding bombs in their clothing. The whole experience was terrifying and humiliating for Hanane. The racist and religiously-motivated attack became even more threatening when the perpetrator told Hanane that 'You're lucky I don't kick you in the uterus and you'll never have a baby again'.

The bus was packed full of passengers and although no-one on the bus intervened, a witness filmed the attack on their mobile phone and uploaded it to Facebook, resulting in the video going viral. After Simone watched the footage, she handed herself in to the police. In court, Simone pleaded guilty to causing racially aggravated distress and was sentenced to a 16-week jail term, suspended for 18 months, and 60 weeks of unpaid work.

(* The case studies included within this chapter are based on real-life hate crimes. A more detailed account of these cases can be found in the report by Hardy and Chakraborti, 2017).

More recently we have also seen increasing levels of scholarly attention devoted to uncovering the targeted violence and abuse experienced by other groups of victims, including people with learning and/or physical disabilities, the lesbian, gay and bisexual population, and **transgender** people. However, there remains a longstanding criticism of conventional hate crime policy which has not been adequately resolved. It is often suggested that hate crime policy creates and reinforces hierarchies of identity, narrowly ascertaining victims as worthy and unworthy of inclusion within the hate crime frameworks. As Mason-Bish (2010: 62) notes:

> ... hate crime policy has been formed through the work of lobbying and advisory groups who have had quite narrow remits, often focusing exclusively on one area of victimisation. This has contributed to a hierarchy within hate crime policy itself, whereby some identity groups seem to receive preferential treatment in criminal justice responses to hate crime.

Activists and campaigners have undoubtedly played a key role in exposing the violence and hostility experienced by certain victim groups, and in stimulating debates and the momentum necessary to influence law formulation and policy enforcement. However, there is a downside to this process; namely, that the parameters of hate crime frameworks are often dependent upon the ability of campaign groups to lobby for recognition. An ever-growing body of research has raised concerns about the lack of recognition and support for a range of victims who are regular targets of violent and intimidatory behaviour, including the homeless (Allison and Klein, 2019), sex workers (Campbell, 2014), people with mental-ill health (Chakraborti et al., 2014), women (Mullany and Trickett, 2018) and members of alternative sub-cultures such as goths, punks and others with a strikingly different appearance (Garland and Hodkinson, 2014). These groups share much in common with the more familiar groups of hate crime victims, as they too are singled out as targets of hostility, specifically because of their 'difference'. However, lacking in either the support of lobby groups or political representation and typically perceived as 'undesirables', criminogenic or less worthy than other more 'legitimate' or historically oppressed victim groups, they are thus excluded from conventional hate crime frameworks. For these marginalised victims, the process of inclusion and exclusion in policy recognition is beyond a conceptual challenge; it is a fundamental human right and equality concern with life-changing consequences. It is for this reason that the steps taken by many police forces to change their policy to monitor additional strands – including attacks against sex workers, alternative subcultures and the homeless – is a welcome development, as is the Law Commission's ongoing review of the scope and effectiveness of hate crime laws in England and Wales which is due to be published in 2021.

Moreover, it is often the more violent and extreme acts of targeted hostility which attract media, political and academic attention, while the experiences and the cumulative harms of the more 'ordinary', everyday forms of abuse, bullying and harassment are underappreciated. During one of our studies we found that 98% of participants had been verbally abused on the basis of their identity, and 54% of these participants experience this form of victimisation repeatedly. A wide range of studies illustrate that hate crime victims encounter repeat victimisation, which manifests itself predominantly through verbal abuse and harassment.

Knowledge link: This topic is also covered in Chapter 5.

—————————————— Case Study 18.2 ——————————————

Racial Abuse

When 26-year-old Grace met Jack she felt as though she had met her soulmate, but over the next six months their relationship was tested. Jack's family and friends took it upon themselves to show their dislike for Grace on the basis of their interracial relationship, by expressing and posting offensive comments which had racist and xenophobic undertones. She received racially abusive messages on her social media which made explicit threats of violence:

> "She's a slitty eyed mental trench gook who needs to be chopped up and binlinered and dumped in the canal."

> "I think we should all get pellet guns and all wait outside her work and shoot the f**k into her."

> "Report it because she's got slanted eyes! Get [name] to sort her out he knows how to get round to these yellow skin freaks."

Frightened that these threats of violence might be acted upon, she reported this hate crime to the police via 101, a non-emergency number which members of the public are encouraged to use.

From the very first interaction that Grace had with the police she was let down. After explaining the nature of her victimisation to the police operator, she found them to be dismissive and unhelpful. Though Grace was told that an officer would follow up on her case, days passed without contact being made which compounded her anxiety. At no point was Grace signposted to support services despite her telling the call handler how much the incident was affecting her. Throughout the investigation the police failed to handle Grace's victimisation with the sensitivity, empathy and seriousness it deserved. The case was not identified or recorded as a hate crime and a decision was taken not to prosecute despite Grace having evidence to support her claims.

Finally, given the ubiquity of internet usage in the contemporary age, people are becoming increasingly connected over online platforms. It is therefore imperative to consider how online space can be used as a vehicle to spread prejudiced and hateful views as in the case study above. Data from 32 police forces in England and Wales reveal a 33% increase in recorded online hate crime against disabled people between 2016/17 and 2017/18. Furthermore, research by Paterson et al. (2018) highlights that 80% of the LGB and/or T and the Muslim participants surveyed had experienced at least one online hate incident. Similarly, the 2017 Stonewall LGBT in Britain report highlighted that one in ten LGB and/or T people have experienced online homophobic, biphobic and transphobic abuse or behaviour directed at them personally in the last month (Bachmann and Gooch, 2017). It is evident that online hate is a growing concern warranting greater attention, as understandings of who commits it and why are in their infancy.

HATE CRIME PERPETRATORS

Much academic endeavour within the field of hate studies has focused upon the processes, forms and impacts of hate crime victimisation. Far less attention however has been paid to the motivations of hate crime perpetrators. While there have been a number of studies on far-right parties, mainly by political scientists, there has been comparatively little criminological scrutiny of the causes and patterns of hate-related offending committed by those who do not identify with such political groups. Official data on the demographics of hate crime perpetrators are equally sparse. Despite the relative paucity of empirical evidence, some significant research studies have generated insights into the profiles of hate crime offenders. The most influential work to date on hate offender profiles was conducted by McDevitt, Levin, Nolan and Bennett (see McDevitt et al., 2002). Based on analysis of 169 hate crime cases investigated by the Boston Police Department, their typology consists of four categories of perpetrators as outlined below:

'Thrill Offenders'

The majority (two-thirds of the cases assessed) of hate crime perpetrators were categorised as 'thrill' offenders. These individuals are commonly teenagers or young males who, acting in a group, commit hate crimes in search of a viscerally exciting experience. Key characteristics of this type of offending include the perpetrator(s) venturing from their neighbourhood in search of someone to target, and selecting victims based on an underlying prejudice towards their group affiliation.

This profile is supported by official statistics in England and Wales which suggest that a significant proportion of hate offenders are under the age of 25. In addition, analysis of data gathered by the Metropolitan Police Service revealed that 76% of 6,426 accused perpetrators were men (Walters and Krasodomski-Jones, 2018). Similarly, a number of academic studies, although focusing on different strands of hate crime, have found that most hate crimes are committed by young males acting in groups (see Walters et al., 2016). The suicide of Fiona Pilkington and her disabled daughter Francesca Hardwick in 2007 was a tragic outcome following seven years of relentless abuse and harassment by thrill-seeking youths in the neighbourhood: see Chakraborti and Garland (2015: ch. 6) for further details about this case).

'Defensive Offenders'

A quarter of the cases reviewed by McDevitt et al. (2002) were categorised as 'Defensive' offenders, who share a similar demographic profile to 'Thrill offenders'. These offenders typically commit hate crimes as a means of 'protecting' their neighbourhood from perceived intruders. Within this context the victim, or more aptly the community to whom the victim is perceived to belong to, is seen to be as posing a threat, whether this is socially, culturally or economically.

Examples of the types of offences committed by 'Defensive' offenders, include the spike in levels of hate crimes targeting Eastern Europeans following the 2016 EU Referendum. Research reveals that victims were singled out because they were speaking in a foreign language, which is a marker of 'difference' that could be perceived as posing some sort of threat. Similarly, the 'Punish a Muslim Day' campaign in 2018 serves as another example. The letters, which were sent to mosques, Muslim-owned businesses and Muslim MPs, stated that 'they have hurt you, they have made your loved ones suffer' and that they 'would like nothing more than to do us harm and turn our democracies into Sharia led police states'. Articulating a defensive rhetoric, the letters claimed that 'only you can help turn things around' and advocated verbally abusing, throwing acid at, torturing and butchering Muslims.

'Retaliatory Offenders'

'Retaliatory' offenders – which accounted for approximately 10% of cases – typically travel to the victim's territory to avenge a previous incident which they perceive the victim, or the victim's social group, to have committed. In the case of both 'defensive' and 'retaliatory' offenders, motivations underpinning hate crime perpetration conform to the framework proposed by Perry (2001), in that hate crimes can be deployed as '**message crime**s', designed to instil a sense of fear and intimidation to victims and the wider community.

Revenge attacks were observed following the Manchester arena bombing in 2017. Greater Manchester Police recorded a 505% increase in **Islamophobic** attacks, with 224 reports of anti-Muslim hate crimes recorded in the month after the attack, compared to 37 during the same period in 2016. In addition, Steven Bishop was found in possession of explosive substances and convicted for plans to detonate a bomb in a mosque to exact 'revenge' for the terror attack. Similarly, in the aftermath of the London Bridge terror attack in the same year, the London Metropolitan Police Service recorded a five-fold increase in Islamophobic attacks, with 20 anti-Muslim incidents recorded per day in comparison with a daily average of 3.5 for 2017. These spikes show that '**trigger**' events of local, national and international significance can influence the prevalence and severity of hate incidents within cyber-space and the physical world (Williams and Burnap, 2015).

'Mission Offenders'

Motivated by an overarching 'mission', these offenders are considered to be hate-fuelled individuals and are often far-right sympathisers. Unwavering allegiance to a bias ideology is more evident here than with the offenders in the other three categories, where engagement in violence is prompted by the need to prove a point, rectify perceived wrongs or exterminate groups who are deemed evil or inferior. Although such offenders are relatively rare, risks of extreme violence are the greatest. David Copeland who perpetrated the 1999 London nail bombings, Anders Behring Breivik who was the instigator of the 2011 Norway terror attacks, and Brenton Tarrant who was the shooter in the 2019 Christchurch mosque atrocities, are perhaps some of the most well-known examples of 'mission' offenders.

Although 'mission' offenders conform to the archetypal idea of a hate crime perpetrator, in reality the vast majority of hate crime offenders fall within the other three categories. The fact that a large proportion of incidents are motivated by a desire for 'thrills' within everyday contexts suggests that much of what we think of as 'hate crime' is worryingly 'routine' from the perspectives of both the offender and the victim. A growing evidence base suggests that many hate crimes tend to be committed by relatively 'ordinary' people in the context of their 'ordinary' day-to-day lives. These offences are not always driven by entrenched prejudice or hate harboured by the perpetrator, but instead are a departure from standard norms of behaviour, an inability to control language or behaviour in moments of stress, anger or drunkenness, or a sense of weakness or inadequacy stemming from various subconscious emotional and psychological processes (Walters et al., 2016). These are all possible reasons influencing hate crime perpetration.

Pause for Thought

Reflecting on what you have read so far, do you think that there are any limitations associated with the typology of perpetrators proposed by McDevitt et al.?

The foundations of much hate crime scholarship and policy have been built on the assumption that these are exclusively majority-versus-minority crimes. However, this interpretation fails to recognise that the types of prejudices and stereotypes which underpin acts of hate crime are not the exclusive domain of any particular group. Racist attacks, for instance, can arise from disputes between members of different minority ethnic groups, while victims of homophobic and transphobic hate crimes are sometimes targeted by religious minorities (Chakraborti et al., 2014). Equally, our reliance on the labels 'victim' and 'offender' assumes dichotomous roles in hate crime offences. This reinforces a de-contextualised picture of some cases, particularly neighbourhood conflicts, where both parties can share culpability for anti-social behaviour which forms the basis for the broader conflict and hate offence (Walters et al., 2016). All of these points are too significant to remain peripheral to the domains of scholarship and policy. We need to resist any temptation to draw overly simplistic conclusions, and instead inform our conceptual and empirical understanding through these multiple realities.

RESPONDING TO HATE CRIME

Within this final section we consider some of the key challenges which need to be addressed within our collective responses to hate crime. These include the limitations of hate crime laws, the difficulties associated with generating high levels of victim satisfaction, and the scope for alternative responses which sit outside of the criminal justice system. As the preceding discussion illustrates, hate crime is a highly complex and divisive subject area. The further we attempt to seek conceptual clarity, the more likely we are to find ourselves confronted with operational challenges. Learning how best to tackle hate crime is a difficult, ongoing task, but one which has formed a unifying theme within contemporary criminological enquiries. Often the responsibility of responding to hate crime is designated to criminal justice agencies. However, as we shall see, this approach can have limited effectiveness in addressing offending behaviour or the support needs of victims.

Many countries around the world have taken steps to implement legislative frameworks to deal with hate crime, enabling the courts to impose enhanced sentences when the underpinning motivation of hostility is proven. Such laws have significant value in terms of their capacity to express collective condemnation of prejudice; to send a declaratory message to offenders; to convey a message of support to victims and stigmatised communities; to build confidence in the criminal justice system within some of the more disaffected and vulnerable members of society; and to acknowledge the additional harm caused by hate offences (Chakraborti and Garland, 2015). Within this context effective legislation and enforcement is important, both for individual freedoms and security, and for cohesive communities. Nevertheless, the principles underpinning the creation of hate crime laws have been contested by academics, lawyers, politicians and the public. This is particularly evident in relation to the symbolic value of hate crime legislation, with critics questioning the capacity of hate crime provisions to have a declaratory and deterrent impact on the general public. Further concerns have been expressed over the effectiveness of such laws to facilitate justice, with hate crime prosecutions declining since 2015/16. Walters et al. (2018) identified that inconsistent application of sentencing provisions in court, alongside limited awareness of available legislative provisions among key legal professionals, were primary factors limiting the effectiveness of hate crime legislation in England and Wales. Moreover, ambiguous definitions of terms including 'motivation' and 'hostility' in the legal guidance heighten difficulties in understanding, and thus proving, what hate crime constitutes (ibid., 2018).

There are also uncertainties associated with the appropriateness of criminal justice responses to punish and to rehabilitate offenders. Hall (2013) provides three criticisms of the use of imprisonment for hate crime offenders. Firstly, prison has limited deterrent value to these offenders. Secondly, prisons are often divided along the lines of race and religious affiliation and may therefore reinforce intolerant attitudes, inadvertently encouraging hate-related activity. And thirdly, the overcrowded prison environment offers little opportunity for the rehabilitation necessary to truly address prejudicial beliefs. Therefore, while imprisonment and the use of enhanced sentences may be entirely appropriate in certain contexts, there are equally many forms and perpetrators of hate crime for which such punishment might not be especially effective.

As outlined earlier on within this chapter, hate crime policy within England and Wales is based upon an inclusive, victim-centred approach which seeks to improve levels of trust and confidence within historically marginalised communities and to increase the numbers of victims coming forward to report hate crime. However, hate crime victims are less likely to be satisfied with the police response both in terms of the fairness and effectiveness of the service provided when compared to victims of non-hate motivated crimes. Based on combined 2015/16 to 2017/18 surveys, just 51% of hate crime victims within England and Wales were found to be very or fairly satisfied with the handling of their case, compared to 69% of general crime victims (Home Office, 2018). Further issues with police responses to hate crime were highlighted as part of the inspection conducted by Her Majesty's Inspectorate of Constabulary and Fire & Rescue Services (HMICFRS) in 2018. While the inspection revealed examples of professional, sensitive and effective practices among officers and staff, it also identified considerable inconsistencies in the service delivered between and sometimes within individual forces (HMICFRS, 2018). Criticisms of the initial response tend to stem from a feeling of not being listened to, not being taken seriously, and not being treated with an appropriate level of decency and empathy.

An emerging body of research challenges prevailing assumptions about hate crime victims' desire for enhanced prison sentences by revealing an overwhelming preference – shared by victims of different violent and non-violent hate crime and from various communities, ages and backgrounds – for the use of community education programmes and restorative interventions as a more effective route to challenging underlying prejudices and preventing future offending (Chakraborti et al., 2014; Paterson et al., 2018). Within one study we found that 82% of survey respondents were in favour of greater use of educational programmes in school, 55% of community 'payback' orders involving voluntary work, 46% of diversity awareness-raising interventions for perpetrators, and 35% of face-to-face mediation between the victim and the offender (Hardy and Chakraborti, 2018). There are promising signs that policy makers are beginning to engage with this empirical evidence as responses to hate crime are becoming less prescriptive and more victim-centred.

Within the UK specifically, there has been a growing recognition of the importance of challenging prejudicial attitudes before they fully develop. Education and early intervention within and beyond the classroom – such as those delivered by Anne Frank Trust, the Sophie Lancaster Foundation, and Show **Racism** the Red Card – assume an important role in raising awareness of the harms of hate. Equally, health and social care services can offer crucial support and treatment for victims, and their capacity to recognise and respond to hate crimes is pivotal given that such crimes often have severe consequences for physical and emotional health and wellbeing. Non-governmental organisations also play a key role by monitoring and reporting incidents, acting as a voice for victims and campaigning for action and improvements to legislation. These developments are illustrative of the need for a holistic, collective approach to hate crime which can facilitate appropriate responses to ongoing problems, effectively rehabilitate hate crime offenders, and crucially, prevent future instances of hate crime.

CHAPTER SUMMARY

- The concept of hate is more complex than many might imagine. With no universal definition, it can be prone to subjective interpretation and poses significant challenges to academics, law makers and criminal justice professionals.
- The impacts of hate crime are substantial in terms of their physical and emotional harms. Incidents extend beyond the primary victim to also affect families, friends, communities and others with shared identity characteristics.

- Recent years have seen an emergence of new knowledge, ideas and policies to tackle forms of targeted violence and hostility. However, several themes remain un- or under-explored. Many frameworks have sidelined acts of hate directed towards groups of 'others' from beyond the five monitored strands, resulting in a hierarchy of victims and a failure to understand 'hidden' forms of hate.
- Similar challenges are evident in relation to existing knowledge on hate crime perpetration. A lack of empirical research, official data and over-simplified assumptions have skewed our understanding of the underlying factors and situational contexts that give rise to offending behaviour.
- There are positive signs of progress with tangible changes for victims of hate. Through a shared commitment to tackling hate, prejudice and targeted hostility in all its guises and to developing sustainable modes of support, such progress can be maintained across the academic and policy domains.

Review Questions

1. What forms can hate crimes take and in what ways can they affect victims, their families and wider communities?
2. What are the benefits and potential challenges associated with the way in which police forces define hate crime?
3. What policy responses have been developed within the UK to deal with hate crime?

GO FURTHER

Books/Book Chapters

1. This book offers a broad and accessible insight into the causes, impacts and responses to hate crime from a UK perspective:

   Chakraborti, N. and Garland, J. (2015) *Hate Crime: Impact, Causes and Responses,* 2nd edition. London: Sage Publications.

2. This second title adopts an international perspective, exploring key theories, concepts, global reflections and responses to hate crime across the world:

   Hall, N., Corb, A., Giannasi, P. and Grieve, D. (2015) *The Routledge International Handbook on Hate Crime.* Oxon: Routledge.

3. The following text offers an in-depth analysis of the lived realities of hate crime, as informed by research undertaken with the largest sample of victims to date:

   Hardy, S. and Chakraborti, N. (2019) *Blood, Threats and Fears: The Hidden Worlds of Hate Crime Victims.* London: Palgrave Macmillan.

Journal Articles

1. Underpinned by empirical evidence, this article outlines the gap that can exist between academia, policy and practice, and explains how victims of hate crime are being failed:

   Chakraborti, N. (2018) Responding to hate crime: escalating problems, continued failings. *Criminology and Criminal Justice,* 18(4): 387–404.

2. This article draws from the author's research evidence to detail the multitude of barriers that can exist to inhibit the reporting of hate crime:

    Hardy, S. (2019) Layers of resistance: understanding decision-making processes in relation to crime reporting. *International Review of Victimology*, Online First.

3. This article builds upon the harms of hate to exemplify how and why incidents of hate can extend beyond the individual victim to generate impact upon whole communities:

    Walters, M. A., Paterson, J., McDonnell, L. and Brown, R. (2019) Group identity, empathy and shared suffering: understanding the 'community' impacts of anti-LGBT and Islamophobic hate crimes. *International Review of Victimology*, Online First.

Useful Websites/Reports

1. This source outlines and explains the criteria for what constitutes a hate offence and how the criminal justice system should respond in England and Wales:

    College of Policing (2014) *Hate Crime Operational Guidance*. Coventry: College of Policing. Available at: https://www.college.police.uk/What-we-do/Support/Equality/Documents/National-Policing-Hate-Crime-strategy.pdf

2. This resource offers a detailed breakdown reported hate crime data from across Europe with accompanying visual aids:

    ODHIR (2019) *Hate Crime Reporting*. Available at: http://hatecrime.osce.org/

3. This academic report offers insight into criminal justice handling of hate crime cases, in addition to information on best practice and direction for future approaches:

    Walters, M. A., Brown, R. and Wiedlitzka, S. (2016) *Preventing Hate Crime: Emerging Practices and Recommendations for the Effective Management of Criminal Justice Interventions*. Brighton: University of Sussex. Available at: http://sro.sussex.ac.uk/id/eprint/64925/1/Interventions%20for%20Hate%20Crime%20-%20FINAL%20REPORT_2.pdf

REFERENCES

Allison, K. and Klein, B. R. (2019) Pursuing hegemonic masculinity through violence: an examination of anti-homeless bias homicides. *Journal of Interpersonal Violence*, 1(1): 1–24.

Awan, I. and Zempi, I. (2018) "You all look the same": non-Muslim men who suffer Islamophobic hate crime in the post-Brexit era. *European Journal of Criminology*, 1(1): 1–18.

Bachmann, C. L. and Gooch, B. (2017) *LGBT in Britain – Hate Crime and Discrimination*. London: Stonewall.

Campbell, R. (2014) 'Not Getting Away with It: Linking Sex Work and Hate Crime in Merseyside'. In N. Chakraborti and J. Garland (eds), *Responding to Hate Crime: The Case for Connecting Policy and Research*. Bristol: The Policy Press. pp. 55–70.

Chakraborti, N. and Garland, J. (2015) *Hate Crime: Impact, Causes and Responses*, 2nd edition. London: Sage Publications.

Chakraborti, N., Garland, J. and Hardy, S. (2014) *The Leicester Hate Crime Project: Findings and Conclusions*. Leicester: University of Leicester.

College of Policing (2014) *Hate Crime Operational Guidance*. Coventry: College of Policing.

Garland, J. and Hodkinson, P. (2014) "F**king freak! What the hell do you think you look like?" Experiences of targeted victimisation among goths and developing notions of hate crime. *British Journal of Criminology*, 54(4): 613–631.

Hall, N. (2013) *Hate Crime*, 2nd edition. London: Routledge.

Hardy, S. and Chakraborti, N. (2017) *Hate Crime: Identifying and Dismantling Barriers to Justice*. Leicester: University of Leicester.

Hardy, S. and Chakraborti, N. (2018) *A Postcode Lottery? Mapping Support Services for Hate Crime Victims*. Leicester: University of Leicester.

Hardy, S. and Chakraborti, N. (2019) *Blood, Threats and Fears: The Hidden Worlds of Hate Crime Victims*. London: Palgrave Macmillan.

HM Government (2018) *Action Against Hate: The UK Government's plan for tackling hate crime – 'two years on'*. London: HM Government.

HMICFRS (Her Majesty's Inspectorate of Constabulary and Fire & Rescue Services) (2018) 'Understanding the difference: The initial police response to hate crime'. London: HMICFRS.

Home Office (2018) *Hate Crime, England and Wales, 2017/18*. London: Home Office.

Home Office (2019) *Hate Crime, England and Wales, 2018/19*. London: Home Office.

Iganski, P. and Lagou, S. (2015) Hate crimes hurt some more than others: implications for the just sentencing of offenders. *Journal of Interpersonal Violence*, 30(10): 1696–1718.

Mason-Bish, H. (2010) 'Future Challenges for Hate Crime Policy: Lessons from the Past'. In N. Chakraborti (ed.), *Hate Crime: Concepts, Policy, Future Directions*. London: Routledge. pp. 58–77.

McDevitt, J., Levin, J. and Bennett, S. (2002) Hate crime offenders: an expanded typology? *Journal of Social Issues*, 58(2): 303–317.

Mullany, L. and Trickett, L. (2018) *Misogyny Hate Crime Evaluation Report*. Nottingham: Nottingham Trent University.

ODIHR (Office for Democratic Institutions and Human Rights) (2009) Hate Crime Laws: A Practical Guide. https://www.osce.org/odihr/36426

Paterson, J., Walters, M. A., Brown, R. and Fearn, H. (2018) *The Sussex Hate Crime Project: Final Report*. Brighton: University of Sussex.

Perry, B. (2001) *In the Name of Hate: Understanding Hate Crimes*. London: Routledge.

Tell MAMA (2018) *Beyond the Incident: Outcomes for Victims of Anti-Muslim Prejudice*. London: Tell MAMA.

Walters, M., Brown, R. and Wiedlitzka, S. (2016) *Causes and Motivations of Hate Crime*. London: EHRC.

Walters, M. and Krasodomski-Jones, A. (2018) Patterns of hate crime: who, what, when and where?, https://www.demos.co.uk/wp-content/uploads/2018/08/PatternsOfHateCrimeReport-.pdf

Walters, M., Owusu-Bempah, A. and Wiedlitzka, S. (2018) Hate crime and the 'justice gap': the case for law reform. *Criminal Law Review*, 12(1): 961–986.

Williams, M. L. and Burnap, P. (2015) Cyberhate on social media in the aftermath of Woolwich: a case study in computational criminology and big data. *British Journal of Criminology*, 56(2): 211–238.

Race and Racialised Crime

19

Tina G. Patel

————————— Learning Objectives —————————

By the end of this chapter you will:

- Understand the social construction of 'race' in matters relating to crime, justice and victimisation.
- Explore the persistent presence of racism within the criminal justice system.
- Develop knowledge on key criminological theories and empirical studies on this subject.
- Be able to critically evaluate the impact of racialised crime.

————————— Framing Questions —————————

1. What purpose does race serve in debates about crime, justice and victimisation?
2. Despite the recognition and addressing of racism within the criminal justice system, how and why does it still exist there?
3. What is the value of criminological contributions for developing our knowledge and practice?
4. Who gains and who loses when crime is racialised?

INTRODUCTION

In introducing the concerns of this chapter, it is important to acknowledge that criminological discussion on the influence of race, processes of racialisation and the impact of racism in matters relating to crime, justice and victimisation, has documented the endemic and persistent problem of bias. This results in practices that (over)focus on particular groups culminating in disproportionate victimisation and injustice. Processes of racialisation had traditionally defined some, specifically those of black Asian and minority ethnic (BAME) background, as innately prone to criminal behaviour. Not only are 'BAME' and other non- (and 'not-quite') 'white' bodies more readily labelled as criminal (or at the very least deviant), but they are also subjected to processes that render them hyper-visible and suspect – regardless of whether they have actually engaged with crime or not.

This chapter will encourage you to examine the ways in which race is socially constructed within discussions relating to crime, justice, and victimisation. Attention will be paid to highlighting how such racialised constructions serve the interests of those who seek to maintain a position of power and authority, as well as sustain a dominant 'white' ideology. In reading the chapter, you will understand the contributions made by critical criminological, anti-racist and activist approaches, specifically Black Criminology, Critical Race Theory, and the Black Feminist Critique. The chapter will also give you knowledge of key empirical research in order to assist your development of an understanding of how racism is able to maintain a stronghold within the criminal justice system, despite various events that have recognised, condemned and addressed racism and racist cultures. Finally, the chapter will invite you to critically evaluate the impact of racialising crime, considering the consequences for key players as well as wider society. Throughout the chapter, key criminological literature, theory, and empirical research will be drawn on – with a particular focus on those that are described as aligned with the critical criminological approach. In addition to knowledge development, this chapter invites you to critically consider the value of criminology for contributing to the achievement of fair and just practices in matters relating to race and racialised crime.

A NOTE ON TERMINOLOGY

Before this chapter goes any further, it would be useful for you to have clarification on my use of terminology. Terminology in this area is flexible, complex, problematic, and open to interpretation (and criticism). Despite there being wider acknowledgement that 'race' remains socially constructed, it nevertheless remains conceptually powerful – a term used by one group to abuse and exploit others. It is something used in very real ways, and has serious consequences in society. For this reason, the term 'race' is used in this chapter. Similarly, the terms 'black Asian and minority ethnic' (BAME) and 'white' are at present popular terms of reference, and are used here accordingly. The terms refer to cultural, ethnic, and politically defined categories, rather than biologically-based ones. That said, these terms should always be problematised. Indeed, there is much work being (and yet to be) done to develop terms of reference so that language is more accurate and representational. They are for now though, the most suitable ones available.

In addition, this chapter henceforth uses the term 'race and racialised crime' to refer to matters of race, racism, racialisation, crime, justice, and victimisation. The adopted term is used as shorthand to refer to this somewhat broad area, whilst attempting to support your focus on the core concerns: the significance of race and its use to determine experiences and outcomes.

It is important to recognise that whichever term is used, they are done so with a sense of uneasiness – they are not perfect, and for reasons beyond the scope of this chapter, often cause (me) discomfort.

───────── Pause for Thought ─────────

Have you ever thought about the language you use in matters relating to race, both in lay interactions and your academic studies?

───────── Student Voice ─────────

"In terms of race, being able to define ourselves in ways of our own choosing is very important. It is a right that should be enabled and protected, especially given that it is part of a deep and meaningful self-identification process. As academics, we can of course guide the development of language used to describe racialised groups, but we must acknowledge that our contribution is neither final nor universal."

(Esra, Second Year Student, PhD Criminology)

MAPPING THE TERRAIN: RACIALISED PROCESSES WITHIN CONSTRUCTIONS OF CRIME

Before a fuller discussion commences, this section will provide you with a review of the scholarly work on race and crime. The contested nature of race has been well documented. Used as a standard of measure long before the term was conceptualised, biological positivist ideas about race which claimed that biologically-based racial difference, or 'hereditary descent', determined one's capabilities and thus position in society. Such work reinforced the popularity of 'scientific racism' and the use of race to explain human civilisation. This is the view that humans are easily categorised according to fixed somatic, psychic and cultural characteristics. These views popularised the creation of racial hierarchies, where those who were considered 'white races' were always placed at the top, whilst 'black races' were always placed at the bottom. This resulted in various practices of human conquest, exploitation and genocide.

Race is considered amongst the social scientific community as something that is socially constructed. It is recognised as a problematic, yet powerful concept that has been used to justify socially- and culturally-based inequalities. Can you think of any examples where race has been used to exploit, control or exert power over another group or groups? In particular, processes of **racialisation** – an 'Other defining process' which uses both racially-based real and imagined biological and/or cultural characteristics, have rendered BAME bodies as problematic, deviant, and criminally suspect. For instance, consider the continued narratives which you may have seen around 'black crime' which are normalised and popularised. These narratives rely on 'culturalist' explanations, i.e. the 'African Caribbean muggers' who lack a father/authority figure, the hyper-sexual 'Asian grooming gangs' for whom sex with their own women was off-limits, or the 'Islamic terrorists' who are backward and irrational. What all these racialised crime explanations do is reinforce a crude idea of BAME groups as unable to meet British (Western) traditions of decency and civility (Murji, 2003: 231).

Today, race is still used to popularise and justify pre-emptive and reactionary practices that are selective and disproportionate. This commonly occurs within the criminal justice system and in matters relating to crime, justice and victimisation. Although race is not real, it nevertheless remains real in consequence and has a real impact in people's lives. Indeed, for some, race is a matter of life and death (West, 2017). Consider here the case of Brazilian Jean Charles de Menezes, who was 'mistaken' for a suspected terrorist, and fatally shot seven times by London Metropolitan Police (UK) officers at Stockwell Underground station on 22 July 2005. More recently there is the case of 46-year-old black African American male, George Floyd, who had an officer from Minneapolis Police Department (USA) kneel on his neck continuously for at least eight minutes, ultimately resulting in his death, and ruled by two autopsies as homicide.

It is important for you to consider the contributions made by the Critical Race perspective, which has highlighted how in practice, we have a situation where racist logic, practices and consequences remain strong. Here, newer forms of racism have replaced the older and unpopular biologically-based ideas about race. Kundnani (2001) refers to this as the 'new popular racism', a particular type of cultural discrimination that is context-specific and popularised as acceptable, even in these supposedly 'post-race' times. It is **'xeno-racism'** – a more complex form of racism that is wrapped in nationalistic and xenophobic sentiments, in other words, a focus on national self-determination and a 'natural' fear of strangers, and includes anti-Traveller/Gypsy sentiments, hostility towards asylum seekers and refugees, anti-Muslim racism and Islamaphobia. The popularity of such 'civilisational racism' is the bedrock of contemporary 'nativist' views on race, culture, difference, and 'the preservation and defence of "our people", "our culture", "our race"' (Sivanandan, 2006: 2). The crime, justice and victimisation agendas are not immune from these views.

CRIMINOLOGICAL CONTRIBUTIONS TO THE STUDY OF RACIALISED CRIME

Writing in the nineteenth century and drawing on contemporary Enlightenment thought, the biological positivist ideas as asserted by Cesare Lombroso (1911), popularised ideas about bodily stigma and criminality. Although scientifically challenged and soundly disputed, the biological positivist ideas today still have a significant body of support and are familiar in lay and socio-political discussions. The biological strand of positivist thinking included the use of race-based characteristics to explain criminal behaviour, arguing for instance that skull formations (or defects) in criminals meant they were animalistic savages. The problem being here that Lombroso's catalogue of defects paralleled features commonly found in dark(er)-skinned members of his sample population, i.e. Sicilians in Italy.

Today, much of the criminological literature in this area has focused on the victimisation of BAME people in lay society, as well as their treatment either as suspects, offenders or victims within the criminal justice system. These data demonstrate the subtle and not-so-subtle ways in which BAME people are stereotyped and discriminated against at hugely disproportionate levels in comparison to their white(r) counterparts, with more recent work focusing on race-based criminalisation in what is often claimed to be a 'post-race' society. See for example the case of the Black Lives Matter movement (https://blacklivesmatter.com/about/).

Case Study 19.1

Trayvon Martin and Black Lives Matter

Trayvon Martin was an unarmed black African American 17-year-old, who in February 2012, was walking back to a relative's apartment after visiting a convenience store. Martin was walking through a Sanford (Florida) neighbourhood which had experienced several robberies earlier that year.

At this time, George Zimmerman, who was a member of the local community watch scheme, saw the unarmed Martin and called the local police to report 'a real suspicious guy' who appeared to be 'on drugs' (Lee, 2013: 154). Despite police advice to await their arrival, moments later Martin was shot in the chest by Zimmerman. Zimmerman was not charged at the time of the shooting by the Sanford Police on the basis (they argued) that there was no evidence to refute his claim of self-defence, and because Florida's 'stand your ground' law provides immunity for the use of force in self-defence. However, following public protest and local community activism, Zimmerman was charged and found guilty of second-degree murder and manslaughter in July 2013. The Black Lives Matter movement emerged, following the Martin case. This is a global organisation whose aim is to highlight and campaign against a racialised violence and anti-black racism. In using the Martin case to demonstrate the fallacy of post-race claims, Lee (2013) notes how race still matters hugely in society today, albeit in different ways from the past. Race matters in the lives of BAME communities who continue to experience discrimination and disadvantage based on the use of implicit racist stereotypes. This racial bias influences perceptions of suspicion and threat, which goes on to impact negatively on how they are perceived and treated in society, both in lay interactions and when encountering institutions. Lee (2013) rightly notes that it would have been highly unlikely that Zimmerman would have perceived Martin to be 'a real suspicious guy' or 'on drugs' if he had been white. It is argued that implicit racial bias exaggerated Zimmerman's fear of Martin (as the black deviant subject) and motivated what seemed to him to be a reasonable decision to use deadly force (Lee, 2013: 101). What is more interesting though – and suitably illustrates the complexity of post-race racism – is the fact that Zimmerman self-identifies as Hispanic and sometimes white Hispanic. The Martin case challenges the idea of a non-racially biased state and illustrates the continued racialised victimisation of black communities.

Pause for Thought

Do you think there is a need for such a movement to be racially defined – in other words, don't *all* lives matter, or are black ones particularly more vulnerable?

In assessing criminological contributions to the study of race and crime, it is necessary to ask yourself the following uncomfortable question: to what extent can the white (male, middle-class) and racist roots of criminology be trusted to provide an accurate, critically reflective and meaningful examination of crime, justice and victimisation issues?

Pause for Thought

One possibility is to consider the call made by Phillips and Bowling (2003: 269) 'to move beyond the so-called "race and crime" debate that has preoccupied us ... the need to refine this debate, extend its parameters, and to raise concerns about the nature of the discipline itself', by developing 'minority perspectives' in criminology. What do you think about the possibility of these suggestions?

The criminological and wider social scientific community's highlighting of how and why crime is racialised, including the impact this has on individuals, communities and the criminal justice system at large, has made important contributions to the legal, policy and practice framework. The broader equality and anti-discrimination legislation in the UK addressing employment and service provision includes the Race Relations Act 1965 (and later 2000), the Racial and Religious Hatred Act 2006, and the Equality Act 2010; and their equivalents in Europe, USA and Australia, such as the Civil Rights Acts of 1964 and 1991 in the USA, and the Commonwealth Racial Discrimination Act 1975 in Australia. In terms of race and racialised crime in the UK, it was the Macpherson Report (Home Office, 1999) – an inquiry into the Metropolitan Police Force's handling of the Stephen Lawrence murder in 1993 – that can be identified as key to raising public awareness and supporting criminological research into racial bias within the criminal justice system, not only in terms of the Lawrence case, but also in terms of wider concerns about the disproportionate (ab)use of stop and search powers and the comparatively higher number of deaths in custody involving BAME people. Famously, Macpherson highlighted the presence and impact of 'institutional racism', i.e. 'the unwitting prejudice, ignorance, thoughtlessness and racist stereotyping expressed' in the attitudes, behaviour and practices of social and political institutions, which then go on to disadvantage minority ethnic people (Home Office, 1999: para 6.34).

The legacy of the Macpherson Report has been contested. Some have claimed that nearly all of its recommendations have been implemented, while others highlight the persistence of racist practices, even in a supposedly post-race society. Thus, efforts to better the situation of BAME people have been accused of being 'tokenistic', disingenuous, and masking continued practices of discrimination. In addition, other crime prevention measures have been introduced within what has been suggested is a period witnessing a newer, more dangerous crime and security threat, i.e. terrorism – and specifically radical Islamic terrorism, which it is argued warrants a different and more serious counter/prevention approach. In combination, these have in many ways reversed the progress made by earlier anti-racist and anti-discriminatory policy.

Now that you have awareness of the subject context, including key perspectives and constitutions, we will consider in more detail the negative consequences emerging from the racialisation of crime, justice and victimisation.

BIAS, OVER-FOCUS AND DISPROPORTIONALITY WITHIN THE CRIMINAL JUSTICE SYSTEM

This section will specifically examine the prevalence of racially-based bias in the criminal justice system. The section will highlight how such bias leads to an over-focus on BAME populations, resulting in disproportionate experiences of victimisation and encounters with criminal justice bodies. As Covington (1995: 547) notes:

> Crime is racialized, for example, when the criminal behaviours of individual black offenders are understood in terms of 'racial traits', 'racial motives', or 'racial experiences'. When traits, motives, or experiences are classified as the property of whole races or racial communities, these conceptions of race assume causal significance in explaining criminal behaviour ... When crime is thus racialized, whole communities or whole categories of phenotypically similar individuals are rendered precriminal and morally suspect.

There has been a long history in criminology and the social sciences where explanations of criminality have been racialised; consider for instance the popularity of biological positivism and biosocial theories of crime (discussed later in this chapter). These theories present BAME bodies as either biologically or culturally deficient – lacking in related values that would otherwise filter criminal or deviant tendencies.

Consequentially, some crimes have been more readily assigned to particular BAME groups – as you no doubt would have witnessed. For example, the 'mugging' moral panic of the 1970s claimed that there was a particular threat posed by the criminal propensities of British-born young males of African-Caribbean background. With no robust evidence, this group were held responsible for a supposed spike in the number of street robberies. Critical commentators highlighted that crime figures were not only grossly exaggerated, but also that the creation of this term (mugging) was entirely delivered within a racialised narrative of street crime. In more recent times, the racialisation of BAME bodies remains, but the ways in and reasons for which have changed. For instance, having been considered 'passive', 'weak' and 'effeminate' for many years, now Asian (brown-skinned) men, following the child sexual exploitation cases that hit England in 2012, have been presented as hyper-sexual predators – groomers and abusers, with a particular tendency for targeting young white girls. On another level, Asian men have also been subjected to processes of racialisation within the 'war on terror' context, resulting in them being seen as a particular type of dangerous body. In this scenario, not only are 'brown' men rendered suspicious in terms of terror-related activity, but *their* type of terror is also considered to surpass that of previous terror groups (see Pantazis and Pemberton's (2009) discussion comparing 'old' and 'new' terror suspects). Aas argues that 'the discursive and political coupling of migration and crime' creates the fearful image of 'crimmigrant bodies' (2011: 337), and that as well as being a racialised category, BAME immigrants are also criminalised in uniquely problematic ways which result in them being subjected to enhanced global and domestic crime control measures. There are also increasing calls being made for a more meaningful consideration to be given to those groups who also sit outside of the centralised white position, what is referred to as those who have 'marginalised white ethnicities', i.e. those who are 'white-ish' in appearance, but also considered 'not quite white' or 'not white enough', for example, the white 'underclass' or 'new' migrants.

Pause for Thought

Do you think everyone experiences racialisation in the same way when it comes to crime and deviance? Or do some groups have it worse than others – and if so, how and why?

To understand the persistent ways in which racist stereotyping and ideology remain, we need to critique the racialised relationships within a white majority society, and consider the structures of power and cultural features of criminal justice bodies. Criminal justice institutions and allied bodies place some in a privileged position of power and authority, able to exercise authority, use force, criminalise people, and shape how society responds to identified problems. Addressing this problem now needs to be the focus of criminological attention.

Student Voice

"The study of race and racialised crime can be difficult. It is therefore important that you have a good system of support in place which can be used to help you cope with any difficulties that you may be exposed to whilst studying or working within this area."

(André, First Year Student, BA (Hons) Criminology)

THEORISING RACE AND CRIME

The chapter now provides you with a breakdown of the key theories on race and racialised crime. This can be broadly divided into three parts: (i) biological positivism; (ii) sociological positivism; and (iii) social constructionism. The roots of biological positivist criminology can be linked to period within the discipline referred to as 'Classical Criminology', which argued that punishment should only be used as a form of social control and deterrence when a social contract (i.e. law, itself reflecting the consensus) was broken. While underpinned by a language of universalism, equality and liberal ideas, Classical Criminology however rested on the basis that laws and social contracts were the result of the free collective will of rational individuals – a status and quality not assigned to subjects of imperial European domination (Rowe, 2012).

Knowledge link: This topic is also covered in Chapter 6.

Pause for Thought

Essentially, the racist roots of criminology became enmeshed as the discipline emerged from the Classical tradition. Later, this became occupied with explaining human behaviour, the outcome being the development of biological (scientific) racism and the Eugenics movement. Ask yourself, how and why did the arguments of biological (scientific) racism persist?

Sociological positivist perspectives developed in the 1970s. With older biological perspectives having been denounced following attempts to move away from the biologically-based racist atrocities of Nazi Germany, biosocial theories started to gain support from some quarters of criminology. Rather than arguing that biology (or race) alone determined criminal behaviour, biosocial theorists such as Herrnstein and Murray (1984) argued that biology, along with social, psychological, and environmental factors, contributed to criminal behaviour. Most powerful was the view that race-based inherited traits, such as a propensity towards aggression (due to high testosterone levels) or low intelligence, along with poverty and a lack of respect for authority (due to problematic family formations), combined to explain the higher proportion of BAME criminality.

Sociological positivism's focus on ecological or environmental causes had appeared in the work of W.E.B. Du Bois (1899), and later Park and Burgess (1925 [1967]), who identified the role placed by geography and urban ecology in crime and offending behaviour, as well as wider social behaviour. This work was later developed by others such as Wilson and Kelling (1982), who considered how neglect, marginalisation and discrimination moved some people from positions of law-abiding status to criminality and delinquency (Rowe, 2012: 30). This later informed race-cultural theories, such as those by Wolfgang and Ferracuti (1967), which sought to explain 'black criminality' with reference to 'unique racial (black) subcultures' (Covington, 1995: 552). Although highlighting the socially defined element of crime and deviance, sociological positivism in many ways reinforced the relationship between race and crime.

Social constructionism advanced on some of the discipline's positivist tendencies in the 1960s, with the 'Outsiders' work of Howard S. Becker (1963) which highlighted the importance of 'labels', bias (racism) and power – ultimately drawing our attention to how these factors combined to explain the over-representation of BAMEs in the criminal justice system. Other social constructionists, e.g. Hall et al. (1978), followed-up with a focus on Labelling Theory, as applied to the idea of 'black criminality' and the racist structures of society and its institutions, such as the criminal justice system. It was because of the emergence of critical criminological, anti-racist and activist approaches, specifically

Black Criminology, Critical Race Theory, and the Black Feminist Critique, that a new approach to the study of race and racialised crime would mark a significant turn in the discipline. Having looked at the historical disciplinary developments and criminological work on the (ab)use of race within the criminal justice system, an examination of newer emerging criminological thinking is needed.

CRIMINOLOGY AND RACE MATTERS: CRIME, JUSTICE AND VICTIMISATION

This section will discuss the contribution and significance of the critical approaches to the study of racialised crime that have developed in more recent times, highlighting in particular the work of Critical Race Theory and Black Feminist Theory. The key concerns of this section ask why is there a need for such critical approaches and can they meaningfully penetrate the 'normative whiteness' of criminology?

There are very real and serious consequences when crime becomes racialised (as well as gendered and classed), both individually and collectively. This includes experiences of enhanced surveillance, heavy-handed over-policing, under-policing and inadequate protection, and disproportionate punishment. This has an impact on feelings of safety as well as corroding the social, psychological, and emotional self. Indeed, let us remember Cornel West's point that for some, race and racism is an everyday matter of life and death (West, 2017: xiii) – as clearly illustrated in the cases of Trayvon Martin and Jean Charles de Menezes. More widely, over-focusing on one group and not on any others, serves to distract and divert attention away from other often more serious crimes, such as acts of corporate criminality. This ensures that the powerful continue to dominate social and institutional structures, and the marginalised, vulnerable and powerless continue to suffer.

Critical approaches to the study of race and racialised crime have emerged and challenged the limitations of mainstream criminology. The central position of Critical Criminology is a belief that crime is inextricably linked to social circumstances, i.e. the current cultural, economic, historical, and political conditions within society, that are experienced on an individual and/or group basis. More specifically, the approach argues that racialised experiences of discrimination, inequality and exclusion explain crime rates. In this vein, the approach started to pay closer attention to (and expose) relationships of power – specifically structural inequalities, discrimination, exclusion, racism and sexism, which the critical criminological strand argued over-criminalises 'poor' and marginalised groups.

Soon after, in the mid-1970s, Critical Race Theory (CRT) emerged and began to comment on how social structures disadvantage the less powerful in society. As an interdisciplinary activist-based movement, CRT explores how race, class and gender combine (or intersect) to shape one's experiences within various social institutions, including the criminal justice system. Here they argue that two key points explain the BAME experience of criminal justice. The first is 'differential racialisation' where different racial groups have qualitatively different experiences within society and several factors, such as depictions in the popular media, inform how they are perceived and treated in terms of criminal justice. Second is 'interest convergence' (aka, 'material determinism') which argues that white ethnic groups manipulate notions of race and racial issues (including, racialised crime control) in order to protect their own material and other interests.

In developing the work of CRT, elements of Black Feminist Theory and Critical Race Feminist Theory have been used in combination to develop a Black Feminist Criminology. The tenets of Black Feminist Criminology are 'interconnected identities, interconnected social forces, and distinct circumstances to better theorize, conduct research, and inform policy regarding criminal behaviour and victimization among African Americans' and other BAME groups (Potter, 2006: 109). In examining these areas more fully, Black Feminist Criminology can assist to understand violence against BAME women, and the structural, cultural and familial influences within this experience (Potter, 2006: 106).

Knowledge link: This topic is also covered in Chapter 8.

Pause for Thought

What are your thoughts on the development and need of a specific branch of Black Feminist Criminology, separate from mainstream Feminist Criminology?

In combination, these critical race approaches have critically examined the racist and discriminatory nature of the criminal justice system, and the impact that this has on social status, positioning, power and the human rights of BAME communities, e.g. Gabbidon et al's (2011) research on black women's experiences of violence, and Mitchell and Davis's (2019) study of formerly incarcerated black mothers. Not only do these 'Black perspectives' provide a critical understanding of race and racialised crime, but they also challenge White hegemonic (Colonialist and Orientalist) ideas about 'black crime' through the offer of a progressive 'minority perspectives criminology' which refines the race and racialised crime debate as well as questions the limitations of the discipline itself. These perspectives also allow for oppression-specific (postcolonial) criminological analysis.

Pause for Thought

Achieving fairness in this area is by no means an easy task. Indeed, do you think race-equality and fairness in matters relating to crime, justice and victimisation can ever be achieved?

The more sceptical among us may suggest that this is impossible given the deeply rooted nature of bias in the criminal justice system and allied bodies. That said, there are critical approaches, such as those mentioned, which are making efforts to influence policy developments in this area. In addition to highlighting the continued post-race practices of racism, this body of work is drawing our attention to the primary and secondary victimisation of those groups who are comparatively under-researched, and making recommendations for governments and legal bodies to ensure that preventative measures and support services are fit for purpose. For instance, see Irene Zempi (2015) (who is featured below) and her research with victims of Islamophobia.

Hear from the Expert

Dr Irene Zempi's Research on Islamophobia

Zempi has studied the experiences of Muslim women and the veil, focusing particularly on their experiences of Islamophobia and victimisation (2015). Using a critical race feminist approach that factors the concept of Intersectionality, Zempi examines how and why veiled Muslim women are perceived as the personification of gender oppression, and how veiled bodies are marked out as dangerous, and a threat to public safety and national cohesion. She argues that the victimisation of veiled Muslim women remains largely 'invisible' in research, as well as falling under the police and local authority 'radar'. This means that victims of gendered Islamophobia often suffer in silence. Moreover, the marginalisation of veiled Muslim women in politics and media contributes to their 'invisibility' and silences their voices. Zempi's work addresses this significant gap in knowledge. Drawing on intersectionality (as a nexus of identities that work together to render certain individuals as 'ideal' targets to attack), her work demonstrates that veiled Muslim women experience gendered Islamophobia both in the 'real' world and in cyber space, due to the intersections between their 'visible' Muslim identity, gender performance and other (real or perceived) aspects of their identity such as age, race/**ethnicity**, (dis)ability, sexual orientation, class and political ideology. In investigating the nature and impact of this victimisation upon veiled Muslim women, their families and wider Muslim communities, Zempi has contributed to understanding the factors that contribute to the under-reporting of this victimisation and the coping strategies which are used by veiled Muslim women in response to their experiences of Islamophobia. This is important knowledge for policy and practice development, and specifically for the police (and other criminal justice agencies), who Zempi argues should employ strategies that will improve veiled Muslim women's confidence such as engaging with them in a religious and culturally sensitive manner, and ensuring that their voices are heard. In this context it is necessary for the police, and for service providers more generally, to receive relevant training on ways to provide high-quality services that meet the religious and cultural needs of veiled Muslim women. Moreover, it is necessary that both policy makers and criminal justice practitioners understand the diversity within the Muslim population which covers ethnicity, nationality and theology, but most importantly, gender. Services need to be flexible and specifically meet the needs of veiled Muslim women, whose experiences differ considerably from those of Muslim men.

To develop critical criminological work on race and racialised crime matters requires more than highlighting how and even why post-race and related discriminations occur. That is not to say that to continue its documentation and discussion is not important. There needs to be emphasis on developing a branch of criminological theory and research impact which works towards improving the lives of those who are susceptible to disadvantage and discrimination. This chapter has encouraged you to consider the development of strong 'minority perspectives in criminology' which would 'be concerned with empirical, theoretical, practical and policy issues and address matters of representation, knowledge production, the historical contextualization of minority experiences in theory development, and the ethical duties of criminologists working within a minority perspective' (Phillips and Bowling, 2003: 269). Specifically, it has been suggested to you that a minority perspective focusing on race and racialised crime, would challenge the ongoing creation and reinforcement of the 'false pathologies' of minority groups as inherently criminal, that have tended to dominate mainstream criminological understanding (Phillips and Bowling, 2003: 271).

This approach would also permit you to more fully examine the marginal and excluded experiences of anyone in a minority status, not just those defined on the basis of race and ethnicity, and in doing so also highlight intersectional experiences, if not support the development of a specific 'intersectional criminology'. It is also an approach that all criminologists can contribute to, on the basis that they do not exploit research participants, e.g. for the purpose of furthering their own career, winning large research grants, or securing publications. This inclusive nature of the minority perspective is in contrast to the calls of 'black criminology' which favours the positionality of a core, essential black experience for undertaking this work (Phillips and Bowling, 2003: 273).

In a similar vein, it would be useful for impact work from criminological and other social scientific research to consider the gains of being influenced by activist and advocacy-based movements, or using action-based methodologies. This can help to ensure that research not only highlights the socio-cultural and political status of minority groups, but also that it changes in real and meaningful ways, their material conditions. Some recent examples of work here include the following case study, which outlines Isakjee and Allen's (2013) work on Project Champion surveillance in Birmingham (UK).

—————————— Case Study 19.2 ——————————

Project Champion and Racialised Surveillance

Known to be predominantly populated by Muslims, residents of the Washwood Heath and Sparkbrook areas of Birmingham (UK) were informed by local crime prevention agencies that there would be just over 200 CCTV cameras erected in the area as part of a general crime-reduction strategy – an initiative welcomed by the residents who themselves had raised concerns about vehicle crime, drugs offences and anti-social behaviour. A short while after the erection of the CCTV, it was discovered that 40 of the cameras were catergorized as 'covert', believed to have been hidden in walls and trees. As questions began to arise about the purpose of the CCTV system, it was revealed that funding for the cameras had come from the government's Terrorism and Allied Matters Fund, whose remit includes the funding of counter-terror projects and prosecution cases regarding terror-related activity. The concern raised by the Washwood Heath and Sparkbrook residents was that not only had this funding and covert camera information not been disclosed to them, but that they felt that Project Champion's real purpose infringed basic human rights, given that it was seen to have been set up in order to spy on members of the Muslim community. Residents also felt that the victim–offender narrative had been reversed, in that Muslims were being rendered criminal, or to be more precise, involved in terror-related activity. The Islamophobic underpinnings of Project Champion was clear: to be Muslim was to be a terrorist, and if not actually, then potentially or in support of it. Following the residents' challenge of what was referred to as 'spy cams', the last of the cameras was finally dismantled in June 2011. In examining the case of Project Champion, Iskajee and Allen (2013: 758) note the power of racist (or Islamophobic) underpinnings in the terror-panic logic, as well as how readily the human rights and civil liberties of British citizens are aggressively attacked within such a logic.

—————————— Pause for Thought ——————————

Ask yourself, is it ever justifiable to use racial or ethnic profiling in security measures?

CHAPTER SUMMARY

The key points and arguments made in the proceeding sections have emphasised how and why matters relating to the **racialisation** of crime, justice and victimisation are now more than ever an important area of criminological attention. To summarise, the key points for you to take from this chapter are:

- Race is not a naturally occurring biological trait. Rather it is a status emerging from a socially constructed process influenced by cultural, economic, historical and political conditions.
- Race is a problematic concept that has been used to justify socially- and culturally-based inequalities. These are most evident in matters relating to crime, justice and victimisation.
- BAME people are continuously presented as innately and unavoidably criminal, even when the reasoning for such claims is problematic or evidently flawed.
- There are very real and damaging consequences when crime is racialised, both individually and collectively.

- Criminology has been dominated by biological and sociological positivist ideas about 'black criminality'. In more recent times, these have been theoretically and empirically challenged by anti-racist approaches taking a social constructionist stand. These include the Critical Criminological Approach, Black Criminology, Critical Race Theory, and the Black Feminist Critique.
- Criminological work has contributed equality and anti-discrimination legislation. However, much work is still to be done to ensure that change is meaningful.
- As well as challenging the racist roots of criminology itself, the critical work on racialised crime today must include an examination of how and why post-race discriminations occur.

Framing questions revisited

This chapter began by giving you four questions to frame your reading and critical reflection of the subject. From the material discussed in this chapter, we can start to formulate answers to these questions, which would be useful also for your further reading into this area.

Review questions

1. What is 'race'? How has it been used to understand crime?
2. To what extent does race influence experiences of crime, justice and victimisation?
3. What is the role of criminology for understanding race and racialised crime?
4. What is the future of race and racialised crime, both in the criminal justice **system** and criminology?

GO FURTHER

To explore more of the ideas discussed in this chapter, there are a number of recommended sources.

Books

1. The first text is a good starting point on the journey of race within the discipline of criminology:

   Rowe, M. (2012) *Race and Crime*. London: Sage.

2. This second text explores how and why criminology should develop an approach that moves away from its white western roots:

   Potter, H. (2015) *Intersectionality and Criminology: Disrupting and Revolutionizing Studies of Crime*. London: Routledge.

3. The following title is an authoritative, yet accessible resource on key developments in race and racialised crime, in relation to claims of a 'post-race' society:

   Patel, T. G. and Tyrer, D. (2011) *Race, Crime and Resistance*. London: Sage.

Journal Articles

1. This argues for the importance for criminology to openly challenge its own biases and racialised privileges:

    Phillips, C. and Bowling, B. (2003) Racism, ethnicity and criminology: developing minority perspectives. *British Journal of Criminology*, 43(2): 269–290.

2. The following article critically discusses the methods used for racialising crime, justice and victimisation:

    Cockbain, E. (2013) Grooming and the 'Asian sex gang predator': the construction of a racial crime threat. *Race and Class*, 54(4): 22–32.

3. The third article provides a clear and accessible outline of racialisation processes in crime matters:

    Covington, J. (1995) Racial classification in criminology: the reproduction of racialized crime. *Sociological Forum*, 10(4): 547–568.

Useful Websites

1. The Institute of Race Relations is a UK-based website offering updated information on race-related research and analysis: http://www.irr.org.uk/
2. The Equality and Human Rights Commission is a UK-based website providing details of work that promotes equality and human rights ideals and laws: https://www.equalityhumanrights.com/en
3. The Black Lives Matter website outlines the work and activity of an international activist-based organization: https://blacklivesmatter.com/

REFERENCES

Aas, K. F. (2011) "'Crimmigrant' bodies and bona fide travellers: surveillance, citizenship and global governance. *Theoretical Criminology*, 15(3): 331–346.

Becker, H. S. (1963) *Outsiders: Studies in the Sociology of Deviance*. New York: Free Press.

Covington, J. (1995) Racial classification in criminology: the reproduction of racialized crime. *Sociological Forum*, 10(4): 547–568.

Du Bois, W. E. B. (1899) *The Philadelphia Negro: A Social Study*. New York: Benjamin Blom.

Gabbidon, S. L., Higgins, G. E. and Potter, H. (2011) Race, gender, and the perception of recently experiencing unfair treatment by the police: exploratory results from an all-Black sample. *Criminal Justice Review*, 36(1): 5–21.

Hall, S., Critcher, C., Jefferson, T., Clarke, J. and Roberts, B. (1978) *Policing the Crisis*. London: Macmillan.

Herrnstein, R. and Murray, C. (1984) *The Bell Curve: Intelligence and Class Structure in American Life*. New York: Free Press.

Home Office (1999) *The Stephen Lawrence Inquiry: Report of an Inquiry by Sir William Macpherson of Cluny*, Cm 4262-I, February.

Isakjee, A. and Allen, C. (2013) 'A catastrophic lack of critical inquisitiveness': a critical study of the impact and narrative of the Project Champion surveillance project in Birmingham. *Ethnicities*, 13(6): 751–770.

Kundnani, A. (2001) In a foreign land: The new popular racism. *Race and Class*, 43(2): 41–60.

Lee, C. (2013) Making race salient: Trayvon Martin and implicit bias in a not yet post-racial society. *GW Law School Public Law and Legal Theory*, paper no. 2013-97 (http://ssrn.com/abstract=2282686).

Lombroso, C. (1911) *The Criminal Man*. New York: GP Putnam's Sons.

Mitchell, M. B. and Davis, J. B. (2019) Formerly incarcerated Black mothers matter too: resisting social constructions of motherhood. *The Prison Journal*, 99(4): 420–436.

Murji, K. (2003) 'Racialization'. In E. McLaughlin and J. Muncie (eds), *The SAGE Dictionary of Criminology*. London: Sage. pp. 231–232.

Pantazis, C. and Pemberton, S. (2009) From the 'old' to the 'new' suspect community: examining the impacts of recent UK counter-terrorist legislation. *British Journal of Criminology*, 49: 646–666.

Park, R. and Burgess, E. (1925) *The City*. (Reprinted 1967) Chicago: University of Chicago Press.

Phillips, C. and Bowling, B. (2003) Racism, ethnicity and criminology: developing minority perspectives. *British Journal of Criminology*, 43(2): 269–290.

Potter, H. (2006) An argument for Black Feminist Criminology. *Feminist Criminology*, 1(2): 106–124.

Rowe, M. (2012) *Race and Crime*. London: Sage.

Sivanandan, A. (2006) Race, terror and civil society. *Race and Class*, 47(1): 1–8.

West, C. (2017) *Race Matters*, 3rd edition. Boston, MA: Beacon Press.

Wilson, J. Q. and Kelling, G. L. (1982) Broken windows. *Atlantic Monthly*, 249(3): 29–36.

Wolfgang, M. and Ferracuti, F. (1967) *The Subculture of Violence*. London: Tavistock.

Zempi, I. (2015) 'Responding to the Needs of Victims of Islamophobia'. In N. Chakraborti and J. Garland (eds), *Responding to Hate Crime: The Case for Connecting Policy and Research*. Bristol: Policy Press, pp. 113–126.

Gender, Crime and Victimisation 20

Nicola Groves

Learning Objectives

After reading this chapter you will be able to:

- Discuss the arguments in favour of taking a gendered approach to the study of victimisation.
- Understand what constitutes gender-based violence (GBV).
- Appreciate the significance of gendering the victim.
- Recognise both feminist and LGBTQ informed approaches when evaluating some key cases and events of GBV.
- Evaluate the arguments *for* and *against* developing criminal reforms for GBV.
- Critically reflect on the concept of 'justice' in the context of GBV.

Framing Questions

1. What are the strengths and limitations of adopting a gendered approach to the study of victimisation?
2. How does criminology consider gender identity when examining gender, crime and victimisation?
3. How can feminist approaches inform our understanding of GBV?
4. What does 'justice' mean in the context of GBV?

INTRODUCTION

This chapter draws attention to the issue of gender, crime and victimisation in the context of gender-based violence (GBV). The chapter is divided into five main parts. 'Mapping the Terrain' lays out the definitions of terms and discusses arguments in favour of taking a gendered approach to the study of victimisation. 'Old wine in new bottles?' then considers the unprecedented visibility of gender-based violence evidenced by #MeToo Movements. 'Sex, Gender, Identity' encourages you to critically analyse the significance of gender identity when considering GBV and how gender identity can shape our understanding of GBV. 'Gendering the Victim' follows, discussing gendered patterns of victimisation and considering 'who does what to whom?' (Hester, 2009). The final section, 'Gendering Justice', examines the meaning of justice and whether increased criminal justice reforms and more law can lead to a better experience for victims of GBV. The summary draws together the key arguments made and provides some concluding considerations.

MAPPING THE TERRAIN

This section will give a brief overview of definitions for the terms 'gender-based violence', 'victim' and 'victimisation', and highlights that the use of such terms is not without controversy. Forms of gender-based violence include, but are not limited to: **domestic abuse**, forced marriage, female genital mutilation, rape, sexual harassment, and murder. Gender-based violence is violence that is directed at a person based on their actual or perceived gender identity or sexuality. Whilst 'violence' has traditional connotations of *physical* abuse, such understandings of violence are outdated and radical feminist approaches in particular have been instrumental in highlighting the multiple dimensions that violence can take, including emotional abuse and harm. GBV can include physical, sexual, verbal, psychological abuse, threats, control and coercion, and can occur in a public or private arena. Feminist approaches argue that gender-based violence results from gender inequalities (**liberal feminism**) and gender oppression (**radical feminism**) in society. Literally speaking, 'anyone' can experience GBV (males, females, non-binary), however this idea fails to take on board feminist theorising that locates the source of the problem in historically-rooted gendered hierarchies, structural and institutional inequalities (Sundari and Lewis, 2018). As this chapter highlights, even a cursory glance at research into GBV illustrates a consistent pattern in which girls and women are more likely victims and boys and men are more likely offenders (Hester, 2009).

Knowledge link: This topic is also covered in Chapter 8.

Over the past fifty years, in seeking to understand and explain the interplay of gender and violence, radical feminist research has specifically focused on violence against women and girls (VAWG) and in so doing has highlighted the gendered nature of crimes such as domestic abuse and sexual violence (Dobash and Dobash, 1980; Kelly, 1988). **Intersectional** theorists (Crenshaw, 1991) have been pivotal in highlighting that gender is not the only social category that can affect victimisation and have pointed to other intersecting identities such as race, ethnicity, class, age, and disability. More recently queer feminism has highlighted the significance of sexual orientation and gender identities in the role of victimisation. In particular, they have highlighted the significance of victimisation for those who do not conform to normative gender expectations and identities (Marinucci, 2016).

Discussing gender-based violence in a chapter entitled *victimisation* is not straightforward. For some, there is more than a semantic unease with discussing gender-based violence, in the same breath as victimisation. It is well documented that feminist scholars have been instrumental in drawing attention to the conceptual tension in naming those who experience gender-related violence as 'victims'. The term 'victim' downplays the agency of women who experience GBV. In relation to domestic abuse and sexual violence in particular, feminist approaches have drawn attention to implicit connotations of passivity, culpability and blame reflected in the traditional and dominant conceptualisation of the term 'victim'. The notion of the passive female victim is resisted in part through the use of 'survivor'. 'Survivor' is an empowering concept, signifying 'the everyday reality of negotiating and coping strategies that women employ in their everyday lives' (Davies, 2007: 182). The empowering nature of the 'survivor' is illustrated by Wood, Rose and Thompson (2018) who consider the recent and growing phenomenon of the 'survivor selfie', whereby victims of domestic abuse upload photos and accounts of their injuries to social media in an attempt to seek online justice. Others suggest that *both* terms, 'victim' and 'survivor', have utility. The combined term 'victim/survivor' is regarded as useful because it recognises the fluidity of women's experiences and the fact that women 'survive' on a daily basis, but also that some do not survive.

Knowledge link: This topic is also covered in Chapter 3.

Some challenge the use of the term 'gender-based violence' itself, suggesting that it can be 'anachronistic, gender-neutral [and] bureaucratic' (Boyle, 2018: 2). Conceptual distinctions have meanings for victims, practitioners, academics, law makers and the general population alike, and can simultaneously inform or misinform what we understand as gender-based violence. Conceptually, the notion of 'continuum thinking' has been instrumental in feminist theorising of gender-based violence (Boyle, 2018). Originally, Kelly (1988) used the notion of 'continuum', to explain women's experiences of sexual violence, ranging from 'everyday' to more 'serious' at either end of the continuum. More recent research which considers so-called 'revenge porn' suggests that such behaviour 'should be understood as just one form of a range of gendered, sexualised forms of abuse which have common characteristics forming … the continuum of image-based sexual abuse' (McGlynn et al., 2017: 25). Such continuum thinking is invaluable in highlighting the links between different forms of gender-based violence.

There are important limitations and distinctions within the umbrella terms 'Violence against Women' (VAW) and 'gender-based violence' (GBV). For Boyle, VAW implies 'women's vulnerability rather than men's responsibility and omits a crucial detail: that this is a movement *against* violence against women' (Boyle, 2018: 2). The same author advocates caution in using the term 'GBV':

> … simply naming gender does not mean that our analysis is gendered … gender-based violence can be a worryingly gender-neutral term which flattens important differences in terms of who is doing what to whom, in which contexts, to which effects and to whose overall benefit. (Boyle 2018: 14)

Boyle (2018) encourages us to be cautious of conflating VAW and GBV. It is important therefore, that you are aware of the use and significance of terminology when considering gender, violence and victimisation.

Pause for Thought

Why is terminology important when considering GBV and victimisation?

Having considered some key definitional, conceptual and political contextual issues, we will continue to show how gender *still* matters. A feminist-informed approach to considering gender-based violence and victimisation follows and we shall return again to conceptualisation and theorising of gender. For now, continue to foreground gender as you read and think about 'who does what to whom?' throughout this chapter (Hester, 2009).

—————————————— Student Voice ——————————————

"Studying gender-based violence has provided me with insight into the deep-rooted reality of gender inequality and has given me a profound awareness of the pervasiveness of violence against women. My own experience of conducting research on the topic of gender-based violence has allowed me to recognise day to day controlling acts and strategies of violence by men which oppress women in many scopes of their everyday life. I believe that research into gender-based violence will provide others with insight into the nature and extent of male dominance and violence over women."

(Olivia, Third Year Criminology student, Leeds Beckett University)

OLD WINE IN NEW BOTTLES: NEW DEBATES OR JUST THE SAME OLD ISSUES?

You will note that this chapter is located in *Part 3: Contemporary Challenges*. It can be suggested that #Metoo, Rape Culture and Transgender people are not new topics, they are old experiences that have been given new space and coverage. In this respect they are 'old wine in new bottles' (Gelsthorpe, 1990). However, it can also be suggested that the official recognition and legal equalities that these issues are achieving is 'new'. In the pages that follow, you are encouraged to critically reflect on long-standing, 'new' and 'progressive' debates about VAW, GBV and gender and victimisation more broadly.

The politicisation of violence against women predates 1960s Second Wave Feminism. African American women activists were fighting white men's sexual abuse of Black women, and the public and legal neglect of it as part of the systematic abuse and oppression of Black women (McGuire, 2011; Phipps, 2018). Radical feminism in the 1960s and beyond was instrumental in bringing public and political attention to the nature, extent and prevalence of gender-related violence, VAWG in particular. Phipps discusses the role of such feminists:

> Brownmiller (1975) and others focused on the 'violence' in sexual violence, conceptualising it as a tool of gender oppression which functioned to preserve male dominance rather than express uncontrolled sexuality (which was the popular belief). (Phipps, 2018: 44)

Over the decades, radical feminist research has revealed domestic violence and abuse, and more recently coercive control (Stark, 2007), as hidden experiences, occurring within a familial setting perceived by many as 'private'. Scholars and activists have highlighted the importance of 'naming and recognising' such violence (Kelly, 1988; Groves and Thomas, 2014) and point out that offenders are not unknown strangers but are primarily 'known men', motivated by a desire for 'power and control' in their intimate relationships. Feminist perspectives view violence against women as directly linked to gender oppression, rather than the misbehaviour of a few aberrant men.

In recent years, the topic of gender and victimisation has been brought to the fore of public consciousness and political debate via the #MeToo, #Times Up, #This Is Not Consent, #I Believe Her and #Mosque Me Too movements. This activism dovetails with decades of work by feminist activists, scholars and policy makers, and responds to highly publicised cases of men's abuse of women and children, such as Jimmy Savile (UK), Harvey Weinstein (USA), the Roman Catholic Church (Great Britain and Ireland) and sexual abuse of children in sport (UK). Modern social media has been used to spread common experiences of suffering around the world, matters that have previously been deemed to be personal, individual and private.

Whilst this increased visibility and the 'calls for action' and self-empowerment may be unprecedented, it has given rise to a victim backlash. We should not be surprised that when victims' voices gain strength and momentum, those in power, threatened by calls for gender justice, use their power to discredit those voices. Examples of victim shaming and blaming are never too far behind self-empowering calls for change. A predicament of 'two steps forward, one step back' is illustrated by the case of Judge Brett Kavanaugh versus Dr Christine Blasey Ford, in Case Study 20.1 below.

Case Study 20.1

Judge Brett Kavanaugh versus Dr Christine Blasey Ford, USA

In July 2018 Judge Brett Kavanaugh, a Republican, was nominated to the US Supreme Court by President Donald Trump. In the following September, at the US Senate Committee, Dr Christine Blasey Ford gave testimony that Kavanaugh had sexually assaulted her at a party in 1982.

The testimony was televised. During her testimony, Christine Blasey Ford appeared composed and credible, but clearly distressed and nervous. Brett Kavanaugh, in contrast, appeared implausible, belligerent, defensive and blamed a left wing, Democratic conspiracy for the situation that he found himself in.

Following the testimony, President Trump proceeded to victim-shame and blame Blasey Ford in a series of tweets which questioned the truth of the allegation, and why she had not told her parents (she was fifteen at the time) or reported her experience to the police.

Following these tweets, at a rally in Mississippi on 2nd October 2018, Trump publicly mocked Blasey Ford's testimony and mimicked her answers to questions and her inability to recall certain details of the alleged sexual assault.

Kavanaugh was appointed to the Supreme Court following these events in a blatant demonstration and assertion of the ruling elite's power to influence public opinion and further publically discredit Blasey Ford.

Pause for Thought

In what way can Kavanaugh versus Blasey Ford be used as evidence of a 'victim backlash'?

The above suggests we should be cautious in interpreting the increased visibility and acknowledgement of gender-based violence as 'progress' in and of itself. Whilst the social media attention given to such issues is undoubtedly welcome, what belies such calls for action are inadequate criminal justice responses to gender-based violence. Such an argument has been put forward by feminist thinkers and activists for over fifty years; it is perhaps the case that the criminological challenges to considerations of gender, crime and victimisation are not necessarily 'new' and instead reflect 'old wine in new bottles' (Gelsthorpe, 1990). Given this caveat, perhaps we need a sharper analysis of gender to enable us to appreciate the complex social realities of gender-based violence.

SEX, GENDER, IDENTITY

A useful starting point is a discussion of gender, gender identity and associated gender expectations, norms and stereotypes.

Feminist theory has been instrumental in defining the difference between 'sex' and 'gender' (Oakley, 1972). The traditional nature/nurture debate has led to the distinction that sex is biologically given and gender is socially constructed. Within this gender framing, some have argued that the social construction of what it means to be female or male is 'accomplished' (West and Zimmerman, 1987; Messerschmidt, 1993) or 'performed' (Butler, 1990) by acting masculine or feminine congruent with one's gender. Messerschmidt (1993) argues that crime can be a way for boys and men to 'do' gender; that they engage in crime to demonstrate their masculinities. Mainstream framings of gender have been primarily based on assumptions of **heteronormativity** and the gender binary of male and female.

In introducing a discussion of gender *identity*, a more nuanced approach to conceptualising gender, sexuality and violence is possible. Feminism has always argued that gender is a social construct rather than a fixed identity. Gender *identity* can be expressed beyond the traditional binary of male and female, and whilst a person's gender identity can correspond to assigned sex-at-birth it can also differ from it. The existence of transgender people suggests that the gender identity of a man or woman does not match the sex-assigned-at-birth; gender can be 'disembodied'. Equally, for those identifying outside of the male/female binary and the associated tropes of masculinity and femininity, gender can be fluid and identities can fluctuate between feminine, masculine, neither or both. Whilst the existence of gender identities is not new, research into gender identity and GBV is a relatively recent addition to the field of criminology and sociology (see for example Donovan and Hester, 2014; Donovan and Barnes, 2020).

Radical feminist research into VAWG has been instrumental in highlighting that girls and women are more likely to experience domestic and sexual violence (Dobash and Dobash, 1980; Kelly, 1988). Whilst the value of such theorising is undeniable, some now argue it neglects men's and LGBTQ people's experiences of violence. A recent commentator suggests that:

> the inter-relationships between gender and violence are more complex and multi-faceted then some models suggest. (Boyle, 2018: 13)

Donovan and Hester (2014) consider how domestic violence in lesbian, gay, bisexual and/or transgender (LGB and/or T) relationships can be shaped by gender, sexuality and age. They point to an unintended consequence of feminist scholarship, a 'public narrative' that describes domestic abuse as a problem between heterosexual men and women. The narrative's overriding assumption is that domestic abuse is only embedded in heteronormative gendered roles in heterosexual relationships (Donovan and Hester, 2014). An impact of this public narrative is that it both leads to and reinforces myths, i.e. it implies that:

- domestic abuse in same-sex relationships is not harmful;
- that women can't be violent;
- if there *is* violence in LGB and/or T relationships then both must be to blame (Donovan and Hester, 2014).

Such observations reflect gendered thinking and help make sense of reported and under-reported patterns and experiences of abuse. Whilst numerically heterosexual women are the largest group reporting domestic abuse (Walby and Towers, 2018), more than one in ten LGB people and one in five trans people and non-binary people faced domestic abuse from a partner in the last year (Bachmann and Gooch, 2018).

In discussing gender identity, we can further usefully consider legal and policy developments. In 2004, the Gender Recognition Act was introduced in the UK. It granted legal recognition for binary transgender adults (eighteen years plus) to officially register a change to assigned-at-birth sex. A decade later, *The Transgender Inquiry Report* (Women and Equalities Committee, 2016) called for protection from discrimination under the Equality Act 2010, for people identifying as non-binary. More recently, in 2018 the UK Government conducted a public consultation aiming to seek views on how to reform the legal gender recognition process. The narratives underpinning these policy developments are controversial, competing and conflicting, and have led to dominant framings of a divisive debate grounded in 'women's rights' versus 'transgender rights'. This polarised debate is brought into sharp relief when considering the case of Karen White (see Case Study 20.2 below).

Case Study 20.2

Karen White

Karen White was a transgender, male-at-birth prisoner who, whilst on remand for raping two women and attacking a neighbour with a knife, was placed in HMP New Hall women's prison in 2017. Whilst on remand, White sexually assaulted two female inmates. During the subsequent trial, White pleaded guilty and was sentenced to a minimum eight and a half years and subsequently sent to a men's prison, HMP Leeds. The Ministry of Justice apologised for placing White into the women's prison, arguing that her previous offending history, which included convictions of sexual offences against women and children, had not been taken into account. (See *BBC News* (2018) 'Trans Inmate Jailed for Wakefield prison sex offences'. Available at: https://www.bbc.com/news/uk-england-leeds-45825838)

In the UK, as it currently stands, transgender prisoners must be sent to a prison that corresponds with their legally recognised gender (demonstrated by a Gender Recognition Certificate) or alternatively demonstrate that they pursue an 'actual life in the gender with which they identify' and have their situation considered by a local Transgender Case Board. In the above case, White entered the UK prison system as a transgender woman, but did not have a Gender Recognition Certificate, nor had she begun to take hormone therapy, so was legally male but presenting as female. The situation was further complicated as White had previous convictions for sexual offending against both children and women. On the one hand, while some argue that the nature of the offence is relevant to where a transgender offender is placed, others suggest that offenders should be imprisoned according to their gender identity, regardless of the actual offence committed.

The imprisonment of transgender offenders in prisons that *do not* corresponded with their gender identity polarises debates. The deaths of transgender prisoners, such as Vikki Thompson (21 years) who in November 2015 was found dead in her prison cell at HMP Leeds, and Jenny Swift (49 years) who in 2016 was found dead in her cell in HMP Doncaster, are examples of transwomen imprisoned in men's prisons. These cases show that this is a challenging area for those concerned with crime, GBV and justice. Research into the impact of gendered prison policies on transgender prisoners in England and Wales remains marginal, although insights from Lamble (2012) provide an important exception to this.

——————————— Pause for Thought ———————————

How can gender identity shape our understanding of GBV?

——————————— Student Voice ———————————

"After studying gender-based violence, I found that in the majority of cases of victimisation women are more likely to be subjected to domestic violence by men. It was interesting to learn about the history of gender inequality in society and the ongoing subordination of women, which is having a negative impact on their experience as victims. From a theoretical perspective I learnt about gender role expectations forced upon men and women and how these expectations have a huge influence on people's behaviour. More recent research has recognised the victimisation of men and same sex individuals which is significant as they have been overlooked."

(Maarya, Third Year Criminology student, Leeds Beckett University)

GENDERING THE VICTIM

We now turn to consider sexuality and gender identity as a cornerstone to social interactions that influence experiences of GBV, victimisation and justice. We do so through a focus on women as victims, men as victims, and LGBTQ as victims.

Women as Victims

Significant gender differences in victimisation can be identified by looking at interpersonal versus non-interpersonal violence.

Research consistently demonstrates that men are more likely to be victims of violence perpetrated in public, whereas women are more likely to be victims of violence perpetrated in private (Croall, 2011: 192). Whilst the distinction between public and private has been fundamental to feminist theorising, making visible so-called 'hidden' crimes, i.e. domestic abuse, this distinction has become less useful for understanding domestic abuse. Recent research into men's increased use of technologies and social media to manipulate, manage and control women, increasingly blurs the boundaries and geographies of the public and private (Lewis et al., 2017). Australian research (Woodlock, 2017) into men's abuse of technology in stalking and domestic violence highlighted that for some victims there was a constant sense that offenders were 'omnipresent' irrespective of the public/private divide. It seems that the gender inequality underpinning gender-based violence in the 'real' world is replicated in cyberspace (Lewis et al., 2017).

Gendered patterns of victimisation not only shed light on geographies of victimisation but also encourage us to ask 'who does what to whom?' (Hester, 2009). A common feature of both men's and women's victimisation is that both are mainly victimised by other men. The difference in identifying who does what to whom, is that whilst men are primarily victims of stranger violence and are more likely to be victimised by a man they do not know, women are more likely to be victimised by a man known to them. Whilst this gendered pattern of victimisation is well rehearsed within feminist theory, myths persist that women are primarily at risk of sexual violence by an unknown man. For many it still remains counter-intuitive that women are more likely to experience rape, sexual violence and abuse by a man known to them, rather than a stranger.

Men as Victims

On the whole men have been marginalised in criminology's consideration of gender-based violence. Christie's (1986) concept of the 'ideal victim' as defenceless, blameless and feminised allowed little room for considering men as victims of gender-based violence. Whilst it has long since been acknowledged that victims do not neatly fit into this 'ideal', men as victims of GBV in many ways remain anathema to this concept.

Knowledge link: This topic is also covered in Chapters 3 and 31.

Feminist research has traditionally considered not GBV per se, but rather VAWG. Under this umbrella term the focus has inevitably been on the victimisation of *women and girls*, to the exclusion of boys and men. Moreover, as shown earlier, men have been identified as perpetrators. More recently, masculinity studies have considered the experience of men as victims of rape. (See Lowe and Rogers, 2017 for a review of the literature.) Just as mainstream criminology justified its lack of attention to 'women as offenders' because they were in the minority, so too has victimology seemingly justified its lack of focus on 'men as victims' of GBV. Against these historical framings of victims, men's experience of gender-based violence have been rendered marginal, but not invisible.

Let's take the example of considering men as victims of domestic abuse. Recent figures suggest that in the UK, in the year ending March 2018, there were an estimated 695,000 male and 1.3 million female victims of domestic violence (ONS, 2018). The gendered nature of such violence is disputed (Walby and Towers, 2018). On the one hand most feminist scholars following Dobash and Dobash (1992) have argued that domestic violence is characterised by an asymmetrical relationship, in which men are the offenders and women victims, whereas family violence theorists such as Archer (2000) suggest that the relationship is symmetrical and that men can be victims too (and that women can be offenders). Johnson (2008) argues that 'types' of domestic abuse exist, each characterised by nuanced gendered patterns of victimisation and perpetration. More recently Donovan and Barnes (2020) considered domestic abuse in LGBT relationships, and the extent to which Johnson's typology can be used to make sense of LGBT victim and perpetrator accounts of abusive behaviours. All of the above research suggests a way forward in understanding the experience of men as victims of domestic violence, be they in heterosexual, gay, bisexual and/or transgender relationships.

LGBTQ as Victims

As men have been marginalised when considering GBV, so too have LGBTQ victims. In the past twenty years research into the experience of LGBTQ victims has grown in the arena of hate crime. A recent survey of 593 lesbian, gay, bisexual and transgender (LGBT) people in the UK found that direct and indirect hate crimes are highly prolific and frequent for LGBT people, and that 'trans people are more likely to experience heightened levels of threat, vulnerability, and anxiety compared with non-trans LGB people' (Walters et al., 2020: 4583).

Knowledge link: This topic is also covered in Chapter 18.

Despite more apparent open societal attitudes about sexuality; homophobia and misogyny endure and the attendant expectations associated with heteronormative constructs of masculinity and femininity continue to pervade. The experience of LGBTQ victims in the UK was brought into sharp relief in June 2019, when a photograph of two women, distressed and covered in blood after an attack on a London night bus, was posted by them on Facebook (see Case Study 20.3).

Case Study 20.3

Melania Geymonat

Melania Geymonat (female, twenty-eight years) and her partner Chris (female, twenty-nine years) had been travelling home on a bus on the evening of 30 May 2019 when a group of young men (between fifteen and eighteen years) shouted abuse and assaulted the couple, after they refused to kiss. Chris suffered a broken jaw and damaged nose and Melania's nose was broken during the assault.

The photograph and incident were picked up globally, leading to expressions of shock, disgust, outrage, sympathy and empathy (and also examples of shaming and trolling). The women remained defiant and argued for their experience to be recognised as not merely homophobic but also misogynistic. They pointed out that the global media interest led them to question who becomes 'visible' as victims. They commented on the publicity that their case received internationally:

> ... it certainly doesn't hurt that we are both white, we are both conventionally attractive ... I think it begs the question: why do we need this sensational, clickability, graphic (image) to engage people in a story like this? ... But I just wonder how other victims of hate crime, how their experience would compare. (Addley, 2019)

Pause for Thought

Are LGBTQ people the forgotten victims of the criminal justice system?

The above case not only serves to illustrate the complex interplay between gender, sexuality, class and age, it also introduces the relatively recent phenomenon of 'survivor selfies' in which victims take photos of their injuries and post them online. Wood et al. (2019) research intimate partner violence (IPV) survivors and their friends who upload photos of their injuries to social media. In so doing they examine:

> ... how the like economy of Facebook can lead to the rapid circulation of survivor selfies to large audiences, and in doing so, generate what we term viral justice: the outcome of a victim's online justice seeking post 'going viral' and quickly being viewed and shared-on by thousands of social media users. (Wood et al., 2019: 1)

Considering this example neatly provides a step into the final section of this chapter which considers the meaning of justice in the context of GBV.

GENDERING JUSTICE

Pause for Thought

What does 'justice' mean for victims of GBV?

There has been increasing theoretical and empirical analysis of justice in the past couple of decades and the different types of justice are well documented elsewhere. Here we consider the meaning of justice in the context of GBV.

Feminist research has been instrumental in highlighting a '**justice gap**' (McGlynn and Westmarland, 2019) when considering the criminal justice response to sexual violence and domestic abuse. The discrepancy between the number of these crimes reported and recorded, and the number which are actually prosecuted and result in a conviction, is indisputable. High attrition rates suggest that many such cases 'drop out' of the criminal justice system (Hohl and Stanko, 2015). Rape victims continue to report that they are not believed (Avalos, 2016) and that they experience secondary victimisation. Despite recent legal reforms in England and Wales, the criminal justice system response to victims of domestic and sexual abuse remains inconsistent and patchy. The persistence of numerous rape myths and stereotypes throws into question the *actual* impact that criminal justice law reform can achieve.

Knowledge link: This topic is also covered in Chapter 22.

Knowledge link: This topic is also covered in Chapter 31.

Pause for Thought

Why are there so few rape convictions in England and Wales?

It is not only *within* the criminal justice system that we can see examples of rape victims receiving less than adequate responses. Poor responses from other institutions are evident. Consider the so-called Warwick University 'Rape Chat' case (see Case Study 20.4). Before you read this example think about the headline. Since when are threats to rape regarded as 'chat'? Such phraseology normalises gendered violence and perpetuates misogyny by referring to it as 'chat'. It is equivalent to suggesting the men's belief that as male students they have the right and entitlement to use power and control to dominate their fellow female students. If a person threatens to kill a person, it is understood as a crime in most jurisdictions. If a person threatens to rape another person, it is defined and excused as laddish 'banter'. (See Phipps, 2018 for a discussion of 'lad culture' and sexual violence against students. See also *'That's* what she said': women students' experiences of 'lad culture' in higher education, NUS, 2012).

Case Study 20.4

The Warwick University 'Rape Chat' Case

This case refers to a group of male and female student friends at Warwick University. In March 2018, one of the female students scrolled through a Facebook group chat that the male students had set up and she came across hundreds of sexually violent, misogynistic and abusive messages that were targeted at her and her friends. The messages included threats of rape, gang rape and female genital mutilation that had been exchanged between the male students over one and a half years. When the female student searched her name it came up hundreds of times and she noticed that the men had

(Continued)

changed their own names to those of notorious serial killers and rapists. The female student and another woman who was mentioned in the Facebook 'chat' put in a formal complaint to Warwick University and an internal investigation was conducted.

What followed raised legitimate concerns about Warwick University's response. The Director of Press, was given the role of leading the investigation and a conflict of interest arose from the outset. The female students were invited to attend a meeting at short notice and were shocked at the accusatory stance that was taken with them.

Having interviewed the female students, eleven male students were interviewed and then over a two-day disciplinary panel meeting a range of punishments were agreed. Initially, this resulted in one student being expelled and given a lifetime campus ban, two further students being expelled and given ten-year campus bans, and two more students were excluded for a year. The male students had the right to appeal and as a result of the appeal process two had their ten-year bans reduced to one year on the grounds of 'new evidence' that the victims were never informed of.

These decisions and the treatment of the female students led to questions being asked about Warwick University's handling of the investigation. Feeling that they had not attained justice one of the female students took to Twitter, and under the #ShameOnYouWarwick drew attention to the university's handling of the case, arguing that it had failed in its support for the female victims.

The 'Warwick University Rape Chat Scandal' featured in a BBC 3 documentary and aired in August 2019.

Pause for Thought

How can universities safeguard against online sexual bullying and threats against students and staff?

Knowledge link: This topic is also covered in Chapter 22.

The underlying concept of justice is key to this case. Hester et al's (2015–2018) ESRC-funded research project, 'Justice, Inequality and Gender-Based Violence', considers how justice is understood, sought and experienced by victims-survivors of GBV. In comparing the meanings of justice for those who experienced sexual violence and domestic violence, the research finds that women want safety, containment (don't do it again) and punishment. In domestic violence cases women use the police to manage their partners' violence, but they were less concerned with punishment as a form of justice. In contrast, in the cases of sexual violence, women were more likely to want the offender convicted (Mulvihill et al., 2018). The findings reveal a nuanced notion of justice that keeps shifting depending on victims-survivors experiences and needs. The research project further analyses what justice means to black and minority ethnic (BME) victims-survivors of GBV (Gangoli et al., 2019). McGlynn and Westmarland's (2019) empirical investigation with twenty victim-survivors of sexual violence, develop the notion of 'kaleidoscopic' justice highlighting its fluid nature and argue that 'it is only by better understanding victim-survivors' perspectives on justice, and embedding the concept of kaleidoscopic justice, that we can begin to address the sexual violence "justice gap"' (McGlynn and Westmarland, 2019: 179). In light of the diverse and multiple meanings of justice for victims of GBV, we now consider whether 'more laws' necessarily lead to 'better' justice for victims.

———— Hear from the Expert ————

Nicole Westmarland, Director, Centre for Research into Violence and Abuse (CRiVA) and Professor of Criminology, Durham University

I have been working as a researcher in the area of violence and abuse for twenty years now, in various positions starting as a research assistant and working my way up to Professor of Criminology and leading a major research centre. One of the highlights of my career was being appointed as Special Advisor to the Joint Committee on Human Rights for their Inquiry into Violence against Women and Girls in 2015. It was really interesting to be able to map what I knew academically onto recommending questions to be asked by the Committee members. It was really useful as well to have a good grounded knowledge of the specialist domestic and sexual violence sector in terms of activists and practitioners as well, so that I could suggest them as witnesses to the Inquiry. I'm not interested in just writing books and articles, I'm interested in changing the world, and both knowledge and action need to go hand in hand for that to happen. The role of Special Advisor felt very connected in that way and it was a great way to make sure specialist knowledge about violence and abuse was being heard within such a powerful institution as Parliament.

TACKLING GBV THROUGH CRIMINAL JUSTICE REFORMS

- Recent criminal justice reforms in England and Wales are evident and there continues to be changes in legislation that impact on gender-based violence, although the laws themselves remain gender-neutral. The Serious Crime Act 2015 (Section 76) deemed controlling and coercive behaviour, which is defined as 'an act or a pattern of acts of assault, threats, humiliation and intimidation or other abuse that is used to harm, punish, or frighten their victim', to be a criminal offence in England and Wales (Home Office, 2015).
- In the same year, the Criminal Justice and Courts Act 2015 (Section 33) created the offence of disclosing private sexual photos or films without consent, and with intent to cause distress; commonly referred to as 'revenge porn' but more recently conceptualised as 'image based violence' (McGlynn et al., 2017).
- In 2019, inspired by the campaigning efforts of Gina Martin, the Sexual Offences Act (2003) was amended to criminalise certain acts of voyeurism commonly referred to as 'upskirting'.
- The Voyeurism (Offences) Act 2019 (Section 67A) criminalises someone who takes a photo or records an image under another person's clothing for their own sexual gratification or in an attempt to cause distress to the victim.

Whether such criminalisation will result in an improved response for victims is contested. In respect of the Serious Crime Act 2015 (Section 76), Walklate, Fitz-Gibbon and McCulloch ask 'is more law the answer?' (2018: 115). Whilst acknowledging the legal reform is 'a legitimate attempt to bring a wider range of abusive behaviours within the remit of the criminal law', they conclude that 'introduction of the offence does little to overcome the difficulties women have long encountered in accessing justice' (2018: 127). Such debates are brought into sharp relief when considering the case of Sally Challen (see Case Study 20.5 below).

—————————— **Case Study 20.5** ——————————

Sally Challen

Sally Challen killed her husband Richard on 14 August 2010 when she struck him with twenty or more blows from a hammer. Challen was charged with murder and her plea to manslaughter on the grounds of diminished responsibility was not accepted and the defence did not argue provocation. On 26 June 2011 Challen was sentenced to life imprisonment with a minimum of twenty-two years, which was reduced to eighteen years at appeal.

In 2017, the feminist campaign group 'Justice for Women' and the human rights lawyer Harriet Wistrich submitted an appeal to the Court of Appeal on the basis of fresh evidence of 'coercive control', namely that Challen had experienced abusive, bullying, belittling and humiliating behaviour from her husband during their forty-year marriage. The legal team were able to develop this new defence as in the years since Challen's trial the Serious Crime Act 2015 (Section 76) made it a criminal offence to exercise 'coercive control' over one's partner.

On 27 and 28 February 2019 the Court of Appeal heard the new evidence and the conviction was overturned and a retrial was ordered, due to take place on 1 July 2019. However, at a hearing before Mr Justice Edis at the Old Bailey, the Crown accepted Challen's plea to the lesser charge of manslaughter and she was sentenced to nine years and four months. The judge ruled that Challen had already served an equivalent sentence for manslaughter on the grounds of diminished responsibility, and as such she was released that same day.

(The Sally Challen case featured in a BBC2 documentary aired in December 2019: https://www.bbc.co.uk/programmes/m000c65v)

—————————— Pause for Thought ——————————

Are increased legal sanctions beneficial to victims of gender-based violence?

CHAPTER SUMMARY

This chapter has explored gender, crime and victimisation with a particular focus on GBV. It has considered criminological understandings of the following:

- The strengths and limitations of adopting a gendered approach to the study of victimisation:
  - ○ Gender-based violence is violence that is directed at a person based on their actual or perceived gender identity or sexuality.
  - ○ There are inherent challenges to discussing GBV *and* victimisation due to traditional conceptualisations of 'victims' as culpable and blameworthy.
  - ○ Recent research asks us to reflect on our use of the term 'gender' as 'simply naming gender does not mean that our analysis is gendered' (Boyle, 2018: 14).
  - ○ It is useful to develop a sharper focus on gender that goes beyond traditional binary conceptualisations of masculinity and femininity.

- The significance of gender identity for understanding experiences of, and responses to, crime and victimisation:

  ○ When considering GBV criminology has traditionally focused on the experience of girls and women as victimised by men.

  ○ Whilst the value of the above theorising is not disputed, this chapter has asked you to consider the marginalisation of men and LGBTQ people's experiences of GBV.

- How feminist approaches inform our understanding of GBV:

  ○ Feminist approaches are central to our understanding of GBV. In recent years there has been unparalleled public interest and 'calls for action' in the development of #MeToo, #TimesUp and #ThisIsNotConsent. A plurality of feminist approaches contribute to knowledge about how gender matters in understanding crime, victimisation and justice.

- What 'justice' means in the context of GBV:

  ○ The Warwick University 'Rape Chat' Case illustrates some of the challenges facing those seeking justice *outside* of the criminal justice system.

  ○ For those seeking justice *within* the criminal justice system feminist research has highlighted a patchy response and the existence of a 'justice gap' (McGlynn and Westmarland, 2019).

  ○ Victims-survivors concepts of justice are not always static nor based on legal understandings of justice; rather the meaning of justice can be fluid and 'kaleidoscopic' in nature (McGlynn and Westmarland, 2019).

Review Questions

1. What are the strengths of taking a gendered approach to the study of victimisation?
2. What is gender-based violence? List some examples.
3. In what way can victims (and offenders) be described as 'gendered' beings?
4. How can feminist and LGBTQ-informed approaches be used to offer a sharper analysis of GBV?
5. What are the arguments *for* and *against* developing criminal justice reforms for GBV?
6. What does 'justice' mean in the context of GBV?

GO FURTHER

Books

1. This useful book provides insight into the nature and extent of domestic violence and offers a conceptual framework in which domestic violence and criminal justice might be better understood:

   Groves, N. and Thomas, T. (2014) *Domestic Violence and Criminal Justice*. Oxon: Routledge.

2. This is a great book and is essential in its consideration of GBV in universities and for considering 'what works' in preventing GBV on campus:

   Sundari, A. and Lewis, R. (eds) (2018) *Gender-Based Violence in University Communities: Policy, Prevention and Educational Interventions*. Bristol: Policy Press.

3. This book provides an accessible account of feminist-informed methodologies used in researching GBV and is great for students wishing to conduct research on domestic and sexual violence:

    Westmarland, N. and Bows, H. (2018) *Researching Gender, Violence and Abuse: Theory, Methods, Action*. London: Routledge.

Journal Articles

1. This is an insightful article which discusses the representational practices of feminist theorising around gender and violence, and ultimately argues for the use of 'continuum thinking' in feminist theorising:

    Boyle, K. (2018) What's in a name? Theorising the Inter-relationships of gender and violence, *Feminist Theory*, 20(1): 1–18.

2. This article suggests limitations to framing women's experiences as 'coercive control' in law and concludes that, in the case of coercive control, more law is not the answer to improving the criminal justice system response to domestic violence:

    Walklate, S., Fitz-Gibbon, K. and McCulloch, J. (2018) Is more law the answer? Seeking justice for victims of intimate partner violence through the reform of legal categories. *Criminology & Criminal Justice*, 18(1): 115–131.

3. This article is based on empirical research with twenty victim-survivors of sexual violence; the authors develop the term 'kaleidoscopic justice' to reflect victim-survivors shifting and evolving experiences of justice:

    McGlynn, C. and Westmarland, N. (2018) Kaleidoscopic justice: sexual violence and victim-survivors' perceptions of justice. *Social & Legal Studies*, 28(2): 179–201.

Useful Websites

1. The following blog, *Talking Research*, features in-depth interviews with prominent academics and researchers who study sexual violence across disciplines. The aim is to make academic knowledge and research on sexual violence accessible. Every Sunday, guests talk about their research, their findings, the process, the challenges and everything else in between: https://talkingresearch.transistor.fm
2. The following website is great for students interested in gender inequalities in the criminal justice system and it highlights the work of the 'Centre for Women's Justice' in bringing forward cases and holding the state to account in relation to VAWG: www.centreforwomensjustice.org.uk
3. The Fawcett Society is the UK's leading charity campaigning for gender equality and women's rights in the home, work and public life, and as such offers useful resources for students interested in gender inequality: www.fawcettsociety.org.uk

REFERENCES

Addley, E. (2019) 'Homophobic attacks must stop, say women assaulted on London bus', *The Guardian*. Available at: https://www.theguardian.com/uk-news/2019/jun/15/homophobic-attacks-must-stop-say-women-assaulted-on-london-bus-chris-and-melania-geymonat [accessed 28 March 2020].

Archer, J. (2000) Sex differences in aggression between heterosexual partners: a meta-analytic review. *Psychological Bulletin*, 126(5): 651–680.

Avalos, L. (2016) Prosecuting rape victims while rapists run free: the consequences of police failure to investigate sex crimes in Britain and the United States. *Michigan Journal of Gender & Law*, 23(1): 1–64.

Bachmann and Gooch (2018) LGBT in Britain: Home and Communities. Stonewall.

BBC News (2018) 'Trans inmate jailed for Wakefield prison sex offences'. Available at: https://www.bbc.com/news/uk-england-leeds-45825838 [accessed 16 July 2019].

BBC News (2019) 'Inside the Warwick University rape chat scandal'. Available at: https://www.bbc.com/news/uk-48366835 [accessed 16 July 2019].

Boyle, K. (2018) What's in a name? Theorising the Inter-relationships of gender and violence. *Feminist Theory*, 20(1): 1–18.

Brownmiller, S. (1975) *Against Our Will: Men, Women and Rape*. London: Penguin.

Butler, J. (1990) *Gender Trouble: Feminism and the Subversion of identity*, New York: Routledge.

Christie, N. (1986) 'The Ideal Victim'. In E. A. Fattah (ed.), *From Crime Policy to Victim Policy*. London: Palgrave Macmillan.

Crenshaw, K. (1991) Mapping the margins: intersectionality, identity politics, and violence against women of colour. *Stanford Law Review*, 43(6): 1241–1299.

Croall, H. (2011) *Crime and Society in Britain*. Harlow: Pearson.

Davies, P. (2007) 'Lessons from the Gender Agenda'. In S. Walklate (ed.), *Handbook of Victims and Victimology*. Cullompton: Willan.

Dobash, R. E. and Dobash, R. P. (1980) *Violence against Wives: A Case against the Patriarchy*. London: Open Books.

Donovan, C. and Hester, M. (2014) *Domestic Violence and Sexuality: What's Love Got To Do With It?* Bristol: Policy Press.

Donovan, C. and Barnes, R. (2020) *Queering Narratives of Domestic Violence and Abuse: Victims and/or Perpetrators?* London: Palgrave.

Gangoli, G., Bates, L. and Hester, M. (2019) What does justice mean to black and minority ethnic (BME) victims/survivors of gender based violence? *Journal of Ethnic and Migration Studies. https://doi.org/10.1080/1369183X.2019.1650010*

Gelsthorpe, L. (1990) 'Feminist Methodologies in Criminology: A New Approach or Old Wine in New Bottles?'. In L. Gelsthorpe and A. Morris (eds), *Feminist Perspectives in Criminology*. Milton Keynes: Open University Press. pp. 89–106.

Groves, N. and Thomas, T. (2014) *Domestic Violence and Criminal Justice*. Oxon: Routledge.

Hester, M. (2009) *Who Does What to Whom? Gender and Domestic Violence Perpetrators*. Bristol: University of Bristol.

Hohl, K. and Stanko, E. (2015) Complaints of rape and the criminal justice system: fresh evidence on the attrition problem in England and Wales. *European Journal of Criminology*, 12(3): 324–341.

Johnson, M. P. (2008) *A Typology of Domestic Violence: Intimate Terrorism, Violent Resistance and Situational Couple Violence*. Hanover & London: University Press of New England.

Kelly, L. (1988) *Surviving Sexual Violence*. Oxford: Polity Press.

Lamble, S. (2012) Rethinking gendered prison policies: impacts on transgender prisoners. *ECAN Bulletin*, Issue 16: 7–12.

Lewis, R., Rowe, M. and Wiper, C. (2017) Online abuse of feminists as an emerging form of violence against women and girls. *British Journal of Criminology*, 57(6): 1462–1481.

Lowe, M. and Rogers, P. (2017) The scope of male rape: a selective review of research, policy and practice. *Aggression and Violent Behaviours*, 35: 38–43.

Marinucci, M. (2016) *Feminism is Queer: The Intimate Connection between Queer and Feminist Theory*, 2nd edition. London: Zed Books.

McGlynn, C., Rackley, E. and Houghton, R. (2017) Beyond 'revenge porn': the continuum of image-based sexual abuse. *Feminist Legal Studies*, 25(10): 25–46.

McGlynn, C. and Westmarland, N. (2019) Kaleidoscopic justice: sexual violence and victim-survivors' perceptions of justice. *Social & Legal Studies*, 28(2): 179–201.

McGuire, D. L. (2011) *At the Dark End of the Street: Black Women, Rape, and Resistance: A New History of the Civil Rights Movement from Rosa Parks to the Rise of Black Power*. London: Vintage Books.

Messerschmidt, J. W. (1993) *Masculinities and Crime*. Lanham, MD: Rowman and Littlefield.

Mulvihill, N., Walker, S.-J., Hester, M. and Gangoli, G. (2018) How is 'justice' understood, sought and experienced by victims/survivors of gender based violence? A review of the literature. https://dx.doi.org/10.5255/UKDA-SN-853338

National Union of Students (2012) *'That's What She Said': Women Students' Experiences of 'Lad Culture' in Higher Education*. London: NUS.

Oakley, A. (1972) *Sex, Gender and Society*. London: Temple Smith.

Office for National Statistics (2018) *Domestic Abuse in England and Wales: Year ending March 2018*. London: ONS.

Phipps, A. (2018) '"Lad Culture" and Sexual Violence Against Students'. In S. Anitha and R. Lewis (eds), *Gender-based Violence in University Communities: Policy, Prevention and Educational Interventions*. Bristol: Policy Press. pp. 41–62.

Stark, E. (2007) *Coercive Control: How Men Entrap Women in Personal Life*. Oxford: Oxford University Press.

Sundari, A. and Lewis, R. (2018) *Gender-based Violence in University Communities: Policy, Prevention and Educational Interventions*. Bristol: Policy Press.

UK Parliament (2015) Serious Crime Act 2015. Available at: http://www.legislation.gov.uk/ukpga/2015/9/contents/enacted

UK Parliament (2019) Voyeurism (Offences) Act 2019. Available at: http://www.legislation.gov.uk/ukpga/2019/2/contents/enacted

Walby, S. and Towers, J. (2018) Untangling the concept of coercive control: theorizing domestic violent crime. *Criminology and Criminal Justice*, 18(1): 7–28.

Walklate, S., Fitz-Gibbon, K. and McCulloch, J. (2018) Is more law the answer? Seeking justice for victims of intimate partner violence through the reform of legal categories. *Criminology & Criminal Justice*, 18(1): 115–131.

Walters, M. A., Paterson, J., Brown, R. & L. McDonnell (2020) Hate Crimes Against Trans People: Assessing Emotions, Behaviours, and Attitudes Toward Criminal Justice Agencies. *Journal of Interpersonal Violence*, 35(21–22): 4583–4613.

West, C. and Zimmerman, D. H. (1987) Doing gender. *Gender and Society*, 1(2): 125–151.

Williamson, E., Aghtaie, N., Bates, L., Eisenstadt, N., Gangoli, G., Hester, M., Matolcsi, A., McCarthy, E., Mulvihill, N., Robinson, A. & Walker, S-J. (2021) *The Justice, Inequalities and Gender Based Violence (GBV) Project: A description of the methodological and analytic approach to phase 3 qualitative interviews with victim-survivors (v-s)*, Unpublished Working Paper, University of Bristol: School for Policy Studies/Bristol Medical School.

Women and Equalities Select Committee (2016) 'Transgender equality: first report of session 2015–16'. Available at: https://www.parliament.uk/business/committees/committeesa- z/commons-select/women-and-equalities-committee/inquiries/parliament-2015/transgender-equality/

Wood, M., Rose, E. and Thompson, C. (2019) Viral justice? Online justice-seeking, intimate partner violence and affective contagion. *Theoretical Criminology*, 23(3): 375–393.

Woodlock, D. (2016) The abuse of technology in domestic violence and stalking. *Violence Against Women*, 23(5): 584–602.

PART IV

CRIMINAL JUSTICE PRACTICE

Social Control

Murray Lee and Alex Simpson

21

Learning Objectives

By the end of this chapter you will:

- Understand the different levels of social control that operate and their contexts.
- Be familiar with the historical development of social control from enlightenment philosophy to contemporary criminology.
- Be able to recognise the relationships between crime, social control and power.
- Understand how forms of governance influence individual and group action.

Framing Questions
---

1. What social forces influence rule making and rule breaking?
2. To what extent does social control reflect existing social inequalities?
3. Do laws and rules reduce offending or is social conformity influenced by other forces?
4. Does investment in dominant social forms and social institutions influence the likelihood of offending?

INTRODUCTION

All societies and individuals within societies are subject to social control. Indeed, social control is a necessary part of every human society. From small nomadic tribes to village settlements to the modern metropolis, social control guides, manages, or coerces individuals to adhere to the rules, values, mores, laws and traditions of any given society. Social control is exercised through a range of social, cultural and legal mechanisms, through individuals, groups, and institutions. These include family, peers, and organisations of the state such as organised religion, schools, workplaces and medical establishments. The desired goal of social control is to maintain conformity to established norms and rules. Hence, the nature of norms and rules will to some extent also dictate the forms and targets of social control, as well as its limits. It follows that the forms, strategies and targets of such controls have varied radically across cultures, amongst societies and throughout history. Such variation reflects the specific social, cultural and economic makeup of the society, particularly expectations of individual freedom, the role of the state, and the mores of values of the culture. Social control is often envisaged as having two specific forms, i.e. formal and informal.

This chapter begins with an overview of the concept of social control, and in particular its emergence from enlightenment and neo-classical philosophy. It then maps some of the key theories and concepts of social control. In outlining these we explore social control from early sociological theories, theories of the metropolis, and later sociological theories, through to criminological conceptions of social control.

MAPPING THE TERRAIN: HISTORICAL DEVELOPMENT

The term 'social control' was first coined by Albion Woodbury Small and George Edgar Vincent in 1894 (p. 328), however its foundations emerged out of political theorists and penologists from the Enlightenment era such as Thomas Hobbes (1651), Cesare Beccaria (1764), and Jean-Jacques Rousseau (1762). These proto-sociological treatises were subsequently expanded upon by the likes of Durkheim (1897), Weber (1904) and Marx (1844).

In *Leviathan* (first published 1651), Hobbes advocated for a strong central government, which would prevent the natural driving passions of each person from claiming a right or licence to everything in the world (2011). To deter this 'war of all against all', people accede to a **social contract** to establish a civil society. While Hobbes felt that humans' natural inclination towards self-interest could be tamed through a strong state, he also argued that laws and punishments were ineffective in regulating everyday conduct. He suggested that negative sanctions were relatively ineffective in many cases, and held that 'no man reproach, revile, deride, or any otherwise declare his hatred, contempt, or disesteem of any other' (2008: 14). For Hobbes, to do so was to facilitate a return to a warring nature. Clearly, Hobbes envisaged a mix of formal and informal social control with the aim of ensuring peace, security and stability.

If ultimately Hobbes' philosophy attempted to strike a balance whereby the state should use its power of social control over citizens sparingly, Baccaria's work continued this theme into the specific realm of punishment and corrections. The most ostentatious display of social control for conduct that a given society considers extremely deviant, is criminal punishment. *On Crimes and Punishments* (first published in 1764) emerged out of the Milan Enlightenment, and was ultimately an inquiry into whether measures of punishment were justifiable and proportionate. Amongst other things it constituted the first critical analysis of capital punishment that demanded its abolition. Beccaria, drawing on Montesquieu, stated in terms of justifiability that 'every act of authority of one man over another, for which there is not an absolute necessity, is tyrannical' (1872: 31). In regard to proportion he argued:

If an equal punishment be ordained for two crimes that injure society in different degrees, there is nothing to deter men from committing the greater as often as it is attended with greater advantage. (1872: 32)

Ultimately, his work is amongst the first to articulate closely calibrated policy levers needed for efficient, effective, and importantly just and proportionate state-sanctioned social control. Levers based on pleasure and pain in that '[p]leasure and pain are the only springs of action in beings endowed with sensibility' (1872: 28). As an early social scientific articulation of social control, the fundamentals of Beccaria's thesis still hold in the purposes of punishment and the utility of deterrence.

Knowledge link: This topic is also covered in Chapter 6.

Whereas this form of societal regulation discusses the imposition of penalties and rewards to regulate deviant behaviour, Rousseau envisaged in his *On the Social Contract*, that we all make compromises to live relatively securely and safely, i.e. that self-interest can be rendered subject to a greater good. People will thus freely and willingly forfeit a portion of their rights, and self-impose a number of duties equally for the stability of society, including the safeguarding of property. Rousseau's image of social control is one, then, where freedom is based upon self-regulation.

As we will see below, many of the themes touched on by these earlier thinkers re-emerge in later discussions on the topic. In time social control would become a theory in its own right.

Knowledge link: This topic is also covered in Chapter 7 which discusses the relation between power and the criminalisation of some forms of behaviour.

EARLY DEVELOPMENTS IN SOCIOLOGICAL CONTROL

Social Control Theory examines the devices employed which limit undesirable behaviour to bring individuals into conformity with the societal norm. Whereas other theories search for the reason why people engage in deviant behaviour and crimes, Social Control Theory tackles the problem in an opposite way by looking at what causes a person to refrain from offending (Akers and Sellers, 2004). Quite simply, it asks the question 'how is social order possible, even though persons choose their actions for themselves?' (Luhmann, 1982: 10). Group members who exhibit 'deviant' behaviour are subjected to various forms of pressure, including shame, coercion, force, restraint and persuasion. In this manner, the theory is notable inasmuch as it inverts the traditional question concerning modernist criminology, i.e. why is it that we do *not* commit crime when, to all intents and purposes, we could. What is stopping us?

One of the first to address this question was the French sociologist Emile Durkheim. Writing as a critique of Hobbes' and Rousseau's theories of a social contract and the centralising force of control, Durkheim (1964) posited that social control is nothing but society itself. In other words, to understand society is to understand the collective binds of solidary, community and, ultimately, the rules of control. Prior to Durkheim's writing, society had been positioned as an *object* or a *thing*, held together by what Rousseau called the *social contract*. By contrast, Durkheim argued that society is a *process*; a flow of common judgements that gives rise to a sense of identity and belonging. Central in this conceptualisation are the shared *minded patterns*, or mental images, that affect the interactions of individuals and impart directives for action as well as give shape to perspectives of reality (Poggi, 2000). These minded patterns would later be subsumed under the concept of *règle* – translated somewhere between 'rule' and 'social norm'. What is important in relation to our discussion, however, is the shift in focus from society being held together by a *decree* or *contract* and towards a collective imagination based on *social likeness* or a *community of beliefs and sentiments* (Durkheim, 1983: 278). What Durkheim ultimately argued is that social control rests on a culturally maintained and normative sense of moral order.

The laws and juridical rules that govern society through sanctions of noncompliance are, on one level, the prime example of how control is asserted and applied across a given society (Poggi, 2000: 88). However, not all anti-social conduct is proscribed by law and not all violations of the criminal code are truly anti-social (Downes and Rock, 2011). Laws are only approximate expressions of the underlying moral order. Furthermore, the motivation for control cannot be reduced simply to calculative rationality, pointing to a broader common morality of legitimacy that runs through society and holds value in the minds of individuals to the extent that motivation becomes compliance (Durkheim, 1964). Even in a society of saints, Durkheim stressed, there would still be 'sinners' since deviance is nothing more than the deviation from a shared moral judgement. In Durkheim's (1983: 229) words, 'every society is a moral society' and each 'society learns to regard its members no longer as things over which it has rights, but as co-operators whom it cannot neglect and towards whom it owes duties'. Not only does modern social order rest on morality, but social control is an essential condition of social order that is internalised as a set of moral judgements within each individual.

Knowledge link: This topic is also covered in Chapter 6.

Knowledge link: Extinction Rebellion is also covered in Chapter 24.

In contrast to Hobbes' and Rousseau's centralised governance of control, Durkheim here establishes a theory of control that exists and is maintained through learned codes of compliance and moral judgements. Within this development, crime is no longer constructed as a 'problem', but instead plays a social function which is 'an integral part of all healthy societies' (Durkheim, 1964: 68). Not only is crime an inevitable presence across all societies, it also serves to maintain and reinforce collective moral sentiment. By marking deviations of normative moral judgements and, in turn, creating a distinct demarcation between the 'normal' and the 'pathological', societies can help affirm a collective sense of belonging and social cohesion throughout society. Crime, then, is as 'useful' as it is 'necessary', bound up with the fundamental conditions that are indispensable to the moral sensibility of any given society. Moreover, deviance helps promote change by challenging established boundaries and promoting new ones. Today, we only have to look at predominant social movements, such as *Extinction Rebellion* or *Black Lives Matter*, to understand how rule breaking can help shift the rules of moral judgement.

The work of Durkheim has been instrumental for developing a critical understanding of control through questions of *solidarity* and *social community*. As society developed towards modernity and ever-shifting, multiple social relations, Durkheim feared a loosening of control:

> The more weakened the groups to which [the individual] belongs, the less he [sic] depends on them, the more he consequently depends only on himself and recognizes no other rules of conduct than what are founded on his private interests. (Durkheim, 1951: 209)

The issue of weakening control as a consequence of social development is a common theme throughout the literature on control. For example, Edward A. Ross (2009 [1901]), one of the first to present social control as a *theory*, argued that, as society developed, impersonal and contractual relations weaken such instincts, creating more self-interested interactions. For Ross, human beings naturally inherit four instincts: sympathy, sociability, a sense of justice, and resentment to mistreatment. In intimate social relations, these attributes are enough to create and maintain a harmonious society. However, facing impending disorder, the response is to implement new social mechanisms.

Central to Ross's (1901) work in theorising control is that society itself holds the 'means' of control. 'Natural', 'pre-modern' communities have, for Ross, been increasingly replaced by 'artificial civilised societies', which, in turn, is necessitated by the rapid urbanisation and industrialisation at the turn of the twentieth century. However, this transformation prioritised controls that maintained safety and stability, usurping instinctive and internal controls. Thus, according to Ross, the more civilised a society becomes, the greater the increase of control exerted by government or the state. In this model, the self-serving individual contradicts the natural purposes of society, and society's purposes are misaligned with those of individuals. In other words, control becomes a libertarian constraint that reduces free will. This position, however, can be contrasted by Charles H. Cooley (1902), who illustrated how an individual becomes absorbed into a society through association. For Cooley, much more like Durkheim than Ross, social control manifests through integration, engagement and association. This model, in turn, views social control as an inherent part of society's functioning, rather than a constructed device.

Whether restrictive, normalising or associative, what emerges is a vision of control that provides a vital social function. Moreover, these early sociological criminologists all raise the same spectre of the shifting relationship of the individual within society amidst the advent of modernity. This focus of the expanding modern metropolis and questions of weakening control leading to a loss of 'rootedness' and 'moral sensibility' was to, as we shall see, shape the evolving discussion on social control.

Pause for Thought

How does Durkheim's conceptualisation of society differ from Rousseau's and how does this impact our understanding of social control?

ECOLOGIES OF CONTROL: THE BIRTH OF METROPOLIS

What we can see in our discussion of Durkheim, touching on Ross and Cooley, is how the shifting nature of urbanisation and rapid advancement of modernity have reshaped how social control is manifest, internalised and upheld. Through the work of Durkheim, we can see the expression of control move away from the spectacular but erratic systems of Hobbesian sovereignty and towards a more socially learned system of internalised judgements that knit a society together. In the face of modernity, Durkheimian social control works to achieve whole new levels of conformity whilst retaining individual autonomy.

The rapid advancement of urban centres in the early part of the twentieth century provided the basis of control; specifically, giving new meaning to themes of distance, proximity, separation, connection and openness. One of the first to address these questions was German sociologist, Georg Simmel. Writing in *the Metropolis and Mental Life*, Simmel argues that the metropolis stands as the key site of modernity and represents the point of intensification:

> The deepest problems of modern life derive from the claim of the individual to preserve the autonomy and individuality of his existence in the face of overwhelming social forces, of historical heritage, of external culture, and of the technique of life. (Simmel, 1997: 174)

In Simmel's work, we can see the metropolis is a space of disaggregation and raises new questions relating to social cohesion through the dualism of distance. According to Simmel, we, the individual, are as much confronted by new social orders of moral *difference* as we are increasingly *distanced* from one another through the power of capital. Simmel's urban characterisation is linked to a sense of social 'rootlessness', which one might associate with Durkheim's *anomie*. Simmel's model of urban disruption and the 'shock of the new' highlights the shifting dynamics placed on communities and individuals swept up by rapid urban expansion and industrialisation.

Knowledge link: This topic is also covered in Chapter 2.

Such themes take us to the 1930s and 1940s writings of the Chicago School – arguably the birthplace of American criminology – and the work of Shaw and McKay. Published in 1942, Shaw and McKay's *Juvenile Delinquency in Urban Areas* is an evocation of Chicago's rapid industrialisation. Perfectly captured in Upton Sinclair's 1906 novel *The Jungle*, urbanisation sees the modern city – or metropolis – emerge as a new ecology, at once disrupting and shaping new systems of social control. Out of their ecological study of Chicago, Shaw and McKay (1942) note two twinned factors influencing social control within urban development; firstly, areas of economic deprivation tend to have high rates of population turnover, and secondly, they are characterised by community heterogeneity.

These two processes, common to early urban development, were assumed to lead to an increased likelihood of social disorganisation and the weakening of control. What we see here, as Bursik (1988: 521) states, is social disorganisation arising from 'the inability of local communities to realise the common values of their residents or solved commonly experienced problems'. In other words, Shaw and McKay show us how rapid urbanisation of the early twentieth century brought a new plurality of social relationships which each contained a distinct moral order. This clash of ideals, values and common sensibilities, much like Simmel before, led to a loss of social orientation, cultural obsolescence, and with it, diminished control.

Shaw and McKay's (1942) ecologies of control may seem humdrum by today's standards and open to critique given the way these can be used to close down debate on multi-culturalism within contemporary communities, but it is important to stress their radicalism of the time. Rather than responding to 'dangers' presented by migrant groups, Shaw and McKay's primary concern was the expansion of industry into communities. Rapid urbanisation had created lasting pockets of social disorganisation. Subsequent ripples of displacement, stemming from 'industrial invasion' as businesses and factories broke out of the centralised business zone into residential communities, led to the loss of social solidarity and disorganisation. Any impact relating to highly mobile immigrant groups being drawn into urban centres is a product of the initial wave of industrial advancement (Snodgrass, 1976). Furthermore, their conclusions pushed back against the predominant assumptions that crime was a product of biological and individual deficiency; an assertion that had dominated criminological debates up to this time and still, especially in public discourse, is difficult to shift. For Shaw and McKay, the enduring characteristic was not within the individual but the neighbourhood itself. After all, their studies had highlighted how neighbourhood crime rates endured over time, despite rapid population turnover. In other words, people came and went, yet neighbourhood characteristics of crime remained relative stable.

Knowledge link: This topic is also covered in Chapter 6.

What we see from Shaw and McKay's work is a focus on population turnover within turbulent communities. It is the chaos and heterogeneity of transition that uncouples individuals from established institutions and which, for Shaw and McKay, affect control. Within this model, the 'security' of primary social relationships and the informal structures of control emanating from surrounding networks, which were so prevalent in Durkheim's work, cannot take root given the constant state of flux. Again, in this approach we see heterogeneity impede a shared cultural belonging and obstruct a collective coming together to solve social goals (Bursik, 1988). Containing echoes of Durkheim's *society as control* thesis, we can witness here how urban development, for Shaw and McKay at least, led to rapid social transformation and disorganisation. As a result, individuals living in affected areas suffer from the loss of a common value system, limited social cohesion, and the weakening of cultural institutions such as family, neighbours, schools and religious organisations.

Case Study 21.1

Boyz in the Hood

John Singleton's 1991 coming of age drama, *Boyz in the Hood*, stands as an exemplar through which social control can be understood. The film follows the lives of three young black men living in the Crenshaw, Los Angeles, and raises critical questions pertaining to race, relationships and violence in the neighbourhood. Crenshaw's work, much like Shaw and McKay's depiction of Chicago, is characterised by rapid urbanisation, economic deprivation, and is all but cut off from the wider social environment. In the 'Hood', we see the emergence of a social order defined by 'values' of masculine aggression and a 'street code' whereby disagreement is commonly settled through violence. Crucially, the enduring characteristic of gang violence and criminality is not necessarily within any individual but the neighbourhood itself.

Within this environment, the film follows the relative pathways of Trey (Cuba Gooding, Jr.), the main protagonist, and his two childhood friends, Doughboy (Ice Cube) and Ricky Baker (Morris Chestnut). Growing up together in 'the Hood', we see how, in the manner of Reiss (1951), each character internalises different levels of 'controls' and develops a sense of morality. While Ricky is the 'All-American' athlete, on the verge of winning a football scholarship to USC, and with it a 'stake in conformity' (Toby, 1957), his half-brother Doughboy has a limited stake, succumbing to petty gang violence to maintain a sense of pride and code of honour. In between is Trey, caught between these two divergent pathways. At a crucial juncture, Trey looks destined to use the code of the street to right the wrongs in his life. However, at the last-minute conformity prevails. Reading through Hirschi's (1969) vision of social control, Trey benefits from a father who strengthens attachments to both family and friends, a strong commitment to and involvement with education that align him with normative expectations as well as limiting the timespan of his engagement with deviance, and a firm belief in the social values he ascribes to.

In both the work of Durkheim (1964; 1983) and Shaw and McKay (1942), we can begin to see the importance of institutions in maintaining a collective utility of compliance so as to establish the norms and moral values of a society. We can also see the shared risks of social disorganisation, which can be broadly linked to Durkheim's anomie, in disrupting these institutions of control and engendering either cultural obsolesce, where previously-held rule systems no longer carry value, or the weakening of ties amongst community members. There is a shared assumption that control relies upon ecological or social stability and that disorganisation will lead to a loss of control. However, this is absent from Simmel's (1955) writing, in which the acceleration and intensification of, especially urban, modernity challenges individuals to become enmeshed in new social groupings, with overlapping or conflicting moral sentiments, necessitating multiple social identities that belie the certainties of modernity. Nonetheless, in reference to crime, the lack of control brought on by urban redevelopment leads to persistent criminal activity, and it is not until communities are able to reorganise and gain a semblance of stability that control can be regained and the crime rate can fall.

While ecological approaches to control remained popular within criminology throughout the early part of the twentieth century and were at the forefront of the emergence of American criminology, the interest in neighbourhoods waned but its popularity has increased once again in the last thirty years (Reiss and Tonry, 1986; Wickes and Hipp, 2018). An enduring question is one of *causality*; it remains unclear whether or not changes in neighbourhood ecology impact social control processes, if those changes impact crime, and in turn, how crime feeds back to influence the nature of community cohesion and with it control (Wickes and Hipp, 2018: 278). In other words, it remains unclear as to whether the relationship between community cohesion and crime is *causal* or simply a *correlation*.

Seeking to address this problem, Bursik argues that crime and control are linked only in as much as shared expectations and informal systems of control are disrupted (Bursik, 1988; Bursik and Grasmick, 1993). This led to Bursik and Grasmick (1993) establishing three levels of control within the community: *the private* in which control is exercised closely by intimate relations; *the parochial* in which control is exercised by neighbourhood residents and predominant institutions; and *the public* which denotes the capacity for neighbourhoods to secure productive services from larger political and economic institutions.

Much like Shaw and McKay before them, Bursik and Grasmick's typology denotes the ways in which control manifests throughout a neighbourhood as well as how, when such systems become weakened, a loss of moral orientation occurs that leads to persistently higher rates of crime within a community. It is not until a process of community reorganisation can take place that control will be reasserted, and crime rates will begin to fall. However, even within this typology, the question of agency is largely diminished. For Sampson (2001), this points to a need to de-emphasise social ties and instead, promote the capacity of individual community members to regulate unwanted behaviour. After all, agency should not be diminished. Communities will always manage, and have always managed, the expectations of behaviour, creating a shared belief as well as a capability for action.

———— Hear from the Expert ————

Rebecca Wickes, Director of the Monash Migration and Inclusion Centre, Monash University

Normative theories of social control and crime have evolved significantly since the early twentieth century, yet core tenets remain relevant in contemporary society. One of the guiding principles of Social Disorganisation Theory, as originally conceptualised by Shaw and McKay, states that social order is achieved when residents share similar values regarding the prevention of crime. This principle remains central to more recent reformulations of this theory. Collective Efficacy Theory, arguably one of the most popular neighbourhood social control theories, contends that crime is lower in neighbourhoods where residents have a working trust of each other and share a willingness to work together when problems arise. The relationship between collective efficacy and lower crime, in particular violence, holds in several advanced western democracies, including the United Kingdom and Australia. Although inner city neighbourhoods may no longer represent the zones of transition as proposed by Shaw and McKay, the pernicious effect of neighbourhood disadvantage on both social control and crime is evident in much of the collective efficacy research. There is also evidence of a reciprocal relationship between disadvantage and social control, such that poverty reduces collective efficacy, which in turn increases poverty at a later time point. A significant departure from traditional ecological social control theories is the proposed relationship between immigration, social control and crime. While some cross-sectional studies find support for the immigration-low social control relationship, longitudinal studies are more equivocal. In different national contexts, scholarship reveals a null or indeed a negative relationship between immigration concentration crime over time, suggesting that immigration concentration may protect against crime. This has been linked to migrants' religious values, family stability, and their motivation to succeed in their new host country. What remains less understood is how these informal social control processes lead to specific actions from individuals that seek to prevent crime or desist from offending. Thus while Durkheim's and later Shaw and McKay's theorising of social control is seen as emanating from shared beliefs, sentiments and moral orientations, the mechanisms which transform these beliefs into social control actions that benefit the collective remain poorly understood.

LATE DEVELOPMENTS IN SOCIOLOGICAL CONTROL

The question of agency brings our discussion to the impact of control upon the individual. This is not to cast an arbitrary distinction, after all Durkheim's questions on society seek to address how it is the community members who act in accordance with a common rule system. This is to place issues of self-control within the spectre of power and to ask, not just how cultural practice and normative expectations operate amongst a collective group, but also 'how stratified social systems of hierarchy and domination persist and reproduce intergenerationally without powerful resistance and without the conscious recognition of their members?' (Swartz, 1997: 6). The answer to this question, as Swartz continues, lies in exploring 'how cultural resources, processes and institutions hold individuals and groups in competitive and self-perpetuating hierarchies of domination' (Swartz, 1997: 6). The intergenerational and individualisable existence of control, therefore, structures action, produces knowledge, and with it taken-for-granted assumptions as well as providing the moral contours that direct social life.

As a corollary to power, individual control needs to be viewed as more than a resource-driven system of action, whereby 'A has power over B to the extent that he can get B to do something that B would not otherwise do' (Dahl, 1957: 203). As Dahl argues, such an assertion is not particularly 'interesting, informative or accurate' since it fails to articulate the detailed sociological, political and economic circumstances in which control is established. Rather, we need to view control as a constructed and maintained force that exists within cultural and institutional norms, but which filters down to include the uncritical habituation of non-resistance and obedience on the part of the individual (Foucault, 1982). It is the enactment of these shared assumptions, expressed as a habitual 'way of being', which imparts a 'normative moral sentiment' and establishes a force to which we submit in our everyday lives (O'Neill, 1986). Again, invoking Durkheim, deviation from this moral sentiment gives meaning to biographical objects such as the criminal. In this context, the marker of criminality holds no ontological reasoning in and of itself but is established through a degree of difference in relation to normative cultural expectations sustained by the production of knowledge (Foucault, 1975).

The importance of control for sociological discussion is paramount. However, Gibbs (1989) goes as far to suggest that it should be the 'central notion' of sociology, i.e. sociology as a discipline would make more sense and be cohesive if it were defined by the study of control. If sociology is the study of societal values and the reproduction of power, then, as Durkheim taught us, control becomes the driving force. By naming the sociological importance of control, Gibbs makes an empiricist argument that aims to make sociology more scientific (Collins, 1990). In this argument, Gibbs distinguishes instances of social control from mere 'reactions to deviance'. Much like Dahl's delineation of power before, Gibbs argues that simple responses to, or the issuing of, orders are not considered an assertion of social control. Rather, Gibbs defines social control as an attempt to cause an individual to do or refrain from doing something through a third party – this could be an actual person, or notions of norms, values and expectations. An example of this is when a victim of harmful behaviour seeks to compel their attacker to stop their criminal conduct by threatening to report the incident to the police. As such, Gibb's version of social control seeks to manipulate behaviour through reference to extraneous justification.

A key discussion of social control in the late twentieth century developed from the work of French scholar Michel Foucault. For Foucault social control could be traced back to how power in society was organised and exercised. Foucault's (1975; 1980) work allows us to conceive of social control not as a result of simply state centred power or control, but rather as a form of power that is exercised throughout the social body via institutions, organisations, and individuals. Unlike Marxism which conceived of social control as a top-down process, or liberalism which sees social control as a necessary evil to balance a free society, Foucault believed that power – and the social control that flowed from such power – operated though mentalities of rule, or what he termed **governmentality**. Governmentality according to Foucault could be defined in three ways, however it is his first definition that is important to us here, namely that it is a modern form of power which is:

> [t]he ensemble formed by the institutions, procedures, analyses and reflections, the calculations and tactics that allow the exercise of this very specific albeit complex form of power, which has as its target: population, as its principal form of knowledge: political economy, and as its essential technical means: apparatuses of security. (Foucault, 1991: 102)

For Foucault governmental power was productive. Through what he termed the micro-physics of power, the individual could be government through their own freedoms (Rose, 1999). The beauty of Foucault's model for understanding social control was that it broke down the dualisms of structure and agency, individual control and societal control, and even formal and informal control. Social control could be decentred in analysis, and rather than being simply a tool of dominance (although it could be that), it could also be the result of other narratives, other discourses. The most efficient form of social control is that which those subjected to it are barely aware of – or feel works in their interests. Take public health discourse under Covid-19. For the most part laws were not required to enlist the public in the largest social control exercise of the twenty-first century. Rather, we followed protocols for the public good as prudent 'free' citizens.

But beyond governmentalities other forms of social control operate through social media. Here, peer-to-peer control and the search for affirmation led to new technologies of the self. Social control that was beyond government and beyond institutionalised governmentalities. Social control in late modernity may need to be understood beyond, not only the state, but also society itself. We could also misquote Bauman (2000: viii) and his case for **liquid modernity** to suggest social control in the twenty-first century also entails an element of 'fragility, temporariness, vulnerability and inclination to constant change. To "be modern" means to modernize – compulsively, obsessively; not so much just "to be", let alone to keep its identity intact, but forever "becoming", avoiding completion, staying underdefined'. From a sociological perspective, understanding social control in the twenty-first century will mean grappling with the complexity of highly connected, complex, technologised societies in a context where truth is relative and meta-narratives have collapsed.

Pause for Review

As society becomes more fragmented and 'liquid', what impact does this have on how social control is organised?

CRIMINOLOGIES OF CONTROL

How then does this sociological discussion of *control* and *power* manifest within the realm of criminology? This is to assert that control imparts a degree of *order* and, without control, *disorder* may ensue. The work of McKay and Shaw highlighted how this operates at an ecological level, while Albert Reiss translated this assertion to the level of the individual and in doing so developed the subject of control into a coherent field of analysis. Reiss (1951) saw the family and the normative moral controls imparted upon individuals being central to keeping juveniles away from deviant lifestyles. He noted that 'a major factor in the development of personal controls is the moral ideal which parents represent and the techniques they use to control their child's behaviour' (1951: 199). In other words, Reiss places the family as the central institution for upholding control and espousing a normative moral sensibility. Delinquency thus ensues as the result of a failure of restraint and the lack of social controls required to produce conformity (Reiss, 1951: 196).

While Durkheim explored the role of control in engendering a social ethic and, in turn, a sense of cohesion, Reiss focuses on how individuals internalise such controls and the consequences of failure. The focus on the family promotes the idea, not unlike social learning theorists, that controls need to be learned (or taught) through socialisation and are a necessary for the development of a sense of morality. Such disciplinary controls were also extended to the school, which Reiss saw as vital to the control of behaviours in relation to societal norms. Quite simply, a measure of submission to such norms was to be obtained through attendance. However, unlike social learning theory, Reiss (1951: 197) argues that 'delinquent' association is a consequence of the lack of personal and social control, not a causal factor in its own right. Reiss (1951: 204) concluded that delinquent behaviour was a result of: ineffective control structures, which is to say, norms and effective techniques in producing conformity; an inability to accept or 'submit' to the control of social groups that enforce conformity; and a lack of or weakened sense of social guidance that comes with a mature ego and flexible responses to social situations. What we have in Reiss's work is a much more normative understanding of individualistic models of control, focusing on individual or parental deficiency. However, little thought is given to the question of *why* individuals may lack – or reject – the strictures of pro-social control. Instead control, obedience and conformity are constructed by Reiss to be an a priori social good without question.

Toby (1957) responded to this problem by introducing the concept of a 'stake in conformity', which serves as a measure for the probability of a person to engage in delinquency. Essentially, he argued that most people refrain from deviant behaviour because they had invested a large portion of their life towards conforming with the norm:

> Youngsters vary in the extent to which they feel a stake in American society. For those with social honour, disgrace is a powerful sanction. For the boy [sic] disapproved of already, there is less incentive to resist the temptation to do what he wants and when he wants to do it. (Toby, 1957: 16)

For Toby, those with few stakes in society, or who have been rejected altogether, are more likely to move away from the norm since they have fewer restraints in terms of reputation or consequence. Without a stake, it is not that individuals have a reduced sense of moral judgement, but that the social costs of exclusion and rejection do not apply in the same way, and therefore individuals are more likely to move away from the norm.

Both Toby's and Reiss's work function to pull the debates of social control away from their macro origins, however both suffer from the issue that offenders are characterised as people who are fundamentally different (lacking in control) from non-offenders (Taylor et al., 1973). Here, Matza (1964) employed the concept of 'drift'. Quite simply, this acknowledges that people do not clearly fit into the categories of conformists and delinquents, but rather opt in and out of the dichotomies. Most 'delinquents' do not engage in delinquency all of the time and many 'law abiding' people still drift into a praxis of deviance from time to time. This was based on Matza's observation of delinquents expressing guilt over their crimes, their respect for law-abiding people, and their ability to return to conformity. They also distinguished between people they were allowed to victimise and not, in the case of crime, showing respect for 'rightful citizens'. Crucial here is that victims of delinquent behaviour are not (or rather, seldom) arbitrary. Rather, group members adhere to their own sense of moral conformity and code of ethics. Unlike subcultural theorists, such as Cohen, Matza argues that many delinquents continue to maintain strong community relations and to a large degree perform the same normative functions as law-abiding citizens. Here, individuals drift in and out of patterns of conformity and delinquency, displaying simultaneous traits of 'weak' and 'strong' social control.

Knowledge link: This topic is also covered in Chapter 30.

The perspective of drift illustrates a constant push and pull within individuals between notions of conformity and delinquency and accentuates often complex and certainly non-linear pathways to deviancy (Box, 1970: 403–404). Whereas Matza acknowledged and gave meaning to the complexity of offenders being *both* law abiding and law breakers, Travis Hirschi, a firm disciple of Durkheim, accepted the ideas of Enlightenment social philosophers, such as Hobbes and Bentham, and saw humans as naturally amoral and pleasure-seeking. In many ways, Hirschi has become the father of social control theory as we understand it today. In his influential book *Causes of Deviancy* (1969), he once again asked the question not of what causes people to commit crime, but rather what keeps people from committing crime every time they have the opportunity to do so? He responded to Durkheim's claim that humans are 'moral beings to the extent that we are social beings' (Durkheim, 1961) by arguing that 'we are moral beings to the extent that we internalise the normal of society' (Hirschi, 1969: 18). In other words, where Durkheim saw control as a corollary to morality, Hirschi posits that individuals are only moral to the extent that they internalise the norms of society.

Hirschi's version of social control theory envisages four aspects in the maintenance of familial and social bonds which prevent deviant behaviour. First is *attachment* to friends, family, colleagues. Second is *commitment* and investment in activities that align with the norm, e.g. educational and career ambitions. Third is *involvement* in activities which strengthens social bonds and limits any remaining time for deviant conduct. Fourth is a *belief* in the group's social values (Siegel and McCormick, 2006). Demonstrating his thesis Hirschi finds 'the child attached to his father is less likely to commit deviant acts. Among those with no delinquent friends and among those with several delinquent friends, the weaker the attachment to the father, the greater the likelihood of delinquency' (1969: 99). Like Matza, his control theory accounts for variations of offending as well as desistance, principally through the strengthening of social bonds. In this manner, not only does his theory propose to explain how crime occurs in the first place, but also asks why patterns of desistance occur at varying speeds. While Hirschi, writing with Gottfredson, would later distance himself from the question of desistance, his work remains prominent in how control is understood, and has been described by Ackers (1994: 115) as the 'dominant theory of criminal and delinquent behaviour for the past twenty-five years'.

CRIMINOLOGICAL TYPOLOGIES OF CONTROL

Sociologists tend to identify two primary forms of social control: informal and formal. Such typologies are useful if somewhat limiting in defining various elements of social control. Informal social control constitutes the internalisation of norms and expectations through complex processes of 'socialisation' – many of which we have discussed above, i.e. a set of processes whereby 'an individual, born with behavioural potentialities of enormously wide range, is led to develop actual behaviour which is confined to the narrower range of what is acceptable for him by the group standards' (Lindzey, 1954: II, 655–692). On the other hand, formal social controls are constituted through the enforcement of laws and regulations imposed by a government, police, schools, and even workplaces. Both forms of social control can also be understood through the sanctions imposed. Informal sanctions may include shame, ridicule, sarcasm, criticism and disapproval. Such informal sanctions operate for example in forms of restorative justice. These tend to have the effect of altering an individual's behaviour through internalised social values, or the reiteration of such values. Informal sanctions check 'deviant' behaviour.

Formal sanctions also reflect society's values and norms. In section 61HE of the *Crimes Act 1900* (NSW) for example, **social norms** in relation to consent in sexual relations are implanted into the legislation. Where affirmative consent serves to exonerate sexual assault (*Crimes Act 1900* (NSW), s61I), it becomes irrelevant in the strict liability for sexual intercourse with a child under the age of 10 (*Crimes Act 1900* (NSW), s66A), and sexual offences against persons with cognitive impairment (*Crimes Act 1900* (NSW), s66F(3)). Social control in these instances are heightened to reflect society's disapprobation of that level of delinquency and the legal sanction likely to follow such behaviour. However, as we have seen in our discussion so far, social control is more than simply that which is derived from police or legal authority but a deeply engrained social sensibility akin to normative and expected behaviour.

Chriss (2012) draws on three formations of social control, i.e. informal, legal and medical. *Informal control* covers areas of interpersonal relations and group living, foregrounding the mechanisms and practices, including but not limited to family, peers, work, media and religion. In other words, these

Knowledge link: This topic is also covered in Chapter 2.

are the ordinary community institutions of everyday life in which individuals and groups conform to a distinct social and moral way of life. Whereas informal control, as the name suggests, rests on moral enforcement through informal institutions, *legal control* deploys the force of the law, police and justice to maintain order. *Medical control* tends to occur only after legal control has acted upon a subject and is characterised by the use of medical personal or knowledge to pacify unsocial behaviour. Closely following Foucault (1982), medical control uses the apparatus of **bio-power** to enforce normative sensitisation through binary categories of 'sickness' and 'health', 'sanity' and 'insanity'. Together, these three typologies of control seek to zoom in on and work between three areas of social experience – relationships, behaviour and the law. Whilst distinct, in practice each of these forms of control intersect with one another to give us a broader picture of social, legal and medical governance over acts of deviance.

CHAPTER SUMMARY

- In outlining the importance of control theory to criminological discussion, we have shown how its origins emerged from the proto-sociological treatise of Hobbes and Rousseau before developing its early sociological origins through Durkheim and Simmel.
- Here, we begin to see the emergence of control in terms of a population and a moralistic social sentiment shared by its members. To this end, social control becomes about identity, and with it, shaping an axis of inclusion and exclusion.
- These themes continued, again through Simmel, but more notably with Shaw and McKay's shift to ecological, or community, concepts of control. The focus here shifted from control as society to the changing nature of industrial relations and the impact this has on communities.
- Disruptions to community bonds through the displacement or invasion of industry overturned the otherwise stable community relations that had existed before, and had dominated much early American criminology, were then revisited in the 1980s and 1990s, noticeably by Bursik and Grasmick (1993).
- Despite the centrality of control in sociology, as seen through Durkheim, Foucault and Gibbs, criminology's biggest disciple of control, Hirschi, all but abandoned his approach in 1990, when he collaborated with Gottfredson to write *A General Theory of Crime*.
- In our discussion, what we have presented is the centrality of control within the disciplines of sociology and criminology. Even if theoretical accounts may slip or vary, the central question being addressed remains one of deviance and why it is that some people do not break normative rules while others do.
- It is a question that runs through nearly all criminological work and, as Gibbs foregrounds, remains central to sociological debates on culture, representation and identity.

Review Questions

1. What are some of the desired goals of social control?
2. What is Rousseau's contract and how does it link to the idea of social control?
3. What do Shaw and McKay mean by 'rapid urbanisation'? What are the social consequences?
4. For Foucault, what underscores and precedes social control?
5. What are Hirschi's four aspects of social control which prevent deviant behaviour?

GO FURTHER

Books

1. The following text provides an alternative and comprehensive introduction overview of social control:

   Chriss, J. J. (2012) *Social Control: An Introduction*. Cambridge: Polity Press.

2. This second text has been a highly influencial critical text on modernity and social control and underpins much contemporary work on the topic:

   Foucault, M. (1975) *Discipline and Punish: The Birth of the Prison*. London: Penguin Books.

3. Matza's text is a key reading in criminology, as it provides both a critique of classical social control theory and a more appreciative theory of juvenile offending:

   Matza, D. (1964) *Delinquency and Drift*, London: John Wiley and Sons.

Journal Articles

1. The following article gives an overview of Hirschi's influential but much critiqued general theory:

   Costello, B. J. and Laub, J. H. (2020) Social Control Theory: the legacy of Travis Hirschi's Causes of Delinquency. *Annual Review of Criminology*, 3: 21–41.

2. Toby's article is a classic in the social disorganisation literature and highly influential:

   Toby, J. (1957) Social disorganization and stake in conformity: complementary factors in the predatory behavior of hoodlums. *Journal of Criminal Law, Criminology, and Police Science*, 48: 12–17.

3. Wickes and Hipp provide a sophisticated contemporary take on neighbourhood dynamics summing up current work in this field:

   Wickes, R. and Hipp, J. R. (2018) The spatial and temporal dynamics of neighborhood informal social control and crime. *Social Forces*, 97: 277–308.

Useful Websites

1. The following website, Oxford Biographies, provides you with an overview of social control: https://www.oxfordbibliographies.com/view/document/obo-9780195396607/obo-9780195396607-0091.xml
2. Revise Sociology provides you with a short plain language introduction to social control: https://revisesociology.com/2020/03/18/what-is-social-control/
3. The Other Sociologist provides you with an understanding of how disobedience to social control can actually be pro-social: https://othersociologist.com/2013/12/08/nelson-mandela-moral-disobedience/

REFERENCES

Akers, R. and Sellers, C. (2004) *Criminological Theories: Introduction, Evaluation, and Application*. Los Angeles, CA: Roxbury Publishing Company.

Appelrouth, S. and Edles, L. D. (2007) *Classical and Contemporary Sociological Theory: Text and Readings*. Thousand Oaks, CA: Pine Forge Press.

Bauman, Z. (2000) *Liquid Modernity*. Cambridge: Polity Press.

Beccaria, C. (1872) *On Crimes and Punishments*. Albany: W. C. Little & Co.

Box, S. (1970) Book review: Becoming Deviant. *Sociology*, 4(3): 403–404.

Bursik, R. (1988) Social disorganization and theories of crime and delinquency: problems and prospects. *Criminology*, 26: 519–552.

Bursik, R. J. and Grasmick, H. G. (1993) Economic deprivation and neighborhood crime rates, 1960–1980. *Law and Society Review*, 27.

Chriss, J. J. (2012) *Social Control: An Introduction*. Cambridge: Polity Press.

Collins, R. (1990) Review: Getting Sociology Under Control. *Contemporary Sociology*, 19(5): 649–652.

Cooley, C. H. (1902) *Human Nature and the Social Order*. New York: Charles Scribner's Sons.

Conger, R. (1976) Social control and social learning models of delinquency: a synthesis. *Criminology*, 14(1): 17–40.

Costello, B. J. and Laub, J. H. (2020) Social Control Theory: the legacy of Travis Hirschi's Causes of Delinquency. *Annual Review of Criminology*, 3: 21–41.

Dahl, R. (1957) The concept of power. *Behavioral Science*, 2: 201–215.

Downes, D. and Rock, P. (2011) *Understanding Deviance*. Oxford: Oxford University Press.

Durkheim, É. (1951) *Suicide: A Study in Sociology*. New York: Free Press.

Durkheim, É. (1961) *Moral Education*. New York: Free Press.

Durkheim, É. (1964) *The Rules of Sociological Method*. New York: Free Press.

Durkheim, É. (1983) *The Division of Labor in Society*, London: Free Press.

Foucault, M. (1975) *Discipline and Punish: The Birth of the Prison*, London: Penguin Books.

Foucault, M. (1980) *Power/Knowledge: Selected Interviews and Other Writings*. Brighton: The Harvester Press.

Foucault, M. (1982) The subject and power. *Critical Inquiry*, 8: 777–795.

Foucault, M. (1991) 'Governmentality'. In G. Burchell, C. Gordon and P. Miller (eds), *The Foucault Effect: Studies in Governmentality* (pp. 87–104). Chicago: University of Chicago Press.

Gibbs, J. (1989) *Control: Sociology's Central Notion*. Chicago: University of Illinois Press.

Gottfredson, M. R. and Hirschi, T. (1990) *A General Theory of Crime*. Redwood City, CA: Stanford University Press.

Hirschi, T. (1969) *Causes of Delinquency*. Berkeley: University of California Press.

Hobbes, T. (2008) *The Elements of Law Natural and Politic*. Oxford University Press, Oxford.

Hobbes, T. (2011) *Leviathan: Parts I and II*. Peterborough, ON: Broadview.

Holland, G. and Skinner B. F. (1961) *The Analysis of Behaviour (The Autoinstructing Program)*. New York: McGraw-Hill.

Lindzey, G. (ed.) (1954) *Handbook of Social Psychology. I. Theory and method. II. Special fields and applications* (2 vols). Boston, MA: Addison-Wesley Publishing Co.

Luhmann, N. (1982) 'Durkheim on Morality and the Division of Labor'. In N. Luhmann (ed.), *The Differentiation of Society* (pp. 3–19). New York: Columbia University Press.

Marx, K. (1975 [1844]) 'Contribution to the Critique of Hegel's Philosophy of Law: Introduction'. In *Karl Marx and Frederick Engels Collected Works*, vol. 3 (pp. 175–187). London: Lawrence & Wishart.

Matza, D. (1964) *Delinquency and Drift*. London: John Wiley and Sons.

Meier, R. F. (1982) Perspectives on the concept of social control. *Annual Review of Sociology*, 8: 35–55.

O'Neill, J. (1986) The disciplinary society: from Weber to Foucault. *British Journal of Sociology*, 37: 42–60.

Poggi, G. (2000) *Durkheim*. New York: Oxford University Press.

Reiss, A. (1951) Delinquency as the failure of personal and social controls. *American Sociological Review*, 16: 196.

Reiss, A. and Tonry, M. (1986) *Communities and Crime: Volume 8, Crime and Justice: An annual review of research*. Chicago: University of Chicago Press.

Rose, N. (1999) *Powers of Freedom: Reframing Political Thought*. Cambridge: Cambridge University Press.

Ross, E. (2009[1901]) *Social Control: A Survey of the Foundations of Order*. London: Transaction Publishers.

Rousseau, J. J. (2003/1762) *On the Social Contract*, translated by G. D. H. Cole. Mineola, NY: Dover.

Sampson, R. J. (1992) Review work: a general theory of crime. *Social Forces*, 71(2): 545–546.

Sampson, R. J. (2001) 'Crime and Public Safety: Insights from Community-Level Perspectives on Social Capital'. In S. Saegert, P. Thompson and M. R. Warren (eds), *Social Capital and Poor Communities* (pp. 89–114). New York: Russell Sage Foundation.

Sampson, R. J. and Laub, J. H. (1993) *Crime in the Making: Pathways and Turning Points through Life*. Cambridge, MA: Harvard University Press.

Shaw, C. and McKay, H. (1942) *Juvenile Delinquency and Urban Areas*. Chicago: University of Chicago Press.

Siegel, L. J. and McCormick, C. (2006) *Criminology in Canada: Theories, Patterns, and Typologies*, 3rd edition. Washington, DC: Thompson.

Simmel, G. (1955) *Conflict: Web of Group-Affiliations*. New York: Free Press.

Simmel, G. (1997) 'Metropolis and Mental Life'. In D. Frisby and M. Featherstone (eds), *Simmel on Culture: Selected Writings* (pp. 174–186). London: Sage Publications.

Small, A. W. and Vincent, G. E. (1894) *Study of Society*. American Book Company: New York.

Snodgrass, J. (1976) Clifford R. Shaw and Henry D. McKay: Chicago criminologists. *British Journal of Criminology* 16: 1–19.

Swartz, D. (1997) *Culture and Power: The Sociology of Pierre Bourdieu*. Chicago: University of Chicago Press.

Taylor, I., Walton, P. and Young, J. (1973) *The New Criminology: For a Social Theory of Deviance*. London: Routledge.

Toby, J. (1957) Social disorganization and stake in conformity: complementary factors in the predatory behavior of hoodlums. *Journal of Criminal Law, Criminology, and Police Science*, 48: 12–17.

Weber, M. (1992/1904–05) *The Protestant Ethic and the Spirit of Capitalism*, translated by T. Parsons, intro by A. Giddens. London: Routledge.

Whyte, W. F. (1943) Social organization in the slums. *American Sociological Review*, 8(1): 34–39.

Wickes, R. and Hipp, J. R. (2018) The spatial and temporal dynamics of neighborhood informal social control and crime. *Social Forces*, 97: 277–308.

Models of Justice 22

Natasha Mulvihill and
Marianne Hester

Learning Objectives

By the end of this chapter you will:

- Be able to identify various models of justice: their characteristics, similarities and differences.
- Recognise that 'justice' for victims can mean different things to different individuals in different contexts.
- Understand specifically how 'justice' may be perceived, sought and experienced by victim-survivors of gender-based violence.
- Consider how knowledge about 'justice' is produced through criminological research.

Framing Questions

1. What individual and social factors do you think may affect how victims of crime and harm perceive, seek and experience justice?
2. As criminologists, we are often focused on the criminal justice system, but how else might victims seek and find 'justice'?
3. How do we know what 'justice' means to victims?

INTRODUCTION

This chapter considers models of justice: their characteristics, similarities and differences. In doing so we draw on the findings of a 30-month research project that explored different models of justice, with a view specifically to understanding how victims of **gender-based violence** (GBV) perceive, seek and experience 'justice'. As well as thinking about what 'justice' for victims means, we also want to encourage you to think about 'how we know what we know' about justice (or anything else for that matter). This is important in encouraging you to approach what you read in criminology critically. We start the chapter by introducing some context to issues of justice and GBV, exploring current definitions of both, and the development of policy approaches in England and Wales to justice for victim-survivors. The so-called **'justice gap'** (see for example Kelly et al., 2005), where victims of GBV often feel mistrustful or dissatisfied with the criminal justice system, is highlighted. We then briefly explain how we identified the models of justice outlined in this chapter (and how, through that searching process, we noted that academic knowledge is always incomplete and indeed may reflect and reinforce particular biases). After outlining the different models, we consider their relevance in light of interview excerpts with victims and survivors of GBV. Overall, the chapter highlights the shortcomings of, and opportunities to improve, our current systems of delivering 'justice' to victims and survivors of GBV.

MAPPING THE TERRAIN

What is 'justice' for victims? For some it relates to the atonement of wrongs and harms caused (McCann, 2016: 113). It is a concept we associate with diverse themes including 'fairness, human rights, just deserts, [...] punishment, moral worth, personal liberty, social obligation and public protection' (Drake et al., 2009: 3). Yet some of these ideas contradict one another: for example, a victim's desire for justice as capital punishment could be said to undermine an offender's human rights. Standpoint is also important: a victim, a family member, an offender, a politician, an academic, or a member of the public, may all have different perceptions of what justice for victims means. Perceptions of justice will also depend on the crime or harm that occurred and the context in which it takes place: for example, a violent and unprovoked attack against a member of the public by an individual experiencing psychosis may lead to calls for a review of mental health care, as well as compensation for the victim and secure treatment of – or better care for – the 'perpetrator'. In other words, while as criminologists we commonly understand justice in terms of 'criminal justice', personal, social, economic, ethical and welfare considerations and needs are also important. Moreover, 'the varieties of justice available to victims [are] politically and culturally diverse' (McCann, 2016: 114) across time and space. For the purpose of this chapter, we take 'justice' broadly to refer to a favoured outcome, remedy or consequence following an incidence of harm.

As noted above, in this chapter, we are interested in exploring specifically what justice means from the perspective of victims of gender-based violence. We use the United Nations' (UN) definition of GBV as primarily 'violence that is directed against a woman because she is a woman or that affects women disproportionately' (United Nations, 1992: General Recommendation, 19(6)). We also recognise GBV as a form of violence rooted in power imbalances and inequality throughout society (see for example Article 3 of the Council of Europe 'Istanbul' Convention, 2011). While we recognise that violence and abuse may be experienced by men and by those under 18, our working definition for the purpose of this chapter includes domestic, sexual and 'honour'-based violence and abuse (including forced marriage) and applies to women of any sexual orientation and adults aged 18 or over. We also include here violence between family members (e.g. from son to mother or mother-in-law to daughter-in-law), abuse mediated through the internet or mobile phones, and stalking and harassment.

Knowledge link: These topics are also covered in Chapter 8 and Chapter 20.

Partly in response to the work of campaigners, researchers, victims and survivors, recent decades have seen an expansion in the use of criminal and civil justice systems to address gender-based violence. In England and Wales, there have been significant reforms to the instruments of justice. These include the advent of new civil measures, such as forced marriage protection orders (the Forced Marriage (Civil Protection) Act 2007), and new criminal statutes, including the criminalisation of repeated or continuous coercive or controlling behaviour perpetrated against an intimate partner or family member (Serious Crime Act 2015). There has also been a policy shift in recognising the needs of victims within the justice process, including the introduction of specialist domestic violence courts, the offer of special measures within the criminal court for victims providing testimony, and the establishment of dedicated and trained units within police forces to deal with, for example, domestic abuse or sexual crimes.

Yet there continues to be gaps:

- First, many victim-survivors of GBV fail to obtain criminal justice. This is evidenced, for example, by significant under-reporting and a high attrition rate of reported domestic abuse and rape cases within the criminal justice system (Hester, 2006; Hohl and Stanko, 2016) or dissatisfaction with the police response when victims do report (Mulvihill et al., 2018).
- Second, there are gaps in understanding how different social identities and inequalities relate to experiences of justice. How, for example, is the experience of reporting to police different for victims of domestic abuse in a same-sex relationship compared to a heterosexual relationship? What is the experience of seeking justice for rape if you have learning difficulties? What are the barriers to justice for a young British woman forced to marry abroad? Are the justice needs of victims of domestic abuse different where the perpetrator is also the father of the victim's children, or are they the same as for victims without children?
- Finally, there are gaps in understanding what 'justice' actually means to victim-survivors of GBV. Such understandings may reach beyond the prevailing formal systems of justice and include restorative justice processes or religious tribunals or more practical responses. From such perspectives, withdrawing from the criminal justice system process, for example, could indicate positive, self-protective choices by victim-survivors who recognise the type of 'justice' on offer is not what, or how, they want (Hester, 2006). It may simultaneously reflect the failures of, and harm incurred by, the prevailing criminal and civil justice systems, and raises the question of what alternatives are available.

Pause for Thought

- Can you think what justice might mean for victims of gender-based violence and the different forms it might take?
- What would the systems that deliver these different forms of justice look like?

To summarise, we have suggested in this opening section that the concept of justice for victims is complex and contested and that the available formal systems for providing 'justice' – the police, the civil and criminal courts, the prison and probation system – can be difficult to access, difficult to navigate, and may not provide 'justice', as appreciated by victims of crime and harm.

In the next section, we will explain how we identified different models of justice from reviewing the work of other scholars. We want to mention this process because it is important in your studies that you consider critically how knowledge is constructed and recognise how criminologists are always building on the work of others. We will then describe the models of justice we identified and consider their characteristics, similarities and differences. Using excerpts from interviews that were carried out with victims and survivors of GBV, we will consider briefly how far these 'theoretical' models of justice can be used to make sense of individual experiences. Finally, we will pull together what we have learnt and consider how this work challenges our understanding of what 'justice' means, how it is sought and experienced by victims, and what questions this raises about the efficacy and appropriateness of the criminal justice system.

Finding Out What 'Justice' Means

When criminologists start researching a topic, they first need to review what is already known and they do that by conducting a '**literature review**'. A literature review requires entering particular search terms and setting other parameters (e.g. identifying dates of publication, format of publication, language etc.) into different online library databases. The researchers then sift through the published work to see what might be relevant to their study. They are interested mainly in academic or other 'reputable' work – so this encompasses peer-reviewed journal articles (where articles are reviewed 'blind' by other experts in the field), academic books and often, for example, research reports by governmental or expert non-governmental organisations.

As expected, the number of items returned through our literature searches was high at over 38,000 results! A team of four researchers spent a considerable amount of time sifting through all this work to decide what was relevant, identifying a final set of about 1,400 items and then categorising each of these publications under different criteria, e.g. date, format of publication, GBV focus, country where research took place, and so on. We also identified what type of justice was being discussed in each publication and this is how we built up the 'models of justice' discussed below.

Before we go on to describe the models, we want to briefly share what we learnt through this exercise of searching for literature. Once we had categorised and mapped out the final set of literature that we identified as relevant, we noticed it had particular characteristics. Here are a few:

- Research conducted within the United States of America (USA) accounted for around half of the literature. Over half of the South Asia category consisted of items relating to India. Few papers related to Africa or Latin America.
- Two thirds of the literature identified were either conceptual/discussion pieces or took a qualitative approach, most often interviews. The majority of the quantitative studies were carried out in the USA and Canada and this work in turn generally focused on domestic abuse.
- Each publication was categorised by principal focus in terms of type of GBV. The vast majority concerned domestic violence and abuse. Sexual violence and abuse accounted for a significant portion of the remaining literature.
- The majority of the literature concentrated on the criminal justice system. Around 8% of publications focusing equally on criminal and civil measures and 3% on restorative approaches (restorative justice is explained further below).

These observations are important in thinking about how knowledge, including criminological knowledge, is often partial. We note how the academic knowledge which gets published in English (the dominant language of publication and at conferences for academics globally) emerges predominantly from Western countries; how issues such as 'honour' abuse and violence, female genital mutilation (FGM) or institutional abuse receive less coverage; and how literature on the criminal justice system dominates discussions of 'justice'.

Models of justice

In this section, we set out the different models of justice which we identified from our final set of literature. Remember that we were interested in understanding the wide landscape of knowledge around 'justice', beyond the formal systems of criminal and civil justice. Here, we briefly evaluate their presentation within the literature. We consider also how we can make sense of these types of justice individually, collectively, and in relation to their value in articulating the justice experiences and perceptions of victim-survivors of gender-based violence.

Table 22.1 Models of Justice Identified

Community justice

Cultural context model

Economic/financial/distributive justice

Effective/affective justice

Egalitarian justice

Feminist jurisprudence/feminist legal thinking

Gender justice

Human rights/Women's rights

Interactional justice

Neo-liberal justice

Parallel justice

Peacemaking

Problem-solving justice

Procedural justice

Restorative justice

Social justice

Therapeutic jurisprudence/therapeutic justice

Transformative justice and participatory jurisprudence

Victims' rights

Community justice

The meaning of 'community justice' within the thirty-four papers identified in this category was diverse. First, it included items which referred to community-based justice initiatives and included discussion on the strengths and limitations of such mechanisms (e.g. sex offender notifications; see Presser and Gunnison, 1999). Second, it referred to arguments that gender-based violence should be treated as a community responsibility, requiring community accountability, and not as an individualised crime. Third, it included work exploring the informal community justice mechanisms or responses within particular minority communities or how minority communities mediate with the formal justice sector. There is clearly some philosophical overlap with the literature on restorative approaches (see below). However, we decided to be led by the terms that authors used – in this case 'community justice' – rather than as researchers impose our own.

Cultural context model

Proposed by Almeida and Lockard (2005) as a model of accountability and empowerment to respond to domestic abuse, the Cultural Context Model (CCM) is rooted in principles of universal human rights and practices that foster a critical consciousness. CCM explicitly challenges patriarchy and racism by placing social justice principles at the centre of domestic abuse interventions. Lichtenstein (2009) proposes CCM as a possible route to addressing the barriers faced by older African American women to reporting domestic abuse to law enforcement in the rural 'deep south' of America. These barriers include a distrust of police stemming in part from the history of racial oppression in the United States and that Black African American women have been accused of betrayal for reporting Black African men.

Distributive, economic or financial justice

Distributive justice is concerned with a socially just allocation of goods and resources. So, for example, this covers the access for victim-survivors of domestic abuse to social housing. Economic and financial justice approaches include, for example, recognition of economic loss (housing, job, credit status, standing in community, confidence) inflicted by the experience of GBV, and the specific tactics of financial control used by abusers.

Effective justice and affective justice

Effective justice is concerned with the technical, procedural and rational features of the justice system. Affective justice is the sense or feeling that justice has been done: it is concerned with the individual and the collective emotional resonance of crime. Brownlie (2003) considers how social anxieties about sexual crimes, where the victims or perpetrators are young people, require a justice response which responds to both the effective and affective dimensions.

Egalitarian model

Song (2007: 9) considers the tension between liberal democracies espousing equal treatment through cultural blindness, and the extent to which 'justice requires special accommodations for cultural minorities under certain circumstances'. She argues that an egalitarian model of justice requires some level of accommodation. The place of 'culture' has been a thorny issue in the development of a justice response to so-called 'honour'-based violence and FGM. For decades, such practices were seen as 'cultural' and therefore justice interventions were deemed unnecessary or complicated to apply. The arguments in Song's paper remind us that the social identities of victims – in terms of, for example, ethnicity, faith and immigration status – may affect both the victim's perceptions and experiences of justice and society's (mis)perceptions of what justice means to individuals who belong to one group or another.

Feminist jurisprudence

Feminist jurisprudence is a philosophy of law based on the political, economic, and social equality of sexes. It starts from the premise that the law has been fundamental to women's historic subordination and is focused on law as both a theoretical enterprise as well as having practical and concrete effects in women's lives. Du Toit (2012), for example, expresses concern about the trend towards gender neutrality within the law, which she says undermines the sexual specificity of rape. Such feminist analysis is a useful means of visibilising the effects of patriarchy within the justice systems of liberal democracies. Too often, we may conceive of 'the law' as operating in a rarefied space, outside and above social power relations. Feminist approaches remind us that patriarchy is a consistent feature of all justice systems.

Knowledge link: This topic is also covered in Chapter 8.

Gender justice

Gender justice can be conceptualised as a human right, calling for every woman and girl being entitled to live in dignity and freedom and to also live without fear of violence, for example. The literature identified citing this model was notably international. A handful of papers focused on the experiences of women during wartime: Durbach and Chappell (2014) for example consider the case for victim reparations for sexual violence during conflict.

Human rights/Women's rights

A human rights-based approach to justice is about empowering people (or women and girls, in the case of 'women's rights') to know and claim their rights. It aims to increase the ability and accountability of individuals and institutions who are responsible for respecting, protecting and fulfilling rights (definition taken from the Scottish Human Rights Commission website, no date). Johnson (2001), for example, considers the formal response of the justice system to domestic violence in Russia, which tends to attribute responsibility to women or position such violence as a private affair. Johnson identifies a political tension concerning gender during the post-communist period around 'whether or not women should have the full rights of citizenship, especially the fundamental right to live free from bodily harm' (2001: 153).

Interactional justice

Interactional justice relates to the experience of justice. Laxminarayan (2012) identifies two parts: receiving adequate information about the justice process ('informational justice') and being treated during the justice process with dignity and respect ('interpersonal justice'). Laxminarayan's research suggests that vulnerable victims of domestic and sexual violence and abuse are experiencing secondary victimisation through interactional injustice. Secondary victimisation can arise during the initial response by police or during cross-examination in court.

Neo-liberal justice

Comack and Peter (2005) consider how the criminal justice system is implicated in broader socio-economic trends and specifically how the neo-liberal value of 'responsibilisation' plays out in sexual assault cases. Through a qualitative analysis of one survivor's story, the authors examine the implications of neo-liberal rationalities for women and child victims seeking justice for sexual violence. This approach could be usefully contrasted with feminist jurisprudence or gender justice above to explore the impact of individualising and de-gendering definitions and experiences of justice.

Parallel justice

The phrase 'parallel justice' is used sometimes within discussions of restorative justice systems, to describe a twin-track process, serving the different needs of victims and offenders and located at both the state and community level. However, the 'parallel justice' model identified within Minallah (2007) refers to resolution processes running outside the formal justice system. Such processes might be referred to as 'traditional' or 'indigenous' and have often evolved within communities over time. They may be seen as preferable where confidence in formal judicial processes is low – because it is seen as costly, time-consuming or undermining traditional power bases (such as the family or community elders), for example. Minallah discusses the impact of *jirgas* or *panchayats* in Pakistan where rape claims have been resolved not by monetary payments, but by pledging in marriage young female relatives of the accused to male members of the victim's family. This justice approach conflicts with the women's rights and gender justice models identified above.

Peacemaking

The peacemaking approach to gender violence is described by Donna Coker (2005), drawing on her work with the Navajo community in the United States. Coker suggests that peacemaking processes may be appropriate for some women who have experienced domestic abuse, but only if those processes meet five criteria. These are: prioritising victim safety over the perpetrator's rehabilitation; offering material as well as social support for victims; working as part of a coordinated community response; challenging gender domination more broadly (as well as how it manifests through violence); and *not* making forgiveness a goal of the process (Coker, 2005). Coker also explores the differences between the Navajo peacemaking model and other so-called 'indigenous' justice systems, a useful reminder of the diversity within this group.

Problem-solving

Originating in the United States and organised around particular themes, such as domestic abuse, drugs or mental health, problem-solving courts are an innovation within the criminal justice system where offenders are tasked with a package of court-supervised measures to address the underlying causes of their behaviour. Castellano (2011) expresses cautious optimism for the development of problem-solving mechanisms but calls for more research into how victims and their families subjectively experience these courts, and how the theory underpinning problem-solving is practically translated into a justice which is acceptable to victims.

Procedural justice

Procedural justice is concerned with the fairness and transparency of the justice process and how decisions are made. It is not focused on outcomes of justice in the same way as, for example, distributive or retributive justice (which focuses on punishing the offender). For example, Hickman and Simpson (2003) explored whether victims of domestic abuse are more likely to re-report if they viewed their previous experience with police as either procedurally fair or achieving their preferred outcome. Notably, while both factors were deemed important, the previous arrest of the offender in accordance with victim preference was a significant predictor of willingness to report again.

Restorative justice

Restorative justice often includes the victim and offender meeting with a third party to talk about the offence or incident, recognising accountability and identifying opportunities for repairing the harm done. A key preoccupation within the current literature is the appropriateness of restorative justice interventions in the context of domestic abuse. There is a concern about the unequal footing of the victim and perpetrator where, for example, there is a history of coercive control which can lead to silencing, acquiescence and fear among victims. However, other work points to the empowering potential of restorative justice for some GBV victim-survivors (see for example McGlynn et al., 2012).

Social justice

Social justice is a broad term based on the concepts of human rights and equality and, in this context, would be concerned with combatting gender discrimination and oppression and securing rights and freedoms for women and men. First (2006), for example, draws on the testimonies of thirteen women survivors of incest to document their route to empowerment by becoming social justice activists. This is a useful reminder of how victim-survivors can seek a broader justice outside the confines of formal court processes and indeed of their own experience. In the Justice, Inequality and Gender-Based Violence project that this work forms a part of, activism and volunteering was an important route to justice articulated in a number of the interviews that we conducted with victim-survivors (see below).

Therapeutic justice or jurisprudence

Therapeutic justice or jurisprudence is a relatively new field. It considers how the law and justice systems can be curative or healing (however defined) for those who engage with its institutions and processes. Of interest here, the approach is concerned with the impact on the emotions, behaviours and mental health of victim-survivors, among others. For example, Wright and Johnson (2012) in the USA explored the efficacy of civil protection orders against domestic abuse perpetrators in alleviating the levels of trauma experienced by victim-survivors. You can see some overlap here with the procedural, interactional and problem-solving models outlined above.

Transformative justice

Transformative justice identifies oppression at the root of all forms of harm, abuse and assault and therefore aims to address and confront those oppressions on all levels. Participatory jurisprudence (Marchetti and Daly, 2007) is a related and radical approach that goes beyond the principles found in restorative justice and therapeutic jurisprudence, to ensure that those involved in court processes are allowed to communicate and participate in a way that inculcates real ownership and engagement. Again, there is commonality with other models discussed here, including social justice and community justice.

Victims' rights

Victims' rights are legal rights afforded to victims of crime. We also include here victim-focused measures. These might include, for example, the right to speak at justice proceedings or the right to give evidence using special measures because of the fear of intimidation. The rights of victims have gained political attention in the UK recently, with the establishment of the Victims' Commissioner in 2013 and updates to the Victims' Code in 2015 to comply with the *European Union Victims' Directive* (see ch. 41 in this volume). Langevin (2010) assesses the effectiveness of the Québec Crime Victims Compensation Act which currently compensates women and children who are victims of sexual violence in the family, although it did not do so at its inception in 1972. The author argues that the time limit for filing a claim for compensation can be hard to meet for victims of familial abuse (given how long it can take victim-survivors to recognise and then feel able to report, particularly if their abuser is still alive and a close family member) and calls for legislative reform. Indeed, the law was changed by the Assemblée Nationale Du Quebec in 2013.

Visual Mapping of the Models of Justice

One way of drawing out the similarities and differences between the theoretical models identified within this set of literature is to consider their respective focus on the victim, the perpetrator and the process aspects of justice (see Figure 22.1). We find that the models identified are concerned overwhelmingly with recognising, empowering or restoring the victim (see the central blue box in Figure 22.1). Less often, models are focused mainly on the perpetrator or mainly on the process of administering and experiencing justice. A number are focused on areas between on the victim and perpetrator *or* on the victim and the justice process (see the blue boxes in Figure 22.1).

Identifying these models of justice informed our research project in a number of ways. We recognised that there are emerging and alternative spaces to 'do justice' for victim-survivors of GBV. There are spaces which engage the wider community (including peacemaking, community justice or restorative justice, for example) or which attend to the practical and emotional impact and outcomes of justice (economic/financial/distributive models, therapeutic justice and interactional justice, for example). We saw more clearly how individuals (and society) may have different and sometimes conflicting expectations from the justice process and how social inequalities may limit the possibilities for justice in different ways. As we shall see below in the discussion of our interviews with victim-survivors of GBV, and as acknowledged above in our discussion on literature searches, these theoretical models are not the final word on justice. But they did provide us with an expansive vocabulary and an indication of the range of issues that need to be considered.

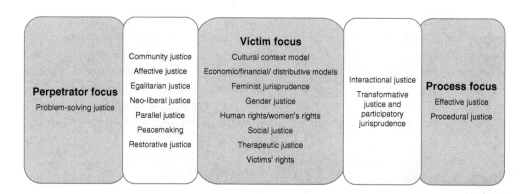

Figure 22.1 Theoretical Models of Justice Organised by Focus on Perpetrator, Victim or Process

---

Pause for Thought

So now we know what the academic literature says about the types of justice sought and experienced by victims of gender-based violence. What should we do next?

The Views of Victims and Survivors

In *Finding out what 'justice' means* above, we noted that the literature on justice that we had found had particular characteristics. We saw that research conducted in the United States dominates English language output; that just over half of the final literature set related to domestic abuse and around a quarter focused on sexual violence and abuse. Around 60% of the literature focused on the criminal justice system, followed to a much lesser extent by civil remedies and an emerging literature on restorative justice.

On a closer reading of our final literature set, we found a further characteristic: only 20 to 25% of the research identified documented the experiences and understandings of justice *as articulated by victim-survivors of GBV themselves*. In the main, the meaning of 'justice' was either conceptualised in the abstract or mediated through different indicators selected by authors. While it is of course the role of criminologists to theorise social life, as feminist researchers, we are also keen in our work to elicit the experiential knowledge of justice from victim-survivors of GBV *in their own words*. This is both to develop the existing academic knowledge base and to inform policy and practice going forward.

Informed in part by the models of justice that we identified in the literature, but also through discussion with a panel of victims and practitioners that we convened to inform this early stage of our research project, we developed a set of questions and a list of participant characteristics and experiences that it was important to collect. These question schedules asked victims and survivors how they perceived, sought and experienced justice in relation to: criminal, civil, family court, restorative justice; mediation and arbitration; informal justice, including family and community processes, revenge; political activism and volunteering; and so on. We went on to conduct 251 interviews with victims of GBV and the case study below provides a selection of quotes from those data.

Case Study 22.1

Victims and Survivors' Views of Justice

"I know [it] seems really odd but I didn't really care what happened to him [...] I honestly did not care. If they'd sent him to prison or whatever, it was irrelevant to me. I didn't even go to the sentencing hearing, couldn't ... I wanted to know that he was ... the only part I wanted to know was: was he allowed anywhere near me?" (Participant A)

"He didn't get justice legally, he didn't get a criminal record, he didn't get arrested for what he did, I don't know what would have happened if I had called the police, I don't know whether they

(Continued)

would have taken him away or whether they would have just given him a warning, I don't know. But my sense of justice is that I'm free from him, and that sense of freedom, it's just priceless, priceless." (Participant B)

"He doesn't accept that there's anything wrong – and that isn't justice to me. Justice would have been a realisation on his part that what he did was utterly dreadful and the impact it had was utterly dreadful – that would be justice to me. You know that he'd get in touch with me and he'd sort of say, 'I've realised, I know now'." (Participant C)

"I don't know, I think justice would be if my husband realised what he has done and he realises what he has lost. I think that would be my justice … and to tell you the truth I am not concerned about justice, I am more concerned about the justice we get after we die… so with our God and everything." (Participant D)

"Now, if anything, actually, I'm more calm about it and don't really feel like I need personal justice in my own case. It makes me sad and upset, and angry that these things happen so frequently, but I feel like we need to fix it on a systems level. I feel like, often, the types of people that do these things have a lot of other things going on in their lives, or have had a lot of other things going on in their lives growing up. That actually, we need to fix the systems that cause these problems, rather than necessarily punish individuals." (Participant E)

The interview excerpts demonstrate the importance for victim-survivors of the *affective* dimensions of justice ('affective', as explained above, relates to feelings and emotions). Two themes recur here and across the wider interview data: first, justice as safety, specifically the removal of the perpetrator; and second, justice as reflective accountability, with the perpetrator understanding the gravity and impact of their behaviour. In terms of the first issue, having the perpetrator 'out of my life, *forever'*, is crucial to many victims because without that assurance, they cannot restore their lives emotionally or practically. Victims spoke of *in*justice where their perpetrator breached a restraining order without sanction, or where the perpetrator was parent to the victim's children and was granted regular access by the courts. Second, an issue for some victim-survivors was a desire to see in their perpetrators' eyes a genuine recognition of the harm they had caused. Such displays of accountability are not required to serve criminal justice (accountability is linked to admission of guilt and conviction) although the use of victim impact statements can ensure the perpetrator hears, if does not respond to, the harm caused. *Restorative justice, peacemaking* and *problem-solving courts* may offer spaces for such victim-perpetrator encounters, although these must be skilfully managed.

Participant E seems to be arguing that at root *social justice* or *transformative justice* is what is needed to prevent future GBV. It is interesting how this participant separates their own justice needs from the wider justice needs of past and future potential victims. It appears that for them, distance of time has made this possible. Current justice systems are strongly focused on individuals and events. Yet it may be that more holistic mechanisms – akin perhaps to the public inquiry, panel or case review – are needed to review broader issues of policy, statutory and professional practice, and to bring about change. Indeed, a common refrain from victim-survivors is "I don't want anyone to experience what I did." Justice for them is preventing future harm to others.

The interviews with victim-survivors also introduced new elements. Participant D, for example, talks of divine justice being her key concern. Other interviewees identified justice as the 'outing' of perpetrators to friends and family, particularly where perpetrators had crafted a charming and respectable public persona. Outing to colleagues and employers was important where the perpetrator was a professional, including where they had abused a position of trust.

CHAPTER SUMMARY

- The aim of this chapter was to identify and explore different models of 'justice' and specifically to understand how 'justice' may be perceived, sought and experienced by victim-survivors of gender-based violence.
- We conclude that 'justice' requires consideration of needs (emotional and practical), rights and inequalities at the individual and social level, the impact of culture and local norms, and both the process *and* outcomes of justice systems.
- We also considered how knowledge about 'justice' is produced through criminological research. In reviewing the existing literature, we found that too often researchers interpret the perceptions and understandings of victim-survivors (in this case, in relation to 'justice'), without attempting to elicit or directly facilitate their voices. This was the aim of our research.
- We noted the dominance of Western research within the 'justice' literature and we acknowledge our reinforcement of that bias by excluding from our literature searches work that was not published in the English language.
- Both cultural bias and the tendency to speak for, rather than to facilitate victim-survivor voices, mean that certain types of knowledge about 'justice' may be missed.
- As students and researchers of criminology, we should be mindful of the gaps and silences within academic knowledge and of the importance of connecting our work to those whose experience we seek to understand.

Review Questions

1. How would you define 'justice'?
2. Why do perceptions and experiences of 'justice' vary between individuals and groups who experience crime and harm and why does this matter?
3. How do we know what we know about 'justice'?
4. When researching crime, harm and justice, why is it important for criminologists to look beyond the criminal justice system?

GO FURTHER

Books

1. The following text provides a thoughtful and wide-ranging exploration of justice systems across the world:

    Drake, D., Muncie, J. and Westmarland, L. (eds) (2009) *Criminal Justice: Local and Global*. Cullompton: Willan Publishing, in association with the Open University.

2. This second text comprehensively explores Indigenous peoples' contact with criminal justice systems in a contemporary and historical context:

    Cunneen, C. and Tauri, J. (2017) *Indigenous Criminology*. Bristol: Policy Press.

3. Finally, Beth Richie's book demonstrates well how intersecting identities (in this case of race, economics and gender) can combine to create barriers to justice for victims of GBV:

    Richie, B. (2012) *Arrested Justice: Black Women, Violence, and America's Prison Nation*. New York: NYU Press.

Journal Articles

Below are some emerging findings from the Justice, Inequalities and Gender Based Violence Project. We recommend readers also select an article cited under the 'Models of Justice' heading above, and also in the reference list, to read in full:

1. Gangoli, G., Bates, L. and Hester, M. (2019) What does justice mean to black and minority ethnic (BME) victims/survivors of gender-based violence? *Journal of Ethnic and Migration Studies*. https://doi.org/10.1080/1369183X.2019.1650010
2. Walker, S-J., Hester, M., McPhee, D. and Patsios, D. (2019) Rape, inequality and the criminal justice response in England: the importance of age and gender. *Criminology and Criminal Justice*. https://doi.org/10.1177/1748895819863095

Useful Websites

1. Further resources and writing on transformative justice can be found at: https://transformharm.org/
2. Rights of Women are a UK campaigning organisation, providing free legal advice and representation to women affected by violence: https://rightsofwomen.org.uk/
3. The Restorative Justice Council is a membership body for restorative practitioners and provides educative resources: https://restorativejustice.org.uk/

ACKNOWLEDGEMENTS

This chapter is evolved from an earlier working paper, Mulvihill, N., Walker, S. J., Gangoli, G. and Hester, M. (2018) *How is 'justice' understood, sought, and experienced by victim-survivors of gender-based violence? A review of the literature*. The authors would like to acknowledge also the work of Dr Andrea Matolcsi, Dr Lis Bates and Sarah-Jane Walker in coding the literature identified.

REFERENCES

Almeida, R. and Lockard, J. (2005) 'The Cultural Context Model: A New Paradigm for Accountability, Empowerment, and the Development of Critical Consciousness Against Domestic Violence'. In N. J. Sokoloff (ed.), *Domestic Violence at the Margins: Readings on Race, Class, Gender, and Culture* (pp. 301–320). New Brunswick, NJ: Rutgers University Press.

Brownlie, J. (2003) An unsolvable justice problem? punishing young people's sexual violence. *Journal of Law and Society* 30(4): 506–531.

Castellano, U. (2011) Problem-solving courts: theory and practice. *Sociology Compass*, 5(11): 957–967.

Cochrane Training (2018) *Cochrane Handbook for Systematic Reviews of Interventions*. [online] Cochrane Training. Available at: https://training.cochrane.org/handbook

Coker, D. (2005) Restorative justice, Navajo peacemaking and domestic violence. *Theoretical Criminology*, 10(1): 67–85.

Comack, E. and Peter, T. (2005) How the criminal justice system responds to sexual assault survivors: the slippage between 'responsibilization' and 'blaming the victim'. *Canadian Journal of Women and the Law*, 17(2): 283–309.

Council of Europe (2011) *Convention on preventing and combating violence against women and* domestic *violence* ('Istanbul Convention'). Available at: https://rm.coe.int/CoERMPublicCommonSearchServices/DisplayDCTMContent?documentId=090000168046031c (accessed 16 October 2017).

Drake, D., Muncie, J. and Westmarland, L. (eds.) (2009) *Criminal Justice: Local and Global*. Devon: Willan Publishing; Milton Keynes: Open University.

Durbach, A. and Chappell, L. (2014) Leaving behind the age of impunity: victims of gender violence and the promise of reparations. *International Feminist Journal of Politics*, 16(4): 543–562.

Du Toit, L. (2012) Sexual specificity, rape law reform and the feminist quest for justice. *South African Journal of Philosophy*, 31(3): 465–483.

First, J. A. (2006) 'Process of empowerment for 13 women incest survivors: Becoming social justice activists'. PhD thesis, Union Institute and University, USA.

Greer, C. and McLaughlin, E. (2012) 'This is not justice': Ian Tomlinson, institutional failure and the press politics of outrage. *British Journal of Criminology*, 52(2): 274–293.

Hester, M. (2006) Making it through the criminal justice system: attrition and domestic violence. *Social Policy and Society*, 5(1): 79–90.

Hickman, L. and Simpson, S. S. (2003) Fair treatment or preferred outcome: the impact of police behaviour on victim reports of domestic violence incidents. *Law and Society Review*, 37(3): 649–676.

Hirschel, D. (2010) The benefits of more 'victim-focused' coordinated community responses to intimate partner violence: A critique of 'The impact of victim-focused outreach on criminal legal system outcomes following police-reported intimate partner abuse', by DePrince A.P. and Belknap J. *Violence Against Women*, 18(8): 897–905; discussion 906–912.

Hohl, K. and Stanko, E. A. (2016) Complaints of rape and the criminal justice system: fresh evidence on the attrition problem in England and Wales. *European Journal of Criminology*, 12(3): 324–341.

Islamic Sharia Council (2010) Data downloaded from website accessed 16 October 2017. Available at: http://www.islamic-sharia.org/statistics/

Johnson, J. (2001) Privatizing pain: the problem of woman battery in Russia. *NWSA Journal*, 13(3): 153–168.

Kelly, L., Lovett, J. and Regan, L. (2005) *A gap or a chasm? Attrition in reported rape cases*. Home Office Research Study 293. London: Home Office Research, Development and Statistics Directorate.

Langevin, L. (2010) The Québec Crime Victims Compensation Act: when the clock is ticking against victims of intra-familial sexual abuse. *Canadian Journal of Women and the Law*, 22(2): 485–503.

Laxminayaran, M. (2012) Interactional justice, coping and the legal system: needs of vulnerable victims. *International Review of Victimology*, 19(2): 145–158.

Lichtenstein, B. (2009) Older African American Women and Barriers to Reporting Domestic Violence to Law Enforcement in the Rural Deep South. *Women & Criminal Justice* 19(4): 286–305.

Marchetti, E. and Daly, K. (2007) Indigenous sentencing courts: towards a theoretical and jurisprudential model. *Sydney Law Review*, 29: 416–443.

McCann, L. (2016) 'Justice and Victims'. In K. Corteen, S. Morley, P. Taylor and J. Turner (eds), *A Companion to Crime, Harm and Victimisation* (pp. 113–115). Bristol: Policy Press.

McGlynn, C., Westmarland, N. and Godden, N. (2012) 'I just wanted him to hear me': sexual violence and the possibilities of restorative justice. *Journal of Law and Society*, 39(2): 213–240.

Minallah, S. (2007) Judiciary as a catalyst for social change. *Pakistan Journal of Women's Studies*, 14(2): 119.

Mulvihill, N., Gangoli, G., Gill, A. and Hester, M. (2018) The experience of interactional justice for victims of 'honour'-based violence and abuse reporting to the police in England and Wales. *Policing and Society*, 29(6): 640–656.

Presser, L. and Gunnison, E. (1999) Strange bedfellows: Is sex offender notification a form of community justice? *Crime & Delinquency*, 45(3): 299–315.

Song, S. (2007) *Justice, Gender, and the Politics of Multiculturalism*. Cambridge: Cambridge University Press.

United Nations (1992) General Recommendation No. 19 (11th session), Violence Against Women, para 6. Available at: http://www.un.org/womenwatch/daw/cedaw/recommendations/recomm.htm (accessed 16 October 2017).

Williamson, E., Eisenstadt, N., Bates, L. and Hester, M. (forthcoming) *Action, Engagement, Remembering: Victims/Survivors of Gender Based Violence and Perspectives on Justice*. Available from: e.williamson@bristol.ac.uk

Wright, C. V. and Johnson, D. M. (2012) Encouraging legal help seeking for victims of intimate partner violence: the therapeutic effects of the civil protection order. *Journal of Traumatic Stress*, 25(6): 675–681.

Partnership and Multi-Agency Working

23

Tackling Domestic Abuse

Pamela Davies

Learning Objectives

By the end of this chapter you will:

- Understand the emergence, potential and persistence of multi-agency working to tackle crime and disorder all within the broader context of crime prevention and community safety.
- Be able to exemplify how, in the context of domestic abuse, multi-agency partnerships operate at local levels.
- Appreciate how innovative multi-agency approaches to tackle domestic abuse seek to prevent victimisation, tackle serial offending and support victims.
- Be able to outline the key challenges inherent in partnership and collaborative working in the specific context of policing domestic abuse.

Framing Questions

1. When and why did multi-agency working begin to characterise ways of tackling social and criminal justice problems?
2. What are the key characteristics that constitute multi-agency working?
3. What common features often hamper effective multi-agency working practice?
4. How are partnership and collaborative approaches to tackling domestic abuse adapting to prevent abuse, tackle serial perpetrators and support victims?

INTRODUCTION

Partnership, collaborative and **multi-agency** working has become a key feature in strategies to tackle crime. Multi-agency strategies and working practices are evident in various sizes, shapes and forms and their reach can extend across continents, national boundaries and regional areas. They also operate at local levels. Indeed, as will be argued in this chapter, it is perhaps the local that matters most in any form of partnership working. The chapter begins by mapping the terrain of partnership and multi-agency working within the broader context of **community safety**. The focus is in the main on England and Wales though you will appreciate that global similarities exist in terms of the core concepts, principles, features and issues that are discussed. The historical commitment to partnership working in the context of community safety over the last three decades is well established and policing partnerships extend across a range of contexts (including corrections, parole, probation) to address a plethora of crime and disorder problems (e.g. child sexual abuse, fraud, organised crime, terrorism, racism). I will illustrate how this now holds true in the context of strategies to combat domestic abuse where multi-agency working has become integral to strategies to combat and 'police' (see below) this stubborn and too often fatal type of abuse. The case example used – the Multi-Agency Tasking and Co-ordination (MATAC) approach to tackling serial perpetrators of domestic abuse – originates at a local level, and serves to show you why local partnerships and collaborative working are central to effective crime prevention and reduction, perpetrator **responsibilisation** and victim support. The chapter then signals how the knowledge and lessons from the local are significant at national, international and global levels. First, we will start by looking at what we mean by community safety. We will trace the emergence of the community safety agenda in the 1980s in England and Wales and the growth of partnership working.

MAPPING THE TERRAIN: COMMUNITY SAFETY - PARTNERSHIPS AND MULTI-AGENCY WORKING

Knowledge link: This topic is also covered in Chapter 24.

As you will have gathered from several chapters in this volume, policing in the twenty-first century goes well beyond the public, police and what police do. The new **plural policing** model is a patch-work mix of **policing** provision. Non-public sector policing provision of policing activities includes marketised and private forms of policing, transnational forms of policing, and policing activities engaged in by citizens themselves (Loader, 2000). Thus, community safety today involves a much more tangled but potentially effective web of partners working together. Before I illustrate this, you should be aware of how community safety has been defined and what its aspirations originally were. Broadly defined community safety is:

> The strategy which seeks to move beyond a police-driven crime prevention agenda, to involve other agencies and generate greater participation from all sections of the 'community'. It has been particularly associated with local 'partnership' strategies of crime and disorder reduction from local authorities. However, it is a capacious phrase, which may also refer to strategies aimed at improving community safety from harms from all sources, not just those acts classifiable as 'crimes'. (Hughes 2006a: 54)

An earlier explanation of community safety, which is widely cited, originates from the Local Government Management Board (LGMB) in 1996. The LGMB described community safety as:

> the concept of community-based action to inhibit and remedy the causes and consequences of criminal, intimidatory and other related anti-social behaviour. Its purpose is to secure sustainable reductions in crime and fear of crime in local communities. Its approach is based on the formation of multi-agency partnerships between the public, private and voluntary sectors to formulate and introduce community-based measures against crime. (LGMB, 1996)

The aspirations of this new ideal were to be about 'rights, opportunities, enhancing "quality of life" and citizenship values ... recognising that crime and victimisation were the direct result of disadvantage, discrimination, social divisions and blocked opportunities' (Squires, 2006: 2). Both of the above definitions stress how crime prevention is a task for the whole community, that a central feature of community safety is partnership working and that the scope of community safety is potentially wide and nebulous. Throughout this chapter, all three of these features will be examined.

As Menichelli (2020) has recently noted, there is extensive literature on community safety. The same author considers what community safety has become and asks what community safety presently encompasses and what community safety partnerships do (Menichelli, 2020: 40). In the next section I will address similar questions under the provocative question 'Whose Community? Whose Agenda?' Before this, however, I will introduce the concept of community safety and outline the emergence of this agenda. The central features of partnership and multi-agency working are also considered. The promised critique of the community safety agenda that unfurled is then provided.

Let us look further then at the advent of community safety, and consider the key milestones that cemented the future of partnership and multi-agency working from the 1980s onwards. The creation of Neighbourhood Watch schemes (the first in 1982), the Five Towns Initiative (launched in 1986) and the Safer Cities Programme (launched in 1988) were forerunners in the shift to a community safety agenda and signalled the first criminal justice-focused partnerships. These developments were spurred on by Home Office Circular 8/84, which stipulated that crime prevention was the responsibility of the whole community. The Safer Communities Report – often referred to as the Morgan Report (Home Office 1991) – recognised the value of partnership working to address the causes of crime. Following the 1998 Crime and Disorder Act, Crime and Disorder Reduction Partnerships (CDRPs) were established to develop multi-agency working within the criminal justice system. Multi-agency crime prevention has been defined as:

> The planned, coordinated response of several social agencies to the problems of crime and incivilities. The movement to multi-agency intervention implies that prevention/corrections services, education, employment, family services, health and housing, and private bodies such as charities and 'business', and at times the 'community' as well as the police all have a role to play in crime prevention. (Hughes, 2006b: 253)

Partnership working is one of the key features that sits at the heart of an effective community safety strategy. The partnerships referred to above became responsible for delivering a local crime and disorder reduction strategy, and thus the new 'community safety' ethos was officially encoded in the new apparatus for tackling and preventing local crime and disorder (Home Office, 1991; Squires, 2006).

These developments saw funding allocated to local communities to tackle local crime problems, and the subsequent proliferation of burglary reduction schemes, the use of physical measures to target-harden and deter offending, and situational crime prevention. The 1990s thus expanded the repertoire of stakeholders in the policing project, increasing community responsibilities and multi-agency collaboration. Into the twenty-first century, Multi-Agency Safeguarding Hubs (MASH) to safeguard children and young people have brought key professionals together to facilitate earlier, and better quality, information sharing, analysis and decision making about how to intervene. In addition, the central plank of strategies to 'risk manage' dangerous offenders in England and Wales has been the use of 'multi-agency public protection arrangements' (MAPPAs). However, as further explained below, such strategies seek to prevent only one 'cluster' of violent or sexual behaviour and do little to tackle serial perpetrators of domestic abuse and protect women from the serious harm they do.

---------------------------- Pause for Thought ----------------------------

Can you identify what principles are at the heart of community safety partnerships?

Whose Community? Whose Agenda?

In 2006, fifteen years after the Morgan Report (mentioned above) was published, and which heralded in a new era of community safety as an alternative to crime prevention, Peter Squires, Professor of Criminology at the University of Brighton, published *Community Safety: Critical Perspectives on Policy and Practice*. A series of questions were the spur for this edited collection. These questions centred on the development, the working model and the achievements of community safety. Below, I have précised these questions into a series of provocative statements about the impact of community safety:

- Community safety policy making has been eclipsed by 'crime and disorder management'.
- Local community strategies may not be sufficient to address national/global criminogenic contexts.
- Community safety has become the new anti-social behaviour enforcement strategy, legitimising racist or xenophobic attitudes.
- The original community safety goals have been subverted by a new corporatist local policy making, prioritising economic regeneration over community values, quality of life and safety.
- The most common community safety investments, and the most money spent are on CCTV projects – illustrating the points above and the unequal weight attached to different community safety interests (see below).
- Not all sections of the population have been equal beneficiaries of community safety – some benefit more and at the expense of others:

  o *Community safety was intended to unearth the hidden and underreported patterns of* victimisation, *such as domestic violence, racial harassment and the victimisation of vulnerable groups*. In reality, relatively few new priorities had emerged. (Squires, 2006: 3–4)

These questions about whether or not the new landscape of community safety was achieving the ideals envisaged were apt when originally posed and remain so today. Since 2006, there has been a plethora of research, much of which has examined these very questions about (in)equality, justice, safety and vulnerability. The critique by Squires in 2006, has thus been extended, and one of the most vociferous sets of critiques concerns questions about whose safety has been privileged and whose has been ignored. We now explore this particular critique of community safety before drilling into efforts to address it.

Whose safety?

Like others (Walklate and Evans, 1999), I have questioned the extent to which an inclusive community safety paradigm has unfolded and have commented on the partiality of the dominant community safety paradigm (Davies, 2008). Community safety has the potential to embrace a wide range of anti-social experiences in its remit. However, by concentrating rather too exclusively upon fear of strangers in public spaces, there is a neglect of risks from those who are known and trusted and reside in our own households and work alongside us.

Radical, feminist and critical perspectives in criminology, following pioneering work in the 1980s, have all exposed the domestic sphere as a key site for the violence and sexual abuse experienced by women and children. These knowledges look beyond what is easily witnessed and at the events that go on behind closed doors which we do not 'see', and as such, they are key to furthering a more inclusive crime prevention and community safety strategy. Walklate and Evans (1999: 138) thus went on to argue for a greater emphasis on families and sets of personal relationships, on local social dynamics, formal and informal networks in communities. In their view, 'close ties' and the 'local' matter such that the meaning of locally formulated policy responses may need to be reinterpreted.

Knowledge link: This topic is also covered in Chapter 8.

Pause for Thought

Think about the aspirations of the new community safety agenda. Were all sections of the population equal beneficiaries of community safety in the 1990s and into the twenty-first century?

In 2006 Squires had alerted us to the failure to prevent those at risk of suffering domestic violence. Subsequent research suggested that for community safety to work more effectively in its aspiration to confront the reality of crime and victimisation, it must acknowledge the dynamics of interpersonal violence and abuse at structural, institutional, local and intimate levels. The chapter now turns to illustrate multi-agency partnership approaches to tackling domestic abuse.

MULTI-AGENCY WORKING TO TACKLE DOMESTIC ABUSE

Responses to domestic abuse cannot be divorced from the social context within which it occurs. Across the globe, there is widespread recognition that domestic abuse is an issue of power and control involving patterns of behaviours that can be physical, emotional, economic and sexual in nature. The dynamics of such abuse are thus connected to the concept of coercive control, which captures the psychological aspects and on-going nature of the behaviour, and the extent to which the actions of the perpetrator control the victim through isolation, intimidation, degradation and micro-regulation of everyday life. In England and Wales, the new offence of 'controlling or coercive behaviour in an intimate or family relationship' under section 76 of the Serious Crime Act 2015 captures these complex dynamics of domestic abuse.

Traditional criminal justice responses and mandated sanctions for offenders from the criminal courts have increasingly been combined with other preventive measures often involving multi-agency approaches to tackling the problem. The increasingly sophisticated response has seen investment in specialist services for women victims of domestic abuse in order to provide better support through to recovery. The commitment to the multi-agency approach has become well established (Davies and Biddle, 2017) and contemporary partnerships are currently grappling with the implications of new definitions of abuse as innovative multi-agency ways of tackling the problem continue to evolve in various jurisdictions and communities.

Tackling domestic abuse through partnership working

Partnership approaches were identified early in the new era of community safety as a way of tackling domestic abuse (Barton and Velero-Silva, 2012). Since the mid-to-late 1980s, there has been increasing reliance on such partnerships to prevent such abuse and protect from it. This tradition is well established in England and Wales. Prior to this, single agency responses were typical with great reliance on the police and their willingness to intervene. There was very little information sharing, particularly between statutory and voluntary agencies. Operating largely within the confines of a traditional criminal justice paradigm which seeks to hold perpetrators to account through legal sanctions and mandated rehabilitation solutions, domestic violence forums proliferated inspired by the 'Duluth approach'. Originating in the early 1980s in Duluth, Minnesota, USA, this intervention adopts the use of the 'Power and Control Wheel' as a tool to understand patterns of abusive behaviour. In the UK, government leadership on domestic violence in the 1990s saw national action plans emerge. By the turn of the century, prompted by a combination of Home Office guidance and legislative requirements to form partnerships to tackle crime and disorder, information sharing became more routinised (Westmarland, 2012). Before continuing on with the remainder of this section and reading the case study below, pause for just a moment.

Pause for Thought

Think about what principles might be at the heart of a multi-agency approach to tackling domestic abuse. What do you think might be the potential challenges for stakeholder partners?

There has been significant economic and political change in the period since multi-agency working became the dominant approach to tackling domestic abuse and as the community safety agenda has matured. These changes have affected partnership working in many areas of social policy and have also affected local agenda setting and commissioning (Davies and Biddle, 2017). Policies adopted since the austerity budget plan of 2010 have changed the way victim support is managed, and in the context of domestic abuse, where the local impact of austerity measures have been keenly felt, these cuts to services have interfaced with women's safety. This has seen collaborative working practices being put to the test, if not severely compromised, risking further marginalisation of domestic abuse victims. Furthermore, from 2014–2015 provision of services for many victims rests with Police and Crime Commissioners, who are also responsible for establishing local policing priorities. Thus, the current climate is a challenging one for partnership work, especially partnership work to tackle domestic abuse where the politico-economic environment is austere and uncertain, taking its toll on local services and where the safety of women and girls has risen to a higher level of priority (Davies, 2018).

The recent legislative changes to the definition of domestic abuse in England and Wales, and looming further changes, follow over two decades of policy reform that sought to implement an integrated strategy to tackle Violence Against Women and Girls (VAWG) more broadly. Significant victim-focused policy reform has occurred. There are many criminal and civil intervention options in England and Wales, and most recently, the shift has been towards the responsibilisation of perpetrators – holding men to account for their actions – where we see preventive ideologies gathering momentum. Part of this package of interventions enables prospective victims to be provided with information about their partners' previous violent behaviour, e.g. legally enforceable short-term protective measures include Protection Notices (DVPNs) and Protection Orders (DVPOs), introduced via the Crime & Security Act (2010). A DVPN precedes the DVPO. The former is an emergency non-molestation and eviction notice which can be issued by the police, when attending a domestic abuse incident, to a perpetrator. Police can use these following a domestic incident to provide short-term protection to the victim when an arrest has not been made but positive action is required, or where an arrest has taken place but the investigation is in progress. DVPOs resemble provisions operating elsewhere in Europe: the Austrian

Protection against Domestic Violence Act 1996 and the German Protection from Violence Act 2002 (Bessant, 2015). Additionally, the Domestic Violence Disclosure Scheme 2014 (DVDS or Clare's Law) provides a framework for members of the public to ask about a person's history of domestic abuse or intimate partner violence. The latter are part of a changing landscape internationally where campaigns are targeting primary prevention at men (Cismaru and Lavack, 2011). Despite such commitments and considerable reforms, too many women are victims, with an estimated 1.2 million in England and Wales experiencing such abuse in any given recent year, and on average two women are killed each week by a current or former partner. In the context of tackling domestic abuse, the story of statutory partnership working to tackle such offending and reduce victimisation has been slow and not yet won. The challenge to effect change remains in the lap of local stakeholders. One such multi-agency approach to tackle serial perpetrators of domestic abuse is described in Case Study 23.1.

Case Study 23.1

The Multi-Agency Tasking and Coordination (MATAC) Approach
What is it and why do it?

Multi-Agency Tasking and Co-ordination addresses the most harmful and serial domestic abuse perpetrators. To effectively tackle domestic abuse we need to deal with the cause – the perpetrators. The aim is to protect victims from harm by encouraging offender behaviour change and disrupting perpetrator ability to commit further offences. The approach is designed to:

- prevent domestic abuse occurring in the first place/limit its reoccurrence;
- ensure victims receive prompt and comprehensive wraparound support where abuse occurs; and
- ensure that perpetrators are held to account.

How did MATAC start and what is it made up of?

MATAC started in November 2014 in a police force in the north east of England. It comprises:

1. A tool to identify the Recency, Frequency and Gravity (RFGV) of offending. The formula is as follows:

   RFGV Risk Model Formula
   Final Score = (Average Recency + Frequency + Maximum Gravity + Serial Victim) / 6
   (max 100) (max 200) (max 100) (max 200)
   This gives a final score out of one hundred

2. The MATAC process (see Figure 23.1 showing a series of steps that lay out what people in each of the relevant agencies should do).
3. A domestic abuse toolkit (see Figure 23.2).
4. Force-wide availability of voluntary Domestic Violence Perpetrator Programmes (DVPPs).
5. Work with housing providers to focus on domestic abuse perpetrators.

At MATAC meetings, actions are determined to manage perpetrators (see Figure 23.1). The toolkit (Figure 23.2) is designed to facilitate prevention, diversion, disruption and enforcement according to the assessment of an engaging/non-engaging perpetrator. A pathway for 'engaging perpetrators' ('green options') is for those who recognise their behaviour is problematic and want to change.

(Continued)

A pathway for 'non-engaging perpetrators' ('red options') is for those who are unwilling to recognise their behaviour is abusive. Perpetrators can be managed in ways that cut across both pathways.

Perpetrators are served a Warning Notice and the process of doing this is risk assessed to ensure all safeguarding precautions are attended to via a harm reduction plan to negate any potential escalation of abuse. It is served by a Domestic Abuse 1:1 worker. The serving of the Notice is accompanied by robust wraparound support for potential victims. The Notice explains that the perpetrator is in the MATAC. It gives information about services and support in the area in which the perpetrator resides, and encourages them to access this support while also giving warnings of actions and tactics that will be used to disrupt them if they do not engage.

Outcomes

An evaluation of the MATAC (Davies and Biddle, 2017) found that for every perpetrator targeted there had been some positive outcomes, including reductions in domestic abuse-related offences, and reductions in reoffending of all offence types. Measures of the RFGV score of perpetrators before they entered the MATAC process against their RFGV score six months after discharge showed reduced scores, and perpetrators still had a lower score six months after being discharged from the MATAC process. In addition, the evaluation found positive outcomes for victims and a reduction of risk to victimisation, with a sustained reduction in perpetrators assessed by multi-agencies as posing a risk of murder or serious harm.

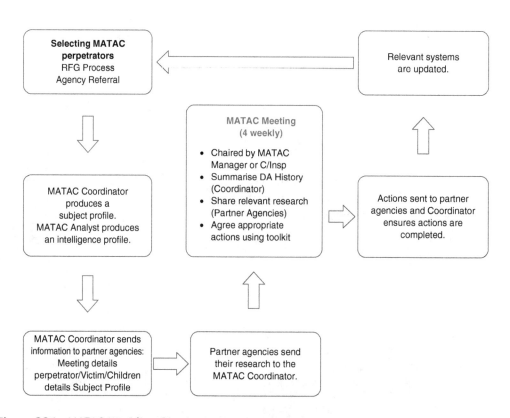

Figure 23.1 MATAC Workflow Chart

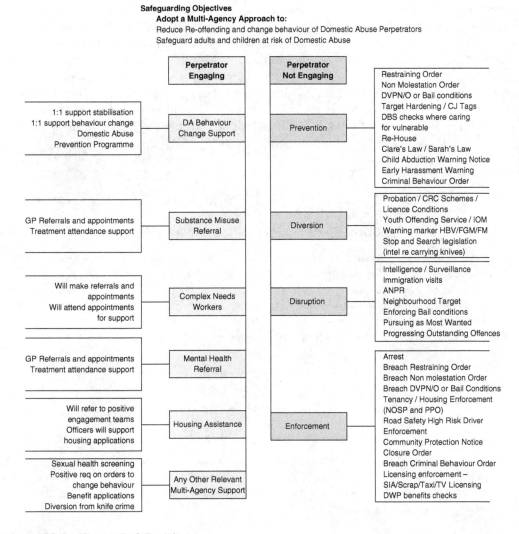

Figure 23.2 The MATAC Toolkit

Pause for Thought

- In light of the failure to reduce domestic abuse and protect victims through mandated criminal justice mechanisms, in what way does the MATAC approach to tackling serial perpetrators signify a different approach?
- What key principles are at the heart of the MATAC approach to tackling serial perpetrators of domestic abuse?

Case Study 23.1 illustrates what community safety has become, what it encompasses, how multi-agency working operates, what can be achieved, and what the challenges are in light of socio-economic, political and policy changes and transformations that have impacted at local levels and within criminal justice and policing institutions.

An important outcome of MATAC is the increased visibility of the perpetrator and the way in which the multi-agency partnership holds perpetrators accountable for their behaviour. This is part of an important broader shift towards prevention and early intervention. The earlier critiques of community safety suggested that an inclusive community paradigm could yet be achieved. MATAC-like innovations prioritise the safety of those who are vulnerable to domestic abuse. They enlist domestic abuse 'knowledge holders' at very local levels. MATAC has been adopted as core business in several police forces and similar multi-agency approaches are evident across England and Wales, including 'make a change' partnerships in Lincolnshire and Sussex and the Drive/Respect partnership now operating in four sites following pilot projects, as explained by Chief Inspector Lisa Gore in the Hear from the Expert Box below.

———— Hear from the Expert ————

Lisa Gore, Chief Inspector South Wales Police

The introduction of Drive in South Wales has been a real catalyst for change in the way we approach domestic abuse. There has been a genuine sea change amongst police and partners away from asking 'why doesn't she leave?' to asking 'why doesn't he stop?'. We have started to put much more focus on the perpetrator and hold them to account for their behaviour, whilst at the same time ensuring that safeguarding and preventing and reducing future risk is everyone's focus. It is genuinely heart-warming to hear feedback from victim/survivors about the positive impact that Drive has had on their lives in making them feel safe.

———— Pause for Thought ————

Drawing on data from the Crime Survey for England and Wales, have a look at the crime patterns for domestic abuse. How can partnership and multi-agency approaches to tackling serial perpetrators of domestic abuse function more effectively through a shared understanding of the gendered nature of domestic abuse?

The follow-on from MATAC in the north of England has been the adoption of a whole system approach (see Figure 23.3). As you can see, this approach involves multi-agency partnerships and collaborations across each of the three themes: i) effective working in the criminal justice system; ii) partnership work with civil and family courts; and iii) multi-agency victim support and offender management. These form the three pillars in the holistic approach designed to provide strategic and integrated actions. The final section of the chapter moves out of the specific context of the MATAC to consider the broader theme of partnership and multi-agency approaches to tackling social problems and crime and victimisation issues. In doing so I highlight some of the key challenges and practical lessons.

PARTNERSHIPS AND MULTI-AGENCY WORKING: CHALLENGES AND PRACTICAL LESSONS

Recent innovations in the policing of domestic abuse illustrate that multi-agency and partnership working remains the cornerstone for tackling this problem. Modern partnerships tend to draw on

VISION

To transform domestic abuse services with a strategic and integrated approach, giving police and partner agencies the ability to truly deliver lasting change and provide a template for all forces and partnerships to deliver on, for the benefit of domestic abuse victims and their children.

Using victim and survivor feedback we focus on:

Prevention and education	Early intervention	Effective engagement with victims	Meaningful consequences for perpetrators

Theme 1 Effective working within the Criminal Justice System	**Theme 2** Partnership work civil and family courts	**Theme 3** Multi-agency victim support and offender management
• Coercive Control Training Programme • DVSA (domestic violence support and assistance) response • Domestic abuse and criminal justice system (DACJS) workers • Independent domestic abuse scrutiny panel • Best practice standards for domestic abuse case work	• Family court proceedings – development of regional corporate police disclosure request process • Family Court Proceedings and domestic abuse self-help materials and online resources • Domestic abuse, civil and family court training for key police personnel • Child and Family Court Liaison (CFCL) workers	• Development of multi-agency safeguarding hubs (MASHs) • Multi-agency tasking and coordination for the most harmful domestic abuse perpetrators (MATAC) • Commissioning of RESPECT accredited voluntary domestic abuse prevention programmes

Figure 23.3 Domestic Abuse: A Whole System Approach

research-informed knowledge and evidence-based policing in addition to the wealth of knowledge held in local communities by a range of stakeholders. Increasingly, the focus of these multi-agency partnerships ensures that a wider community is protected and those responsible for the abuse are held to account. Such innovations in partnership and multi-agency working illustrate how far the community safety agenda has travelled since the criticisms levelled at the developments in the first decade of the twenty-first century. This shift signifies a move away from enforcement towards safeguarding (Menichelli, 2020), and the widening of the community safety agenda in the last ten to fifteen years.

Whilst the benefits and outcomes of effective multi-agency and partnership working are many and positive – including protections and support for some of the most vulnerable and their capacity to engender attitudinal and cultural change – there are a number of common problems that seem inherent in criminal justice multi-agency partnerships. The MATAC and the Whole Systems Approach (DAWSA) illustrate that where there are shared visions to reduce domestic abuse via tackling serial perpetrators, protecting and supporting victims, and preventing future victimisation, new partnerships can be less wedded to the criminal justice paradigm and more committed to a holistic approach. Preventing victimisation from domestic abuse, safeguarding victims and responsibilising perpetrators is becoming embedded and normalised at the local level (Davies, 2020). This is not to deny there are challenges and practical lessons that can be learned from new partnerships and collaborative work with stakeholders in multi-agency fora. A summary of some of the common stakeholder challenges is listed below, together with various illustrations of these challenges encountered in process evaluations with the stakeholders, and research that has been conducted into the effectiveness of these.

Stakeholder Challenges

- Identification of all key partners and the 'right' representative/s – those partnerships that are required by law may suffer from partners being forced to coordinate (see Case Study 23.2, point ii). Too many partners can be cumbersome, too few may mean there are gaps in terms of key parties being members. A dedicated individual and deputy ensures continuity. Members must have and be able to share information. Some partnerships are mandated whilst others are not. In the early days of multi-agency partnerships police tended to lead partnerships and be a partner in them. Though other agencies now also lead safeguarding partnerships, police tend to be very much the engaged partner (very visible, vocal and active). This can engender power struggles and recognition of differential power relations in partnerships remains important (Crawford and Jones, 1995).

- Leadership and governance structures – strong and passionate leadership where the aims and values of the partnership are at the heart of the ambition tend to impact positively on effective working. Sometimes sceptical leaders become ardent converts and this is a positive outcome in and of itself! There are links between effective leadership and challenges around communication, shared values, and the confidence and buy-in of all partners.

- Shared vision and goals – having a common agreed and shared vision and common goal keeps the focus even in times of heated debate around the table (see Case Study 23.2, point i). This is clear in Figure 23.3 where the vision is clearly articulated and forms the umbrella under which all ways of working to tackle domestic abuse sit. The challenge of sticking to shared goals is often referred to in terms of partner 'buy-in'.

- Communication – there are various dimensions to this and links to other stakeholder challenges. Being a partner involves bringing information to the table for sharing and speaking out (see Case Study 23.2).

- Effective methods of identifying problems – this might be problems with the way the partnership is working and may mean there are other challenges that are impacting on identifying problems related to the goals and aims of the partnership. In the MATAC the police RFGV risk model formula was adapted from a slightly different RFG model, such that it was tailored to identify specific problem perpetrators. However, there was not sole reliance on this police-owned tool. Effective methods of identifying perpetrators included receipt of information from other partners such as housing providers and health professionals.

- Effective referral mechanisms – ineffective referral mechanisms may relate to a single partner who must be open to changing their practice, or it may be due to poor communications between stakeholders. The effectiveness of referral mechanisms can also change over time and in light of socio-economic and political issues that require cuts or compliance with new policies and procedures.

- Effective feedback mechanisms – in the context of both mandatory and non-mandatory multi-agency partnerships in the crime and justice context, effective feedback mechanisms tend to be crucial to safeguarding. Any non- or poor communication can result in enhanced risks and knowing this can reduce confidence amongst stakeholders. As with the challenge of establishing and operationalising effective referral mechanisms, ineffective feedback mechanisms may relate to a single partner who must be open to changing their practice and again, feedback mechanisms can also change over time and in light of socio-economic and political issues that require cuts or compliance with new policies and procedures. There is an onus on stakeholders to be fully abreast of any changes in their area that might have a knock-on effect on how the partnership operates, such that there is no slippage that negatively impacts on feedback mechanisms.

- Information sharing – some stakeholders may lag behind others in respect of knowing what they can safely and legally share with others. This can slow down partnership work and the tracking and processing of on-going case management and risk assessments.

- Bespoke interventions in accordance with risk, harm, need and motivation to change – the range, level and access to interventions available in local areas may vary and change over time. There may be eligibility criteria that rule out some interventions or prioritise some 'clients'. What is available can also change over time and in light of socio-economic and political issues that require cuts. This might result in what is often referred to as a 'postcode' lottery. Requirements to be compliant with new legislation, policies and procedures around risk for example can affect the bespoke nature of interventions.

- Tailored specialist advice, advocacy and wraparound support for different groups and individuals – the challenges here are similar to some of the above. Tailored support will depend on matching needs to services and support at the local level and this is a common problem in that mismatches or no match can result. In some instances this can result in deficient support or none at all and serious consequences can ensue.

- Flexible and adaptable models and resources – institutions, organisations and agencies are (sometimes stubbornly) wedded to their own cultures, practices and procedures, and this can inhibit the provision of flexible and adaptable, bespoke and tailored interventions. Though austerity cuts are often blamed, there can also be organisation and institutional inertia which inhibits imaginative and different ways of working and adapting (see Case Study 23.2, point iii).

- Tangible products, e.g. toolkits, training packages, resources – clearly articulated products and knowledge of them, including regular updates as changes are made make several of the other potential challenges less so (see Figure 23.2 as a good example). Handbooks can also be developed and updated with various appendices providing reminders of the toolkits and resources for all stakeholders.

- Confidence and engagement of stakeholders – these challenges may be linked to one another or may be singularly challenging. There are also links between these issues and the need to ensure there is a shared vision and goal as well as having the right representatives (see above). These challenges may be ameliorated through workforce development strategies and training (see below).

- Workforce development/training – the roll-out of partnerships must go wider than just those partners that literally come to the table in the multi-agency forum. Sharing of information is otherwise inhibited. Those representatives who do come to the table are professionals who need to be properly equipped to be there and to engage in the pooling of information.

- Scepticism and conflict – scepticism may arise because other challenges have become evident such as the lack of a shared vision and common goals. Scepticism can be exacerbated by a lack of confidence and/or by concerns about safety, security and risk such that there are perceptions (real or not) that the vulnerable are not being adequately safeguarded or they are being put in harm's way and subject to greater risk. This can escalate from scepticism to concern and even conflict. This then becomes a major threat to the stability of the partnership. There are several ways in which this can be resolved and this involves tackling some of the issues listed above. However …

- Partnership work is hard work. Those who have close knowledge of particular partnerships have witnessed this over twenty-five years ago and much more recently too. Crawford and Jones suggest it is important to recognise the existence of conflict and manage and regulate it through constructive debate and in an accountable manner: 'Conflict may be the healthy and desirable expression of different interests' (Crawford and Jones, 1995: 31). I have also reported on:

  ○ *The healthy mix of scepticism evident in partnership working means that collaboration is hard work. Stakeholders from charities and statutory bodies must find a way of working such that they become 'critical allies'.* (Davies, 2020)

--- **Case Study 23.2** ---

Improving Multi-Agency Coordination: Overcoming the Barriers to Communication

Finney's (2002) article explores the relevance and roles of communication processes in the failure of a multi-agency Drug Action Team (DAT) to function and coordinate effectively. The author reports on four themes that explain the difficulties experienced by the DAT representatives. These are:

1.   the nature of the task for which the representatives meet;
2.   the implications of mandated (forced) coordination;
3.   the features of modern bureaucratic organisations;
4.   the characteristics of multi-agency relations.

The major practical lessons learned from this research are:

*   the team must agree a pressing problem exists – it must focus on the task and clearly define its remit at the earliest opportunity, to focus and direct further activities;
*   participants need to remain open-minded as individuals and as a group to prevent narrow 'either/or' ideological barriers forming;
*   action (practical activities) must be committed to and engaged in early to motivate further decision making;
*   the prerequisites of effective coordination (as highlighted above) must be publicised so as to be present in the minds of participants;
*   within participating organisations:

    o   upward communication must be facilitated to equip senior-level representatives with the information they need to make informed decisions and to enlighten concerns brought to the multi-agency meeting forum;
    o   downward communication must also be facilitated to ensure ground-level staff have faith that their work and experiences are acknowledged at the strategic level, and that whole organisations are working towards one common overarching goal;

*   leaders must acknowledge their role as being crucial for the balance of formality with informal relations, for ensuring agencies are not excluded from participation and that representatives are not silenced by more powerful others, and for structuring communications by adequately preparing for meetings and circulating appropriate materials (Finney, 2002: 43–44).

Source: Derived from Finney, A. (©2002) Improving multi-agency coordination: overcoming the barriers to communication – a case study. *Crime Prevention and Community Safety*, 4: 33–45. Reproduced by kind permission of Springer Nature.

CHAPTER SUMMARY

By now it will be clear that partnership and multi-agency working has become mainstream in efforts to tackle safety, crime, justice and policing problems and a host of other social issues. The vocabulary of community safety is perhaps less evident this century as compared with the latter years of the twentieth century. The shift has been towards safeguarding, though this sits alongside the enduring concept of risk and criminological critique, and debate now focuses on the various dimensions to the uneasy nexus between risk and vulnerability. In summary:

- The ideals of 'Community Safety' are laudable but in practice there has been very slow change in terms of whose safety is prioritised.
- Not all sections of the population have been equal beneficiaries of community safety.
- The global context is important but the local matters most in partnership and multi-agency working – this is especially the case in tackling domestic abuse.
- Understanding the dynamics of interpersonal violence and abuse is important – gender matters in multi-agency partnerships and collaborations to tackle serial perpetrators of domestic abuse.
- Recent MATAC-like partnerships are developing the professional response to domestic abuse and support for victims at the same time as they are increasing perpetrator visibility and holding them accountable for their behaviour.
- The community safety model has shifted from a model confined to crime and disorder to a broader model defined by the safeguarding of the vulnerable.
- Multi-agency and partnership working remains important in the policing of a wide range of social problems.
- There are challenges and barriers to effective multi-agency working:
  - poor communication is a common feature to ineffective partnership working;
  - socio-economic and political flux and uncertainty means partnership must evolve and adapt – often very swiftly – especially at local levels.
- Research suggests there are features common to successful partnerships that can be replicated. These include having a shared vision and goal, effective co-ordination and communication, agreement about actions, clearly owned responsibilities, and strong, dedicated and passionate leadership.
- Austerity measures have impacted on established ways of multi-agency working, provoking innovative collaborative partnerships underpinned by evidence-based policing.

Review Questions

1. What did the shift from 'crime prevention' to 'community safety' signify?
2. What is the relationship between community safety, partnership and multi-agency working?
3. To what extent does the MATAC approach to tackling serial perpetrators of domestic abuse enshrine the key principles of multi-agency and collaborative working?
4. In efforts to enhance safety and security, why does the local matter?
5. Why is multi-agency and partnership working a continuous challenge?

GO FURTHER

Books/Book Chapters

1. This edited book contains a collection of chapters that draw on a range of research about the contexts and direction of community safety initiatives:

   Hughes, G., McLaughlin, E. and Muncie, J. (eds) (2002) *Community Safety: New Directions*. London: Sage.

2.   This chapter outlines the birth of 'community safety' in England and Wales as well as traditional understandings of crime prevention before addressing the contemporary issues:

Van Ginneken, E. (2017) 'Community Safety and Crime Prevention'. In P. Davies, J. Harding and G. Mair (eds), *An Introduction to Criminal Justice* (pp. 189–207). London: Sage.

3.   This chapter offers an overview of the multi-agency approach to policing. It includes two case studies. The first explores multi-agency responses to violence against sex workers, and the second considers the multi-agency approach taken to policing wildlife crime:

Wyatt, T. and Laing, M. (2017) 'Policing as part of a Multi-agency Approach'. In P. Davies, J. Harding and G. Mair (eds), *An Introduction to Criminal Justice* (pp. 229–243). London: Sage.

Journal Articles

1.   The following article considers the origins of the community safety discourse and develops a critical analysis of it:

Squires, P. (1999) 'Criminology and the "Community Safety" Paradigm: Safety, Power and Success and the limits of the Local'. *The British Criminology Conferences: Selected Proceedings*, Volume 2. Papers from the British Criminology Conference, Queens University, Belfast, 15–19 July 1997. M. Brogden (ed.).

2.   Based on an evaluation study of a community safety intervention in the south-west Dublin suburb of Tallagh, this article confirms the import of 'the local' in matters of community safety, one key theme being the role of community safety workers' local knowledge and autonomous action within the local authority structures:

Bowden, M. (2017) Community safety, social cohesion and embedded autonomy: a case from south-west Dublin. *Crime Prevention and Community Safety*, 19(2): 87–102.

3.   For those wanting to follow up on multi-agency working to tackle gendered violence, this article explores the role of socio-cultural factors in child sexual abuse and sexual violence in British South Asian communities. It argues that effective ways to combat these problems depend on the family/community, charity and statutory sectors working together:

Gill, A. K. and Harrison, K. (2019) 'I am talking about it because I want to stop it': child sexual abuse and sexual violence against women in British South Asian communities. *British Journal of Criminology*, 59(3): 511–529.

Useful Websites

1.   This Police Foundation website contains links to several reports about multi-agency working in the context of policing and case management:

http://www.police-foundation.org.uk/publication/multi-agency-case-management/

2.   The following is the website of the College of Policing. Though the site is steered towards those working in the police service in England and Wales it contains a range of useful reports and online research resources:

https://www.college.police.uk/Pages/Home.aspx

3. This website contains a report on a Home Office-funded project to better understand multi-agency information-sharing models as well as links to other resources:

https://www.gov.uk/government/publications/multi-agency-working-and-information-sharing-project

REFERENCES

Barton, H. and Valero-Silva, N. (2012) Policing in partnership. *Public Sector Management*, 26(7): 543–553.

Bessant, C. (2015) Protecting victims of domestic violence – Have we got the balance right?, *The Journal of Criminal Law*, 79(2): 102–121.

Cismaru, M. and Lavack, A. M. (2011) Campaigns targeting perpetrators of intimate partner violence. *Trauma, Violence and Abuse*, 12(4): 183–197.

Crawford, A. and Jones, M. (1995) Inter-agency cooperation and community-based crime prevention. *British Journal of Criminology*, 35(1): 17–33.

Davies, P. (2008) Looking out a broken old window: community safety, gendered crimes and victimisations. *Crime Prevention and Community Safety: An International Journal*, 10(4): 207–225.

Davies, P. (2011) Post-emotional man and a community safety with feeling. *Crime Prevention and Community Safety: An International Journal*, 13(1): 34–52.

Davies, P. (2018) Tackling domestic abuse locally: paradigms, ideologies and the political tensions of multi-agency working. *Journal of Gender-Based Violence*, 2(3): 429–446.

Davies, P. (2020) Partnerships and Activism: Community Safety, Multi-Agency Partnerships and Safeguarding Victims in J. Tapley and P. Davies (eds) *Victimology: Research, Policy and Activism*. London: Palgrave Macmillan.

Davies, P. and Biddle, P. (2017) Implementing a perpetrator focused partnership approach to tackling domestic abuse: the opportunities and challenges of criminal justice localism. *Criminology & Criminal Justice*, 18(4): 468–487.

Edwards, A. (2013) 'Learning from Diversity: The Strategic Dilemmas of Community Based Crime Control'. In G. Hughes and A. Edwards (eds), *Crime Control and Community*. London: Routledge. pp. 140–166.

Finney, A. (2002) Improving multi-agency coordination: overcoming the barriers to communication – a case study. *Crime Prevention and Community Safety*, 4: 33–45.

Home Office (1991) *Safer Communities: The Local Delivery of Crime Prevention through the Partnership Approach*. Report of the Standing Conference on Crime Prevention (The Morgan Report). London: Home Office.

Hughes, G. (2006a) 'Community Safety'. In E. McLaughlin and J. Muncie (eds), *The SAGE Dictionary of Criminology*. London: Sage. p. 54.

Hughes, G. (2006b) 'Multi-agency Crime Prevention'. In E. McLaughlin and J. Muncie (eds), *The SAGE Dictionary of Criminology*. London: Sage. p. 253.

Loader, I. (2000) Plural policing and democratic governance. *Social & Legal Studies*, 9: 323–345.

Local Government Management Board (1996) (with ADC/AMA and ACC) *Survey of Community Safety Activities in Local Government in England and Wales*. July.

Menichelli, F. (2020) Transforming the English model of community safety: from crime and disorder to the safeguarding of vulnerable people. *Criminology & Criminal Justice*, 20(1): 39–56.

Squires, P. (ed.) (2006) *Community Safety: Critical Perspectives on Policy and Practice*. Bristol: Policy Press.

Walklate, S. and Evans, K. (1999) *Zero Tolerance or Community Tolerance? Managing Crime in High Crime Areas*. Aldershot: Ashgate.

Westmarland, N. (2012) 'Co-ordinating Responses to Domestic Violence'. In J. M. Brown and S. L. Walklate (eds), *Handbook on Sexual Violence*. London: Routledge. pp. 287–307.

Policing

Ben Bradford

24

Learning objectives

By the end of this chapter you will:

- Understand the contribution police make to social order.
- Critically consider the place of 'crime-fighting' in police activity.
- Consider what might be the most pressing challenges currently facing the police.
- Understand the nature of police-community relations and why this is such an important issue.
- Explore the different ways police activity can be directed and controlled.

Framing Questions
---

1. Who are the police – and what is policing?
2. Is fighting crime the main job of the police?
3. What are the most important challenges facing the police today?
4. How can we ensure police powers are used appropriately?

INTRODUCTION

Police are a ubiquitous feature of modern life. All states have a police organisation – some have many – and all territories except, arguably, Antarctica, are at least nominally governed by police. In large parts of the world, police are a familiar part of people's everyday experiences, particularly if they come from a marginal, excluded or socially denigrated group, class, or race. In a country such as the UK, most residents will experience meaningful encounters with police officers at least a few times in their lives: as a victim of crime, witness to an accident, suspect in an offence, or in some other capacity. Some will interact with the police far more frequently. Moreover, images and stories abound in fictional and non-fictional media that make police and policing culturally salient – often highly so – in ways that are independent of personal experience.

Yet the ubiquity of the police is also by and large a product of the modern era. Most human societies, across most of history, have functioned without an institution similar or even approximating to what we now call police. Despite the fact that almost all those societies conducted *policing* – activity oriented towards reproducing normative social order – the police, as a separate organisational entity and embodiment of the effort to maintain social order, are in historical terms a very recent development.

An account of the journey from 'there' to 'here' is beyond the scope of the current chapter. But underlining that police are at once a seemingly inevitable feature of essentially all present-day polities and a particular socio-cultural development of remarkable recency, directs attention to some necessary, and fundamental, definitional questions; and also cautions against overly simplistic or circular answers to fundamental questions such as *what is policing,* and *who are the police*. Much of the work of producing social order (which we can label 'policing') is conducted by actors, organisations, and social practices other than police. And it also turns out that police organisations are involved in a range of activities far wider than the crime-fighting function usually assigned to them.

The pages that follow flesh out these points to provide a general account of the institution of police, most specifically relating to the situation in the United Kingdom but also relevant to many other 'developed' and 'less-developed' democracies. From here the chapter proceeds as follows. First, by way of mapping the terrain, I provide answers to the two questions posed above. Second, discussion moves on to the contribution of police to social order, and the relationship between police work and crime. Third, I outline some of the central challenges facing police organisations at the current point in time (and indeed into the future), before, fourth, turning to the foundational relationship between police and policed. The chapter concludes with some thoughts on the governance of police.

MAPPING THE TERRAIN

Who then are the police, and what is policing? At the most fundamental level policing concerns the production and reproduction of social order – the enforcement of 'various types of rules and customs that promote a defined order in society' (Brodeur, 2010: 130), or what can otherwise be called **social control**. Almost any human behaviour might under specific circumstances serve to generate and reproduce social order, but social control is usually envisaged as the effort to prevent or address *threats* to this order and thus as a more limited set of behaviours. Social control is, in addition, best defined as activity on the part of or involving the presence and actions of specialist organisations and collaborative efforts: 'the *organised* ways in which society responds to behaviour and people it regards as deviant, problematic, worrying, threatening, troublesome or undesirable' (Cohen, 1985: 1–2, emphasis added).

Knowledge link: This topic is also covered in Chapter 21.

On this account, the police and other criminal justice agencies, but also fire and rescue, schools, hospitals and psychiatric units, social security systems, private security providers, and many other actors, are all involved in some form of policing. The police do not hold a monopoly in social control activity. Yet, equally, police activity is clearly wider than merely providing a response to deviant or problematic people or events. Most police organisations have a wide remit, ranging from guardianship roles that at least hint at the idea of social control, e.g. via the deterrence of crime, to responding to accidents, missing persons and other situations not usually considered as threats, at least in the way outlined above. It therefore makes sense to distinguish between policing, which is conducted by many actors, and police work, activity carried out by the police. And police work is concerned not only with threats but also with *ruptures,* situations where something has gone wrong or someone is out of place; those famously described by Bittner (1990) as situations wherein 'something is happening that ought not to be and about which someone had better do something now!'.

If this is police work, who are the police? A minimal definition might refer to the fact that while many organisations and actors are involved in policing, the police are state-funded specialists in this role; those, as Bittner argued, whom we turn to when something, anything, has gone wrong. Other agencies – local councils, fire and rescue, hospitals, social services etc. – have specific social control functions, but the police have a much more general and indeed unspecified power, i.e. the ability to act in almost any situation where a threat or rupture has occurred or is occurring, and to intervene proactively to try to prevent such events transpiring. Only the police can seek to arrest an offender, mediate in a neighbourhood dispute, guard a high-profile location, respond to a traffic accident, *and* search for a lost child. Police can thus be defined as 'a state agency with the omnibus mandate of order maintenance' (Bowling et al., 2019), and, it might also be noted, crucially representative of the state's effort to maintain social order within the territory it governs.

The ability to use force is, arguably, the other defining feature of the police. Brodeur (2010) notes that other state and non-state actors (e.g. prison guards, mental health nurses, private security) can use force in a limited set of situations, and of course this is the raison d'être of the armed services, although here force is (primarily) projected outside the territory of the state. But only police are able to use force *as and when* they see fit and *within* that territory. The uniqueness of this ability is accentuated by (a) the fact that, at least under the British system, it is vested in individual officers, and (b) that this power is in an important sense limitless. Police are able to do *whatever is necessary*, up to and including the use of deadly force, to assert their will in a given situation. While this power is plainly also constrained by law and regulation, it nevertheless exists. The police are a 'morally troubling' institution because police officers can, and do, use violence to achieve their aims.

THE CONTRIBUTION OF POLICE TO SOCIAL ORDER

The account provided above raises two important questions relating to the relationship between police and notions of social order, and it is to these we now turn. First, what is meant by social order, and how might we conceive of police contributing to it? One might be referring here to the actually existing order within a particular social context, and the particular forms and structures of power, wealth, influence and security which define vertical and horizontal relationships within it. Perhaps the most common way to think about order in these terms is to define and describe the relational hierarchies of gender, age, ethnicity, class, health etc. that structure a society, and to consider the boundaries of that society, who is 'in' and who is 'out'. If one has in mind this version of social order, then the role of the police is to maintain already existing power relations and hierarchies, and to control membership of the group (society) they structure.

Pause for Thought

- Is this how you see police and police work?
- What evidence can you think of to back up your argument?

Social order can also be seen in more general or abstract terms – as a state distinct from disorder, the existence of stability or, more concretely, a set of social structures and processes, based on widely shared norms and values, that serve to regularise human behaviour within a given context. Under this conception police activity enables us to go about our lives, for example by providing protection from crime and anti-social behaviour, and by creating the space for civil society to flourish.

Crucially, police in a country such as the United Kingdom are engaged in maintaining *both* types of order. Police activity is concerned with protecting people from the predations of others, investigating crime, arresting offenders, providing guardianship and so on (what Brodeur, 2010, calls 'low' policing). This fulfils the basic need for the state to protect its members, but also in a wider sense enables personal freedom and civic activity. Yet police are also concerned with protecting the state from its members (i.e. us – this is what Brodeur calls 'high' policing), and with sustaining the currently existing system of social order. Not everyone can live the life they choose, and the police are deeply implicated in processes of social ordering that empower some individuals and groups at the expense of others.

The second question concerns the success and importance of the police's contribution to social order. There are, again, two distinct understandings of this issue. On the one hand, it can be argued that the police are integral to the reproduction of social order. Police activity serves to systematically repress and exclude those at the bottom of various social hierarchies, and the possibility for reforming or overthrowing the existing order would be very much greater in the absence of (effective) police. This account is of course useful in understanding policing in some autocracies and dictatorships, where the regime relies on overt and covert policing to retain power. But there is also much to suggest that these functions and outcomes can also be ascribed to police in liberal democracies. Equally, police can be positioned as effective enablers of social interaction and commerce (Jacobs, 2016). On this account, they are a vital part of the effort to maintain and reproduce widely shared norms of behaviour, and, in the most positive understandings, ethical values.

On the other hand, it can be argued that police activity is only tangentially connected with the reproduction of order, or at least that other institutions are much more important in this regard. Hierarchies of race, class and so on are maintained by other structures and processes of domination – such as political ideologies – which ensure the continuance of existing power relations. While police may indeed be repressive they are not essential for the maintenance of the system within which they are embedded. Equally, it is plausible to suggest that general social order is maintained with little input from the police. Here, factors such as trust between citizens, and between citizens, institutions, and the state, are far more important, and the main role of the police is to deal with situations that fall through the cracks of other larger, more important and more efficacious systems of ordering and control.

In reality, the contribution of the police to social order falls somewhere between the poles outlined above. It is readily apparent that the social control activity engaged in by police is only one factor contributing to the reproduction of social order, and in many or even most cases other actors and processes will indeed be more important. One need only think of the importance of the institutions of family, school and work for shaping individual and group behaviour to realise that most social ordering is conducted outwith the ambit of the police. That said, police activity does provide effective social control at some times and in some places, whether this is through crime reduction or the suppression of political dissent (see Key Event: Policing Extinction Rebellion below).

Key Event: Policing Extinction Rebellion

The policing of protest presents a crucial test of the arguments presented in the preceding paragraphs. People living in a democracy have a right to protest, the exercise of which has led to fundamental social change. To the extent that police work with protestors to ensure a peaceful and safe outcome to proceedings they can be seen as enabling protest and the change it might herald. Yet, the policing of protests has often taken a negative, even repressive, turn, with police officers acting to shut down protests in ways that have been heavily criticised, both at the time and subsequently. In such circumstances the charge that police are functioning to protect the established order is hard to ignore.

Consider the two major Extinction Rebellion (ER) 'events' in London in 2019. While over 1,000 protestors were arrested during the first in April (getting arrested was a deliberate aim for many), policing was nevertheless relatively restrained. While officers acted continuously to deal with disruption caused by the protestors, for example by removing people who had glued or chained themselves to buildings or public transport, the protests as a whole were allowed to continue despite loud complaints from businesses, politicians and others. Perhaps partially in response to these complaints the second event, in October, was policed significantly more aggressively, culminating in the use of Section 14 of the Public Order Act 1986 to ban all ER protests in London. This allowed officers to move on – on pain of arrest – camps of protestors and those linked to ER not actively causing disruption. Intriguingly, the High Court ruled in November 2019 that use of Section 14 for these ends was unlawful because it went beyond the powers laid out in the 1986 Act. The practical implications of this ruling were limited, since the protests had already been successfully disrupted, but it nevertheless constituted a sharp rebuke to the MPS.

Police Work and Crime

The discussion thus far has largely avoided mention of the activity often considered synonymous with police work, i.e. crime fighting. That police are primarily and most importantly crime fighters, and spend – or at least should spend – most of their time in this function is an idea held by many politicians, the press, and arguably large sections of the public, as well as the police themselves. It is striking, therefore, that the empirical evidence points in an entirely different direction – most police work has little or nothing to do with crime. Brodeur (2010: ch. 5) outlines an evidence base, formed from studies of police time-use conducted in many different times and places, which converges on the fact that police spend between a third and half of their time dealing with directly crime-related issues, with most estimates at the lower end of that range. Other common activities include answering other calls for service, patrol work and problem solving in relation to events not directly concerning crime, responding to accidents and other emergencies, guardianship roles, and indeed a list of behaviours entirely in line with Bittner's definition of police above. Police can be called upon to deal with *anything and everything* that threatens social order, and are thus engaged in a (very large) set of activities that merely includes crime as one element.

There are three important provisos here. First, while activity such as dealing with disputes, traffic duty, and guardianship functions (and associated paperwork) might not be directly related to crime, this is not a neat distinction, and can very rapidly become much more crime focused in particular situations. A more expansive view, which attends to the possible implications of an argument between neighbours or a faulty tail-light, might conclude that the police spend much more time dealing with crime than seems immediately apparent. Second, specialist officers and units clearly *do* spend much or even all of their time dealing specifically with crime. Third, it may be the case that while police officers spend most of their time in activity other than crime fighting it might still be the most *important* thing they do; this, though, raises some interesting questions about how to gauge the relative importance of, say, dealing with a spate of burglaries, attending a serious traffic accident, or guarding a high-profile public event. Drawing a hierarchy of the need and importance of police activities can be difficult (see for example Sherman et al., 2016).

The effectiveness of police in dealing with crime is also hotly debated. There is once more a marked dissonance between political and cultural debates around police work, which tend to stress a fundamental link between police activity and levels of crime, and research on this question, which tends towards the idea that any such association is rather tenuous. Take, for example, the basic correlation between police numbers and crime, which is often simply assumed in policy discussions but for which the evidence is decidedly ambiguous (see Case Study 24.1).

Case Study 24.1

Police Numbers and Crime

At the time of writing, the Conservative Government elected in 2019 is seeking to make good its promise to hire 20,000 new police officers in England and Wales over a three-year period. Many political platforms over the years have been built on the promise to deliver more police and thus cut crime (e.g. Murray and Malik, 2019); such policies assume, implicitly or explicitly, a causal link between the two. But much research questions this assumption. The existence and 'presence' of a police organisation almost certainly has an effect on crime rates, as documented in relation to police strikes and other situations where the police have been totally removed from a situation (Sherman, 2003), and conversely in circumstances where sudden 'shocks', such as a terrorist attack, have led to radical increases in the number of officers in particular locations (e.g. Di Tella and Schargrodsky, 2004). However, marginal effects from increasing police numbers on crime have been much more difficult to identify (although see Bradford, 2011). It is far from clear that simply increasing the number of police officers in, say, a city, will automatically reduce the level of crime. Many criminologists accordingly stress that what is important is not how many police officers there are but what they are doing.

Even when the focus switches to the behaviour of officers rather than simply their number there is uncertainty around the efficacy of various tactics and deployments. On the one hand the evidence-base surrounding police patrol work is strong. While it seems clear that 'random' routine patrol is ineffective in cutting crime (Telep and Weisburd, 2012), there is good evidence that **hotspots policing**, where resources are targeted at high-crime micro-locations, does have such an effect, at least in the short term (Weisburd et al., 2012). There is similarly good evidence that tactics and policies such as **Problem Oriented Police** (POP) and **focused deterrence** can prevent offending (College of Policing, n.d.a). On the other hand, the evidence in relation to many other modes and methods of policing is much weaker, and often almost entirely absent. Many studies, for example, conclude that stop and search, an emblematic police power, has only a very marginal effect on crime (e.g. Bradford and Tiratelli, 2019).

It is important to note that individual investigations can be highly effective, and many offenders are brought to justice as a result of police action. In the UK the conviction rate for murder, for example, tends to be high (e.g. ONS, 2018) (although the conviction rate for other serious crimes is much lower, the most notorious example being rape; see Angiolini, 2015). What is much less clear is whether, outside some specific areas of activity, police have any general effect on levels of crime and offending. This points to a further feature of much police work: that police are often able only to provide proximate, short-term solutions to the problems that confront them. To put it another way, police officers can be highly effective in dealing with individual crimes, problems or dilemmas, but frequently lack the wherewithal to provide longer-term solutions. Officers can arrest and process an individual in relation to a specific offence, or prevent crime in the short term by targeting crime hotspots. But *on their own* they have only a very limited ability to influence the environmental and social contexts that provide opportunities for crime and shape the decision-making processes of potential offenders. It is for this reason, among others, that many police organisations and much police research now concentrate on partnership and collaboration, as police work with other agencies and organisations to try to bring about longer-lasting change (Ayling et al., 2010).

Knowledge link: This topic is also covered in Chapter 23.

CURRENT AGENDAS AND FUTURE CHALLENGES

The section above sketched out who the police are and, in broad brush terms, what they do. The discussion now moves on to consider police activity in a little more detail, with a particular emphasis on some of the current and future challenges faced by police in the United Kingdom, and indeed elsewhere.

Police activity was for many years dominated by what Sherman (2013) has termed the three Rs,— Random patrol, Rapid response and Reactive investigations. 'Traditional policing' revolved around the provision of more or less random patrols, originally on foot but from the 1960s onwards increasingly in cars; providing as rapid response as possible to calls for service; and reactively investigating crimes notified by victims, witnesses, and others. In addition to basic order maintenance work, the focus was on so-called 'volume' crime – burglary, theft, assault, theft of and from vehicles, and so on.

While many current police organisations would reject the idea that they conduct random patrols, a version of the three Rs still dominates much of their practice. Patrols may be more targeted in nature, and investigatory work often sits alongside more proactive models such as POP. But the basic functions of maintaining a presence 'on the streets', providing assistance when called upon, and investigating crime, remain core police activities. This both motivates and structures the variety of police work described above, since what officers encounter while in public facing situations, and the calls for service they receive – two of the three Rs – are in important ways beyond their control, being often determined by others and having no necessary link with crime.

This variety of police work, and the fact that it is largely generated by other actors, provides one of the central challenges currently facing many police organisations. In the UK, austerity measures instituted after the 2008 financial crash, and over the longer term by neoliberal economic 'reform', have resulted in the withering away of social services – social security nets, youth services, mental health services, and so on. The police have always been the service of last resort, there to provide basic assistance when no-one else can or will (this is often what it means to 'call the police'). But this role has expanded as other services have declined, often with the effect of shifting police attention increasingly onto issues that seem far removed from their crime-fighting image. The paradigmatic example is mental health, with estimates suggesting that between 20 and 40% of police time is spent dealing with issues that have a mental health element to them (i.e. dealing with individuals, across a wide range of situations, who have some sort of mental health issue) (Home Affairs Select Committee, 2015: 8). A variety of partnership working and other policies have been instigated, in some places at least, to help police deal with this issue (Kane et al., 2018), and mental health has always been a factor in ordinary police work. But the sheer extent of the problem has caused significant concern inside and outside the service because, put bluntly, police officers are not mental health professionals.

Partly as a result of dissatisfaction with the predominantly reactive, 'band-aid', style of policing outlined above, which seems ill-suited to providing long-term solutions to problems of crime and disorder, there is an increasing emphasis on developing more proactive, targeted, modes of police work. The clearest expression of this trend is the Evidence-Based Policing (EBP) movement. Derived from the model of evidence-based medicine, EBP seeks to create a situation where 'police officers and staff create, review and use the best available evidence to inform and challenge policies, practices and decisions' (College of Policing, n.d.b). Key to this approach is what Sherman (2013), in a direct coun-terpoint to the 3Rs, has called the 3Ts: Targeting, Testing and Tracking. The underlying idea is that police should seek to identify issues which are already causing harm or have the potential to cause harm in the communities they serve, and develop tailored approaches to address them, hopefully in ways that halt significant harm *before* it occurs. This marks a significant shift from hitherto reactive modalities, not least in as much as it suggests police should be far more active in selecting their own 'high-priority targets' (ibid.: 7) and shifting resources towards them.

Closely linked to EBP is the move towards predictive policing specifically and data-driven policing in general (Brayne, 2017). The allure here is obvious. If the police can more accurately map, and even better predict, the distribution of crime, then their activities can be far better targeted, increasing effectiveness, efficiency and, perhaps, circumventing any need to provide longer-term solutions (since problems will consistently be 'nipped in the bud'). However, few if any forces in the UK have fully integrated predictive policing into their practice (see Case Study 24.2 below).

—————————————— Case Study 24.2 ——————————————

Kent Police and Predpol

Kent Police was an early adopter of predictive policing in the UK. In 2013 it entered into a contract with Predpol, one of the leading organisations in this field. Predpol provides proprietary software that attempts to identify the times and locations where crime is most likely to occur and help police develop systems to send officers to those locations to prevent it. However, it was reported in 2018 that Kent Police were withdrawing from the project. Senior officers noted that while the package was good at identifying where offences might occur, it was hard to ascertain whether it had had any effect in reducing crime overall (BBC, 2018).

At the present point in time it is perhaps more accurate to speak of the promise of data-driven policing rather than the reality, but there seems little doubt that predictive technologies will be increasingly used in the future. This seems set to generate significant debate and discord, as predic-tive policing raises many ethical and political challenges (e.g. relating to racial bias within predictive systems) that are far from being resolved and which may become even more acute as these types of technologies are taken up (Ferguson, 2017). Predictive policing, for example, seems likely to concen-trate police activity in more deprived areas – which have higher levels of some types of crime – with significant implications for residents (positive and negative).

—————————————— Pause for Thought ——————————————

What do you think might be the potential benefits and pitfalls of predictive policing?

Police, Governance and Geography

Alongside a focus on the 3Rs, police organisations have traditionally been bound to the territory of state and nation, and are indeed representative, physically and symbolically, of the state apparatus of which they are part. Closely tied to government and regimes of law, police were confined to specific territories, although some level of police cooperation across borders has a long pedigree (the first informal international police cooperation can be traced back to at least 1914; see Andreas and Nadelmann, 2006). However, globalisation and the digital revolution have had profound implications for the way policing is done and for the objects of police work.

Police officers are, first, increasingly required to work across borders, as global flows of people, material and data challenge the idea that the nation-state can be policed solely by its own sovereign agency. Mechanisms for cross-border cooperation and global policing have proliferated, particularly in the European Union, which has a number of cooperation frameworks in place as well as advanced mechanisms for policing the borders themselves. On a more informal basis, police organisations across the world are constantly talking to one another, sharing knowledge, expertise, and sometimes even personnel.

Second, the digital revolution is arguably *the* greatest challenge facing police in the third decade of the twenty-first century. Growth in the use of the internet and related technologies, which now permeate almost every aspect of life, has thrown up demands unthought of thirty, even twenty, years ago. These range from: practical issues relating to evidence collection, processing and presentation in an era where investigation of one sexual offence can involve sifting through hundreds of thousands of texts, emails and social media messages; through cyber-enabled crimes such as cyber-bullying, an explosion of illegal pornography and myriad new fraud offences; to entirely new cyber-dependent crimes like hacking and denial of service attacks, and the enormous opportunities for crime presented by the Internet of Things.

Knowledge link: This topic is also covered in Chapter 12.

But perhaps the most significant shift here is precisely that of *territory*. Many of the human behaviours police deal with are no longer tied to particular geographic spaces, or indeed any physical place at all, but exist at least partly in the virtual realm, the physical underpinnings of which – server farms, tech companies – may be located in remote jurisdictions. This poses profound challenges for organisations which, notwithstanding globalisation and cross-border cooperation, remain so closely tied to particular nation-states and, most especially, legal jurisdictions. Few if any police organisations governed by the rule of law have yet solved the riddle of how they, as specialists in social control activity, can deal with Nigerian '419' scams or the activities of Russian 'troll farms'. Indeed few have even tried, indicating what is potentially the real lesson here. These are issues traditional police organisations cannot deal with, at least alone, requiring far greater cooperation with other state- and non-state stakeholders in 'networked' or 'nodal' systems (Wall, 2007). They also raise the question of whether the police *should* be the agency to deal, in particular, with cyber-dependent crime. While they may take some sort of lead in driving responses, other actors – Internet Service Providers, banks, tech companies – are far better placed, and indeed have a duty to, undertake the actions required. The crime potentiality of the digital revolution may thus be highlighting some important limits to police power, and is at the very least throwing up situations where they are simply incapable of acting alone.

Pause for Thought

Who, if anyone, is currently responsible for policing the internet? And who, if anyone, should be?

There is one area in which police involvement in, or binding to, the boundaries of the nation-state has increased in recent years: the policing of borders. The advent of mass immigration, in the UK and elsewhere, has heralded far greater police involvement in border maintenance work. This may be at the actual physical border or, in a country such as the UK where there is a separate non-police border agency (Border Force), at virtual, internal, borders (Weber, 2013), where police are making increasingly stringent efforts to identify and remove immigrants who did not enter in the legally sanctioned manner, have over-stayed, or are engaged in activity that mandates removal. This process can often involve working closely with immigration agents during routine police work (e.g. in custody suites), and can be heavily racialised (Parmar, 2019).

POLICE AND PUBLIC

The discussion above underlines that the police do not exist or function in a vacuum, but rely fundamentally on other actors. For example, they are often described as the 'gatekeepers' of the criminal justice system, implying close, symbiotic (but also at times fraught) relationships with prosecutors, the wider legal profession, courts, probation services, and others. As emergency first-respondents, police must work with fire and rescue and paramedics in sometimes extreme circumstances. And the advent of the digital revolution implies an increasingly close relationship with technology companies and others who have otherwise unavailable expertise in relevant domains. Police have always relied on relationships of these kinds, and the need to work in partnership with other agencies and stakeholders will only increase in the future. The most important relationship for police, however, is undoubtedly with the various publics they both serve and govern, and it is to this we now turn.

There are two fundamental and interconnected reasons for the importance of police-community relations. First, police rely on the public for information and cooperation. Most of the crimes they become aware of are reported by victims, witnesses or others. The subsequent cooperation of these individuals is needed if those crimes are ever to be detected and brought to court. More broadly, the intelligence on which good police work relies often comes from similar sources; and across the range of police functions (e.g. at public order and sporting events, road-traffic accidents, or during neighbourhood problem-solving activities) the active or at least passive cooperation of ordinary people is needed for any police activity taking place to be successful. To put it another way, police officers can usually deal very well with a few troublemakers in a given context (however 'trouble' is defined) if everyone else there either cooperates or at least allows them to act. But if widespread cooperation and/or consent is absent, police action becomes difficult if not impossible.

Second, the **legitimacy** granted to police by the public is foundational to their ability to function in the kinds of ways we have come to imagine they should. The British policing model, for example, is built around the notion of consent, and Peel's famous (and apocryphal) principles, with their emphasis on the idea that 'the police are the public and the public are the police', are frequently invoked as the guiding principles underlying police activity (Jackson et al., 2013). On this account, widely shared within and beyond police organisations, the *willing support* of the public is needed if police officers are to be able to fulfil their roles and duties in morally and ethically desirable ways. The consent of the policed is needed for police to function at any level of effectiveness, and in the long run to exist at all. The need for legitimacy therefore limits the power of the police, and a dialectic involving the assertion of authority and the quest for legitimacy can be seen as a fundamental factor structuring police activity and the outcomes it produces.

Crucially, a wealth of empirical evidence suggests that this legitimacy, and the public trust on which it is founded, stem most importantly from people's assessments of **procedural justice**. People attend, that is, to the fairness of the activities and processes used by police officers, and when they perceive these to be fair – which means here transparent, neutral and clearly explained decisions, and interpersonal treatment that is respectful, dignified and honest – they are more inclined to trust those officers and grant them legitimacy (Tyler, 2006; Tyler and Jackson, 2014). Unfairness across these dimensions has the reverse effect, because it indicates that police officers do not value those they are interacting with, see them as outsiders warranting exclusion, and/or are behaving outside widely shared norms and values. Other aspects of police activity may be important in generating trust and legitimacy in certain times and places, for example their effectiveness in dealing with crime and disorder, or the fairness of the outcomes they provide. But almost all studies conducted in developed democracies have concluded that procedural justice is the single most important factor, at least in terms of assessments of police activity that feed into trust and legitimacy (see Figure 24.1).

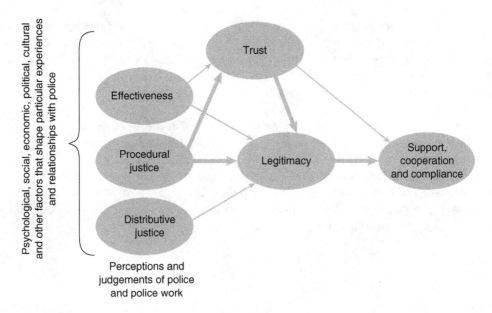

Figure 24.1 A Model of Public Trust and Police Legitimacy

----------- **Hear from the Expert** -----------

Inspector Dan Popple, West Midlands Police

Policing is complex and often undefined. We're there to support victims, investigate crime, find missing people and much more. We are faced with making decisions in very difficult situations. Police officers have a unique role in society: we can take away a person's liberty, use force (sometimes deadly) and stop and search someone simply because we suspect them of carrying something illegal. Police officers want to do a good job, we want to help the public, but sometimes we don't get it right, and in those interactions we risk jeopardising our legitimacy.

I have been a frontline officer my whole career, but I now work on the West Midland's Police Fairness in Policing Team. It is not a normal role in policing, but it is an important one. Prior to that I had no knowledge of the foundations of police legitimacy: I believed the public wanted to see me walking the beat or conducting search warrants; and I had never heard of procedural justice, or questioned, for example, whether it mattered how I did a stop and search.

I joined the Fairness in Policing team because I was drawn to the ambition of improving police-public relations whilst working alongside academics. At first it was a very steep learning curve, but expressions like 'legitimacy' and 'organisational justice' soon became common language to me.

(Continued)

We developed a structure which meant every department was asked to focus on ways to improve fairness for their staff and the community. At the same time, we also focused on activities known to be controversial with our public such as stop and search. I am proud of the work we are doing with stop and search, where we are developing ways to capture feedback and asking our officers to reflect on their encounters.

Legitimacy is a golden thread running through all policing, and I've come to realise that what we do *and* how we do it really does matter.

Knowledge link: This topic is also covered in Chapter 19.

The relationship between police and minority groups – particularly racial and ethnic minorities – is a constant feature of any debate on police-community relations. Studies from many parts of the world have shown that (a) police attention is disproportionately directed towards people from some minority groups, (b) that this is down to a mixture of personal, institutional and structural racism or bias (Bowling et al., 2019), and (c) results in significantly less trust in police, and lower levels of legitimacy, within the communities affected (Jackson et al., 2013). It is important not to over-generalise – in the UK, for example, people from some ethnic minority groups tend to have higher levels of trust than those from the white British majority (Bradford et al., 2017). But the consistency of the overall pattern may reveal something important about the nature of police work. To police is in a fundamental sense be to patrol the borders of inclusion, to determine whose presence in a particular context is acceptable and whose is not, and/or to restore the *status quo ante*. It is not surprising, given endemic structural and other forms of racism, that police attention is drawn to groups whose social, cultural, economic and political presence is uncertain, contested, or even denied.

Pause for Thought

If ethnicity can be an important variable shaping people's experiences of police and therefore trust and legitimacy, what do you think might be others? Are they universal, or context dependent?

Police-public relationships are, then, based on values concerning how power should be used and how authorities should treat those they govern. This is why people from minority groups experiencing excessive forms of policing have less trust – they see police power misapplied. Moreover, people living in countries such as the UK seem to think of police officers not in instrumental terms, but morally and indeed symbolically. When it comes to forming trust and legitimacy, that is, they tend to ask not "are police reducing crime?" but "are they behaving in the right way?" and "are they representing a set of values I share?" The police represent dominant social orders in important ways, and this structures how people construe and react to police work. When people think about the 'police' they then are often also thinking about 'nation', 'state' and 'community', and their relation to these categories. All this has implications for how we think about governance and the vexed question of controlling the police. It is to this point I now turn.

GOVERNING THE POLICE – HOW TO WATCH THE WATCHERS

The huge range of legal powers vested in police, their variety and potential intrusiveness and, of course, the ability to use force, mean that the question of controlling this power is never far away from any discussion of police work. Yet, rarely does any definitive answer present itself, and indeed it is perhaps best to conceive of a variegated mosaic comprised of the controls, limits and processes surrounding and embedded in police organisations and police work, the success of which varies over time and context. Moreover, elements of this mosaic can exist in some tension with the needs and desires of the police themselves, which are often directed towards the aggregation of more powers, the more extensive use of existing powers, and/or the circumventing of controls and transgression of limits for principled (as in the case of 'noble cause corruption') or nefarious ends.

This mosaic of control has five important elements, although it is not limited to them. First and foremost, police organisations are governed by law, and there are elaborate legal frameworks around particular elements of police work. However, empirical studies throw up an uncomfortable fact – that it is often better to think of the law as enabling police action rather than constraining it (Bowling et al., 2019). Suffice to say, the law and legal regulation provide a necessary but not sufficient system of controls, checks and balances on police behaviour.

Second, there are extra-legal modes of bureaucratic, social and cultural regulation within police organisations. These include reward and disciplinary schemes, training and development, and informal cultural practices that direct behaviour in certain ways. An important issue here is the extent to which these processes can pull in different directions. The classic, somewhat hackneyed but still relevant example here is that of the experience of recruits, who are given one version of how policing should be conducted during training, and quite another when they join their new colleagues 'on the streets'.

Third, there are the various forms of direct democratic oversight and governance placed around and above police organisations. In the UK the paradigmatic example is the office of Police and Crime Commissioner, a single elected official with strategic control and oversight of a particular police force. This form of governance almost always exists in a state of some tension: police officers need to be subject to democratic control but also separate from it, not least in order to avoid tyranny of the majority dilemmas (the enforcement of popularly supported interventions that undermine the fundamental rights of minority populations).

Fourth, and distinctly, there is the need for police officers to retain legitimacy, which, recall, is founded on public perceptions of fairness and justice. These facts may function together to place important limits around police activity: despite their power, the police cannot simply do what they want. If the public become aware of widespread malfeasance or unjust behaviour, police may be forced to change, or run the risk of a fundamental loss of legitimacy.

Fifth, and finally, there are the controls that are internal to police officers themselves. These might stem purely from personal ethics and morality, and most police organisations attempt to recruit people with the right 'character' for the job. Equally, however, intrinsic motivations to behave in appropriate ways and avoid the abuse of power can be encouraged – or inhibited – by organisational structures and processes. A significant strain of policing research has recently opened up around the idea of **organisational justice**, which can be seen as a direct counterpart to the idea of procedural justice outlined above. There is much evidence to suggest that officers who feel fairly treated at work are, for a variety of reasons, more likely to engage in normatively desirable modes of activity and less likely to abuse their power (Trinkner et al., 2017). This shifts the emphasis onto police managers who, it increasingly seems, need to do much more to manage internal *relationships*, as opposed to just rules and regulations.

CHAPTER SUMMARY

- The police are a state-funded specialist social control institution, engaged in protecting the established social order by means much wider than simply 'fighting crime'.

- The extent of the contribution police make towards this end is unclear, but police work does play a role. In the absence of a relatively well-functioning police service, crime would be higher and security more tenuous; and the established order would be less well protected and more subject to challenge.
- Police can therefore promote social change, by helping to create a baseline of security that frees people to act in ways that would otherwise be unavailable to them. Yet, the police can also inhibit social change, by serving too closely the status quo and established hierarchies and interest groups. They both threaten and protect freedom, not least because the powers needed to do the latter can so easily be misused.
- The relationship with the *policed* is central to understanding the role, place and success of the police. All else equal, police work that generates, sustains or at least does not undermine positive relations with the communities within which it is conducted can be seen as successful; conversely, styles and modes that damage trust and legitimacy, regardless of what other outcomes they produce, are inherently problematic.
- Police officers must foster other relationships in order to conduct crime-fighting and other modes of activity. As police work becomes ever more clearly focused on these relationships, their quality and the broader outcomes they produce should become important ways of thinking about what good police work looks like, and the kinds of outcomes it can be expected to produce.

Review Questions

1. Who are the police?
2. What is the primary function of the police?
3. What are three important challenges currently facing police in the UK?
4. Why is the relationship between police and public so important?
5. How can we ensure police activity is constrained within appropriate boundaries?

GO FURTHER

Books

1. This is the definitive account of the history, status, activities and as the name suggests politics of British policing; the new edition also widens the focus to include global issues:

   Bowling, B., Reiner, R. and Sheptycki, J. (2019) *The Politics of the Police* (5th edition). Oxford: Oxford University Press.

2. A great counterpoint to *The Politics of the Police*, this book takes a more analytical approach and also covers the wider range of organisations involved in policing:

   Brodeur, J-P. (2010) *The Policing Web*. Oxford: Oxford University Press.

3. This book comprises one of the fullest accounts yet of the sources and consequences of public trust and police legitimacy:

   Jackson, J., Bradford, B., Stanko, B. and Hohl, K. (2013) *Just Authority? Trust in the Police in England and Wales*. London: Routledge.

Journal Articles

1. The following article provides an in-depth sociological account of how police use 'big data':

   Brayne, S. (2017) Big data surveillance: the case of policing. *American Sociological Review*, 82(5): 977–1008.

2. This second article is a definitive account of the need for and promise of evidence-based policing:

   Sherman, L. W. (2013) The rise of evidence-based policing: targeting, testing and tracking. *Crime and Justice*, 42(1): 377–451.

3. The following is an excellent overview of police legitimacy, ranging from definitional issues to empirical investigation:

   Tyler, T. R. and Jackson, J. (2014) Popular legitimacy and the exercise of legal authority: motivating compliance, cooperation and engagement. *Psychology, Public Policy and Law*, 20(1): 78–95.

Useful Websites

1. College of Policing (n.d.) *Crime Reduction Toolkit*, is an extremely useful tool for those interested in evidence-based policing: https://whatworks.college.police.uk/toolkit/Pages/Toolkit.aspx
2. The following is the final report of the President's task force on 21st-century policing: https://www.themarshallproject.org/documents/2082979-final-report-of-the-presidents-task-force-on
3. The following is a wide-ranging evaluation and set of recommendations for policing in the twenty-first century. *Does stop and search reduce crime?* A report published by the Centre for Crime and Justice Studies. It is arguably the first robust, wide-ranging, evaluation of whether use of this 'iconic' power has any effect on crime: https://www.crimeandjustice.org.uk/publications/does-stop-and-search-reduce-crime

REFERENCES

Andreas, P. and Nadelmann, E. (2006) *Policing the Globe: Criminalization and Crime Control in International Relations*. Oxford: Oxford University Press.

Angiolini, E. (2015) 'Report of the independent review into the investigation and prosecution of rape in London'. London Metropolitan Police Service and Crown Prosecution Service.

Ariel, B., Sutherland, A., Henstock, D., Young, J., Drover, P., Sykes, J., … and Henderson, R. (2017) 'Contagious accountability': a global multisite randomized controlled trial on the effect of police body-worn cameras on citizens' complaints against the police. *Criminal Justice and Behavior*, 44(2): 293–316.

Ayling, J., Grabosky, P. and Shearing, C. (2010) *Lengthening the Arms of the Law*. Cambridge: Cambridge University Press.

BBC (2019a) 'Kent Police stop using crime predicting software'. Available at: https://www.bbc.co.uk/news/uk-england-kent-46345717 (last accessed 12/12/19).

BBC (2019b) 'Recruitment of 20,000 new police officers to begin "within weeks"'. Available at: https://www.bbc.co.uk/news/uk-49123319 (last accessed 22/10/19).

Bittner, E. (1990) *Aspects of Police Work*. Boston, MA: Boston University Press.

Bowling, B., Reiner, R. and Sheptycki, J. (2019) *The Politics of the Police* (5th edition). Oxford: Oxford University Press.

Bradford, B. (2011) 'Police numbers and crime – a rapid evidence review'. Report prepared for Her Majesty's Inspectorate of Constabulary.

Bradford, B., Sargeant, E., Murphy, T. and Jackson, J. (2017) A leap of faith? Trust in the police among immigrants in England and Wales. *British Journal of Criminology*, 57(2): 381–401.

Brayne, S. (2017) Big data surveillance: the case of policing. *American Sociological Review*, 82(5): 977–1008.

Brodeur, J-P. (2010) *The Policing Web*. Oxford: Oxford University Press.

Cohen, S. (1985) *Visions of Social Control: Crime, Punishment and Classification*. Cambridge: Polity Press.

College of Policing (n.d.a) Crime Reduction Toolkit. Available at: https://whatworks.college.police.uk/toolkit/Pages/Toolkit.aspx (last accessed 12/12/19).

College of Policing (n.d.b) What is evidence-based policing? Available at: https://whatworks.college.police.uk/About/Pages/What-is-EBP.aspx (last accessed 12/12/19).

Di Tella, R. and Schargrodsky, E. (2004) Do police reduce crime? Estimates using the allocation of police forces after a terrorist attack. *American Economic Review*, 94(1): 115–133.

Ferguson, A. G. (2017) *The Rise of Big Data Policing: Surveillance, Race, and the Future of Law Enforcement*. New York University Press.

House of Commons Home Affairs Committee (2015) Policing and mental health: Eleventh Report of Session 2014–15. London: HMSO.

Jackson, J., Bradford, B., Stanko, B. and Hohl, K. (2013) *Just Authority? Trust in the Police in England and Wales*. London: Routledge.

Jacobs, J. (2016) 'Police, the Rule of Law and Civil Society: A Philosophical Perspective'. In B. Bradford, B. Jauregui, I. Loader and J. Steinberg (eds), *The SAGE Handbook of Global Policing*. London: Sage.

Murray, K. and Malik, A. (2019) 'Contested Spaces: The Politics of Strategic Police Leadership in Scotland'. In P. Ramshaw, M. Silvestri and M. Simpson (eds), *Police Leadership*. London: Palgrave Macmillan.

ONS (2018) *Homicide in England and Wales: Year ending March 2018*. London: Office for National Statistics.

Parmar, A. (2019) Policing migration and racial technologies. *British Journal of Criminology*, 59(4): 938–957.

Sherman, L. W. (2003) 'Policing for Crime Prevention'. In L. W. Sherman et al. (eds), *Preventing Crime: What Works, What Doesn't, What's Promising*. A report to the United States Congress.

Sherman, L. W. (2013) *The Rise of Evidence-Based Policing: Targeting, Testing and Tracking*. Chicago: University of Chicago.

Sherman, L. W., Neyroud, P. W. and Neyroud, E. (2016) The Cambridge crime harm index: measuring total harm from crime based on sentencing guidelines. *Policing: A Journal of Policy and Practice*, 10(3): 171–183.

Skogan, W. G., Van Craen, M. and Hennessy, C. (2015) Training police for procedural justice. *Journal of Experimental Criminology*, 11(3): 319–334.

Telep, C. W. and Weisburd, D. (2012) What is known about the effectiveness of police practices in reducing crime and disorder? *Police Quarterly*, 15(4): 331–357.

Trinkner, R., Tyler, T. R. and Goff, P. A. (2016) Justice from within: the relations between a procedurally just organizational climate and police organizational efficiency, endorsement of democratic policing, and officer well-being. *Psychology, Public Policy, and Law*, 22(2): 158.

Tyler, T. R. (2006) *Why People Obey the Law* (2nd edition). New Haven, CT: Yale University Press.

Tyler, T. R. and Jackson, J. (2014) Popular legitimacy and the exercise of legal authority: motivating compliance, cooperation and engagement. *Psychology, Public Policy and Law*, 20(1): 78–95.

Weber, L. (2013) *Policing Non-Citizens*. Abingdon: Routledge.

Weisburd, D., Groff, E. R. and Yang., S-M. (2012) *The Criminology of Place: Street Segments and Our Understanding of the Crime Problem*. Oxford: Oxford University Press.

The Crown Prosecution Service

25

Joanne Clough

---------------- Learning Objectives ----------------

By the end of this chapter you will:

- Understand the historical background to the system of public prosecutions.
- Appreciate the role of the Crown Prosecution Service in England and Wales and its key personnel.
- Gain an understanding of the duties of a Crown Prosecutor.
- Be able to critically consider the complexities and challenges of an independent, state prosecution system.

---------------- Framing Questions ----------------

1. Is the rationale behind an independent, state-operated prosecution service without logic?
2. Critically analyse the current organisational structure of the CPS and consider how, if at all, you might modify or update it.
3. Should the CPS be the official legal representative for the victims of crime, or is it preferable that there is some distance between the two?
4. Is it appropriate that private individuals can still bring prosecutions in certain situations?

INTRODUCTION

The prosecution is the legal party with responsibility for presenting a case against an accused person in a criminal trial. This is the case in both common law adversarial systems such as within Canada, Australia and the UK, and in civil law inquisitorial systems, such as France, Germany and Brazil. It is typical for the prosecutor, i.e. the legal representative of the prosecution, to represent the government, or the State, hence they are independent from the actual victim of the offence.

There were approximately 1.38 million defendants prosecuted in the UK in 2018 (Criminal Justice System Statistics Quarterly: December 2018, 2020). Until around 1880, it was the victim of a crime who had to either personally prosecute the alleged offender before the courts, or if they could afford it, to instruct a lawyer to represent them. Between 1880 and 1986, the police took over responsibility for prosecuting criminal offences. By the late 1980s, amidst concerns that there should be separate agencies for investigating and prosecuting criminal offences, the **Crown Prosecution Service (CPS)** was created. Its team of legally qualified solicitors and barristers now undertake the day-to-day conduct of prosecuting offenders in the courtroom.

In this chapter, you will explore the history behind the formation of the CPS, understand the personnel who work within the CPS, and find out more about the evolving functions of CPS lawyers. You will see that the CPS lawyer is more than simply the solicitor or barrister who is a trial advocate on behalf of 'the State'. They are also responsible for advising the police, for determining whether and with what offence to **charge** a suspect, and for recommending out of court disposals, designed to divert appropriate offenders away from the criminal justice system. The CPS has responsibility for ensuring the victims of crime are treated fairly, kept up to date with the progress of the case, and understand why certain decisions are taken by the CPS in relation to the case. You will note, however, that while proper ethical and procedural standards are set by CPS policy makers, external pressures often provide challenges to meeting and maintaining these standards.

MAPPING THE TERRAIN

Historically, in England and Wales, a criminal was brought to justice by a private citizen. During the eighteenth century, around 80% of prosecutions were conducted by either the victim of a crime or someone acting on the victim's behalf, with most prosecutors being men (Hay, 1983: 167). A formal prosecution could be avoided if the matter was considered insignificant, or if the offender engaged in community action, such as paying the victim money to compensate a theft or being thrown into the town pond by way of public humiliation. The cases that were prosecuted, were dealt with in front of a single magistrate sitting informally in his parlour or a local tavern, or before two magistrates sitting more formally in the petty sessions court. The private individual, as prosecutor, could take more serious matters, such as those that could be used to set an example, to a higher court. The poor tended not to prosecute offences due to the cost of bringing a case to court. Even the organisation of local prosecution associations, consisting of up to fifty individuals, usually farmers and businessmen, whose subscription fees financed the prosecution of anyone offending against their number, was not enough to widen access to justice. In 1778, legislation was passed to allow costs to be awarded to any prosecutor who secured a conviction aiming to encourage appropriate prosecutions from all in society (Emsley, 2010).

During the nineteenth century, the criminal process became more formalised, with the introduction of trial by magistrates without jury, and the creation of stipendiary magistrates to deal with cases requiring more legal expertise. As a result, both the prosecutor and the defence were often represented by solicitors. Law reformers began to argue that England needed a system of public prosecution, like that which was already operating in Scotland and across Europe, in order to overcome the reluctance of victims to prosecute crime due to fear or a lack of funding. It was felt this would also discourage vexatious prosecutions by those who held a grudge and had enough money to satisfy it.

After the creation of the Metropolitan Police in 1829, police officers were permitted to take on prosecutions if the magistrates refused to finance a prosecution privately. Consequently, by the mid-nineteenth century, the police became the main prosecutors before the courts, mainly in prosecutions for public order, public decency, public safety matters, and petty theft (Emsley and Storch, 1993). The police also began to step in to prosecute for those who were too poor to afford it and for those with lesser social status, such as women. The legal profession disliked the police acting as prosecutors as they lacked legal expertise and tended not to put their case forward in an impartial manner.

In 1845, the Criminal Law Commission reported that prosecutions were 'loose and unsatisfactory' and were 'frequently performed unwillingly and carelessly' (Grieve, 2013), hence public prosecutors were cited as the solution. A growing profession of solicitors, fearful of losing a vital source of income, presented the biggest opposition to several Bills, seeking to create a public prosecution system, but which were rejected by Parliament throughout the 1850s and 1870s. There were also fears that the State prosecuting offences would be too expensive and would impinge upon individual liberties. However, the prevailing view was that the proposed new police force with the responsibility of preventing crime, clearly also encompassed the responsibility to prosecute perpetrators of crime. Hence, the Prosecution of Offenders Act 1879 was enacted to create a **Director of Public Prosecutions** (DPP), with a remit to determine the prosecution of difficult and important cases, with the assistance of the Treasury Solicitor. The DPP's role, at this stage, was mainly advisory (Hay, 1983), with limited resources, no department of his own and only one assistant and three clerks to help him (Grieve, 2013).

By the start of the twentieth century, there was still no formal system of State prosecutions run by State officials. Prosecutions were generally conducted by the professional police force, who investigated the offence, decided on the charges and, even where counsel was instructed to present the case in court, remained the final decision makers as to whether the case was to be proceeded with (Grieve, 2013). By 1962, concerns were raised by a Royal Commission that it was not appropriate for police officers to both investigate and prosecute cases due to a fear that the police were not impartial. The criminal justice system at this time was described as 'haphazard, inefficient and often arbitrary and unfair' (Grieve, 2013: 3). The Commission therefore recommended that all police forces should have separate legal departments within which prosecuting solicitors would work to take police cases to court.

In 1978, a wider review of the prosecution system took place, prompted by an inquiry into the failings of the police in the investigation and prosecution of the Maxwell Confait murder case (Robins, 2019). Chaired by Sir Cyril Philips, the Royal Commission on Criminal Procedure (The Philips Inquiry, 1981) reported that police officers who investigated alleged offences could not always be relied upon to make fair decisions as to whether to prosecute offenders. It was thought that as officers had a vested interest in being seen to arrest and then successfully hold the arrested person to account, they proceeded with inappropriate prosecutions, resulting in cases being thrown out of court for a lack of evidence, or in ignorance of evidence that would have resulted in an acquittal. It was found that the police officer investigating a case, whether deliberately or otherwise, naturally forms a view about the guilt of the suspect and from there, can be inclined to shut their mind to other evidence that undermines that view. Alternatively, they can overestimate the strength of the evidence already gathered, hence without oversight, these flaws in the system provided an opportunity for police corruption. It was also suggested that different police forces across the country were making inconsistent prosecution decisions. The Philips Inquiry therefore repeated the earlier recommendation that police forces should no longer investigate *and* make prosecution decisions, except for the most minor of crimes and regulatory offences.

Case Study 25.1

The Philips Enquiry, 1981

The Philips Enquiry found that police bias regarding the value of their case and their views on who had committed it, led to over-charging: 43% of Crown Court acquittals were as a result of the prosecution having insufficient evidence to create a **prima facie case** against the accused.

In 1983, a Government White Paper took the recommendation a step further by proposing the creation and organisational structure of a national prosecution service answerable to the DPP, to provide more consistency and independence (Home Office, 1983). These two significant reports set the scene for the introduction of what are considered to be the two modern pillars of criminal justice: the Police and Criminal Evidence Act 1984 and the Prosecution of Offences Act 1985.

THE CROWN PROSECUTION SERVICE

The Prosecution of Offences Act 1985 (POA 1985) was enacted on 23 May 1985, creating an independent, State run, and State funded, prosecuting service for England and Wales – the Crown Prosecution Service (CPS). The POA 1985 provided the legislative structure within which the CPS was to operate, with the aim of separating the functions of investigating and prosecuting crime, so that the police, as investigators, would act independently from the CPS, as prosecutors. The CPS was believed to be able to provide a counterbalance to the increased police powers within the newly enacted Police and Criminal Evidence Act 1984, which governs the procedures for criminal investigations and the treatment of suspects. In 1986, the CPS finally became operational, bringing England and Wales in line with Scotland, which had an independent Procurator Fiscal prosecuting separately from the police since the eighteenth century by virtue of the Criminal Procedure Scotland Act 1701.

Pause for Thought

To what extent do you consider the reforms to the system of prosecuting offenders over the years, were influenced by political or institutional demands?

What does the CPS do?

The Crown Prosecution Service prosecutes criminal cases that have been investigated by the police and several other investigative organisations in England and Wales. Today these other organisations include, the National Crime Agency, the UK Border Agency, Her Majesty's Revenue and Customs (HMRC), and the Department for Work and Pensions (DWP). It is the CPS's duty to ensure that the right person is prosecuted for the right offence, and, where possible, to bring offenders to justice. Prosecutors must act fairly, objectively and independently of the police and of the government when making decisions and when prosecuting cases, ensuring that the **Code for Crown Prosecutors** (see below), which sets out the basic standards for making case decisions, is followed.

The CPS work closely with the police, courts, the Judiciary and other partners to deliver justice. In so doing, prosecutors must follow the legal guidance provided within the "Statement of Ethical Principles for the Public Prosecutor" (the Statement). In particular, they must adhere to the highest professional standards as set out in section 3.1 of the Statement as follows:

a. exercise the highest standards of integrity and care;
b. not conduct the prosecution of a case which is beyond their competence, knowledge or experience;
c. take reasonable steps to maintain and enhance their professional knowledge and skills and keep themselves well-informed and aware of relevant legal developments;
d. strive to be, and to be seen to be, consistent, independent, fair and impartial;
e. preserve professional confidentiality at all times, subject to the requirements of the law;
f. serve and protect the public interest; and
g. respect the right of all people to be held equal before the law - prosecutors must never act in a way that unjustifiably favours or discriminates against particular individuals or interests.

Figure 25.1 Professional Standards of the CPS

Source: Derived from 'Statement of Ethical Principles for the Public Prosecutor, URL: https://www.cps.gov.uk/legal-guidance/ethical-principles-public-prosecutor-statement. Reproduced under the Open Government License v2.0, URL: http://www.nationalarchives.gov.uk/doc/open-government-licence/version/2/.

CPS Personnel

The Prosecution of Offences Act 1985 (POA 1985) provides for the organisational structure of the CPS and outlines the responsibilities of each of the key roles. Currently, the CPS has fourteen operational areas, and each is headed by a Chief Crown Prosecutor (CCP) with responsibility for a team of prosecutors, case workers and administrative staff. Each CPP is supported by an Area Business Manager. There is also a virtual fifteenth area, namely CPS Direct, also headed by a CCP, which provides charging

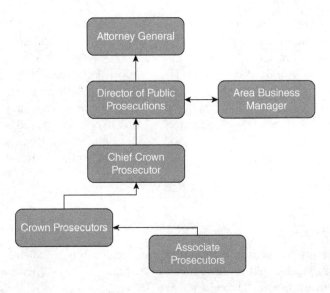

Figure 25.2 The Organisational Structure of the CPS

Source: Derived from: https://www.cps.gov.uk/ (circa 2019).

Reproduced under the Open Government License v2.0, URL: http://www.nationalarchives.gov.uk/doc/open-government-licence/version/2/.

advice and decisions to all police forces and other investigators across England and Wales 24 hours a day, 365 days a year. So, who are the personnel within this organisation and what do they do?

The Attorney General

The **Attorney General** (AG) is the Crown's chief legal advisor who has several independent public interest functions. They have oversight of the Law Officer's departments including the CPS, the Serious Fraud Office, Her Majesty's Crown Prosecution Service Inspectorate and the Government Legal Department. In this role, the AG safeguards the independence of prosecutors, but they have limited practical involvement in the day-to-day running of the CPS.

The Director of Public Prosecutions (DPP)

The DPP is the head of the CPS (POA 1985, s.1(1)(a)), appointed by the AG, and discharging their functions under the superintendence of the AG (POA 1985, s.3(1)). The DPP must be a barrister or solicitor with at least ten years' experience (POA 1985, s.2). The DPP has responsibility for the conduct of criminal proceedings instigated by the police force and all other investigative agencies within their remit (see below). The duties of the DPP include the following (POA 1985, s.3(2)):

- Taking over the conduct of all criminal proceedings instituted by or on behalf of a police force, or the National Crime Agency.
- Advising police forces on all matters relating to criminal offences as considered to be appropriate.
- Appearing for the prosecution when directed by the court to do so on certain types of appeal case.
- Discharging such other functions as may from time to time be assigned to them by the AG.

The DPP has the power to discontinue any proceedings they have responsibility for, or to take any other step in relation to those proceedings including the bringing of an appeal and the making of representations in respect of applications for bail (POA 1985, s.15(3)). In addition, the DPP is responsible for issuing and updating a Code for Crown Prosecutors (POA 1985, s.10), to provide guidance on general principles to be applied when making decisions about prosecutions. This includes principles about: determining whether proceedings for an offence should be instituted; or, where proceedings have already started, whether they should be discontinued; what charges should be preferred; and representations to be made about mode of trial in any magistrates' Court case. The eighth and most recent version of the Code was published in October 2018 and is available to view on the cps.gov.uk website.

Crown Prosecutors

The DPP may designate any barrister or solicitor within the CPS to be a Crown Prosecutor (CP) (POA 1985, s.1(3)). A CP may represent the CPS in the courts to prosecute cases. They have 'all the powers of the Director as to the institution and conduct of proceedings but shall exercise those powers under the direction of the Director' (POA 1985, s.1(6)). If the DPP's consent is required to take a particular step in a case, a CP may give such consent as delegated by the DPP (POA 1985, s.1(7)). There is a Chief Crown Prosecutor designated to each CPS area (POA 1985, s1(4)).

The DPP is also empowered by the Act to appoint persons who are not members of the CPS to institute or take over the conduct of criminal proceedings (POA 1985, s.5(1)), e.g. they may instruct an agent barrister to prosecute on their behalf. The appointed person has all the powers of a CP but has to exercise those powers subject to any instructions given to them by the DPP (or a CP acting on the DPP's behalf). In practice the volume of CPS work in the magistrates' courts is such that some has to be delegated to barrister and solicitor agents under this power, however the agent must obtain authority from a CPS lawyer before taking steps in relation to any case, e.g. offering no evidence or accepting a **bind over**. By contrast, in the Crown Court, Counsel instructed to prosecute on the CPS's behalf has much more independence when it comes to presenting the case and does not require such stringent permissions to be obtained.

Associate Prosecutors

It is possible to also appoint staff who are not legally qualified (POA 1985, s.7A) and these individuals are known as 'Associate Prosecutors' (AP). They are permitted to represent the CPS in bail applications and other pre-trial applications such as requests for adjournments. They may conduct trials in cases involving non-imprisonable summary offences.

The Functions of the CPS

Having looked at the various personnel within the CPS, we now turn to the role of the CPS, as outlined within the Code for Crown Prosecutors and which encompasses much more than simply appearing before the court as an advocate for the police. The CPS essentially has four key functions:

- Making decisions on whether to prosecute and for which offence.
- Prosecuting offences in the courts.
- Determining whether a case is suitable for an 'out of court disposal'.
- Advising the police.

We will now look at each of these in more detail.

The decision to prosecute

The CPS took over the job of making decisions on charging suspects in all but the most minor road-traffic and regulatory offences, following the recommendations of the Philips Inquiry in 1981 (see above). CPS lawyers were considered to have the legal expertise to properly analyse the strength of the evidence, as well as the independence from the case to consider the evidence objectively. A few years later, it was found that too many low-level offences were being considered by the CPS prosecutors and this introduced a degree of delay while lawyers dealt with every case that was investigated by the police (Grieve, 2013). In 2012, the list of low-level crimes that could be dealt with and charged by the police, without the need for a prosecutor's decision, was increased, to remove this inefficiency, hence the CPS now manage only the charging decisions of the more serious and complex cases.

In the current system, after the police have arrested a suspect and completed an investigation, they will bring them before the Custody Sergeant of the police station where they are detained for a decision on whether to charge. In all but the least serious cases, the Officer investigating the case consults with a CPS prosecutor who decides whether there is enough evidence to **charge** the person and if so, with what offence. As there are strict limits on the amount of time a suspect can be held in custody before charge, the Custody Sergeant may release the suspect on bail under s.37(7) Police and Criminal Evidence Act 1984, to allow sufficient time for the prosecutor to make a charging decision in accordance with the 'Full Code Test'.

Figure 25.3   The Full Code Test

Source: Derived from 'The Code for Crown Prosecutors', URL: https://www.cps.gov.uk/publication/code-crown-prosecutors. Reproduced under the Open Government License v2.0, URL: http://www.nationalarchives.gov.uk/doc/open-government-licence/version/2/.

The Full Code Test

Knowledge link: This topic is also covered in Chapter 26.

The decision on whether to charge a suspect is based on the 'Full Code Test' as outlined in the Code for Crown Prosecutors (CPS, 2018; part 4). The Full Code Test should usually be applied when all outstanding reasonable lines of inquiry have been pursued (CPS, 2018: para 4.3). There are two stages to the Full Code Test, both of which must be satisfied before a charge can be laid:

The evidential stage   This is the first stage in the decision to prosecute. A Crown Prosecutor must be satisfied that there is enough evidence against the defendant to provide a 'realistic prospect of conviction' on a charge. This is an objective test which means that an objective, impartial and reasonable jury or bench of magistrates, properly directed in accordance with the law, will be more likely than not to convict the defendant of the offence alleged (CPS, 2018; para 4.7). It is a different test from the one that the court will apply when determining guilt at trial; a court should only convict if it is 'sure' of a defendant's guilt, which is a much higher test to establish.

In applying the evidential test, prosecutors must consider the following:

- Can the evidence be used in court?
- Is the evidence reliable, i.e. relevant and accurate?
- Is the evidence credible?
- Is there any other material that might be obtained through further reasonable lines of enquiry which could affect the prospects of conviction?

If a case does not pass the evidential stage, it must not go ahead, no matter how important or serious it may be (CPS, 2018: para 4.6).

The public interest stage   If a case passes the evidential stage, the CP must then determine whether a prosecution is needed in the public interest. This means the prosecutor will only proceed with the prosecution if the public interest factors tending in favour of prosecution outweigh the public interest factors against prosecution (CPS, 2018: para 4.10). Alternatively, the prosecutor may consider that the public interest is best served by offering the offender the opportunity to have the matter dealt with by an out-of-court disposal (see below) instead of taking the matter to court (CPS, 2018: para 4.10).

In determining whether the public interest test is satisfied, a CP must consider the following matters: the seriousness of the offence; the culpability of the suspect; the harm caused to the victim; the suspect's age and maturity; the impact on the community; whether prosecution is a proportionate response to the offending; and whether sources of information need protecting (CPS, 2018: para 4.13). The prosecutor must weigh these factors fairly and evenly. Some factors may increase the need to prosecute but others may suggest that another course of action would be better, e.g. issuing a caution. The CPS may only start or continue a prosecution if a case has passed both stages of the Full Code Test.

Pause for Thought

In a speech to the Legal Action Group in 2013, former DPP, Sir Keir Starmer QC MP, considered the decision not to prosecute in circumstances where there is enough evidence to do so. He said:

> "Prosecutorial discretion is a good thing. It takes the edges off blunt criminal laws; it prevents injustice; it provides for compliance with international obligations; and it allows compassion to play its rightful part in the criminal justice response to wrongdoing."(Starmer, 2013)

- If you were the victim of an offence, how would you feel about being told that the case does not meet the Full Code Test and therefore the suspect cannot be charged?
- Would you feel different if the offender had been offered an out of court disposal, after admitting the offence and after you were consulted about such an outcome?

The prosecution of offences in court

Under the Prosecution of Offences Act 1985 s.3(2) it is the DPP's duty to take over the conduct of all criminal proceedings instituted by a police force, once a decision to charge has been made. Under Rule 7.2 of the Criminal Procedure Rules, a case must be started by a 'prosecutor'. Thereafter, it is for the Crown Prosecution Service, utilising the evidence gathered by the police, to prove the case against the accused. The standard of proof required for a conviction in a criminal court is proof beyond reasonable doubt, i.e. the court must be 'sure' of the offender's guilt. The CPS have different considerations to bear in mind throughout the various stages of prosecuting an offender as set out below:

Knowledge link: This topic is also covered in Chapter 26.

Bail When the case is first brought before the court after charge, the CPS lawyer must deal with bail. Once charged, an offender must either be held in custody for the next available court or the police may grant bail, either with or without conditions (PACE 1984 s.47); the latter aims to reduce the number of suspects detained for the courts overnight. The police or the CPS may oppose or agree bail at court and it is the job of the prosecutor to make representations to the Court as to whether the accused can be granted bail, conditionally or otherwise. The Court is able to impose conditions that allay any concerns the Prosecution (or police) may have about the offender committing further offences on bail, contacting the witnesses in the case, or failing to attend court for trial including conditions of residence, reporting to a police station, curfews or no-contact with witnesses (see provisions within the Bail Act 1976).

Disclosure of evidence For the weeks following the first hearing, and upon the defendant entering a not guilty plea, the case is fully prepared for trial. Under the Criminal Procedure and Investigations Act 1996, an accused person is entitled to full disclosure of the case against them so they can also prepare their defence. This means that the police, through the CPS, must disclose, i.e. provide to the defendant, all the evidence that they propose to use at trial to secure a conviction; known as 'used material'. In addition, the police must disclose any 'unused material' which meets the statutory test of either undermining the case for the prosecution or assisting the case for the defence. Unused material is any information which the police have gathered during their investigation, and which they must log item by item on a 'Schedule of Unused Material', but which they do not propose to use to prove their case. Although the duty is on the police to manage the evidence and to keep the disclosure of evidence under constant review, it is more often the prosecutor that manages this process, the CPS lawyer having the most detailed knowledge of proceedings for the duration of the prosecution.

If the police do not disclose evidence to the CPS, this can make a case look stronger than it really is. Things that can be missed from disclosure schedules include important matters such as information that suggests the accused was somewhere other than the scene of the crime at the time of the incident. Equally, the police rarely have the time, training or inclination to keep up their disclosure duties (Sanders and Young, 2012) and once the investigation has concluded, the officers move on to the next case, leaving the CPS lawyers to deal with the matter. The Criminal Cases Review Commission, in their Annual Reports of 1999/00 and 2003/04, reported that non-disclosure of evidence was the third most common reason for a wrongful conviction; one mistake or omission from just one person within the disclosure chain, could be fatal to a case.

Case Study 25.2

'Making it Fair: A Joint inspection of the disclosure of unused material in volume Crown Court cases', CPS, July 2017

A joint inspection of prosecution disclosure was carried out by HM CPS Inspectorate and HM Inspector of Constabulary in 2017. It noted 'significant failure' across both the police and CPS (CPS, 2017: 1.4). Police compliance with disclosure was rated either 'poor' or 'fair' across 78% of cases that were reviewed; the figure for the CPS compliance was 77%. Consequently, the 2017-18 Annual Report and Accounts of the CPS acknowledged that their standards of disclosure, the 'cornerstone of justice', had not always been met, and highlighted the implementation of the Joint National Disclosure Improvement Plan between the CPS, the National Police Chiefs' Council and the College of Policing. A review of their disclosure manual was undertaken to take account of changes to the criminal justice system, and the fact that more digital material was being used in criminal investigations. The report also stated that each CPS area had agreed a joint local disclosure improvement plan, hence a National Disclosure Forum was established jointly chaired by the CPS and police, and including representatives from the Law Society, the Bar Council and the Criminal Bar Association, defence solicitors and the judiciary, designed to keep the process under a state of continuous evaluation. These measures, designed to improve the compliance with disclosure procedures, forced the effective disclosure of evidence to be a key priority for the CPS, and it appears from more recent annual reports, that matters are now improving.

Trial   When the case comes to court to be tried, it is also the role of the Prosecutor to present the evidence to the court in order that the magistrates or jury may determine whether the offender is guilty or not guilty. The prosecutor will open the case (outline the facts and the evidence to be presented), will question the prosecution witnesses and present prosecution evidence, will cross-examine the defendant and defence witnesses, and will ensure that the defence lawyers are following the procedural rules of court. A prosecutor will also be required as advocate at other court hearings to present the case for the prosecution, e.g. to outline the facts of the case at a sentencing hearing following a guilty plea or verdict, or to deal with any queries the court has in preparation for trial.

Knowledge link: This topic is also covered in Chapter 26.

Pause for Thought

Not every offender will pursue their case to trial. According to Sanders (2010), approximately 60% of Crown Court defendants and 92% of magistrates Court defendants either plead guilty to the offence charged or they are found guilty after a trial in which they failed to turn up and give evidence. Zander and Henderson (1993) found that over 10% of guilty pleaders in the Crown Court claimed to be innocent, indicating that sometimes offenders may plead guilty when the evidence is not against them. Consequently, where the evidence points to the guilt of an offender, or sometimes when it does not, but the offender wishes for the matter to 'go away', the prosecution can secure a conviction easily with a guilty plea.

Do such convictions skew the rate of 'successful' prosecutions for the CPS?

Out of court disposals

Rather than taking a case through the formal prosecution route, the CPS can choose one of several methods to 'divert' a suspect from the courtroom. For example, if a suspect makes a full admission to an offence in police interview, there is sufficient evidence to provide a realistic prospect of conviction (i.e. satisfies the evidential test – see above) but if the CPS determine that it is not in the public interest to prosecute, an offender can be cautioned. Cautioning is considered much more cost and time effective than taking the case to court; it both clears up the crime report while dealing with the offender swiftly and justly. The caution, whether simple or conditional, is recorded on the offender's police record, and normally only one simple caution will be permitted per adult. Young offenders can receive a reprimand for a first offence and a final warning for a subsequent or first, more serious, offence. A caution, reprimand or warning can be taken into account as previous wrongdoing when sentencing in subsequent prosecutions. Note that this system is currently under review.

Knowledge link: This topic is also covered in Chapter 27 and Chapter 28.

Advising the police

The final function of the CPS is to advise the police in their investigations. Every criminal offence is made up of several 'elements', all of which must be proved before a conviction can be secured. The CPS, with their legal expertise, plays an important role in advising the police as to whether there is a gap in the evidence such that a particular element of an offence cannot be proven. Equally, CPS lawyers can advise the police if a particular piece of evidence is admissible or inadmissible in court, for example, because the rules relating to the investigation and gathering of evidence contained within the Police and Criminal Evidence Act 1984 have not been complied with, or because an evidential legal rule states that the evidence cannot be used in court. In turn, this assists the police in building the strongest possible case against the accused and together, the police and CPS are able to secure the safest convictions for those responsible for criminal offences.

Lawyers for the victim

Underlying all four functions of the CPS is the fact that someone, a victim, is affected by the criminal activity. In a criminal trial, a defence lawyer represents the accused so you would be forgiven for thinking that the CPS lawyer represents the victim. However, the CPS does not act for victims or their families in the same manner as solicitors act for criminal clients as it is the public interest that guides the prosecutor's work (CPS, 2018: 4.14). While the CPS helps to get justice for the victim, it is the State and not the victim per se, who brings the case against the accused person. Nevertheless, the CPS lawyer is the person presenting the case on behalf of the victim and the CPS aims to 'treat all victims and witnesses with respect and understanding throughout the justice process' (cps.gov.uk).

Knowledge link: This topic is also covered in Chapter 3.

The Code of Practice for Victims of Crime (MOJ, 2015), which was part of a wider Government strategy to put victims first within the criminal justice system, sets out a minimum standard of approximately twenty entitlements that must be provided to victims of crime by various organisations in England and Wales, including the CPS. In order to meet the requirements of the Victims Code, the CPS set up Victim Liaison Units (VLU) which have the responsibility of informing victims about CPS decisions to charge and/or discontinue a case, and who will signpost victims to the review procedure where necessary. If a victim is unhappy at a CPS decision not to charge, to discontinue or to bring proceedings to an end, they are able to utilise the Victim's Right to Review Scheme in order to have the decision reviewed.

Case Study 25.3

R v Killick [2011] EWCA Crim 1608

In Killick, the Court considered the rights of a victim of crime to challenge a CPS decision not to prosecute and determined that: victims have a right to seek a review in such circumstance; victims should not have to seek recourse to judicial review; and the right to a review should be made the subject of clear procedure and guidance with set time limits. As a result of this case, the Victim's Right to Review Scheme was launched by the CPS to make it easier for victims to seek a review of qualifying CPS decisions made on or after 5 June 2013.

In addition to providing a witness statement detailing the incident in question, a victim is entitled to give a Victim Personal Statement (VPS), allowing them the opportunity to explain the effect that a crime has had on them. This can include details about the physical, emotional or financial impact of the offence, whether the victim is considering claiming compensation and whether there are concerns about the accused being released from custody. The court must consider a Victim Impact Statement before sentencing an offender, and the victim is entitled to attend court to read it out, if they choose to do so. In a murder case, where the accused is acquitted after trial, the relatives of the murder victim are entitled to enhanced support from the CPS and the police.

Special measures

The thought of giving evidence in a courtroom at trial is a daunting prospect for many victims and witnesses, particularly those who were subjected to violent or sexual offences. In order to assist, the CPS have produced a guide to help witnesses prepare for giving evidence (see cps.gov.uk). For those who are considered to be vulnerable or intimidated, a range of 'special measures' under Part II of the Youth Justice and Criminal Evidence Act 1999, can be put in place to ensure the experience of giving evidence is as comfortable as it possibly can be. This will be considered by the CPS lawyer with responsibility for the case, who will make an application to the Court to decide what special measure, if any, can be put in place. The measures available to assist witnesses to give evidence include the following: giving evidence via a live TV link; video-recorded evidence; giving evidence from behind a screen; and giving evidence in private.

Knowledge link: This topic is also covered in Chapter 26.

In the 2014–15 Annual Report and Accounts of the CPS, in which it was stated that only 65% of victims were 'very' or 'fairly' satisfied with the service they received from the CPS, the DPP decided that one of its four strategic objectives for the following year was to make their service to victims and witnesses central to everything they did. The key measures implemented to improve the victim experience included:

- reducing the number of cases that were lost due to victim issues;
- improving the communication to victims utilising the newly written 'Speaking to Witnesses at Court' guidance;
- reviewing and acting on reports from the Victim's Commissioner and Inspectorate relevant to the CPS's work.

As a result of the new approach to supporting victims and witnesses at court, the CPS later reported, in their 2016–17 Annual Report, that over 95% of witnesses were very satisfied or satisfied with the service provided by the CPS. Nevertheless, the campaign to improve the victim experience continues.

Private prosecutions

Although the CPS conducts most prosecutions, it is still possible to prosecute an alleged wrongdoer as a private individual. Private prosecutions are cases which are initiated by a private citizen or organisation which is not acting on behalf of the police or other prosecuting authority. Usually this will happen where the CPS or the police are not interested or able to conduct the prosecution, so it is a means by which a victim of a crime can get justice for wrongdoing against them. A private prosecution takes the same form as a normal criminal trial; put simply, the case is not brought by the CPS, but instead by a lawyer acting on behalf of the private individual (or the private individual themselves).

A private prosecution is commenced by the individual applying to the magistrates' Court by a process known as 'laying an information'. After this, the court will issue a summons to secure the attendance of the accused at court (Criminal Procedure Rules 2005: Rule 7.2). Some private prosecutions are in fact brought by public authorities. For example, the Royal Society for the Prevention of Cruelty to Animals (RSPCA) privately prosecute animal welfare cases. The police privately prosecute minor road traffic offences and Local Authorities privately prosecute dog fouling or truancy matters. Other agencies who prosecute privately include the Probation Service (for breaches of probation orders), the Driver and Vehicle Licensing Agency (DVLA) (for driving licence offences), and TV Licensing (for using a TV without a licence).

—————————— **Case Study 25.4** ——————————

Christopher Davies

One notable private prosecution in the 1990s, involved the case of serial rapist Christopher Davies who sexually assaulted two different sex workers at knifepoint after they had visited his home. The first woman was a tattooed biker, who was told by police that she would never get justice in court. The second woman was attacked a year later. She was working in the porn industry in order to raise money to support her disabled husband. The CPS refused to take the cases to court due to insufficient evidence so the two women, working together with the English Collective of Prostitutes (ECP) and Women Against Rape, gathered a legal team to work **pro-bono** on the private prosecution of Davies. After three and a half years, in 1995, the case was tried before the courts, and Davies was convicted. This became the first private prosecution for rape in England and Wales (Garland, 2019).

CHAPTER SUMMARY

The Crown Prosecution Service (CPS) was created in 1986 in order to separate the bodies who investigate and who prosecute criminal offences, amidst concerns that there was a lack of impartiality on the part of the police who, prior to this date, undertook both roles:

- The CPS is headed by the Director of Public Prosecutions, who has responsibility for a team of Crown Prosecutors and Associate Prosecutors in each CPS area.
- The main roles of the CPS are to advise the police on investigation and charge, to litigate criminal allegations through the criminal courts, and to protect the interests of the victims of crime.
- A Prosecutor must follow the guidance in the Code for Crown Prosecutors when fulfilling their duties.
- It is possible to bring a private prosecution against an offender, in particular in cases where the police or the CPS decide not to prosecute.

————————— Review questions —————————

1. What are the main functions of the Crown Prosecution Service?
2. Explain the components of the Full Code Test in determining whether to charge a suspect.
3. What role does the victim play in the prosecution of offenders? What can the victim not expect from the process?
4. Does the CPS have to charge a suspect in every case? If not, what alternatives do they have?
5. Does a victim have any options in a situation where the CPS decide not to prosecute?

GO FURTHER

Books/Book Chapters

1. For a real-life account of the CPS in action in the criminal justice system, see:

   The Secret Barrister (2018) *Stories of the Law and How It's Broken*. London: Picador, ch. 4.

2. For further information on the early history of the prosecution system in the UK, see:

   Emsley, C. (2010) *Crime and Society in England 1750–1900*, 4th edition. Harlow, UK: Pearson Education Limited, ch. 8.

3. For more analysis on the theory behind the creation of the CPS and the ways in which the findings of the Philips Inquiry were implemented, see:

   Home Office (1983) *An independent prosecution service for England and Wales* (Cmnd 9074). London: HMSO.

   and

   McConville, M., Sanders, A. and Leng, R. (1991) *The Case for the Prosecution*. London: Routledge.

Journal Articles

1. For more analysis on the theory behind the creation of the CPS and the ways in which the findings of the Philips Inquiry were implemented, see:

   White, R. M. (2006) Investigators and prosecutors or, desperately seeking Scotland: Re-formulation of the 'Philips Principle'. *Modern Law Review*, 69(2): 143–182.

2. For a critical analysis of the CPS guidance on the handling of victims and witnesses, see:

   Baki, N. and Agate, J. (2015) Too much too little too late? Draft CPS guidance on speaking to witnesses. *Entertainment Law Review*, 26(5): 155–159.

3. For a more in-depth consideration of prosecuting domestic abuse, see:

   Porter, A. (2018) Prosecuting domestic abuse in England and Wales: Crown Prosecution Service 'working practice' and New Public Managerialism. *Social & Legal Studies*, 28(4): 493–516.

Useful Websites

1. To access the Code for Crown Prosecutors, the CPS Annual Reports and further information about the CPS duties towards victims of crime and witnesses, go to: www.cps.gov.uk
2. Her Majesty's Crown Prosecution Service Inspectorate (HMCPSI) is the independent organisation with responsibility for inspecting, assessing and reporting on the operations of the CPS. For more information on their work, go to: https://www.justiceinspectorates.gov.uk/hmcpsi/
3. A summary of the 1998 review of the CPS, the Glidewell Report, is available at: https://assets.publishing.service.gov.uk/government/uploads/system/uploads/attachment_data/file/259808/3972.pdf

REFERENCES

Crown Prosecution Service (2009) *Statement of Ethical Principles for the Public Prosecutor*. Available at: https://www.cps.gov.uk/legal-guidance/ethical-principles-public-prosecutor-statement (accessed 10 February 2021).

Crown Prosecution Service (2017) *Making it Fair: A Joint inspection of the disclosure of unused material in volume Crown Court cases*. Available at: www.justiceinspectorates.gov.uk/cjji/wp-content/uploads/sites/2/2017/07/CJJI_DCS_thm_July17_rpt.pdf (accessed 24 October 2019).

Crown Prosecution Service (2018) *The Code for Crown Prosecutors*, 8th edition. Available at: https://www.cps.gov.uk/sites/default/files/documents/publications/Code-for-Crown-Prosecutors-October-2018.pdf (accessed 22 September 2019).

Emsley, C. (2010) *Crime and Society in England 1750–1900*, 4th edition. Harlow, UK: Pearson Education Limited.

Emsley, C. and Storch, R. D. (1993) Prosecution and the police in England since 1700. *Bulletin of the International Association for the History of Crime and Criminal Justice*, 18: 45–57.

Garland, E. (2019) *The Legal System Failed Two Sex Workers – So They Took Their Rapist to Court*. Available at: https://www.vice.com/en_uk/article/ne8md8/sex-workers-first-private-prosecution-rape-uk (accessed 5 November 2019).

Grieve, D. Rt Hon. (2013) *The Case for the Prosecution: Independence and the public interest*. Delivered on 13 March 2013. Available at: www.gov.uk/government/speeches/the-case-for-the-prosecution-independence-and-the-public-interest (accessed 3 July 2019).

Hay, D. (1983) Controlling the English prosecutor. *Osgoode Hall Law Journal*, 21: 165–186.

Home Office (1983) *An independent prosecution service for England and Wales* (Cmnd 9074). London: HMSO.

Ministry of Justice (2015) *Code of Practice for Victims of Crime*. Available at: https://assets.publishing.service.gov.uk/government/uploads/system/uploads/attachment_data/file/476900/code-of-practice-for-victims-of-crime.PDF (accessed 23 October 2019).

Ministry of Justice. (2020) *Criminal Justice System Statistics Quarterly: December 2018*. Available at: https://www.gov.uk/government/statistics/criminal-justice-system-statistics-quarterly-december-2018 (accessed 11 March 2020).

Robins, J. (2019) *Cases that Changed Us: Maxwell Confait*. Available at: https://www.thejusticegap.com/cases-that-changed-us-maxwell-confait/ (accessed 12 March 2020).

Royal Commission on Criminal Procedure (1981) (Cmnd. 8092). London: HMSO.

Sanders, A. (2010) 'The Nature and Purposes of Criminal Justice: The Freedom Approach'. In T. Seddon and G. Smith (eds), *Regulation and Criminal Justice*. Cambridge: Cambridge University Press.

Sanders, A. and Young, R. (2012) 'From Suspect to Trial'. In M. Maguire, R. Morgan and R. Reiner (eds), *The Oxford Handbook of Criminology*, 5th edition. Oxford, UK: OUP.

Starmer, K. (2013) Legal Action Group Annual Lecture. Available at: http://www.lag.org.uk/media/145594/lag_annual_lecture_2013_transcript.pdf (accessed 11 January 2020).

Zander, M. and Henderson, P. (1993) 'Crown Court Study', *Royal Commission on Criminal Justice*, Research Study No. 19. London, UK: HMSO.

STATUTES

Criminal Procedure and Investigations Act 1996
Police and Criminal Evidence Act 1984
Prosecution of Offences Act 1985

CASE

R v Killick [2011] EWCA Crim 1608

The Court System in England and Wales

26

Kayliegh Richardson

Learning Objectives

By the end of this chapter you will:

- Have developed an understanding of the court structure that exists in England and Wales.
- Learn about the role that victim-survivors play in different types of legal proceedings and how they may be represented.
- Have developed an understanding of 'choice' in type of proceedings.
- Learn about Litigants in Person.
- Examine the problem of cross-examination in domestic abuse cases and the measures that can be used to protect victim-survivors during court proceedings.

Framing Questions

1. Do the same procedural rules apply to all courts regardless of type of case, i.e. civil, criminal or family?
2. How do the procedural court rules protect the human rights of a victim-survivor and alleged perpetrator of domestic abuse during court proceedings?
3. Do the procedural court rules allow both parties in court proceedings to give oral evidence to their full potential?

INTRODUCTION

In this chapter you are going to learn about the court structure that exists in England and Wales. You will also learn about some of the different procedural rules that apply within the different court systems. This will be discussed within the context of domestic abuse proceedings, as an example of one of the main types of proceedings that can span across the different court jurisdictions. The chapter will provide you with the opportunity to reflect on the overall purpose of a court system and an understanding of why individuals may be reluctant to engage with the criminal justice system. It will also provide you with an insight into how court processes can be manipulated by perpetrators to further abuse and intimidate victim-survivors.

MAPPING THE TERRAIN

First we provide an introduction to the role that the courts play within the overarching English legal system and an overview of how laws are made.

In England and Wales we have a **common law** legal system. This system was originally developed by Henry II in 1154 after concerns were raised about the inconsistent approach being taken by each of the king's courts across the land. The term 'common law' derived out of the concept that the law should be 'common' to all. Under this system, the law is developed by judges deciding cases and laying down binding case precedents. The principle of 'stare decisis' was developed, which simply means that courts are bound by the previous decisions of other courts higher up the hierarchy from themselves (and in some cases, courts of the same level; see Figure 26.2 for a diagram highlighting the hierarchy of the courts). The development of this system allowed for a more consistent and predictable approach in applying and developing the law of England and Wales.

Historically, judge-made law was the primary method of developing new laws. Nowadays, Parliament also contribute to the development of the law through the creation of **legislation**. Judges now more commonly see their role as interpreters of legislation, rather than primary developers of the law itself. Other examples of common law systems include those of Australia and Canada. This can be contrasted with a civil law system, where the primary source of the law is a written set of rules known as codes. The role of the judge in a civil law system will be to interpret the case in front of them rigidly in line with the appropriate code. Most of mainland Europe has a civil law system, specific examples being France and Germany.

An example of judge-made law in England and Wales is the offence of murder, which was developed through a series of cases, rather than by Parliament laying down legislation, as can be seen in Figure 26.1. To this day, the definition of murder is not set out in any statute, although the defences to murder (explanations accepted in law that may lead the court to find that no offence has been committed) are in the figure below.

On a very basic level, we think of the court system as a means of punishing wrongful behaviour, correcting injustices and protecting those who need it. However, academics such as Richardson and Speed (2019) and Bishop and Bettinson (2017) have written at length about the risk of re-victimisation during the court process and that the process can be used to further perpetrate control or abuse. This has been a particular concern in domestic abuse proceedings. For example, a perpetrator of abuse may seek to embarrass or intimidate the victim-survivor during questioning or to increase the costs of legal representation for the victim-survivor by drawing out the length of proceedings as a means of **economic abuse**.

In light of concerns about the way in which domestic abuse proceedings have been dealt with throughout the court system, and the lack of effectiveness of the existing protections afforded to victim-survivors of domestic abuse, the government issued a public consultation, 'Transforming the

Knowledge link: This topic is also covered in Chapter 3.

> **First definition of Murder – Sir Edward Coke (Institutes of the Laws of England, 1797):**
> "Murder is when a man of sound memory, and of the age of discretion, unlawfully killeth within any county of the realm any reasonable creature in rerum natura under the king's peace, with malice afore-thought, either expressed by the party, or implied by law."

> **Gibbins and Proctor (1918) 13 Cr App R. 134:**
> The actus reus of murder can be committed either through an act or an omission e.g. starvation.

> **R v Vickers [1957] 2 Q.B. 664 & R v Cunningham [1981] UKHL 5:**
> Held that express malice afore-thought is where there is an intention to cause death and implied malice afore-thought is where there is an intention to cause grievous bodily harm.

> **Dpp v Smith [1961] A.C. 290:**
> Defined grievous bodily harm a "really serious harm".

> **R v Moloney [1985] 1 All E.R. 1025:**
> When considering "foresight", a Judge should invite the Jury to consider two questions:
> 1. "was death or really serious injury in a murder case a natural consequence of the defendant's voluntary act?"
> 2. "did the defendant foresee that consequence as being a natural consequence of his act?"

Figure 26.1   Developing the Offence of Murder

Approach to Domestic Abuse', in March 2018. Following this consultation process, the Domestic Abuse Bill was drafted. The Bill was reintroduced to the House of Commons in March 2021, following a delay due to the 2019 General Election. The Bill received Royal Assent (i.e. completed all parliamentary stages and became an Act of Parliament) on 29 April 2021. This is now known as the Domestic Abuse Act 2021. Some of the concerns that the Bill aimed to rectify and some of the main changes implemented under the Act are addressed in this chapter.

THE COURT STRUCTURE IN ENGLAND AND WALES

Having considered the role that the courts play in making laws in England and Wales, we now move on to consider the different types of courts that exist and the hierarchies within them.

The court system within England and Wales can be crudely divided into three main streams:

- Criminal courts
- Civil courts
- The family court

In addition, there is also a tribunal system, dealing with issues such as employment disputes and appeals against decisions by government departments (including immigration and welfare benefits appeals). The example drawn on throughout this chapter is the different types of domestic abuse proceedings and the courts that are of relevance in these types of proceeding are thus foregrounded.

Within each court system is a hierarchy of courts, designed to hear appeals from the courts below. The Supreme Court sits as the highest court within the jurisdiction of England and Wales and can hear cases on any area of law. (See Figure 26.2 for a diagram of the court structure in England and Wales.)

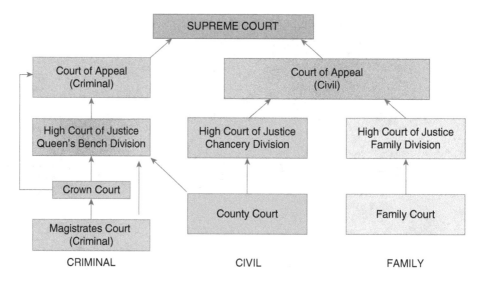

Figure 26.2 The Court Structure in England and Wales

Each court system has its own set of procedural rules: the Criminal Procedure Rules for the Criminal Courts (blue in Figure 26.2), the Family Procedure Rules for the Family Court (green in Figure 26.2) and the Civil Procedure Rules for the Civil Courts (orange in Figure 26.2). Whilst there are some similarities between the procedural rules in each of these courts, there are also major differences. This is particularly evident in domestic abuse cases and some of these procedural differences are highlighted within this chapter.

As well as different procedural rules, each court system has its own evidential standard that must be reached before an order can be made. The evidential standard of proof in criminal proceedings is that the offence has been committed 'beyond reasonable doubt' and the burden for meeting this standard falls on the prosecution. In other words, everyone begins with a presumption of innocence (that the offence has not been committed by the defendant) and the Crown Prosecution Service (CPS) which you will learn about later in this chapter must prove to the judge or jury hearing the case that an offence has been committed to the point where they no longer have any reasonable doubt about it.

Knowledge link: This topic is also covered in Chapter 25.

—— Case Study 26.1 ——

Criminal Court Case Study Example

Person A has been accused of assaulting person B on a bus.

Person A provides the explanation that they tripped over when the bus came to a sudden stop and accidentally struck person B.

If the Judge hearing the case believes that Person A's version of events is reasonably plausible then they must find Person A not-guilty, even if they are not fully convinced by it.

In contrast, the standard of proof in civil and family proceedings is 'on the balance of probabilities' and the burden of proving their case to this standard falls on the individual or organisation making the application to the court. This includes cases that involve criminal elements but are being heard within the civil or family courts, such as child protection proceedings or domestic abuse injunctions.

Case Study 26.2

Family Court Case Study Example

Person A is accused by their partner, Person B, of assaulting them and is asking the court to make an order to prevent Person B from returning to the family home.

Person B denies assaulting Person A.

The only evidence available to the court is each person's version of events.

The judge must weigh up each version of events and determine which version they believe more.

If the judge believes Person A's version is more probable and that they need the protection of the court, then they should make the protective order.

Lando (2009) argues against the difference in evidential standard, claiming that having a higher standard of proof in criminal proceedings provides less of a deterrent against committing offences. If the threshold were lower, there would be an increased chance of prosecution and therefore, according to Lando's theory, an increased level of deterrence. The generally accepted justification for the difference in evidential standard of proof, however, is the severity of the sentences available to the criminal courts compared to the potential consequences of civil/family proceedings.

Where there are two concurrent sets of proceedings running side by side, one in the family/civil courts and one in the criminal courts, this difference in standard can lead to an outcome that appears, on the face of it, to be unfair for one party.

Taking child protection proceedings as an example: criminal proceedings may be brought against a parent for physically abusing their child, but the only purpose of those proceedings is to decide if an offence has been committed and what punishment is required. This does not remove a child from that parent's or parents' care. If it is decided that the child is not safe to remain in the care of that parent or parents, the Local Authority will need to initiate their own proceedings in the family court to ask permission to remove the child from the home and place them somewhere safe. These proceedings will often run at the same time but may have very different outcomes. There may be insufficient evidence to meet the criminal standard of proof that an offence has been committed. However, there may be sufficient evidence to meet the lower civil standard of proof, thereby allowing the court to make an order that a child be permanently removed from that parent's care. In cases such as this, the justification addressed above for the difference in standard does not hold strong. Many people would argue that removing a child permanently from a parent's care is as severe, if not more severe, than a prison sentence.

Pause for Thought

Should there be a difference in evidential standard required depending on the type of case and potential consequences?

Domestic abuse cases are another type of case that can be dealt with by the criminal, civil or family courts. See Figure 26.3 for examples of the different domestic abuse related proceedings that may take place within each court system.

Legal Options for Victims of Domestic Abuse in England

Criminal Justice System
- Offences Against the Person 1861
- Offences of controlling or coercive behaviour – Serious Crime Act 2015
- Domestic Violence Protection Notice/Domestic Violence Protection Order
- Restraining Order
  – Protection from Harassment Act 1997
- Offence of forcing someone to marry
  – The Anti-social Behaviour, Crime and Policing Act 2014
- Offence of Female Genital Mutilation (FGM) or a failure to protect from FGM
  – Female Genital Mutilation Act 2003

Family Proceedings
- Application under the Children Act 1989
- Non-Molestation Order – Family Law Act 1996
- Occupation Order – Family Law Act 1996
- Forced Marriage Protection Order
  – Family Law Act 1996
- Female Genital Mutilation Order
  – Female Genital Mutilation Act 2003

Civil Proceedings
- Injunction – Protection from Harassment Act 1997
- A claim under Protection from Harassment Act 1997
- Personal injury claim for Trespass to the Person
- A Criminal Injuries Compensation Claim

Figure 26.3 Legal Options for Victim-Survivors of Domestic Abuse in England

Historically, criminal proceedings were only available in a domestic abuse case where there was evidence of physical abuse, resulting in a possible conviction under the Offences Against the Person Act 1861. For non-physical domestic abuse, victim-survivors were almost entirely reliant on bringing their own proceedings in the civil or family courts for an Injunction Order. Even where a victim-survivor could obtain an Injunction Order against the perpetrator, prior to 2007 breach of such an order was not a criminal offence. In 2014, there was a move towards criminalisation of a wider range of domestic abuses when the offence of forcing someone into marriage was introduced. In the same year, the police were given the power to issue a Domestic Violence Protection Notice (often abbreviated to DVPN) and apply for a Domestic Violence Protection Order (DVPO) on behalf of a victim-survivor of domestic violence.

The most notable change came the year after with the introduction of the Serious Crime Act 2015, which made it an offence to 'repeatedly or continuously engage in behaviour towards another person B that is controlling or coercive' if the perpetrator and the victim-survivor are 'personally connected' (Section 76, Serious Crime Act 2015). This change shifts the emphasis such that other features of domestic abuse are captured. The revised legislation allows the police to arrest an individual for abusive behaviour that falls short of actual physical assault and has therefore broadened police powers in domestic abuse cases.

Knowledge link: This topic is also covered in Chapter 20.

However, there is still an uphill battle in persuading a judge or jury 'beyond reasonable doubt' that an offence has been committed. Non-physical abuse can be very difficult to evidence and, as will be addressed in the next section, reliance will often be placed on the strength or otherwise of a victim-survivor's own account (provided either in a written statement or directly in oral evidence to the court).

THE PROCESS OF LEGAL PROCEEDINGS

Having considered the different types of proceedings that may occur in a domestic abuse scenario we now consider how those proceedings practically take place, including the role that the victim-survivor plays and how they are represented. As a criminology student, this is important for you to consider because these processes can have an impact on how willing an individual is to engage with the criminal justice process, an issue that will be analysed in detail below.

The Role of the Victim-Survivor in Proceedings

Criminal proceedings are brought by the CPS, rather than the victim of the crime themselves. The role of the victim-survivor is as a **complainant**, and where they are willing to support the action, as a witness for the prosecution.

This contrasts with the way in which criminal proceedings are brought in other jurisdictions across the world including Russia and even some European countries. In Russia, in most domestic abuse proceedings (except for the most serious offences relating to torture or murder), the onus lies with the victim-survivor to bring their own proceedings without any support from the State. In Germany, the position is a hybrid between the English and Russian position. A publicly-funded prosecutor is instructed to bring the case on behalf of the victim-survivor but they can take a more active role in proceedings as a 'subsidiary prosecutor' if they so wish. These three contrasting positions raise the question as to whether the role of the victim-survivor in criminal proceedings should be simply as a witness or whether they should play a more active role in the proceedings.

Pause for Thought

Is relegating a victim-survivor to the status of a 'prosecution witness' necessary to protect them or could it be argued that we are in fact taking the control away from them and potentially increasing trauma?

In civil or family proceedings, the victim-survivor is responsible for bringing their own proceedings as either a **claimant** or an **applicant**. They are responsible for organising their own legal representative, and unless they are eligible for legal aid, privately funding the cost of that representation, together with any court fees that are payable. This can be very expensive and if the applicant is unable to meet that expense, it can be a confusing and intimidating process to tackle alone.

Choosing Between Different Types of Proceedings

The range of proceedings available gives victim-survivors something of a choice between either supporting the CPS with a criminal prosecution or pursuing protection and/or compensation through the civil/family courts. They could of course always do both. Hirschel and Hutchinson (2003) support this notion of choice, arguing that the victim-survivor is best positioned to decide whether criminal prosecution is an appropriate way forward in their case. Richardson and Speed (2019) agree that a choice of proceedings is 'potentially a very powerful tool and puts the control back in the hands of the victim', but only if they are fully informed about all the legal options available to them.

It is worth remembering that not all victim-survivors will have this 'choice' due to the difference in evidential standards of proof highlighted earlier in this chapter. There may simply not be enough evidence for the police to take action or for the CPS to progress a case to court. This is not unheard of in domestic abuse proceedings, where victim-survivors could have been subjected to abuse for years without seeking assistance or notifying anyone. Indeed, in cases of controlling or coercive behaviour, they may not have even self-identified as being in an abusive relationship.

According to the latest ONS crime survey, almost 50% of domestic abuse-related cases heard in the criminal courts are not progressed due to evidential difficulties arising from the victim-survivor not supporting the action (Domestic abuse in England and Wales: year ending March 2018). In contrast, the number of applications to the family court for non-molestation orders (which must be applied for directly by the victim-survivor) is increasing year on year.

Pause for Thought

Why might victim-survivors prefer to seek their own protection through the family courts, rather than supporting a prosecution through the criminal courts?

Hear from the Expert

Professor Vanessa Bettinson - Professor of Criminal Law and Criminal Justice at De Montfort University

Professor Bettinson has written extensively about mechanisms for domestic abuse protection, prevention and intervention. Her recent work focuses on comparative approaches to tackling coercive and controlling behaviour:

> Victim retraction and non-attendance in domestic violence cases is considerably higher when compared with other criminal cases. The literature has identified a number of factors affecting complainant decisions to withdraw from the trial process, including fear of retaliation by the **defendant** or their relatives, a desire to continue with the relationship, and dissatisfaction with, or fear over, the court process. (Bishop and Bettinson, 2017)

Professor Bettinson's view is that "More work needs to be done to ensure prosecuting authorities are proactive at bringing charges and activism is needed to ensure proper enforcement of the law. Enforcement should not include a reliance on witness compellability that can interfere unnecessarily with victim autonomy. Compellability can reduce a victim's likelihood to reach to the criminal justice system in future and therefore leave them in a dangerous situation. Prosecution raises issues of victim autonomy and prosecution authorities should be engaging with other domestic violence agencies to ensure that a criminal justice response is being pursued at the right time for the victim."

Other reasons why an individual may not engage with the criminal justice process could also include:

- negative perceptions/lack of trust of the police.
- a lack of police understanding of non-violent domestic abuse and how it may present. Alongside the introduction of the offence of controlling or coercive behaviour in 2015, national police guidance was produced. This guidance made it clear that the police should be taking action in those

cases, even where there is no evidence of physical violence. However, in their 2018 report, the Home Affairs Committee have suggested that, despite this guidance, there continue to be concerns about the way in which domestic abuse claims are being dealt with by the police. Confidence in the police may remain low if incidents continue to ignore coercive control.

- that not all victim-survivors want the perpetrator to be arrested/sent to prison. There may be financial reasons why they do not want this, for example if they are relying on the perpetrator's income to meet mortgage payments. They may not want to involve the police in their domestic abuse incident and risk the perpetrator losing the income that is allowing them to make those payments.
- the lack of privacy in criminal proceedings. Criminal Courts are usually open courts, which could be intimidating for a victim-survivor, particularly if there are 'supporters' of the alleged perpetrator who choose to sit in the public gallery. In contrast, family proceedings will generally be heard in private, which provides an advantage in cases that involve such sensitive issues.

It is therefore clear to see why a victim-survivor may be reluctant to support a police action and/or criminal proceedings. However, without early legal advice victim-survivors will not know that there are other options available to them through the family or civil courts and may therefore choose to take no action at all. We now go on to consider the impact that the legal aid cuts have made on the ability of victim-survivors to obtain this legal advice.

THE RISE OF LITIGANTS IN PERSON

When the Legal Aid Sentencing and Punishment of Offenders Act (LASPO) was introduced in 2012, drastic cuts were made to legal aid across all areas of law but civil and family cases were particularly affected. LASPO put an end to eligibility based on financial criteria alone. Now there are strict 'means', 'merits' and evidential tests to obtain public funding for legal cases. In family law cases, legal aid eligibility was restricted to public law cases (e.g. where the local authority commences court proceedings), child abduction cases, or private law cases where evidence of domestic abuse or child abuse can be presented. In the latter case (evidence of domestic abuse or child abuse), the evidence itself will not qualify an individual and financial eligibility must also be established. It should also be noted that this will only make the victim-survivor potentially eligible for public funding, not the alleged perpetrator.

The hope had been that this would lead to an increase in people using Alternative methods of Dispute Resolution (ADR) such as mediation, rather than resorting to court proceedings. However, the government failed to consider that most referrals to ADR come from solicitors. Without access to legal advice about the benefits of ADR, use of mediation fell and court proceedings continued to rise, with more individuals choosing to represent themselves. These self-represented litigants have become known more commonly amongst the legal profession as 'Litigants in Person' (LiPs).

In the period January to March 2019, 81% of family law cases (not including public law cases) involved at least one party without representation. In 38% of cases, neither party had representation (Family Court Statistics Quarterly: January–March 2019). To highlight the impact of LASPO, this position can be contrasted with the statistics immediately prior to the legislation being implemented, where at least one LiP was present in 69% of cases (12% lower than the 2019 statistics) but in only 12% of cases did neither party have representation (24% lower than the 2019 statistics). Where one party has representation and the other party does not, this can lead to accusations of 'inequality of arms'.

─────────────── **Case Study 26.3** ───────────────

MG and JG v JF [2015] EWHC 564

Case summary: This case involved two women who were in a civil partnership (MG and JG) and who had arranged to have a child with a man (JF). The arrangement was that the child would live with MG and JG but would have contact with JF. Unfortunately, after a while this arrangement broke down and family court proceedings were initiated. The child was entitled to publicly-funded representation but none of the parents were eligible for legal aid so they had to fund their own legal costs, including the instruction of reports by two psychologists and representatives for the court hearings. Despite increasing the mortgage on their house by £20,000 to pay legal costs, MG and JG soon ran out of money and therefore requested that JF fund their outstanding legal costs (including representation for them at the final court hearing).

Case outcome: JF was ordered to pay 80% of the two applicants' legal costs, as well as funding his own representation. The judge hearing the case acknowledged that this could be perceived to be 'grossly unfair' but stated 'that is where the government has left him. It is a sorry state of affairs'. He went on to state that the inequality in representation would otherwise lead to 'a gross inequality of arms, and arguably a violation of their rights under Articles 6 and 8 of the European Convention on Human Rights and Article 47 of the European Charter of Fundamental Rights'.

─────────────── Pause for Thought ───────────────

Is it fair that one party in legal proceedings should have to fund the legal costs for both parties, even when they are not the person who initiated the court proceedings?

With no changes to the legal aid position on the immediate horizon, LiPs are likely to remain a consistent feature in the civil and family courts. Consideration therefore needs to be given to how proceedings can, and should, be adapted and we do this below.

THE PROBLEM OF DIRECT CROSS-EXAMINATION

Let us consider the process where one or both parties are trying to give evidence to the court without the benefit of a lawyer to represent them.

In civil or family proceedings, if the parties are not able to reach an agreement, then the proceedings may become 'contested' (in other words, one party is asking the court to make an order and the other party is saying that the order is not necessary or that a different order is more appropriate). In this scenario, the parties may both be required to give oral evidence to the court. They will first give their 'evidence in chief' by either simply confirming the evidence set out in their previous written statements or through their representative asking them questions. The other side will then be given the opportunity to challenge or pick holes in this evidence by asking 'cross-examination' questions. This process will also take place in the criminal courts if the defendant pleads 'not guilty' to an offence.

This is a skilled but relatively straightforward process if both parties have representatives. However, the problem comes in cases where one or both parties does not. In these circumstances, they may be expected to conduct this process themselves.

In their longitudinal study of court proceedings pre- and post-LASPO, Trinder and Hunter (2015) found that 'cross-examination is beyond the capacity of most LiPs' regardless of levels of education or professional experience. They gave the example of one case in which 'a highly vulnerable father managed to ask only one question in his cross-examination of a key witness before drying up, despite prompting and support from the judge'.

The position is even more concerning in domestic abuse proceedings. It must be remembered that, at this stage, no findings are likely to have been made by the court and therefore the allegations before the court are just that: 'allegations', not facts. The person being accused of perpetrating domestic abuse must therefore be given the opportunity to defend themselves. Without this, they cannot be said to be exercising their rights under Article 6 of the Human Rights Act (the right to a fair trial). Equally, the individual who alleged the domestic abuse must be protected against potential further abuse, controlling or coercive behaviour that could be provoked via this process.

Pause for Thought

Can a fair outcome be achieved if both parties do not have access to legal advice and representation?

Let us now look at how cross-examination works in practice, firstly in the criminal courts and then in the family courts.

The Criminal Courts

Since the introduction of the Youth Justice and Criminal Evidence Act 1999, a defendant in a case involving a sexual offence will be prevented from directly cross-examining a complainant (section 34). Under section 35 of the same Act, there are similar provisions in place prohibiting direct cross-examination of child complainants and child witnesses. For offences where there is no express legislative prohibition in place, such as domestic abuse offences, the court retains discretion under section 36 of the Act to make an order that the defendant cannot directly cross-examine the victim-survivor. If the defendant is prohibited from conducting direct cross-examination, either by way of an express legislative prohibition or due to an order of the court, the court can appoint a lawyer to conduct this cross-examination on their behalf.

The Family Courts

Historically, direct cross-examination has been permitted in the Family Courts in all family law cases. However, the number of cases in which this arises has been exacerbated due to the increase in LiPs discussed previously. In November 2017, Part 3A Family Procedure Rules and Practice Direction 3AA were introduced to provide guidance to the judiciary in dealing with these cases and the ways in which a vulnerable party/witness could provide their evidence to the court.

Key Guidance

Paragraph 5.5 of Practice Direction 3AA

'In all cases in which it is proposed that a vulnerable party, vulnerable witness or protected party is to be cross-examined (whether before or during a hearing) the court must consider whether to make participation directions, including prescribing the manner in which the person is to be cross-examined'.

These provisions did not introduce a complete prohibition on direct cross-examination in the same way that the provisions in the Youth Justice and Criminal Evidence Act did in the criminal courts. This complete prohibition is something that esteemed members of the judiciary such as Sir James Munby (previous President of the Family Court) and Mr Justice Hayden have been arguing is necessary for many years now. In his annual lecture to The Wales Observatory on Human Rights of Children and Young People (2015), Sir James Munby summed up the position by stating 'in the family justice system we are obliged to tolerate what in the Crown Court would be forbidden: the cross-examination of an alleged victim by an alleged perpetrator, a process which can sometimes amount, and on occasions quite deliberately, to a continuation of the abuse'.

Instead, the provisions in Practice Direction 3AA maintain judicial discretion as to how to deal with cases where an alleged perpetrator of domestic abuse is unrepresented and wishes to cross-examine the other party. In the author's experience, a common approach taken by the family courts is to direct the alleged perpetrator to file a written list of cross-examination questions with the judge in advance of the court hearing. The judge will then be responsible for identifying if those questions are suitable, before putting those questions to the party or witness. This was also the position in the criminal courts prior to 1999. The difficulty with this proposed solution is that a LiP will have had no training in the rules of cross-examination and may therefore not be clear as to what questions will or will not be appropriate.

Concerns have been raised about the expansion of the judge's role in cases such as the above, including by the judiciary themselves. In Re H [2006] EWHC 3099, Judge Roderic Wood stated 'For my part, I feel a profound unease at the thought of conducting such an exercise in the family jurisdiction, whilst not regarding it as impossible. If it falls to a judge to conduct the exercise it should do so only in exceptional circumstances'. The judge is supposed to have a neutral role presiding over the hearing, listening to both parties' positions and then delivering a judgement. It is easy to see how a judge who becomes entangled in the process of cross-examination could be perceived to no longer be playing neutral role. Judge Roderic Wood also pointed out how far the family courts were falling behind the criminal courts in this area, and urged the government to introduce statutory provisions mirroring the 1999 Act.

Case Study 26.4

RE B (A CHILD) (PRIVATE LAW FACT FINDING – UNREPRESENTED FATHER), D V K [2014] EWHC 700

Case summary: This case involved private law children proceedings about a three-year-old boy. The mother in those proceedings raised several allegations, including that the father had raped her. The father denied this allegation. The court felt that this allegation was so serious that a determination needed to be made as to whether 'on the balance of probabilities' this had happened before a determination could be made as to what contact, if any, was in the child's best interests.

A fact-finding hearing was therefore directed with this purpose. The problem was that the mother was eligible for legal aid and therefore had a representative for those proceedings, whereas the father was not eligible and did not have a representative to conduct cross-examination on his behalf.

The position in the Family Courts (where the case was heard): There was no legislative prohibition on direct cross-examination. The father was therefore not entitled to a court appointed representative. Judge Wildblood, who was allocated the case, considered the different methods available to progress cross-examination in the absence of representation. The judge described the prospect of personally conducting the cross-examination on behalf of the father as insufficient 'in meeting the justice of the case'. The judge referred the case to the legal aid agency and asked them to consider granting the father public funding. In this case, the legal aid agency later agreed to provide funding for the father. However, this was due to the father issuing a claim for Judicial Review with the assistance of the Public Law Project, rather than directly because of Judge Wildblood's request.

If the allegations had been heard in the Criminal Courts: The allegations would have fallen under Section 34 of the Youth Justice and Criminal Evidence Act 1999. Direct cross-examination would therefore have been automatically prohibited without any court determination being necessary, and a representative would have been appointed by the court if the father chose not to instruct one himself.

Despite the media attention surrounding this and concerns even being raised by the then Prime Minister, Theresa May, the government did not seek to consult with the public on this specific issue as part of their 2018 consultation 'Transforming the Response to Domestic Abuse'. Instead, a very vague statement was included which said that 'The government is committed to addressing this issue and will legislate to give family courts the power to stop this practice as soon as legislative time allows'.

Despite only asking questions about cross-examination in the criminal courts, it is telling that the responses to the consultation 'overwhelmingly focused on family proceedings' and were 'unanimous on the need to give family courts the power to stop unrepresented perpetrators of abuse directly cross-examining their victims'. Because of this public outcry, a provisions have now been included at sections 31Q – 31Z of the Domestic Abuse Act 2021 prohibiting 'cross-examination in person in family proceedings' in defined circumstances. This includes where one of the parties to the proceedings has been convicted of a specified offence, received a caution for such an offence or is currently charged with such an offence. It also applies where one of the parties is protected from the other party by an injunction or where they have other evidence of domestic abuse perpetrated by the other party. If none of those circumstances applies, the court still has discretion to prohibit direct cross-examination (similar to the discretion they currently have under Practice Direction 3AA, discussed above) and should consider the alternatives to direct cross-examination also set out within the Act.

There are other measures that could be used to help prevent re-victimisation and further trauma being incurred during the courts process, as will now be considered in the next section.

SPECIAL MEASURES

In the family and civil courts, it is not uncommon for the first hearing to take place in Judge's Chambers. These are small office-like rooms, where both parties (and their representatives, if they have them) sit across a small table from the judge. This can be very intimidating for a victim-survivor of domestic abuse who will be expected to sit in close proximity to the alleged perpetrator of the abuse. Whilst

Knowledge link: This topic is also covered in Chapter 25.

criminal proceedings are likely to be heard in much larger courtrooms, this does not necessarily mean that they will be any less intimidating for a victim-survivor. They will still be able to see the alleged perpetrator when they are giving evidence to the court. As noted earlier, they may also be confronted with friends and family of the perpetrator sitting outside the courtroom or in the public gallery.

There are protective measures that can be put in place with the aim of making the proceedings less intimidating for the victim-survivor or witness. These are called 'special measures'. Special measures can include:

- physical screens that prevent the victim-survivor/witness from seeing the alleged perpetrator and/ or the public gallery;
- providing evidence via a live video-link or pre-recorded interview;
- giving evidence in private.

In addition to formal 'special measures', there is also a range of less formal mechanisms that can be used to protect vulnerable witnesses whilst at court. These include:

- separate entrances;
- separate waiting areas.

Prior to the introduction of the Domestic Abuse Act 2021, it was at the discretion of the judge to decide whether special measures would be granted. When deciding whether to grant special measures, the judge would balance the improvement that will be made to the quality of the witness evidence by implementing the measures, against the risk of inhibiting the other party from testing that evidence.

Under the Domestic Abuse Act 2021, a statutory presumption has now been created setting out that special measures should be granted to victims of domestic abuse because 'the quality of [a victim's] evidence and participation in proceedings is likely to be diminished by reason of vulnerability'.

Whilst this is certainly a step forward, concerns have been raised about the availability and quality of the equipment needed to implement special measures. In his '16th View from the President's Chambers', Sir James Munby spoke of his own experience of presiding over cases where special measures directions had been made. He described video link facilities as being a 'disgrace' and gave the example of everything in a video link appearing 'in such a bright blue shade as to remind me of *Avatar*'. The most concerning thing about this example is he was talking about the facilities in the Royal Courts of Justice in London. It can therefore only be imagined how poor the quality is in much smaller courts around the country. He talked about his own regional court having no available screens and no video link.

Acknowledging these problems, the government laid out a grid of non-statutory commitments, which included:

- improving 'the court environment, with new waiting areas designed to ensure victim safety';
- 'a new court design guide focusing on accessibility for the most vulnerable';
- increasing 'the number of privacy screens that are available to allow vulnerable victims and witnesses to give evidence without being seen by the defendant or the defendant's family;
- revising 'legal guidance on special measures so that victims and witnesses can better understand what help might be available'.

The grid of commitments does not specify whether these improvements will be limited to the criminal courts or whether improvements will be made to all courts. However, the use of the phrase 'defendant or defendant's family' seems to indicate that at least the third commitment will be to the criminal courts alone. No time estimate was provided as to when these improvements will be completed or how they will be funded.

In summary, special measures can be a valuable tool in allowing a victim-survivor to fully participate in court proceedings but their availability and quality are currently inconsistent.

CONCLUSION

As has been demonstrated in this chapter, despite hearing cases involving similar (sometimes identical) issues, the approaches taken by the criminal, civil and family courts are very different. In the words of Sir James Munby (2016), 'the family justice system lags woefully behind the criminal justice system' when it comes to the ways in which vulnerable people give evidence to the court. Looking at this from a criminology perspective, it could be argued that the current system is turning a blind eye to the re-victimisation of victim-survivors of domestic abuse.

CHAPTER SUMMARY

- Laws in England and Wales can be made in two ways: Parliament passing legislation (written laws) or Judges making decisions on cases.
- There are three main court streams (civil, family and criminal), each with their own set of procedural rules.
- A higher evidential test is applied before a conviction can be made in the criminal courts compared to that required before an order can be made in the family/civil courts.
- The role of the victim-survivor in criminal proceedings is to be a witness for the prosecution who will be represented by the Crown Prosecution Service (a state-funded agency).
- Victim-survivors can seek their own protection through the family courts (regardless of whether there are ongoing criminal proceedings).
- Legal aid cuts have led to an increase in people having to represent themselves in civil and family proceedings.
- 'Special Measures' can be put in place to make court proceedings less intimidating for victim-survivors of domestic abuse but their availability and quality vary across different courts.

Review Questions

1. What is a common-law legal system?
2. What role will a victim-survivor of domestic abuse play in criminal proceedings?
3. Can a perpetrator of domestic abuse directly question a victim-survivor in court proceedings?
4. Give three examples of practical steps that could be taken to allow a victim-survivor to give evidence to a court without feeling intimidated.

GO FURTHER

Books

1. The following title explains how laws are made and applied in England and Wales:

    Slapper, G. (2017) *The English Legal System,* 18th edition. London: Routledge.

2. This second text explains the basic concepts of criminal procedure in England and Wales:

    Sprack, J. (2019) *A Practical Approach to Criminal Procedure*, 16th edition. Oxford: Oxford University Press.

3. This final book considers a range of socio-legal perspectives about domestic abuse:

    Hilder, S. and Bettinson, V. (2016) *Domestic Violence: Interdisciplinary Perspectives on Protection, Prevention and Intervention.* Basingstoke: Palgrave Macmillan

Journal Articles

1. This journal article considers the use of Independent Domestic Violence Advisors to support victim-survivors of domestic abuse within specialist court formats:

    Taylor-Dunn, H. (2016) The impact of victim advocacy on the prosecution of domestic violence offences: Lessons from a realistic evaluation. *Criminology and Criminal Justice*, 16(12): 21–27. Available at: https://doi.org/10.1177%2F1748895815599581

2. This journal article considers the impact of the legal aid cuts on family court proceedings:

    Richardson, K. and Speed, A. (2019) Restrictions on legal aid in family law cases in England and Wales: creating a necessary barrier to public funding or simply increasing the burden on the family courts? *Journal of Social Welfare and Family Law*, 41(2). Available at: https://www.tandfonline.com/doi/full/10.1080/09649069.2019.1590898

3. This looks at the approach to criminalising domestic abuse in England, when compared to Russia, considering the possibility of re-victimisation in both jurisdictions:

    Richardson, K. and Speed, A. (2019) Two worlds apart: a comparative analysis of the effectiveness of domestic abuse law and policy in England and Wales and the Russian Federation. *Journal of Criminal Law.* Available at: https://journals.sagepub.com/doi/10.1177/0022018319858478

Useful Websites

1. This document sets out the responses to the government consultation 'Transforming the Response to Domestic Abuse', the first draft domestic abuse bill and a grid of government commitments. HM Government, *'Transforming the Response to Domestic Abuse: Consultation Response and Draft Bill'* (2019): https://assets.publishing.service.gov.uk/government/uploads/system/uploads/attachment_data/file/772202/CCS1218158068-Web_Accessible.pdf
2. A charitable organisation campaigning for better protection for female victims of domestic abuse and gender-based violence: https://www.womensaid.org.uk/
3. A similar organisation to Women's Aid but focusing on male victims of abuse: https://www.mankind.org.uk/
4. A blog written by students at Northumbria Law School, highlighting family law and access to justice issues: https://afamilyaffairsite.wordpress.com/

REFERENCES

Bishop, C. and Bettinson, V. (2017) Evidencing domestic violence, including behaviour that falls under the new offence of controlling or coercive behaviour. *The International Journal of Evidence and Proof*, 22(1): 3–29.

Hirschel, D. and Hutchinson, I. (2003) The voices of domestic violence victims: predictors of victim preference for arrest and the relationship between preference for arrest and revictimization. *Journal of Crime and Delinquency*, 49(2): 313–336.

House of Commons Home Affairs Committee (2018) 'Domestic Abuse, Ninth Report of Session 2017–19'. Available at: https://publications.parliament.uk/pa/cm201719/cmselect/cmhaff/1015/1015.pdf

Joint Committee on the Draft Domestic Abuse Bill (2019) 'Draft Domestic Abuse Bill: First Report of Session 2017–19'. Available at: https://publications.parliament.uk/pa/jt201719/jtselect/jtddab/2075/207502.htm

Lando, H. (2009) Prevention of crime and the optimal standard of proof in criminal law. *Review of Law & Economics*, 5(1): 33–52.

Ministry of Justice (2019) 'Family Court Statistics Quarterly, England and Wales: January to March 2019'. Available at: https://assets.publishing.service.gov.uk/government/uploads/system/uploads/attachment_data/file/811693/FCSQ_January_to_March_2019_final.pdf

Munby, Sir James (2016) 'Statement from the President of the Family Division, Sir James Munby: Cross-examination of vulnerable people'. Available at: https://www.judiciary.uk/announcements/president-of-the-family-division-sir-james-munby-cross-examination-of-vulnerable-witnesses-in-the-family-court/

Munby, Sir James (2017) '16th View from the President's Chambers: Children and vulnerable witnesses: where are we?', *Family Law*.

Office for National Statistics (2018) 'Domestic abuse in England and Wales: year ending March 2018'. Available at: https://www.ons.gov.uk/peoplepopulationandcommunity/crimeandjustice/bulletins/domesticabuseinenglandandwales/yearendingmarch2018#outcomes-of-domestic-abuse-related-offences

Richardson, K. and Speed, A. (2019) Two worlds apart: a comparative analysis of the effectiveness of domestic abuse law and policy in England and Wales and the Russian Federation. *Journal of Criminal Law*. Available at: https://journals.sagepub.com/doi/10.1177/0022018319858478

Trinder, L. and Hunter, R. (2015) Access to justice? Litigants in person before and after LASPO, *Family Law*, 535.

Out of Court Disposals and Diversion

27

Paul Biddle, Lyndsey Bengtsson
and Aaron Amankwaa

Learning Objectives

By the end of this chapter you will:

- Be able to list what Out of Court Disposals are available for adults aged 18 and over.
- Be able to describe the circumstances in which each Out of Court Disposal is appropriate.
- Understand the origins of and philosophical justifications for Out of Court Disposals.
- Understand the development of Out of Court Disposal policy and practice and the associated key debates.

Framing Questions

1. What are Out of Court Disposals?
2. Can you describe the difference between a simple caution and a conditional caution?
3. What led to the introduction of the two-tier framework?
4. Can you describe the essential characteristics of the Northumbria Police Conditional Caution Framework and the aims behind it?

INTRODUCTION

─────────────── **Case Study 27.1** ───────────────

Alex – Conditional Caution

Alex is a first-year undergraduate student who went out with friends to a nightclub party as part of freshers' week. At the party, Alex got drunk and was engaged in an affray with another student on the street outside the club. He threw a heavy stone that smashed the windshield of a parked car. The police arrived at the scene and arrested the two students who had no previous conviction or arrest records. Due to the minor nature of the crime and background of the students, the police, in consultation with the owner of the car, decided to resolve the case via a conditional caution. Alex was given a conditional caution to attend an alcohol intervention workshop and compensate the owner of the car. The second student was also issued a conditional caution to attend a victim awareness workshop to learn about the effects of crime. The conditional caution offered an opportunity for the students to be dealt with without registering a criminal record that may affect their future job prospects.

In this chapter you will learn about Out of Court Disposals (OOCDs), such as the **conditional caution** example in Case Study 27.1, for adults aged 18 and over. The chapter will provide you with knowledge and a critical understanding of OOCDs and associated policy, practice and debates. You will learn about the scope, origins of and philosophical justifications for OOCDs and the development of OOCD policy and practice in the subsequent sections. The chapter also includes a synthesis of existing research findings and key debates to help you to understand the effectiveness of, and key issues associated with, OOCDs.

As illustrated in the introductory example (Case Study 27.1), OOCDs enable early intervention to divert offenders from the criminal justice system to support their rehabilitation. OOCDs relate to the critical criminal justice concepts of victim satisfaction, effective resolution and the prevention of reoffending (Glen, 2017). These concepts, and other terminology, are explained in the next section in order to aid your understanding of OOCDs. As explained below, victims may be involved in both the decision making in relation to the use of some OOCDs and what, if any conditions can be attached to the OOCD. It is important to note that there is an alternative, more critical narrative around the development of OOCDs which we discuss later in this chapter.

MAPPING THE TERRAIN

OOCDs are alternatives to formal charges and are designed to allow the police to effectively respond to low-level (and often first time) offending (Ames et al., 2018). They are based on a body of evidence suggesting that certain less severe punishments, which are personalised, can be more effective in reducing recidivism (i.e. committing further crimes following a conviction for another crime) than going to trial (Slothower, 2014). OOCDs aim to deliver a simple, swift and proportionate response to low-risk offending, such as minor theft (Office for Criminal Justice Reform, 2010). They also aim to reduce the number of times that courts deal with minor cases, involving crimes where the perpetrator accepts responsibility (however, as discussed later in this chapter, use of some OOCDS does not require admittance of responsibility by an offender) (Criminal Justice Joint Inspection, 2011).

Pause for Thought

On reflection of the above, what do you notice about the nature of OOCDs?

As already illustrated above, OOCDs encompass interventions that are designed as alternatives to prosecution at court. Before we present information about each type of OOCD, we explain some terminology to help you understand the operation of OOCDs. Some OOCDs can be used to deal with what are called **'either way', summary and non-indictable offences**. Non-indictable or summary offences are less serious offences dealt with in Magistrates Courts *either before a judge or magistrates* (e.g. most motoring offences and minor criminal damage). The 'either way' offences are triable either on indictment *before a judge and jury* or summarily *before a Magistrate judge* (Ministry of Justice, 2015). Indictable offences are more serious offences and are dealt with by Crown Courts. Table 27.1 below summarises the different OOCDs. It is important to remember that some OOCDs discussed in this chapter enable the use of **restorative justice** (RJ). This is because RJ aims to repair damage and harms to victims and to hold offenders accountable in ways that provide an opportunity for making amends (Zehr and Mika, 2003; Johnstone, 2011). This is generally achieved through meetings between victims, offenders and other parties (Wood, 2015).

Knowledge link: These topics are also covered in Chapters 25 and 26.

Table 27.1 Summary of OOCDs

Type of OOCD	Brief Description	Legislation
Simple Cautions	A formal caution given by the police that has no conditions attached, used for summary and some 'either-way' offences.	Criminal Justice Act (2003) Criminal Justice and Courts Act (2015)
Conditional Cautions	A caution for a summary-only offence given by police that has specific conditions attached, which the perpetrator must obey.	Criminal Justice Act (2003) The Legal Aid, Sentencing and Punishment of Offenders (LASPO) Act 2012
Community Resolutions	Community resolutions are voluntary, with both offender and victim agreeing to their use. They enable a range of interventions to be undertaken (including restorative justice) focused on repairing harm caused by the offence.	Anti-Social Behaviour, Crime & Policing Act (2014)
Penalty Notices for Disorder (PNDs)	PNDs give the police (and other designated individuals) power to levy fines at pre-determined levels for a range of offences.	Criminal Justice and Police Act (2001)
Cannabis Warnings	A warning given by the Police to someone found to be in possession of cannabis with no evidence of intent to supply.	Misuse of Drugs Act (1971)
Khat Warnings	A warning given by the police to someone found to be in possession of khat with no evidence of intent to supply.	Criminal Justice and Police Act (2001) Misuse of Drugs Act (1971)
Fixed Penalty Notices (FPN)	FPNs are issued by the police and other authorised individuals to deal with a range of offences. Different offences attract different levels of fine.	Fixed Penalty Offences Order (2013) Road Traffic Safety Act (2006) Road Traffic Offenders Act (1988)

This section outlined the definition of OOCDs and the different types used in England and Wales. In the next section, you will learn about the characteristics of the different types of OOCDs and their applications.

DESCRIPTION OF EXISTING TYPES OF OOCDS

As previously mentioned, the current OOCD framework consists of seven different disposal types. This section describes each one in further detail.

Simple Cautions

A simple caution is a formal warning given by the police to persons aged 18 and over when it is not in the public interest to prosecute for low-level, mainly first time, offending. They are given only for non-indictable offences and potentially some 'either-way' offences, when a person admits the offence and agrees to accept the caution. A simple caution is given only if the decision maker is satisfied there is sufficient evidence to provide a realistic prospect of conviction if the offender were to be prosecuted. Victim views on the use of a simple caution should be sought prior to use, but the decision to impose a simple caution rests with the police and/or the Crown Prosecution Service (CPS). Simple cautions are not generally used in cases involving domestic violence, unless the alternative would be no further action due to a lack of evidence (Ministry of Justice, 2015).

Conditional Cautions

Conditional Cautions (CCs) can be used for summary-only offences dealt with by Magistrates Courts, where the offender is 18 and over, admits the offence, and accepts the conditions attached to the caution. Conditional Cautions provide an opportunity to:

- offer a proportionate response to low level offending;
- make reparation to victims and communities;
- divert offenders away from the criminal justice system at an early opportunity into rehabilitative services;
- punish offenders by means of a financial penalty.

Section 23 of the Criminal Justice Act 2003 sets out the requirements that must be met before a Conditional Caution may be given. Formal guidance on when to offer a CC is contained in the Code of Practice for Adult Conditional Cautions 2013 and the Directors Guidance on Adult Conditional Cautions. There must be evidence that the offender has committed an offence and therefore a prospect of conviction at court. Authority levels for the issue of a CC are dependent on the gravity level of the offence. The decision to issue a CC for an indictable offence can only be made following authorisation by a Police Superintendent and the CPS. For summary and minor 'either-way' offences (which are triable at either the magistrates or Crown Court) they are decided upon by a Police Sergeant, with serious 'either-way' offences decided by a Police Inspector. For serious 'either-way' offences the decision to offer a CC must be made by the police Superintendent and the CPS. The decision maker must determine that there is sufficient evidence to issue a CC. Where the offender denies the offence or raises a defence it would be inappropriate to offer a CC.

Conditional Cautions are so-called because, unlike Simple Cautions, they include specific conditions to which perpetrators must adhere to avoid future prosecution for the offence admitted. Conditions can be rehabilitative (conditions designed to modify offender behaviour that leads to reduced reoffending), reparative (conditions that result in the offender repairing the damage they have done in some way), and/or include an element of punishment. Examples of rehabilitative conditions include attendance at substance misuse services, or engagement with services designed to help offenders to tackle other problems such as gambling addictions or debt problems. Reparative conditions may include an apology, financial compensation and unpaid work. Restrictions can be placed on the CC where they contribute towards rehabilitation and these may include limiting who offenders may contact, locations they can visit, and activities they can participate in. Punitive conditions may include payment of financial penalties (Ministry of Justice, 2013).

The effect of the CC should be explained to the offender together with a warning that a failure to comply with the conditions may result in prosecution at court. The offender must sign a document which sets out the details of the offence and the conditions attached to their caution, their admission that they have committed the offence, and their consent to the CC.

Victim views on the use of a CC should be considered in the decision making and condition-setting process. Victim agreement must be obtained in any case where direct reparation or Restorative Justice (RJ) processes are being considered (where a meeting is arranged between the victim and offender with the goal to discuss the harm caused by the crime) or where the victim is directly involved in some way. Outside of this requirement, decisions to give a CC and the conditions to be attached lie with the decision maker (e.g. the relevant police officer). CCs can only be used for hate crime or partner domestic abuse in exceptional circumstances and with the CPS authority (Ministry of Justice, 2013; Glen, 2017).

Knowledge link: This topic is also covered in Chapter 22.

Community Resolutions

Community Resolutions (CRs) are used to deal with lower-level crime or incidents for summary-only offences, and are not used for intimate partner domestic abuse. They can be used only for offences that are admitted by the offender. Victims' views must be sought about the use of a Community Resolution, but victim consent is not required to proceed if a supervisory police officer agrees to the use of a CR. The offender must have no relevant offending history and CR records for the same or similar offences in the last 12 months in most circumstances. Conditions and options available within a CR include words of advice about the behaviour from a police officer, an apology (in person or in writing), repairing the damage, and paying for the loss caused. Restorative Justice is also an option and this brings those harmed by crime and those responsible for the harm into communication, enabling everyone affected by a particular incident to play a part in repairing the harm and finding a positive way forward. RJ, within a CR, is voluntary for both the victim and offender and the offender must have admitted responsibility for the harm caused (Association of Chief Police Officers, 2012; Glen, 2017).

Penalty Notices for Disorder (PNDs)

PNDs are a type of fixed penalty notice that is available to the police, Trading Standards Officers and other accredited persons in England and Wales for a specified range of penalty offences. Offences include wasting police time, some types of misuse of electronic communication, words or behaviour likely to cause harassment, alarm or distress, drunk and disorderly behaviour in a public place, destroying or damaging property (under £300) and retail theft (under £100). Additional offences also include a breach of a fireworks curfew, the sale or attempted sale of alcohol to a person who is drunk, a range of alcohol offences related to those under 18, possession of a Class B or C controlled drug, some forms of trespass and littering. Penalties are either £60 or £90 depending on the seriousness of the offence. Admittance of guilt is not required for use of a PND. Victims' views on their use should be sought before a decision to use a PND is made but the decision to administer a PND rests with the relevant officer (Ministry of Justice, 2014).

Cannabis Warnings

Cannabis warnings are given, as an alternative to arrest, to individuals aged 18 and over, found to be in possession of a small amount of cannabis, when there is no evidence of intent to supply to others (Association of Chief Police Officers, 2007). They are used to deal with adults caught in possession of cannabis, a Class B drug under the Misuse of Drugs Act 1971, where it is obvious that it is in the offender's possession for personal use, not for intent to supply or dealing.

Khat Warnings

Khat warnings are available for use with those aged 18 and over who are found to be in possession of a small amount of khat and where there is no evidence of intent to supply this to others (Association of Chief Police Officers, 2014). Khat is a Class C drug under the Misuse of Drugs Act 1971, and is defined in Part IV of Schedule 2 as 'the leaves, stems or shoots of the plant of the species Catha edulis'.

Fixed Penalty Notices (FPNs)

FPNs can be issued to deal with a range of offences, including certain minor motoring offences, littering, fly-tipping, dog control offences, noise offences, abandoned vehicles, nuisance parking and some waste offences. FPNs may be issued without an admission of guilt. Different authorities have powers to issue FPNs for specific offences. Those able to issue FPNs include local authorities, relevant police officers, the Environment Agency and the National Park Authority. Different offences attract different levels of fine that are paid by the perpetrator (Gov.uk, 2019; The Sentencing Council, 2020).

Pause for Thought

In this section, you learned about the nature of the different types of available OOCDs in England and Wales: what does the analysis reveal about the England and Wales criminal justice system?

The next section will examine the appropriateness of OOCDs.

REFLECTIONS ON THE APPROPRIATENESS OF OOCDS

Knowledge link: This topic is also covered in Chapter 6.

There are different views about OOCDs and their legitimacy appears highly contingent (i.e. support for OOCDs is based on specific circumstances and wider views of justice).

OOCDs are argued to be an appropriate, speedy and certain response to minor, first-time offending. OOCDs may enable reparation by an offender, deliver victim satisfaction and reduce unnecessary costs, whilst also reducing reoffending (Ministry of Justice, 2010). Allen (2017) argues that OOCDs can reduce labelling, act as a deterrent, and divert offenders into treatment and support which may address the underlying causes of their offending.

However, there are criticisms of OOCDs. Allen (2017) notes some criminal justice professionals argue offenders may accept a Caution (a type of OOCD) when they are not guilty and without understanding the implications for their criminal record. It has been argued that OOCDs may marginalise courts' roles in the criminal justice process. Concerns have been raised about the development of a 'cautions culture', whereby OOCDs are used inappropriately widely (including as a response to serious offences and repeat offenders) due to a lack of appropriate police judgement, resources and training (Donoghue, 2014; Slothower, 2014; HMCPSI & HMIC, 2015; House of Commons Home Affairs Committee, 2015; Gibbs, 2017; Ames, 2018). However, a decline in the recent use of OOCDs, linked to legislation to limit their use (e.g. the Criminal Justice and Courts Act, 2015), suggests any over-use of Cautions is being addressed. It has been argued that interventions associated with OOCDs are too limited and the extent to which the principles of restorative justice are reflected in OOCDs has been questioned (Westmarland et al., 2017; Ames, 2018).

Public opinion about OOCDs is based on a variety of interrelated factors including age, gender, level of education, experience of victimisation, perceptions of current crime levels, and views of criminal justice policy. Additional important factors are public perceptions of procedural justice (an individual's views of the criminal justice process and their role within it) and police effectiveness (an individual's views about outcomes achieved) (Pfeiffer et al., 2005; Spiranovic et al., 2012; O'Sullivan et al., 2017). This adds further complexity to discussions of the appropriateness of OOCDs which requires acknowledgement.

Knowledge link: This topic is also covered in Chapter 24.

Evidence indicates some public support for less punitive responses, which are found within the OOCDs, for certain groups (e.g. juvenile offenders and those with mental health issues), in certain circumstances (e.g. first-time offenders), and for lower level offending (Miller and Applegate, 2015; Mowle et al., 2016). Research studies illustrate public support for some of the interventions associated with OOCDs, including compensation, restitution, community work, and interventions that are seen to act as a warning to offenders to change their behaviour to avoid a future harsher criminal justice response (Roberts and Stalans, 2004). It is nevertheless critical to understand that the public retain an attachment to punitive approaches (Payne et al., 2004; Roberts and Stalans, 2004; Mackenzie et al., 2012).

The diversity of OOCDs and their application creates a complex patchwork of options that are delivered in an environment where public opinion on punishment is not only clearly nuanced, but also inconsistent, ill-informed and which includes both retributive and rehabilitative preferences (Payne et al., 2004; Cook and Lane, 2009). Given the different views of OOCDs and evidence suggesting public support for them is highly contingent on a range of aforementioned factors, it is important that OOCDs are used in ways that the public deem appropriate if they are to be seen as a legitimate and proportionate response. Otherwise they may be seen as interventions resulting in 'soft justice', with the public perceiving OOCDs as delivering unduly light outcomes relative to the offence in question, which risks eroding public confidence in them (Allen, 2017).

In this section, you have learned about the supportive and critical arguments associated with OOCDs. In the next section, you will learn about the development of OOCDs in England and Wales.

Case Study 27.2

Sarah - Application of OOCDs

Sarah is a single mum of two who is struggling to pay her bills and provide food for her toddlers. She found her neighbour's wallet on the street one morning and used the money in it to pay her bills. She also bought groceries from a convenience shop using the neighbour's contactless card which was also in the wallet. Overall, she spent £500 using the money and the contactless card.

(Continued)

Sarah has no previous convictions, and following an assessment of the case, she was issued a conditional caution to pay back the money. As part of the conditional caution, she was directed to a charity for financial support and was able to repay her neighbour.

Although the conditional caution was completed, the victim felt the conditional caution was not proportionate to the stress and anxiety they had felt during the period. On the other hand, Sarah found the conditional caution very helpful and was positive that she will not reoffend again.

Pause for Thought

The case example (Case Study 27.2) illustrates the varied opinions about the application of OOCDS. What are your thoughts on the outcome of the case study?

DEVELOPMENT OF THE ENGLAND AND WALES OOCD REGIME

The last decade (2008–2018) saw a decrease in the number of OOCDs administered by the police from approximately 660,000 to 229,000 individuals (Ministry of Justice, 2018). Cases disposed of by cautions (cautions for either summary non-motoring offences or indictable offences declined by 78%, from 350,000 to 75,300). For PNDs, there was a decrease by 88.7%, from 200,000 to 22,700. Cannabis/khat warnings declined from 110,000 to 20,000. Separate data on community resolutions demonstrated a decreasing trend from 120,000 to 101,000 (Ministry of Justice, 2018). This decline has been attributed to changes in policy and practice around the application of OOCDs, following concerns about inappropriate and inconsistent implementation (Whitehead, 2009; Sosa, 2012; Ministry of Justice, 2018).

At the same time, there has also been concerns raised about the perceived overuse of OOCDs, and more generally, criticism levelled at the complexity of the framework (Neyroud, 2017). Sosa (2012) highlighted the use of OOCDs for unsuitable offences (e.g. sexual offences and persistent offenders) and it has been argued that there remains scope to make OOCDs more transparent, streamlined, and focused on reparations to victims and the rehabilitation of offenders (Glen, 2017). It has been a matter of debate for a number of years as to where the boundary should lie between the use of OOCDs and court prosecution (Steer, 1970). As Neyroud (2017) highlights there are (potentially) competing considerations in reducing reoffending, victim confidence in the criminal justice system, an efficient process, and the wider public confidence in the criminal justice system. For the CJII (2011), a strategy is required that 'works to improve victim satisfaction, reduce reoffending and provide value for money'.

Pause for Thought

On reflection of the above, what strategy do you think could achieve a reduction in reoffending and increase victim confidence?

Subsequently, between 2013 and 2014, the Ministry of Justice conducted a consultation exercise with stakeholders and practitioners regarding OOCDs (Ministry of Justice, 2014). This confirmed the prevailing view that the OOCD system was confusing and there was a lack of transparency. A House of Commons Home Affairs Committee report, published in 2015, criticised the inappropriate and inconsistent use of OOCDs, arguing this undermined public confidence. For example, although OOCDs target first-time minor offenders, there were instances where individuals with a previous conviction were given a caution. The report argued for a simplified system of OOCDs, with greater scrutiny provided to ensure the use of OOCDs is appropriate and consistent across police forces and offences (House of Commons Home Affairs Committee, 2015).

A more recent review of the effectiveness of OOCDs suggests they may be more effective in achieving their outcomes than court prosecutions. Neyroud (2018) found effective outcomes among low harm/risk offenders. Further, OOCDs with conditions (such as conditional cautions and community resolutions) appeared to have a positive impact on the reduction of harm such as domestic violence. Gaps were identified which included limited data for a direct comparison of OOCDs with conditions and those without conditions, and a lack of data to demonstrate the effectiveness of gender-specific OOCD approaches.

Such criticism has spurred the ongoing development of OOCD policy and practice towards a more streamlined regime. Given that support for interventions associated with OOCDs depends on a range of factors discussed above, it is crucial that these are reflected in OOCD-related policy and practice if OOCDs are to avoid being perceived as delivering 'soft justice'.

This complexity, alongside the critique of OOCDs, led to the recommendation of a streamlined two-tier framework which is focused on conditional cautions and community resolutions. In November 2013, the Justice Secretary announced a trial in three police force areas. This new two-tier approach was underpinned by the following assumptions: cost effectiveness, appropriate condition setting and management, victim satisfaction and just treatment of offenders (Neyroud, 2017). The pilot involved three police forces ceasing the use of Simple Cautions, Cannabis Warnings, Khat Warnings and PNDs, and instead focusing on Conditional Cautions and Community Resolution. The three police forces were also allowed to use Conditional Cautions for offences involving domestic violence and hate crime in limited circumstances where previously Simple Cautions could have been applied. In this section, we have explored the development of OOCDs over the last decade. The next section details the nature of a recent pilot study and its key outcomes.

PILOT OF THE TWO-TIER FRAMEWORK

This section will provide you with an overview of how the two-tier framework was delivered in a pilot study and its impact in relation to the status quo. The framework was piloted between November 2014 and October 2015 (Ames et al., 2018). As stated earlier, the framework is distinguished from the status quo (i.e. the seven-OOCD framework) by the provision of only two types of OOCDs: a top-tier conditional caution and a lower-tier community resolution. One of the key distinctions between Conditional Cautions and Community Resolutions is that offences under Conditional Cautions must have a prospect of conviction when prosecuted in court. The pilot was carried out to understand the cost and (potential) impact of the framework before rolling it out across England and Wales. Ames et al. (2018) provide an evaluation of the process, impact and economics of the framework against the status quo.

Generally, the evaluation study identified differences in how the two-tier framework was delivered. Three operational delivery models were identified which can be described as follows:

1. Centrally organised delivery model (CODM)
2. Condition review delivery model (CRDM)
3. Flexible delivery model (FDM)

The first model, CODM, operated under dedicated teams for the OOCD types and. was governed by locally adapted central guidance on the administration of the disposals. There was also a system in place to review all conditions under the OOCD types. The main difference between the CRDM and the CODM was the lack of dedicated teams. The FDM, on the other hand, lacked all three elements across the police force. In the economic evaluation, Ames et al. (2018) found that the implementation cost for the CODM force (<£0.1m) was lower than the CRDM (£0.3m) and FDM (£0.5m) forces. This suggests the CODM may be cost-saving. However, the total cost of operating the two-tier framework was found to be ~70% higher than the status quo. This was attributed to an increase in the use of CCs, the additional costs of providing interventions for offenders, the cost implications of non-compliance, and a loss of revenue.

In the pilot, four types of conditions were administered under the CCs and CRs:

1. Rehabilitative (e.g. alcohol intervention programme)
2. Reparative (e.g. compensation or payment for a damaged property)
3. Restrictive (e.g. restriction on access to public spaces)
4. Punitive conditions (e.g. a fine)

Ames et al. (2018) found that reparative and restrictive conditions were more common under the two-tier framework, which was attributed to their ease of administration. The qualitative process evaluation (involving 74 interviews with criminal justice professionals and victims) found wide support for the two-tier framework. The perceived benefits of the framework were the enhanced simplification and transparency of the new system, victim engagement and communication, and promotion of desistance. However, a key challenge that was highlighted in the interviews was the lack of resources to support the system.

The impact evaluation analysed quantitative data from the pilot areas. This was compared to data from other selected police forces that operated the status quo (referred to as a counterfactual area/force). There was no statistically significant difference in the number of OOCDs administered by the pilot areas (13,643: 59% CRs and 41% CCs) and the counterfactual areas (13,273: 55% CRs, PNDs and Cannabis/Khat Warnings and 45% Simple/Conditional Cautions) from November 2014 to October 2015. There was also no difference between the pilot and counterfactual areas in proven reoffending within three months. These results suggest the impact of the two-tier framework may be comparable to the status quo. However, this may require further evaluation to make firm conclusions.

Hear from the Expert

Cerys Gibson, PhD Researcher, Nottingham University

The current system of out-of-court disposals was developed in a piecemeal fashion, with concerns about appropriate decision making and consistency in their use within and between police forces (Criminal Justice Joint Inspection, 2011). It has also been criticised as unnecessarily complicated and difficult for the public and practitioners to understand (Home Affairs Committee, 2014; Ministry of Justice, 2014). The Ministry of Justice, College of Policing and National Police Chiefs' Council therefore developed a new two-tier system of out-of-court disposals to replace the current model. This new structure would reduce the number of out-of-court disposals to two: a Community Resolution and a Conditional Caution. This aims at simplifying the system of out-of-court disposals, improving victim satisfaction and providing early intervention to prevent reoffending. It also aims to increase diversion from the formal criminal justice system, reducing the significant costs of court time (National Police Chiefs' Council, 2017; Neyroud, 2018).

This new approach was piloted between 2014 and 2015 in three police forces: West Yorkshire, Leicestershire and Staffordshire. A process and impact evaluation was published in 2018 which concluded that there was no improvement in reoffending rates for offenders in the pilot areas. The economic evaluation also quantified the cost of operating the new framework as higher than the status quo (Ames et al., 2018).

Eleven forces have thus far adopted the two-tier system, but this has resulted in inconsistency between forces. In its recent White Paper on sentencing, the Ministry of Justice stated that it planned to put the two-tier system of out-of-court disposals on a legislative footing, ensuring that all police forces use the same framework for out-of-court disposals (Ministry of Justice, 2020). This would mean, in the next few years, the police will use two statutory OOCDs and not PNDs, simple cautions, cannabis or khat warnings, though some deferred prosecution pilot schemes will remain in place.

In this section, the two-tier framework delivered in the pilot study was explored and the key outcomes from the evaluation of the framework were highlighted. In the next section, you will learn about a new and innovative Revised Conditional Caution Framework (RCCF) that has been developed by Northumbria Police.

NORTHUMBRIA POLICE REVISED CONDITIONAL CAUTION FRAMEWORK

In 2016, Northumbria Police reviewed their OOCD framework to develop an appropriate strategy to implement the two-tier framework. This separate initiative led to the design of an innovative and simplified OOCD model called RCCF. The model is mainly focused on the top-tier Conditional Caution OOCD. The RCCF was piloted between 2017 and 2018 to understand its effectiveness and inform movement to the two-tier framework. In this section, you will learn about the characteristics of this model and its conceptualised benefits to the criminal justice system.

Like the pilot programme, the RCCF administers rehabilitative, reparative, restrictive and punitive conditions aimed at enhancing victim satisfaction and reducing reoffending by addressing the root cause of offending behaviour. Under the RCCF, offenders are referred to programmes called conditional caution pathways that are designed to address their specific offending behaviour. There are six RCCF pathways:

1. Women's pathway
2. Victim Awareness pathway
3. The Veterans' pathway
4. Unpaid work
5. Alcohol and Drug Triage Assessment and alcohol brief intervention
6. ABC (alcohol behaviour change)

The Women's pathway is exclusively designed for female offenders. They are required to attend and complete an assessment at a local women's hub within twenty-eight days of receiving the caution. The hubs are run by an external partner agency, Changing Lives, who provide motivational interventions for the women. These interventions are designed to be gender-sensitive and trauma-informed. Further, they are tailored to meet each individual woman's needs. The aim of the programme is to help divert women from further offending. The assessment covers areas such as substance misuse, self-management skills, health, social networks/relationships, accommodation and offending. The 'Hear From the Expert' Box below provides an overview of the impact of the Women Specific Conditional Caution Scheme (WSCCS) from a student researcher perspective.

——————————— **Hear from the Expert** ———————————

Student Researcher Experience of the Northumbria RCCF

"The scheme gives women the opportunity to get help with other factors present in their lives that may be impacting on their offending. This includes domestic abuse, mental health, drugs and alcohol, and financial issues. As needs assessments are carried out by an experienced voluntary sector organisation in a women-only setting, it provides a safe space for women to access any help they may need as an alternative to being dealt with by the criminal justice system. Many women who have accessed the scheme have continued to receive ongoing support after the initial timeframe of the conditional caution has passed."

(Sophie Mitchell, PhD Researcher, Northumbria University)

The Victim Awareness pathway (V-Aware) is a programme for male offenders which must be completed within twelve weeks of receiving the conditional caution. In this programme, the offender participates in a three-and-a-half hour interactive and scenario-based session where they reflect on the impact of their offending behaviour on the victim and others, as well as the consequences of repeat offending. It is aimed at men who have committed a range of lower-level offences who would benefit from an educational and behaviour change programme.

The Veterans' pathway is a programme for ex-HM Forces involved in the criminal justice system and those at risk of offending. The conditional caution requires the offender to complete an assessment of their offending-related needs within twenty-eight days. The programme is run in partnership with an external organisation, Project NOVA, which is specialised in supporting veterans. The assessment covers areas such as substance misuse, housing, welfare assistance, financial advice and support, anger management, domestic abuse, mental health, and employment support. The offenders are referred to specialist agencies based on their specific needs, and they may extend their intervention with NOVA on a voluntary basis for up to twelve months on completion of the conditional caution.

The unpaid work pathway requires the male offender to complete a seven-hour session of supervised unpaid work within twenty-eight days of receiving the conditional caution. Unpaid work is also known as Community Payback, which was previously only available through the courts. This programme is also available under community resolutions. It is a punitive condition that benefits the community. However, the offender is expected to learn valuable practical and life skills which can support a reduction in their reoffending. The types of work under this programme are mainly conservation and environmental work, such as cutting back overgrowth, tree planting, litter picking, painting and decorating and garden maintenance for elderly residents.

Under the Alcohol or Drug Triage Assessment and alcohol brief intervention pathway, the male offender must complete an assessment of their substance misuse within twenty-eight days of receiving the conditional caution. For those misusing alcohol, an educational alcohol brief intervention is also required. This and the ABC programme are for those who have committed an offence whilst under the influence of drugs or alcohol. The intervention is administered by locally commissioned treatment agencies that are available in each local authority area. As part of the condition setting, the offender is required to complete an Alcohol Audit Assessment Tool. Those scoring between 0–15 (low or increasing risk) are referred to the ABC course, whilst those scoring 16– 20+ (harmful drinking or dependency) receive a triage assessment and alcohol intervention.

The Alcohol Behaviour Change pathway is a self-funding programme (£45) that must be completed by the male offender within twelve weeks of receiving the conditional caution. The programme runs in a similar format to a speed awareness course. It targets offenders who may benefit from an educational and motivational change course. Topics covered under this programme include the impact of drinking on health, alcohol and the law, individual and community risks.

The RCCF pathways are partly informed by existing research and patterns of offending. Several studies suggest that the needs of female offenders are more complex than those of male offenders (Bartlett et al., 2015; Gobeil et al., 2016; Rodermond et al., 2016). The substance/alcohol misuse pathways are supported by research evidence that suggests an association between recidivism and substance/alcohol misuse (Wheelhouse, 2008; Hancock et al., 2012). Available statistical data shows that veterans exhibit certain characteristics such as psychological/mental disorders and substance misuse which may lead to offending behaviour (Short et al., 2018). For some specific offences, limited studies have considered the potential of using unpaid work and victim awareness interventions (Gottschall et al., 2015; Pamment, 2016).

The pathway delivery model may be a more structured and simplified OOCD compared to the status quo. However, there is a need for an evaluation of its effectiveness and how it may inform the roll-out of the two-tier framework across England and Wales. An evaluation study was recently commissioned in collaboration with Northumbria University and has yet to be published by the Force. The findings from the study will allow policy makers and stakeholders to make an informed decision about the most appropriate OOCD framework. The 'Hear from the Expert' Box below provides insights into the experience of one researcher on the evaluation of the RCCF.

Hear from the Expert

Researcher Experience

For Researcher A, the streamlined OOCD framework has a positive prospect to address the root causes of offending behaviour:

> "Our research found positive results for all the evaluation outcomes: efficiency of the implementation process, victim satisfaction, and reoffending rate. One of the biggest challenges we identified from our research is the sustainability of the framework. There is a need for an allocation of adequate resources to support the programme. We observed that, in some cases, offenders may benefit from a more individualised or continuous intervention, but this was not possible due to resource constraints."

When asked about the potential implementation challenges of the streamlined framework, Researcher B wrote that the current police culture and public (victim) attitudes may affect the success of the programme:

> "On the one hand the programme may be beneficial, but there are concerns among officers and stakeholders that conditional cautions may be disproportionate to the adverse impact crimes may have on victims, a view that describes out of court disposals as 'soft justice'. I think we will need more counterfactual research to clearly demonstrate the actual benefits (and risks) of the streamlined framework. This will help influence the police culture and public attitudes to the framework."

CHAPTER SUMMARY

In summary, this chapter introduced the out of court and diversion regime in England and Wales. There is currently a shift from the seven-OOCD framework towards a more simplified two-tier framework. This shift is due to concerns about the inconsistencies and complexity of the seven-OOCD framework. The characteristics of the new framework are summarised below:

- The two-tier framework is made up of two types of OOCDs: conditional cautions and community resolution.
- The aims of these OOCDs are to enhance victim satisfaction, support minor offenders to change their offending behaviour, and reduce the risk of reoffending.
- Available evidence on the two-tier framework shows both positive gains and challenges in implementing the regime.
- Whilst views on the simplicity and transparency of the two-tier framework are encouraging, its cost implications may be higher than the status quo.
- Three models of delivering the two-tier framework have been identified from existing research. Of these, a centrally organised delivery model was associated with lower implementation costs.

In a more recent development, Northumbria Police has developed an OOCD model, called the Revised Conditional Caution Framework, which appears to be research-informed and more simplified. Whilst the overall impact of the two-tier framework has yet to be demonstrated, it is anticipated that the proposed OOCDs will lead to a revolution in policing and criminal justice that will move towards the promotion of desistance.

REVISITING THE FRAMING QUESTIONS

1. What are Out of Court Disposals?

Out of Court Disposals are interventions that are designed as alternatives to formal charges and prosecution at court.

2. Can you describe the difference between a simple caution and a conditional caution?

A simple caution is a formal caution given by the police that has no conditions attached, whilst a conditional caution includes specific rehabilitative, reparative, punitive and restrictive conditions which must be fulfilled by the offender.

3. What led to the introduction of the two-tier framework?

The key reasons for the introduction of the two-tier framework are: 1) concerns about the overuse of the previous out of court disposals; 2) inconsistencies in the use of the different OOCD types by police forces, including their use for unsuitable offences; and 3) the potential of the two-tier framework to improve victim satisfaction, reduce reoffending, and provide value for money.

4. Can you describe the essential characteristics of the Northumbria Police Conditional Caution Framework and the aims behind it?

The Northumbria Police Conditional Caution Framework consists of seven intervention pathway programmes that are aimed at enhancing victim satisfaction and reducing reoffending by addressing the root cause of offending behaviour. The seven pathways include a women specific pathway, a victim awareness pathway, a veterans' pathway, an unpaid work pathway, an alcohol and drug triage assessment and alcohol brief intervention pathway, and an alcohol behaviour change (ABC) pathway.

Review Questions

1. Briefly outline and discuss the four types of conditions that may be attached to a conditional caution.
2. Compare and contrast fixed penalty notices and penalty notices for disorder.
3. Discuss the factors that may impact on public opinions about the appropriateness of Out of Court Disposals.
4. Evaluate the pros and cons of the seven-OOCD and two-tier OOCD frameworks.
5. Compare the operational delivery models for the two-tier OOCD framework.

GO FURTHER

Books/Book Chapters

1. Chapter 2 in the following text includes a reflective discussion of Penalty Notices for Disorder:

   Bell, E. (ed.) (2011) *Criminal Justice and Neoliberalism.* Basingstoke: Palgrave Macmillan.

2. Pages 419–421 in the following title provide an introduction to the use and impact of cautions:

   Elliott, C. and Quin, F. (2017) *English Legal System.* Harlow: Pearson.

3. Chapter 8 in the following text includes a discussion of the financial/equity implications of financial penalties included within some Out of Court Disposals:

   Grover, C. (2008) *Crime and Inequality.* London: Routledge.

Journal Articles

1. The following article reflects on the potential to integrate restorative justice interventions into conditional cautions and why integration can be problematic:

   Braddock, R. A. (2011) Rhetoric or restoration? A study into the restorative potential of the conditional cautioning scheme. *International Journal of Police Science and Management,* 13(3): 195–210. https://journals.sagepub.com/doi/pdf/10.1350/ijps.2011.13.3.251

2. This second article explores how the police implement Out of Court Disposals and how implementation can be made as effective as possible:

   Slothower, M. (2014) Strengthening police professionalism with decision support: bounded discretion in Out-of-Court Disposals, *Policing,* 19(4): 353–367. https://academic.oup.com/policing/article-abstract/8/4/353/1563780?redirectedFrom=fulltext

3. This third article provides a perspective from those who receive alternatives to court:

Snow, A. (2019) Receiving an on the spot penalty: a tale of morality, common sense and law abidance. *Criminology & Criminal Justice*, 19(2): 141–159. https://journals.sagepub.com/doi/pdf/10.1177/1748895817738556

Useful Websites

1. The link below will take you to a publication that is essential reading to understand what developments have taken place in the area of Out of Court Disposals and the evaluation results of a pilot study of the two-tier framework: https://assets.publishing.service.gov.uk/government/uploads/system/uploads/attachment_data/file/718947/adult-out-of-court-disposal-pilot-evaluation.pdf

2. This second link will take you to a website where you will find a report that presents findings from an evaluation of an initiative that aimed to use restorative justice within cautioning: https://restorativejustice.org.uk/resources/proceed-caution-evaluation-thames-valley-police-initiative-restorative-cautioning

3. The following link will take you to some essential reading to help you appreciate key debates surrounding the use of Out of Court Disposals in England and Wales and whether there should be a reform of the criminal justice system: https://policyexchange.org.uk/wp-content/uploads/2016/09/proceed-with-caution-2.pdf

4. This final link will take you to the Code of Practice governing the use of Conditional Cautions in England and Wales and as such is essential reading for the circumstances in which Conditional Cautions are used: https://assets.publishing.service.gov.uk/government/uploads/system/uploads/attachment_data/file/243436/9780108512162.pdf

REFERENCES

Allen, R. (2017) 'Less is more – the case for dealing with offences out of court'. London: Transform Justice.

Ames, A., Di Antonio, E., Hitchcock, J., Webster, S., Wong, K., Ellingworth, D., Meadows, L., McAlonan, D., Uhrig, N. and Logue, C. (2018) *Adult Out of Court Disposal Pilot Evaluation – Final Report*, Ministry of Justice Analytical Series.

Association of Chief Police Officers (2007) *Guidance on Policing Cannabis – Use of Cannabis Warnings*. London: Association of Chief Police Officers.

Association of Chief Police Officers (2012) *Guidelines of the use of Community Resolutions (CR) Incorporating Restorative Justice*. London: Association of Chief Police Officers.

Association of Chief Police Officers (2014) *National Policing Guidelines on KHAT Possession for Personal Use Intervention Framework*. London: Association of Chief Police Officers.

Bartlett, A., Jhanji, E., White, S., Harty, M. A., Scammell, J. and Allen, S. (2015) Interventions with women offenders: a systematic review and meta-analysis of mental health gain. *Journal of Forensic Psychiatry & Psychology*, 26: 133–165. https://doi.org/10.1080/14789949.2014.981563 (accessed 07.02.2020).

Cook, C. L. and Lane, J. (2009) The place of public fear in sentencing and correctional policy. *Journal of Criminal Justice*, 37: 586–595.

Criminal Justice Joint Inspection (2011) *Exercising Discretion: The Gateway to Justice: A study by Her Majesty's Inspectorate of Constabulary and Her Majesty's Crown Prosecution Service Inspectorate on cautions, penalty notices for disorder and restorative justice*. England.

Donoghue, J. C. (2014) Reforming the role of magistrates: implications for summary justice in England and Wales. *The Modern Law Review*, 77(6): 928–963.

Gibbs, P. (2017) The end of the 'cautions culture?' *The Justice Gap*. https://www.thejusticegap.com/end-cautions-culture/ (accessed 7.2.2020).

Glen, S. (2017) *Charging and Out of Court Disposals: A National Strategy*. London: National Police Chiefs' Council.

Gobeil, R., Blanchette, K. and Stewart, L. (2016) A meta-analytic review of correctional interventions for women offenders: gender-neutral versus gender-informed approaches. *Criminal Justice and Behavior*, 43: 301–322. https://doi.org/10.1177/0093854815621100

Gottschall, S., Greiner, L., Brown, S. and Serin, R. (2015) Value, challenges, and solutions in incorporating victim impact awareness in offender rehabilitation: the results of qualitative interviews with stakeholders. *Victims & Offenders*, 10: 293–317. https://doi.org/10.1080/15564886.2014.949959

Gov.uk (2019) 'Fixed penalty notices: issuing and enforcement by councils'. https://www.gov.uk/guidance/fixed-penalty-notices-issuing-and-enforcement-by-councils (accessed 02/07/2019).

Hancock, J., Fearon, C., McLaughlin, H. and Fielden, B. (2012) Policing the 'Drugs Intervention Programme' (DIP): an exploratory study of the Southern UK policing region. *Policing*, 6: 431–442. https://doi.org/10.1093/police/par059

HMCPSI HMIC (2015) *Joint Inspection of the Provision of Charging Decisions*. Home Affairs Committee, *Out-of-Court Disposals Fourteenth Report of Session 2014–15 Report* (HC 2015, 799).

House of Commons Home Affairs Committee (2015) *Out-of-Court Disposals: Fourteenth Report of Session 2014-15: Report together with formal minutes*. London: HMSO.

Johnstone, G. (2011) *Restorative Justice: Ideas, Values, Debates*. London: Routledge.

Mackenzie, G., Spiranovic, C., Warner, K., Stobbs, N., Gelb, K., Indermaur, D., Roberts, L., Broadhurst, R. and Bouhours, T. (2012) Sentencing and public confidence: results from a national Australian survey on public opinions towards sentencing. *Australian and New Zealand Journal of Criminology*, 45: 45–65.

Miller, R. N. and Applegate, B. K. (2015) Adult crime, adult time? Benchmarking public views on punishing serious juvenile felons. *Criminal Justice Review*, 40: 151–168.

Ministry of Justice (2010) *Breaking the Cycle: Effective Punishment, Rehabilitation and Sentencing of Offenders*. London: HMSO.

Ministry of Justice (2013) *Code of Practice for Adult Conditional Cautions*. London: Ministry of Justice.

Ministry of Justice (2014a) *Out of Court Disposals: Consultation Response*. London: Ministry of Justice.

Ministry of Justice (2014b) *Penalty Notices for Disorder*. London: Ministry of Justice.

Ministry of Justice (2015) *Simple Cautions for Adult Offenders*. London: Ministry of Justice.

Ministry of Justice (2018) *Criminal Justice Statistics Quarterly, England and Wales, July 2017 to June 2018 (provisional)*. London: Ministry of Justice.

Mowle, E. N., Edens, J. F., Clark, J. W. and Sorman, K. (2016) Effects of mental health and neuroscience evidence on juror perceptions of a criminal defendant: the moderating role of political orientation. *Behavioural Sciences and the Law*, 34: 726–741.

National Police Chiefs' Council (2017) *Charging and Out of Court Disposals, A National Strategy*. www.npcc.police.uk/Publication/Charging%20and%20Out%20of%20Court%20Disposals%20A%20National%20Strategy.pdf (accessed 30.01.2020).

Neyroud, P. (2018) *Out of Court Disposals Managed by the Police: A Review of the Evidence*. National Police Chief's Council. https://www.npcc.police.uk/Publication/NPCC%20Out%20of%20Court%20Disposals%20Evidence%20assessment%20FINAL%20June%202018.pdf

Office for Criminal Justice Reform (2010) *Initial Findings from a Review of the Use of Out-of-Court Disposals*. London: HMSO.

O'Sullivan, K., Holderness, D., Hong, X. Y., Bright, D. and Kemp, R. (2017) Public attitudes in Australia to the reintegration of ex-offenders: testing a belief in redeemability (BiR) scale. *European Journal on Criminal Policy and Research*, 23: 409–424.

Pamment, N. (2016) 'Realising the Potential: The Research Evidence Base for Unpaid Work'. In N. Pamment (ed.), *Community Reparation for Young Offenders: Perceptions, Policy and Practice*. London: Palgrave Macmillan. pp. 29–55. https://doi.org/10.1057/9781137400468_3 (accessed 7.2.2020).

Payne, B. K., Gainey, R. R., Triplett, R. A. and Danner, M. J. E. (2004) What drives punitive beliefs? Demographic characteristics and justifications for sentencing. *Journal of Criminal Justice*, 2: 195–206.

Pfeiffer, C. and Windzio, M. (2005) Media use and its impact on crime perception, sentencing attitudes and crime policy. *European Journal of Criminology*, 2: 259–285.

Roberts, J. V. and Stalans, L. J. (2004) Restorative sentencing: exploring the views of the public. *Social Justice Research*, 17: 315–334.

Rodermond, E., Kruttschnitt, C., Slotboom, A.-M. and Bijleveld, C. C. (2016) Female desistance: a review of the literature. *European Journal of Criminology*, 13: 3–28. https://doi.org/10.1177/1477370815597251

Short, R., Dickson, H., Greenberg, N. and MacManus, D. (2018) Offending behaviour, health and wellbeing of military veterans in the criminal justice system. *PLOS ONE*, 13: e0207282. https://doi.org/10.1371/journal.pone.0207282

Slothower, M. (2014) Strengthening police professionalism with decision support: bounded discretion in Out-of-Court Disposals. *Policing*, 19(4): 353–367.

Spiranovic, C. A., Roberts, L. D. and Indermaur, D. (2012) What predicts punitiveness? An examination of predictors of punitive attitudes towards offenders in Australia. *Psychiatry, Psychology and Law*, 19(2): 249–261.

Sosa, K. (2012) *Proceed with Caution: Use of Out-of-Court Disposals in England and Wales*. London: Policy Exchange.

Spiranovic, C. A., Roberts, L. D. and Indermaur, D. (2012) What predicts punitiveness? An examination of predictors of punitive attitudes towards offenders in Australia. *Psychiatry, Psychology and Law*, 19: 249–261.

The Sentencing Council (2019) *Penalty notices – fixed penalty notices and penalty notices for disorder*. https://www.sentencingcouncil.org.uk/explanatory-material/magistrates-court/item/out-of-court-disposals/5-penalty-notices-fixed-penalty-notices-and-penalty-notices-for-disorder/# (accessed 02.7.2019).

Westmarland, N., Johnson, K. and McGlynn, C. (2017) Under the radar: the widespread use of 'Out of Court Resolutions' in policing domestic violence and abuse in the United Kingdom. *British Journal of Criminology*, 58(1): 1–16.

Wheelhouse, P. (2008) 'Intervention with Drug Misusing Offenders and Prolific and other Priority Offenders'. In *Resource Material Series No.74: Work Product of the 135th International Senior Seminar: Promoting Public Safety and Controlling Recidivism Using Effective Interventions with Offenders: An Examination of Best Practices*. Tokyo: United Nations Asia and Far East Institute, pp. 65–82.

Whitehead, T. (2009) 'Repeat offenders are escaping court with on-the-spot fines'. https://www.telegraph.co.uk/news/uknews/law-and-order/6048581/Repeat-and-seriousoffenders-are-escaping-court-with-on-the-spot-fines.html (accessed 1.7.2019).

Wood, W. R. (2015) Why Restorative Justice will not reduce incarceration. *British Journal of Criminology*, 55: 883–900.

Zehr, H. and Mika, H. (2003) 'Fundamental Concepts of Restorative Justice'. In E. McLaughlin, R. Fergusson, G. Hughes and L. Westmarland (eds), *Restorative Justice: Critical Issues*. London: Sage Publications. pp. 40–43.

Non-Custodial Sentencing

28

George Mair

Learning Objectives

By the end of this chapter you will:

- Be able to understand what non-custodial sentences are.
- Grasp how they differ from each other.
- Understand how they are used by the courts.
- Be able to critically reflect on the key issues facing non-custodial sentences.

Framing Questions

1. What are non-custodial sentences for?
2. Can they compete with custody in any meaningful sense?
3. Do non-custodial sentences have a future?

INTRODUCTION

This chapter will explore the use of **non-custodial sentences** for offenders aged 18 and above. It will describe what these sentences are and how they differ from each other, as well as from a prison sentence. Their place in the sentencing tariff will be explored, and their use over time and how they are being used currently will be examined with regard to both the Crown Court and the magistrates' courts. Non-custodial sentences have – on the whole – been marginalised in the criminological literature; prisons are a much 'sexier' topic to study as they represent the most serious sentence that a court in England and Wales can pass on an offender. But it needs to be emphasised from the start that by far the majority of individuals found guilty in the courts receive a non-custodial sentence (more than three-quarters of those sentenced in 2018). And it should also be noted that relatively recently – perhaps over the last twenty years or so – probation-based sentences have been receiving far more attention than previously. This is to a great extent a result of the massive changes that probation has been subjected to since 1991. Without non-custodial sentences it is no exaggeration to claim that the current criminal justice system would be unsustainable.

Knowledge link: This topic is also covered in Chapter 29.

The overall aim of this chapter is to bring home to you the significance of non-custodial sentences. They are at least as effective as, are considerably cheaper than and (even at their most **punitive**) far more humane than a custodial sentence. As I write (January 2020) they stand at a crossroads with key political decisions awaited that will define their future. I firmly believe that the use of non-custodial sentences should be encouraged, and by the end of the chapter I hope that you will agree (for a complementary view see Mair, 2017).

MAPPING THE TERRAIN

So what are non-custodial sentences? Crudely, they are anything that is not a prison sentence. But it is important to bear in mind that the number and type of non-custodial sentences have changed considerably over the years. The probation order, for example, was introduced in 1907; the community service order in 1972. Attendance centre orders appeared in the 1948 Criminal Justice Act. A suspended sentence order was introduced in 1967. The 1991 Criminal Justice Act introduced the combination order and the curfew order. The drug treatment and testing order appeared in 1998. None of these seven non-custodial sentences exist now. And the probation service as a whole has changed dramatically over the last thirty years – as we will discuss below.

In the 1980s England and Wales probably had a wider range of non-custodial sentences than most countries, yet 'the policy of proliferation was not a conspicuous success' (Ashworth, 2015: 337). To a greater or lesser degree, all of them aimed at diverting offenders from a custodial sentence but all of them failed to do this effectively because in the end they were all perceived as 'soft options' when compared to custody. Sentencers, therefore, found it difficult to use them instead of a prison sentence. To make matters worse the development of non-custodial sentences has been fragmentary and lacks any consistency (see, for example, Mair, 2016 for the development of probation; and Halliday, 2001 for the sentencing framework generally), which means that it remains unclear how they should be used and who they should be used for. The primacy of prison as the only 'meaningful' court sentence distorts how we perceive non-custodial sentences.

Currently, the main sentences available to the courts are as follows (roughly in order of punitiveness):

- Imprisonment
- Suspended sentence of imprisonment (SSO)
- Community order (CO)
- Fine

- Compensation order
- Conditional discharge
- Absolute discharge

This chapter is concerned with all of these *with the exception of imprisonment*. This raises two important issues. First, it should be emphasised again that despite the centrality of prisons to criminological research, imprisonment is only one sentence of the seven main dispositions available to the courts. Second, legally, the Suspended Sentence Order (SSO) is a custodial sentence; the offender is sentenced to a period of imprisonment which is then suspended for a period of time, and if the offender does not offend during that time and complies with any requirements of the SSO, the whole of the sentence is served in the community. It is, therefore, certainly debatable whether the SSO should be counted as a non-custodial sentence. For the purposes of this chapter, however, that is how the SSO will be treated.

There are also a number of 'Other' sentences that are available, such as restriction orders, hospital orders, recognizances and bind overs, but these are rarely used and will not be discussed here.

Pause for Thought

How many forms of non-custodial sentences do the courts need?

WHAT DO THE VARIOUS NON-CUSTODIAL SENTENCES LOOK LIKE?

The *Absolute Discharge* is the least serious court sentence, and is only used for the most trivial offences where the court decides that although the offender is guilty there would be no benefit to inflicting punishment. The sentence requires nothing of the offender, and it is the only court sentence where it can accurately be said that – following its imposition – the offender 'walked free from court'.

The *Conditional Discharge* is a slightly more serious sentence in that it requires the offender not to commit any further offence within a period specified by the court, which can be up to three years. If this condition is breached and another offence is committed, then the offender will be dealt with not only for the new offence but also for the one for which the conditional discharge was originally imposed. This sentence, then, represents a clear warning to the offender.

The *Compensation Order* was introduced in 1972. This is where the offender is ordered by the court to pay a specified sum of money to the victim of his/her crime to compensate for the loss suffered. The courts are expected to consider making a compensation order where the victim has suffered any harm or loss; and since 1982 they have been expected to prioritise compensation before a fine when the offender cannot afford to pay both. The compensation order can be used as an ancillary measure alongside another sentence, or it can be the sole order passed by the court. Unlike the fine (see below) compensation paid by the offender goes to the victim, not the state.

The *Fine* is by far the most popular sentence used by the courts. It can be imposed for almost any offence (except murder) and has been claimed by Ashworth to be

> ... the ideal penal measure. It is easily calibrated, so that courts can reflect differing degrees of gravity and culpability. It involves no physical coercion and is non-intrusive, since it does not involve supervision, or the loss of one's time. It is largely reversible, in the event of injustice. Indeed, it is straightforwardly punitive, uncontaminated by other values ... (2015: 346)

In the Crown Court, there is no limit to the amount of money that an offender can be fined. And this is now the case in the magistrates' courts since the Legal Aid, Punishment and Sentencing of Offenders Act 2012 abolished the maximum of £5,000 that had been in place. Fines are assessed according to the seriousness of the offence and in the magistrates' courts a band system is used to calculate the level of the fine:

Table 28.1 Fine Bands

Starting Point		Range
Fine band A	50% of relevant weekly income	25-75% of relevant weekly income
Fine band B	100% of relevant weekly income	75-125% of relevant weekly income
Fine band C	150% of relevant weekly income	125-175% of relevant weekly income

The *Community Order* (CO) was introduced in the Criminal Justice Act 2003 and was made available to the courts in 2005. Essentially, it replaces the old-style probation-based sentences such as the probation order, the community service order and the like. The CO is made up of a number of requirements (see Table 28.2) and has to comprise at least one. In 2018, 92% of COs had one or two requirements and the average was 1.5. It has a maximum length of three years and the 2003 Act specifies that it

Table 28.2 Requirements for the Community Order and the Suspended Sentence Order

Rehabilitation activity (up to 36 months; 24 months maximum for the SSO)

Unpaid work (40-300 hours to be completed within 12 months)

Attendance centre requirement (12-36 hours with a maximum of 3 hours per attendance; only for those aged up to 25)

Prohibited activity e.g. if offences took place at football matches, the offender could be banned from attending any matches (up to 36 months; 24 months maximum for the SSO)

Programme (length to be expressed as the number of sessions)

Alcohol treatment, which is aimed at dealing with alcohol dependency (up to 36 months; 24 months maximum for the SSO; offender's consent is required)

Drug rehabilitation (up to 36 months; 24 months maximum for the SSO; offender's consent is required)

Mental health treatment, where, if offending is related to mental health issues, the offender can access appropriate help (up to 36 months; 24 months maximum for the SSO; offender's consent is required)

Residence, where the offender must live at a place specified by the court (up to 36 months; 24 months maximum for the SSO)

Curfew, where the offender is required by the court to be in a particular place for certain times (up to 12 months and for between 2-16 hours in any one day; if a stand-alone curfew requirement is used, there is no probation involvement)

Exclusion, where the offender is banned from entering a certain area or place, e.g. a particular street or shop (up to 24 months)

Foreign travel prohibition (up to 12 months)

Alcohol abstinence and monitoring, which is aimed at addressing issues relating to alcohol misuse (up to 120 days)

Electronic monitoring (length as long as the requirement where compliance monitoring is required)

should only be imposed if the offence is 'serious enough' to justify its use, or in cases where a minor offender has been dealt with previously by a fine with regard to three or more previous convictions, and the current offence does not pass the seriousness criterion. The requirements applied should be the most suitable for the offender and commensurate with the seriousness of the offence. Since 2013 it has been mandatory for all COs to have a punitive requirement or a fine, unless there are exceptional reasons not to do so.

Pause for Thought

- Are there any requirements that you feel should be added to the list in Table 28.2?
- Or any that might be taken off?

The *Suspended Sentence Order* (SSO) blurs the boundaries between custody and non-custodial sentences. Legally, as noted earlier, it is a custodial sentence, but if all goes well, it will be served in the community. The SSO can be applied when a custodial sentence of between 14 days and 24 months has been imposed. On the face of it, the SSO looks very similar to the CO insofar as it is made up of the same requirements (in 2018, where requirements were used, 89% of SSOs had one or two, with the average being 1.7). However, there are several differences: first, whereas the CO has a maximum length of 36 months, the SSO has a maximum of 24 months; second, since 2012 the SSO can be made without any requirements; and third, there is provision for the SSO to be reviewed periodically by the courts which could lead to strengthening or relaxing of the requirements. Because it is a custodial sentence, the SSO has to pass the custody threshold: custodial sentences should only be applied when the offence is 'so serious' that neither a fine nor a community sentence can be justified. In principle, both the CO and the SSO can act as alternatives to custody, although whether they do so in practice is another matter.

As you should have noticed, the non-custodial sentences described are very different from each other and involve varying degrees of punitive bite: there is a considerable difference between a conditional discharge of 12 months; an SSO with three requirements, e.g. 240 hours unpaid work, an exclusion requirement of 18 months and an alcohol abstinence and monitoring requirement of 120 days; and a fine of £500. The 2003 Criminal Justice Act set out five aims of sentencing, although it did not prioritise these and it is left up to individual sentencers to decide how they might apply to their sentences:

- Punishment
- Crime reduction
- Reform and rehabilitation
- Protection of the public
- Reparation

Pause for Thought

How do you think that the various non-custodial sentences map onto the aims of sentencing?

Having looked at what non-custodial sentences are, in the next section of the chapter we will explore how they are used by the courts.

HOW ARE NON-CUSTODIAL SENTENCES USED?

Not surprisingly, given their different levels of punitiveness, non-custodial sentences are used for different kinds of crimes. In 2018 a total of 1,172,456 sentences were passed on adults (18+) and companies and Table 28.3 shows how these were distributed. The fine is by far the most commonly used sentence; it is used almost 12 times as often as imprisonment or the community order. Indeed, non-custodial sentences as a whole make up more than nine out of ten sentences imposed – even though it is prisons that both criminological research and media interest focus upon.

Table 28.3   Court Sentences (2018)

Sentence	No.	%
Imprisonment	77,485	6.6
SSO	42,699	3.6
CO	77,913	6.6
Fine	916,507	78.2
Compensation order	4,828	0.4
Conditional discharge	38,232	3.3
Absolute discharge	3,742	0.3
Other	10,989	0.9

Knowledge link: This topic is also covered in Chapter 26.

But because they deal with different kinds of offences (the Crown Court with more serious and magistrates' courts with the less serious), the distribution of sentences differs according to court type, as Table 28.4 shows.

Table 28.4   Sentences by Court Type (2018)

Sentence	Crown Court No.	%	Magistrates' courts No.	%
Imprisonment	40,678	59.5	36,807	3.3
SSO	16,623	24.3	26,076	2.4
CO	5,557	8.1	72,356	6.6
Fine	1,346	2.0	915,161	82.9
Compensation order	45	0.1	4,783	0.4
Conditional discharge	982	1.4	37,250	3.4
Absolute discharge	71	0.1	3,671	0.3
Other	3,054	4.5	7,935	0.7
Total	68,356	100	1,104,100	100

The first thing to note about Table 28.4 is that the sentence most commonly imposed by the Crown Court is imprisonment; non-custodial sentences only make up 40.5% cent of sentences used in the Crown Court, and if for the moment we exclude the SSO (remember, it is a custodial sentence), then only 16.2% of sentences in the Crown Court are non-custodial. In the magistrates' courts, on the other hand, only 3.3% of sentences are custodial; 96.7% are non-custodial. Indeed, more than eight out of ten magistrates' courts' sentences are fines. Why is this the case? Quite simply, it is because the magistrates' courts deal with relatively minor offences, and the harshness of the sentence should reflect the seriousness of the crime, taking into account the culpability of the offender, the harm done, and any mitigating and aggravating factors. So less punitive sentences are used in the magistrates' courts and therein lies the significance of non-custodial sentences.

It is worth noting several other points from Table 28.4:

- The high proportionate use of the SSO in the Crown Court, although magistrates use this sentence more often in absolute terms. Indeed, the success of the SSO (in terms of its use by the courts) has led to several efforts to curb its growth (see below).
- The very low use (less than 5% of sentences in both courts) made of compensation orders, conditional discharges and absolute discharges – although conditional discharges are imposed more often than custody in magistrates' courts. There would appear to be considerable scope to make greater use of such sentences, particularly in the magistrates' courts.
- The huge disparity in the use of the fine between the two types of court; as noted above, this is a direct result of the kinds of offences dealt with in each court.
- The relatively low use of the CO in both courts. In 2010, 18% of Crown Court sentences were COs, while the figure in the magistrates' courts was 9.7% – a disturbing development if the decline in COs continues.

We can get an even better idea about how non-custodial sentences are used by looking at the kinds of offences they are used for; Tables 28.5a and 28.5b show this for the Crown Court and the magistrates' courts respectively.

Table 28.5a   Crown Court Sentences by Offence Group 2018 (%)

	Custody	SSO	CO	Fine	Compensation	Conditional discharge	Absolute discharge	Other
Violence	18.8	16.7	12.5	3.9	24.4	7.3	14.1	17.3
Sexual	7.6	3.6	5.6	0.4	2.2	0.7	11.3	6.8
Robbery	5.5	1.1	1.0	0.1	-	0.1	1.4	2.3
Theft	17.3	9.7	11.9	2.9	13.3	9.0	5.6	7.7
Criminal damage and arson	1.0	0.8	0.8	0.4	6.7	1.0	1.4	2.0
Poss. of weapons	6.7	7.7	5.5	0.9	-	4.8	2.8	6.3
Public order	4.8	6.8	9.2	3.7	2.2	8.1	8.4	6.3
Fraud	3.0	7.1	5.7	2.1	11.1	4.7	4.2	2.3
Drugs	17.3	16.3	12.7	22.1	-	22.9	11.3	14.3
Summary offences	3.3	8.3	12.8	32.8	37.8	30.9	19.7	12.9
Other	14.6	21.8	22.2	30.8	2.2	10.5	19.7	21.8
Total No.	40,678	16,623	5,557	1,346	45	982	71	3,054

Table 28.5b Magistrates' Courts' Sentences by Offence Group 2018 (%)

	Custody	SSO	CO	Fine	Compensation	Conditional discharge	Absolute discharge	Other
Violence	10.1	10.3	5.8	0.2	1.8	2.0	1.0	2.7
Sexual	0.5	0.8	0.7	-	0.1	0.1	-	0.2
Robbery	-	-	-	-	-	-	-	-
Theft	35.6	23.3	17.7	1.0	31.1	23.3	4.3	17.7
Criminal damage and arson	0.3	0.4	0.4	-	1.1	0.3	0.2	0.3
Poss. of weapons	5.1	8.8	2.7	0.1	-	0.5	0.1	0.7
Public order	7.3	5.5	4.2	0.3	0.9	1.9	1.4	5.0
Fraud	1.2	2.9	2.9	0.1	1.3	1.7	0.1	0.7
Drugs	1.7	1.7	3.2	1.4	-	10.5	3.7	9.1
Summary offences	33.5	41.8	59.5	96.3	62.8	57.6	86.8	50.4
Other	4.7	4.4	2.9	0.6	0.8	2.1	2.3	13.2
Total No.	36,807	26,076	72,356	915,161	4,783	37,250	3,671	7,935

In the Crown Court, it is clear that not only are non-custodial sentences (with the exception of the SSO) rarely used, but when they are they are most commonly imposed for **summary** (less serious) **offences**. They still have a small role to play in dealing with **indictable offences** in the Crown Court, but it is in cases where the crime is not particularly harmful or there are strong **mitigating factors** (such as age, the crime is a first offence, or there is clear evidence of remorse for any harm caused). The SSO – with its threat of custody – is almost three times as likely to be used in the Crown Court as the CO. I set out below the kinds of offences that are dealt with by the courts.

Types of Offences

- Indictable offences are the most serious and are dealt with in the Crown Court.
- Triable either way offences are those which can be tried in either the Crown Court or the magistrates' courts.
- Summary offences, which constitute the great majority of crimes, can only be tried in the magistrates' courts.
- In line with the usual conventions, in this chapter when I refer to indictable offences, I mean both indictable and either way offences.

It is in the magistrates' courts, where summary offences comprise the vast majority of cases, that non-custodial sentences are most significant. Almost one million fines were imposed by magistrates in 2018, virtually all of them for summary offences. More than nine out of ten compensation orders were for theft or summary offences; and conditional discharges followed the same pattern. The absolute discharge was mostly made in cases of summary offences. Because it is magistrates who deal with summary offences – almost 90% of cases heard in the magistrates' courts are summary, compared to only 6.7% in the Crown Court – it is they who make use of these low-level sentences.

While magistrates use the CO far more often than the Crown Court, they also use them mostly for summary offences. This is not exactly what such sentences were meant for. At the time of the

CO's introduction, the Sentencing Guidelines Council emphasised that the CO could be used as an alternative to a custodial sentence (Sentencing Guidelines Council, 2004). The sentences that the CO replaced – the probation order and the community service order – both aimed to deal with offenders who had committed indictable offences. Yet three-fifths of COs made by magistrates are for summary offences; ten years earlier, in 2008, the figure was 51.7%, so there has been a significant rise in the use of the CO for summary offences by magistrates. In the Crown Court there has been a similar trend in the use of COs – from 9.3% for summary offences in 2008 to 12.8% in 2018. This is a worrying development for a sentence that aims to deal with relatively serious offenders; and it also points to an especially disturbing development in sentencing – that it is becoming more punitive, despite crime having fallen during the last twenty years.

The SSO lies in a no-man's land between the CO and custody. On the one hand, as I have noted, it is legally a custodial sentence, and this may account for its popularity in the Crown Court where its use dwarfs that of the other non-custodial sentences combined, and it is imposed for indictable offences in more than nine out of ten cases. On the other hand, it acts very much as a CO if the offender complies with it and this may be why it is used as often as it is by magistrates who are legally constrained in their use of custody and might fall back on the SSO. Magistrates may also be attracted to it by its threat of custody if there is any failure to comply – a threat which is not present with the CO. Indeed, 42% of SSOs imposed by magistrates are for summary offences – again, I would argue, a sign of punitiveness, although it should be noted that in 2008 the figure was 51%. The SSO has certainly proved popular with sentencers – perhaps too popular. Its use was twice that predicted a year after its introduction, and there was a proposal that the Criminal Justice and Immigration Bill in 2007 should contain a clause exempting the SSO from use for summary offences; a clause that was removed prior to the Bill's enactment (Mair, 2011). And in 2018 the Chair of the Sentencing Council sent a circular to the courts instructing sentencers to restrict their use of the SSO and to use COs instead (*Guardian*, 22 April 2018); it will be interesting to monitor whether this has any impact.

What about longer term trends in use? Are non-custodial sentences being used more often or less often (bearing in mind that there has been a long-term decrease in the number of cases coming to court)? Tables 28.6a and 28.6b show developments over the last ten years in the Crown Court and magistrates' courts respectively.

Use of the SSO – the most punitive of the non-custodial sentences – has increased between 2008–2018 in both courts, although its popularity has dropped back a little in the last few years. The CO has lost considerable ground in the Crown Court, from 16.7% in 2008 to 8.1% in 2018, and its use has also decreased in the magistrates' courts. This is a rather troubling development. It has been claimed by the Centre for Justice Innovation (2018) that the decreasing use of the CO is to a large extent the result of sentencers losing trust in probation due to the problems that have been caused by the split in probation between the National Probation Service and Community Rehabilitation Companies (CRCs – these are the private companies, that at the time of writing, carry out the bulk of work with offenders who receive COs and SSOs). Government proposals (Ministry of Justice, 2019a) for a further restructuring of probation might improve matters or might not. Neither compensation nor the absolute discharge show much change. The conditional discharge seems to be losing ground in both courts. The fine has seen some growth in the magistrates' courts, but this is because of increased use for summary offences: in 2008, 94.7% of fines in the magistrates' courts were imposed for summary offences, while in 2018 this figure had increased to 96.3%.

Overall, non-custodial sentences – with the exception of the SSO – are used for less serious offences, and the popularity of the CO, the compensation order, and both discharges seems to be declining. All of which suggests that we are becoming more punitive when it comes to dealing with offenders.

Table 28.6a Sentences in the Crown Court 2008–2018 (%)

	2008	2009	2010	2011	2012	2013	2014	2015	2016	2017	2018
Custody	55.2	54.7	51.6	55.4	56.0	56.3	55.1	54.3	56.6	58.2	59.5
SSO	20.3	21.4	22.0	21.6	22.5	25.2	27.0	28.3	27.6	27.6	24.3
CO	16.7	16.7	18.5	16.4	15.8	13.1	12.0	10.8	8.3	6.8	8.1
Fine	2.7	2.5	2.5	2.0	1.9	2.2	2.1	2.4	2.2	2.1	2.0
Compensation	0.2	0.1	0.1	0.1	-	-	-	-	-	-	0.1
Conditional discharge	2.9	2.7	3.1	2.5	2.0	1.5	1.9	1.9	1.8	1.5	1.4
Absolute discharge	0.1	0.1	0.1	0.1	0.1	0.1	0.1	0.1	0.1	0.1	0.1
Other	1.9	1.8	2.1	1.9	1.6	1.6	1.8	2.2	3.4	3.6	4.5
Total No.	86,009	92,129	99,744	99,985	88,730	84,626	84,921	85,994	81,152	75,193	68,356

Table 28.6b Sentences in the Magistrates' Courts 2008–2018 (%)

	2008	2009	2010	2011	2012	2013	2014	2015	2016	2017	2018
Custody	3.9	3.6	3.8	4.0	4.1	4.1	3.9	3.6	3.7	3.7	3.3
SSO	2.0	2.1	2.2	2.3	2.3	2.6	2.7	2.9	3.0	2.9	2.4
CO	9.7	10.1	10.3	10.4	9.6	8.7	7.4	7.5	6.9	6.7	6.6
Fine	74.0	75.9	74.3	73.9	74.8	75.2	77.2	78.4	80.2	81.0	82.9
Compensation	0.7	0.6	0.4	0.5	0.6	0.8	0.5	0.4	0.4	0.4	0.4
Conditional discharge	6.5	6.0	6.7	6.7	6.7	6.6	6.1	5.4	4.5	4.0	3.4
Absolute discharge	0.6	0.5	0.5	0.5	0.5	0.6	0.4	0.7	0.4	0.4	0.3
Other	2.5	1.2	1.7	1.6	1.4	1.4	1.7	1.0	0.9	0.9	0.7
Total No.	1,187,557	1,233,228	1,191,725	1,149,324	1,093,555	1,056,318	1,099,255	1,132,209	1,133,559	1,107,673	1,104,100

--------------------------------- Pause for Thought ---------------------------------

What might be the reasons for us becoming more punitive?

The increasingly punitive nature of sentencing is a major challenge facing non-custodial sentences, but there are other issues too which pose serious threats to their long-term viability and these will be considered next.

Key Issues for Non-custodial Sentences

It would probably be possible to come up with a wide range of challenges that face non-custodial sentences, but I focus in the remainder of the chapter on four that I consider to be the most significant: effectiveness, the deeply embedded view that they are a 'soft option', the endless restructuring that has bedevilled the probation service over the last thirty years or so, and particularly the privatisation of probation.

1. Effectiveness

While you cannot simply compare the reconviction rates for different sentences because levels of risk are different for those who receive different sentences, the reconviction rates associated with low-level sentences are consistently lower than those for prison (Ministry of Justice, 2019b). The twelve-month reconviction rate for absolute/conditional discharges is 14.9%; for fines it is 25.7%; for COs it is 33.9%; for an SSO with requirements it is 33.0%; and for an SSO without requirements it is 47.1%. The overall rate for custody is 48.3%, although for those with sentences of less than twelve months it is 64.3%. Non-custodial sentences are also much less costly than prison: in 2017/18 the cost of a prisoner for twelve months was £37,453 (House of Commons Library, 2019), while the most recent data (2012/13) for the cost of a CO/SSO is £4,305, which is significantly cheaper than custody. Fines and discharges cost nothing – indeed, the fine makes money. Prisons are also far more likely than non-custodial sentences to be associated with various harms, e.g. violence, mental illness, domestic problems, unemployment, drug abuse. Using these indicators of effectiveness, then, non-custodial sentences would seem to be a success and could surely be used more than they are. That non-custodial sentences are effective cannot be emphasised enough.

2. The 'soft option'

The notion that probation is a 'soft option' has lingered around like a bad smell since the probation order was introduced in 1907 (Mair and Burke, 2012). And if that was the case, then it followed that less demanding sentences such as fines and discharges were even 'softer' on offenders. This had a number of consequences. First, it confirmed prison as the 'tough' option and one that would really punish offenders, so that any other sentence was seen as weak. It does not help that 'non-custodial sentences' as a collective term for all those court disposals that are not prison, privileges custody. Second, a great deal of policy effort has been expended over the years to try to 'toughen up' probation-based sentences (e.g. the introduction of community service in 1972, of day centres in 1982, of the combination order and the curfew order in 1991, of the need to have a punitive requirement or a fine in COs in 2013), partly to try to rid them of their 'soft option' image, and partly in order that they might thereby act as alternatives to custody and relieve pressure on numbers in custody (Mair, 2013). Neither objective has had much success and it could well be argued that by making probation-based sentences 'tougher', they run the risk of losing what makes them unique. Non-custodial sentences are by no means soft options: a fine can have punitive bite if the offender does not have much money; a community order with several requirements can be very demanding; an SSO carries the threat of imprisonment. We need to rid ourselves of the negative connotations of the 'soft option' image and understand non-custodial sentences as appropriate and effective ways of dealing with the vast majority of offenders.

3. The endless restructuring of the probation service

Since the middle of the 1980s a number of government policy interventions have destabilised and fragmented the probation service. The service may have been somewhat complacent about its position and there is little doubt that there was inconsistent practice, but government initiatives have made matters much worse. At least since 1984, when the Statement of *National* Objectives and Priorities was published (Home Office, 1984; emphasis added), the possibility of moving towards a national service rather than having fifty-four individual probation services appeared. Such a development had much in its favour: a number of individual, quasi-autonomous services did not encourage consistency of practice, and government increasingly felt that it lacked control over what probation did. Over the years, government began to take control over probation's finances (moving to 100% central-government funding), probation's programmes (with a policy of accredited programmes), recruitment and training (by first scrapping, then redefining the process), and even how services organised partnership working (see Mair and Burke, 2012). Much closer working between probation and prisons was encouraged (Home Office, 1998). Eventually, in 2001, a National Probation Service (NPS) with a National Director was introduced, reducing the number of probation areas to forty-two and turning the service into a full-fledged criminal justice agency by moving its civil work functions to a separate organisation (the Children and Family Court Advisory and Support Service). The NPS scarcely had time to bed down before it was merged with the prison service to become part of the National Offender Management Service (NOMS) in 2004. Probation's role in NOMS was never clarified as Judith McKnight pointed out in her Bill McWilliams Memorial Lecture in 2008 (McKnight, 2009) and it was increasingly marginalised. On 1 April 2017, Her Majesty's Prison and Probation Service (HMPPS) replaced NOMS. But perhaps the most significant structural change for probation was privatisation.

4. Privatisation

The privatisation of criminal justice has been going on seriously since 1992 when Wolds prison was privatised and there are currently thirteen private prisons. For probation, the process can be seen to have begun with an increasing emphasis on partnership working from the beginning of the 1990s, and with the introduction of electronic monitoring of curfews from 1995. The Carter Review (2003) proposed the introduction of contestability into the provision of probation services – a recommendation accepted by government. In February 2015, the arrangements whereby the National Probation Service organised and operated services for offenders sentenced to community orders and suspended sentence orders were ended, and twenty-one Community Rehabilitation Companies (CRCs) took over most (around 70%) of probation work. The NPS was left with risk assessment, the preparation of court reports and the supervision of high-risk offenders; while the CRCs took over work with medium and low-risk offenders. Fundamental issues were brushed aside in the rush to privatise. What damage might be done to the value-base of probation work with a clear shift from an altruistic approach to a more commercially-driven business model? Where precisely does accountability lie with the CRCs which are private companies? What about the fragmentation that might occur between a public, national service and a number of private companies? Were the CRCs financially viable (and eight out of twenty-one CRCs went into administration early in 2019)?

A number of official reports have firmly condemned the privatisation of probation (House of Commons Justice Committee, 2018; National Audit Office, 2019; HM Chief Inspector of Probation, 2019). In July 2018, the government announced that it would be terminating existing contracts with CRCs in 2020 rather than 2022. And in 2019 plans were published for a further reduction of probation areas to twelve regions, proposing that all offender manager work would come under a national probation service but that all key services – such as unpaid work or accredited programmes – would be undertaken by the private or voluntary sector (Ministry of Justice, 2019a). In other words, there would still be fragmentation and privatisation would still be significant, neither of which is likely to strengthen the confidence of sentencers and make them use the CO more often. For all those who have argued that probation should revert completely to being a public service it looks as if privatisation is here to stay for better or worse.

CHAPTER SUMMARY

Although they have been marginalised and are often ignored, it would be difficult to deny that non-custodial sentences play a crucial role in how we deal with offenders:

- Despite our longstanding love-affair with prison, it is non-custodial sentences that are used to deal with the vast majority of offenders – because the vast majority of offences that are committed are relatively minor.
- While there may be some scope for making more use of non-custodial sentences in the Crown Court, this will always be limited by the serious nature of offences which are dealt with in the higher courts.
- There is some worrying evidence that over the last decade the use of non-custodial sentences has decreased in the Crown Court – especially if we ignore the SSO – and this is particularly disturbing with regard to the community order.
- With regard to the magistrates' courts, at first glance it looks as if non-custodial sentencing has grown, but this is because of the increase in the use of the fine for summary offences – and again there is a decline in the community order.

There are significant challenges facing non-custodial sentences, and it is imperative that these are resolved satisfactorily in order to ensure a less punitive and more effective criminal justice system. Given the new government's commitment to tougher sentencing announced on 21 January 2020, it will be interesting to see how non-custodial sentences fare in the coming years.

Review Questions

1. How significant are fines as court sentences?
2. What are the key differences between the community order and the suspended sentence order?
3. How would you describe trends in the use of non-custodial sentences?
4. What are the key challenges facing non-custodial sentences?

GO FURTHER

Books/Book Chapters

The three chapters specified below all cover, in slightly different ways, non-custodial sentences and how they are used. Reading all three will provide an excellent overview of the topic:

1. Ashworth, A. (2015) *Sentencing and Criminal Justice*, 6th edition. Cambridge: Cambridge University Press. (See ch. 10, 'Non-custodial sentencing'.)
2. Cavadino, M., Dignan., Mair, G. and Bennett, J. (2020) *The Penal System*, 6th edition. London: Sage. (See ch. 5, 'Punishment in the community'.)
3. Easton, S. and Piper, C. (2016) *Sentencing and Punishment: The Quest for Justice,* 4th edition. Oxford: Oxford University Press. (See ch. 10, 'Punishment and rehabilitation in the community'.)

Journal Articles

1. This first article offers a European perspective on day fines and how they work:

    Drapal, J. (2018) Day fines: a European comparison and Czech malpractice, *European Journal of Criminology*, 15(4): 461–480.

2. The following article examines the origins of the community order and how it has been used by the courts:

    Mair, G. (2011) The community order in England and Wales: policy and practice. *Probation Journal*, 58(3): 215–232.

3. The third article provides a compelling argument about reclaiming the fine as a serious court order:

    O'Malley, P. (2009) Theorizing fines. *Punishment and Society*, 11(1): 67–83.

Useful Websites

1. The following is the website of the Ministry of Justice which is responsible for prisons, probation and the courts. The website contains statistics that are published regularly on the use of sentences, as well as information about research. All data used in the chapter are taken from Ministry of Justice statistics: www.gov.uk/government/organisations/ministry-of-justice
2. The following is the website of HMPPS – Her Majesty's Prison and Probation Service – and contains information about probation: https://www.gov.uk/government/organisations/her-majestys-prison-and-probation-service
3. This final website is the website of the Sentencing Council for England and Wales. As well as sentencing guidelines, it contains information about how judges and magistrates decide what sentence to impose: https://www.sentencingcouncil.org.uk/

REFERENCES

Ashworth, A. (2015) *Sentencing and Criminal Justice*, 6th edition. Cambridge: Cambridge University Press.

Carter, P. (2003) *Managing Offenders, Reducing Crime*. London: Home Office.

Centre for Justice Innovation (2018) *Renewing Trust: How We can Improve the Relationship between Probation and the Courts.* London: Centre for Court Innovation.

Halliday, J. (2001) *Making Punishment Work: Report of a Review of the Sentencing Framework for England and Wales.* London: Home Office.

Her Majesty's Chief Inspector of Probation (2019) *Annual Report.* Manchester: HMIP.

Home Office (1984) *Probation Service in England and Wales: Statement of National Objectives and Priorities.* London: Home Office.

Home Office (1998) *Joining Forces to Protect the Public.* London: HMSO.

House of Commons Justice Committee (2018) *Transforming Rehabilitation.* Ninth Report of Session 2017–19. London: House of Commons.

House of Commons Library (2019) *UK Prison Population Statistics.* London: House of Commons Library.

Mair, G. (2011) 'The community order in England and Wales: policy and practice'. *Probation Journal,* 58(3): 215–232.

Mair, G. (2013) 'Community Sentences'. In A. Hucklesby and A. Wahidin (eds), *Criminal Justice,* 2nd edition. Oxford: Oxford University Press. pp. 162–180.

Mair, G. (2016) "A difficult trip, I think': The end days of the probation service in England and Wales?' *European Journal of Probation,* 8(1): 3–15.

Mair, G. (2017) 'Community Sentences'. In J. Harding, P. Davies and G. Mair (eds), *An Introduction to Criminal Justice.* London: Sage. pp. 284–303.

Mair, G. and Burke, L. (2012) *Redemption, Rehabilitation and Risk Management: A History of Probation.* London: Routledge.

McKnight, J. (2009) 'Speaking up for probation', *Howard Journal,* 48(4): 327–343.

Ministry of Justice (2019a) *Strengthening Probation, Building Confidence: Response to Consultation.* London: Ministry of Justice.

Ministry of Justice (2019b) *Proven Reoffending Tables (annual average), January 2017 – March 2017.* London: Ministry of Justice.

National Audit Office (2019) *Transforming Rehabilitation: Progress Review.* HC 1986. Session 2017–19. London: National Audit Office.

Sentencing Guidelines Council (2004) *New Sentences: Criminal Justice Act 2003 – Guideline.* London: Sentencing Guidelines Council.

Prisons

Kate Herrity and Jason Warr

Learning Objectives

By the end of this chapter you will:

- Be able to identify and challenge the myths and dominant assumptions about prisons.
- Think critically about the nature and purpose of the prison.
- Recognise and explore the complexity of the prison as a system of social organisation and social control.
- Familiarise yourself with the broad history of, and differing scientific approaches to, research in prisons.

Framing Questions
---

1. Where does our information about prisons come from?
2. What is prison for?
3. Do prisons do what society wants them to do?

INTRODUCTION

Prisons are complex places. Designed to contain, punish, and re-make those who are subject to moral and criminal censure. Prisons are often dirty, drug-infused, violent environments. Everything bad about prisons has grown worse over the last decade. People in prison, on both sides of the keychain, are less safe than they have been at any other point since records began (Ministry of Justice, 2019a). Yet they remain our paradigmatic form of punishment. How can we begin to understand such places?

Not only are prisons strange but the stuff of everyday life inside is also largely hidden from view. What do you know about prison? How do you know it? How does what you know shape what you think about prisons? This chapter will help you to think critically about a number of issues relating to the prison in order to develop your understanding as criminologists. The chapter is organised into three related sections, Spectacle, Space, and Science, designed to help you explore some of the core themes in contemporary prisons studies. *Spectacle* allows us to consider the role of the prison in changing ideas about the form and functions of punishment. Considering prison *Space* encourages thinking about the ways the prison is physically constructed and experienced in daily life. The notion of order, and its ruptures, has long preoccupied prison studies as have attempts to examine its conditions through the absence or presence of **legitimacy**. *Science* foregrounds the ways in which underlying assumptions about our relationship with the social world (**ontology**) colour assumptions about what can be understood of the prison, and how it can be understood (**epistemology**). Though we largely focus on England and Wales we maintain a sensibility to the importance of the wider literature.

MAPPING THE TERRAIN

Understanding of the prison has changed over the last fifty years. Sociological, cultural, and spatial shifts in criminology have informed much of that change (Hayward, 2012) (see the section on space below). This has resulted in a move away from understanding the prison as a place of legal punishment to exploring it as a place of constrained sociality; a distinct social world, separated from the rest of society. Focusing on constraint and social life, allows us to further explore power and its effects on, and within, the occupational and social ecologies of the prison. Power shapes every element of the social and occupational lives of those existing within, and to some degree, beyond the prison wall (Crewe, 2009).

Prisons have their own rules and regulations, economies, cultures, problems, tensions, and conflicts. Those we consign there eat, sleep, toil, suffer, and dream, cheek by jowl with strangers, with little or no escape, often confined to a cell for 20+ hours a day (HMIP, 2019). In England and Wales, we send tens of thousands of people to prison every year. The prison population has increased by over 70% in the last thirty years from a population of 45,000 in 1990 to over 83,000 (Ministry of Justice, 2019b). We imprison increasing numbers of our fellow citizens, and for longer periods. To what end? They do not keep people safe, they do not reduce reoffending, nor act as a deterrence for primary offending (Chalfin and McCrary, 2017). They are also extraordinarily expensive, costing the government nearly £3billion a year (HMPPS, 2019). As Marsh and colleagues (2009) conclude, given that they seem to fail at their most basic functions, they make little economic sense. Yet we continue to build more.

Intersections of structural inequality in society are amplified within prisons. 31% of women and 27% of men in prison were taken into care as children compared to 2% of the general population; 53% of women and 27% of men in prison suffered abuse as a child compared to 20% in the general population; a significant percentage of the women who enter prison have been subject to continued violence in both domestic and relational contexts; and 81% of women and 67% of men who enter prison were without a job in the period leading up to their incarceration compared to only 8% of employment-aged adults in wider society (Prison Reform Trust, 2019: 20). More than half of those released from prison have no settled accommodation to go to (Ministry of Justice, 2018). The same structural inequalities exist when we look at the issues of race. The Lammy Review (2017) highlights that structural and institutional racism in wider society is not only replicated but also amplified within prisons and the criminal justice system. People from Black and minority ethnic (BAME) categories make up 14% of the general public, but over 27% of the prison population: 'there is greater disproportionality in the number of Black people in prisons here than in the United States' (Lammy, 2017: 3). A figure even more inflated amongst young people in custody where those categorised as BAME make up 40% of the population. Young Black men are over-represented within these statistics, as are those from the Roma and Travelling communities, demonstrating the need to differentiate the experiences of those within the 'BAME' category rather than conflating them.

Knowledge link: This topic is also covered in Chapter 19.

In order to understand this disproportionate representation, we need to look beyond the figures. Coretta Phillips (2012) notes that exploration of the ways in which race is written into prison practices reveals important insights into the realities of the relationship between racism and the prison. Behind the headline data presented above, there are many intersections of inequality to explore (for example see the report on women in custody by Baroness Jean Corston, 2007, and the ten-year follow-up in 2017). How can we start to develop a criminological understanding of such places? To begin, we must explore the complex entanglement of power, political ideologies, economic factors, social, racial, and gendered inequalities, geographies, and cultures that make up our prisons. First, we turn to the place of the prison in popular imagination (*Spectacle*), the changing ideas about the wider social functions of punishment and the impacts of this on how we understand the prison and life behind its walls. We then go on to discuss ideas relating to the physical prison and prison society (*Space*), before considering the ways in which different assumptions about the world and how we know manifest in treatments of the prison (*Science*).

SPECTACLE

Prisons represent a paradox. What occurs within them is largely hidden from our collective gaze, yet they are potent symbols – a spectacle – in our popular imagination. Most of us have no direct experience or knowledge of its realities. Most of us have never heard the harsh clang of the prison door as it closes behind us, or been forcibly locked into close bodily proximity with complete strangers. Nor have many experienced the continual intimate surveillance of power in prison spaces. So, where do popular conceptions of prison come from? In the main they are forged by the media that we consume.

Knowledge link: This topic is also covered in Chapter 5.

One problem with this is inaccurate representation, and the assumptions they can produce. Many ideas about prison come from films, TV productions, and 'reality' shows which proliferate on entertainment media. *The Shawshank Redemption, Orange is the New Black, Inside the World's Toughest Prisons*, the news, and a host of other examples shape our understanding. The media acts as a powerful tool in both informing and misleading on issues of crime and punishment. This is especially true when it comes to prisons, where the audience rarely has real-world knowledge with which to inform understanding of the images they consume (Bennett, 2006). We become penal voyeurs, passively absorbing myths, misrepresentations, and stereotypes that are neither contextualised nor interrogated (Ross, 2015). This creates a 'constructed reality' of the prison in our minds (Surette, 1997), which in turn informs our opinions and assumptions. Often there is a distinction between the myths/stereotypes evident in film/TV and those in news media. This creates two sets of ideas on prison life: on the one hand depictions of an overly brutal environment, on the other the portrayal of prison as a 'holiday camp'. The contrast between these constructed realities, and the opinions and assumptions upon which they are built, creates a conflict between what we want, need, and imagine the prison to be.

The prison has long held fascination in the public imagination. In *Discipline and Punish: The Birth of the Prison* (1977: 14), Michel Foucault begins by exploring how the 'great spectacle of physical punishment' – the public theatrics of torture-as-punishment – began to disappear in the West in the first half of the nineteenth century. The notion that it was important for the public to bear witness to the punishment of wrongdoing began to fade from ideas of justice. The denial of this spectacle of punishment was made manifest in the great walled edifices of the Victorian prisons. Stony monoliths stood in the centre of towns and cities acting as constant reminders of the consequences of wrong-doing. The public no longer saw the episodic punishment enacted on the body of the wrongdoer, but were constantly subjected to the spectacle of these imposing institutions in their everyday lives.

In the twentieth and twenty-first centuries this visual role of the prison faded. Prisons were removed from the everyday gaze of the citizenry (Jewkes et al., 2017) and moved to remote and isolated locales in the countryside. They were often located in former industrial areas where these newer institutions could soak up the economic slack of lost industries. The consequence of this was that the prison no longer operated as a spectacle of punishment and justice. This created a vacuum in the public perception of punishment, but the need for accompanying spectacle remained (Maratea and Monahan, 2013). Into that vacuum stepped the media-constructed realities of the prison. One popular myth is the representation of the prison as 'a holiday camp' where people are given Xboxes and three hot meals a day. These myths are either not true or based on partial truths. For example, three hot meals a day ceased to be a reality in England and Wales in the mid-1990s. Instead people in prison are furnished with a breakfast pack (often containing one of those miniature-sized cereal packets usually found within a multipack), they receive a cold lunch of a roll, a packet of crisps, and a piece of fruit, at about 11.30–12, and their one hot meal of the day at about 16.30 before evening lock-up. The conflict between fictionalised images of the prison as a place of violence and suffering on film and TV on the one hand, and on the other, news media portrayals of lawless 'holiday camps', partially account for the stubborn persistence of these myths. This creates a tension that disrupts our idea of the prison as a site of justice.

The headline in Figure 29.1 draws on the 'media-constructed realities of prison' alluded to above, by referring to 'Sky sports' and '18-rated DVDs' as illustrations of what is identified as a 'cushy' life.

As with the media-fuelled public fear of crime (Reiner et al., 2003), this tension is exploited by politi-cians pursuing popular, authoritarian crime-control policies, to harness assumed **punitivist** sentiment in the public (Campbell, 2015). Chris Grayling's actions following his appointment as the Secretary of State for Justice (2012 to 2015) exemplify this. He released a series of news briefings to the *Daily Mail* in which he stated that he would stop prisons in England and Wales being 'Holiday Camps' (Slack, 2012) and 'Cushy' (Doyle, 2013: see also Figure 29.1). In making claims about harshening prison conditions, he used the news media as a platform to create a spectacle of 'tough' punishment and exploit the grow-ing penal populism that had developed in the West (Pratt, 2007). The purchase of this spectacle relied upon not only public ignorance of the realities of prison life but also the ways in which prison spaces are configured through the culture of punishment in the public's consciousness (Brown, 2009). Brown argues that representations of the prison do cultural 'work' in validating them in the public imagi-nation, but in ways which obscure its pains. This simultaneously cements the idea of prisons whilst creating a further layer of public ignorance about their realities. This exploitation of public ignorance, cultural perception, and appeals to popular punitivist sentiment, is a recurring theme in British poli-tics. From Michael Howard's 'Prison Works' in the early 1990s (Brown, 1993) to New Labour's 'Tough on Crime' in the mid-2000s (Newburn, 2007), to today's prisons of austerity (Ismail, 2020), the prison has been utilised as a political tool with which to appeal to the public (see Tonry, 2004; Maratea and Monahan, 2013).

Pause for Thought

How might you go about getting underneath these popular representations of the prison?

Convicts 'will be denied Sky Sports and 18-rated DVDs'

END OF A CUSHY LIFE IN PRISON

By **Jack Doyle**
Home Affairs Correspondent

PRISONERS will be forced to work to end the culture of 'holiday camp' jails.

They will also be denied access to Sky Sports and 18-rated DVDs and will no longer win privileges simply for keeping out of trouble.

Instead, offenders will start their life behind bars adhering to a spartan regime, wearing prison uniform and having to earn any perks.

Only by hard work or study will they be allowed television, full access to the gym, the right to wear their own clothes and to be able to spend any money they earn in the prison shop. Inmates who wreck cells, start fires or damage prison property will be forced to pay compensation.

Announcing the shake-up in an interview with the Daily Mail yesterday, prisons minister Jeremy Wright said: 'Prison is there to punish, it's not there to be comfortable.

'It's there to be somewhere you don't want to go back to and what we are doing in changing the regime is to make sure that message is there and heard loud and clear.

'But it's also a place where we expect rehabilitation to happen. We expect people to do those things that make it less likely when they come out that they reoffend.'

Inmates used to get full entitlements simply by avoiding violence; if you 'kept your nose clean and didn't punch the officers', said Mr Wright.

But, in future, offenders will go on a new entry regime for the first fortnight of their sentence, during which they will have to wear uniform and be denied TV and use of the shop.

They will be required to join a work programme, education or drug rehabilitation course or some other purposeful activity. To mirror life outside, the 'working day' in prison will be extended to

Turn to Page 2

Figure 29.1 Example of Media-Constructed Reality of Prison

As criminologists, our task is to look beyond popular stereotypes to seek the truths of prison life. The first place to start is by looking at the social and cultural aspects of the prison in order to see (and hear) what goes on there. The legacy of a rich tradition of **ethnography** in prisons research manifests in the continued focus on capturing their intricate lifeworlds (e.g. Drake et al., 2015). However, before we explore some of that literature it is important to gain some understanding of the foundations of prison research. There have traditionally been two branches of criminological thought applied to the prison. These are i) that the determinants of social organisation in the prison are imposed through a series of deprivations (the Deprivation Model) introduced by Gresham Sykes in his book *Society of Captives* (1958), or that ii) they are imported into the prison by those who are held there (the Importation Model) introduced by Irwin and Cressey (1964). These two texts, alongside Goffman's *Asylums* (1961) and the work of Foucault (1977), have done much to determine our understanding of prison and life therein.

Sykes (1958) notes that there are as many prisons as there are prisoners (experience is subjective). Nevertheless, he argues that underlying those individual experiences are a set of five core deprivations or pains. These are: the deprivation of liberty – the loss of freedom; the deprivation of security – being subject to intrusive threats to personal safety; the deprivation of **autonomy** – the core aim of the prison is to secure compliance and this is achieved by removing the power to make personal decisions (e.g. what you eat and when); the deprivation of heterosocial relationships – being forced into a circumstance where the majority of one's life is spent in a (institutionally defined) single-sex environment; and finally, the deprivation of goods and services – where access to everything from healthcare and medication to food and clothing is constrained. Sykes argues that these deprivations fundamentally shape the social life of the prison. In some regards he, like Goffman (1961) who we will return to, present the prison as something approaching a closed system where the social life and cultures that exist are 'indigenous' to those prisons.

Case Study 29.1

A Tragedy at HMP Bronzefield

During the early hours of Friday 27th September 2019, a woman in HMP Bronzefield gave birth, alone, without any medical care, in her cell. The baby died before help could be summoned. An ambulance was not called to the prison until 08.30 in the morning after unlock. Throughout that time the woman suffered alone.

Syke's account of the pains of imprisonment was published in 1957, but this example illustrates the enduring relevance of his work. This woman was unable to summon help as she was not free to do so. She had no autonomy, lacking control over her care and body. In turn, this limited her security because she was unsafe and exposed to medical danger, a danger which proved fatal for her baby, and she did not have access to the same level of goods and services as she would on the outside because she could not access medical care and support.

In contrast to Sykes' (1957) identification of imprisonment as characterised by a series of deprivations, John Irwin (a former prisoner) and Donald Cressey (1964) took a different approach to understanding prison life. Building on the earlier work of Clemmer (1958), they argued that prison subcultures (norms, values, practices, and hierarchies) are imported by those imprisoned there. They said this occurs because the prison is not a closed system. People move in and out of prisons all the time, making a purely indigenous culture impossible. The prison cultures that we see replicate and reflect the criminal and non-criminal subcultures outside. Specifically, they argued there was a combination of three distinct subcultures which comprise the 'inmate code': the Thief Culture based on ideas of loyalty, honour, and toughness imported by professional criminals and thieves; the Convict Subculture as imported by those raised in state institutions (care homes, juvenile detention centres) who have an individualised, exploitative, and mercenary attitude to others; and finally, a marginal but legitimate sub-culture imported by those who largely adhere to the norms and law-abiding values in wider society. Irwin and Cressey hold that it is the competition and accommodation between these subcultures, against the backdrop of the institution, which create the 'prisoner' culture.

These Importation and Deprivation models of explanation, and the tensions between them, provide the foundation upon which much of the research on prisons has been built. However, in the last thirty years there has been an explosion in ethnographic research into prisons and prison society which has developed our understanding of what it means to be in a prison. Our knowledge of what a prison is, what it does and the varied experiences of being 'inside' is much deeper. It is this new knowledge to which we now turn and which will allow you to move further beyond the 'mediated spectacle' (Maratea and Monahan, 2013) of prison that shapes the thinking of wider society.

Space

Rather than thinking of the prison as a given thing, it is useful to think about the ways it comes to inhabit the particular roles it occupies in our social, cultural, and economic conscience. The prison exists on various planes of human experience simultaneously, on plans and maps, in practices of daily life which shape and remake its meaning, as well as through ideas such as those represented in the media. As discussed above, the prison is both politically configured, as a site for enforcing social control (Durkheim, 1900), and a figurative site on which those political ideas and cultural representations play out. Additionally, it is a physical space where people live and work, a place where particular relationships between people and environment are imposed. One aspect of these relationships, central to prison studies, is the way social behaviour is regulated; the problem of order (Sparks et al., 1996).

From the 'reforming penitentiaries' of the nineteenth century, shaped by monastic ideas of repentance, to the Titan megaliths of today, designed on economies of scale and cost-saving, different eras of penal policy are embodied in the stone, brick, and mortar of the prison (Jewkes and Johnston, 2007). As Carl Cattermole (2019: 6) explains, 'Nineteenth century prisons look like dilapidated castles, twentieth-century prisons look like broken down leisure centres and twenty-first century prisons look like Amazon storage warehouses'. In this sense architectures of confinement refers to both the literal manifestation of ideas into the shape, form and 'feel' of spaces, and the multitude of agencies, policies and practices which sustain the logics of incarceration. When Cattermole refers to the modern day 'Amazon warehouse' prison, he makes parallels with work which foregrounds political economy as a basis for the logics of incarceration (see Rusche and Kirchheimer, 1939; DiGiorgi, 2013; Melossi and Pavarini, 2018). In a capitalist society the central function of the prison is to meet the requirements of the labour market. Prisons come to resemble factories, imposing specific forms of routine and ritual to remould the individual to the demands of the workplace. In a late modern capitalist and globalised society, where social order and the control of labour and labour movement is an ever-increasing concern of governments, prisons have come to reflect and resemble large-scale warehouses.

Prisons are concerned with inducing compliance in those held within, in order to deter disorder or attempted escape. However, social order in prison is a most vexatious problem (Sparks et al., 1996). How do you get people in prison to comply with the rules when they don't want to be there? Liebling and Arnold (2004: 291) define prison order as 'the degree to which the prison environment is structured, stable, predictable and acceptable'. This problem was thrown into stark relief in the late 1980s with a series of significant riots across the prison estate (culminating in the riot at HMP Strangeways), followed by a number of high-profile escapes. Two branches of thought emerged from subsequent criminological inquiry. One focused on Situational Control measures and the other, legitimacy, on how compliance is rooted in the quality of social relationships and the degree to which this secures acceptance of authority.

The Situational Control model was based on the idea that 'behaviour can only be understood in terms of an interaction between the characteristics of an actor and of the environment in which an act is performed' (Wortley, 2002: 3). An example of this would be installing a number of locked gates to control the 'flow' of people within the prison. Environmental factors become key in the control of those within that environment. From this premise emerged the idea that to both create and maintain order in the prison, situational control measures should be employed. Based on **rational actor** and **routine activity** logics, bars, gates, razor wire, cameras, and physical architectures of segregation and controlled movement (flow) can significantly vary the behaviour of people in prisons in ways that impose control. However, as Carrabine (2005) notes, exclusive reliance on these situational control measures can prove impractical, exponentially expensive, and often fail.

Legitimacy is concerned with how power and authority are experienced, and responded to, by those who are subjected to that power (Liebling and Arnold, 2004). In order for those in prison to adhere to the authority of their captors they must accept that authority as just. It is a truism of prison life that order relies upon the acquiescence of those imprisoned (Sykes, 1958). In the wake of mass disorder, the 25-day takeover of HMP Strangeways, and the disturbances at 20+ other establishments, an inquiry was held to establish the causes. This became known as the Woolf Report (Woolf and Tumin, 1991). It is to the twelve main recommendations that people principally refer when they talk of the 'decency agenda', a set of ideals for prison policy and management which remain influential. The inquiry concluded that a key component in the disorder was a collective sense of injustice in the manner in which prisons were being run. In the wake of the Woolf Report there were a number of studies conducted in prisons specifically focused on order. The most significant of these was Sparks et al's (1996) *Prisons and the Problem of Order*. They noted that to understand prison order, both the interaction between those locked in as well as the manner in which the prison is run on a day-to-day basis – the regime – must be examined. It is in the delivery of that regime and the way rules are implemented where judgements of fairness/justness (legitimacy), and consequently acceptance of those rules, are determined. For Sparks et al. (1996), and Liebling and Arnold (2004), prison order is dependent on these judgements. Perceptions of unfairness and unjustness lead to legitimation crises, and a breakdown of order.

This notion of legitimacy (and the related concept of procedural justice; see Jackson et al., 2010) and prison order has dominated criminological understandings of the prison in the last twenty-five years. Like all dominant theoretical perspectives this has shaped the way the prison can be understood. The basis for assuming order rests on the acceptance of authority relying on a particular, top down, understanding of power in the prison. For Sykes (1958) power is a more diffused and variegated aspect of social life, forming the stuff of everyday navigations and negotiations within the prison social world. This more nuanced account of how power operates in prison more closely echoes Mathiesen's (1990) discussion of what has now become known as 'soft power' (Crewe, 2009). Here, soft power relates to how authority is founded on the micro-interactions between staff and those inside. The staff perspective provides a useful means of understanding this. As Carrabine (2004: 30) notes:

> the microsociology of prison life is profoundly asymmetrical. In practically every account the analytical gaze is skewed toward prisoners. Whilst this can illuminate the pains, degradations and so forth experienced by the confined, it tells us little about how the powerful are able to be powerful.

In *The Prison Officer*, Alison Liebling and colleagues (2011) explore how prison officers use discretion as part of a broader repertoire of techniques of authority and control. Discretion here refers to a flexible use of authority in the application of prison rules to ease social relations. These techniques are evident in different approaches to prison officer work (Tait, 2011). For a deeper consideration of the emotional labour and demands of the prison working environment see Crawley (2004). There are a number of approaches to examining the stark power relations that pervade prison life, not all of which rest on a purely relational conception of power, but extend to interactions between people and place. It is to these issues we now turn.

The use of movement as a means of imposing social control and compliance is a frequently overlooked aspect of the argument presented in *Prisons and the Problem of Order* (Sparks et al., 1996). Sparks et al. argue that the least controversial example of 'control movement' (1996: 273) is the forced movement of people from one location to another within the prison (inter-wing movements) for disciplinary reasons. They identify movements between prisons, without the consent or against the wishes of the individual concerned, as a source of considerable resentment. For the person subject to the move this can have profound implications, particularly if they are moved to an undesirable location – specifically if the prison is not well thought of, or more pertinently, if it is far away from the person's external support networks. The threat of being moved when or where you don't want is a source of great anxiety – one which is used a great deal in prison. This foreshadows recent innovative contributions to prison studies from beyond criminology, most notably **Carceral Geography**, which places the matter of mobilities at the centre of the carceral project (Moran et al., 2013).

This adds an important contribution to our understanding of how power is enacted upon the imprisoned body, not only between carceral spaces but also within carceral space (see Warr, 2020b on forced moves, otherwise known as 'Ghosting').

These new perspectives prompt us to think differently about prison spaces and the textures of social life within them. As Crewe et al. (2014) assert, prisons are not monolithic but rather comprised of an array of interconnected sites distinguished by the behaviour – and consequently the 'feel' or emotional geography – conducted within them. Atmospheres within the library, kitchens, and cells are distinct from that of the landings. Such considerations heighten awareness of the relationships between places of incarceration and those beyond, e.g. the home, the city. The point here, is to alert you to different ways of thinking about prison spaces both in terms of everyday life inside and the relationships between spaces within and beyond the prison walls. Carceral geography invites us to make these connections between place and space, offering a means of disrupting assumptions of the separateness of prison as a 'total institution', instead emphasising the porousness of its walls. Erving Goffman coined the term 'total institution' in *Asylums* (1961). He argued total institutions are characterised by their occupants being cut off from the outside world for prolonged periods, and sharing rituals and routines which both reinforce the separateness of these spaces and accustom occupants to life within them. The significance in this lies both in how we understand the experience of these spaces and the nature of their social function. Foucault (1977) echoed this similarity between different institutional spaces: a carceral continuum:

> Is it surprising that the cellular prison, with its regular chronologies, forced labour, its authorities of surveillance and registration, its experts in normality, who continue and multiply the functions of the judge, should have become the modern instrument of penality? Is it surprising that prisons resemble factories, schools, barracks, hospitals, which all resemble prisons? (Foucault, 1977: 228)

Carceral geography disrupts the notion of impermeable walls, emphasising instead the degree to which people traverse the prison boundary not only physically, but also in terms of culture, e.g. music and art (Turner, 2016). In the sense that Goffman and Foucault were exploring the various operations of power, and the impact on the individual, this qualification arguably has limited importance. Its significance lies in forging deeper connections in thought and practice between the prison and its wider environment, as well as the various planes of existence on which these connections are experienced. More contemporary work extends this reconfiguration of focus on space and social life. These contributions to knowledge illuminate the ways in which identities – particularly of young, Black males – are interwoven with notions of place and belonging to forge inescapable connections between urban spaces and the prison (Wacquant, 2001). Prison looms disproportionately large in the lives of these communities (see the case study below; for a US context on this subject see Shabazz, 2015).

———— Case Study 29.2 ————

Terraformed: Young Black Lives in the Inner City

... How does this relate to the lived experiences of being poor in an affluent world, of feeling trapped and stuck? The sense of loss is palpable when your people (parents, siblings, friends), are removed from your life in some way or another; dead, deported, in custody, or incarcerated. These types of losses are so commonplace that when young Black Londoners make a

(Continued)

reference to someone being "in", they don't mean at home, they mean in prison. Families are ruptured and friendships are constrained by rules of association, local policies and processes. (White, 2020: 3)

Joy White powerfully illustrates the ways in which the prison comes to feature in the ebb and flow of daily life and its practices. How prison features in our lived experiences is, to a huge extent, shaped by who we are. As we have illustrated, young, Black people are over-represented within the criminal justice system. As a result, their relationships between the spaces through which they pass and the prison are more pronounced, policed and restricted. As a budding criminologist it is important that you take account of the ways in which marginalised groups experience criminal justice differently, and listen to the voices of those we too often overlook.

Science

Prison research is not static, nor does it come from a singular perspective. It is an evolving practice that involves a wide range of approaches. Thinking about prison spaces in the way explored above, carves out room to think about how prison is experienced as a particular environment by those who live and work within it. Such thinking adds nuance to considerations of how prison spaces are distinct ecologies; comprised of unique combinations of individuals and their relationships both to one another and the particular prison environment. Toch (1993) proposes that sensitivity to the way prison environments are more or less survivable is linked to more successful outcomes for the prison. This scientific approach centres the needs of the imprisoned individual. These ideas contrast with those focusing on a broader-scale, aggregate approach to minimising 'risk' as well as those who assume those entering the prison system are deficient in some way.

In *Risk Society: Towards a New Modernity* (1992), Ulrich Beck argues that in the wake of the Second World War, Western societies became increasingly dominated by ideas of risk and its management (practices which seek to define and control future outcomes, through the collation and analysis of statistical information). The predominance of scientific rationality in Western politics meant ever greater, more sophisticated, practices of risk identification, measurement, and management became the defining feature of modern societies. This scientific rationality has come to permeate every element of the contemporary prison (Clear and Cadora, 2001). The move away from moral and clinical judgement of wrongdoers, to mechanisms of classification based on ideas of 'dangerousness' characterised the 'New Penology' (Feeley and Simon, 1992). This was accompanied by a shift from seeing the individual in terms of their crime, to classifying and scoring them for potential future offending based on a generalised understanding of offending within population-level statistics. Classifying an individual in this way presents a logical fallacy known as the Ecological Fallacy (inferring information about an individual from statistics about the population to which the individual belongs) (Warr, 2020a). In relation to prisons this has manifested in the entrenchment of what has become known as 'Managerialism' – where policy has been geared towards top down strategic planning, target-setting, performance measurement, risk identification and management (Liebling and Crewe, 2013). This 'managerialism', with its focus on 'imagined' individualised prisoners and the risk they are perceived to represent (Carlen, 2008), still dominates everyday prison practices.

Politicians have utilised the idea of the prison as a tool for gaining political popularity, which is reflected in a particular way of thinking about the prison. This is in part due to what Pratt (2007) has referred to as the 'New Punitiveness', whereby the desire for, and popularity of, penal sanctions to solve societal problems has become a key factor of modern capitalist societies. This has led to a symbiotic relationship between the expanding scope of criminal law, increasing harshness of sentencing – especially with drug laws (see Koram, 2019) – and the public appetite for prisons and punishment. As Cohen (1985) notes, the penal net has widened and its mesh thinned as less people are aided by social welfare and instead 'captured' by the criminal justice system (Garland, 2001). One consequence of this is the phenomenon of 'mass incarceration'. Mass incarceration led to an explosion in the development, construction, and use of prisons, most notably within the US – who now house a quarter of the world's prison population – but also in England and Wales. Just as in the US, where mass incarceration has led to the widespread marginalisation, criminalisation and imprisonment of ethnic and specifically Black minorities (see Schoenfeld, 2018; Mitchell, 2019), the increased use of imprisonment as the paradigmatic form of punishment in England and Wales has disproportionately affected minority groups.

Knowledge link: This topic is also covered in Chapter 30.

Risk, the 'New Penology', the 'New Punitiveness', and the problems of structural and institutional racism have been compounded by an overt adoption of criminological positivism within the criminal justice system. This form of positivism proposes that the 'criminality' inherent to the offending of individuals is caused by some latent defect of morality, psychology, or personality. This 'defect', which renders the individual 'dangerous' and a substantial 'risk', must be addressed by the criminal justice system. Here we see the connection between the disciplinary concepts of risk and rehabilitation (Warr, 2020a) coupled with the individualisation that occurs within the 'managerial' prison. We tend to think of rehabilitation in health or medicalised terms – a change that allows the individual to return to a former, 'healthy' self. In England and Wales, where modes of rehabilitation are often experienced as underfunded, superficial, and unlikely to affect any form of change (Bullock and Bunce, 2020), we must ask what rehabilitation means in the context of the prison. Is rehabilitation about some conception of returning to a healthy self, is it a means of addressing the risk that a person is perceived to represent, or is it a further means of creating compliance? These are complex questions but if we are to understand the prison then we need to think critically about such terms and associated practices.

Knowledge link: This topic is also covered in Chapter 6.

The issues of 'race' and racism are a sharp lens through which to explore these complexities and the 'science' of risk and rehabilitation in the prison context. Performances of Blackness (cultural representations of varying Black identities) are often misjudged, or judged negatively, within prison settings. As a result, these become factors of risk in and of themselves (Liebling and Williams, 2018). This racialisation of risk is a continuation of the racist and positivist myths and tropes of 'Black criminality' (Gilroy, 1987; see also Ewing, 2016). Black men in particular, though this also applies to other ethnicities, are often framed as more violent and predatory then their white counterparts, even when committing analogous offences. Positivism collapses the complex causal elements of crime to individualistic and latent criminogenic factors. Blackness becomes aligned with risk and danger. These tropes of Blackness/ethnicity and risk, impact on how ideas of 'rehabilitation' are imposed upon people of colour within the prison. There is an inherent 'whiteness' in behavioural expectations interwoven with conceptions of rehabilitation built into 'treatment programmes' delivered in prisons in the West (Smith and Campbell, 2019). Different ethnicities are not only judged more harshly in terms of risk (see Earle and Phillips, 2013) but they are also judged through a lens of 'whiteness' in assessments of treatment and rehabilitation. Acknowledging the deep structural and institutional racism this constitutes, enables us to challenge the very sciences that both construct disciplinary systems of risk and rehabilitation, and are implicit to our understanding of the prison.

Science is not fixed, but rather evolves through internal critique and revision. One of the most significant leaps in understanding has emerged from feminist critique. In *Papa's Discipline* (1982) Pat Carlen explored how traditional constructions and disciplinary practices of the prison imposed paternalistic ideas of 'womanhood' on imprisoned women. In doing so, the prison established a broad and complex framework of constraining influences, including medical ones, that not only judged women for their offending, but also for their deviation from perceived and approved forms of femininity. Women were being punished in very different ways to men, e.g. their adherence to social norms in terms of 'feminine' appearance and the degree to which they were considered to have failed as "good" mothers. This revolutionised prison studies, forcing a recognition that punishment is not gender neutral. For women, imprisonment is not only more damaging and painful but compounds multiple vulnerabilities (Carlen and Worrall, 2004). These vulnerabilities are forged at the intersections (Crenshaw, 2012) between gender, race, class, poverty and prison, creating new, gendered pains of imprisonment (Corston, 2007). This work extended our understanding of both the deprivation and importation models and provided the foundation of the United Nations Rules for the Treatment of Women Prisoners and Non-custodial Measures for Women Offenders (known as the Bangkok Rules; see United Nations, 2010). This set of rules was designed to minimise the use of imprisonment for women and where that was not possible to attempt to mitigate the very gendered pains identified. In England and Wales these rules, much like many of the recommendations set out in the Corston Report, have yet to be implemented in any significant way.

———— Case Study 29.3 ————

'Sensing' the Prison

Here are two excerpts from a Sensory Criminology blog (www.sensorycriminology.com) by Dr Jason Warr, entitled *The Power of Touch* (2020), on how we need to extend our scientific enquiries about the prison and include differing notions of 'expertise':

"As a prisoner you are forced to endure the touch of powerful others on a daily basis. There is little gentleness, no thoughtfulness, no comfort to these touches. In the texture of this touch is woven the matrices of penal power that you, as a prisoner, are now forced to endure. You are subjected to multiple bodily violations of person and privacy on a daily basis. Leaving the wing, leaving the workshop, gym, exercise yard, library, education department, medical wing, every breach of a portal means you are subject to a search, a rub down. More hands, unwanted hands, rubbing, pawing, at you.

So many have had lives blighted by prolonged and continual abuse of every physical description. How do they experience the coerced nakedness, the unwanted touch, the imposition of powerful hands? What consequence does inflicting this breach of bodily autonomy have, what long-term effects on psyche and self? What does it do to those who do the searches? Does it desensitise them to the laying of hands on powerless others? Do they even recognise the powerlessness of the 'other'? This is a sensory practice/experience that we, as a society, inflict on tens of thousands of our citizens every single day – yet we have little understanding of what effect this may have. We perhaps need to think about that ..."

Another set of important critiques came from Abolitionist perspectives. **Abolitionism** emerged in the UK in the 1970s. Its main aim is not the reform of prisons, but their end. This has led people to dismiss the work associated with it as ideological and utopian (Ryan and Ward, 2015). However, one of the central themes of abolition is to focus on the harms that prison causes to both individuals and society. As Mathiesen (1990) notes the central function of the prison (punishment) is to impose harm. However, the harms done by imprisonment often extend further than acknowledged. They harm the individual morally, emotionally, psychologically, often physically, relationally, occupationally, and socially. Imprisonment often represents a rupture to familial and social bonds. The person will often lose their home and future employment opportunities become severely limited. This means that imprisonment is often a disproportionate punishment for those who are subject to it (most are imprisoned for non-violent offences; see MoJ, 2019b). Abolitionists present us with two critical questions: i) given the harms represented by imprisonment should we seek less harmful alternatives, both for those subjected to it and for society more broadly? ii) do we as criminologists contribute to those harms through our work on prisons (see Brown and Schept, 2017)?

The critiques represented here have fundamentally challenged and developed our knowledge of prisons. New ways of researching prison from Convict Criminology (Earle, 2016) to Sensory Penalities (Herrity et al., 2021) are emerging. This evolution furthers our knowledge to include: Foreign Nationals in prison; LGBTQIA+ people's experiences in prison; imprisonment and children/childhood; trans and non-binary prisoners; autism and neuro-diversity; self-harm, suicide, and death; violence in prison; prison architecture; families and motherhood; diet and nutrition; arts, philosophy, technology, and education in prison. There is more to explore, and additional, different questions to be asked. This is where you come in. As new criminologists it is your role to push the science of prisons research and ask new questions, challenge what we know, and forge new understandings.

CHAPTER SUMMARY

- The prison has a unique place in our cultural, political, and social imagination. Interrogating how it comes to occupy this position requires us to engage with the various aspects of existence with which it is intertwined.
- The prison is a physical environment, but one whose meaning is remade through everyday practices, political constructions and cultural representations.
- Our purpose was to encourage you to think about how the prison retains such a potent hold over our imaginations, and to examine what this tells us about the social function of punishment as well as the purpose of prison: the spectacle.
- We sought to evoke your imaginations as to how daily life inside is experienced: space,
- To critically engage with how the ways this can be thought about are shaped both by the questions we ask, and the ways we ask them: science.
- Having expanded your understanding of what the prison is, we encourage you to question why this is important?

Review Questions

1. What factors contribute to public ignorance about the realities of prison life?
2. What are the implications of considering the prison as either a closed institution or a porous one?
3. In what ways does thinking about the prison through the lens of 'New Penology' shape our understanding?
4. Are there problems in the way we generate knowledge about the prison? What are these?

GO FURTHER

Books

1. The following is an interesting collection of essays exploring prison spaces from perspectives beyond criminology:

   Moran, D., Gill, N. and Conlon, D. (2013) *Carceral Spaces: Mobility and Agency in Imprisonment and Migrant Detention*. Surrey: Ashgate.

2. This second text is a collection of short articles detailing the intricacies of prison life from the perspective of someone who served a life sentence. It is important to see how those who end up in prison experience life there:

   James, E. (2003) *A Life Inside: A Prisoner's Notebook*. London: Atlantic Books.

3. This final text is an important, critical examination of changing relationships between society and prison and what this means for how we understand why we punish the way we do:

   Scott, D. (2013) *Why Prison?* Cambridge: Cambridge University Press.

Journal Articles

1. The following is a classic article exploring the particular pains of imprisonment for a number of women in a Scottish prison:

   Carlen, P. (1982) Papa's discipline: an analysis of disciplinary modes in the Scottish women's prison. *The Sociological Review*, 30(1): 97–124.

2. This second article explores the ways in which urban and prison spaces are bound up with black masculinities:

   Shabazz, R. (2009) 'So high you can't get over it, so low you can't get under it': Carceral spatiality and Black masculinities in the United States and South Africa. *Souls: A Critical Journal of Black Politics, Culture and Society*, 11(3): 276–294.

3. This short article explores the implications of sensory methods for the process of knowledge production as well as the impact on relationships in the field and what this means for the purpose of criminology (in relation to prisons):

   Herrity, K. (2020) 'Some people can't hear, so they have to feel …': Exploring sensory experience and collapsing distance in prisons research. *ECAN Bulletin*, No. 43: 26–31. https://howardleague. org/wp-content/uploads/2020/01/ECAN-Autumn-2019-final-draft-2.pdf

Useful Websites

1. EAR Hustle: podcast about prison life produced at San Quentin State Prison by former inmate Earlonne Woods and former inmate Antwan Williams, along with Nigel Poor, an artist who volunteers at the prison: https://www.earhustlesq.com/
2. PRT podcasts: a timely series of blogposts charting a range of experience of imprisonment and associated issues from the perspective of service users: http://www.prisonreformtrust.org.uk/WhatWeDo/Projectsresearch/Prisonerpolicynetwork/Podcasts

3. SensoryCriminology: a blog to accompany the book, *Sensory Penalties*, exploring the sensory experience of places of punishment around the world: https://sensorycriminology.com/blog-feed/blog/

REFERENCES

Beck, U. (1992) *Risk Society: Towards a New Modernity*. London: Sage Publishing.

Bennett, J. (2006) The Good, the Bad and the Ugly: The Media in Prison Films. *The Howard Journal of Criminal Justice*, 45(2): 97–115.

Brown, C. (1993) 'Howard seeks to placate "angry majority": Home Secretary tells party that balance in criminal justice system will be tilted towards public', *The Independent*. https://www.independent.co.uk/news/uk/howard-seeks-to-placate-angry-majority-home-secretary-tells-party-that-balance-in-criminal-justice-1509088.html

Brown, M. (2009) *The Culture of Punishment: Prison, Society, and Spectacle*. New York: New York University Press.

Brown, M. and Schept, J. (2017) New abolition, criminology and a critical carceral studies. *Punishment & Society*, 19(4): 440–462.

Bullock, K. and Bunce, A. (2020) 'The prison don't talk to you about getting out of prison': on why prisons in England and Wales fail to rehabilitate prisoners. *Criminology & Criminal Justice*, 20(1): 111–127.

Campbell, C. M. (2015) Popular punitivism: finding a balance between the politics, presentation, and fear of crime. *Sociology Compass*, 9(3): 180–195.

Carlen, P. (1982) Papa's discipline: an analysis of disciplinary modes in the Scottish women's prison. *The Sociological Review*, 30(1): 97–124.

Carlen, P. (2008) 'Imaginary Penalties and Risk-Crazed Governance'. In P. Carlen (ed.), *Imaginary Penalties*. Cullompton, Devon: Willan Publishing. pp. 1–25.

Carlen, P. and Worrall, A. (2004) *Analysing Women's Imprisonment*. Cullompton, Devon: Willan Publishing.

Carrabine, E. (2004) *Power, Discourse and Resistance: A Genealogy of the Strangeways Riot*. Aldershot: Ashgate.

Carrabine, E. (2005) Prison riots, social order and the problem of legitimacy. *British Journal of Criminology*, 45(6): 896–913.

Cattermole, C. (2019) *Prison: A Survival Guide*. London: Penguin Random House, Ebury Press.

Chalfin, A. and McCrary, J. (2017) Criminal deterrence: a review of the literature, *Journal of Economic Literature*, 55(1): 5–48.

Clear, T. R. and Cadora, E. (2001) 'Risk and Correctional Practice'. In K. Stenson and R. R. Sullivan (eds), *Crime, Risk and Justice: The Politics of Crime Control in Liberal Democracies*. Cullompton, Devon: Willan Publishing.

Clemmer, D. (1958) *The Prison Community* (2nd Edn). Chicago, Il: Holt, Rinehart and Winston.

Cohen, S. (1985) *Visions of Social Control*. Cambridge: Polity Press.

Corston, J. (2007) *A Report by Baroness Jean Corston of a Review of Women with Particular Vulnerabilities in the Criminal Justice System*. London: Home Office.

Crawley, E. (2004) *Doing Prison Work: The Public and Private Lives of Prison Officers*. Cullompton, Devon: Willan Publishing.

Crenshaw, K. W. (2012) From private violence to mass incarceration: thinking intersectionally about women, race, and social control. *UCLA Law Review*, 59(6): 1418–1473.

Crewe, B. (2009) *The Prisoner Society: Power, Adaptation and Social Life in an English Prison*, Clarendon Studies in Criminology. Oxford: Oxford University Press.

Crewe, B., Warr, J., Bennett, P. and Smith, A. (2014) The emotional geography of prison life. *Theoretical Criminology*, 18(1), 56–74.

DiGiorgi, A. (2013) 'Prison and Social Structures in Late Capitalist Societies'. In D. Scott (ed.), *Why Prison?* Cambridge: Cambridge University Press. pp. 25–43.

Doyle, J. (2013) 'End of a cushy life in prison', *Daily Mail*. https://www.dailymail.co.uk/news/article-2316840/Convicts-denied-Sky-Sports-18-rated-DVDs.html

Drake, D. H., Earle, R. and Sloan, J. (2015) *The Palgrave Handbook of Prison Ethnography*. London: Palgrave Macmillan.

Durkheim, E. (1900) 'Two Laws of Penal Evolution, *Cincinnati Law Review*, Vol. (38)'. In D. Melossi (ed.) (1998), *The Sociology of Punishment*. Dartmouth: Ashgate. pp. 285–308.

Earle, R. (2016) *Convict Criminology: Inside and Out*. Bristol: Policy Press, University of Bristol.

Earle, R. and Phillips, C. (2013) 'Muslim is the New Black': new ethnicities and new essentialisms in the prison. *Race and Justice*, 3(2): 114–129.

Ewing, A. (2016) In/visibility: solitary confinement, race, and the politics of risk management. *Transition*, Vol. 119: 109–123.

Feeley, M. M. and Simon, J. (1992) The new penology: notes on the emerging strategy of corrections and its implications. *Criminology*, 30(4): 449–474.

Foucault, M. (1977) *Discipline and Punish: The Birth of the Prison*. London: Allen Lane.

Garland, D. (2001) *The Culture of Control: Crime and Social Order in Contemporary Society*. Chicago: University of Chicago Press.

Goffman, E. (1961) *Asylums: Essays on the Social Situation of Mental Patients and Other Inmates*. Garden City, NY: Anchor Books.

Gilroy, P. (1987) 'The Myth of Black Criminality'. In B. Spalek (ed.), *Ethnicity and Crime: A Reader*. Maidenhead: Open University Press. pp. 113–123.

Hayward, K. J. (2012) Five spaces of cultural criminology. *British Journal of Criminology*, 52(3): 441–462.

Herrity, K. Z., Schmidt, B. and Warr, J. (2021) *Sensory Penalities: Exploring the Senses in Spaces of Punishment and Social Control*. Bingley: Emerald Publishing Limited.

HMIP (2019) *Her Majesty's Inspectorate of Prisons in England and Wales Annual Report 2018–19*. London: Justice Inspectorates.

HMPPS (2019) *Her Majesty's Prison and Probation Service Annual Report and Accounts 2018–19*. London: Ministry of Justice.

Irwin, J. and Cressey, D. (1964) 'Thieves, Convicts, and the Inmate Culture'. In H. Becker (ed.), *The Other Side*. New York: Free Press. pp. 225–247.

Ismail, N. (2020) The politics of austerity, imprisonment and ignorance: a case study of English prisons. *Medicine, Science and the Law*, 60(2): 89–92.

Jackson, J., Tyler, T. R., Bradford, B., Taylor, D. and Shiner, M. (2010) Legitimacy and procedural justice in prisons. *Prison Service Journal*, 191: 4–10.

Jewkes, Y. and Johnston, H. (2007) 'The Evolution of Prison Architecture'. In Y. Jewkes (ed.), *Handbook on Prisons*. Abingdon: Routledge. pp. 174–196.

Jewkes, Y., Slee, E. and Moran, D. (2017) 'The Visual Retreat of the Prison: Non Places for Non People'. In M. Brown and E. Carrabine (eds), *Routledge International Handbook of Visual Criminology*. Abingdon: Routledge. pp. 293–304.

Koram, K. (2019) 'Introduction: The War on Drugs and the Global Colour Line'. In K. Koram (ed.), *The War on Drugs and the Global Colour Line*. London: Pluto. pp. 1–20.

Lammy, D. (2017) *The Lammy Review: An Independent Review into the Treatment of, and Outcomes for, Black, Asian and Minority Ethnic Individuals in the Criminal Justice System*. London: Ministry of Justice.

Lefebvre, H. (1991) *The Production of Space*, Oxford: Blackwell Publishing.

Liebling, A. and Arnold, H. (2004) *Prisons and Their Moral Performance: A Study of Values, Quality and Prison Life*, Clarendon Studies in Criminology, Oxford: Oxford University Press.

Liebling, A. and Crewe, B. (2013) 'Prisons Beyond the New Penology: The Shifting Foundations of Prison Management'. In J. Simon and R. Sparks (eds), *The SAGE Handbook of Punishment and Society*. London: Sage. pp. 283–307.

Liebling, A., Price, D. and Shefer, G. (2011) *The Prison Officer*, 2nd edition, Cullompton, Devon: Willan Publishing.

Liebling, A. and Williams, R. J. (2018) The new subversive geranium: some notes on the management of additional troubles in maximum security prisons. *British Journal of Sociology*, 69(4): 1194–1219.

Maratea, R. J. and Monahan, B. A. (2013) Crime control as mediated spectacle: the institutionalization of gonzo rhetoric in modern media and politics. *Symbolic Interaction*, 36(3): 261–274.

Marsh, K., Fox, C. and Hedderman, C. (2009) Do you get what you pay for? Assessing the use of prison from an economic perspective. *Howard Journal of Criminal Justice*, 48(2): 144–157.

Mathiesen, T. (1990) *Prison on Trial*, London: Sage.

Melossi, D. and Pavarini, M. (2018) *The Prison and the Factory: Origins of the Penitentiary System* (40th anniversary edition). London: Palgrave Macmillan.

Ministry of Justice (2018) Freedom of Information request 180915001 by Vicki Cardwell. Available at: https://www.whatdotheyknow.com/request/homelessness_on_release_from_pri#incoming-1240602

Ministry of Justice (2019a) *Safety in Custody Statistics Quarterly: Update to December 2019*. London: Ministry of Justice.

Ministry of Justice (2019b) *Offender Management Statistics Quarterly: October–December*. London: Ministry of Justice.

Mitchell, O. (2019) 'The Paradox of a Black Incarceration Boom in the Era of Declining Black Crime: Causes and Consequences'. In J. D. Unnever, S. L. Gabbidon and C. Chouhy (eds), *Building a Black Criminology: Race, Theory, and Crime*. Abingdon: Routledge. pp. 343–368.

Moran, D., Gill, N. and Conlon, D. (2013) *Carceral Spaces: Mobility and Agency in Imprisonment and Migrant Detention*. Surrey: Ashgate.

Newburn, T. (2007) 'Tough on crime': penal policy in England and Wales. *Crime and Justice*, 36(1): 425–470.

Phillips, C. (2012) *The Multicultural Prison: Ethnicity, Masculinity and Social Relations Amongst Prisoners*. Oxford: Oxford University Press.

Pratt, J. (2007) *Penal Populism*. Abingdon: Routledge.

Prison Reform Trust (2019) *Bromley Briefings Winter Full Fact File*. London: PRT.

Reiner, R., Livingstone, S. and Allen, J. (2003) 'From Law and Order to Lynch Mobs: Crime News Since the Second World War'. In P. Mason (ed.), *Criminal Visions: Media Representations of Crime and Justice*. Cullompton, Devon: Willan Publishing.

Ross, J. I. (2015) Varieties of prison voyeurism: an analytic/interpretive framework. *The Prison Journal*, 95(3): 397–417.

Rubin, E. L. (2001) The inevitability of rehabilitation, *Law and Inequality: Journal of Theory and Practice*, 19(2): 343–378.

Rusche, G. and Kirchheimer, O. (1939) *Punishment and Social Structure*. New York: Columbia University.

Ryan, M. and Ward, T. (2015) Prison abolition in the UK: they dare not speak its name? *Social Justice*, 41(137): 107–119.

Schoenfeld, H. (2018) *Building the Prison State: Race and the Politics of Mass Incarceration*. Chicago: University of Chicago Press.

Shabazz, R. (2015) *Spatialising Blackness: Architectures of Confinement and Black Masculinity in Chicago*. Springfield: University of Illinois Press.

Slack, J. (2012) 'I'll stop our jails being like holiday camps, says new minister for justice', *Daily Mail*. https://www.dailymail.co.uk/news/article-2205824/Ill-stop-jails-like-holiday-camps-says-new-minister-justice.html

Smith, P. and Campbell, C. (2019) 'Race and Rehabilitation'. In J. D. Unnever, S. L. Gabbidon and C. Chouhy (eds), *Building a Black Criminology: Race, Theory, and Crime*. Abingdon: Routledge. pp. 369–394.

Sparks, R., Bottoms, A. E. and Hay, W. (1996) *Prisons and the Problem of Order*. Oxford: Oxford University Press.

Surette, R. (1997) *Media, Crime, and Criminal Justice*, 2nd edition. Belmont: West/ Wadsworth.

Sykes G. M. (1958) *The Society of Captives: A Study of a Maximum Security Prison*. Princeton, NJ: Princeton University Press.

Tait, S. (2011) A typology of prison officer approaches to care. *European Journal of Criminology*, 8(6): 440–456.

Toch, H. (1993) *Living in Prison: Ecologies of Survival* (new edition). Washington, DC: American Psychological Association.

Tonry, M. (2004) *Punishment and Politics: Evidence and Emulation in the Making of English Crime Control Policy*. Cullompton, Devon: Willan Publishing.

Turner, J. (2016) *The Prison Boundary: Between Society and Carceral Space*. London: Palgrave Macmillan.

United Nations (2010) *The United Nations Rules for the Treatment of Women Prisoners and Non-custodial Measures for Women Offenders ('the Bangkok Rules')*, General Assembly. New York: United Nations. https://www.ohchr.org/Documents/ProfessionalInterest/BangkokRules.pdf

Wacquant, L. (2001) Deadly symbiosis: when ghetto and prison meet and mesh. *Punishment & Society*, 3(1): 95–133.

Warr, J. (2020a) 'Always gotta be two mans': lifers, risk, rehabilitation, and narrative labour. *Punishment & Society*, 22(1): 28–47.

Warr, J. (2020b) *Ghost in the Sweatbox*. https://sensorycriminology.com/2019/12/15/ghost-in-the-sweatbox/

Warr, J. (2020c) *Forensic Psychologists: Prisons, Power, and Vulnerability*. Bingley: Emerald Publishing Limited.

White, J. (2020) *Terraformed: Young Black Lives in the Inner City*. London: Repeater Books.

Woolf, H. and Tumin, S. (1991) *Inquiry into Prison Disturbances 1990–1991*. London: Home Office.

Wortley, R. (2002) *Situational Prison Control: Crime Prevention in Correctional Institutions*. Cambridge: Cambridge University Press.

Youth Crime and Youth Justice

30

Tim Bateman

---------- Learning Objectives ----------

By the end of this chapter you will:

- Understand that youth crime and youth justice are social constructs.
- Understand that how Youth Offending is conceptualised has implications for the way that children who break the law are treated.
- Explore some of the dynamics that have shaped the historical development of youth justice and how these are manifested in the legal structures for youth justice, including the courts, the minimum age of criminal responsibility, and the mechanisms by which services are delivered.

---------- Framing Questions ----------

1. What is meant by the youth justice system?
2. What does it mean to say that youth crime is a social construction?
3. What are the different ways in which youth crime can be conceptualised and what might the implications of such conceptualisations be?

INTRODUCTION

In this chapter you will be introduced to some of the complexities that arise when thinking about youth justice. You will be encouraged to challenge commonly held assumptions that underpin discussions of youth crime, children who commit offences and how society responds to youthful lawbreaking. In thinking about those challenges, the main focus will be England and Wales, although you will on occasion be signposted to what happens in Scotland where things are done very differently.

Terminology is important. Throughout the chapter we will refer to 'youth crime' and 'youth justice', expressions which are deployed in the UK, and some other parts of the world. It is important to be aware when looking at the wider literature that you will find other terms adopted. 'Juvenile delinquency' and 'juvenile justice' are common alternatives. Perhaps more controversially, we have chosen to refer, in what follows, to those people who are processed by the youth justice system as 'children', reflecting their status under the United Nations Convention on the Rights of the Child (UNCRC) and the fact that they are entitled to the same safeguards and protections as other children, irrespective of their criminal behaviour. Other expressions, which may denote the same population – such as 'young offenders', 'juveniles' or 'youth' – are avoided, since, in the view of the author, they are stigmatising, but you may come across them in other writings.

We will first map the terrain, considering the argument that youth justice is a social construct, before moving on to consider how changes to the court system can help us understand the ways in which constructions of Youth Offending have changed over time. We will then proceed to look at the age of criminal responsibility, exploring what it tells us about changing attitudes to children who offend. The manner in which youth justice interventions have been delivered at different points in history is also investigated. Finally, the chapter concludes with a discussion of how youth crime is measured.

MAPPING THE TERRAIN: YOUTH CRIME AND YOUTH JUSTICE AS CONTINGENCIES

This section introduces the idea that how we understand offending by children is socially constructed. It is tempting to imagine that youth crime and youth justice are relatively straightforward concepts; to presuppose that youth crime is simply offending by individuals who happen to be aged under eighteen and that the youth justice system is that part of the criminal justice apparatus that processes, and punishes, children when they offend. In some respects, arrangements in England and Wales do conform to, and thereby encourage, such expectations. The trial process for children is broadly similar to that for adults, although proceedings are, in the main, conducted in a specially adapted youth court. The mechanisms by which a sentence is selected also mirror, to a large extent, those which apply in the adult arena, although the available range of disposals have different names.

However, it is important that these surface similarities do not lead you to conclude that youth justice can be adequately represented as just a specialist part of the wider system. Such a conclusion would involve a substantial oversimplification of the nature of youth crime and how responses to it have developed.

Let us take two examples. First, to the extent that the youth justice system deals with lawbreaking by children, there is the obvious question of the age boundaries to which these different arrangements apply. Legislation in most jurisdictions (but not all) specifies the minimum age at which children are considered legally liable for their actions and thereby subject to criminal proceedings. Most people would consider it inappropriate that a three-year-old who broke another child's toy could be prosecuted for criminal damage, even if their actions were deliberate. This minimum age of criminal responsibility (MACR) varies considerably from one country to another. In England and Wales this important age threshold is ten years, but you will find that this is low by international standards and frequently subject to criticism for this and other reasons (Bunn and Brown, 2018).

Moving to our second example, it is important to understand that the youth justice apparatus in England and Wales is just one of a range of possible approaches (McAra, 2010). As noted above, in many respects, the treatment of child 'offenders' in this jurisdiction mirrors arrangements for adults who break the law: the youth justice system and adult justice system are, if you like, in *vertical* alignment. In Scotland, however, a close neighbour, youth justice is best understood as being in *horizontal* alignment with other elements of services for children who require state intervention. While in England and Wales, care proceedings and criminal justice proceedings are distinct, that is not so north of the border where children who offend and those who require care and protection are dealt with through the same process. In Scotland, the children's hearing system, where decisions are made by a panel of community volunteers, deals with both care and crime, at least for children below the age of 16. Children who offend are not therefore subject to court proceedings as they are in England and Wales (Burman and McVie, 2017).

But variation is not simply found across geographic boundaries; arrangements within a single jurisdiction are not static. They change over time, sometimes quite rapidly. What was taken for granted as being a core element of youth justice practice a few years ago, may no longer be regarded as an appropriate response to youth crime.

Stephen Case (2018:1) has argued persuasively that youth justice can best be understood as a 'constructed reality': responses to youth crime are largely determined by how Youth Offending is defined and explained. These definitions and explanations are 'dynamic, contested and contingent' (Case, 2018:1). They change over time within single jurisdictions and may vary significantly, at the same time, from one place to another.

Student Voice

Thoughts on social construction

"At first, I really struggled with the idea that Youth Offending is a social construction, because it is about the crimes that young people commit. Either they do or they don't. It was only when I was given some concrete examples that I began to understand what people were getting at. When I realised that society chooses whether a particular piece of behaviour is counted as a youth crime or not; and those decisions make a real difference to how youth justice operates." (Pauline, Level 4, BA Criminology)

Pause for Thought

Think about the differences between the youth justice system in Scotland and in England and Wales. What do you think they suggest about how children in trouble are conceptualised?

THE COURT: A BAROMETER OF CHANGING APPROACHES TO YOUTH OFFENDING

Now that you have been introduced to the contingent nature of youth justice, let us move on to explore in more detail how these questions of definition and explanation have influenced the development of responses to children in trouble in England and Wales. We start with the court system – arguably one of the most important structural frames around which the rest of the edifice is constructed.

The juvenile court was established in 1908 by the Children Act of that year, providing for the first time a separate venue for dealing with children's lawbreaking. Given the discussion in the previous section, it is important to consider the circumstances in which the new court emerged to tease out what it tells us about how youth crime was viewed at the time. Until the mid-nineteenth century, the criminal justice framework and available punishments were identical whatever the age of the defendant, provided they were over the MACR – seven years of age. There was no separate youth justice provision, although there was some mitigation of punishment to allow for youth (Arthur, 2010). The gradual development of specialist custodial facilities for children throughout the second half of the century signified that attitudes were changing.

An 1835 report by the House of Lords Select Committee on Gaols argued that it was not appropriate to continue confining children alongside adult offenders when they were sentenced to custody. The Committee based its conclusions on the increasingly prevalent view that the lack of separate custodial provision for children was counterproductive since it subjected them to the baleful influence of 'more experienced delinquents [leading to] increasing criminality' (cited in Stack, 1979: 390). Three years later in 1838, Parkhurst Prison was opened as a custodial establishment for boys, presaging the development of a range of distinct institutions for children in trouble that included reformatories and industrial schools (Arthur, 2010). The process was however a long one: it was not until 2000 that all children in custody were placed in establishments distinct from adults'.

In retrospect, it is possible to see such developments as a response to what Muncie (2015: 51) calls the 'discover[y of] juvenile delinquency', reflecting wider concerns about the threat that children of the poor represented to the social order in the wake of rapid urbanisation and the upheaval of industrialisation. This 'discovery' involved, for the first time, a recognition that adolescence was a distinct developmental stage, and raised a potential contradiction. Teenagers were considered as a social threat distinct from that posed by adults; at the same time, distinguishing adolescents from adults also focused attention on their vulnerability and society's responsibility to safeguard them. These two competing dynamics – children conceived of as both a risk and as being at risk – had repercussions beyond the criminal justice system. Think for instance about the contemporaneous development of Factory Acts that prescribed the conditions under which children could work, and Education Acts that increasingly mandated children's attendance at education (Hendrick, 2015).

The emergence of youth crime as a distinct social problem required an increasingly differential treatment of children who engaged in it. The establishment of the juvenile court can be seen as a natural emanation of these processes; part of a programme of reform that signalled a shift in how children were viewed by society. Such developments were not unique to England and Wales: the first juvenile court in the world was established some years earlier, in Illinois in 1899, and most developed Western countries had introduced a similar mechanism within twenty years (Arthur, 2010). Moreover, the juvenile court was not an isolated innovation. The Probation of Offenders Act 1907 had already introduced probation as a statutory function, and provided for a specialist body of probation staff with a remit to work primarily with children (Arthur, 2010). This amalgam of specialist courts, staffing and custodial establishments has prompted many commentators to argue that it is only possible to identify a youth justice system from the first decade of the twentieth century onward (Bateman, 2019).

The new court differed from its adult counterpart not just in terms of the age of those processed: it also dealt with care-related cases as well as those involving children who broke the law (Gelsthorpe and

Morris, 1994). The dual function provided a systemic acknowledgement, not just that children should be treated separately from adults, but also that there was a link between the child's circumstances and youthful lawbreaking. The new arrangements thereby manifested an understanding of youth crime as a symptom of underlying welfare need, and a perception that the function of youth justice intervention was, at least in part, to address the root causes. Such an approach is frequently described in the literature as the welfare model (Hazel, 2008). This is not to suggest that the inception of the juvenile court was indicative of any abandonment of the notion that children in trouble should be held to account. Indeed the court was designed as a mechanism for the 'rescue as well as the punishment of juveniles' (Gelsthorpe and Morris, 1994: 951).

While the juvenile court did legitimise responses to youth crime that attempted to address welfare concerns, it also retained elements of a justice paradigm: the view which holds that what distinguishes children who break the law from their disadvantaged peers is that they have offended, and it is this transgression which warrants state intervention through the justice system. The notion of proportionality – the idea that the punishment should fit the crime – is thus central to the justice model (Hazel, 2008). It is possible to view the history of youth justice in England and Wales as oscillating between justice and welfare without ever adopting a consistent alignment with either one of those ideal types. The welfare and justice paradigms are described in Table 30.1.

Most discussions of youth justice start by distinguishing between welfare and justice approaches. Each model offers a different conception of how youth crime should be understood and accordingly has implications for the nature of youth justice interventions.

Table 30.1 Key Concepts: Welfare and Justice Paradigms

The Nature of Youth Crime	
Welfare	Offending is a symptom of underlying welfare need and the backgrounds of children in trouble and those in need of care and protection are similar.
Justice	Offending is behaviour that contravenes criminal legislation. Not all children in need commit crime and what distinguishes those who offend from those who require protection is that the former have broken the law while the latter have not.

The Role of Youth Justice	
Welfare	To focus on the child's needs. Interventions should aim to tackle the root causes of offending.
Justice	To focus on deeds. Interventions should be proportionate to the seriousness of the offending.

For fifty or so years after the establishment of the juvenile court, welfarism was increasingly in the ascendant (Arthur, 2010). The Children and Young Persons Act (CYPA) 1933 introduced a requirement that all courts, in cases involving children, should have regard to the welfare of the child. By the early part of the 1960s, the Labour Party seriously contemplated the abolition of the juvenile court and its replacement by a 'family council' composed of social workers and other child experts who would make the relevant decisions as to what happened to children who broke the law (Bottoms, 2002). The boundary between care and crime would in the event of such a reform have been completely elided, and the transition to a pure welfare model completed. These radical proposals, however, met with significant political opposition, and the juvenile court survived (Thorpe et al., 1980).

A similar dynamic in Scotland did lead to the abolition of criminal proceedings for children below the age of sixteen years, and its replacement by a system of children's hearings, outlined earlier in the chapter. In 1964, the Kilbrandon Committee, adopting a clear welfare stance, argued that:

the needs of children in conflict with the law did not differ from the needs of children who required welfare and protection and proposed that these needs should be met through a single system. (Vaswani et al., 2018: 12)

The report's recommendations were put into statute two years later.

Pause for Thought

Reflect on how differently youth justice has developed in two parts of the UK since the 1960s and the implications for how children in trouble are treated.

In England and Wales, the CYPA 1969 fell a long way short of the abolition of the court, but it did contain measures which manifested a continued welfarist orientation. In particular, it introduced care orders and supervision orders as sentences for offending in the hope that more punitive disposals, including custody, would wither. But in retrospect, it is clear that this was the welfare model's highpoint.

The mid-1970s onwards saw the rise of what has been termed a 'back to justice' movement, critical of the welfare approach which it alleged was responsible for increasing levels of criminalisation of children for minor infractions of the law. The argument was predicated on the idea that if the rationale for youth justice intervention was addressing welfare need, it would inevitably lead to larger numbers of children being drawn into the youth justice arena so they could benefit from such support – a process known as **net-widening**. There was, it was further contended, an associated process of up-tariffing. Children subject to welfarist interventions, such as the newly created supervision orders, often continued to offend, thereby legitimising more intensive penalties, including those, such as care orders and custody, which involved removal from home (Bottoms and Kemp, 2006). Despite benevolent intent, therefore, the hybrid welfare system ushered in by the CYPA 1969, did not, it was argued, necessarily operate in the child's best interests.

Knowledge link: This topic is also covered in Chapter 21.

This critique had some statistical support: between 1974 and 1978, the number of children convicted rose from 79,300 to 96,000. Custodial sentencing of children grew correspondingly. Expectations that care orders and supervision would supersede the use of child imprisonment proved misplaced (Allen, 1991).

You might anticipate that a justice model involves harsher treatment of children but such a correlation is not inevitable. The justice-based practice of the late 1970s and the 1980s was informed by a commitment to 'minimum intervention', the idea that contact with the criminal justice system was damaging for children and should be avoided wherever possible (McAra and McVie, 2015). It was further argued that most children grow out of crime as they mature; those with welfare needs requiring intervention should be supported through the social care system rather than criminalised (Rutherford, 1992). Such arguments had a profound impact: child convictions fell from 89,900 in 1980 to 24,600 in 1991, accompanied by a sharper decline in custodial sentences from 7,500 to 1,400 (Bateman, 2019).

The shift in philosophy had implications for the court. The Children Act 1989 established a new family proceedings court (later renamed the family court) to deal with care matters, leaving the juvenile court to focus on criminal cases. The youth justice framework was accordingly modified to reflect the increasingly dominant perception that youthful lawbreaking should be understood, and treated, as distinct from other expressions of childhood disadvantage (Curtis, 2005). The final statutory change of note followed shortly after the juvenile court was shorn of jurisdiction over care matters. The Criminal Justice Act 1991 changed the name to the youth court and extended the upper jurisdiction from seventeen to eighteen years. The measure was partly a response to the UK becoming a signatory to the UNCRC, but also reflected a growing consensus that adulthood commenced at eighteen. Let us now consider age-related issues in more detail.

Pause for Thought

Does it surprise you that child imprisonment rose as youth justice shifted in a welfarist direction, but fell once there was a back to justice movement? How can this be explained?

THE MINIMUM AGE OF CRIMINAL RESPONSIBILITY

The juvenile court initially had jurisdiction in criminal proceedings for children aged seven years or older. Younger children were deemed not criminally liable for their actions; any compulsory intervention would accordingly come through care proceedings. In adopting seven years as the MACR, the Children Act 1908 was simply reflecting existing practice, based on common law assumptions dating from the end of the seventeenth century (Bendalli, 2000). But in the context of the new court, it reflected a rather different understanding of childhood. In earlier periods, seven had been the age above which children tended to take on adult roles, with the various rights and responsibilities that implied (Bendalli, 2000). Given the changes described earlier in the chapter, such a conception of the point at which childhood ended no longer fitted social expectations that children should be excluded from the workplace and subjected to mandatory education until they were considerably older. The juvenile court provided a solution to this tension: it allowed the retention of a MACR established in a period very different from that at the start of the twentieth century by locating it within a new court system which acknowledged that childhood extended well beyond seven years of age.

Over the next sixty years, the MACR rose progressively, albeit in small increments. The CYPA 1933 provided that children younger than eight years could not be prosecuted; the MACR was further raised in 1963 to ten, where it currently stands (Bateman, 2012). These increases were a recognition that younger children were entitled to greater protections than society had previously afforded them, and were also consistent with shifts that increasingly saw youth crime as a welfare issue.

Although there have been no further changes in the MACR since 1963, the impetus that had underpinned the rises was not fully exhausted. In addition to the measures described above, the CYPA 1969 contained provision to raise the MACR to fourteen years (Bottoms, 2002). It was however never implemented and the legislation was repealed in 1991 as the shift back to justice consolidated. No government since has given serious consideration to increasing the age of criminal responsibility (Bateman, 2012).

Table 30.2   Key Events: Changes to the Minimum Age of Criminal Responsibility 1908-2019

Children Act 1908	MACR set at 7 for new juvenile court in line with common law
CYPA 1933	MACR raised to 8, alongside the introduction of the welfare principle
CYPA 1963	MACR raised to 10
CYPA 1969	MACR raised to 14 but the provision was never implemented and was repealed in 1991
Crime and Disorder Act 1998	Abolition of doli incapax, the presumption that children below the age of 14 years did not know the difference between right and wrong - represented an effective lowering of the MACR for many children

As noted previously, the justice model that emerged in the wake of the CYPA 1969 was characterised by diversionary impulses which sought to keep children out of the system wherever possible. It became clear that a justice paradigm was equally consistent with a harsher philosophy following what has been called the 'punitive turn' in the wake of the moral panic triggered by the murder of two year old James Bulger by two ten year old boys in 1993 (Muncie, 2008). (See Case Study 30.1 below.) A hardening attitude to children in trouble saw a dramatic climb in the number of children entering the court system and a 90% increase in child imprisonment over the course of the decade (Bateman, 2017). Net-widening, it transpired, was compatible with both welfare and justice precepts.

———— Case Study 30.1 ————

The Murder of James Bulger

In February 1993, two-year-old James Bulger was taken from a shopping centre in Merseyside by two ten-year-old boys, Jon Venables and Robert Thompson. James was tortured and killed by the boys who left his body on a railway track. Venables and Thompson were convicted of murder and sentenced to **Detention at Her Majesty's Pleasure**, the equivalent of a mandatory life sentence for adults.

The case generated substantial public interest and Venables and Thompson were vilified in the press. A headline in the *Sun* newspaper, for example, read 'The devil himself couldn't have made a better job of these two fiends', and when the boys were sentenced, the *Daily Mail* asked 'How do you feel now, you little bastards?'

The case is widely thought to have contributed to the punitive turn in youth justice. In the same year as the murder, the government announced that it would introduce new secure training centres for children as young as twelve years. Previously, no child below the age of fifteen could be sentenced to custody in the youth court.

———— Pause for Thought ————

Reflect on the fact that Jon Venables and Robert Thompson were young children themselves who were only just above the age of criminal responsibility. What do you think would have happened if they had been aged nine at the time of the incident?

When New Labour took office in 1997, the government's primary concern was to 'nip offending in the bud' through early youth justice intervention (Home Office, 1997). The Crime and Disorder Act (CDA) 1998 introduced a series of reforms to deliver this aim. Prior to the Act, the principle of *doli incapax* had afforded a degree of protection to children aged between ten and thirteen years, by requiring the prosecution to adduce evidence not only that they had committed the alleged offence, but also that they knew that their behaviour was seriously wrong rather than just naughty or mischievous. The CDA abolished *doli incapax*, a doctrine of seven hundred years' standing, on the grounds that it was 'contrary to common sense' (Home Office, 1997: paragraph 4.4). Consistent with the government's 'get tough' ethos, this constituted in effect a lowering of the MACR by making it significantly easier to prosecute children under fourteen.

The subsequent reluctance to review the MACR is curious. It is contrary to a broad consensus shared by academics and youth justice policy experts alike, and clearly at odds with the UK's obligations as regards children's rights. The UN Committee on the Rights of the Child (2019: paragraph 37) has confirmed that signatories to the UNCRC should increase their MACR to 'at least 14 years of age'. A low MACR is also indicative of what Goldson (2009: 518) calls a problem of 'intra-jurisdictional integrity'. While children are held fully responsible for their criminal behaviour from the age of ten, in other areas of social policy, safeguards or limitations on responsibility kick in much later. For instance, children are not regarded as sufficiently mature to purchase alcohol or tobacco until they attain eighteen years; they cannot consent to sex until the age of sixteen but can be prosecuted, and imprisoned, for sexual offences six years earlier (Bateman, 2012).

The MACR, just as the court framework, is an instructive signifier of how children who break the law are conceptualised. Unsurprisingly, this in turn helps to determine the nature of the agencies responsible for youth justice interventions. It is to this issue that we now turn.

Pause for Thought

Why do you think that the MACR is set so low? Might it suggest that children who offend do not enjoy the same protections that apply to others of the same age?

THE DELIVERY OF YOUTH JUSTICE

How youth crime is viewed at any point in time has implications for the professionals tasked with the delivery of youth justice interventions. We have already seen that the formal separation of childhood offending from that of adults led to the emergence of a specialist profession, in the form of probation, with a responsibility to work with children. But as welfarist presumptions strengthened, and the role of probation expanded into the adult arena, responsibility for youth justice fell to local authority children's departments when they were established by the Children Act 1948; youth justice in effect became a function of social work 'blurring the distinction between young offenders and children in need of protection' (Arthur, 2010: 14).

This blurring did not survive the return to justice. The late 1970s witnessed the emergence of specialist juvenile justice teams (later youth justice teams) intent on replacing welfarist principles with a commitment to minimum intervention, advocacy on behalf of children in trouble, and evincing a 'crusading zeal' (Allen, 1991: 49) against the use of child imprisonment.

The tougher climate of the 1990s yielded further change. The CDA 1998 introduced a requirement on local authorities to establish a **Youth Offending Team** (YOT) with statutory responsibilities for supervising children in conflict with the law. YOTs are multi-agency bodies involving those– including police, probation, health and education – who prior to the Act had no role in supervising youth justice interventions. The change was a deliberate attempt to undermine the culture associated with youth justice teams, which the government of the day charged with excusing youth crime (Home Office, 1997). In addition, while considerations of welfare and justice continued in play, another model had emerged. The minimisation of risk, rather than traditional goals of rehabilitation or retribution, increasingly became a major tenet of the criminal justice landscape. Risk management established itself as the dominant rationale for youth justice intervention (Case, 2018). The risk factor paradigm is described in more detail in the following paragraph.

The **risk factor paradigm**, is concerned to identify the risk factors associated with a child's offending so that these can be addressed. In contrast to the welfare model, it is more concerned with reducing the risk the child poses rather than addressing the child's needs; in contrast to justice principles, the level and nature of intervention are predicated on the nature and extent of risk – what the child might do rather than what they have done. It thus tends to undermine the concept of proportionality.

YOT practice was moulded in accordance with these new priorities. **ASSET**, a mandatory youth justice framework, developed by the **Youth Justice Board** (YJB) (newly established by the CDA), required practitioners to assess children against twelve domains of risk and develop intervention plans that addressed identified risk (Baker et al., 2011). Although not logically equivalent, the risk paradigm tended to reinforce punitive practice. As Muncie (2006: 781) puts it, 'risk is increasingly associated with pathological constructions of wilful irresponsibility, incorrigibility and family/individual failure'. It is certainly true that risk-averse practice led to substantial rises in breach action as practitioners returned children to court for failing to comply with the increasingly onerous conditions of their court orders, in turn feeding the growing custodial population (Hart, 2011).

More recently, the worst excesses of the punitive turn have abated. Since 2008 there has been a rediscovery of diversion: behaviour that would have resulted in a formal sanction is now more frequently diverted from the youth justice system. Levels of child imprisonment have also declined sharply (Bateman, 2017). ASSET has been replaced by **AssetPlus**, designed to balance risk alongside 'consideration of a young person's needs, goals and strengths' (Baker, 2014). The YJB (2018) has declared itself in favour of a 'child first, offender second' philosophy, a far cry from its vision four years earlier which endorsed a system where 'more offenders are held to account for their actions' (Youth Justice Board, 2014a: 4). Such developments mark something of a return of welfarist sentiments, although, at the current time, the degree to which practice at the local level has shifted to adopt this new ethos varies considerably (Smith and Gray, 2018). Nonetheless, they have prompted questions as to whether the YOT model continues to be most appropriate mechanism for youth justice services. Byrne and Brooks (2015), for instance, contend that New Labour's youth justice architecture is outdated and should be replaced by an integrated service for vulnerable young people. You can see here the beginning of a potential cycle: the delivery of youth justice interventions through integrated services would entail a re-blurring of the distinction between children who offend and those in need.

Table 30.3 Key Events: Changes to the Delivery of Youth Justice Services 1907-2019

Probation of Offenders Act 1907	Introduced probation as a statutory function to work primarily with young people in the justice system in the first instance
Children Act 1948	Established local authority children's departments, allowing youth justice to become largely a function of social work
Late 1970s	The establishment of juvenile justice teams, comprised of specialist social workers and youth workers, reflecting a shift from welfare to justice principles
Crime and Disorder Act 1998	The establishment of YOTs and the YJB, leading to the introduction of standardised youth justice assessments

---

Pause for Thought

What are the practical implications of adopting, as the YJB has done, a child first, offender second philosophy?

MEASURING, CONSTRUCTING AND RECONSTRUCTING YOUTH CRIME

By now you should appreciate that how youth crime is conceptualised impacts on the treatment of children who offend and how interventions are delivered. You will also know, from arguments rehearsed elsewhere in this volume, that criminologists frequently consider crime to be a social construct. Combining these two insights implies that conceptions of youth crime are also key to determining trends in Youth Offending.

The first step in the argument is straightforward. Victim surveys, such as the Crime Survey for England and Wales (CSEW), are regarded as the best measure of the volume of offending (Office for National Statistics, 2019) since they are not subject to variations in police practice, or levels of detection, but they tell us little about *youth* crime because they focus on the experiences of victims and offer no information on perpetrators. As a consequence, it is not possible to determine what proportion of the total volume of offending can be attributed to children. It is only possible to measure youth crime where it has been detected (Bateman, 2017).

Knowledge link: This topic is also covered in Chapter 4.

But this poses a problem since, as we have already seen, different approaches to children in trouble can lead to radically different practice in terms of whether particular children are diverted from, or channelled into, the youth justice system. Net-widening, for example, will lead to increases in the level of detected youth crime; conversely, diversionary approaches that substitute informal, or no action at all, for formal sanctions will give the impression that youth crime is falling (Bateman, 2015). We have already seen examples of these two processes from data in relation to the number of children convicted in the 1970s and 1980s respectively.

More recent statistics need to be interpreted through the same lens. In 2008, 124,744 children received a caution or conviction for an indictable offence; the equivalent figure in 2018 was 19,158 (Ministry of Justice/Youth Justice Board, 2019), a reduction of 84%. At least some of this decline is likely to reflect a genuine fall in the underlying level of children's lawbreaking: CSEW figures show that overall victimisation has fallen over the period, and measurements of other forms of children's problematic behaviour, such as drinking alcohol or taking drugs, indicate reducing levels of risk-taking and offending is prone to follow a similar trajectory (Bateman, 2017). But it seems highly unlikely that changes in children's behaviour could account for trends recorded in the official data. This is especially true given that the rapid contraction occurred immediately after a short-term, but sharp, rise as shown in Figure 30.1.

These abrupt oscillations are readily explained as consequences of changes in the treatment of children who break the law, in turn a manifestation of shifting approaches to Youth Offending. As noted above New Labour was inclined to a tough approach to law and order, and in 2002 established a target to increase the number of offences that received formal sanction by 250,000 by March 2008. Although the measure did not distinguish between youth and adult offending, it had a disproportionate impact on the former because children were previously more likely to receive an informal response from the police and therefore offered greater scope for a shift to formal outcomes. The target was met, in other words, by criminalising large numbers of children who would otherwise have been diverted (Morgan, 2009). It is this dynamic that is shown in the early years of the above chart.

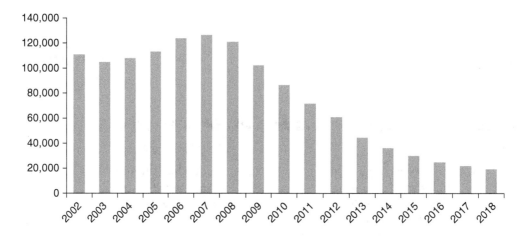

Figure 30.1 Detected Youth Crime: 2002-2018 (Indictable Offences)

By 2008, the punitive imperative that had characterised youth justice for more than a decade was largely spent and diversion once again became the preferred strategy. This about-turn was triggered by a new target that required a reduction in the number of children entering the youth justice system for the first time, so-called first-time entrants (FTEs), of 20% by 2020 (Home Office, 2008). The target was in fact met within one year and between 2008 and 2018 FTEs declined by 86% (Ministry of Justice/ Youth Justice Board, 2019). It is this fall that explains the downward trajectory shown in the latter part of Figure 30.1.

Again, you can see how changes in police practice would achieve this result: children who would previously have been cautioned or charged for low-level offending were no longer formally sanctioned. This process was facilitated by the introduction of a new range of disposals, most notable community resolutions, which did not constitute a criminal record and were not therefore counted as youth crimes (Youth Justice Board, 2014b).

———— Hear from the Expert ————

Because measuring youth crime is complex, researchers have to be cautious about how they talk about the trends displayed in crime statistics. I remember a few years ago being cited in a national newspaper as saying that the number of **'grave crimes'** committed by children had more than doubled, when that is not what I meant at all. What I had intended to say was that because the youth justice system had become more punitive, courts were more likely to regard offences as being serious than they had previously. As a result, the number of cases that were sent to the crown court, as grave crimes, had more than doubled.

Such complexities do not mean that researchers can say nothing about trends in youth crime. Rather we just need to be aware of the different dynamics that influence the figures for detected crime. Doing so allows us to explain why youth crime appears to rise and fall at different periods. For instance, government targets, as explained above, can have a significant impact on the police and other youth justice agencies which in turn can determine whether or not a particular piece of behaviour receives a formal response; whether it becomes a 'youth crime'.

In this final section, we have established that the way that youth crime is understood at any point in time, does not just influence how children in trouble are conceptualised and how they are treated. It can also help to determine how much youth crime there is. Moreover, the volume of youth crime is itself a factor that determines how society responds to youth justice issues. Where youth crime is seen to be rising, that might generate a more punitive environment for children who offend; conversely, when youth crime falls, society may become more tolerant of children's infractions of the law.

Pause for Thought

To what extent can the level of detected youth crime be explained by government policy?

CHAPTER SUMMARY

Let us recap what we have learned:

* The treatment of children in trouble is determined by how adolescent criminality is conceptualised in any period.
* We have seen that the most common typology involves contrasting welfare and justice models, although other conceptualisations, including the risk paradigm discussed above, are increasingly important.
* It is often assumed that a welfare approach will be associated with a more lenient treatment of children in trouble; while precepts of justice will lead to harsher responses, but this is an oversimplification. During the 1970s, welfarist sentiments tended to encourage net-widening and higher levels of child imprisonment; more recently, incipient welfarism has coincided with high levels of diversion.
* Equally, the justice model is consistent with a commitment to minimum intervention (as during the 1980s) as well as increasing levels of criminalisation (such as followed the punitive turn).
* Measuring youth crime is particularly problematic because classification depends upon the culprit being apprehended: youth crime is by definition *detected* youth crime.
* But figures for the latter only capture incidents that attract a formal youth justice disposal and whether this threshold is crossed depends upon a range of factors, including the nature of responses to youthful lawbreaking.
* Such responses may change rapidly, leading to abrupt fluctuations in the volume of Youth Offending. Youth crime will tend to fall when diversionary impulses are to the fore. Conversely, net-widening, where it occurs, will tend to be associated with increased Youth Offending.

Pause for Thought

Think back to the framing questions at the beginning of the chapter. Consider how you might answer each question on the basis of the above bullet points.

----------------------------- Review Questions -----------------------------

1. What are the differences between welfare and justice models of youth justice and the risk factor paradigm? What sorts of response to children in trouble does each imply?
2. Why has the MACR not risen for more than fifty years?
3. Is the Youth Offending team model outdated?
4. Is detected Youth Offending a reliable indicator for the level of children's lawbreaking?

GO FURTHER

Books

1. The following is a recent text focused on youth justice. It looks at the development of youth justice in England and Wales as a 'constructed reality':

    Case, S. (2021) *Youth Justice: A Critical Introduction*, 2nd edition. London: Routledge.

2. This second text provides a collection of chapters on different youth justice-related topics, by leading scholars in the field:

    Goldson, B. and Muncie, J. (eds) (2015) *Youth Crime and Justice,* 2nd edition. London: Sage.

3. A comprehensive overview of youth justice, within the context of wider criminological theory, is offered in:

    Muncie, J. (2021) *Youth and Crime,* 5th edition. London: Sage.

Journal Articles

1. The following article is a critique of the current low MACR in England and Wales:

    Arthur, R. (2012) Rethinking the criminal responsibility of young people in England and Wales. *European Journal of Crime, Criminal Law and Criminal Justice,* 20(1): 13–29.

2. This is a discussion of recent trends in youth justice, with an explanation of why detected youth crime is falling:

    Bateman, T. (2014) Where has all the youth crime gone? Youth justice in an Age of Austerity. *Children and Society,* 28(5): 416–424.

3. The following describes recent research into the divergent nature of youth justice practice across England:

    Smith, R. and Gray, P. (2018) The changing shape of youth justice: models of practice. *Criminology and Criminal Justice.* Available at: http://dx.doi.org/10.1177/1748895818781199

Useful Websites

1. *The National Association for Youth Justice*: https://thenayj.org.uk/. This is the website of a campaigning charity focused on youth justice issues. Reports include the State of youth justice 2020,

a comprehensive overview of recent trends and developments in England and Wales: https://thenayj.org.uk/cmsAdmin/uploads/state-of-youth-justice-2020-final-sept-(1).pdf

2. *The Alliance for Youth Justice*: https://www.ayj.org.uk/. This is the website of an umbrella organisation for charities with an interest in youth justice. You can sign up for a free monthly youth justice news bulletin here: https://www.ayj.org.uk/newsletter.

3. *The Youth Justice Board for England and Wales*: https://www.gov.uk/government/organisations/youth-justice-board-for-england-and-wales. This is the website of the arm's length non-governmental body created by the Crime and Disorder Act 1998. The site includes a youth justice resource hub which contains a range of relevant resources: https://yjresourcehub.uk/. The site also has a link to youth justice statistics which are published every year: https://www.gov.uk/government/statistics/youth-justice-statistics-2019-to-2020.

REFERENCES

Allen, R. (1991) Out of jail: The reduction in the use of penal custody for male juveniles 1981–1988. *Howard Journal of Criminal Justice*, 30(1): 30–52.

Arthur, R. (2010) *Young Offenders and the Law*. London: Routledge.

Baker, K. (2014) *AssetPlus Rationale*. London: Youth Justice Board.

Baker, K., Kelly, G. and Wilkinson, B. (2011) *Assessment in Youth Justice*. Bristol: Policy Press.

Bateman, T. (2012) *Criminalising Children for No Good Purpose: The Age of Criminal Responsibility in England and Wales*. London: National Association for Youth Justice.

Bateman, T. (2015) 'Trends in Detected Youth Crime and Contemporary State Responses'. In B. Goldson and J. Muncie (eds), *Youth Crime and Justice*, 2nd edition. London: Sage. pp. 67–82.

Bateman, T. (2017) *The State of Youth Justice: 2017*. London: National Association for Youth Justice.

Bateman, T. (2019) 'Responding to Youth Offending: Historical and Current Developments in Practice'. in P. Ugwudike, H. Graham, F. McNeill, P. Raynor, F. S. Taxman and C. Trotter (eds), *The Routledge Companion to Rehabilitative Work in Criminal Justice*. Abingdon: Routledge. pp. 718–728.

Bendalli, S. (2000) 'Children, Responsibility and the New Youth Justice'. In B. Goldson (ed.), *The New Youth Justice*. Lyme Regis: Russell House Publishing. pp. 81–95.

Bottoms, A. (2002) 'On the Decriminalisation of the English Juvenile Courts'. In J. Muncie, G. Hughes and E. McLaughlin (eds), *Youth Justice: Critical Readings*. London: Sage. pp. 216–227.

Bottoms, A. and Kemp, V. (2006) 'The Relationship between Youth Justice and Child Welfare in England and Wales'. In M. Hill, A. Lockyer and F. Stone (eds), *Youth Justice and Child Protection*. London: Jessica Kingsley. pp. 139–157.

Burman, M. and McVie, S. (2017) 'Scotland'. In S. H. Decker and N. Marteache (eds), *International Handbook of Juvenile Justice*, 2nd edition, Cham: Springer.

Bunn, S. and Brown, P. (2018) *Age of Criminal Responsibility*. Postnote number 577. London: Parliamentary Office for Science and Technology.

Byrne, B. and Brooks, K. (2015) *Post-YOT Youth Justice, What is Justice?* Working Papers 19/2015. London: Howard League.

Case, S. (2018) *Youth Justice: A Critical Introduction*. London: Sage.

Curtis, S. (2005) 'The Welfare Principle'. In T. Bateman and J. Pitts (eds), *The RHP Companion to Youth Justice*. Lyme Regis: Russell House Publishing. pp. 53–58.

Gelsthorpe, L. and Morris, A. (1994) 'Juvenile Justice 1945–1992'. In M. Maguire, R. Morgan and R. Reiner (eds), *The Oxford Handbook of Criminology*. Oxford: Oxford University Press. pp. 949–993.

Goldson, B. (2009) 'Difficult to understand or defend': a reasoned case for raising the age of criminal responsibility. *Howard Journal for Criminal Justice*, 48(5): 514–521.

Hart, D. (2011) *Into the Breach: The Enforcement of Statutory Orders in the Youth Justice System*. London: Prison Reform Trust.

Hazel, N. (2008) *Cross-national Comparison of Youth Justice*. London: YJB.

Hendrick, H. (2015) 'Histories of Youth Crime and Justice'. In B. Goldson and J. Muncie (eds), *Youth Crime and Justice*, 2nd edition. London: Sage, pp. 30–36.

Home Office (1997) *No More Excuses: A New Approach to Tackling Youth Crime in England and Wales*. London: Home Office.

Home Office (2008) *Youth Crime Action Plan*. London: Home Office.

McAra, L. (2010) 'Models of Youth Justice'. In D. Smith (ed.), *A New Response to Youth Crime*. Cullompton, Devon: Willan Publishing. pp. 287–317.

McAra, L. and McVie, S. (2015) 'The Case for Diversion and Minimum Necessary Intervention'. In B. Goldson and J. Muncie (eds), *Youth Crime and Justice*, 2nd edition. London: Sage. pp. 119–136.

Ministry of Justice (2019) *Criminal Justice Statistics Quarterly, England and Wales, Year ending December 2018*. London: MoJ.

Ministry of Justice/Youth Justice Board (2019) *Youth Justice Statistics: England and Wales*. London: MoJ.

Morgan, R. (2009) The quiet revolution: the rise and rise of out-of-court summary justice. *Criminal Justice Matters*, 75: 5–6.

Muncie, J. (2006) Governing young people: coherence and contradiction in contemporary youth justice. *Critical Social Policy*, 26(4): 770–793.

Muncie, J. (2008) The 'punitive turn' in juvenile justice: cultures of control and rights compliance in Western Europe and the USA. *Youth Justice*, 8(2): 107–121.

Muncie, J. (2015) *Youth and Crime*, 4th edition. London: Sage.

Office for National Statistics (2019) *Crime in England and Wales: year ending March 2019*. London: ONS.

Rutherford, A. (1992) *Growing out of crime: the new era*. 2nd edition. Winchester: Waterside Press.

Smith, R. and Gray, P. (2018) The changing shape of youth justice: models of practice. *Criminology and Criminal Justice*. Available at: http://dx.doi.org/10.1177/1748895818781199

Stack, J. A. (1979) Deterrence and reformation in early Victorian social policy: the case of Parkhurst Prison, 1838–1864. *Historical Reflections*, 6(2): 387–404.

Thorpe, D. H., Smith, D., Green, C. J. and Paley, J. H. (1980) *Out of Care: The Community Support of Juvenile Offenders*. London: George Allen and Unwin.

UN Committee on the Rights of the Child (2019) *Children's Rights in Child Justice Systems*. General Comment 37. Geneva: United Nations.

Vaswani, V., Dyer, F. and Lightowler, C. (2018) *What is Youth Justice? Reflections on the 1968 Act*. Glasgow: Centre for Youth and Criminal Justice.

Youth Justice Board (2014a) *YJB Corporate Plan 2014–17 and Business Plan 2014/15*. London: Youth Justice Board.

Youth Justice Board (2014b) *Youth Out-of-Court Disposals: Guide for Police and Youth Offending Services*. London: Youth Justice Board.

Youth Justice Board (2018) *Strategic Plan 2018–2021*. London: Youth Justice Board.

Victims, Witnesses and the Criminal Justice System

31

Pamela Davies and Ian R. Cook

--------- Learning Objectives ---------

After reading this chapter you will:

- Understand the challenges and implications of defining victims and witnesses.
- Be able to describe and explain the changing role of victims and witnesses within the criminal justice system in England and Wales.
- Be familiar with the support and assistance for victims and witnesses provided by the public and voluntary sectors.
- The journey of victims and witnesses through the criminal justice system.

--------- Framing Questions ---------

1. To what extent are victims and witnesses given a central role in the criminal justice system?
2. Do the special provisions for victims and witnesses ensure that they are treated fairly?
3. What are the problems with matching victims' services with victims' needs?

INTRODUCTION

Victims of crime and witnesses of crime have not always been a priority for those in the criminal justice system or academia. In different parts of the world, the criminal justice system has stood accused of treating both groups as a means to an end – a successful conviction – as well as compounding, causing or ignoring harms. Over many years, support has been limited for victims and witnesses with their needs rarely considered. Academics interested in crime, broadly defined, have not usually concentrated on the experiences of victims or witnesses. Indeed, victims are often peripheral figures within criminological accounts while witnesses are rarely mentioned.

Knowledge link: This topic is also covered in Chapter 3.

Things have arguably improved, however. More and more academics – many calling themselves 'victimologists' – have centred their work on victims and victimisation. Many criminology degrees now have victimology modules. The study of witnesses remains far patchier admittedly. Also, different criminal justice systems have introduced measures to support victims and witnesses, often alongside rhetoric that boasts of both groups being placed at the 'centre' or 'heart' of the criminal justice system. This shift within the criminal justice system is in part the result of the work of activist groups campaigning for the rights and needs of victims and (to a lesser extent, once more) witnesses.

This chapter examines the relationship between victims, witnesses and the criminal justice system. We explore two important themes. Under the first, we explore the evolving role of victims and witnesses in the criminal justice system in England and Wales. Under the second, we review public and voluntary sector support and assistance for victims and witnesses. To do this, we draw on academic research on victims and witnesses and use a variety of examples. The all-too-prevalent and stubborn cases of interpersonal violence problems of rape and domestic abuse are concentrated on. The next section opens the discussion by considering how victims and witnesses have been defined and what the implications of those definitions are. Next, we examine the evolving role of victims and witnesses in the criminal justice system in England and Wales and further afield. Following this, we critically consider the journeys of victims and witnesses through the criminal justice system, looking at three issues: **attrition** (i.e. cases dropping out), **secondary victimisation**, and through a case study of Victim Support, the provision of services by voluntary organisations.

MAPPING THE TERRAIN: CONCEPTUALISING VICTIMS AND WITNESSES

Defining and identifying victims of crime is not straightforward. Indeed, definitions of the term **victim** are controversial and range from a narrowly defined victim *of crime* to more expansive conceptualisations that are inclusive of those who have suffered harm and injustice. Walklate, for instance, provides an expansive definition, identifying a victim as 'an individual who has suffered some kind of misfortune' (2007: 27). Definitional issues are also considered in Chapters 3 and 27, and suffice to say here that the label 'victim' is often contested and struggled over.

One such struggle revolves around who *qualifies* as a victim. Many academic victimologists agree with the Norwegian criminologist Nils Christie (1986) who reasoned that the treatment of victims by the criminal justice system is often linked to whether they are deemed to qualify as an 'ideal victim' or not. **Ideal victims** are those who are most readily given the complete and legitimate status of being a victim. Such victims attract this status because they are perceived to be vulnerable, defenceless and clearly innocent. They are, therefore, worthy of a sympathetic and compassionate response including support and compensation. Many victimologists, nevertheless, are weary of the popular belief in the ideal victim, and the treatment of those who do not qualify.

Societal expectations about who qualifies as a victim, as well as how a victim should behave, can have very real consequences not only for victims but also for those called upon as witnesses. Close to Christie's notion of the ideal victim is Cole's (2007) concept of the 'true victim'. Cole argues that a true victim is a 'noble' victim who suffers in silence; they refrain from gathering sympathy or publicly displaying weakness. They command their own fate and do not exploit their injuries, and their victimisation must be immediate, concrete and without any doubt. Such expectations are especially problematic for those suffering harm where there are no third-party witnesses – for example, those who experience domestic abuse. Thus, taking the definitional and labelling controversy further, many feminists prefer to use the term *survivor* rather than victim (see following paragraph). From a feminist perspective, 'survivor' denotes a more active and positive image of women who overcome harmful experiences. This status challenges perceptions of the female victim as passive, helpless, powerless, blameworthy or victim-prone, and complements discussion about the negotiating and coping strategies women employ to live their daily lives.

Knowledge link: This topic is also covered in Chapter 8.

While criminologists have spent time thinking about who or what a victim is, few criminologists have considered who or what a **witness** is. The *Oxford Dictionary of English* provides some assistance, however. It defines 'witness' not only as a *noun* – 'a person who sees an event, typically a crime or an accident, take place' – but also as a *verb* – to 'see (an event, typically a crime or accident) happen'. The emphasis is on sight, hence the synonym 'eyewitness'. As with a victim, a witness is usually understood *relationally* – that is, in relation to the other people and things involved in the event(s).

The state has also sought to define a witness. The Crown Prosecution Service, for instance, defines a 'witness' as a person who stands up in court to state what they know after taking an oath to tell the truth (Crown Prosecution Service, 2017). Meanwhile, section 52 of the Domestic Violence, Crime and Victims Act 2004 also gives a comprehensive outline of who should qualify as a 'witness'. Central to this definition is the idea that witnesses are those who can assist in criminal proceedings.

Since the late 1990s, there has been an emphasis in England and Wales on identifying, and providing services for, a particular group of witnesses: Vulnerable and Intimidated Witnesses (VIMs). Following the Youth Justice and Criminal Evidence Act 1999, these two groups are eligible for 'special measures'. These allowances can include screens in the courtroom to prevent the defendant and the witness seeing each other, and allowing the defendant to give evidence via a live video link from somewhere outside the court room. In guidance from the Ministry of Justice (2011: 5), intimidated witnesses are defined as 'those whose quality of evidence is likely to be diminished by reason of fear or distress'. The guidance states that in determining whether a witness should be included in this category or not, the court should consider several issues:

Knowledge link: This topic is also covered in Chapter 26.

- The nature and alleged circumstances of the offence.
- The age of the witness.
- Where relevant:

  - the social and cultural background of the witness;
  - the domestic and employment circumstances of the witness;
  - any religious beliefs or political opinions of the witness.

- Any behaviour towards the witness by:

  - the accused;
  - members of the accused person's family or associates;
  - any other person who is likely to be either an accused person or a witness in the proceedings.

The guidelines, furthermore, list the following as vulnerable witnesses:

* Those under 18.
* Those who suffer from a mental disorder (as defined by the Mental Health Act 1983).
* Those who have a significant impairment of intelligence and social function.
* Those who have a physical disability or disorder.

Victims of sexual offences and human trafficking as well as witnesses of knife and gun offences are also entitled to special measures unless they wish to opt out. As we can see with the special measures for VIMs, qualification and classification as a particular type of witness and/or victim play an important role in shaping service provision in the criminal justice system and, potentially, in making experiences at court more bearable.

The criminal justice system relies on victims and witnesses in several ways, including reporting crimes and furnishing the police – often gatekeepers to the criminal justice system – with information to build evidence for a court case. However, not all victims and witnesses report incidents to the police for a variety of reasons as we know from successive sweeps of the British Crime Survey and more recently the Crime Survey for England and Wales. Thus, those 'on record' as victims and witnesses within the criminal justice system are only a small and distorted proportion of those suffering misfortune.

Pause for Thought

Definitions of 'victim' and 'witness' vary. Why is this and why does it matter?

Having considered definitional issues surrounding 'victims' and 'witnesses' we will now consider the role of these key players in the criminal justice system.

THE ROLE OF VICTIMS AND WITNESSES IN THE CRIMINAL JUSTICE SYSTEM

A commonplace critique of the criminal justice system in England and Wales is that it has marginalised victims and witnesses, taken them for granted, and given little attention to any rights or needs that they may have. This is not a new criticism. Indeed, Kearon and Godfrey (2007: 30) argue that victims of crime in the UK were disempowered in the 1840s, becoming 'less able to initiate prosecutions, or control the court process', with their role in court reduced to 'witnesses to a case brought in the *public interest'*. The conflict became one between the prosecution and the defendant, where the offence was committed against the Crown. In Christie's (1977) words, this involves 'stealing' the conflict from the victim. Rock (2007: 38) elaborates further on these ideas when he portrays the victim of crime as:

> the 'forgotten person' who appeared only as a witness, an applicant for compensation or a complainant or *alleged* victim until the conclusion of a trial. The prime conflict at law did not touch significantly on the victim: it was deemed to be between two parties only, the prosecution and the defendant, and the individual victim merely provided evidence of an offence that, for all practical purposes, was committed not so much against him or her but against the collectivity in the form of the Crown, the State or the community. Private wrongs were a matter for tort and civil procedure[.]

Given the functional importance of crime victims to the operation of the criminal justice system in England and Wales, and their crucial role in providing evidence, it is perhaps surprising that it was not until the post-war period that the first significant mechanisms were introduced to support direct victims. This began with the introduction of a criminal injuries compensation scheme in 1964 whereby selected victims could – and still can – claim financial compensation from the state. Its website announces that 'we can compensate blameless victims of violent crime, or people whose loved ones have died as a result of violent crime'. Requiring 'blameless' applicants to have reported the crime to the police, the scheme adds extra characteristics – of responsibility and dutifulness – to Christie's notion of the ideal victim.

Since 1964 there have been numerous developments and alterations in the provision of support and assistance for victims of crime. Some of these are listed in the next section (in Table 31.1). The state's increased focus on the needs of the victims corresponds with the emergence of a victims' movement in the UK and other parts of the world during the latter part of the twentieth century. This movement was in reaction to the marginalisation of victims in the criminal justice system and, in part, recognition of the under-reporting of victimisation. The victims' movement also corresponded with, and blurred with, the 'second wave' feminist movement. The latter raised awareness of the victimisation of women in the home and of women's experiences of sexual violence and campaigned for such violence to be recognised by the criminal justice system and society more widely. England and Wales have not been alone as these movements also gathered pace elsewhere. As Sebba (2001: 36) notes, lobbying by feminists and organisations devoted to victim assistance was:

> instrumental in the intensive barrage of victim-related legislation and policy reform which were insti-
> gated in the 1980s and 1990s [...] and included the granting of procedural rights to victims in the course
> of the trial process (and subsequent proceedings), victim-oriented sentencing dispositions such as resti-
> tution, the introduction of state compensation boards and victim assistance programmes.

Supportive provisions and victim assistance schemes are now provided in most jurisdictions across the world, all of which have differing relationships to their respective criminal justice systems. Some victim services are at arm's length from, or fully independent of, the government, some are provided under statute, and some are run by voluntary groups and charities. How victims access and experience these supportive provisions is explored in the next section.

Focusing predominately on the UK, both Kearon and Godfrey (2007) and Rock (2007) demonstrate that the victim has in effect been reinvented as a witness or, worse still, a tool of the criminal justice system. That being said, Fyfe (2005: 514) reminds us that victims rather than witnesses became the primary focus of the early reforms:

> [D]espite the incontrovertible importance of witnesses, their role in the criminal justice system has,
> until recently, largely been taken for granted. Witnesses were rarely given any preparation or assistance
> in relation to their appearance at court, despite the fact that giving evidence in court and being cross-
> examined can be intimidating and distressing experiences. Moreover, they frequently had to endure long
> waiting periods in court buildings where they risked encounters with the accused and their supporters.
> Nevertheless, the concerns of witnesses were largely invisible to policy-makers. Unlike victims, who
> were gradually becoming recognised as needing and deserving government assistance, witnesses had
> not achieved the same status.

In bringing this section on the role of victims and witnesses in the criminal justice system to a close we introduce the concept of 'procedural justice'. We do so in order to consider whose interests are being served and supported as the role of victims and witnesses changes and as support and assistance have evolved. Simply put, procedural justice equates to fair treatment. Procedural justice emphasises the fairness of the process by which decisions are made (Elliott et al., 2014). In the following sections, we review the extent to which support and provisions are introduced and adapted to meet the wants and needs of victims and witnesses. We also consider how these same developments can be seen rather differently, not as primarily in the interests of victims and witnesses but as efficiency measures designed to improve the smooth running of the criminal justice system and please the voting public. Our review of developments, therefore, highlights a shift from activist to market-driven services and support (Hall, 2020).

EVOLVING SUPPORT AND ASSISTANCE FOR VICTIMS AND WITNESSES OF CRIME

As noted above, the criminal justice system in England and Wales – echoing most of its counterparts in other parts of the world – has traditionally shown scant regard for the needs of victims and witnesses of crime. However, many changes have been introduced aimed at 'rebalancing' the system. Criminal justice policies in different countries have been mobilised to bring the victim and witness (more) centre stage with new policies introduced and old ones repackaged accompanied by claims that they meet the needs and rights of victims and witnesses. However, the 'rights' of the victim in penal procedure in common law countries such as England and Wales, Australia, Canada, New Zealand and most of the USA, are largely limited to that of witness for the prosecution, though changes have recently seen the granting of participatory rights for crime victims as part of a concerted endeavour to bring the victim to the forefront. Some of the changes made in recent years, such as the measures to protect witnesses in court, seem to have improved the victims' position, yet victimological commentators remain sceptical about the extent to which policies advocated in the name of the victim are a good thing (Davies, 2015).

Entitling Victims and Witnesses

As Table 31.1 shows, a series of changes in the criminal justice system have taken place in England and Wales repositioning the victim and the witness in recent decades. A key development, and a catalyst for further changes, was the publication of the *Victims Charter: A Statement of the Rights of Victims of Crime* (Home Office, 1990). It claimed to set out for the first time the entitlements and rights of victims of crime. A revised version was published by the Home Office six years later in 1996. Its new subtitle – *A Statement of Service Standards for Victims of Crime* – gave a more realistic summary of the actual contents. The vocabulary used had shifted from 'rights' to 'service standards'. Nevertheless, the introduction of the Victims Charter was a key landmark development which acknowledged the importance of the victim in securing justice.

The Victims Charter was revised several times throughout the 2000s before becoming the *Code of Practice for Victims of Crime*. The latest version at the time of writing – from 2015 – takes the form of a 104-page document comprising twenty entitlements for victims of crime. To comply with the Victims' Rights Directive of the European Union (that Member States had to adhere to from 2015), the 2015 Code broadened its focus away from only victims of 'recordable' offences (Hall, 2017). Entitlements in the 2015 Code include: being informed about certain developments in the police investigation (e.g. when a suspect is arrested and charged and any bail conditions imposed); the option of a court familiarisation visit; and the ability to enter court through a different entrance from the suspect and sit in a separate waiting area where possible. As the case study below highlights, victims also have certain entitlements to write and potentially read out a Victim Personal Statement in court. The language of the *Code of Practice for Victims of Crime* is revealing, however, with the words 'entitled' and 'entitlements' appearing continually throughout the document, with far less references to 'duties' and 'duty'. If we take the Victims Code as an approximate indicator of the current state of victim-oriented policy, rights-based vocabularies remain noticeably absent.

Table 31.1 Important Developments in Support and Assistance for Victims and Witnesses of Crime in England and Wales

Date	Development
1964	Criminal Injuries Compensation Board set up to administer Criminal Injuries Compensation Scheme (CICS) for victims of violent crime
1972	First UK Women's Aid refuge set up in Chiswick, London
1974	First Victim Support project set up in Bristol
1976	First UK Rape Crisis Centre opened in London
1986	Childline established
1987	First Home Office funding for Victim Support
1989	Victim Support launched the first victim/witness in court project
1990	Home Office Victims' Charter published
1991	Home Office fund Victim Support's Crown Court Witness Service
1996	Victims' Charter (revised 2nd edition) published
1999	Home Office funding to establish the Witness Service in Magistrates' Courts
2001	Victim Personal Statements (VPS) introduced
2003	Victim Support provides a Witness Service in all criminal courts
2005	*The Code of Practice for Victims of Crime* published
2007	The Witness Charter published
2015	Revised *Code of Practice for Victims of Crime* published and the rolling out by the European Union of new rules setting out binding rights for victims that Member States are obliged to adhere to

Case Study 31.1

Key Development: Victim Personal Statements

Introduced by the New Labour government in 2001, the Victim Personal Statement appeared in the *Code of Practice for Victims of Crime* for the first time in 2013 (Hall, 2017). Their role is summarised in the 2015 version:

A Victim Personal Statement (VPS) gives you an opportunity to explain in your own words how a crime has affected you, whether physically, emotionally, financially or in any other way. This is different from a witness statement about what happened at the time, such as what you saw or heard. The VPS gives you a **voice** in the criminal justice process. However, you may not express your opinion on the sentence or punishment the suspect should receive as this is for the court to decide (Ministry of Justice, 2015: 21, bold in original).

(Continued)

Often termed 'Victim Impact Statements' in other jurisdictions, they originated in California in 1976 and have become one of many criminal justice policies that have circulated internationally (McMenzie et al., 2019). They are available to victims in several jurisdictions, especially those with common law such as Aotearoa New Zealand, Australia, Canada, Northern Ireland and Scotland. In England and Wales, victims are eligible to make a statement at any time prior to sentencing, and should a suspect be found guilty, they can request that it is read aloud or played in court before a decision on the sentencing is reached. The victim is able to decide if they want to read it aloud themselves or have someone else read it on their behalf, while the judge or magistrate is allowed to take this into account when determining the sentence.

There have been concerns about the low numbers of people who are actually offered (and have written) a VPS in England and Wales (Hall, 2017). Equally, questions have been raised in different parts of the world about the effect of the VPS on the objectivity of the court, unnecessarily raising the expectations of victims, and statements leading to harsher sentences (O'Connell, 2016). Nevertheless, the VPS has been praised for giving the victim 'a voice' in the courtroom (beyond their role as a witness), reducing their feelings of helplessness, and improving their confidence in the criminal justice system (O'Connell, 2016).

Pause for Thought

If you were a victim of crime and had reported it to the police, would you write a Victim Personal Statement? If so, would you read it aloud in court? Would your answers to these questions depend on the type of victimisation you experienced?

Service provision for witnesses in England and Wales has lagged behind those of victims. This is best illustrated by the development of the first Witness Charter seventeen years after the original Victims Charter. The original Witness Charter (Office for Criminal Justice Reform, 2007) outlines thirty-four 'standards of care', informing both defence and prosecution witnesses of what they should expect from the different criminal justice agencies and from lawyers involved in the case. These were reduced and revised into twenty-one standards of care in the 2013 version (Ministry of Justice, 2013b). Notably, none of these standards of care mention witness protection. As Case Study 31.2 demonstrates, witness protection is an important – and necessarily secretive – element of the state's services for selected witnesses of crime.

Case Study 31.2

Key Provision: Witness Protection

There is little public knowledge about witness protection in the UK. This is no surprise given the secrecy surrounding it. What we can be clear on is that the Metropolitan Police created the UK's first Witness Protection Unit in 1978 and similar schemes elsewhere were subsequently established. Since 2013 these have been orchestrated by the UK Protected Persons Service (UKPPS) which sits within the National Crime Agency. According to their website, the UKPPS has a remit to provide 'protection to people judged to be at risk of serious harm where the protection arrangements required by the individual are not available to the local police force or referring agency'.

Witness protection is not mentioned in the 2013 Witness Charter. The UKPPS website states that the protection provided is bespoke, and from the outside, protection seems to centre around the resettlement of those at risk of serious harm. As one anonymised official working in witness protection interviewed on a 2015 edition of *Newsnight* (2015) noted, 'our best tool [...] is miles on a map. So if you lived in Dover, we could look at somewhere miles and miles away'.

The UKPPS is often promoted as being a tool in the 'fight' against organised crime. Here, it is seen as a means of providing more willing and less intimidated witnesses for the prosecution which could increase conviction rates. Interviewed in *The Independent* (2010, n.p.), the head of the Greater Manchester Witness Protection Unit – named only as Kim – said:

> For some people it is positive experience. Some people have had their lives blighted by crime or have spent their lives involved in criminality. Those people can see it as an opportunity for a fresh start with people who can advise them in how to turn their lives around.

Yet Kim also acknowledges that it 'can be very traumatic for people'. Indeed, this chimes with Fyfe and McKay's (2000: 88) assessment that witness protection is 'a profoundly disorienting and destabilizing personal experience'. Through their research as well as reports in the media, those on witness protection have aired concerns about their safety, the difficulties of breaking social ties, and the challenges of maintaining a new identity. One participant, 'Rachel', interviewed in the *Guardian*, reasoned that 'I feel like a fraud every day [...] My name is not my name. I cannot tell anybody. I have nothing to fall back on. I live in shock' (Booth, 2018: n.p.). Like Rachel, there have been other service users who have been critical of the management of witness protection, with criticism of the information about the scheme given to them before participating and the services subsequently provided for them (see also *File on 4*, 2012).

Pause for Thought

What are the pros and cons of participating in witness protection? Do the positives outweigh the negatives?

Justice for Victims and Witnesses?

Restorative justice is now available to many victims of crime in England and Wales. Although it is notoriously difficult to define, in the context of support for victims of crime, restorative justice can be viewed as a process of dialogue between victim and offender, in which the victim describes their feelings about the crime and the harm caused as a result, and from this they both develop a plan to repair the harm done. Unlike many other criminal justice mechanisms, it 'gives victims a voice'. As the 2015 Victims Code outlines, all victims are entitled to receive information on restorative justice and it is potentially available to all victims of crime at all stages of the criminal justice process, although there are local differences in service provision. While it is technically available for all victims, there is controversy around its use for certain offences including domestic violence, sexual assault and hate crime.

Despite progressive moves such as the introduction of restorative justice, it seems that victims and witnesses of crime in England and Wales continue to occupy a position defined by their perceived need rather than by any notion of rights (Goodey, 2005). Significantly, the various incarnations of the Witness Charter and the Victims Code cement procedural justice. They give neither witnesses nor victims 'enforceable rights, but merely permits them to complain if the service obligations are not met' (Wolhuter et al., 2009: 5). Thus, in bringing this section on the evolving support and assistance for victims and witnesses of crime to a close, we return to the concept of procedural justice to summarise how the provisions that have emerged over the last half a century or so might be interpreted from a victim/witness perspective. The rhetoric and language of 'entitlements', the concerns with giving victims a voice and treating victims and witnesses with respect and dignity, seem to amount to what Elliott and colleagues (2014: 590) term the 'relational criteria' of procedural justice. That is:

> politeness, concern for rights, treatment with dignity and respect, expression and consideration of views, neutrality of decision-making process, addressing needs and concerns, doing the right thing by the victim, explanation of reasons for police actions, and police trustworthiness.

Such justice is not rights-based justice as such, but one conceived in terms of a more limited *procedural fairness*.

EXPERIENCING THE CRIMINAL JUSTICE SYSTEM

With the developments above in mind, how do victims and witnesses experience the criminal justice system in England and Wales? There is no homogeneous experience; every victim and witness is different as are their interactions and perceptions of the criminal justice system. That said, both the Victims Code and Witness Charter attempt to capture a typical 'journey' through the criminal justice system so as to provide clarity to victims and witnesses. The Victims Code (Ministry of Justice, 2015) suggests there are five stages that victims will encounter if their case goes to court: reporting the crime; police investigation; charge and pre-trial hearings; trial; and after the trial. In a similar fashion, the Witness Charter (Ministry of Justice, 2013a) is structured according to a journey a witness might take through the criminal justice system, focusing on the police investigation, pre-trial arrangements, arriving at the courtroom, speaking in court, and post-trial. A close reading of both documents, however, show the journeys of victims and witnesses are not homogeneous: there are exit points along the way, and there is the availability of special entitlements for certain groups such as vulnerable and intimidated witnesses.

Other factors, some of which are related to the defining of victims and witnesses (as noted earlier) and their respective roles in the criminal justice system, contribute to these differential experiences. We now explore two issues that affect the journeys of many victims and witnesses through the criminal justice system. Both are under-acknowledged within the Witness Charter and Victims Code. They are the processes of attrition and secondary victimisation.

Attrition

Attrition in criminal justice refers to the 'drop out' of cases. In rape cases, attrition is stubbornly problematic. Hester (2013) notes that rape cases can drop out at any one of three stages: at police involvement and investigation, during CPS involvement, or at court. Her research into rape cases and the criminal justice system in the North East of England found that three quarters of the cases dropped out at the police stage, with many of these involving very vulnerable victims such as those with extensive mental health problems. Measures to protect rape victims in court (who fall into the 'vulnerable victim' category) seem to be having little impact on the attrition rate for rape victims. Perceptions of the 'credible' ideal victim on the one hand, and 'non-credible' culpable victim who 'precipitated' their rape on the other, appear firmly entrenched and reinforced by so-called 'rape myths'. Rape myths are commonly held beliefs about rape that are ill-informed and misconceived. Such myths suggest that women: lie about rape and make false allegations; want, enjoy and provoke rape; can prevent rape; should put up a fight and show signs of struggle; sustain genital injuries; and are less traumatised by rape by a non-stranger. More broadly, concerns remain about the impact of special measures in relation to all crime types on attrition rates, and 'victim blaming' attitudes continue to thrive in the criminal justice system in England and Wales.

Secondary Victimisation

Secondary victimisation refers to the further harm caused to victims of crime as a direct result of their participation in the criminal justice system. It is often emotional or psychological, and is not necessarily a deliberate act. As noted by Wolhuter et al. (2009: 47), it can take several forms including insensitive questioning, poor communications, and the cross-examination process.

On the one hand, it is clear that the Witness Charter and the Victims Code try to encourage practices by criminal justice practitioners and agencies that limit secondary victimisation for victim-witnesses, even if they do not use the phrase 'secondary victimisation'. On the other hand, scholars have argued that there are systematic faults with the criminal justice system that create the conditions for secondary victimisation to take place. Wolhuter et al. (2009), for example, point to two systemic problems. The first is the 'institutional culture' of criminal justice agencies that combine a 'crime-control focus on "catching criminals" or obtaining convictions' with some prejudices and stereotypes towards marginalised groups in society, meaning that the needs of victims and witnesses are sidelined, especially those from certain parts of society (2009: 48). The second is the common law adversarial system that repositions the victim as a witness and views the crime as a crime against the state rather than against the victim. This system uses the principle of orality whereby all evidence must be produced in court and it must be orally introduced (Goodey, 2005). Under this system, the courtroom can be particularly difficult for victims and witnesses:

> During the trial itself the English adversarial process involves a contest between the prosecution and the defence in which cross-examination is the primary weapon. Defence counsel resort to tactics under cross-examination designed to undermine the prosecution or attack the credibility of the witness. This experience of cross-examination has been regarded as one of the more traumatic forms of secondary victimisation, particularly in rape trials[.] (Wolhuter et al., 2009: 48)

Taking the example of rape, victims and witnesses are often known to one another and there are usually no bystanders or independent witnesses, and their status as victim/witness/perpetrator becomes indistinct and blurred to magistrates, jury and judge in a court of law rendering victimhood difficult to prove. Often the victim is the sole witness. Scholars have highlighted how defence lawyers in the adversarial system use aggressive questioning in order to expose 'untruths' in a victim's testimony, and often call into question the victim's lack of consent to sex by referencing past sexual behaviours (Lees, 1997; see also Rock, 1991). Though the witness is entitled to be treated with dignity and respect under the Victims Code and the Witness Charter, the criminal justice system in England and Wales also acknowledges the rights of the defendant to a fair trial. This is sometimes represented as a balancing act between the rights of the victim and those of the accused (Goodey, 2005). In these scenarios, victims may fail to meet the ideal victim criteria and risk being discredited as non-credible witnesses and undeserving victims. The common law adversarial approach to criminal justice has tended to adopt the 'ideal victim' and a similar 'ideal witness' approach to testimony in court.

Pause for Thought

- When does being a victim and being a witness overlap?
- What issues might this raise in the journey through the criminal justice system?

VICTIMS, WITNESSES AND THE PROVISION OF SERVICES BY THE VOLUNTARY SECTOR

Recent decades have witnessed the increasing involvement of a range of voluntary organisations in the provision of services and support for victims and witnesses of crime in England and Wales. This shift echoes the development of services for victims and (less so) witnesses by the voluntary sector in other countries. Voluntary organisations such as Victim Support, Childline and Rape Crisis are important providers of support for victims and witnesses in England and Wales, operating not-for-profit, staffed predominately with volunteers, and given varying degrees of support and funding from state bodies.

In this section, we explore the work of Victim Support (VS) in England and Wales, how it has changed over the years, and how it became politicised. VS was initially set up in Bristol in 1974, and by the early 1980s it had become an extensive network of local schemes across England and Wales with a central headquarters in London (Simmonds, 2013). Reacting against a void in dedicated victim services, VS focused their energies on using volunteers to visit victims of crime. 'Their role', as Simmonds (2013: 203) notes, 'was to offer emotional support and practical assistance within a few days of the crime occurring – in other words they provided an outreach service offering crisis intervention'.

Though a charity, VS was long funded through government grants. In the financial year 2013/14, for instance, its income was £50.2 million of which £39.4m was from the Ministry of Justice (Victim Support, 2014): 1987 was a landmark year here as this was when central government started to provide significant funds for VS (Hall, 2017). VS was appealing to the Conservative administration at the time and their successors as, among other things, they shared a belief in creating 'active citizens' who would help each other (Wolhuter et al., 2009).

VS has changed considerably since its inception. Three changes are worth noting. The first is its movement away from focusing on victims of burglaries in its early years – due in part to the police's reluctance to refer more serious crimes to a volunteer-dominated organisation (Simmonds, 2013) – towards the delivery of services for a range of victims and witnesses of all types of crime. With regard to victim services, emphasis has remained on providing emotional support and practical help for victims of crime, irrespective of their age or whether the crime has been reported or not. Well into the twenty-first century, they continue to provide 'the sticking plaster for many victims in the aftermath of crime' (Goodey, 2005: 104).

A second key change was the incorporation of services for witnesses of crime. Between 1989 and 2015 VS delivered the Witness Service, piloted first in selected Crown Courts then extended to all criminal courts in England and Wales by 2003. VS provided emotional support and practical help for prosecution and defence witnesses as well as their family and friends (Wolhuter et al., 2009), with the aim of making the experience of being in court less daunting and confusing. As part of this, they arranged pre-trial courtroom tours, supported witnesses during the trial, and provided witnesses with private waiting areas in court.

The third change is their recent reduced involvement in service provision for victims and witnesses. This change stems largely from a fundamental shift, beginning in the mid-2010s, in the allocation of public money for victim and witness services. As part of this, services were categorised as being national or local. Nationally, the Ministry of Justice commissioned a witness service, a homicide service, support for victims of human trafficking, and support for victims of rape through rape support centres. Locally, the elected Police and Crime Commissioners (PCCs) were given the responsibility to award contracts for other victim services within their constituencies. The message from central government was clear: services for victims should be economically competitive and, in many instances, decided locally (Hall, 2018). The repercussions for VS were significant. Their preferential status began to slip as, while they continue to deliver victims services in many PCC areas, in others they have been replaced by other (often voluntary) organisations. Furthermore, nationally they are no longer publicly funded to deliver services for witnesses. As of April 2015, Citizens Advice – another voluntary organisation – is now running the Witness Service.

Despite all these changes, voluntary organisations including VS continue to play an important role in delivering services for victims and witnesses. However, as we can see with the example of VS, their services, funding and relationship with government are subject to continued transformation within an increasingly competitive environment. While the local flexibility and accountability might be something to celebrate, questions remain about whether a disintegrated and increasingly neo-liberal service market is the way forward. Hall (2020) also provides food for thought when he notes that 'on the whole larger charities still tend to dominate this new "marketplace" of supply for victim services and thus we are far from a return to the more activist-based support base for victims of crime seen before the rise of Victim Support as a national "preferred supplier"'.

The above review of service provisions emanating from the voluntary sector rounds off our broader review of victims, witnesses and the criminal justice system. We will now summarise the key issues and arguments made across this chapter.

CHAPTER SUMMARY

- Within criminology, there has been increased attention paid to the experiences of victims and (less so) witnesses of crime.
- The act of defining victims and witnesses influences how they are treated by the criminal justice system.
- We can point towards several positive developments regarding the treatment of victims in the criminal justice process such as the increased availability of restorative justice to many victims of crime in England and Wales.
- A question remains as to whether the state in England and Wales has provided victims and witnesses with meaningful rights.
- Service provision and protections for witnesses in England and Wales have lagged behind those of victims.
- Service provision for victims and witnesses in England and Wales has become increasingly market-driven and less activist-driven in recent years.
- Voluntary organisations such as VS play an important role in delivering services for victims and witnesses.
- In their journey through the criminal justice system, some victims may experience secondary victimisation.
- For some crime types including serious form of interpersonal violence and abuse, there are stubbornly high attrition rates.

Review Questions

1. What policies to support victims and witnesses have been introduced in England and Wales since the 1980s? Have policy makers done enough to meet the needs of victims and witnesses of crime?
2. How and why has the development of services and support for witnesses seemingly lagged behind those for victims in England and Wales?

FURTHER READING

Books

1. This is a student-friendly, accessible introduction to the study of victims and victimology. As an edited collection, it introduces the key perspectives and debates via contributions from many of the key scholars in the field:

   Davies, P., Francis, P. and Greer, C. (2017) (eds) *Victims, Crime and Society: An Introduction*, 2nd edition. London: Sage.

2. This edited collection is for those wanting to extend their reading on victimisation. It pays close attention to the role of social difference within victimisation and the responses to victimisation by the criminal justice system:

   Walklate, S. (ed.) (2018) *Handbook of Victims and Victimology*, 2nd edition. London: Routledge.

3. This is well-written textbook that examines the subjects and experiences of victimisation, the theoretical debates within victimology, and the service delivery for victims of crime:

   Wolhuter, L., Olley, N. and Denham, D. (2009) *Victimology: Victimisation and Victims' Rights*. London: Routledge-Cavendish.

Journal Articles

1. This article traces the history of present-day court culture thereby contextualising the difficulties of engaging victims, witnesses and defendants in the criminal courts:

   Kirby, A. (2017) Effectively engaging victims, witnesses and defendants in the criminal courts: a question of 'court culture'? *Criminal Law Review*, 12(12): 949–968.

2. Paul Rock provides a compelling account of the position of witnesses in the courtroom. While it was written prior to the introduction of the Witness Charter, it makes us wonder whether the experience of witnesses in court remains much the same:

   Rock, P. (1991) Witnesses and space in a Crown Court. *British Journal of Criminology*, 31(3): 266–279.

3. In this article, the geographer Nick Fyfe provides a fascinating analysis of the experiences of intimidated witnesses and the measures designed to reduce their vulnerability:

   Fyfe, N. (2005) Space, time and the vulnerable witness: exploring the tensions between policy and personal perspectives on witness intimidation. *Population, Space and Place*, 11(6): 513–523.

Useful Websites

1. This following website provides useful information on what victims and witnesses can expect at different stages of the criminal justice system in England and Wales. This ranges from the reporting of a crime to after a trial. It also provides access to resources such as the latest versions of the Victims Code and Witness Charter and information on compensation offered to victims of crime: www.victimandwitnessinformation.org.uk/

2. Victim Support is an independent charity that supports people affected by crime or traumatic events, aiming to provide the support they need and the respect they deserve: www.victimsupport.org.uk

3. The World Society of Victimology is an international resource and platform for academics, scholars and practitioners. Its website has useful links to related websites in several countries: www.worldsocietyofvictimology.org

REFERENCES

Booth, R. (2018) 'Police have ruined my life, says woman living in witness protection', *Guardian*, 12 May.

Christie, N. (1986) 'The Ideal Victim'. In E. A. Fattah (ed.), *From Crime Policy to Victim Policy*. London: Macmillan. pp. 17–30.

Christie, N. (1977) Conflicts as property. *British Journal of Criminology*, 17(1): 1–15.

Cole, A. (2007) *The Cult of True Victimhood*. Stanford, CA: Stanford University Press.

Crown Prosecution Service (2017) https://www.cps.gov.uk/victims-witnesses (accessed 13.01.2020).

Davies, P. (2015) Victims: continuing to carry the burden of justice. *British Society of Criminology Newsletter*, 76: 16–17.

Elliot, I., Thomas, S. and Ogloff, J. (2014) Procedural justice in victim-police interactions and victims' recovery from victimisation experiences. *Policing and Society*, 24(5): 588–601.

File on 4 (2012) BBC Radio 4, 1 April.

Fyfe, N. (2005) Space, time and the vulnerable witness: exploring the tensions between policy and personal perspectives on witness intimidation. *Population, Space and Place*, 11(6): 513–523.

Fyfe, N. and McKay, H. (2000) Witness intimidation, forced migration and resettlement: a British case study. *Transactions of the Institute of British Geographers*, 25(1): 77–90.

Goodey, J. (2005) *Victims and Victimology: Research, Policy and Practice*. Harlow: Pearson.

Hall, M. (2017) *Victims of Crime: Construction, Governance and Policy*. Basingstoke: Palgrave Macmillan.

Hall, M. (2020) 'Police and Crime Commissioners and Victim Service Commissioning: From Activism to Marketisation?' In J. Tapley and P. Davies (eds), *Victimology: Research, Policy and Activism*. London: Palgrave.

Hester, M. (2013) *From Report to Court: Rape Cases and the Criminal Justice System in the North East Executive Summary*. Bristol: University of Bristol.

Home Office (1990) *The Victims Charter: A Statement of Rights for Victims of Crime*. London: Home Office.

Home Office (1996) *Victims Charter: A Statement of Service Standards for Victims of Crime*. London: Home Office.

Independent (2010) 'Special report: Life in witness protection', *The Independent*, 10 September.

Kearon, T. and Godfrey, B. S. (2007) 'Setting the Scene: A Question of History'. In S. Walklate (ed.), *Handbook of Victims and Victimology*. Cullompton, Devon: Willan Publishing. pp. 17–36.

Lees, S. (1997) *Ruling Passions: Sexual Violence, Reputation and the Law*. Buckingham: Open University Press.

McMenzie, L., Cook, I. R. and Laing, M. (2019) Criminological policy mobilities: understanding the movement of the 'Swedish model' to Northern Ireland. *British Journal of Criminology*, 59(5): 1199–1216.

Ministry of Justice (2011) *Achieving Best Evidence in Criminal Proceedings: Guidance on Interviewing Victims and Witnesses, and Guidance on Using Special Measures*. London: Ministry of Justice.

Ministry of Justice (2013a) *Code of Practice for Victims of Crime*. London: Ministry of Justice.

Ministry of Justice (2013b) *The Witness Charter: Standards of Care for Witnesses in the Criminal Justice System*. London: Ministry of Justice.

Ministry of Justice (2015) *Code of Practice for Victims of Crime*. London: Ministry of Justice.

Newsnight (2015) BBC Two Television, 14 August.

O'Connell, M. (2016) 'Victim Impact Statements'. In K. Corteen, S. Morley, P. Taylor and J. Turner (eds), *A Companion to Crime, Harm and Victimisation*. Bristol: Policy Press. pp. 245–247.

Office of Criminal Justice Reform (2005) *The Code of Practice for Victims of Crime*. London: Office of Criminal Justice Reform.

Office of Criminal Justice Reform (2007) *The Witness Charter: Our Promise to You*. London: Office of Criminal Justice Reform.

Rock, P. (1991) Witnesses and space in a Crown Court. *British Journal of Criminology*, 31(3): 266–279.

Rock, P. (2007) 'Theoretical Perspectives on Victimisation'. In S. Walklate (ed.), *Handbook of Victims and Victimology*. Cullompton: Willan. pp. 37–61.

Sebba, L. (2001) On the relationship between criminological research and policy: the case of crime victims. *Criminal Justice*, 1(1): 27–58.

Simmonds, L. (2013) Lost in transition? The changing face of Victim Support. *International Review of Victimology*, 19(2): 201–217.

Victim Support (2014) *Trustees' Annual Report 2013/14*. London: Victim Support.

Walklate, S. (2007) *Imagining the Victims of Crime*. Maidenhead: Open University Press.

Wolhuter, L., Olley, N. and Denham, D. (2009) *Victimology: Victimisation and Victims' Rights*. London: Routledge-Cavendish.

PART V

BECOMING A CRIMINOLOGIST

Being a Criminologist and Doing Real World Criminological Research

32

Jamie Harding

─────────────── Learning Objectives ───────────────

After reading this chapter you will be able to:

- Choose an appropriate research question for a study.
- Make an informed choice between quantitative, qualitative and mixed methods approaches to research (as appropriate to your research question).
- Put into practice appropriate methods of sampling and data collection.
- Identify the form of data analysis that is likely to be most appropriate.
- Identify the ethical challenges presented by a research project and the most appropriate steps to meet these challenges.

─────────────── Framing Questions ───────────────

1. How can I choose a research question that it is feasible for me to answer?
2. What are the big decisions that I need to make about methodology before considering the practical questions?
3. What are the advantages and disadvantages of different forms of data collection?
4. What do I do with my data once I have collected it?
5. How do I conduct research in an ethical manner?

INTRODUCTION

If you have been following the chapters in this text chronologically you will have become very familiar with what it is to be a criminologist, the research topics and questions that we are interested in, and the vast variety of research that falls within the scope of criminological inquiry. Research methods are crucial to our understanding of crime and matters associated with it. This chapter will help you both to conduct your own research, should you have the opportunity to do so, and to evaluate the claims made by others about their studies. You will be taken through the main stages of a research project, beginning with your choice of research question followed by major decisions that must be made about the methodological approach, then considering practical questions such as how to collect the data and who to collect it from, and finally the options that are available for analysing the data.

MAPPING THE TERRAIN

Researching the social world is central to the discipline of criminology and social science research skills are critical for any criminology student. Good, robust, methodologically and ethically sound research can add to our understanding of the social world and provide important new insights into many issues, including crime and victimisation. For example, domestic violence and abuse (or intimate partner violence) was a crime that was regarded as being of little significance, and one that required a minimal police response, before the groundbreaking research of Dobash and Dobash (1979). Their study demonstrated that women were most at risk of violence from their partner, that the violence was linked to assumptions about marriage that focused on male needs and male control, and that the sources of 'help' that women turned to often left them alienated and victimised. In contrast, bad research methods can have catastrophic effects: for example, Donna Anthony, Sally Clarke and Angela Cannings were all wrongly convicted of killing their children, largely on the basis of the flawed use of statistics at their trial by 'expert witness' Sir Roy Meadow (see Batty, 2005, https://www.theguardian.com/society/2005/jul/15/NHS.uknews1). Statistical research in particular can be highly political – Boris Johnson's rise to prime minister was based partly on the role that he claimed to have played in bringing down knife crime statistics when he was Mayor of London (Buchan, 2019, https://www.independent.co.uk/news/uk/politics/boris-johnson-london-murder-crime-rate-incorrect-commons-speech-a9020826.html). Understanding research methods is crucial to evaluating claims such as these, and to ensuring that any research that you conduct contributes, albeit in a very small way, to our understanding of crime and criminology. The first step in most research projects is to identify an appropriate research question.

Knowledge link: This topic is also covered in Chapters 3, 8 and 23.

RESEARCH QUESTIONS

Most students will use a **deductive approach** to undertake their research, where they read the literature about a topic and then decide on a research question that can add to what is already known about that topic. The alternative, inductive approach – which starts with data collection and considers the literature on the topic at a later stage – is one that is rarely used for a first research project. Choosing an appropriate research question (or research questions) is hugely important to any piece of deductive research. Green (2016: 46–49) suggests that a good research question should be:

- interesting – if the researcher is not interested in what they are doing, it is virtually guaranteed that they will not pursue the task with any enthusiasm;
- relevant – addressing the question should potentially contribute something useful to our understanding of social phenomena;

- feasible – boundaries should be placed around the research to ensure that there is a realistic prospect that it can be successfully completed;
- ethical – ethical issues are discussed below;
- concise – the question should be as precisely worded as possible;
- answerable – it must be capable of being answered by a piece of social research.

Research questions can be descriptive or explanatory. Some of the elements that De Vaus (2002: 23) suggests that should be included in a descriptive research question are:

1. the time frame;
2. the geographical location;
3. whether the researcher is interested in comparing and specifying patterns for sub-groups;
4. how abstract the researcher's interest is.

So an example of a descriptive research question might be 'What are the feelings of safety or fear of crime among male and female university students when walking home to city centre Halls of Residence after midnight on Friday and Saturday nights?'.

Explanatory research questions examine whether one factor has an impact on another. So, for example, Maguire et al. (2019) undertook research to answer the question 'Did the implementation of community policing in Gonzales, a distressed Caribbean community, reduce fear of crime and increase perceptions of safety?'. The answer that the author's reached to the question was that, in the initial stages, community policing in Gonzales seemed to increase fear and had no effect on perceptions of safety. However, as the community policing approach developed and became more effective, fear decreased and the people of Gonzales experienced greater feelings of safety. This study demonstrates that, no matter how much we long for a simple and straightforward answer to our question, the answer is usually less definitive and more complex than we had hoped!

When thinking about your own research question, it is particularly important to choose one that is realistic, given the time and other resources that you have available. Students often experience frustration when there is a research question that they are very keen to answer but where this is not an achievable goal. In many cases, you may need to settle for a research question that is adapted from one used in a published study. To take one example, Hutton, Whitehead and Ullah (2017) found that specifically trained faith-based volunteers had reduced the risk of unsafe alcohol consumption practices – such as pre-loading and binge drinking – among young people in Adelaide, Australia. You might conduct a piece of research to address the research question 'For a group of young people who I went to school with, which sources of advice and information would they be most likely to use in relation to practices such as pre-loading and binge drinking?'.

The nature of the research question has a major influence over the methodology and methods that are chosen for the research study.

CHARACTERISTICS OF QUANTITATIVE RESEARCH

A key decision to make in any research project is one between quantitative and qualitative methodology. This is often thought of in fairly practical terms, i.e. quantitative studies tend to collect broad information from large numbers of respondents, while qualitative studies tend to collect more detailed information from smaller numbers of respondents. However, these approaches derive from different underlying principles about the nature of social science and how research should be conducted.

Some of the characteristics that Bryman (1988: 21–40) links to a quantitative approach are discussed below, with my examples added. These are followed by a key case study, showing how quantitative principles were put into practice in one piece of research:

- Measurement: quantitative methodology seeks to measure social phenomena in a similar manner to natural phenomena such as heat. In addition to the amount of crime, researchers have sought measures for phenomena as diverse as satisfaction with the criminal justice system (Hope, 2015) and the amount of time that detectives spend investigating crimes (Fallik, 2018).
- Causality: although we cannot produce the same sort of 'laws' as the natural sciences, e.g. that heating water to 100 degrees Celsius at sea level will always produce steam, quantitative researchers seek to identify some factors that make others more likely. For example, research has consistently shown that people who define their ethnic origin as 'mixed race' are more likely to be victims of crime than people who class their ethnic origin as 'White' (Phillips and Bowling, 2017: 194).
- Generalisation: the quantitative researcher does not just want to find what is true for the people who are subjects of the research, but to generalise to others. So **random samples** are favoured because they facilitate statistical inferences to the population (this is discussed further below).

———— Case Study 32.1 ————

Example of a Study with Classic Quantitative Characteristics – Gang Membership

One study that demonstrated the key quantitative characteristics of causality, measurement and generalisability concerned gang membership. Researchers used a measurement of the extent to which a young person was involved in a gang that had been developed in English-speaking countries – based on answers to six questions such as 'Which of the following best describes the ages of people in your group?' – and sought to apply it to Latin America. They then considered whether membership of gangs increased the amount of deviant behaviour that young people were involved in (or whether the reverse relationship was true, i.e. that young people who were involved in substantial delinquent behaviour were more likely to join gangs). They concluded that the questions used to measure gang membership needed to be adjusted if they were to be applied to non-English-speaking countries, but with modifications it could help to predict delinquency among individuals and groups (Rodriguez et al., 2017: 1165–1184).

CHARACTERISTICS OF QUALITATIVE RESEARCH

Qualitative research takes as its starting point a belief that reality is socially constructed: different world views are created as people place experiences within their own social, cultural, historical and/or personal context: actions cannot be understood outside of this context. Instead of one, single objective reality, there are different forms of reality constructed by different people (Hennink et al., 2011: 14–15). Some of the characteristics and underlying principles of qualitative research that are identified by Bryman (1988: 50–69) are presented below with my examples:

- Ethogenics: individual actions can often only be understood by considering them as part of a wider 'episode' in an individual's life. If we see, or have an account of, the whole of an episode then we can begin to identify the belief system that has led a person to act in a particular way.

So confrontations between supporters of different football clubs can often best be understood by considering the history of rivalry between the clubs, and sometimes also between the areas in which they are based.

- Understanding perspectives: qualitative researchers are committed to 'seeing through the eyes' of others. The researcher must seek to understand, although not necessarily to share, the point of view of those being studied. So, for example, Sleath and Brown (2019: 519) studied Integrative Offender Management, a government initiative designed to co-ordinate the work of different agencies with responsibility for offenders. They found through qualitative **interviews** that there was a range of perspectives on this approach among their respondents: for example, some professionals and offenders saw it as limiting the opportunities for reoffending but one offender believed that it increased the risk of reoffending once the surveillance was finished.

- Description and contextualism: qualitative researchers believe it is important to view human behaviour in context so describing the scene, or understanding the background to the problem, is essential if we are to understand what is going on. So, for example, Holdaway's (1983: 1) study of policing begins with a description of Hilton, the area covered by the police station at the centre of his research:

> Two years before my research began in the mid-1970s a social survey of the area identified its housing conditions as the worst in the borough; only about one-fifth of the 53,000 people who lived in Hilton had exclusive access to hot water, a bath and an inside lavatory. In the central area of the subdivision, it was estimated, one family in six was headed by a single parent, and 9 per cent of families had four or more children.

MIXED METHODS RESEARCH

Given that quantitative and qualitative research are based on such different methodologies, it is sometimes suggested that they cannot be combined within one research project (Spicer, 2012: 480). However, writers such as Moses and Knutsen (2007: 293–294) argue that the distinction between the two approaches is an unhelpful one and that many studies will include elements of both quantitative and qualitative methods – a mixed methods approach. Spicer (2012: 485) suggests that combining methods can facilitate asking a wider range of questions than would be the case if just one approach was used.

One example of a study that made good use of both quantitative and qualitative methodology is a piece of research that examined the use of various measures to tackle the perceived anti-social behaviour of young people. This research was conducted in four Community Safety Partnership areas: two London boroughs and two cities in the North of England. Quantitative data was collected by identifying all the young people in the area who – within a two year period – had received an Anti-Social Behaviour (ASB) warning letter, signed an Anti-Social Behaviour Contract (ABC), or been made the subject of an Anti-Social Behaviour Order (ASBO). Qualitative data took the form of interviews with staff of Youth Offending services, together with young people and parents who they had worked with (Lewis et al., 2017: 1233 –1234).

Pause for Thought

Many students choose their methodology - usually qualitative methodology - for perfectly sensible practical reasons, e.g. they don't feel comfortable using numbers and/or they cannot contact many potential respondents. However, it is important to think about the implications this has for the broader questions

(Continued)

to be addressed by your research. To illustrate this, identify an area where you would like to conduct research. How would you approach this if you were guided by the key quantitative aim of establishing causality, and what would you do differently if you were instead seeking to see through the eyes of others (the main concern of the qualitative researcher)?

ETHICS

Ethics should be a central concern for anyone who is planning a research project; a student wishing to conduct their own research will have to go through an ethical review process within their own university and may have to go through a further process with any organisation that they are working with. There are a number of factors that make research into criminological questions particularly challenging ethically: crime is a sensitive issue, victims and offenders can both be vulnerable, there may be safety issues for the researcher and there would be a major ethical dilemma if a respondent were to disclose to the researcher information about a crime that was not yet known to the police.

To help to tackle difficulties such as these, the British Society of Criminology has devised a code of ethics for research (http://www.britsoccrim.org/docs/CodeofEthics.pdf); some of the key points for researchers are as follows:

1. Ensure that they minimise potential harm to research participants, protecting and respecting their rights: this is particularly important because, as noted above, criminologists quite often ask respondents about sensitive issues. Whatever the topic of your research, you should consider carefully any potential harm that may be accidentally caused to participants.

2. Minimise risk to themselves: in the past criminologists have been involved in some highly dangerous pieces of research, e.g. Patrick (1973) joined in with the activities of a violent gang. No ethics committee would permit such research today – and rightly so – and even projects that include less obvious risks to the researcher are likely to involve questions about safety. So, for example, if you were interviewing young people at a Youth Offending service, you would need to consider where the interviews were to take place, how easy it would be to let staff know if you felt threatened during an interview, etc.

3. Ensure that participants give freely informed consent in all but exceptional circumstances. The code identifies research that has exposed racism and other social harms as the types of circumstances that would justify an exception. However, in most other types of study, the research should be explained fully to participants before they make a decision as to whether to take part. Particular care should be taken when conducting research with children or anyone else whose understanding of what they are consenting to may be limited. Of course, this principle cannot be applied to the analysis of documents or visual data – it would clearly be impractical to ask all the actors taking part in a detective drama if the show can be analysed.

4. Be aware of the particular ethical issues that are involved in conducting research via the internet (an example of such a study is discussed below). In particular, researchers should avoid making the assumption that because someone had posted something on the internet, there are therefore no restrictions on its use for research purposes. There are no definitive rules on this but one which has been adopted by my university, and which seems sensible, is that information can be used freely when there is no password protection. However, other types of online information, e.g. on the area of Facebook to which friends need to be invited, should be used only with the express permission of the person who provided it.

Of course, the specific ethical issues that are raised by a project depend on practical questions such as from whom data is collected and how – these are the questions that are considered in the next sections.

SAMPLING

A key practical concern in any research project is where to collect data and/or who to collect it from. In some cases, you will be able to collect data from every unit in the group or population that is of interest. The word 'unit' is used here because it is important to remember that it is not always people that are sampled – a sample can be chosen of annual reports, crime stories on the television news, burglar alarms, etc. However, in most cases, students collect data from people and it may be possible to approach the entire population that is of interest, e.g. you may be able to interview all the staff in a Youth Offending Service who work with Youth Offender Panels. While collecting data from the entire population is ideal, there will be many cases, usually involving larger groups, where resources are insufficient for this to be possible. So the alternative is to choose a sample, which means that you must decide which units of the population to collect data from (and which units not to collect data from).

Quantitative researchers often prefer to use **random sampling** for two reasons: it takes any subjective element out of selection and so prevents possible bias and it makes possible the use of **inferential statistics** (which are discussed further below). There are several types of random samples that involve slightly different procedures, but all of these give every unit in the population an equal chance of being selected. The first two are:

1. A simple random sample, where every unit in the population is given a number and then the numbers to appear in the sample are chosen using a random number table or program, such as the one at www.random.org
2. A systematic random sample which involves giving every unit in the population a number and then choosing numbers at regular intervals (e.g. every tenth person). The important point when conducting this type of sample is that the starting point is chosen using random numbers. For example, if you are choosing every tenth person, you should choose at random whether the first person to be included is person 1,2,3,4,5,6,7,8,9 or 10.

The advantage of these two forms of random sample is that they require no prior knowledge of the population. However, the researcher has no control over the characteristics of the sample so that it may be unrepresentative according to key factors, e.g. a population with an even gender split may produce a sample that is 70% male. A random sampling method that provides a way past this difficulty, albeit requiring more work and more knowledge of the population, is a stratified random sample. This is created by slightly amending the systematic sampling method so that (for example) all the women's names are listed first, followed by all the men's. This ensures that the sample is representative in terms of gender, but it is still a random sample, because everyone has an equal chance of selection. This is not an ideal example, because it assumes that no one in the population has a gender identity other than 'male' or 'female' and that gender can be derived from someone's name. The level of knowledge that is required of the population is one of the key disadvantages of stratified random sampling (see De Vaus, 2002: 71–77).

Qualitative researchers, who are less concerned with generalisation, tend to use techniques that are often discussed under the broad term **purposive sampling**. This process is quite deliberately subjective, with the researcher choosing those respondents who will best fit the purpose of the research. Some of the commonly used purposive sampling strategies, which are identified by Patton (2002, cited in Flick, 2009: 122 and with my examples added) include:

- **Selecting extreme or deviant cases** – an approach used when it is thought that sampling the extremities may give the best understanding of the field as a whole. So a researcher wishing to examine the changing impact of the demands of policing with age might select the youngest and oldest police officers within a particular area to collect data from.
- **Seeking maximum variation in the sample** – this approach seeks to demonstrate the range of differences within the population. So, for example, a study of the attempts of former prisoners to re-settle into the community might seek the maximum variation between sample members in terms of length of sentence, strength of family ties, level of skills relevant to the labour market, and so on.
- **Criterion sampling** – this involves choosing all sample members according to some specific criterion. So, for example, Carpenter et al. (2016) undertook research into the manner in which non-suspicious deaths were dealt with by Australian professionals. Their research took place in one jurisdiction, where they interviewed 34 coronial professionals – coroners, forensic pathologists, coronial nurses, etc. These staff were all selected on the basis of having long experience in their role (Carpenter et al., 2016: 700).

In practice, many students have no realistic alternative to choosing another type of sample, i.e. a convenience sample. As its name suggests, this means collecting data from the people you have easiest access to, namely your family, friends and contacts. Collecting data from such a sample clearly reduces the difficulties with access, although it in no way dilutes your ethical obligations to your respondents. One obvious difficulty with this approach is that the respondents are being chosen for reasons of convenience rather than because they are most likely to contribute data that could help to answer the research question.

It is important to note that there are many circumstances – for example, when collecting data from criminal justice professionals – where a request to contact your sample may be refused, or only agreed after a lengthy period of negotiation. This factor should be considered when planning your research.

———————————————— Pause for Thought ————————————————

- If it is necessary to choose a sample of people from a population, why is it so important to use the most appropriate sampling method?
- What could be the consequences of choosing the sample according to inappropriate criteria?

QUANTITATIVE METHODS OF DATA COLLECTION

The most frequently used forms of data collection in quantitative studies involve the use of surveys. The same questions are usually asked of all respondents, most of the questions are closed, responses are placed into pre-set categories, and data is produced in relation to the aggregate of responses (e.g. 77% said 'yes' and 23% said 'no'). The main formats in which surveys can be administered are discussed below, together with a brief discussion of the advantages and disadvantages of each.

Structured Face-to-Face Interviews

There tends to be a higher response rate when conducting face-to-face interviews than when conducting surveys by other formats. Other advantages are that the interviewer can ensure that the correct person is responding, can restate questions that have been misunderstood, and can look for non-verbal clues as to the accuracy of the information (e.g. they should notice if the interviewee is distracted and suggest that they conduct the interview at another time). However, face-to-face interviews carry a high risk of conscious or unconscious interviewer bias, are very time-consuming, and raise issues about personal safety if conducted in the interviewees' homes.

Structured Telephone Interviews

The most obvious advantage of conducting structured interviews by telephone is their low cost because there is no travelling time involved; they can also be conducted at a faster pace than face-to-face interviews and carry less risk of bias, because the respondent is not able to pick up visual clues from the interviewer. However, there is a corresponding disadvantage in that the interviewer cannot record the non-verbal reactions of respondents. In addition, it is difficult to discuss very personal subjects over the telephone, particularly when the respondent has to state their answer rather than tick a box or point to an answer on a response card.

Samples for telephone interviews were once chosen by selecting households from telephone directories and then ringing their landline. Directories are no longer used and many people opt not to have a landline but to communicate only by mobile telephone which makes telephone sampling more difficult for households. However, in studies of professionals, industrial managers or commercial firms it can safely be assumed that all sample members will be accessible by a landline telephone. In addition, some studies chose samples of mobile telephone numbers by randomly selecting the digits although this, of course, means that the researcher cannot choose a stratified sample. Almost all companies that conduct political opinion polls now collect data through telephone interviews (adapted from De Vaus, 2002: 122–130).

Online Questionnaires

The advent of online surveys has transformed the way in which survey data is collected, with numerous organisations developing easy to use software. The advantages of online **questionnaire**s include that they can be completed anonymously (tracing a computer is usually impossible without the assistance of a law enforcement agency) and can be completed by the respondent as and when they have time. In addition, they have the unique advantage that the data does not need to be typed into a program such as SPSS (see below), although the process of transferring the data from the online survey program to the data analysis program can be a tricky one.

Disadvantages of conducting surveys online include there being no opportunity to explain a question to a respondent who appears to have misunderstood. In addition, they are not suitable for groups who do not use the internet or do not feel comfortable when doing so. However, it can be ensured that questions are answered in the required order, by only allowing progress to one question when another has been answered.

The use of online surveys can be helpful when working with hard to reach groups, and/or dealing with sensitive issues, because of the extra level of anonymity that they provide. Respondents are particularly likely to answer questions about attitudes or opinions when they are responding online. For example, Miles-Johnson (2016: 609–611) sought the views of transgender people about the police via an online questionnaire. His research demonstrated a further advantage of online questionnaires, i.e. that they are easy to distribute via a link – the link was shared via various online groups used by the transgender community.

PRACTICALITIES OF QUANTITATIVE DATA COLLECTION

Writing questions is a more difficult task than many students expect and it is good to provide your-self with some guidance by looking at the types of questions that other people have written, or even to include some existing scales of questions in your own data collection, where these fit with your research and are freely available. It is important to conduct a **pilot study** – a mini-practice before the real thing – in any piece of research, as this can help to identify unexpected difficulties. This is particularly important in a quantitative study where you may not realise that a question has been wrongly worded or misunderstood until you have large numbers of inaccurate responses, as I have found out to my cost! For example, you might ask the question 'Do you feel that punishments for robbery are too lenient, about right, or too harsh?' with a follow-up question 'Please could you give reasons for you answer?'. If a respondent to your pilot says that punishments are too lenient and gives the reason 'Because having your home broken into makes you feel anxious every time you go out', then you may decide that the question needs to be prefaced with an explanation of the differ-ences between robbery and burglary. Including such an explanation in the main study will avoid a situation where you collect large amounts of data, but are unable to use it because you are unsure which crime it relate to.

QUALITATIVE METHODS OF DATA COLLECTION

The data collection methods that are most commonly used in qualitative research are outlined below, together with the reasons for using them and the issues they raise.

Interviews

Qualitative interviews differ from those in quantitative studies in that they seek to elicit detailed answers to questions from respondents, so there are more open questions and more opportunities for the researcher to ask follow-ups that are not planned in advance. Hennink et al. (2011: 110) suggest that 'In-depth interviews are thus primarily used when seeking to capture people's individual voices and stories'. Qualitative interviews require a researcher to spend a substantial amount of time with each respondent and thus are resource intensive. In addition, they do not provide the same opportuni-ties to explore collective understandings that are offered by **focus groups** (see below).

Interviews can take many different forms. Semi-structured interviews are likely to be appropriate in many research situations and are recommended for the new researcher because, as their name suggests, they provide some structure and guidance, without taking the standardised approach of the quantita-tive interview. You have a guide to follow when collecting the data, which includes a number of broad questions or topics, with plenty of potential to ask follow-ups.

The unstructured interview appears on the surface to operate in a similar manner to a conversation. The interviewer may have a single question that they begin with, and would then ask follow-up ques-tions based on the response to the first one, or they may have notes of a number of points that they wish to raise in the course of the interview (Bryman, 2008: 438). However, this list of points is shorter than would be the case for a semi-structured interview. Unstructured interviews tend to produce the 'richest' data but are very time-consuming to analyse, as it may be difficult to find commonalities between different interviews.

Life history interviews focus on the life of one person, or one part or period of their life. Life experi-ences are examined in a more holistic way than with other types of interview: breadth of topics covered is likely to be sacrificed for depth of information. Life history interviews can be semi-structured or unstructured but they lend themselves particularly well to an unstructured approach, with the researcher allowing the respondent to give their narrative as they see best (Fielding, 2006: 159–161; Hesse-Biber and Leavy, 2011: 133–134).

Focus Groups

Wilkinson (2011: 168) defines focus group research as:

> ... a way of collecting qualitative data, which usually involves engaging a small number of people in an informal group discussion (or discussions), 'focused' around a particular topic or set of issues.

The distinguishing feature of a focus group is the interaction between the group members; individuals are often required to explain to others why they hold particular views and this can give a greater insight into the reasoning behind the opinions held. Disagreement may demonstrate the strength with which individuals hold their convictions (Oates, 2000: 187).

Bloor et al. (2001: 5–6) note that focus groups also have a role in relation to exploring shared understandings. This point is illustrated by Onifade's (2002) finding that police officers from minority ethnic groups were more likely to acknowledge racism when the data was collected through focus groups rather than individual interviews.

Interaction between respondents has disadvantages because the researcher has a limited amount of control: it may be difficult to prevent the discussion from drifting into areas that are not relevant. In addition, there are some situations in which focus groups are clearly not a suitable method of data collection. They are unlikely to be effective when collecting data on sensitive topics or for institutional contexts where people may not be willing to express their views in front of each other. They are also unlikely to produce useful data where personal narratives are required or the participants strongly disagree with each other (Liamputtong, 2011: 8).

Documentary Analysis

Wharton (2006: 79) defines documentary analysis as:

> The detailed examination of documents produced across a wide range of social practices, taking a variety of forms from the written word to the visual image.

Documentary analysis can be a particularly attractive option for students due to the difficulties of gaining access to data by other means. For example, students are unlikely to gain ethical agreement to interview offenders about their views of life in prison. So the option that may be realistically available to you is to analyse the documents produced by prisoners and ex-prisoners about their experiences. Examples are the blog kept by Ben Gunn and the articles written by Erwin James, which were subsequently compiled into books.

Of course, there are limitations to such forms of data analysis, most notably that it is only the more literate prisoners and ex-prisoners who write about their experiences, while many more would be able to contribute if the data were collected verbally. However, it may well be that this is the only option open to you.

If you wish to understand the views of professionals working in the criminal justice area, the number of documents that are available for analysis is much greater and includes:

- political manifestos and documents produced by government departments, most notably the Home Office and the Ministry of Justice in England and Wales, the Justice Department in Scotland, and the Justice and Home Affairs Council of the European Union;
- reports of criminal justice inspectorates such as HM Inspectorate of Constabulary and HM Inspectorate of Probation. Also their international equivalents, such as the Swedish Parliamentary Ombudsman, whose areas of oversight include the prison and probation service;
- documents produced by pressure groups such as Justice for Women and the Howard League in the UK and groups that operate elsewhere, such as the Arizona Justice Project;
- newspaper articles on issues related to crime.

Such documents can also form part of the literature review, so documentary analysis often blurs the boundaries between literature and data. Although others may disagree, my own view is that any document on which original data analysis is undertaken should be considered to be a piece of primary data. Methods of data analysis are discussed further below.

Digital Data Collection

As was noted above, the internet has opened up new possibilities for research, albeit with some ethical challenges, through the use of internet surveys and other forms of data collection. One example of a study that collected data via the internet was that of Banks (2012), who examined 'advantage play' subculture. 'Advantage play' involves a number of legal strategies by which individuals seek to make money from online gambling, e.g. accepting a free bet on an outcome from one company, and then betting on an alternative outcome with another company, with the amount of the second bet chosen to ensure a profit whichever outcome occurs.

The researcher joined an online forum of advantage players; personal exchanges and group discussion online provided 1,791 forum 'threads' of discussion for analysis (Banks, 2012: 176). Areas covered by the research included 'savage' gambling sites that are involved in theft of payments (usually by simply not paying out when a player had 'won'), identity theft and money laundering. Advantage players reported on, and discussed, these sites online (Banks, 2012: 177–178).

Pause for Thought

- Are interviews thought of as the 'default' option for collecting data?
- Do you think this is justified or should researchers give more consideration to other data collection methods?

DATA ANALYSIS

Once you have all the data that you need, or all the data that you can collect, the next task is to analyse it. The methods of analysing quantitative data are very different from those that are used to analyse qualitative data.

Analysing Quantitative Data

Knowledge link: This topic is also covered in Chapter 4.

The existence and availability of large datasets such as the Crime Survey for England and Wales mean that it is possible to conduct research where the researcher does not collect any data themselves but performs their own analysis of a dataset that is already in existence: this is known as **secondary analysis**. An example of a piece of research such as this is MacQueen and Norris's (2016) secondary analysis of the Scottish Crime and Justice Survey. The survey asked respondents whether they had experienced domestic abuse and if so whether the police knew about this abuse. However, no one had previously undertaken an analysis of the factors that had an influence on whether abuse became known to the police. MacQueen and Norris undertook secondary analysis of the dataset collected in 2008–2009 which showed that abuse was more likely to come to the attention of the police if the victim was female, if they did not have employment, if the abuse took place on multiple occasions, and if children had witnessed the abuse. In contrast, the police were less likely to find about abuse if the victims were young, male, and/or in employment.

Many of the large quantitative datasets that are available for secondary analysis have been created using random samples. The selection of such samples facilitates the use of inferential statistics, which examine how likely it is that a pattern observed in a random sample will also be evident in the population from which the sample is drawn. Take, in a hypothetical example, an online survey of a random sample of students about their attitude to Class A drugs. In the sample, female students are more likely to support the provision of heroin to addicts in controlled environments (sometimes referred to as 'shooting galleries'). An inferential statistical test called the chi-square test of independence can then measure the likelihood that this gender difference would also have been observed had the questionnaire been distributed to the entire student population.

However, many of the quantitative datasets that are collected as part of research projects are not suitable for using inferential statistics. This may be because data has been collected from everyone in the population which means that there is no need to make inferences. Alternatively, the researcher may have collected data from a large number of people but not a random sample – for example, as noted above, students often collect data from their friends and other people they have contacted through social media. In this case, rather than using inferential statistics, the research output should use **descriptive statistics**, i.e. those that describe what is going on in a dataset such as the mean and median of the answer to a numerical question, and data displays such as frequency tables and crosstables.

So, for example, I collected some data from students at my university about their feelings of safety on campus. Ninety-six students completed online questionnaires but the sample chosen was not a random one. So I could have presented some of the findings as shown in the case study below.

Case Study 32.2

Example of Findings Using Descriptive Statistics

Of the 96 students who completed questionnaires, 69 (72%) defined themselves as female, 26 (27%) as male, and one (1%) as other. The ages of respondents ranged from 18 to 57, with the mean being 22.18 and the median being 20.

Twenty-six respondents said that, while they had been a student, they had experienced difficulties caused by someone else's anti-social behaviour (ASB). When asked whether the difficulties had now been resolved, the responses of these 26 students are shown in Table 32.1.

Table 32.1 Whether Difficulties with ASB Resolved

Response	Frequency
Yes	6
Partially	7
No	4
Don't know	4
No answer given	5
Total	**26**

As is shown in Table 32.2, women were slightly more likely to have experienced anti-social behaviour but the difference was small.

Table 32.2 Crosstable of where experienced ASB by gender identity

		Gender identity			
		Female	Male	Other	Total
Difficulties from ASB	Yes	17 (25%)	8 (31%)	1 (100%)	26
	No	52 (75%)	18 (69%)	0 (0%)	70
	Total	**69**	**26**	**1**	

Statistics are usually produced within universities using the Statistical Package for Social Sciences (SPSS). This is a user-friendly program and one which most universities pay the price of a licence for. However, most organisations outside universities do not buy the licence so, if you are interested in a career in research but not at a university (e.g. as an analyst with a police force), it would be worthwhile to learn to use the alternative package R, which is available free of charge.

Approaches to the Analysis of Qualitative Data

While there are quite specific 'rules' that apply to the analysis of quantitative data (e.g. that inferential statistics should only be used with random samples, as noted above), the analysis of qualitative data is more subjective and any number of approaches can be taken. Some of these approaches are listed briefly below:

- **Comparative analysis** involves comparing and contrasting data collected from different respondents until no more new themes or issues arise.
- **Content analysis** is an approach where the researcher works systematically through each **transcript**, looking to see how often certain factors (which are recorded by codes) arise. When applied to the analysis of documents, content analysis is often assumed to be quantitative in nature, and there is clearly an element of counting when this approach is applied to interview or focus group transcripts. However, decisions about the uses of codes and systems of coding involve subjective judgements and consideration of the meanings of the speaker (Dawson, 2009: 119–125).
- **Thematic analysis** is perhaps the most commonly used form of qualitative data analysis and has a degree of overlap with both comparative and content analysis. As its name suggests, thematic

analysis involves looking for the ideas, opinions or experiences that are most frequently discussed in the data. So, for example, Burrows and Powell (2014) undertook thirty-six telephone interviews with trial prosecutors in Australia, seeking to establish how interviews with child witnesses in child sex abuse cases could be improved. They sought to identify themes from the interviews. For example, a comment that 'The absolute fundamentals that need to be nailed down are identify and act' was placed with other comments into the thematic category 'Focus questions on elements of the offence' (2014: 193). This theme was one of the three most important to emerge from the interviews, alongside the need to clarify inconsistencies and ambiguities in the account and to consider how the child would present in the eyes of the jury (2014: 196–203).

Hear from the Expert

My colleague, Nathan Stephens-Griffin, describes the analysis that he is undertaking of life history interviews with environmental activists who discovered that they had been spied on by undercover police officers:

"The difference between biographical research, or at the least the method I am using, and the more traditional qualitative interview is that on the one hand I am doing that classic thematic analysis of looking for the key themes that are coming up in the individual interviews and then across several interviews – what are the thematic connections? – so a simple thematic analysis. But I'm also looking for what Norman Denzin calls 'turning point moments'. So we might intuitively assume that the moment that you learn that someone is an undercover police officer would be a turning point moment in your life. That hasn't always been the case when I've spoken to people but it is an example, when you talk to someone about their experiences, of the type of moment that I am looking for. Moments, changes and significant events that have changed their world view and mean that they have taken a different path."

Student Voice

Here is some good advice from students who conducted research as part of their undergraduate dissertations:

Anna Johnson, whose research concerned the #Me Too movement:

"Make sure you are passionate about the topic you choose.

You've got to start early – just get ahead – start thinking about the literature you are going to use, start gathering your data, because that just takes so much time."

Robert Guy, who examined the psychological impact of prison on offenders:

"Think from the very start what your potential conclusions could be … you have to look at your question … what data do I need to form an argument?"

On reaching a 'neutral' conclusion: "It's not something that you should worry about necessarily, I don't think, because it's better to write 'I don't know' than to shoehorn something in …"

CHAPTER SUMMARY

- Selecting an appropriate research question is an essential step before beginning data collection in any deductive research project.
- Key decisions that need to be made in the course of a research project are whether to use a quantitative, qualitative or mixed methods approach, who to collect the data from, how to collect the data and how to analyse it.
- These are questions that you should consider carefully when conducting your own research and also when evaluating the research of others.
- In many cases, there is no right or wrong answer as to which is the best approach; this is an area where you need to use your own judgement.
- The ability to make good and ethical decisions to enable you to answer a specific research question is one way to demonstrate that you have become a criminologist.

──────── Review Questions ────────

1. What are the characteristics of a good research question?
2. What are the most likely reasons for choosing quantitative or qualitative methodology?
3. Why is a convenience sample often the only option that is available to students and what limitations does this create?
4. In which circumstances are focus groups the most appropriate form of data collection?
5. What are the advantages and disadvantages of using online questionnaires?

GO FURTHER

Books

1. If you would like to read a more detailed overview of the process of criminological research than there is space to provide in this chapter, I recommend this edited collection with a number of excellent contributions on different aspects of the research process:

   Davies, P. and Francis, P. (eds) (2018) *Doing Criminological Research*, 3rd edition. London: Sage.

2. Space has not allowed a discussion of ethnography in this chapter, and it is an ambitious approach for an undergraduate student to consider, but this book provides an excellent introduction:

   Treadwell, J. (2020) *Criminological Ethnography*. London: Sage.

3. As online questionnaires become an increasingly common tool in all forms of social science research, a clear guide to the process is very important and this is provided by:

   Valerie, M. S. and Ritter, L. A. (2012) *Conducting Online Surveys*, 2nd edition. London: Sage.

4. The book that I recommend most strongly to guide you on quantitative data analysis, because it includes a very strong section on the descriptive statistics that students are most likely to use, is:

   Argyrous, G. (2011) *Statistics for Social Research,* 3rd edition. London: Sage.

5. Students often struggle with the practical steps involved in analysing qualitative data; a step-by-step guide is provided by:

    Harding, J. (2017) *Qualitative Data Analysis from Start to Finish,* 2nd edition. London: Sage.

Journal Articles

1. For an example of a piece of criminological ethnographic research, which highlights the practical constraints that any research in this form is likely to face, see:

    Blaustein, J. (2016) Community policing from the 'bottom up' in Sarajevo Canton. *Policing and Society*, 26(3): 246–269.

2. There was not sufficient space to discuss one form of qualitative data analysis (discourse analysis) in this chapter, but a good introduction, which demonstrates effectively how the language used can help us to understand qualitative data, is:

    Hirtenfelder, C. (2016) Masking over ambiguity: suburban Johannesburg police reservists and the uniform fetish. *Policing and Society,* 26(6): 659–679.

3. Another topic that could not be covered in this chapter is the application of content analysis to images. For an excellent example of how this could be put into practice, with a very clear description of the process that was undertaken, see:

    Jolicoeur, J. R. and Grant, E. (2018) Form seeking function: an exploratory content analysis evaluation of the imagery contained in law enforcement agency police officer recruitment brochures. *The Police Journal: Theory, Practice and Principles*, 91(4): 339–355.

Useful Websites

1. Many students find the process of putting together surveys difficult, but much helpful information (e.g. on methods, software and question types) is provided by the UK Data Service at: https://www.ukdataservice.ac.uk/use-data/guides/methods-and-software-guides
2. The Crime Survey of England and Wales is frequently referred to in criminological discussions, and provides many examples of key methodological decisions that must be made in surveys, so I recommend the guide to its methodology which can be found at: https://www.ons.gov.uk/peoplepopulationandcommunity/crimeandjustice/methodologies/crimeandjusticemethodology
3. The Scottish Centre for Crime and Justice Research has discussions both of research projects and some of the methodological issues that underlie them: https://www.sccjr.ac.uk/themes/research-methods-and-criminological-theory-2/

REFERENCES

Banks, J. (2012) Edging your bets: advantage play, gambling, crime and victimisation. *Crime Media Culture*, 9(2): 171–187.

Batty, D. (2005) *The Guardian*. Available at: https://www.theguardian.com/society/2005/jul/15/NHS.uknews1 (accessed 13 April 2021).

Bloor, M. (2011) 'Addressing Social Problems through Qualitative Research'. In D. Silverman (ed.), *Qualitative Research*, 3rd edition. London: Sage.

Buchan, L. (2019) *The Independent*, https://www.independent.co.uk/news/uk/politics/boris-johnson-london-murder-crime-rate-incorrect-commons-speech-a9020826.html (accessed 13 April 2021).

Bryman, A. (1988) *Quantity and Quality in Social Research*. London: Routledge.

Bryman, A. (2008) *Social Research Methods*, 3rd edition. Oxford: Oxford University Press.

Burrows, K. S. and Powell, M. (2014) Prosecutors' recommendations for improving child witness statements about sexual abuse. *Policing and Society*, 24(2): 189–207.

Carpenter, B., Tait, G., Quadrell, C. and Thompson, I. (2016) Investigating death: the emotional and cultural challenges for police. *Policing and Society*, 26(6): 698–712.

Dawson, C. (2009) *Introduction to Research Methods*. Oxford: How To Books.

De Vaus, D. A. (2002) *Surveys in Social Research*, 5th edition. London: Routledge.

Dobash, R. E. and Dobash, R. (1979) *Violence Against Wives: A Case Against the Hierarchy*. New York: Free Press.

Fallik, S. W. (2018) Detective effort: what contributes to arrests during retrospective criminal investigations? *Policing and Society*, 28(9):1084–1104.

Fielding, N. G. (2006) 'Life History Interviewing'. In V. Jupp (ed.), *The SAGE Dictionary of Social Research Methods*. London: Sage.

Flick, U. (2009) *An Introduction to Qualitative Research*, 4th edition. London: Sage.

Green, N. (2016) 'Formulating and Refining a Research Question'. In N. Gilbert (ed.), *Researching Social Life*, 4th edition. London: Sage.

Hennink, M., Hutter, I. and Bailey, A. (2011) *Qualitative Research Methods*. London: Sage.

Hesse-Biber, S. N. and Leavy, P. (2006) *The Practice of Qualitative Research*. London: Sage.

Hesse-Biber, S. and Leavy, P. (2011) *The practice of qualitative research*. 2nd edition. Los Angeles, California: SAGE Publications.

Holdaway, S. (1983) *Inside the British Police: A Force at Work*. Oxford: Basil Blackwell.

Hope, T. (2015) *We Need a Different Crime Survey*. London: Centre for Crime and Justice Studies. https://www.crimeandjustice.org.uk/resources/we-need-different-crime-survey

Hutton, A., Whitehead, D. and Ullah, S. (2017) Can positive faith-based encounters influence Australian young people's drinking behaviours? *Health Education Journal*, 76(4): 423–431.

Lewis, S., Crawford, A. and Traynor, P. (2017) Nipping crime in the bud: the use of antisocial behaviour interventions with young people in England and Wales. *British Journal of Criminology*, 57: 1230–1248.

Liamputtong, P. (2011) *Focus Group Methodology*. London: Sage.

MacQueen, S. and Norris, P. A. (2016) Police awareness and involvement in cases of domestic and partner abuse. *Policing and Society*, 26(1): 55–76.

Maguire, E. R., Johnson, D., Kuhns, J. B. and Apostolos, R. (2019) The effects of community policing on fear of crime and perceived safety: findings from a pilot project in Trinidad and Tobago. *Policing and Society*, 29(5): 491–510.

Miles-Johnson, T. (2016) Perceptions of group value: how Australian transgender people view policing. *Policing and Society*, 26(6): 605–626.

Moses, J. M. and Knutsen, T. L. (2007) *Ways of Knowing: Competing Methodologies in Social and Political Research*. Basingstoke: Palgrave Macmillan.

Oates, C. (2000) 'The Use of Focus Groups in Social Science Research'. In D. Burton (ed.), *Research Training for Social Scientists*. London: Sage.

Onifade, D. (2002) The Experience of Black/Minority Ethnic Police Officers, Support Staff, Special Constables and Resigners in Scotland. Edinburgh: Scottish Executive Central Research Unit. Available online at: http://www.scotland.gov.uk/Publications/2002/06/14841/5304 (accessed 23 May 2012).

Patrick, J. (1973) *A Glasgow Gang Observed*. London: Eyre Methuen Ltd.

Phillips, C. and Bowling, B. (2017) 'Ethnicities, Racism, Crime and Criminal Justice'. In A. Liebling, S. Maruna and L. McAra (eds), *The Oxford Handbook of Criminology*, 6th edition. Oxford: Oxford University Press.

Rodriguez, J. A., Santiago, N. P., Birkbeck, C. H., Crespo, F. and Morillo, S. (2017) Internationalising the study of gang membership: validation issues from Latin America. *British Journal of Criminology*, 57: 1165–1184.

Sleath, E. and Brown, S. (2019) 'Staff and offender perspectives on Integrated Offender Management and the impact of its introduction on arrests and risk of reoffending in one police force region. *Policing and Society* 29(5): 511–529.

So-kum Tang, C., Wong, D., Cheung, F. M. C. and Lee, A. (2000) Exploring how Chinese define violence against women: a focus group study in Hong Kong. *Women's Studies International Forum*, 23(2): 197–209.

Spicer, N. (2012) 'Combining Qualitative and Quantitative Methods'. In C. Seale (ed.), *Researching Society and Culture*. London: Sage.

Wharton, C. (2006) 'Document Analysis'. In V. Jupp (ed.), *The SAGE Dictionary of Social Research Methods*. London: Sage.

Wilkinson, S. (2011) 'Analysing Focus Group Data'. In D. Silverman (ed.), *Qualitative Research*. London: Sage.

Transitioning from Undergraduate Study of Criminology to Further Study and Your Working Life

33

Michael Rowe and Pamela Davies

Learning Objectives

By the end of this chapter you will:

- Be able to provide an overview of the opportunities for further study and volunteering as you mature as a graduate of criminology.
- Be able to outline the range of career paths and the work performed by those with a professional link to criminology.
- Be able to identify key features of a criminological career.
- Be able to identify skill sets and experiences that inform criminological careers.

Framing Questions

1. Can you reflect on your undergraduate studies and assess your strengths and weaknesses in respect of disciplinary knowledge and understanding, intellectual and professional skills and your personal values and attributes?
2. Are you considering further study and/or gaining relevant workplace experience?
3. Do you have a strong sense of what you would like your future career to be?

(Continued)

4. What comes to mind if you are asked to think about what 'a criminologist' does?
5. What skills have you honed through studying criminology and which of these are directly transferable to the world of work?

INTRODUCTION

As the rest of the chapters in this book amply illustrate, criminology is an academic discipline of considerable breadth, depth and variety. It is an eclectic body of work, drawing upon traditions within economics, sociology, psychology, biological science, cultural and media studies, law, political science, philosophy, theology and beyond: which explains Barak's (1994) characterisation of criminology as a 'dynamic discipline'. It is sometimes argued that criminology is not a discipline in the traditional sense: it has no core agreed canon of thinkers, or texts that are widely recognised as central. Methodological variation is also a feature, and the topics and issues addressed by criminologists are similarly diverse. This diversity and dynamism is further reflected in the notion that criminology is a 'rendezvous discipline' (Rock, 1986) since a range of perspectives and intellectual traditions coalesce around issues of crime, offending, law, victimisation and so forth, but do so without escaping the moorings of their parent discipline. A political scientist might share with a theologian and a sociologist an interest in empirical questions about why people obey the law, but they arrive at the question with different sets of conceptual and methodological tools of analysis. Similarly, a psychologist and an engineer might share a concern with the design of crime prevention technology but subsequently return to their core discipline and work on topics that do not mutually overlap.

The remainder of this chapter seeks to bring alive ways in which the knowledge and skills you have developed as a criminologist can inform your future professional practice. In doing this we draw upon a series of testimonials we have captured through an informal survey of a range of people in various professional roles that have some link to the discipline. In seeking to identify some of the options that emerge from our discussion you are encouraged to reflect on your studies to date, your present circumstances and ambitions, and your future prospects and goals. Through all of this we emphasise that the breadth and variety of the criminological imagination means that there cannot be a comprehensive overview. There is no single blueprint for a criminological career. One professional expert we consulted, Charlotte Harris, Executive Director of the British Society of Criminology (BSC), provides testimony that, in her (and our) opinion, criminology is an academic and eclectic discipline of considerable breadth, depth and variety:

> ... criminology is a relatively new discipline and some people think it is still the child of sociology, social policy, law or (to the general public) psychology, I prefer to look at it slightly differently and think of criminology as the parent of all disciplines ...

The discussion below continues by considering the growth in academic study in the UK and elsewhere. The range of sectors and roles in which criminology graduates practice is outlined in a discussion of 'what criminologists do', and this is followed by an exploration of some of the underlying intellectual and professional skills that many of those must have in these different roles. We continue by encouraging you to reflect upon these skill sets, and in doing so emphasise that many of these are practices that you are developing through your university studies. Our expert testimonials show that good communication skills are a central feature and that engaging with diverse partners and audiences is a feature of many of the professions that criminology graduates tend to enter. The role that placement and volunteering opportunities play, which might be available within your programme of study, is reviewed briefly. The chapter then identifies potential career prospects by considering some of the typical employment destinations for criminology graduates. We round off the discussion by reflecting on what we consider some of the most important features of a career in criminology, whatever shape that might take. In doing this we emphasise the importance of developing the critical thinking skills acquired in your programme of study, and the benefits of engaging in 'real world' applied work with agencies, campaign groups, support services and researchers. We highlight the possibilities of pursuing your personal values through professional work, and the tantalising opportunities that criminology can offer you for adventure and voyage through your career.

SETTING THE SCENE: THE GROWTH AND VARIETY OF CRIMINOLOGY

In their review of the state of the discipline of criminology in the UK recently, Harris and colleagues (2019: 137–138) found:

> that in the newer … institutions where criminology has grown fastest, this growth has been accompanied by a flourishing array of new specialisms and perspectives (questions of culture, identity, harm and environment; post-colonial and border studies; critical race perspectives) which have enriched and broadened the criminological curriculum.

It is perhaps more common for a textbook such as this to offer some introductory definition of its subject matter and at the beginning of the first chapter rather than in the final section. We return to these founding debates, though, because they underpin a key theme that emerges from this collection in relation to what it means to professionally practise criminology. You may very well have a preconceived image in your mind of what a criminologist is and what they do. In our experience as academics we tend to find that most people's notion of a criminologist is of someone, probably with a background in psychology, who acts as some form of offender profiler helping police with their investigations. Of course, there are many people who do offer such expertise and who do work with offenders in a clinical environment, but criminological practice encompasses, as you will see below, a much broader and eclectic range of work.

Knowledge link: This topic is also covered in Chapter 1.

In order to develop this point, and drawing on what you will have read in the preceding chapters, one of the first points to note is that the professional experts that we refer to in the discussion below operate in very different organisational working environments. Some of them work in what are sometimes referred to as the 'blue shirt' occupations at the heart of the criminal justice and legal system: police, probation, and prison officers and staff. Although the blue uniforms might no longer be of the traditional type, it is clear that many criminology graduates find work in these 'offender management' professions. At our university we found that around one in four entrants to our criminology programmes stated that they wanted to pursue a career in policing, and it is estimated that around 40% of police officers have a university-level qualification. In recent years the College of Policing has overseen the introduction of the Police Education Qualifications Framework (PEQF) that requires new entrants to have undertaken a first degree in policing. More widely, though, you will see that the criminologists we have consulted work for the civil service, policy-making organisations, large multi-national publishing firms, charitable organisations working with disadvantaged and marginalised groups, professional organisations, and higher education institutions.

Your transition through your undergraduate studies in criminology may have been full-time or part-time, it may have been interrupted deliberately or through necessity, it may have come straight after your 'A' level studies at school or college, it may have been after a gap year, it may have involved study abroad, you might have been a mature student, you might have had caring or family responsibilities, you may have been in full-or part-time employment previously, you might have worked your way through your studies to supplement your loan, you may have done paid or voluntary work before, and you may be clear about where you are headed next or you may still be contemplating your future as a criminology graduate. Whatever your story, your transition from studying through graduation and beyond will probably be a major milestone in your personal and working life. In this section we start by considering what criminologists do by drawing on further testimony from our survey of professionals. We then allude to some of the key sources of information that you may already have consulted about your employment and job prospects as a graduate of criminology. We do not reproduce these – they are easily accessible online – but use them to draw your attention to the headline data about criminology graduate leavers, including information relating to work and earnings. The chapter drills into the intellectual and professional skills and qualities that give you a competitive edge to secure graduate employment, and the placement and volunteering experiences that will not only prove intrinsically rewarding but will likely also further your criminological career. In doing so we pause on the need for sound communications skills, the ability to work effectively with others, the need for you to maintain your curiosity and be inquisitorial, and to nurture your critical thinking skills and criminological imagination at the same time as you become increasingly self-aware and confident in your personal value system which will help you maintain a healthy work-life balance.

WHAT DO CRIMINOLOGISTS DO?

From here on in this chapter we draw on the words of a variety of colleagues. In 1986, Paul Rock conducted a census of all the 160 British university departments and institutes in which criminology might then be found. He described a small and insular professional community, noting that:

> British criminology itself is the work of only 200 or so scholars … they know one another, they educate one another, they sometimes marry one another, they read each other's works and they gossip about each other. (Rock, 1988: 65-67)

Since the 1980s, the growth of criminology has been significant. As a discipline, we have experienced twenty-five years of rapid expansion – especially in the area of undergraduate teaching provision – and much of that growth has been in the 'post-92' universities: 108 Higher Education Institutions (HEIs) offered criminology courses in 2018 (The Complete University Guide, 2019), less than the number identified by Rock in 1986, although the number of scholars teaching criminology has increased significantly. In 2018/19 the British Society of Criminology (BSC) undertook a national survey on criminology teaching and research in the UK in order to seek information on how criminology is taught and researched today. Findings from that survey confirmed the 'fragmentation' of criminology, as evidenced by the way criminologists are situated within different departments and by the ways in which universities organise their criminology staff. Rock's sentiments may remain broadly true, though the more recent survey reports significant diversity (gender, ethnicity, EU/Global origins) with staff bases growing in keeping with the continued proliferation of criminology-related provision and the student appetite for these programmes of study. Changes in technology and broader patterns of globalisation have reduced insularity since the 1980s. Not only do criminal justice policy entrepreneurs work in diverse countries around the world, so too do the political and media – and academic – debates circulate transnationally.

The work done by those who responded to our small-scale survey described work in many different sectors. The extracts below are used from just four respondents respectively from the publishing, charity, private and higher education sectors. A number of people were somehow involved in research and publishing, either as academics, policy makers, or as the extract from Natalie Aguilera (who helped commission and edit this book) illustrates, as publishers:

> My role is focused on managing the Criminology, Sociology and Politics books lists, commissioning new titles and working closely with authors to produce the very best textbooks for students' and lecturers' needs. In order to do this, I need to manage a variety of internal and external relations, project manage products from initiation through to launch, and conduct market research to inform product development or strategy.

Others involved more directly as criminal justice practitioners also characterised their work in terms that demonstrate the wide variety of roles that they fulfil and the different sectors in which their careers have unfolded. Lisa Boyack, Service Manager, Women and Criminal Justice North East, described her work in these terms:

Knowledge link: This topic is also covered in Chapter 23.

> I have worked for Changing Lives [a Third Sector organisation] for over ten years, leading and developing services for women involved in the Criminal Justice System (CJS). I lead a team of twenty staff and volunteers covering a range of services including early intervention and diversion from Court, to interventions for those with complex needs and more entrenched in offending, working within the community and custody ... Previously [my role] was varied including providing intensive outreach supporting women wherever they were – custody, in their homes, in community venues; assisting them to access services, attending Safeguarding and Multi Agency Risk Assessment Conferences (MARAC), safety planning, accessing accommodation, assessing the risk of harm, conviction and needs, attending Court, motivating compliance with Court Orders and Licence conditions. I have had numerous CJS roles including Probation Officer, Addictions Worker with the Police, Housing Support, and providing support to young people and children at risk of offending.

Many contributors identified the important role that research work plays in their everyday working lives. For academic researchers, this work is often done for funding bodies or external clients but also informs the development of university teaching materials. Dr Alexandria Bradley, Lecturer in Criminology at Leeds Becket University, outlined how her academic research work impacts on her teaching and students, as well as those who might directly commission work:

> I am also an active researcher exploring the implementation of trauma-informed practice across the UK prison service. Another aspect of my job involves publishing my research, and I am currently busy writing my first book. I am also very lucky that I can embed my research within my teaching practice. I have written multiple modules based on the contemporary prison and desistance research with which I am currently involved. This means that my students benefit from current debates and discussions and this is the most meaningful teaching experience for me as a lecturer.

Some criminologists are self-employed as consultants or independent researchers. Others are variously engaged in social enterprise. For those working in private sector consultancy, such as Adrian Beck (who left academia after a long career), research activity can directly impact 'real world' practice. Here, he describes his work as a specialist in security management and crime prevention in the retail sector:

> I have taken on a more consultative/policy-oriented role, working with a wide range of businesses in the retail industry to help them better understand and manage the various types of crime and loss they experience. This has included large-scale projects looking at issues such as how businesses define loss, the risks posed by the growing use of self-scan checkouts, and evaluating the impact of a range of technologies, such as video analytics, facial recognition and RFID tags.

WHAT INTELLECTUAL AND PROFESSIONAL SKILLS AND EXPERTISE DO CRIMINOLOGISTS POSSESS?

To a great extent all undergraduate criminologists are equipped with a similar set of intellectual and subject-specific transferable skills and cognitive abilities. In England and Wales, the skills and abilities that students of criminology are expected to possess are set out in the Criminology Subject Benchmark Statement (QAA, 2019). The professional skills you have acquired will enable you to work autonomously both as students and in subsequent employment (see Table 33.1). Despite the breadth of roles, organisations and experiences that your degree in criminology might lead you into, our survey of professional criminologists suggests that some key skills and expertise emerge across the board. Below we pick out some of these key skills as identified by the experts. We will outline these and try to encourage you to think about your own strengths. How do your skills differ from those of your fellow graduates? How have you developed your skills set, how can you further tailor it, and what are the areas that you might want to develop?

Table 33.1 Transferable Skills of a Criminology Graduate

As a graduate you are skilled and competent in a range of practices:

locating, retrieving, managing and analysing appropriate secondary data and evidence

describing, summarising and interpreting quantitative data

reporting the results of quantitative and qualitative analyses, including using appropriate graphical methods

generating and evaluating evidence

taking account of the complexity and diversity of the ways in which crime is constituted, represented and dealt with

assessing the merits of competing theories relevant to crime, victimisation and responses to crime and deviance

assessing the merits and diversity of objectives of competing responses to crime, deviance and harm, including the protection of human rights

assessing how public criminology translates into policy

gathering, retrieving and synthesising data and information

making ethical judgements about methods and published research

making reasoned arguments

using computer-based technologies

working collaboratively

interpreting quantitative data

interpreting qualitative evidence and texts

developing the ability to reflect in critical and constructive ways on their own learning.

Source: Criminology Subject Benchmark Statement QAA (2019). Reproduced with permission of QAA.

Knowledge link: This topic is also covered in Chapter 4.

Many of the technical skills which criminology students possess are generic to all social sciences, and academic study more widely. These include written and oral communication skills, time planning and management, working productively in a group, and presenting data and evidence in an appropriate format for a variety of audiences. Beyond this important set of presentational skills, criminology graduates have also demonstrated that they are able to evaluate evidence of diverse kinds and draw appropriate conclusions and identify policy and operational responses. To do this, they draw on an extensive range of methodological, bibliographic, and computing skills.

Table 33.2 The Top 10 skills Employers Look for in Graduates

1.	Commercial awareness
2.	Communication
3.	Teamwork
4.	Negotiation and persuasion
5.	Problem solving
6.	Leadership
7.	Organisation
8.	Motivation and determination
9.	Ability to work under pressure
10.	Confidence

Pause for Thought

- Can you think of examples of these, that you could provide in an interview?
- Consider the component characteristics of each skill. Teamwork, for example, could include delegating tasks, working collaboratively, and a positive leadership approach. Thinking in this way might help you identify skills you had not previously considered.
- What areas might you improve on? What opportunities might be available for you to do this?

In the context of policing related content within criminology – for example, problem-solving or evidence-based approaches – research skills are directly relevant to a career in the police. Should you choose to do so, you may use your undergraduate degree in criminology to engage in further study as a degree holder entrant to the police. As you will see from the extracts below, communications skills, experience of working effectively and collaboratively with others, and maintaining your inquiring mind and critical thinking skills, are key features of much of our professional experts' work.

Knowledge link: This topic is also covered in Chapter 6.

COMMUNICATION

A key skill, our respondents often noted, was an ability to be able to communicate effectively, and with diverse audiences. Of course, many of those who work within the criminal justice system interact and communicate with individuals presenting difficult backgrounds and behaviour. Thus, Tracy Eadie, who works for a charity supporting older people in the criminal justice system, suggested particular skill-sets and understanding:

> You need to be non-judgemental to do this role, if you stop and think about some of the crimes the people you work with have carried out it may be a challenge for some. Other skills you need to work in this kind of environment are empathy (without being manipulated), prisoners have lots of time on their hands to think of ways to manipulate and they're very good at it and recognise a 'soft touch' so it's good to be aware and adhere to professional boundaries.

As noted in the above, the ability to communicate without being judgemental is a tricky skill to master when you are also striving to engage in critical thinking. Lecturer Alexandria Bradley explains:

> Being able to work in a non-judgemental way is crucial when working within the Criminal Justice System. This can also help when working with any individual at all, to support your understanding of their lives, their truth, and to challenge your own preconceptions.

You might recognise from your own experiences as a student, that many of the academic criminologists we surveyed reported they had to 'wear many hats' in terms of engaging with different audiences. Being able to communicate with people from different backgrounds was an important emphasis in Dr Giuseppe Maglione's overview of his work as a Senior Lecturer in Criminology at Edinburgh Napier University, although he also contrasted this with working in solitude:

> Being a lecturer, and an academic in general, requires multiple social interactions, everyday, with students, colleagues, practitioners and also the general public. I really love spending time with professionals - listening to the challenges they meet is at least as stimulating as having research meetings with colleagues. I quite enjoy the social nature of my job, even though I recharge my batteries by losing myself in the library, in solitude and silence, something I always recommend students to try.

The variety and range of engagement that criminologist practitioners identify in their own work reflects the importance, in many criminology (and other) degrees, of embedding 'transferable skills' within the university curriculum. Completing group projects, delivering oral and visual presentations and so forth, are designed into programmes so that our graduates can transition to careers where skills such as those identified by Alice Weedy, Senior Research Assistant at Northumbria University, are centrally important:

> The ability to work with others is crucial within my job role as I work within a team of researchers, all of whom produce both individual and collaborative work. Outside of my direct team I am required to work alongside academics across the university and professionals within the police and other criminal justice organisations. I believe that one of the most potent skills is the ability to communicate. This is beneficial during studying but also within a job in criminology, whether this is with research participants, academics or senior levels of the CJS.

VARIETY - IN YOUR EMPLOYMENT OPPORTUNITIES AND IN YOUR WORKING ENVIRONMENT

Working across public, private and voluntary organisations and with multiple partners not only requires good communication skills but it also provides, our respondents often suggested, for a varied, exciting and interesting professional environment. Studying criminology might not lead clearly into a single career path, but it certainly provides opportunities for a dynamic career. In terms of her day-to-day activity, Charlotte Harris, Executive Director of the British Society of Criminology, explained her role in these terms:

> I have been Executive Director of the British Society of Criminology for the last ten years. The BSC is a learned society and while the Executive Director role is mainly managing the business - the BSC is a registered company and charity - and many learned societies employ administrators in this role, the BSC has always favoured criminologists. So, although I audit the finances, compile accounts and annual reports, and deal with the Pension Regulator and PAYE (the UK income taxation system for those of you lucky enough not to know), I also use my criminological knowledge to get involved in policy issues - drafting

consultation responses, representing criminology on academic fora, and networking with criminologists working in many fields and countries. Outside my main job, I have acted on Advisory Groups including for the Police Federation and the RNIB. Although it is now some time ago since I finished my PhD, I still receive two or three emails a year from families of those killed in French jurisdictions asking for my assistance and advice in navigating the inquisitorial judicial system.

This variety is also reflected in the extent to which our respondents outlined that they had, at various stages in their careers, moved across and between sectors. Indeed, this was a feature of Charlotte's career too:

I completed my undergraduate thesis on detective fiction and in my subsequent years as a journalist liked covering court and police stories. Somewhere along the line, I served as a Special Constable. Like others in this book, my career path was not finely programmed and I worked in public and community relations in the police and then in the Cabinet Office before joining criminology proper by taking the famous Cambridge MPhil. I then worked in police research before getting my nerve up to start a PhD - a comparative study of murder investigation in France and England.

For Kate Burns this also involved international moves:

I am a Lecturer in Criminology at Monash University in Melbourne, Australia. This role is extremely varied but essentially involves teaching, research and other leadership activities. Before I became an academic, I worked in the civil service in the UK developing criminal justice policy in a variety of areas. These are quite different roles but my criminology degree has been essential to both careers.

Hannah Bows, also an academic, similarly describes her job as varied:

I am a socio-legal academic, which means my research and teaching cut across law, criminology and sociology, with a particular focus on violent and sexual offences against older people and the links between ageing, crime and victimisation. My job now involves conducting research, applying for grants to conduct future research, presenting research to academic and non-academic audiences (for example at conferences or events), writing research findings up for publication in peer-reviewed journals as well as non-academic platforms such as blog and media sites, and teaching students in the broad area of criminal law. I also supervise students to undertake undergraduate and postgraduate dissertations and doctoral studies. So, my job is varied and no two days are exactly the same!

CAREER DESTINATIONS AND EMPLOYMENT

The BSC survey 2018/19 reported that criminology academic staff research interests and local community links provide a wealth of knowledge of the diversity of career opportunities that exist for future criminal justice professionals. These included excellent connections with constabularies and PCCs, the local Youth Offending Service, CPS and Courts (Magistrate & Crown), Prisons Service, Violence Reduction Unit, PIRC, Children's Panel/Hearing System, Community Safety, Victim Support, Rape Crisis, Local Authority (various Departments), Secure Units for Young People.

What do official sources report about your likely career destinations and employment? Firstly, we highlight the main headlines about educational outcomes for criminology graduates and thereby indicate a range of job specifications. Secondly, we drill into person specification-type qualities and skill set requirements for particular avenues of employment as a graduate of criminology. This is where you are guided towards tailoring your own criminological achievements and ambitions towards the world of professional work and a rewarding and satisfying career.

The main official agency with responsibility for data in the higher education sector in the UK is the Higher Education Statistics Agency (HESA). HESA data are used in a variety of ways and by a range of other bodies including Higher Education Institutions such as universities. Discover Uni is one such source of information about higher education. It draws data together from the National Student Survey (NSS), the Destinations of Leavers from Higher Education (DLHE) and Longitudinal Educational Outcomes (LEO) as described below. Students in their final year of study in the university sector in England and Wales will be familiar with the NSS. This is an annual survey where students provide feedback about their course. The results are used by universities and colleges to improve the learning experience as well as helping applicants to decide between courses and institutions. Data from HESA thus feed into various league tables as complied by other bodies and are used alongside other types of data such as those derived from the annual NSS.

HESA currently publish data from the Graduate Outcomes survey. The survey asks graduates about the nature and extent of their employment or other activity at the point it is conducted. If participants are working, it asks about the type of job, the sector and the salary. The most recent data come from those who graduated in the 2016–17 academic year. Alongside this, the LEO dataset uses government tax records to assess earnings three years after graduation. This means that, at the time of writing, the most recent earnings data are from 2015–16 and 2016–17 tax records, and the data currently displayed are for the earnings of those who graduated in 2011–12 and 2012–13. The newly developed model – the Graduate Outcomes Survey – for the collection of graduate destinations data records data from 2017–18 onwards and is designed to reflect recent changes in the HE sector and the graduate labour market. The first experimental statistics from the new survey were published in the summer of 2020. The statistics show the activities of graduates from the 2017–18 academic year fifteen months after completion of a HE course.

Given that the official sources of information have been subject to changes in survey design and methodology over recent years the data, as noted above, are not comparable and data from the newly developed Graduate Outcomes Survey are only beginning to emerge. However, drawing on these sources, we present below a flavour of the main headlines about criminology graduate leavers and about criminology leavers outcomes in terms of work and earnings. Those interested in employment that utilises skills in research and quantitative surveys and methodologies and statistical analysis may be interested in exploring HESA's web pages.

Ninety per cent of criminology graduates are in employment, further study or are working and studying six months after graduating (AGCAS, 2020).

PLACEMENTS AND VOLUNTEERING: IMPACT

As in many subject areas, criminology degrees often include provision for students to take a placement as a formal part of their programme. Of course, the nature of these provisions varies and sometimes are complemented by other opportunities for students to undertake voluntary work related to their studies outside the formal programme of study. It might be that such options are worth taking up, and the extra time this entails might have some association with a better academic performance. The Graduate Outcomes Survey data show that students who take a full-year placement as part of the studies tend to achieve a higher degree classification. Recent DHLE data suggest that 86% of those who undertook a placement graduated with a 'good' honours degree, compared to 79% of those who did not take a placement. A 'good' degree is defined in these terms as one with a final percentage score of sixty or over.

Of the 86% who undertook a placement year and graduated with good honours, 49% achieved a first-class honours degree in comparison to only 28% of those with no placement. Of course there are no guarantees that completing a placement will lead to a higher academic grade; the relationship underpinning those data might not be causal. It would appear, though, that with a placement experience you are more likely to:

- be employed after graduation;
- be employed at graduate level;
- be in a professional role;
- have a higher salary.

Those in professional roles who had undertaken a placement during their studies earned 22% more than those who did not undertake a placement, equating to circa £5k in real terms.

Table 33.3   Top 10 Reasons for Doing a Placement

1.	Graduate with work experience
2.	Develop new technical skills
3.	Develop workplace skills
4.	Earn money – most full-year placements are paid
5.	Find out if your career choice is right for you
6.	Make connections in industry
7.	Possibility that you may receive a graduate job offer if you impress
8.	Apply theoretical knowledge in the real world
9.	Gain first-hand experience of the recruitment and selection process
10.	Gain ideas for your final year project

In addition to the above, you will stand out from the crowd – relevant work experience is crucial.

Several of our respondents – academics and practitioners – have mentioned their volunteering activities as they describe their career, the experiences and influences that led to their career, and their job satisfaction today. Dr Helen Jones, Communications and Membership Coordinator, British Society of Criminology, reflects on what her volunteering led to:

> My teaching and research following this continued to be varied and led to a number of opportunities to teach and research in the USA, Sweden, and even Mongolia. Criminology has taken me around the world to conferences and to invited speaking engagements. Did I know back in my volunteering days that I would do all this? No, it's been quite a voyage.

EMPLOYERS

In addition therefore, to the major employers listed earlier, there are other organisations, agencies, sectors and departments who recruit employees with criminology graduate skill sets. These job opportunities are multiple and varied and the financial rewards can vary significantly. If you have restrictions on where in the world or country you want to work or are able to seek work, you can narrow your search parameters by scouring the jobs market in specific areas. This will often mean doing some research to find out what the names of regional or local organisations, agencies, charities, security industries and law practices are.

A great number of professional job titles exist that are directly related to your criminology degree as the above indicates and as the contributions from our various contributors also show. Graduate Prospects (AGCAS, 2020) lists the following:

- Civil Service administrator
- Community development worker
- Crime scene investigator
- Detective
- Police officer
- Prison officer
- Probation officer
- Social worker
- Youth worker

The website goes on to list further jobs where your degree would be useful:

- Adult guidance worker
- Border Force officer
- Charity officer
- Counsellor
- Housing manager/officer
- Local government officer
- Paralegal
- Political risk analyst
- Social researcher
- Solicitor

The same website also stresses that it is possible to work in a range of social welfare posts, such as mental health support and drug rehabilitation, housing (as housing officers or in outreach support roles), as homelessness officers, and in refugee and victim support/counselling. Other areas of work include criminal intelligence, social work, counselling, teaching and research. Specific posts advertised by the charity Changing Lives for example include a Community Fundraising and Communications Co-ordinator, Sessional and Assistant Support Workers, Team Leaders, Family, Youth and Complex Domestic Abuse and Therapeutic Support Workers.

Other employers are those with staff involved in victim recovery and support. While some of these might be well-known national organisations there are also numerous local outfits working in different sectors across the country. For example, Changing Lives is a nationwide charity that runs specialist services and over 100 projects across England. Staffed by 600 dedicated staff they help people experiencing homelessness, domestic violence, addiction, long-term unemployment to make a positive change – for good. In the Newcastle-upon-Tyne and Tyne and Wear region this charity is commissioned to run women's community hubs for women involved in the criminal justice system and those at risk of offending. There are local hubs in Sunderland, North Tyneside, Blyth, Ashington, Newcastle West, Gateshead, Newcastle East, and South Tyneside. These hubs are safe, women-only, spaces. Each of the community hubs seek to engage those women whose offending is not at a serious level and who may be effectively diverted from further offending. Women will be supported using approaches which are gender-sensitive and trauma-informed. Lisa Boyack's work as referred to below is a good example of employment that enables her to impact upon policy and practice.

ENQUIRY AND CRITICAL THINKING

Where can your criminological imagination take you? You might already be aware that a key skill developed in many areas of study at university is that of critical thinking. In your academic work you are expected to interrogate the assumptions, challenge orthodox 'common sense', and be able to critically review evidence and information. Treadwell and Lyne's (2019) collection explores 50 'facts' about crime and criminology that many hold to be self-evident but in practice turn out, in many cases, to be more nuanced and complex than we might assume. In their introduction they caution that in examining these common myths:

> We ask our readers, therefore, to approach the text here with a critical mind, undertaking an objective evaluation of what is presented in order to form their own views and judgements, because we would suggest that this is the very essence of studying crime, criminal justice and criminology as an academic subject.

When we asked colleagues: What would your advice be to a 21-year-old graduate of a criminology programme? Professor Adrian Beck wrote:

> My advice to graduates is twofold: remember that a criminology qualification is as much about developing a critical mindset as it is about acquiring knowledge about the subject – a questioning mind will always lead you in far more interesting directions.

In response to our question about what skills have helped our colleagues in their role, Dr Giuseppe Maglione wrote:

> Being critical, which is more than a skill. It means approaching the world with a good degree of methodological suspicion, challenging what is taken for granted, uncovering its roots and rationales, led by a commitment to support those who are more vulnerable in our societies. This approach has aided me to generate outcomes I've been proud of, and combined with passion, a good dose of humour and patience, helps me on a daily basis with what I do.

Throughout this text we have sought to provide you with content that is 'introductory' in the sense that you are not expected to have extensive prior knowledge in order to engage with and understand the various topics we have addressed. At the same time, we have sought to provide material that stretches your thinking and is critically and intellectually robust. From an educational perspective these skills are important for your academic development and success. Our respondents often drew attention to the role that such approaches had for their longer-term careers. Publishing editor Natalie Aguilera, for example, spoke of the value of:

> ... the ability to draw together, analyse and critically evaluate information which has been crucial in all manner of ways, from conducting market research in order to develop a new book proposal to writing reports. Numeracy skills are also key to creating budgets, managing costs, and analysing sales and financial data.

In the context of an academic career it is unsurprising perhaps that these skills are valued in terms of the research and the teaching responsibilities criminologists are tasked with. More widely, for example, in contemporary police education in much of England and Wales, practitioners are encouraged to develop 'reflective practice'. This is a useful approach for students too – and you would benefit from thinking critically about your approach to learning and your studying habits. Alexandria Bradley spoke about the importance of this practice to her academic career:

> An important skill which I feel has benefitted my research, practice and teaching, is reflective thinking. To become thoughtful within your practice and approach towards people, will benefit your personal development. Reflective thinking enables a continuous cycle of interaction, reflection, conceptualisation and application. This can help you to improve and reflect upon your engagement with people and your academic practice.

One of our partners in collaborative projects, Lisa Boyack, reported on her job satisfaction, what she looks for as a recruiter, and she also commented on the range of opportunities:

> I too enjoy spotting and nurturing talent in the CJS. The two main things I look for when recruiting are the ability to engage and experience. Being personable and empathic is vital to positively influence and change others' behaviour. This can be a difficult field to enter, volunteering is an excellent way to gain experience and demonstrate commitment. I would advise graduates entering this field to widen your job search, there are many opportunities outside of the 3Ps - Probation, Prison and Police.

EFFECTING CHANGE: MAKING A DIFFERENCE

Hannah Bows is an academic who works with lots of organisations in the course of her research that she hopes will have real-world benefits:

> I often work with statutory bodies such as the police and Crown Prosecution Service, to conduct research which they commission or to work alongside them as partners in developing new research projects to address issues or pressing questions which can help them improve their work. This is known as 'impact' - where your research has a benefit beyond just producing new evidence, and in a tangible way is used by organisations and people outside of academia.

To maintain her real-world research she explains:

> I continued to volunteer with organisations outside of academia; I am currently the Chair of Age UK Teesside [since 2015] and I sit as a magistrate on my local bench [since 2018]. These roles provide me with an opportunity to develop new skills but also to see the wider impact of the issues I research. For example, I gain a deeper understanding and appreciation of the impact of criminal law (which I research and teach) by sitting in court several times each month administering justice - I see the way the criminal law affects individuals and families which extends beyond what I can learn from simply researching these issues.

Hannah's doctoral and post-doctoral research focused on older people as victims of sexual violence. As social scientists, criminologists will often focus their research on under-represented communities in order to help their voices to be heard and as part of their mission to effect change through academic advocacy. Tracy Eadie is a Senior Partnerships & Training Consultant for RECOOP (Resettlement and Care of Older ex-Offenders and Prisoners), a charitable organisation which employs a host of staff to support older individuals with convictions:

Supporting older people within the criminal justice system is at the heart of what my job entails and the charity I work for is one of only a few who focus on this population. 'Older' means anyone who is aged over 50 within criminal justice and whilst some over 50s are fit and healthy, the vast majority are not. Prisons were not built with older prisoners in mind, many are Victorian, often beautiful elaborate buildings, at least in part, but not for those older people who live inside. My job is to work with prisons (primarily) and help them find solutions to the limiting environment for someone who is older. The limits of course are not just environmental, the regime itself doesn't consider age, health or disability and many older prisoners spend far too much time isolated in their cells, with very little to occupy their minds and bodies. Since 2010, RECOOP, the charity I work for, have found innovative solutions that support older prisoners during their time in prison as well as preparing them for life after release. It's a really interesting and rewarding job.

Sana Ilyas is a Victim Care Co-ordinator, Restorative Justice Practitioner and a Safeguarding Lead in Victims First Northumbria UK. She too describes how she supports under-represented communities:

I aim to encourage victims of hate crime to access support in the criminal justice system and to build a trust with under-represented communities. Being a student, I learnt that law can only be enforced if a legal professional is eager to work with the community to maintain and enforce law. My passion to connect with communities, and to work for, and with, the victims of crime has led me to initiate the following activities in North East:

- a rape and sexual abuse awareness event for BME women in North East.
- conducting awareness-raising sessions on: criminal law in UK, crime prevention, hate crime, sexual violence crimes, domestic abuse, honour-based violence and forced marriages within schools, colleges and universities, refugees and asylum seekers and LGBTQ groups.
- drop-in sessions for the disabled and visually impaired community groups.
- worked as a presenter for a local radio for three years to connect with communities, and to initiate community discussion regarding social issues.
- currently I am a member of the PCC's led community focus group and Northumbria police's Hate Crime Strategic groups.

PERSONAL VALUES AND YOUR WORK-LIFE BALANCE

Katie McBride, Lecturer in Criminology and Criminal Justice, University of Plymouth, reflects on how her studies have shaped the way she absorbs and responds to events around the world and close to home:

Criminology informs the way I design and develop my teaching and research. But more than that, it informs the way I see the world. After studying criminology at university, when I am now reading the newspaper or watching the news, I am more attuned to the injustices in the world and have a greater understanding of not only criminal justice but also politics, power relations, race and gender. Justice is an issue that impacts all of our lives, and so having that criminological knowledge allows for deep interrogation of the world around us.

Anita Dockley, research director at the charitable body the Howard League for Penal Reform, told us how she has also found a good fit between her personal values and working passions:

It was not just my academic studies that influenced my career choice, I was always interested in people, social justice and politics. My out-of-work activities reflected this and helped shape my worldview. Ultimately, I wanted to make a difference. At first it was about enabling people to be active, fulfilled members of their communities, but I soon realised that it was equally important to seek systemic and structural change. If you look at what the Howard League advocates you will rarely see it challenging individual actions, but instead we focus on policies and practices. I have stayed with the charity because opportunities emerged with the charity's growth and personal circumstances, but I also realise that it's my commitment to penal reform, social justice, and my close alignment with the Howard League's values.

When I thought about a career after university, I would never have imagined I would be a penal reformer. I did know I wanted to work in a field that focused on enabling people to be active citizens. I was lucky that a job that matched my world view was advertised where I could hone my knowledge and skill-base accordingly, but more than anything I followed my passion.

ADVENTURE! VOYAGE! FOLLOW YOUR PASSION!

Another theme explicitly mentioned by several of our respondents was that their passion for criminology had opened up unexpected opportunities and exciting prospects in later careers. To some extent this stems from the breadth of the subject matter. Criminology (as you read at the start of the chapter) comes into close alignment with many elements of life: political, cultural and media, medicinal and theraputic, punishment and detection. Clearly, this means that you can – perhaps with a degree of good luck – take lecturer Kate Burns' advice to 'follow your passion'. The boundless possibilities are also a reflection of the shift to more diverse service provisions away from the 'Three Ps' (mentioned earlier) into an era where the 'criminal justice system' is characterised by the diversity of provision and engagement with many other agencies and sectors. Kate Burns reflected on this, with the following advice:

Follow your passion! The exciting thing about a criminology degree is that graduates have so many varied career choices. Go where that drive takes you. A criminology degree gives you the foundational knowledge to make a difference in your community and wider society but this can be applied within criminal justice systems, within government or non-government organisations, the private sector and beyond.

CHAPTER SUMMARY

In the first chapter of this book, on 'Being a Criminologist', our colleague Linda Asquith noted that 'being a student of criminology is exciting, rewarding, challenging, and occasionally, emotional'. We have extended this observation throughout this chapter and sought to show how those features continue to describe the various career paths available after graduation. While the chapter has provided some insight into potential employment paths our wider goal has been to sketch some of the broad characteristics that underpin these varied careers. We have also tried to identify key skills and expertise, and to show that many of these are embedded within degree programmes. Most likely you have been able to recognise that you have already developed some of these skills. We hope that the vitality and range of criminology is demonstrated through all of the chapters included in this book. The range of intellectual traditions, issues and debates, methodologies and approaches is broad, which is part of what makes criminology such an engaging and exciting discipline. All of those characteristics extend through criminological careers and we hope that you have developed your thinking about where your academic studies might take you in the future.

Review Questions

1. In what ways has your understanding of potential criminological careers changed in response to this chapter?
2. What are the key features and skills that underpin the range of careers discussed here?
3. Which of these skills do you already have, and which could you develop further?
4. Where would you like your criminological studies to take you? What comes next?

FURTHER READING

Books

1. If you are considering a career in the police, prisons, probation, the courts or youth justice sector, this book may be useful:

   Ragonese, E., Rees, A., Ives, J. and Dray, T. (2015) *The Routledge Guide to Working in Criminal Justice: Employability Skills and Careers in the Criminal Justice Sector*. London: Routledge.

2. The following book explores the politics of crime and the relationship between social science and public policy. It confronts questions about the value of criminology, the collective good criminological inquiry might promote, and how its practitioners engage with politics and public policy:

   Loader, I. and Sparks, R. (2011) *Public Criminology?* Abingdon: Routledge.

Journal Articles

1. For those interested in becoming a police officer, this article usefully explores the historical backdrop to the emergence of the new Police Education Qualifications Framework (PEQF) and accompanying entry routes into policing which embed evidence-based policing:

   Ramshaw, P. and Soppitt, S. (2018) Educating the recruited and recruiting the educated: Can the new Police Education Qualifications Framework in England and Wales succeed where others have faltered? *International Journal of Police Science & Management*, 20(4): 243–250. doi:10.1177/1461355718814850

2. This short paper takes a brief historical tour to consider what the term 'criminology' encompasses and how criminology is identified. Published in 2003, its final sentence ponders the following question: 'How long before secondary school students can take an A-level in criminology?'.

   Bowling, B. and Ross, J. (2006) A brief history of criminology. *Criminal Justice Matters*, No. 65, Autumn: 12–13.

3. Academic staff and students alike will gather an insight into the current state of discipline and how and where it is taught from reading this article:

   Harris, C., Jones, H. and Squires, P. (2019) How criminology is taught and researched today. *Papers from the British Criminology Conference and the British Society of Criminology*. www.britsoccrim.org ISSN 1759-0043; Vol. 19 Paper.

Useful Websites

Employability is a university-wide responsibility. The following document, 'Defining and developing your approach to employability', is a framework which has been developed by the Higher Education Authority (HEA) which provides a process for reflecting on and addressing employability provision in a systematic and holistic manner. It is aimed at Higher Education Institutions (HEIs), but you may be interested to know more about the context in which your own employability is considered during your undergraduate studies:

Cole, D. and Tibby, M. (2013) Defining and embedding your approach to employability: a framework for higher education institutions. Higher Education Academy. Available at: https://www.heacademy. ac.uk/system/files/resources/employability_framework.pdf, (accessed 27 January 2021).

The websites of various criminology societies across the world are useful resources and you might consider becoming an early career member. Such societies are hubs of disciplinary knowledge promoting the study and understanding of the subject and its wider impact by bringing together those involved in research, teaching, policy making, practice.

1. The American Society of Criminology: https://asc41.com/
2. The Asian Criminological Society: http://www.acs002.com/
3. The Australian and New Zealand Society of Criminology: https://anzsoc.org/
4. The British Society of Criminology: https://www.britsoccrim.org
5. Criminological Society of Africa: http://www.crimsa.ac.za/index.html
6. The European Society of Criminology: https://www.esc-eurocrim.org/
7. The Higher Education Statistics Agency: https://www.hesa.ac.uk/about
8. Discover Uni: https://discoveruni.gov.uk/about-our-data/#data_sources
9. AGCAS Graduate Prospects: https://www.prospects.ac.uk/careers-advice/what-can-i-do-with-my-degree/criminology

REFERENCES

Barak, G. (1994) *Varieties of Criminology: Readings from a Dynamic Discipline*. Westport, CT: Praeger.

Harris, C., Jones, H. and Squires, P. (2019) 'How Criminology is Taught and Researched Today'. *Papers from the British Criminology Conference and the British Society of Criminology*. www.britsoccrim.org ISSN 1759-0043; Vol. 19 Paper.

Rock, P. (1988) 'The Present State of Criminology in Britain'. In P. Rock (ed.), *A History of British Criminology*. Oxford: Oxford University Press.

The Complete University Guide (2019) https://www.thecompleteuniversityguide.co.uk/courses/search/undergraduate/criminology

Treadwell, J. and Lynes, A. (2019) *50 Facts Everyone Should Know About Crime and Punishment: The Truth Behind the Myths*, Bristol: Policy Press.

Glossary

'Five Strands' Colloquial name for the five categories of hate crime – race or ethnicity, faith, disability, sexual orientation and gender identity – monitored by criminal justice agencies in England and Wales.

'Groupthink' A behaviour where consensus-seeking becomes so dominant that it tends to override individual thinking (Janis, 1971).

'Law and order' politics A phrase used by Hall et al. (2013) to refer to a political turn in the 1970s wherein governments came to focus on criminal justice as a way of demonstrating their legitimacy and underscoring their authority. This came, Hall et al. (2013) argue, during a time where this legitimacy and authority were particularly under threat due to the global economic crisis and the related growth of social inequality.

'Real Life' Crime Programming Emerging in the 1980s, a highly popular media format that seeks to lay bare the work of criminal justice agencies, often through as-live or documentary film footage. There is huge variety within this, with some programmes taking a distinct pro-criminal justice line, and others being highly critical of criminal justice personnel and processes. What they share is a reliance on testimonial accounts, direct 'on the ground' reporting, and conventions from documentary film.

'Trigger' Event A particular event or moment that is the catalyst for a reaction.

Abolitionism A significant body of work and thinkers who emphasise the need to abolish, e.g. prisons due to the harms they inflict.

Actus Reus The physical act of committing a crime (compared to the mens rea which is the mental element required).

Age-crime curve The age-crime curve is the observation of the relationship between age and crime; that is the number of people involved in offending increases during adolescence, peaks around the late teenage years and early twenties, and subsequently decreases sharply. It is one of the 'facts' of criminology however, some recent observations of the relationship note that it is changing; becoming flatter and wider.

Aetiology The study of causes and origins. The search for answers to questions such as why do things occur and why do things function in the way they do?

Alternative Subcultures Music and style-based subcultures, such as punk or goth, that are characterised by distinctive modes of dress and 'darker' musical styles which are separate from mainstream culture.

Analysis Analysis is the act of studying something to learn more about it, and identify the core issues of a topic.

Anthropocene A (proposed) geological epoch that indicates the period of significant human impact on the natural environment, such as climate change.

Applicant The person who applies for an order in family proceedings. In a domestic abuse case this is likely to be the victim-survivor.

ASSET/ASSETPlus Standardised assessment tools for youth justice, introduced by the Youth Justice Board that are designed to measure risk of reoffending. ASSET was replaced by ASSETPlus in 2014 in an attempt to combine assessments of risk and need.

Asylum Seeker Someone who has fled persecution in their home country and is seeking permanent refugee status.

Atavistic Reverting to or characterised by our primordial or ancient ancestors.

Attorney General The State's chief legal advisor with several independent public interest functions. This individual is normally also a Member of Parliament.

Attribution The process of ascribing an activity/features of an activity to a person or group to ascertain the origin of it.

Attrition The process whereby cases and complainants 'drop out' of the legal process due to barriers and filtering mechanisms in the legal system from the initial report to the police to prosecution.

Autonomy Control of one's self.

Bias Crime A term sometimes used to describe hate crime in the United States.

Bind Over Where a person has entered into a recognizance (a court acknowledged agreement) to perform an act, e.g. to prosecute, to give evidence, or to 'keep the peace'.

Biodiversity The range of plant and animal life in a particular habitat. Because of the way that ecosystems reproduce themselves, a high level of biodiversity is necessary for the sustainability of species.

Bio-Power A form of political power that operates at the level of the population rather than the individual, but has the effect of guiding individual conduct and decision making.

Britain First A far-right political party founded in 2011 by former members of the British National Party.

Capitalism A system for organising the economy and social relationships based on the private accumulation of capital. Key features of capitalist systems include private ownership of property, a wage labour system, and markets in which most of the commodities and common resources can be sold for profit.

Carceral Geography A geographical focus on aspects of incarceration.

Cautionary Tale A paradigm for studying media coverage of crime. Cautionary tales marginalise the behaviour of the victim or would-be victim of crime. Women tend to be the target of such reporting, and they are warned to be more aware, to stay alert, and to adapt their behaviour in light of a perceived threat.

Charge An accusation of an offence. A charge sheet is the document prepared by the police to indicate the accusations against an accused.

Chivalrous   Being especially courteous, usually applied in relation to male behaviour toward women.

Citizen Journalist   An amateur news-maker, who records events and incidents first-hand, often by photographing or video-recording these on mobile phones, but also via blogs or social media posts. Citizen journalists often provide direct insights into what's happening during riots, protests, and/or incidents of police brutality.

Claimant   The person making a claim to the court in civil proceedings, e.g. to claim compensation.

Class Actions   A legal term used to describe cases in which a large number of litigants seek compensation in a civil court. Class actions can be initiated against corporations to pursue damages for the harm they have caused to workers or the community.

Climate Change   Changes to the earth's climate that are considered to be caused by changes in the atmosphere. Conventional wisdom suggests that climate change is the result of human activity such as human-caused pollution.

Code for Crown Prosecutors   The CPS policy document which provides guidance on general principles to be applied when making decisions about prosecutions.

Coercive Behaviour   An act or pattern of acts of assault, threats, humiliation and intimidation or other abuse that is used to harm, punish, or frighten their victim.

College of Policing   Provides training and development of police officers and staff, and sets professional standards for policing in England and Wales.

Colonialism   The acquisition and rule of overseas territories by a nation state.

Common Law   A legal system based on the decisions of judges and led by custom, rather than written laws.

Community Resolution   Is an out of court disposal that is used for low-level offending, allowing police officers to use their professional judgement when dealing with such offenders in a proportionate way.

Community Safety   The concept of community-based action to inhibit crime and harms from all sources such that all members of the community are safe.

Complainant   The person who is making a 'complaint' that the law has been broken in a criminal case, usually the victim of the crime. They will also usually be the main witness for the prosecution.

Conditional Caution   An out of court disposal that requires an offender to comply with a condition in order to avoid prosecution at court.

Conditional Caution Pathway   Where an offender is referred to a particular programme designed to address the specific cause of the offending behaviour and increase victim satisfaction.

Controlling Behaviour   A range of acts designed to make a person subordinate and/or dependent by isolating them from their sources of support, exploiting their resources and capacities for personal gain, depriving them of the means needed for independence, resistance and escape, and regulating their everyday behaviour.

Corporation   A profit-making organisation that is permitted to act as a single entity or 'corporate person' and is recognised as such in law.

Crime Concentration   The number of crimes experienced by each victim on average.

Crime Count   The total number of crimes committed in a given area.

Crime Rate   The number of crimes per 100, 1,000, or 100,000 population or potential targets.

Crime Repetition   At least one victim experiencing at least two crimes.

Crime Statistics   Provide statistical measures of the crimes in societies.

Crime Victimisation Surveys   Contain information about crimes experienced by the general population.

Criminal career   A criminal career is the longitudinal sequence of offences committed by an individual offender. The concept is intended as a means of structuring the longitudinal sequence of criminal events associated with an individual in a meaningful way.

Critical Consumption   In the context of organised crime, critical consumption may be understood as instances where consumers boycott goods and services from businesses/organisations they suspect are linked to or supported by organised crime groups. Instead, consumers are encouraged to direct their custom to businesses/organisations who do not have links to organised crime. This acts as a form of grassroots resistance against mafia-type and other organised crime groups.

Crown Prosecution Service (CPS)   The CPS is the organisation that prosecutes criminal cases investigated by the police in England and Wales.

Cultural History   An approach to examining the past through the lens of culture (media, music, etc.) that is concerned with the circulation of ideas and their impact on experience.

Cyber Crime   The use of networked computers or internet technology to commit or facilitate the commission of crime.

Decency Agenda   A set of ideas about ensuring a decent quality of prison life emerging in the wake of the Woolf Report.

Deductive Approach   An approach to research that begins with what is already know about the chosen topic through existing literature and, from this, identifies a research question to be answered or a hypothesis to be tested.

Defendant   The person who is being accused of having committed an offence in criminal proceedings. If they plead 'not guilty' they will be 'defending' themselves against the allegations.

Democratic Football Lads Alliance (DFLA)   A right-wing movement with an anti-Islam and Muslim agenda based within the United Kingdom.

Dependency Theory   A theoretical tradition that explained global inequalities during the mid-twentieth century as arising from economic exploitation by western countries.

Deprivation Model   A way of thinking about prison culture as one dominated by a series of pains and losses (deprivations).

Descriptive Statistics   Methods of presenting quantitative data that summarise and show what is going on in the dataset.

Deserving Victims   Those individuals and groups easily able to attain the label of victim deserving of our compassion and sympathy.

Desistance   Desistance refers the cessation of offending. This is not a discrete event but rather a process. However developmental and life-course criminologists will often consider a person's last offence as their point of desistance.

Detention at Her Majesty's Pleasure   The sentence which courts must impose where a child is convicted of murder. It is the functional equivalent of a mandatory life penalty for adults: the court sets a minimum period which must be served in custody before the subject can apply for parole. Once released, the individual is subject to statutory supervision for the remainder of their life.

Deterrence The theory that the risk of being caught and punished will deter people from committing crime.

Deviancy Amplification Spiral A schema for understanding how the media amplifies and promotes deviance, used by Cohen (2011) in his study of moral panics. A low-level act of deviance is amplified in the media, responded to punitively by a control culture, leading to those censured to feel increasingly alienated and hostile, and thus more prone to further, more serious forms of deviance.

Director of Public Prosecutions The head of the CPS whose duties are outlined in the Prosecution of Offenders Act 1985, s.3(2).

Domestic Abuse Any incident or pattern of incidents of controlling, coercive, threatening behaviour, violence or abuse between those aged 16 or over who are or have been intimate partners or family members regardless of gender or sexuality. The abuse can encompass but is not limited to: psychological, physical, sexual, financial, and emotional.

Ecocide Human activity that causes extensive damage to ecosystems and/or harms the health and wellbeing of a species (including humans). Ecocide refers to ecosystem damage based on the immediate effects of pollution or to cumulative threats such as climate change.

Ecological Justice The idea that justice systems and processes should apply not just to human victims but also to the environment and non-human nature (e.g. animal victims).

Economic Abuse Any behaviour that has a substantial adverse effect on the survivor-victim's ability to (a) acquire, use or maintain money or other property, or (b) obtain goods or services.

Either Way Offense An offence triable either in the magistrates court or crown court.

Environmental Justice This term refers to the distribution of environments in terms of access to and use of natural resources. It is most frequently concerned with the disproportionate effects of environmental harm felt by minority groups and indigenous peoples and other vulnerable groups.

Epistemological Differences Differences in values and culture between dominant and subordinate groups. In postcolonial theory, it is claimed that those in developing societies have a distinctive epistemology.

Epistemology/Epistemological The branch of philosophy concerned with how we know what we know and our justification for claims to knowledge.

Essentialism A form of analysis in which social phenomena are understood not in terms of the specific conditions of their existence, but in terms of some presumed essence or interest.

Ethics A branch of philosophy that deals with moral principles and how to live a good life.

Ethnicity A collective that share common cultural characteristics, i.e. religion, language, or nationality. It has been accused by some of being used as a euphemism for race.

Ethnocentrism Using value and standards in your own culture to assess other cultures; only being interested in your own society.

Ethnography A means of studying social life by observing and immersing oneself in daily living.

EU Referendum Commonly referred to as 'Brexit', the 2016 referendum saw the United Kingdom elect to withdraw from the European Union by way of a democratic vote.

Evaluation Evaluation is the process of examining the strengths and weaknesses of an idea or issue.

Extremism Agendas or actions of an individual or group that are extreme in nature, usually underpinned by an ideological, political or religious cause.

Far-Right An affiliation with the extreme right on the political spectrum.

Focus Group A form of data collection that involves bringing people with a common bond together to discuss specific issues.

Focused Deterrence A strategy to intervene with high-risk groups and individuals to prevent future crimes, primarily violence. It combines incentives (access to services) with deterrence (strict legal consequences for offending) and efforts from community members to monitor and support those involved.

Folk Devil The group that becomes the focus and repository for public concern and official censure during a moral panic.

Forced Labour Any work or services that people are forced to perform against their will.

Foreign National An individual who is the citizen of a country that is different from the one they are residing in.

Gender-Based Violence (GBV) Abuse and harm directed against a woman because she is a woman, or that affects women disproportionately.

Gentrification A process by which a traditionally working-class area is transformed, and its inhabitants displaced, through a sudden influx of money, affluent residents, and businesses.

Globalisation The process by which the world is becoming interconnected economically and through the media.

Governmentality An approach to the study of power that focuses on how individuals internalise rules of governance as a positive system of behaviours, as opposed to being handed down from a sovereign power.

Grassroots Action, activism or initiatives which take a 'bottom-up' approach, usually consisting of collective action from a group as opposed to a formal, structural or institutional response.

Grave Crimes A technical term that determines which court has jurisdiction. Children's offending is tried in the youth court unless it is deemed so serious that it is a grave crime. In such cases, the child is transferred to the crown court where longer custodial sentences become available.

Green Criminology The study of green crimes and green harms and the study of behaviour that impacts negatively on non-human nature and ecosystems.

Green Victimology An arm of victimology that examines the plight of non-human species as victims, and victims (both human and non-human) of pollution and wider environmental harms.

Gypsy A Romany ethnic group whose members are often defined in terms of their nomadic lifestyle, cultural values and traditions as opposed to their race or origin.

Hate Crime Acts of violence, hostility, and intimidation directed towards people because of their identity or perceived 'difference'.

Hegemonic Prevailing influence exerted by a dominant group.

Her Majesty's Inspectorate of Constabulary and Fire & Rescue Service (HMICFRS) Formerly Her Majesty's Inspectorate of Constabulary (HMIC), HMICFRS independently assesses the quality of police forces and fire and rescue services.

Heteronormativity Assumes that a heterosexual society, based on the gendered binary of male and female, is 'the norm'.

Hierarchy of Victimhood/Victimisation Where victims are placed on a scale whereby those most deserving of our sympathy are placed at the top and those most blameworthy and undeserving are placed at the bottom.

Historicising Understanding past crimes in historically specific ways.

Homelessness Rough sleeping but also covers a number of other situations in which people can be considered to lack permanent accommodation.

Homophobia An irrational fear, dislike or hatred of lesbian, gay or bisexual people.

Hostility Behaviour that is unwelcoming, threatening, and often violent or intimidating to some degree.

Hotspot Policing Involves the targeting of resources and activities to those places where crime is most concentrated. It is based on the premise that crime and disorder is not evenly spread, but clustered in small locations.

Hyperviolence Media depictions of violence that are especially gratuituous, graphic, and disturbing. The tendency is for such depictions to suggest that violence is random and animalistic, rather than socially-patterned.

Ideal Enemy A person who is easy to dislike and resent, and can be used by the populist press and politics to conform to fears and stereotypes and marginalise certain groups.

Ideal Victim A term coined by Christie (1986) to capture the key characteristics that make some people more readily recognised as victims. These characteristics draw particular attention to presumptions of weakness and innocence.

Ideology A set of beliefs, values, principles, and objectives by which an individual defines their distinctive political identity and aims (Drake, 1998).

Image Based Sexual Violence The non-consensual creation and/or distribution of private, sexual images and the non-consensual creation of sexual imagery, e.g. photos and videos created by means of upskirting, forms of voyeurism and sextortion, or recordings of sexual assaults. It also covers perpetrators threatening to share images, commonly part of a pattern of coercive behaviour in abusive relationships.

Importation Model A way of thinking about prison culture as being constructed from ways of life brought into the prison by those held there.

Indictable Offence An offence that is triable in the crown court.

Indigenous Peoples The original inhabitants of territories acquired through colonisation. These include Aboriginal peoples in Australia, and native peoples in the USA and Canada.

Individualism A general term for values in modern societies that favour individual choice and freedom. This can be contrasted with collective or communal values in traditional societies.

Inferential Statistics Techniques that involve testing the likelihood that a pattern that is seen in a random sample will also be seen in the population.

Intersectionality A theoretical framework used to understand how individual, social and political identities combine in a complex manner or overlap to create experiences of marginalisation, discrimination and privilege.

Interview   A method of data collection that involves a one-to-one interaction between the researcher and the respondent. In quantitative research, interviews are structured; in qualitative studies they can be unstructured or semi-structured, and/or can deal with a life history or part of it.

Intolerance   An unwillingness to accept other people, groups, views, beliefs or behaviours.

Islamophobia   Prejudice towards, or hatred of, Islam or those of the Muslim faith.

Joint Enterprise   A legal doctrine that enables a person to be held liable for another person's crime if they have knowingly assisted or encouraged the crime or agreed to act with the primary offender for a common purpose.

Justice   Refers broadly to a favoured outcome, remedy or consequence following an incidence of harm.

Justice Gap   The gap between the justice needs, hopes or expectations of victim-survivors and the actual justice experienced.

Law Commission   A statutory independent body created by the Law Commissions Act 1965 to keep the law under review and recommend revisions where needed to the UK government.

Lecture   A lecture is a large group session where the lecturer provides information to the students, introducing and explaining key ideas. Usually, the lecturer talks and the students listen and take notes.

Left Realism   A reaction within critical criminology to a perception that the Left in criminology has failed to take crime seriously, allowing the political Right to take centre stage within law and order policies. Left Realism focuses on relative deprivation as well as the need to ensure that policing and crime prevention are democratically controlled.

Legislation   Written laws created by Parliament.

Legitimacy   The conditions and extent to which authority is morally accepted, and in criminal justice is often applied to institutions in relation to decency, fairness and trustworthiness.

Liberal Feminism   A liberal feminist approach that sees men and women as equals and that legal mechanisms must be used to ensure such equality.

Liberalism   A very broad political and moral philosophy based upon the freedom and liberty of the sovereign individual. There is a wide range of 'liberalisms' that span across the political spectrum.

Literature Review   A summary of previous research on a topic, which helps researchers to understand existing knowledge and potential gaps.

Liquid Modernity   Captures the idea that modern societies are complex and everchanging, and that rapid technological advancement creates challenges for social cohesion and stability.

Longitudinal   The same respondents are surveyed at different periods of their lives.

Macpherson Report   A UK report which, in 1999, set out the findings of the Inquiry established following the murder of Stephen Lawrence, whose conclusions made reference to the problem of institutional racism within the police service of England and Wales.

Malware   Short for malicious software. It is designed to infiltrate a computer system or mobile device without the owner's consent to gain access within the device, steal valuable/sensitive information, or damage data.

Mean Number of Crimes   The average number of crimes per person, per year, per place, or other denominators.

Mens Rea   A concept in criminal law that recognises an individual must have knowledge that their action or lack of action would cause a crime to be committed. *Mens rea* is a latin phrase that means a 'knowing' or 'guilty' mind.

Message Crime   A hate crime designed to send a hostile or intimidating message to other members of the victim's identity group or community.

Migrant Worker   A term used to describe a person engaged in a remunerated activity in a state of which they are not a national.

Misogyny   Hatred towards women or a belief in male superiority.

Mitigation/Mitigating Factors   Factors that the court takes into account when sentencing and which will lead to a lesser sentence; these could include age, no previous criminal history, remorse.

Modern Slavery   Under the Modern Slavery Act 2015, modern slavery includes the following: human trafficking, slavery, servitude, and forced or compulsory labour.

Modernisation Theory   A theoretical tradition in sociology that believes the whole world must develop like industrialised, western countries.

Moral Panic   Erupting suddenly, moral panics are periods of intense and disproportionate concern. They focus on a group and/or incident that is perceived to be deeply deviant and a threat to the moral order (see '**folk devil**'). The societal reaction involves exaggerated, distored media coverage and, usually, a punitive response from law makers, police, and courts.

Multi-Agency   A caucus of different stakeholders such as service providers, agencies, teams of professionals, other practitioners and sometimes victim/survivors who work together to address regional and/or local social problems and issues such as crime, victimisation and harm.

Multifunctional Actors   Linked to the notion of prosumers, illicit markets are increasingly populated by actors who play more than one role. Instead of the traditional supplier-consumer distinction, individuals can – thanks to advancements in technology and communication – now be producers, suppliers and consumers according to their subjective needs and desires.

Multiple Victimisation   Multiple criminal incidents experienced by either a person or a place.

National Action   A UK far-right neo-Nazi terrorist organisation founded in 2013 concerned with ultra-nationalism.

National Referral Mechanism   This is the framework used in the UK for identifying victims of trafficking, and ensuring they receive appropriate care via the government's contract with The Salvation Army.

Neoliberalism   A form of liberalism that advocates conditions of economic freedom, commodification of vital public services, and rigorous private property rights. Requires a strong state to maintain, preserve, or create these conditions.

Net-Widening   The process by which suspects are drawn into the criminal justice system for behaviour which would previously have been dealt with outside that system.

Non-Custodial Sentence   All sentences available to the courts that do not involve imprisonment (whether or not the suspended sentence order should be counted is a moot point).

Non-Governmental Organisations (NGOs)   These not-for-profit organisations exist independently from any government but deliver policy, regulatory or public service functions.

Office for Democratic Institutions and Human Rights (ODIHR) The human rights institution of the Organization for Security and Co-operation in Europe (OSCE), tasked with assisting OSCE member states in meeting their commitments in the field of human rights and democracy.

Onset In developmental and life-course criminology, onset refers to the start of a particular behaviour. Researchers measure the onset of many things including: antisocial behaviour; self-reported offending; and first contact with the criminal justice system.

Ontological Insecurity If ontology generally refers to an individual's sense of 'being' in the world, then ontological insecurity denotes a pervasive sense of personal anxiety caused by the unravelling and destabilisation of social structures and cultural norms.

Ontology The branch of philosophy concerned with the nature of being, existence and reality. It deals with questions around what things exist and to what extent we can say that they exist.

Order In the context of prison, this refers to how predictable and steady the daily routine is.

Organisational Justice Refers to employee perceptions of fairness in the workplace. These are often classified into four different categories: distributive, procedural, informational, and interactional.

Persistence Persistence refers to continuity in behaviour (antisocial behaviour or offending). In developmental and life-course criminology researchers examine the factors which increase the likelihood that someone will continue offending over time.

Phenomenology The study of people's subjective experience on its own terms; the goal being to better understand the underlying structures, rules and emotions that guide behaviours and actions.

Pilot Study A practice piece of research before the main study which tests out practical issues such as whether respondents understand the questions.

Plural Policing The patchworked mix of policing provision which includes non-public sector policing provision of policing activities.

Polarisation Division or extreme opposition in beliefs.

Policing A matrix of organisations, agencies, bodies and practices that are concerned with the regulation of crime and social order.

Populist A political approach that appeals to lay-people within society adopting the stance of being for the people, as opposed to the elite or established powerful groups.

Postcolonial Theory A theoretical tradition in the social sciences and humanities concerned with experiences and identity politics in ex-colonies.

Postmodernism An intellectual view developed in the mid to late twentieth century within various disciplines, including the arts, philosophy, and architecture, which departed from modernist ideologies during the late nineteenth and early twentieth century.

Poststructuralism A theoretical position popularised among historians by philosophers such as Michel Foucault during the 1970s. It focuses on the analysis of discourse (particularly in terms of perception), exploring the plurality and instability of meaning among individuals and groups, and across time and space.

Prejudice Biased attitudes or feelings towards others based upon perceptions held about their social grouping.

Premeditated Crime A term sometimes used interchangeably with 'cold-blooded crime', premeditated crime involves careful planning and preparation. Because of the planned nature of them, premeditated crimes are seen as more serious than 'crimes of passion' and tend to be subject to more severe punishment.

Prevalence Rates   The number of victims per 100, 1,000, or 100,000 population or potential targets.

Prima Facie Case   Literally means 'of first appearance'. A case in which there is enough evidence to support the allegation, and the evidence will stand unless there is evidence to rebut the allegation. If a party who bears the burden of proving an issue in court does not raise a 'prima facie case', the other party can submit there is no case to answer and the matter can thereafter be dismissed.

Pro Bono   Latin phrase for 'free' and used to denote the free giving of legal advice and services.

Procedural Justice   Theory focuses on the way agencies interact with the public, and how those interactions shape perceptions of legitimacy and authority, willingness to obey the law, and crime-related behaviour. Procedural justice is based on four central principles: dignity and respect, 'voice', neutral decision making, and trustworthy motives.

Prospective longitudinal study   This is a study that follows a group of the same individuals, over time. They are often similar at the start because they have been born at a particular time or attended a particular school. Criminologists follow individuals to see how various factors affect the likelihood of offending or related behaviours.

Prosumers   This term is often used in the context of technological developments, as part of which individuals who purchase and consume products are now increasingly able to produce and/or design these products also. In the context of illicit marketplaces, various technological advancements in recent years have meant individuals are increasingly able to produce illicit goods such as drugs as well as consume those products.

Protective factor   Protective factors mitigate or eliminate the influence of risk factors. For example, while poverty may be a risk factor for crime, its effect is reduced by the presence of protective factors such as high levels of parental monitoring and strong attachments to school.

Punitive   A fairly broad term covering how much punishment is involved in a court sentence, e.g. a five-year prison sentence is more punitive than a six-month term; a community order with three requirements lasting eighteen months is more punitive than one with a single requirement lasting twelve months.

Punitivist   Having a particular focus on punishment.

Purposive Sampling   A method of selecting from a population in which the researcher uses their own judgement to determine which cases (usually people) are included and which are excluded.

Questionnaire   A form of data collection in which a respondent is presented with questions (either by post or online) which they respond to without any direct contact with the researcher.

Racialisation   Those social relations where racial meanings are found. The term recognises the socially constructed nature of race, and its social significance regarding power and privilege.

Racism   Prejudice towards, or hatred of, people on the basis of their perceived race or ethnic background.

Radical Feminism   A feminist approach which identifies patriarchy as fundamental in underpinning and perpetuating women's gender oppression in society.

Random Sampling   A method of selecting from a population in which every case (usually a person) has an equal chance of selection and the researcher has no control over who is in and who is out of the sample.

Rational Actor   The idea that an individual is motivated by a cost/benefit analysis of action.

Recidivism   Committing further crimes following a conviction for another crime.

Recovery and Reflection Period   This 45-day period is granted to people who have been referred into the National Referral Mechanism and judged to be a potential victim of trafficking. They are granted government-funded victim support services during this time (recovery) and encouraged to think about whether they would like to engage with the police (reflection).

Refugee   A person who has been forced to leave their country to escape persecution, war or natural disaster.

Relativism   The belief that there is no objective moral truth, and that morality exists only in relation to particular societies and cultures in specific historical contexts. See MacIntyre (1984) for more.

Repeat Crime Rates   The number of crimes which occurred against the same victim or target per 100, 1,000, or 100,000 population or potential targets.

Repeat Victim Rates   The number of victims or targets that experienced two or more crimes per 100, 1,000, or 100,000 population or potential targets.

Rescue Industry   A growing network of social helpers who have taken it upon themselves to save women from what they perceive to be the horrors of the sex industry.

Responsibilisation   The process where agencies or individuals are rendered responsible for a task or required to 'own' behaviour.

Restorative Justice (RJ)   This type of justice focuses on repairing the harm done, rather than punishment. RJ proposes processes of mediation and conferencing.

Rickrolling   Internet trolling which links uses to the 1987 song 'Never Gonne Give You Up' by Rick Astley.

Risk factor   A risk factor is something that increases the likelihood of an outcome occurring. For example, poverty is a risk factor for criminal behaviour. It does not mean that all poor people become criminals but rather that poverty increases the likelihood of that occurring.

Romanticism   A theoretical tradition in the social sciences and humanities that has a positive view of the world before industrialisation and the modern state.

Routine Activity Theory   The idea that crime occurs when you have a motivated individual, a suitable target and the absence of a capable guardian, and is linked to ordinary, day-to-day behaviour.

Secondary Analysis   The analysis of an existing dataset in order to address a new research question.

Secondary Victimisation   Used to refer to the harm that can be inflicted by the criminal justice system (any of the agencies or professionals) on the victim of crime.

Self-Report Offending/Delinquency Surveys   A measure based upon self-confessed accounts of the prevalence, severity or nature of illicit behaviour.

Seminar   A seminar is a small group session where students will discuss their ideas relating to a set reading or topic. It is also an opportunity for students to ask questions about the topic, and to clarify their understanding.

Sex Worker   Someone who provides sexual services for some form of payment.

Sexist   Treating women less favourably due to their sex or gender; discriminatory, prejudicial or stereotypical treatment.

Sexual Orientation   The general attraction felt towards people of one sex or another, or both.

Sharia   Islamic law derived from religious text.

Sloganisation   Politicians and/or news-makers' transformation of complex political or policy messages into catchy, simplistic soundbites.

Social Contract   An actual or hypothetical contract, or agreement, between the individual and the State.

Social Control   Refers to the social processes through which the behaviour of individuals or groups is regulated.

Social History   A historical approach developed during the 1960s that seeks to understand the experiences, working patterns, and community formation of ordinary people (also known as 'history from below').

Social Identity   An individual's social identity (sense of who they are) depends on the groups to which they belong (Tajfel et al., 1979).

Social Norms   Mores, unwritten rules of behaviour, considered acceptable in a group or society.

Species Justice   This considers the broader responsibility that man owes to other species as the dominant species and the cause of most harm caused to animals and the environment.

Stonewall   An organisation with offices in England, Scotland and Wales which campaigns in the interests of lesbian, gay, bisexual and transgender people.

Structural Limitations   Limits placed on a practical response to a problem (such as a law or policy) that are caused by structural rather than political or individual circumstances. For example, when economists refer to the structural limitations on employment, they mean unemployment is caused by structural economic reasons and cannot therefore be solved simply by training people or offering incentives to individuals.

Subaltern   This is a term used (typically within postcolonial theory) to describe people who are socially, politically and geographically marginal from the hegemonic power structure.

Summary Offence   An offence (usually of a less serious magnitude) triable only in the magistrates court.

Symbolic Interactionism   A sociological perspective that suggests our understanding of the world is a result of a constant negotiation of the meanings we attribute to it.

Tabloid Adversarialism   The tendency for certain news outlets to criticise government policy and push for more punitive, harsher official responses. In some cases, reporting has an anti-establishment tone. The rhetoric of tabloid adversarialism overlaps with that of penal populism, and together these have become a key feature of public debate in the late twentieth, early twenty-first century.

The Chain of Evidence   Ensures the preservation and integrity of any information that is collected by accounting for the actions of individuals or location of evidence. It requires the evidence gatherer to record any individuals who checked, accessed, or changed the information or locations and the reasons why. The times and dates of these events must also be recorded. Failing to preserve the chain of evidence could make it inadmissible in court or have its integrity challenged.

Transcript   The typed record of an interview or a focus group.

Transgender   Someone who has adopted the lifestyle and behaviour of another gender without undergoing surgery. Can also be used as a broad term to cover both transgender and transsexual people.

Transnational Crime   Crime that is conducted across national borders, such as human trafficking and terrorism.

Transportation The practice in Britain and other European countries during the nineteenth century of sending criminals to their remote colonies.

Travellers Communities of people with distinctive lifestyles, traditions and cultures that set them apart from the sedentary population. Often used as a collective term to describe a range of groups, including Irish, Scottish and New Travellers, Gypsies and Roma people.

Tutorial A tutorial is usually a one-to-one meeting with a member of staff to discuss your progress and any problems you might be encountering on the course.

Undeserving Victims Those individuals and groups unable to attain the label of victim and who struggle to gain recognition for the harm they have suffered.

United National Trafficking Protocol This is a shorthand name given to the United Nations Protocol to Prevent, Supress and Punish Trafficking in Persons, especially Women and Children.

Verstehen First articulated in the work of the German sociologist, Max Weber, at the start of the twentieth century, *verstehen* denotes the subjective or appreciative understanding of others' actions and motivations.

Victim The label 'victim' is contingent, complex and dynamic. Rock (2002) suggests 'victim' is an identity and a social artefact that is constructed by different actors in different contexts. It is usually now associated with crime but also relates to someone suffering some kind of misfortune.

Victimisation The process or occurrence of becoming a victim.

Victimisation Risk The proportion of the population experiencing a crime.

Victimisation Survey A methodological tool used to measure the extent and patterning of victimisation by surveying a random sample of the population and asking them questions about their experiences of victimisation.

Victimology The scientific study of the extent, nature and causes of criminal victimisation, and its consequences for the persons involved.

Volume Crime Types Any crime which, through its volume, has a significant impact on the community and the police's ability to tackle it.

Witness A witness to crime is a person who might report a crime to the police or tell the police about what they know. They may stand up in court to state what they know about the crime after taking an oath to tell the truth.

Xeno-Racism A newer type of cultural racism that combines different types of discrimination, such as anti-Muslim racism, Islamaphobia and xenophobia, to produce racialised zones of inclusion/exclusion.

Xenophobia An irrational fear or hatred of those from another country.

Youth Justice Board for England and Wales Established by the Crime and Disorder Act 1998, the YJB is responsible for advising government on youth justice issues and providing guidance for YOTs.

Youth Offending Team A statutory partnership responsible for the delivery of youth justice services in the community. Established by the Crime and Disorder Act 1998, YOTs must have representation from the police, probation, education, health and children's services.

Zemiology An academic discipline concerned with the study of social harms. It emerged as a critique of the notion of crime and of criminology as a discipline, arguing that it should form a new discipline distinct from criminology.

Index

CPSIA information can be obtained
at www.ICGtesting.com
Printed in the USA
JSHW041524190622
27055JS00002B/51